The Rise and Fall of Turkey's Democrat Party

More than sixty years after Turkey's Democrat Party was removed from office by a military coup and three of its leaders hanged, it remains controversial. For some, it was the defender of a more democratic political order and founder of a dominant center-right political coalition; for others, it ushered in an era of corruption, religious reaction, and subordination to American influence. This study moves beyond such stark binaries. Reuben Silverman details the party's establishment, development, rule, and removal from power, showing how its leaders transformed themselves from champions of democracy and liberal economics to advocates of illiberal policies. To understand this change, Silverman draws on periodicals and archival documents to detail the Democrat Party's continuity with Turkey's late Ottoman and early republican past as well as the changing nature of the American-led Cold War order in which it actively participated.

Reuben Silverman is a researcher focused on Turkey. He is the author of *Turkey's Ever Present Past: Stories from Turkish Republican History* (2016), *Politics in Turkey: Parties, Politicians and the Struggle for Power* (2018), and *Borderline Personalities: Lives at the Political, Social, and Geographic Edges of Modern Turkey* (2021).

Cambridge Middle East Studies has been established to publish books on the nineteenth- to twenty-first-century Middle East and North Africa. The series offers new and original interpretations of aspects of Middle Eastern societies and their histories. To achieve disciplinary diversity, books are solicited from authors writing in a wide range of fields including history, sociology, anthropology, political science, and political economy. The emphasis is on producing books affording an original approach along theoretical and empirical lines. The series is intended for students and academics, but the more accessible and wide-ranging studies will also appeal to the interested general reader.

A list of books in the series can be found after the index.

The Rise and Fall of Turkey's Democrat Party

The Cold War and Illiberalism, 1945–60

Reuben Silverman
Independent Scholar

CAMBRIDGE
UNIVERSITY PRESS

CAMBRIDGE
UNIVERSITY PRESS

Shaftesbury Road, Cambridge CB2 8EA, United Kingdom

One Liberty Plaza, 20th Floor, New York, NY 10006, USA

477 Williamstown Road, Port Melbourne, VIC 3207, Australia

314–321, 3rd Floor, Plot 3, Splendor Forum, Jasola District Centre, New Delhi – 110025, India

103 Penang Road, #05-06/07, Visioncrest Commercial, Singapore 238467

Cambridge University Press is part of Cambridge University Press & Assessment, a department of the University of Cambridge.

We share the University's mission to contribute to society through the pursuit of education, learning and research at the highest international levels of excellence.

www.cambridge.org

Information on this title: www.cambridge.org/9781009604451
DOI: 10.1017/9781009604482

When citing this work, please include a reference to the DOI 10.1017/9781009604482

First published 2026

A catalogue record for this publication is available from the British Library

A Cataloging-in-Publication data record for this book is available from the Library of Congress

ISBN 978-1-009-60445-1 Hardback

For my mom, Jenepher Reeves, and my dad, Charles Silverman

Contents

Figure and Map

Acknowledgments

Unlike my previous books, this one is not a collection of short pieces that I wrote as the mood struck me: it began as my dissertation. It required extensive time for research and revision, and it would not have been possible without the aid of a great number of people and institutions who offered me intellectual, emotional, and financial support.

First and foremost, I want to thank my advisors at UC San Diego, Hasan Kayalı and Michael Provence, whom I've always been able to rely on during and since my PhD program. Similarly, I want to thank Paul Levin and Jenny White, who generously gave me the opportunity to develop this book as a postdoctoral researcher at Stockholm University's Institute for Turkish Studies (SUITS). It would not exist without your support.

At both these universities, I also owe thanks to many other people whose support meant a great deal to me. At Stockholm, I was lucky to work regularly with Kimberly Michele Parke as well as İmren Borsuk and Samuele Abrami. (And Isa Blumi, though our paths did not cross in person.) I also had the privilege to attend great seminars, fikas, and dinners and meet many lovely colleges. While there are too many to name, let me at least highlight some people whom I had the pleasure of chatting with over my two years in Stockholm: Matilda Baraibar, Kelly Biddle, Pontus Blüme, Zigne Edström, Jonathan Feldman, Torkel Gure, Karl Gustafsson, Johannes Hartvigson, Maria Hellman, Yeonju Jung, Jennifer Lundgren, Aryo Makko, Enrique Antonio Mejia, Klara Melin, Steven Miller, Axel Nordenstam, Magnus Petersson, Gonzalo Pozo Martin, Mark Rhinard, Shefali Roy, Karina Shyrokykh, Anthony Smythe, Lydia Theresa Wachs, and Maria Wendt. And pride of place must go to Thomas Jonter, whom I kept encountering in the wild, which is to say at various cafes. In the case of San Diego, I've thanked many people before in my dissertation and other books, so here I'll just emphasize some whom I've kept in contact with during this book project: Taylor Gray, Güliz Kuruoğlu, Patrick Patterson, Johanna Peterson,

Jeremy Prestholdt, Dimitrios Stergiopoulos, Barış Taşyakan, Paul Tchir, and Mirna Wasef.

In addition to colleagues, there are several institutions and individual donors that provided crucial support for my research. These include Suzanne Weissman, who helped fund summer research in 2015; UCSD itself, which gave me a Frontiers of Innovation Scholars Program scholarship, covering a year in Istanbul, 2017–18 (and, it should be mentioned, I could not have secured such an interdisciplinary award without support from Richard Biernacki in the Sociology Department); the United States government, which awarded a Fulbright Student Fellowship in Istanbul for 2018–19 (and Ayhan Aktar, who not only sponsored me, but also took me to some of the best fish restaurants I have ever eaten at); the Institute of Turkish Studies, which awarded a Heath Lowry Distinguished Fellowship for 2019–20; and the UCSD History Department, which gave a dissertation year writing fellowship. Without such support, I could not have traveled to Istanbul to do research. Moreover, without steady employment as a TA in UCSD's Making of the Modern World writing program, I could not have maintained financial stability in daily life. Thanks are due, therefore, to Heidi Keller-Lapp and Eberly Barnes for their repeated confidence in me. (Likewise, to Nir Shafir for his willingness to have me as his TA in his fascinating classes during my final year as a graduate student.)

As this book has passed from the manuscript to the submission to the revisions stage, I have also felt gratitude to the people at Cambridge University Press and its associated firms who have guided me through the process: Natasha Burton, Maria Marsh, Rosanna Barraclough, Natasha Whelan, Jodie Mardell-Lines, Gabriel Sam Antony, Chris Jackson, the anonymous reviewers who took time to consider the book, and many others with whom I never directly spoke. During this time period, I have also been fortunate to find work with the devoted, caring people at the Refugee Development Center in Lansing, Michigan.

While researching and writing, I was privileged to meet with a handful of individuals who either participated in the history discussed in this book or contributed to the historiography of which it is a part. These include former leaders of the Democrat Party's Youth Arm, Hüsamettin Cindoruk and Ertuğrul Mat, and the scholars Feroz Ahmad and Cem Eroğul, whose accounts of the Democrat Party remain my favorites five decades after publication. Though I believe that this book offers new insights that will be of interest to readers, it cannot but stand in the shadow of their classic works. I am honored that they all graciously offered me their time and attention.

Beyond immediate colleagues and scholarly idols, there is the category of people who read my work and (I hope) enjoy it. This is always incredibly important to me since it is what makes all the effort worthwhile. Even though some of the following people may not read everything I put out, I know they read *some* of the things and that makes the rest worthwhile: Sinem Adar, William Armstrong, Nick Ashdown, Jared Conrad-Bradshaw, Josef Burton, Nikos Christofis, Nicholas Danforth, Howard Eissenstat, Ryan Gingeras, Suzy Hansen, Zeynep Karataş, Halil Karaveli, Reşat Kasaba, Selim Kuru, Kenny Laurie, Evan Pheiffer, Onur İşçi, Joakim Parslow, James Ryan, Bilge Yesil, Amberin Zaman, and the writers at Turkey Recap.

Then there are those friends I am fortunate enough to see every few years, from before this book was even a vague idea up to the present day. Whether or not there are more books and more opportunities to thank them, this is a pretty good occasion. These include the good friends I made in Seattle, such as Mark Aoyama and Naveen Ahmed Aoyama, Eric Gowdy and Kat Davidson, Keegan Hartman, Matt Rigsby and Allison Suess, and Ryan Sluman and Claudia Li; in San Diego, such as Foster Chamberlain, Gözde Emen Gökatalay, Semih Gökatalay, Peter Braden, Kevan Malone, and Jordan Mylet; and in Istanbul, such as Olga Alexopoulou, Amer Arab, Sheri Cavazos, Jessica Davis, Tyler Denison, Jordan Duquette, Ebru Ezberci, Matthew Ghazarian, Çiğdem Gürleyük-Jorgensen, Michael Jorgensen, Aslı Karaduman, Lars Larsson, Hollie Longmore, Robert Llyod, Sveta Nekrasova, James O'Halloran, Mary O'Halloran, Ben Platt, Eamonn Quinn, Alex Segall, Selin Selçuk, James Smart, Gamze Tekin, Pam Taticek, Amanda Towle Quinn, Chris Wall, and Luke Webb. In recent years, I have even added relatives to this list: Durak, Gülnür, Nermin, and Balkan. They join the ranks with Deborah and Dane.

Most of all, of course, I must thank my wife, Özlem Yılmaz, and my parents, Jenepher Reeves and Charles Silverman. Without their support and love I cannot imagine having written this book.

Note on the Text

Turkish contains a number of letters not found in English: these include two of most vowels (a/â ı/i o/ö u/ü) in which the undotted version is generally pronounced broadly and the dotted version is pronounced more tightly – imagine the distinction between the English words "bow" and "boot" (in the case of o/ö) and "butt" and "butte" (in the case of u/ü). With ı/i the distinction is comparable to the sounds resembling "uh" and "ee." A pair of consonants (ç and ş) represent the longer sounds of "ch" and "sh." The consonant c is pronounced like the English j. And one consonant (ğ) is not pronounced at all; instead, it extends the length of the vowel behind it. For example, President Erdoğan's name should be pronounced "Air-dough-wan."

Three letters (q, x, and w) are used in Kurdish but are not part of official Turkish and, thus, not allowed on IDs, etc. Even so, they are a common daily sight. (In 2013, opposition leader Kemal Kılıçdaroğlu jokingly wondered if the prime minister had ever been to the WC.)[1] In English-language publications, something similar happens: Turkish letters are excluded, meaning that a name like Kılıçdaroğlu is written as "Kilicdaroglu," causing American broadcast news reporters and my father considerable pronunciation trouble.

In general, I have followed *International Journal of Middle East Studies* (IJMES) guidelines for translation and transliteration, but with a few idiosyncratic choices. A few are worth mentioning:

- Most important, the *Demokrat Parti* (DP) is translated throughout as "Democrat Party." Grammatically, however, it should be "Democratic Party" – and this makes sense, given that it intentionally alludes to the United States political party. The main reason I avoid this translation is that Turkey subsequently had a "*Demokratik Parti*" formed in 1970 by partisans of the dissolved *Demokrat Parti*.

[1] Meriç Tafolar, "Başörtüsünde herkes yönetmeliğe uymalı," *Milliyet*, October 4, 2013.

- Although I use the full, English name for Turkish political parties, organizations, etc. (e.g., Republican People's Party), I use Turkish acronyms (e.g., CHP) rather than English ones (e.g., RPP) as some scholars do. For non-Turkish entities (US, USSR, FRG, etc.), I have used the English acronym.
- In translating the titles of frequently referenced books, journals, and newspapers I give the *Turkish name in italics* and the (English name in parentheses). Thereafter, I use the Turkish name. An example would be the DP's official paper *Zafer* (Victory).
- I often include the (*Turkish version of a word in parentheses and italics*) when I think the term has particular resonance in Turkish. For example, statism (*devletçilik*).
- Finally, I have used Turkish letters/spellings for Turkish place-names in almost all cases (for example, İzmir rather than Smyrna or Izmir). I refer to Thessaloniki as Salonika until 1912, when it became part of Greece. In spite of those choices, I use "Istanbul" rather than İstanbul in the main text.

All translations and errors in this book are my own (though I still thank Özlem Yılmaz for trying to save me from the worst mistakes). Ultimately, I have tried to strike a balance such that a reader who does not know Turkish will not be completely lost and a reader who does know Turkish will not be overly annoyed. God willing (*inşallah*), I have approached that goal!

Abbreviations*

Abbreviation	Name (English)	Name (Turkish)
AKP	Justice and Development Party	*Adalet ve Kalkınma Partisi*
AP	Justice Party	*Adalet Partisi*
CENTO	Central Treaty Organization	
CHP	Republican People's Party	*Cumhuriyet Halk Partisi*
CMP	Republican Nation Party	*Cumhuriyetçi Millet Partisi*
DP	Democrat Party	*Demokrat Parti*
ECA	Economic Cooperation Administration	
EEC	European Economic Community	
EPU	European Payments Union	
FOA	Foreign Operations Administration	
FRG	Federal Republic of Germany	
FRUS	*Foreign Relations of the United States*	
HP	Freedom Party	*Hürriyet Partisi*
IBRD	International Bank for Reconstruction and Development	
IMF	International Monetary Fund	
İTC	Committee of Union and Progress	*İttihat ve Terakki Cemiyeti*
MTTB	National Turkish Student Union	*Milli Türk Talebe Birliği*
NATO	North Atlantic Treaty Organization	
OEEC	Organisation for European Economic Co-operation	
SCF	Free Republican Party	*Serbest Cumhuriyet Fırkası*
SEATO	Southeast Asian Treaty Organization	
TMO	Soil Products Office	*Toprak Mahsülleri Ofisi*
UK	United Kingdom	
UN	United Nations	
US	United States of America	
USSR	Union of Soviet Socialist Republics	

* Abbreviations for archives and other sources are in the Bibliography

Map 0.1 Turkey in 1950 (adapted by author from cografyaharita.com).

Introduction

In May 2003, several months after he became prime minister of Turkey, Recep Tayyip Erdoğan addressed a gathering of the Justice and Development Party (AKP) at the seaside resort town of Tekirova. He stressed to attendees that they were part of a political movement that was unburdened by the ideological baggage of other, contemporary parties. "There might be those among us [who once had] connections to other political parties," he conceded. "But now we've left that shirt outside. We see ourselves as the continuation of the Democrat Party. We want to embrace the 70 million [people in Turkey]."[1] This was not the first or last time Erdoğan would invoke the Democrat Party (DP), which came to power after winning Turkey's first relatively free and fair national elections on May 14, 1950. In 2023, for example, despite calls to delay voting due to a devastating earthquake, he decided to hold the elections on the same day as part of an effort to reinforce the link between the parties in the minds of voters.

The DP's 1950 victory ousted the Republican People's Party (CHP), which had ruled the country since its founding almost three decades earlier. DP-led governments under Prime Minister Adnan Menderes would go on to rule Turkey until 1960, when the party was removed from power in a military coup. For Erdoğan and his allies, the DP represented an alternative to the top-down nation-building project of the early Turkish republic. It represented the possibility of a more authentic political and social system rooted in traditional values rather than imported Western understandings of secularism or culture. The coup that ended DP rule was, from this perspective, part of a persistent effort to deny the will of the Turkish nation. In office, Erdoğan often associated himself with Menderes, the party's dominant figure, who was

[1] Abdullah Karakuş, "Milli Görüş'ü ...," *Milliyet*, May 17, 2003, 16.

prosecuted and hanged following the coup. On the anniversary of Menderes's execution, following his own election as mayor of Istanbul, Erdoğan attended the annual memorial service.[2] As prime minister and, eventually, president, Erdoğan oversaw the remaking of Yassıada, the island where Menderes and other DP leaders had been imprisoned and prosecuted, into "Democracy and Freedom Island," part memorial museum, part convention center.

At the grand opening of the redesigned island, held on May 27, 2020, the sixtieth anniversary of the coup, Erdoğan reminded his audience and the youth of the nation what the DP had represented:

> The period of Turkey's transition to multiparty political life is very important … After the sickness and death of our Republic's founder, Gazi Mustafa Kemal [in 1938], the single-party regime of the CHP descended upon the country like a nightmare. The development drive that had been started following our War of Independence [1919–1922] was consciously blocked by the single-party mentality; one by one, works that had progressed came to naught. You youths should learn well here of dear departed Menderes's decade of 1950–60; you should learn well of the progress Turkey made in ten years … While Menderes, may he rest in peace, was making our nation happy, raising the national income by three times and equipping the country with dams, roads, housing, and industrial facilities, some were becoming uncomfortable … they tried to overturn the national will with threats, pressure, guns, and, when it came to it, blood … These putschists, who create vassal lands for the imperialists, are, at the same time, providing [fuel for the fires] of division in our country … From returning the call to prayer to its essential [Arabic] to opening mosques to protecting the thousand-year accumulation of the Turkish language: they saw the Democrat Party's answers to the requests of the nation as a slap in the face.[3]

In his denunciation of coups, Erdoğan was alluding to a 2016 coup attempt that he and the AKP had confronted as much as he was referring to the *actual* historical experiences and accomplishments of the DP. Nonetheless, the speech was in keeping with the ways in which Erdoğan as well as many scholars and journalists have discussed the DP in recent decades.[4] Whether intended as criticism or praise, accounts

[2] "'Menderes, demokrasi …,'" *Cumhuriyet*, September 18, 1995, 5.

[3] "Demokrasi ve Özgürlükler Adası'nın Açılış Töreni'nde Yaptıkları Konuşma," T. C. Cumhurbaşkanlığı, May 27, 2020, available: www.tccb.gov.tr/konusmalar/353/120308/demokrasi-ve-ozgurlukler-adasi-nin-acilis-toreni-nde-yaptiklari-konusma.

[4] Soner Çağaptay, *The New Sultan: Erdogan and the Crisis of Modern Turkey* (London: I. B. Tauris, 2017), 27; Hannah Lucinda Smith, *Erdoğan Rising: The Battle for the Soul of Turkey* (London: William Collins, 2019); Hakan Yavuz, *Erdoğan: The Making of an Autocrat* (Edinburgh: Edinburgh University Press, 2021), 78.

during the past two decades have frequently emphasized a connection between the AKP and DP. The points of similarity can vary, including liberalism, conservatism, populism, use of religious rhetoric, emphasis on rapid development, clientelism, nationalism, or hypocrisy, but the link is present regardless.

The ease with which a present-day political party is associated with one so distant in time may stem from the way binaries are frequently used to explain Turkey. There is, of course, the popular trope of Turkey as a country "torn between East and West," but in academic work, we can also see these divides. In the 1950s and 1960s, scholars presented Turkey as the realization of a century-long process of modernization and secularization. Modernity was itself defined by binaries between tradition and progress, religious authority and secular authority, rural and urban lifestyles. According to the sociologist Niyazi Berkes, for example, efforts by Ottoman officials to bring about this modern society had led to a "bifurcation of culture."[5] Similarly, the sociologist Şerif Mardin argued that the subsequent imposition of secular institutions by Mustafa Kemal Atatürk and his allies in the state administration had helped turn the country's "periphery" into "the center of a counter-official culture."[6] Younger scholars in the 1960s and 1970s, drawing on Marxism and the concepts of dependency and world systems theory, also divided up the world, arguing that Turkey had been exploited by Western, capitalist countries, turned into a "satellite" of greater powers, and shunted into the economic semiperiphery to be exploited for its resources.

For most of these scholars, the DP, like the AKP after it, empowered a particular side of these binaries. For Berkes, "The [DP] governments of the 1950s gave free rein to all sorts of obscurantism under the guise of restoring the freedom of religion and in the name of democracy."[7] For Mardin, the DP "was a party that speculated with a political ideology which it thought would be strongly supported by the rural masses and by their patrons."[8] Through this cynical tactic, the DP became, in the eyes of the periphery, "the incarnation of the ideal government, a government

[5] Niyazi Berkes, *The Development of Secularism in Turkey* (London: C. Hurst & Co., 1998 [1964]), 509. For other accounts of modernization in Turkey, see Daniel Lerner, *The Passing of Traditional Society* (New York: Free Press, 1958) and Bernard Lewis, *The Emergence of Modern Turkey*, 2nd ed. (Oxford: Oxford University Press, 1968 [1961]).

[6] Şerif Mardin, "Center–Periphery Relations: A Key to Turkish Politics?" *Daedalus* 102, no. 1 (1973), 187.

[7] Berkes, *The Development of Secularism in Turkey*, 503.

[8] Mardin, "Center–Periphery Relations," 184.

with truly popular roots which had been the secret dream of the Turkish countryside for centuries and constituted the motive force of its struggle with the representatives of the bureaucracy."[9] To young Marxist radicals, even these harsh assessments were insufficient. To political scientist Cem Eroğul, the DP was the party of the "compradors" – the "parasitic" classes – and "to think that a country under imperialism's exploitation will be able to develop itself by means of those classes who placed it in that exploitive order was nothing other than foolishness."[10] Similarly, İsmail Cem İpekçi saw the party as composed of hypocrites who sought the support of "those opposed to Westernization" while engaging in "Westernizing actions wholly on the side of private capital."[11] Although none of these authors presented the DP in a favorable light, they all shared the belief with Erdoğan that binary oppositions were essential to understanding Turkey and that the DP was primarily associated with one side in these divisions.

This book is hesitant to embrace such binaries. While the divisions that scholars emphasize are real enough to affect the lives of people in Turkey, these divides are multiple and crosscutting. Picking one as "a key to Turkish politics" may be presuming too much. Instead, I present an account of the DP, its role in Turkey's democratization, and its engagement with the emerging Cold War order that is mindful of the divides in Turkey, which constrained and directed the actions of DP leaders, but that also acknowledges the party's ability to transcend those divides – or, at least, embody their multiple contradictions. DP leaders could be both patriots *and* compradors. For all their self-dealing, they were also intent on extracting benefits for the people of Turkey from the American-led Cold War order. They could be both victims *and* perpetrators. After the 1960 coup, they were prosecuted en masse, held in prison for several years, and, in the case of three leaders, executed. Yet some of these same

[9] Şerif Mardin, "Opposition and Control in Turkey," *Government and Opposition* 1, no. 3 (1966), 383–384.

[10] Cem Eroğul, *Demokrat Parti: Tarihi ve İdeolojisi* (Istanbul: Yordam Kitap, 2013 [1970]), 241, 262.

[11] İsmail Cem (İpekçi), *Türkiye'de Geri Kalmışlığın Tarihi*, 4th ed. (Istanbul: Cem Yayınevi, 1974 [1970]), 336. In his career as a writer and politician, İsmail Cem did not use his last name (İpekçi), perhaps to distinguish himself from family members who were prominent as movie studio heads and newspaper editors. Moreover, his family was part of the Dönme minority community (see Chapter 3, n. 142). Because it is his last name, I have included it in parentheses, but it is worth noting that his conservative critics often treated his choice as a devious plot to conceal his identity (Reuben Silverman, *Borderline Personalities: Lives at the Political, Social, and Geographic Edges of Modern Turkey* [Istanbul: Libra Yayınevi, 2021], 213–219).

leaders had approved repressive measures, most likely including violent, coordinated attacks against political opponents and minority communities. They could be both democrats *and* autocrats. The party was led by men who had created a single-party system, challenged it, and, soon enough, taken steps to reimpose aspects of it.

This book presents a portrait of the DP that encompasses these contradictions while also emphasizing DP leaders' connections to the domestic political order that preceded them and to the international order of the 1950s. In doing so, I offer an alternative to accounts of the DP that present its policies as a betrayal of some clearly defined set of foundational principles undergirding the Republic of Turkey. In the first place, policies regarding foreign alliances, religion, ethnic nationalism, and domestic business interests during the single-party period were hardly consistent, whether under Mustafa Kemal Atatürk or İsmet İnönü. Policies changed owing to domestic politics and international conditions. Under the DP, the situation was no different. Like their predecessors, DP governments sought to develop Turkey's national economy, maintain social stability, and inculcate a sense of shared national belonging. Even the defense of Turkey's security – which critics would argue the DP subordinated to American interests – remained a stated goal of its leaders. The aims remained largely unchanged; it was the opportunities and, consequently, the strategies that differed. Multiparty democracy was one such strategy.

Democratization and De-democratization in Turkey

Like Turkey itself, "democracy" cannot be understood in binary terms. It is a process that ebbs and flows; a set of institutions (and relations to those institutions) that can be arranged, rearranged, and removed. Analytically, this imprecision can be frustrating, but the clarity promised by most definitions proves to be an illusion when applied to Turkey and similar real-world examples. Even using political scientist Adam Przeworski's minimalist definition that "Democracy is a system in which parties lose elections," where participants accept "devolution of power from a group of people to a set of rules," is unsatisfying.[12] Although it tells us that Turkey "became" a democracy in 1950, when the DP took

[12] Adam Przeworski, *Democracy and the Market: Political and Economic Reforms in Eastern Europe and Latin America* (Cambridge: Cambridge University Press, 1991), 9–14.

power from the CHP, it does not tell us whether Turkey was *still* a democracy on the eve of the 1960 coup.[13] Furthermore, it does not account for how people at the time perceived events. Perhaps students, journalists, opposition politicians, and the military were wrong in their alarmism over DP policies, but people seldom wait until social scientists' conditions are fully met before deciding to act.[14] In other words, while winning and losing elections is an essential element, the presence of institutions that reassure losers is also vital. But are democracies only legitimate if losers are content? Must their demands be reasonable? And, if so, reasonable to whom?

This much is certain: over the course of the 1950s, people in Turkey lost confidence in existing political institutions – the existing "set of rules" – to produce satisfying results. Critics of the DP government were frustrated with the winner-take-all nature of the electoral system, which provided the DP with majorities in parliament completely out of proportion to its share of the vote. They were also worried that independent voices in the press and academia were being silenced. They demanded a *liberal* democracy in which clear sets of rules constrained majorities. They called for checks and balances, such as a supreme court, and autonomy for universities and the media. Yet DP leaders were also dissatisfied with the existing democratic order. They felt that it provided the opposition with too many opportunities to misuse its freedoms, accusing the DP of promoting reactionary religious views and minimizing the DP's accomplishments. DP leaders wanted an *illiberal* democracy that placed new limits on the system, limiting oversight of their actions and silencing the voices of opponents. Liberal critics sought to restrict democracy, to favor minority rights; the DP sought to eliminate checks and balances on democracy, to ensure the smooth implementation of the majority will. Both these aims required restrictions on democratic institutions, an active effort to de-democratize the political system.

[13] The difficulty of pinpointing when a democracy becomes an autocracy in the absence of a clear indicator (e.g., a ruling party refusing to accept the results of an election) has led political scientists to develop concepts like "competitive authoritarianism" (Steven Levitsky and Lucan Way, *Competitive Authoritarianism: Hybrid Regimes after the Cold War* [Cambridge: Cambridge University Press, 2010], 5).

[14] In later work, Przeworski and coauthors put much greater emphasis on the importance of "alternation," arguing that a winning party must also eventually lose and leave office for a country to be confidently judged as democratic. In fact, the DP is specifically referenced to illustrate this point (Adam Przeworski, Michael Alvarez, José Antonio Cheibub, and Fernando Limongi, *Democracy and Development: Political Institutions and Well-Being in the World, 1950–1990* [Cambridge: Cambridge University Press, 2000], 25–27).

Turkey's troubled experience of democracy in the 1950s is not unique. As this book shows, it stemmed from compromises made during the process of democratization in the mid 1940s. Turkey's transition from an authoritarian system to a rule-based, democratic one occurred after splits within the ruling elite led its factions to reach out to other groups in society to secure their own position.[15] While the governments of the single-party period made use of support from landowners, merchants, and other powerful groups in society, they did not depend on them. The appeal of the DP, by contrast, was its promise to rule in greater consultation with them. Party leaders consistently resisted efforts to tax the agriculture sector and offered significant subsidies. The state was directed to serve people's interests rather than their best interests.

The democratic institutions that ultimately emerged were the result of negotiations between the ruling group and other groups in society. Yet, as Przeworski argues, the institutions of the democracies that emerge from such negotiations bear "institutional traces" of the authoritarian regime.[16] In Turkey, the persistence in government of politicians from the former ruling elite and their reliance on institutions from the authoritarian period increased the likelihood of a return to illiberal, authoritarian methods of governance.[17] Institutions that supported democratic politics – for example, laws allowing substantial freedom of the press and assembly – could easily be revised by a simple, unchecked, parliamentary majority.

In addition to thinking about democracy in Turkey in terms of the presence or absence of institutions, there is the question of how people experienced these institutions. The political scientists Guillermo O'Donnell and Philippe Schmitter, for example, define "democracy" in terms of "the *right* to be treated by fellow human beings as equal with respect to the making of collective choices and the *obligation* of those

[15] Przeworski, *Democracy and the Market*, 57.

[16] Ibid., xi. For a more recent discussion of the transition from authoritarian regimes to democracies, see Michael Albertus and Victor Menaldo, *Authoritarianism and the Elite Origins of Democracy* (Cambridge: Cambridge University Press, 2017).

[17] *Authoritarian* and *illiberal* are distinct terms, but the distinction can easily blur. Authoritarian is often treated as synonymous with nondemocratic. Levitsky and Way, for example, define "*full authoritarianism* as a regime in which no viable channels exist for opposition to contest legally for executive power." Illiberal regimes, by contrast, can tolerate elections – or, as Fareed Zakaria puts it, they "do better on political liberties than on civil ones." Yet how far can civil liberties be restricted before contesting power is no longer "viable"? (Zakaria, "The Rise of Illiberal Democracy," *Foreign Affairs* 76, no. 6 [1997], 23–24; Levitsky and Way, *Competitive Authoritarianism*, 6–7.)

implementing such choices to be equally accountable and accessible to all members of the polity."[18] But, under DP rule, did access to institutions and decision-making become more equal and inclusive? Were DP leaders more accountable to the public? Certainly, more people participated in elections, rallies, and local political clubs, but whether they did so as "equals" or as part of traditional hierarchies is less clear. As we will see in discussions of provincial and national politics, many of the DP's leading figures were familiar faces. Even the institution of elections, which the DP glorified, cannot be taken as synonymous with greater public inclusion in decision-making. According to sociologist Reşat Kasaba, "the Democrats and their successors elevated the formal procedures of democracy, in particular the act of voting, to a very high level of esteem."[19] Once the voting was finished, however, Democrats argued that the "national will" (*milli irade*) had been expressed and that the elected government now represented the whole nation regardless of individual dissent.

Again and again, we will see DP governments and officials act in an imperious manner, not always different from the preceding regime, but now justified on the grounds that they had won the election. Such behavior is typical of "populist" politicians who, as political scientist Nadia Urbinati describes, use elections "as a strategy to reveal a majority that, in their mind, already exists in the country … [they use] elections as plebiscites that serve to prove to the public the force of the winner, rather than to assess the various representative claims."[20] In other words, DP leaders cared only about securing a majority. In victory, they did not feel obligated to implement their policies with any concession to the 41–45 percent of the population that supported the opposition. Their style of governing – already questionable if judged by the standards of O'Donnell and Schmitter – became even less "democratic" after 1957, when the party won a majority in parliament according to the electoral rules it had established, but only a plurality of the actual vote. The party leaders' unwillingness to govern with some acknowledgement of this result led to further instability.

[18] Guillermo O'Donnell and Philippe Schmitter, *Transitions from Authoritarian Rule: Tentative Conclusions about Uncertain Democracies* (Baltimore: Johns Hopkins University Press, 1986), 7.

[19] Reşat Kasaba, "Populism and Democracy in Turkey, 1946–61," in *Rules and Rights in the Middle East: Democracy, Law, and Society*, ed. Ellis Goldberg, Reşat Kasaba, and Joel S. Migdal (Seattle: University of Washington, 1993), 55.

[20] Nadia Urbinati, "Political Theory of Populism," *Annual Review of Political Science* 22 (2019), 6.10.

For DP leaders, democracy was important, but sustaining it was not their primary concern. It was but one of the institutional arrangements with which they were familiar. For example, President Celal Bayar, one of the party's founders, had been involved in political activity for over fifty years by 1960. In his youth, he had been a member of an underground organization whose intention was to restore a constitutional monarchy. Once it seized power, he became a high-ranking official. During the War of Independence, he organized an armed resistance movement, drawing on support from bandits and paramilitary organizations to expel the Greek army and protect the empire. After the establishment of a republic in 1923, he served the single-party regime as head of the country's leading bank; as minister of the economy during a period of state-led development; and, briefly, as prime minister. Finally, he had been the leader of an opposition movement that sought power through elections. People's priorities change throughout their lives, but there is no reason to assume Bayar's reliance on democratic institutions during the late 1940s and 1950s meant that he had wholly renounced other ways of gaining or maintaining power. His political strategies – and those of other Democrats – were influenced by the domestic and international conditions they faced. And, in the period this book considers, those conditions were connected to the early years of the Cold War.

Turkey and the United States-Led Cold War Order

Most of the DP founders spent their formative years as citizens of the Ottoman Empire. As the sociologist Karen Barkey argues, the Ottoman imperial order, at its most successful, was organized on a "hub-and-spoke" model with an imperial center connected through "distinct compacts" to intermediaries who represented various peripheral groups. Crucially, it was "regularly subject to negotiations over the degree of autonomy of intermediaries in return for military and fiscal compliance."[21] This model is also helpful for considering the United States-led Cold War order into which DP leaders integrated Turkey. While the American Cold War order was not "imperial" in precisely the terms Barkey uses, it was certainly "negotiated." And, as with democracy itself, the nature of the Cold War was never static.

During the DP's fifteen years of existence, the Cold War order changed dramatically. US policymakers had not developed a

[21] Karen Barkey, *Empire of Difference: The Ottoman Empire in Comparative Perspective* (Cambridge: Cambridge University Press, 2008), x, 9.

comprehensive approach to the postwar world in the years 1945 to 1947. In the words of historian Melvyn Leffler, US strategy in these years was "inchoate" and "vague."[22] Diplomats and bankers worked to create institutions like the United Nations (UN) and International Monetary Fund (IMF), which would undergird a new liberal international order, but from country to country, policies varied. In Japan, the United States empowered unions and civil society; in Vietnam, the United States helped reimpose European rule; in China, the United States backed a domestic, anti-communist regime. In Turkey, faced with threats from the Union of Soviet Socialist Republics (USSR), leaders of the ruling CHP and of the opposition DP sought to align themselves with the emerging liberal order, which offered the possibility of security. "In the absence of reliable information about America's basic intentions," political scientist Hakan Yılmaz argues, "the best shot of the Turkish leaders was to design their strategy of winning American support on the basis of America's revealed ideals."[23] These included an emphasis on liberal democracy, free trade, and, increasingly, anti-communism.

By the late 1940s, fears of Soviet expansion in Europe, Iran, the Mediterranean, and East Asia led the United States to develop a more consistently anti-communist approach. The United States intervened in elections, provided military aid, and promoted international security alliances. In Japan, the United States now followed a "reverse course" policy of supporting conservative politicians.[24] This was, in fact, an increasingly common policy around the world. In Italy and France, for example, the United States backed the expulsion of Communists from coalition governments. The Communist victory in China in 1949, followed by the outbreak of the Korean War in 1950, led the United States (and its allies) to adopt even stronger anti-communist postures at home and abroad. Amid these events, governments in Turkey, led by both the CHP and DP, pushed for their country's inclusion in the North Atlantic Treaty Organization (NATO). They also liberalized trade laws, thereby economically aligning Turkey with members of the security alliance.

[22] Melvyn Leffler, "The Emergence of an American Grand Strategy, 1945–1952," in *The Cambridge History of the Cold War*, vol. I: *Origins*, ed. Melvyn Leffler and Odd Arne Westad (Cambridge: Cambridge University Press, 2010), 87.

[23] Hakan Yılmaz, "Democratization from Above in Response to the International Context: Turkey, 1945–1950," *New Perspectives on Turkey* 17 (1997): 8–9.

[24] Yong Wook Lee, "The Origin of One-Party Domination: America's Reverse Course and the Emergence of the Liberal Democratic Party in Japan," *Journal of East Asian Affairs* 18, no. 2 (2004): 371–413.

By 1952, Turkey had become part of the American-led economic and security order. But this order was not fixed. Over the course of the 1950s, contradictions emerged and new challenges arose, reordering institutions and the relationships that sustained them. These challenges were economic (e.g., depressions and the question of how to fund rapid economic development schemes), environmental (e.g., unfavorable harvests and the question of how to sustainably expand agriculture), political (e.g., decolonization and the question of how to include newly independent states), and social (e.g., human rights and the question of how regimes might pursue economic liberalism without, necessarily, cultural liberalism).

The initial, uncertain years following World War II led many regimes to allow greater democracy – Turkey, of course, but also countries such as Guatemala and Italy democratized to the extent that they held more competitive elections than had been attempted for decades.[25] The challenges of the 1950s, however, led many regimes to de-democratize in order to maintain stability and their own grip on power. In Turkey and elsewhere, these aims were seldom viewed as distinct. Left-wing and Communist parties calling for radical change were often purged from state institutions and the wider society. Whereas the "revealed ideals" of the immediate postwar years emphasized liberal democracy and free trade, those of the 1950s emphasized anti-communism above all else. The United States not only supported coups carried out in the name of anti-communism (e.g., in Iran and Guatemala), but it also offered tentative support to revolutionary regimes that refrained from wholeheartedly supporting communism (e.g., in Egypt). Anti-revolutionary interventions aimed at reducing or eliminating democratic institutions were also supported if they promised stability (e.g., in France and Pakistan).

An important difference – at least conceptually – between the US-led order and the "hub and spoke" model of the Ottoman Empire was that the spokes of the US-led order were in communication with each other. Not only did leaders in Turkey, France, or Pakistan have relations with the United States, but they also had relations with one another. Turkish leaders and the public were aware of events in other countries. They discussed the events and took lessons from them. This give-and-take between members of the US order, both with the United States and with

[25] James Dunkerley, "Guatemala since 1930," in *The Cambridge History of Latin America*, vol. VII: *Mexico, Central America and the Caribbean*, ed. Leslie Bethell (Cambridge: Cambridge University Press, 1990), 217–221.

each other, is crucial to understanding the changing nature of the Cold War order, or even present-day international relations. As biographer Şevket Süreyya Aydemir has suggested, by the late 1950s Prime Minister Menderes was "in search of a new regime … and this regime would be something resembling [Charles] De Gaulle's new democracy in France," where the former general had been invited to develop a new presidential system following a military uprising.[26] In other words, restricted democracy or outright authoritarian rule was becoming an accepted norm and model among US allies.

In addition to sensing the shifting political norms of the American-led Cold War order, DP leaders clearly perceived its negotiated nature. They sent Turkish citizens to fight and die in the Korean War, supported US and British initiatives in the Middle East, and opened their economy to foreign investment. In return, they expected concessions. Again and again, they pushed American, British, and German officials for loans, aid, and support in international institutions. They rejected calls to cut domestic spending by pointing to the sacrifices they made for the common cause. Often these maneuvers worked, all or in part. Sometimes, of course, they failed. (This was not, after all, the "Turkish-led Cold War order.") Yet such was the nature of negotiation. The failure of DP leaders to consistently squeeze funds or support out of their allies was not evidence that Turkey was wholly subordinated to US dictates. Within the Cold War order, there was significant room for regimes to maneuver and extract benefits.

Prior to 1945 and the transition to multiparty politics, Turkey's leaders had also driven hard bargains with their peers in other states. But Turkey's strength in these negotiations was that no one was sure which side Turkey would take: Germany's? Britain's? The USSR's? In the period 1945–47, this ambiguity all but disappeared, and with the commitment to fight in Korea in 1950, Turkey's choice was clear. Negotiations since have begun with the assumption that Turkey is a dependable ally, one worthy of significant concessions. And while changes in the subsequent seven decades have strained relations, Turkey remains a country whose support is deemed worth cultivating.

Scholarship and Sources

Politicians, whether sensing themselves to be living amid grand events or hoping to shape the way they are remembered, often take the time to

[26] Şevket Süreyya Aydemir, *Menderes'in Dramı?* 7th ed. (Istanbul: Remzi Kitabevi, 2000 [1969]), 275.

record their memories for posterity. This is seldom the case with leaders of the DP. Some of this reticence was a legal matter: "Law 38," passed in 1962, prohibited "speech, writing, news, reports, images, drawings or other means and methods" that made "baseless and unjust" criticisms of the military's May 27 "Revolution," questioned the decisions of courts, or praised those who had been sentenced in connection with the Revolution. The punishment could range from a one- to five-year sentence. It remained in force until May 1969.[27] Yet, even years later, the silence persisted. Memoirs of party leaders and secondary accounts of the party devote nearly all their space to the party's struggle for power from 1945 to 1950 and/or the indignities its members suffered in prison after 1960.[28] By leaving such a conspicuous lacuna, DP memoirists have allowed their critics to shape the historical narrative.

The first scholarly accounts of the DP were produced in the late 1950s and early 1960s by researchers who had directly experienced DP's

[27] *Resmi Gazete* (RG), March 7, 1962, 6837–6838; RG, May 30, 1969, 14.

[28] Samet Ağaoğlu's *Arkadaşım Menderes: İpin Gölgesinde Günler* (My Friend Menderes: Days in the Shadow of the Noose) (Istanbul: Yapı Kredi Yayınları, 2011 [1967]), devoted only 78 out of 204 pages (38 percent) to the DP's decade in power, and Celal Bayar's *Başvekilim Adnan Menderes* (My Prime Minister Menderes), ed. İsmet Bozdağ (Istanbul: Tercüman Gazetesi, 1986 [1969]), devoted only 67 out of 171 pages (39 percent). Yet the trend generally continued after 1969 in such books as Orhan Cemal Fersoy's *Bir Devre Adını Veren Başbakan: Adnan Menderes* (A Prime Minister Who Gave an Era Its Name: Adnan Menderes) (Istanbul: Garanti Matbaası [1971]), which devoted 31 of 606 pages (5 percent), and Cemal Kutay's interview/biography *Üç Devirden Hakikatler: Celal Bayar'ın Yazmadığı ve Yazmayacağı* (Truths from Three Eras: What Celal Bayar Did Not Write and Will Not Write) (Istanbul: Alioğlu Yayınevi, 1982), which devoted 12 of 320 pages (4 percent). Memoirs that buck this trend include Rıfkı Salim Burçak's *On Yılın Anıları* (A Decade's Memoirs) (Ankara: Nurol Matbaacılık, 1998), which devotes 95 percent of its 788 pages (though this was not published until 1998, whereas his 1979 book *Türkiye'de Demokrasiye Geçiş* (Transition to Democracy in Turkey) (Ankara: Olgaç Yayınevi, 1979) did not discuss the party's time in office at all), and Mükerem Sarol's *Bilinmeyen Menderes* (The Unknown Menderes), vol. I (Istanbul: Kervan Yayınları, 1983), which gives 85 percent of its 975 pages to the 1950s, but was published in 1983 (and devotes more of its attentions to political squabbles than to policy). Independent of these examples, there is also an extensive literature on the trials of DP politicians that occurred on the island of Yassıada from 1960 to 1961. Though there are dozens of books one could cite, the following selection gives a flavor: Nazlı Ilıcak's *16 Yıl Sonra Salim Başol'u Yargılıyoruz* (Sixteen Years after, We Judge Salim Başol) (Istanbul: Tercüman, 1977); Rıfkı Salim Burçak's *Yassıada ve Öncesi* (Yassıada and Its Background) (Ankara: Çam Matbaası, 1976) and *İdamların İçyüzü* (The Inside Story of the Executions) (Ankara: Demokratlar Klübü Yayınları, 1997); Mithat Perin's *Yassıada Faciası: 27 Mayıs Darbesinden İdamlara Kadar İşkence Altında Ezilenlerin Dramı* (The Yassıada Tragedy: The Drama of Those Crushed by Torture from the May 27 Coup to the Executions) (Istanbul: Dem Basım Yayım A. Ş., 1990); Tevfik İleri's *Yassıada ve Kayseri Günlükleri* (Yassıada and Kayseri Diaries) (2003); and Doğan Yurdakul and F. Cengiz Erdinç's *Adalet Savaşçısı: Menderes'in Avukatı Burhan Apaydın'ın Anıları* (Warrior for Justice: The Memories of Menderes's Attorney Burhan Apaydın) (Istanbul: Kırmızıkedi, 2012).

decade of rule. In most cases, these authors were critical of Marxism and actively searching for alternative theories of modernization that could explain how "non-Western" countries like Turkey might develop toward liberal, capitalist democracy. The DP's illiberal methods of rule combined with its disregard for the advice of economic experts had alienated many of these scholars by the time of the party's removal. Thus, early accounts by Kemal Karpat (1959), Bernard Lewis (1961), Walter Weiker (1963), and Richard Robinson (1963) tended to criticize the DP, often in harsh terms, for its lack of commitment to secular, liberal values.[29] Some of these scholars were historians, producing accounts that covered the early 1800s to the 1950s; others were sociologists and political scientists focused on the post-Ottoman era. In all cases, their discussions of the DP drew on their own memories, coupled with statistics and interviews they had collected. Only Karpat was something of an outlier, in that he drew heavily on newspaper archives as well.

While the source base did not expand in the subsequent decades, the frameworks for understanding (and finding fault with) the DP grew more diverse. These frameworks tended to reflect trends in academia. For example, a new generation of scholars, often those educated in France during the late 1950s and 1960s, was less hostile to Marxist theories. They did not start from the premise that a liberal, capitalist order was desirable or that a party like the DP, dominated by landlords and bankers, could create a just order. Like the modernization theorists a decade earlier, scholars in the 1960s and 1970s, such as Doğan Avcıoğlu, Cem Eroğul, İsmail Cem (İpekçi), and Stefanos Yerasimos, were generally political scientists and sociologists rather than historians.[30] While Eroğul and Feroz Ahmad relied on major newspapers, most scholars stuck to statistics and more sweeping accounts. Rather than blame Turkey's stymied democratization on unfavorable conditions, such as lack of education, rapid urbanization, and insufficient access to capital, they placed the blame for these conditions on the "comprador"

[29] Kemal Karpat, *Turkey's Politics: The Transition to a Multi-Party System* (Princeton: Princeton University Press, 1959); Lewis, *The Emergence of Modern Turkey*; Walter Weiker, *The Turkish Revolution 1960–1961: Aspects of Military Politics* (Washington: The Brookings Institute, 1963); Richard Robinson, *The First Turkish Republic: A Case Study in National Development* (Cambridge, MA: Harvard University Press, 1963); Berkes, *The Development of Secularism in Turkey*.

[30] Doğan Avcıoğlu, *Türkiye'nin Düzeni: Dün, Bugün, Yarın I* (Istanbul: Tekin Yayınevi, 1996 [1969]); Aydemir, *Menderes'in Dramı?*; Eroğul, *Demokrat Parti*; Cem [İpekçi], *Türkiye'de Geri Kalmışlığın Tarihi*; Stefanos Yerasimos, *Azgelişmişlik Sürecinde Türkiye III: I. Dünya Savaşından 1971'e* (Istanbul: Gözlem Yayınları, 1976); Feroz Ahmad, *The Turkish Experiment in Democracy, 1950–1975* (Boulder: Westview Press, 1977).

bourgeois class that dominated politics. In the case of Şevket Süreyya Aydemir (*Menderes'in Dramı*), the finger was pointed even more directly at the specific personalities of the DP leaders themselves.[31]

From the mid 1970s onwards, scholars' attention turned to the task of bringing "the state back in" to their accounts and placing it in contrast to "society." Marxist-inspired scholars considered the state as an institution over which economically determined social classes struggled. For example, Çağlar Keyder argued that the DP's victory had ushered in "full class rule," enabling the bourgeoisie to take control of the state.[32] Scholars with a more Weberian bent analyzed how DP leaders had played on cultural (as opposed to economic) divisions in society to gain power. The most important example was sociologist Şerif Mardin, whose center–periphery thesis was also used by influential political scientists like Ergun Özbudun, Metin Heper, and Sabri Sayari.[33] Mardin described a social cleavage dating back to the mid 1800s, which "provided a nation-wide basis of allegiance for a party operating at the national level – the DP."[34] Though Mardin, personally, had been a critic of the DP, this framing of the party as a champion of the marginalized was in line with its leaders' self-presentation.

The severity of Turkey's 1980 coup led many scholars to question past military interventions (e.g., 1960) as well as the "Kemalist certainties" of the single-party era, which coup leaders praised. In this context, the DP's challenge to single-party rule and its ouster were considered more sympathetically. In addition to the memorialization of executed DP leaders

[31] Sina Akşin also notes the ongoing "uneasiness" and "bad temper" of Menderes and Bayar despite the DP's successes (*Kısa Türkiye Tarihi* [Istanbul: İş Bankası Kültür Yayınları, 2016 (2007)], 250).

[32] Çağlar Keyder, "The Political Economy of Turkish Democracy," *New Left Review* 115 (1979), 3–44. Keyder's arguments are further elaborated in his book *State and Class in Turkey: A Study in Capitalist Development* (New York: Verso, 1987). A similar argument can be found in Halil Karaveli's *Why Turkey Is Authoritarian: From Ataturk to Erdogan* (London: Pluto Press, 2018), 107.

[33] Mardin, "Center–Periphery Relations"; Ergun Özbudun, *Social Change and Political Participation in Turkey* (Princeton: Princeton University Press, 1976); Metin Heper, "The Recalcitrance of the Turkish Public Bureaucracy to 'Bourgeois Politics': A Multi-Factor Political Stratification Analysis," *Middle East Journal* 30, no. 4 (1976): 485–500; Sabri Sayarı, "The Turkish Party System in Transition," *Government and Opposition* 13, no. 1 (1978): 39–57. For discussions of the center–periphery thesis, see Onur Bakiner, "A Key to Turkish Politics? The Center–Periphery Framework Revisited," *Turkish Studies* 19, no. 4 (2018): 503–522, and Paul T. Levin, "Reflections on Şerif Mardin's Center–Periphery Thesis," *Turkish Studies* 24, nos. 3–4 (2023): 617–639.

[34] Mardin, "Center–Periphery Relations," 187.

beginning after 1987, the popular television program *32. Gün* (32nd Day) broadcast a ten-part documentary series titled *Demirkırat* in 1991 ("Demirkırat" or "Iron-Grey-Horse" being the nickname of the party, a reference to a famous steed from folklore).[35] While the episodes covering the DP's time in office were hardly favorable, the episodes leading up the 1950 election presented the DP in heroic terms, and the episodes covering its prosecution and punishment conveyed a sense of pathos.

The political and economic conditions of the 1980s, 1990s, and 2000s, characterized by export-oriented restructuring of the economy, post-Cold War globalization, and capitalist triumphalism, also tended to elevate the significance of the DP in people's minds. As the party that first consolidated Turkey's position within the Western order, it now seemed to be a harbinger. Accounts published since the late 1990s by Hakan Yılmaz, Mustafa Albayrak, John Vanderlippe, Cemil Koçak, Tanel Demirel, Mogens Pelt, and Reem Abou El-Fadl emphasize the role of international relations.[36] Unlike Marxist accounts from the late 1960s, which emphasized Turkey's dependency on the United States, these accounts present Turkish politicians as active foreign policymakers. In many cases, these scholars draw on a wider range of materials than did their predecessors. Archival materials from Turkey, the United States, and the United Kingdom (UK) are now combined with memoirs, newspapers, and parliamentary records.

Intellectuals' reconsideration of the "state" and the "nation" following the 1980 coup led scholars to look beyond Ankara and Istanbul to understand how the creation and consolidation of the republic were experienced. Furthermore, the electoral success of the Islamist political movement in the 1990s led scholars to question the nature and appeal of the republic's secular policies. As the party associated with moderating the strict secularism of the early republic, the DP (or at least its era)

35 James Meyer, "Memory and Political Symbolism in Post-September 12 Turkey: A History of the May 27th Debate" (Master's thesis, Princeton University, Princeton, 2001), 22–29.

36 Yılmaz, "Democratization from Above"; Mustafa Albayrak, *Türk Siyasi Tarihinde Demokrat Parti, 1946–1960* (Ankara: Phoenix Yayınevi, 2004); John Vanderlippe, *The Politics of Turkish Democracy: İsmet İnönü and the Formation of the Multi-Party System, 1938–1950* (Albany: SUNY Press, 2005); Cemil Koçak, *İkinci Parti: Türkiye'de İki Partili Siyasi Sistemin Kuruluş Yılları, 1945–1950*, vol. I (Istanbul: İletişim Yayınları, 2010); Tanel Demirel, *Türkiye'nin Uzun On Yılı: Demokrat Parti İktidarı ve 27 Mayıs Darbesi* (Istanbul: İstanbul Bilgi Üniversitesi Yayınları, 2011); Mogens Pelt, *Military Intervention and a Crisis of Democracy in Turkey: The Menderes Era and Its Demise* (London: I. B. Tauris, 2014); Reem Abou El-Fadl, *Foreign Policy as Nation Making: Turkey and Egypt in the Cold War* (Cambridge: Cambridge University Press, 2019).

become more intriguing to scholars.[37] Works by anthropologist Michael Meeker and historian Gavin Brockett may be the most influential in this regard.[38] Both focused on the provinces rather than the capital. Meeker considered how Ottoman traditions and local alliances persisted and shaped local political culture. Brockett popularized the idea of using provincial newspapers as a means of understanding Turkish history from a more bottom-up perspective. In the subsequent decade, provincial studies of the DP have become incredibly common.[39] At the same time that many scholars are trying to understand the DP at the grass roots,

[37] Key works on Turkey during the 1950s include Cangül Örnek, *Türkiye'nin Soğuk Savaş Düşünce Hayatı* (Istanbul: Can Yayınları, 2015); *Türkiye'nin 1950'li Yılları*, ed. Mete Kaan Kaynar (Istanbul: İletişim Yayınları, 2015); Begüm Adalet, *Hotels and Highways: The Construction of Modernization Theory in Cold War Turkey* (Stanford: Stanford University Press, 2018); Nicholas Danforth, *The Remaking of Republican Turkey: Memory and Modernity since the Fall of the Ottoman Empire* (Cambridge: Cambridge University Press, 2021); Sarah-Neel Smith, *Metrics of Modernity: Art and Development in Postwar Turkey* (Berkeley: University of California Press, 2022).

[38] Michael Meeker, *A Nation of Empire: The Ottoman Legacy of Turkish Modernity* (Berkeley: University of California Press, 2001); Gavin D. Brockett, *How Happy to Call Oneself a Turk: Provincial Newspapers and the Negotiation of a Muslim National Identity* (Austin: University of Texas Press, 2011). See also: Horst Unbehaun, *Türkiye Kırsalında Kliyentalizm ve Siyasal Katılım: Datça Örneği: 1923–1992* (Ankara: Ütüpya Yayınları, 2005).

[39] The increase in provincial studies is clearly connected with the rapid expansion of Turkey's university system. Dozens of universities have been established in the past two decades as part of a concerted government effort to open an institution in every province. As a result, there are more opportunities for academic works focused on local history. For example: Zehra Arslan, "Demokrat Parti Dönemi'nde Trabzon, 1950–1960" (PhD diss., Karadeniz Teknik Üniversitesi, Trabzon, 2011); Mehmet Pınar, "Van'da Demokrat Parti Teşkilatlanması," *Atatürk Dergisi* 2, no. 2 (2013): 31–55; Fatma Aydın, "Demokrat Parti İktidarı Uygulamalarının Bir Taşra Kenti Basınına Yansımaları: Balıkesir Örneği, 1950–1960" (PhD diss., Balıkesir Üniversitesi, Balıkesir, 2013); Süleyman Akkuş, "Demokrat Parti Aydın Milletvekilleri ve TBMM'deki Faaliyetleri, 1950–1954" (PhD diss., Adnan Menderes Üniversitesi, Aydın, 2016); Béatrice Garapon, "Aux origines de la Turquie conservatrice: Une sociologie historique du Parti démocrate, 1946–1960" (PhD diss., L'université de Bordeaux, 2017); Ercan Bolat, "Demokrat Parti Dönemi Mersin (İçel) Milletvekilleri ve Meclis Faaliyetleri, 1950–1960" (Master's thesis, Ömer Halisdemir Üniversitesi, Niğde, 2017); Fikret Avcı, "Demokrat Parti (DP) İktidarı Döneminde Malatya: Şehir, Siyaset ve Toplum, 1950–1960" (PhD diss., İnönü Üniversitesi, Malatya, 2018); Bayram Akça and Osman Köse, "Demokrat Parti Dönemi'nde Muğla'da Siyasi Hayat," *Sosyal ve Beşeri Bilimler Araştırmaları Dergisi* 41 (2018): 161–185; Gülten Madendağ, "Demokrat Parti Döneminde Adana'da Gündelik Hayat" (PhD diss., Sakarya Üniversitesi, Sakarya, 2018); Aymelek Şenel, "Demokrat Parti İzmir İl Örgütü, 1946–1960: Muhalefetten İktidara Bir Siyasal Partinin Yerel Politikası" (PhD diss., Manisa Celal Bayar Üniversitesi, Manisa, 2018); Çağrı Pişkin, "Demokrat Döneminde Nevşehir" (Master's thesis, Nevşehir Hacı Bektaş Veli Üniversitesi, Nevşehir, 2019); Filiz Gemici, "Demokrat Parti Dönemi Adapazarı-Sakarya, 1950–1960" (PhD diss., Sakarya Üniversitesi, Sakarya, 2019); Emrah Gemicioğlu, "Demokrat Parti Döneminde Hakkâri'de Siyasal Yaşam ve Yapılan Kamu Harcamaları, 1950–1960" (Master's thesis, Van Yüzüncü Yıl Üniversitesi, Van, 2021);

others have begun considering its leading personalities in more detail.[40] Though certainly "top-down" accounts, these works fill a gap in the existing literature. Moreover, their focus on party leaders can be supplemented by recent works that draw on archival material to focus on the DP parliamentary group and organizational aspects of the party such as fundraising.[41]

This book draws inspiration from all this scholarship in an attempt to recover some sense of what DP leaders thought (or at least *claimed*) they were doing during their ten years in power. I have relied on periodicals connected with the party and archival documents, including the transcripts of parliamentary group meetings. Incorporating such materials is a significant contribution to existing literature on the party. Even the best scholarship on the DP has tended to rely on periodicals that became critical of it (publications like *Cumhuriyet* [Republic], *Vatan* [Homeland], and *Forum*) or ones that were directly tied to opposition

Esra Karataş, "Demokrat Parti Döneminde Adana'da Siyasal Hayat, 1950–1960" (Master's thesis, Mersin Üniversitesi, Mersin, 2021); Oğulcan Yücebaş, "Demokrat Parti Döneminde Menemen, 1950–1960" (Master's thesis, İzmir Kâtip Çelebi Üniversitesi, İzmir, 2021); Tuğba Tamküpeli, "Edirne Siyasi Tarihinde Demokrat Parti Dönemi, 1950–1960" (Master's thesis, Tekirdağ Namık Kemal Üniversitesi, Tekirdağ, 2021); İsmail Kocakaya, "1950–1960 Yılları Arasında Demokrat Parti Döneminde Biga" (Master's thesis, Çanakkale On Sekiz Mart Üniversitesi, Çanakkale, 2021); Hasan Karakuzu, "Demokrat Parti Dönemi'nde Zonguldak, 1950–1960" (Master's thesis, Nevşehir Hacı Bektaş Veli Üniversitesi, Nevşehir, 2021); Murat Akgümüş, "Kayseri in the Period of the Democrat Party, 1950–1960" (PhD diss., Erciyes Üniversitesi, Kayseri, 2023); Fatih Kıyıcı, "Demokrat Parti Döneminde (1950–1960) Erzurum'da Iktisadi Hayat" (PhD diss., Atatürk Üniversitesi, Ankara, 2024).

40 For example: Erkan Şenşekerci, *Türk Devriminde Celal Bayar (1918–1960)* (Istanbul: Alfa Yayınları, 2000); Şerif Demir, *Türk Siyasi Tarihinde Adnan Menderes* (Istanbul: Paraf Yayınları, 2010); Rasim Koç, *İdam Sehpasındaki Dışişleri Bakanı: Fatin Rüştü Zorlu* (Istanbul: Ötüken, 2010); Atiye Emiroğlu, *Hasan Polatkan* (Ankara: Nobel Yayın, 2011); Abdurrahman Bozkurt, *Tevfik İleri Cumhuriyetin İkinci Eğitim Mimarı* (Istanbul: İdil, 2012); A. Yavuz Ergun, *CHPli Menderes, 1931–1945: Tek Parti Dönemi'nde Adnan Menderes'in Siyasi Yaşamı* (Istanbul: Boyut, 2017); Erol Yüksel, *Milli Mücadele'den 27 Mayıs'a Bir Siyasetçi: Refik Koraltan* (Ankara: Atatürk Araştırma Merkezi, 2018); Hacı Veli Gök, "Demokrat Parti Döneminin Önemli Bir Siması: Namık Gedik ve Siyasi Faaliyetleri" (PhD diss., İstanbul Üniversitesi, Istanbul, 2020).

41 Kaan Cem Geniş, "Demokrat Parti'ye Yapılan Bağışlara Dair Kayıtlar (1950–1960)," *Atatürk Dergisi*, 9, no. 1 (2020): 73–96; Haydar Temür, *Demokrat Parti'de Parti İçi Muhalefet, 1946–1960* (Istanbul: Tarih Vakfı Yurt Yayınları, 2022); Yunus Özdurğun, "Demokrat Parti iktidarı Hakkındaki Mali Yolsuzluk Iddialarının Yassıada Yargılamalarına ve Dönemin Siyasetine Yansımaları" (PhD diss., Van Yüzüncü Yıl Üniversitesi, Van, 2022); Fatma Eylem Çoban, "Demokrat Parti Döneminde Hükümet-Iş Adamı Ilişkileri" (PhD diss., Dokuz Eylül Üniversitesi, Izmir, 2022); Cemil Koçak, *Demokrat Parti İktidârı (1950–1960), I: Demokratlar ve Halkçılar,1950–1954* (Istanbul: Timaş Yayınları, 2024).

(like *Ulus* [Nation] or *Akis* [Echo]). Even more thorough accounts of the party usually stick to its "official" DP paper, *Zafer* (Victory).[42] There are arguments in defense of these choices. For example, opposition papers had high circulations and often published news that the ruling party would have preferred to ignore. With such reasons in mind, I have referred to them as well. But I am also interested in what DP leaders said and wrote, how members justified their actions and presented issues to the public. Though these sources are often (if not inherently) self-serving, I am skeptical that they are fundamentally less useful than more commonly used sources, which also have biases and glaring hypocrisies.

This book also considers documents from government archives in Turkey, Britain, and the United States. In the case of Turkey, there are only limited documents available for the 1950s. Nonetheless, I draw on what is available: reports, statistics, and court records of the DP's prosecution in 1960–61. As for foreign diplomatic material, I draw on the statistics these sources provide, as well as their accounts of negotiations with Turkish leaders. Despite my reliance on these sources, I find their limitations to be quite clear: not only do foreign officials lack inside knowledge of DP policymaking, but they consistently assert their own biased interpretations. The "Leading Personalities in Turkey" reports published by the British embassy in Ankara illustrate the pleasures and perils of foreign archives. These annual reports give thumbnail biographies of over one hundred important political and military figures. The gossipy quality of their prose is entertaining. DP parliamentarian and *Havadis* (Events) editor Bahadır Dülger is "[r]ather ponderous and not overbright … a heavy but forceful speaker." Turkey's first female lawyer, Süreyya Ağaoğlu, is "a mischievous tale-bearer and must be treated with caution as she is alleged to work for the Turkish police." Parliamentarian and newspaper-owner Mükerrem Sarol is "universally disliked and, although intelligent, is politically and morally dishonest." And opposition journalist Metin Toker, although "fearless," is "basically not very bright."[43]

Yet these descriptions often reveal more about the British diplomats than about their subjects. Foreign Minister Fatin Rüştü Zorlu, for

[42] Originally started by DP supporters Zeki Rıza Sporel, Yusuf Ziya Öniş, Mahmut Baler, Kâzım Arın, and İhsan Doruk in 1949, *Zafer* was eventually bought out by the party itself. At the time of the 1960 coup, shares were held by: the party (940,000); journalist Mümtaz Faik Fenik (25,000); Halim Alanyalı (20,000); athlete/businessman Zeki Rıza Sporel (10,000); and İzmir tobacco merchant Haydar Dündar (5,000) (Korkmaz Alemdar, *İletişim ve Tarih* [Istanbul: İmge Kitabevi Yayınları, 1996], 138).

[43] See Bernard Burrows to Selwyn Lloyd, "Leading Personalities in Turkey," August 18, 1959, British National Archives, Foreign Office (hereafter FO) 371/144740.

example, is “ruthless and cynical, but highly able and conscientious to the point of fanaticism in upholding Turkish interests. His knowledge of economics is limited, but he has great faith in his own quick decisions.”[44] Here, as elsewhere in British archives, we find contempt masking an inability to wring concessions from Turkish officials. US diplomats likewise (albeit with less flowery language than their British peers) conflate support for US national interests with a sound “knowledge of economics.” Zorlu may well have been uninformed in matters of economics, but not because British diplomats tell us so.

Reading traditional sources with this skepticism is important, given the lack of equivalent archival material on the Turkish side during the 1950s. The majority of documents made available to researchers at the Prime Ministerial Archives in Ankara and Istanbul are rather anodyne notices of promotions, requests for permission to travel abroad, and the like. And though, I am certain, some keen future researcher will approach these in an innovative manner, the randomness of the available digitalized documents makes it difficult to assess how representative they even are. The most tantalizing documents currently available, the troves of documents compiled for the post-coup trials held on the island of Yassıada, which contain fascinating details of DP corruption, are similarly unsystematic and likely favor material that casts the DP in the worst light while leaving its critics largely unblemished. Moreover, these files illustrate the precarious nature of archival access: the Yassıada files simply disappeared from the digital database around mid 2020, only to reappear a year or so later without explanation.

Outline of the Book

This book is deeply indebted to generations of scholars, writing in English and Turkish, who have studied the DP and, more broadly, Turkey in the 1950s. Each chapter presents new material – or new juxtapositions of old material – with the hope that even experts on the topic will come away with new insights. The six chapters present a chronological account of the DP, its leaders, and their efforts to achieve their domestic political ambitions in the context of an emerging Cold War order. Chapter 1 looks at the biographies of the DP’s four founders up through the establishment of the party in early 1946. Each of these founders (Celal Bayar, Refik Koraltan, Fuad Köprülü, and Adnan

44 Ibid.

Menderes) played an important role in politics long before breaking with the single-party regime. While most accounts of modern Turkish history note the fact that these men had once been members of the regime, few accounts give more than thumbnail sketches.[45] By contrast, this chapter emphasizes the extent of their involvement in the politics of both the late Ottoman Empire and early Republic of Turkey, crafting the economic, educational, and legal institutions of the state.

Chapter 2 covers the years in which the DP challenged the ruling CHP by looking at some of the young activists whose enthusiastic efforts helped the party achieve victory. These activists include Samet Ağaoğlu, a well-connected bureaucrat and intellectual, who played a key role in promoting the DP as a "liberal" party seeking to limit the role of the state. The chapter also looks beyond ideological battles in Istanbul and Ankara to consider the ways in which the party took shape in the provinces, specifically Balıkesir and Malatya (see Map 0.1). The first was a province on the west coast with a majority Sunni/Turkish population and long-standing connections with European markets; the second was an eastern province, oriented toward Syria in the Ottoman period, with a sizeable Kurdish/Alevi population.[46] In both cases, we see

[45] There are a few notable exceptions to this generalization, such as Kemal Karpat ("Actors and Issues in Turkish Politics, 1950–1960: Prototypes and Stereotypes," *International Journal of Turkish Studies* 17, nos. 1 and 2 [2011]), but his discussion remains focused on the leaders' individual psychology, drawing heavily on the works of Şevket Süreyya Aydemir (*Menderes'in Dramı?*) and Cihad Baban (*Politika Galerisi: Büstler ve Portreler* [Istanbul: Remzi Kitabevi, 1970]). Yüksel Taşkın (*Anti-Komünizmden Küreselleşme Karşıtlığına Milliyetçi Muhafazakar Entelijansiya* [Istanbul: İletişim Yayınları, 2007]) devotes about six pages (91–96) to the lives of Bayar and Menderes as a means of introducing his larger argument that they and the conservative parties that followed them "contributed more to rooting Kemalist reforms in society than did the voluntarism of the republican cadres" (95). Morgens Pelt gives thumbnail descriptions of the four leaders in the space of two pages but tends to emphasize their limited role in the creation of the republic compared with "prominent CHP personalities" (*Military Intervention*, 12–13). Reem Abou el-Fadl (*Foreign Policy as Nation Making*) moves through these connections in four-and-a-half pages (78–83), mostly focusing on Bayar, with a few mentions of Menderes and a gesture toward Koraltan and the Ağaoğlu family. And though Cemil Koçak's detailed account (*Demokrat Parti İktidârı (1950–1960) 1*) emphasizes that the central leaders of the DP were the "inheritors" of the Unionists, doesn't elaborate on their past connections (655).

[46] Anthropologist Jenny White describes Alevis as "a non-Sunni syncretistic Muslim minority that cross-cuts Kurdish and Turkish ethnic designations." More precise definitions are hard to come by. An expert like David Shankland may emphasize the centrality of Shia religious texts like the *Buyruk* (Command) as a basis of commonality among Alevis, while another expert like Elise Massicard may suggest that even this work lacks a common interpretation. Widespread practices like not fasting during Ramazan, not praying five times daily, holding mixed-gender ceremonies, and preferring to focus on mystical contemplation have led to accusations that Alevis are not "real" Muslims. These accusations encourage discrimination and persecution (David Shankland, *The*

that political parties were closely allied with wealthy landowners and that differences in affiliation tended to depend on which local faction had established a closer relationship with the state circa 1946. In other words, while intellectuals like Ağaoğlu promoted the DP as an anti-statist party, in tune with the liberalism of the postwar era, we see from early on that, at the provincial level, supporters were more concerned with *who* controlled the state.

The remaining chapters focus on the DP's years in power. Chapter 3 covers the party's first term in office (1950–54), focusing on two aspects of this period: first, its leaders' consolidation of power; and second, the ways in which their economic policies of lower taxes, expanded credit, and increased investment depended on close relations with the United States. To secure economic and military aid, DP leaders sent soldiers to fight in the Korean War and continuously reminded US officials of Turkey's strategic value. Drawing on diplomatic archives from the United States, Britain, and Turkey, this chapter reveals the dynamics of these negotiations. Moreover, the chapter shows how control of economic policymaking was a crucial arena of intraparty power struggles, both among the top leadership and at the provincial level. Again, looking at examples from Balıkesir and Malatya, we see how tensions increased between the parties during the early 1950s. We also see how the DP's control of government allowed it to steer projects toward provinces that it controlled and penalize provinces that rejected it.

Chapter 4 and Chapter 5 focus on the middle years of DP rule (1953–58), when economic conditions ceased to favor the party. A slump in global demand reduced Turkey's access to foreign exchange, while the government's expansionary monetary policies encouraged inflation. Economic policy became an electoral liability as much as a strength. Facing domestic criticism, DP governments limited the bounds of public dissent in schools, the media, and political organizations. These efforts to constrain institutions that provided checks and balances on the government constituted an active policy of de-democratization. At the same time, the party's leaders played international creditors off against

Alevis in Turkey: The Emergence of a Secular Islamic Tradition [London: Routledge, 2003], x; Elise Massicard, *Türkiye'den Avrupa'ya Alevi Hareketinin Siyasallaşması* [Istanbul: İletişim Yayınları, 2005], 175–176; Jenny White, "Islam and Politics in Contemporary Turkey," in *The Cambridge History of Turkey*, ed. Reşat Kasaba [Cambridge: Cambridge University Press, 2008], 359).

one another and sought access to additional credit. Chapter 4 ends in November 1955, as frustration among DP parliamentarians reached a breaking point, leading liberal members of the party to resign and triggering a crisis that brought down Prime Minister Menderes's cabinet – if not the prime minister himself.

Chapter 5 covers the period between the DP's 1955 political crisis and its greatest financial crisis (a devaluation and bailout in 1958). During this period, Prime Minister Menderes and his allies sought to sustain their economic policies while also retaining political power. Achieving these goals required marginalizing intraparty critics and silencing the media, academics, and the opposition. Unlike in previous chapters, however, we see DP leaders' gambits either failing outright or achieving less than satisfactory results. US and European creditors took a harder line with the government; radical political movements gained popularity in neighboring states such as Syria and Iraq; and turnout in the 1957 elections fell, such that the DP won with only a plurality of the vote. By the summer of 1958, a currency devaluation and bailout were no longer avoidable. Only the uncertainty caused by a revolution in Iraq enabled the DP to secure comparatively favorable terms in negations.

Chapter 6 focuses on the DP's final two years in power (1958–60), which followed a loan restructuring agreement with Western creditors. During these years, DP leaders attempted to implement unpopular economic policies while still holding on to power. Their main tactic was to create and promote the "Homeland Front," a mass political organization (ostensibly distinct from the DP) that would draw the public together to face the challenges of the moment. Though many people did join willingly, the government also relied on high-pressure tactics and propaganda to encourage participation. During this same period, the government increased pressure on the opposition through both legislation and extralegal actions like mobilizing mobs to attack opposition leaders and their facilities. These illiberal – and, often, illegal – methods were, I argue, part of a more general shift toward illiberal, less democratic norms of governance among American Cold War allies in the late 1950s. By 1960, however, the DP's authoritarian actions had alienated important domestic groups, including academics, bureaucrats, and military officers, which led to its removal from power on May 27.

Taken together, these chapters give an overview of the DP's "rise and fall" that emphasizes the role of leading figures in the party at the national and provincial levels, highlighting these leaders' connections to the single-party era and the ways in which those connections shaped their actions during the 1950s. During the years 1945–60 changing international conditions served to empower particular political coalitions in Turkey and produce dramatic changes, but these factions and the developments they wrought were part of a longer history. In highlighting continuities, this book unsettles binary accounts of the DP and, more generally, of Turkey's political history.

1 Young Ottomans: The Origins of the Democrat Party, 1908–1946

Ali Adnan was a teenager when he first met Mahmut Celal, general secretary of the Committee of Union and Progress (İTC) in the province of İzmir. Though he had no formal role in the government, as a leading "Unionist" Celal was part of a political organization, spread throughout the Ottoman Empire, which had seized control of the state in 1913. Adnan was part of a group of students who had come to the general secretary to request that the government do something to limit the spread of Christian missionary activity at foreign-run private schools. From the perspective of these students, the missionaries were contributing to the disintegration of the empire; its former Balkan provinces, now independent, Christian-dominated states, had attacked in 1912 and seized substantial territory. Fearing massacres, large numbers of Muslim refugees were fleeing to territories still under Ottoman control. Rulers of the empire were now perceiving the empire's Christian subjects as a potential fifth column, and missionaries as tantamount to spies.

How precisely Celal responded to Adnan and the other students is unclear. As he would later recall, he made efforts to investigate the issue and saw to it that a few "zealous Christian teachers" were replaced, but the Ottoman government was bound by its treaties with foreign governments and had little ability to regulate missionary activity.[1] Even at the time, however, these treaty obligations did not deter the actions that Unionist officials and their networks throughout the empire were taking against Christian subjects. Even before Celal was appointed general secretary in 1913, Unionists in coastal regions had been enforcing a boycott on non-Muslim (primarily Greek) businesses and organizing attacks on non-Muslim Ottoman subjects, pressuring them to flee their homes. By uprooting the empire's Greek subjects in this manner, Unionist government officials hoped to create a set of facts on the ground that would be favorable to them in advance of either a population

[1] Bayar, *Başvekilim Adnan*, 21–22.

exchange or the outbreak of yet another war. Celal was closely involved in these activities, which helped force out 130,000 Greeks by the summer of 1914.[2] Under pressure from European states and the Orthodox Patriarchate to halt these expulsions, the Unionist interior minister, Talat, toured the Aegean region, ostensibly to stop the attacks. When Celal met his superior near İzmir to discuss the issue, he informed Talat, "As you wish, sir, the forced migrations that were hoped for have ended because none remain to leave."[3]

The students' desire to limit missionary activity along with the ongoing boycotts and attacks on Greek-owned businesses were part of a larger effort by the Unionist government and Ottoman elites to preserve the state. Yet, in doing so, they were actively redefining who belonged to that state and what activities were permitted within its borders. These were not new debates: many Ottoman policymakers had been skeptical of the favorable terms of trade and concessions of legal sovereignty that imperial rulers had made to European merchants and states. But the events of the early 1900s gave matters a new urgency. The Italian invasion of Ottoman Libya, followed by the Balkan Wars, had empowered policymakers who spoke of establishing a "national economy," free from foreign control.[4] As war spread to all of Europe and the Middle East, Unionist leaders pursued these efforts with a murderous vigor. In İzmir, one of the most populous and diverse provinces in the empire, Celal focused on "Turkifying" industries. In the aftermath of World War I, both he and Adnan would play an active role in fighting off invading Greek and Italian armies and, in their own ways, establishing the economic, social, and political order of the Republic of Turkey. In 1945 – now bearing the surnames Bayar and Menderes – they would join with two other men who had come of age in the last years of the Ottoman Empire, Fuat Köprülü and Refik Koraltan. Together, they would establish the DP.

As the meeting between a young Celal Bayar and an even younger Adnan Menderes suggests, the creation of the DP was rooted

[2] Şenşekerci, *Türk Devriminde*, 13. For discussion of the pressures placed on coastal Greek populations in the first half of 1914, see Nicholas Doumanis, *Before the Nation: Christian–Muslim Coexistence and Its Destruction in Late Ottoman Anatolia* (Oxford: Oxford University Press, 2012), 148–152; Emre Erol, *The Ottoman Crisis in Western Anatolia: Turkey's Belle Epoque and the Transition to a Modern Nation State* (New York: I. B. Tauris, 2016), 110–193; Ryan Gingeras, *Fall of the Sultanate: The Great War and the End of the Ottoman Empire 1908–1922* (Cambridge: Cambridge University Press, 2016), 97; Hans Lukas Kieser, *Talaat Pasha: Father of Modern Turkey, Architect of Genocide* (Princeton: Princeton University Press, 2018), 175–177.

[3] Kutay, *Üç Devirden Hakikatler*, 56.

[4] For a discussion of efforts to create a "national economy," see Zafer Toprak, *Türkiye'de Milli İktisat, 1908–1918* (Istanbul: Doğan Kitap, 2012 [1982]).

in decades-long relationships and political struggles. While the founders were certainly representative of powerful groups, including businessmen and landlords, that had grown disenchanted with the single-party regime, they were also individuals who brought a lifetime of experience to bear on their choices and actions. By weaving together an account of the final years of the empire and early years of the republic with the intersecting paths of their lives, we see that the sudden emergence of multiparty democracy in Turkey in 1945 was part of a longer process of state formation. And, to the extent that democratization and Turkey's participation in the Cold War order were driven by economic and political conditions, those conditions were shaped by particular people, with their hopes, dreams, ambitions, and enmities.

Democrats as Unionists, 1908–1923

The eldest of the DP's founders, Mahmut Celal, was born into a family deeply affected by the changes occurring in the nineteenth-century Ottoman Empire. His father, Abdullah Fehmi, was a product of the mid century reformist movement, educated at the *Darülmuallimin*, an Istanbul teachers' college established in 1846 by some of the empire's leading officials. After graduation, he had returned to his Balkan hometown of Berkofca (Berkovica), where he taught at a secondary school established in the 1860s by another leading reformer, Midhat Paşa. He married and had two children there, but the family was forced to flee during the Russo-Ottoman War of 1877–78. They resettled in Umurbey, a village in the coastal province of Hüdavendigâr. Celal was born there in 1883. Like many Muslim subjects, he and his family experienced both Ottoman leaders' efforts to reform imperial institutions and their inability to guarantee security in western regions. These experiences inculcated in people like Celal a concern with strengthening state power so that it could provide security, particularly for its Muslim subjects, who had no foreign state like Russia or Great Britain to defend them.

Though his father was an educator, Celal never completed more than a secondary education. After a brief stint in Istanbul at age twelve, he returned to Umurbey to complete his basic education. His father taught him a bit of Arabic and French. According to one biographer, he longed throughout these years to move to the nearby urban center of Gemlik, or even the provincial capital of Bursa.[5] After finishing secondary school, he

[5] Şenşekerci, *Türk Devriminde*, 22–23.

worked in Gemlik alongside his uncle, a local judge. The two worked in the administration of the Regie, the European-controlled tobacco monopoly, which collected Ottoman farmers' production as a means of paying off the empire's large, international debts. In his youth, Celal's uncle had been a member of secret political organizations that advocated for constitutional government and economic sovereignty.[6] Through this uncle, Celal developed similar interests. He also become friends with a local bookseller who gave him copies of recent publications by "Young Turks," who advocated for a return to constitutional rule.

Celal moved to Bursa and began taking classes to master aspects of the local silk trade. These included advanced French and Arabic so that he could deal with merchants from the Levant. Soon, he found a clerical job at the local branch of Ziraat Bankası (Agricultural Bank). In 1903, at the age of twenty, he married into the well-connected İnegöllüzâde family. The marriage drew Celal into international financial networks. His new uncle-in-law, for example, was involved in establishing the local branch of Deutsche Orient Bank, at which Celal soon worked.[7]

Orient Bank was the third major German commercial bank to be established in the Ottoman Empire since 1888. Thereafter, German involvement in the empire had increased significantly. German banks began purchasing Ottoman bond issues and investing in capital-intensive projects like railways. Though France remained the empire's main creditor, the German share of Ottoman debt was rising quickly and would soon surpass that of the United Kingdom.[8] For some political activists, German support for the empire's autocratic system was a reason to be

[6] Aydemir, *Menderes'in Dramı?* 153–154; Şenşekerci, *Türk Devriminde*, 23. In the 1870s, Celal Bayar's uncle had been a follower of Ali Suavi, one of the more radical thinkers among the group of intellectuals called "Young Ottomans." In the 1860s and 1870s, they challenged the economic liberalism and bureaucratic rationalization efforts of the preceding generation. Suavi, in particular, emphasized religious belief as the basis for concepts of justice, equality, and constitutional rule. He died in a raid on the imperial palace following the suspension of the constitution. Bayar's uncle took part as well. For discussions of Ali Suavi, see Şerif Mardin, *The Genesis of Young Ottoman Thought: A Study in the Modernization of Turkish Political Ideas* (Princeton: Princeton University Press, 1962), 360–384; Deniz Kılınçoğlu, *Economics and Capitalism in the Ottoman Empire* (London: Routledge, 2016), 135–136; Berna Turnaoğlu, *The Formation of Turkish Republicanism* (Princeton: Princeton University Press, 2017), 74–76.

[7] Şenşekerci, *Türk Devriminde*, 26–27.

[8] V. Necla Geyikdağı, *Foreign Investment in the Ottoman Empire: International Trade and Relations, 1854–1914* (London: I. B. Tauris, 2011), 100–108. According to Şevket Pamuk, Germany's share of Ottoman debt rose from 11.7 percent in 1890 to 15 percent in 1898 to 21 percent in 1914; the UK's share declined from 23.1 percent to 17.9 percent to 14 percent in these same years (*The Ottoman Empire and European Capitalism* [Cambridge: Cambridge University Press, 1987], 74–75).

suspicious; for others – especially military officers – there was much to admire about Germany regardless of its support for the sultan.[9]

The issue of dependence on foreign powers was but one set of tensions within the "Young Turk" opposition movement in the early 1900s, when Celal became formally involved in underground political organizing. In 1907, he joined a constitutionalist group, the abovementioned Committee of Union and Progress (i.e., the İTC). By 1908, he had become its general secretary for Hüdavendigâr. As the Unionist representative for the empire's second-most populous province, he was well-placed when the organization forced the sultan to restore constitutional rule in 1908.[10] When an uprising in 1909 briefly removed the Unionists from power, Celal traveled the region, recruiting fighters to march on Istanbul and reinstate the organization.

In June 1912, Unionists were again forced from office by a military uprising. This political instability in Istanbul, combined with an ongoing war to defend Trablusgarp (modern Libya) from an Italian invasion, encouraged Balkan states to attack the empire's western provinces in October 1912. Mounting defeats served as a pretext for the Unionists to once again force their way into power in January 1913. Though, they succeeded in retaking some European territory, their government had little choice but to accept large territorial losses. When fighting in the Balkans ended with the Treaty of Constantinople in September 1913, the Kingdom of Greece was left in control of the city of Salonika, where the Unionist organization had been based, and multiple islands within reach of important Ottoman territories on the Anatolian mainland.

While the five years between the Unionists' initial revolution and their seizure of power in 1913 were marked by extensive territorial losses and political unrest, they were also a time of cultural renaissance. The government initially reduced censorship and allowed the formation of political organizations. Ideas that an earlier generation of Ottoman students

[9] According to Naci Yorulmaz, many German officials in 1908 feared a loss of influence following the reinstatement of the constitution. Kaiser Wilhelm II and military leaders, however, correctly predicted that their connections with the Ottoman officer corps would enable them to maintain influence. Especially after 1909, when the civilian Unionist leaders were ousted from power and were forced to rely on Unionist officers, Germany's position grew more secure (*Arming the Sultan: German Arms Trade and Personal Diplomacy in the Ottoman Empire before World War I* [London: I. B. Tauris, 2014], 230–236).

[10] In 1906–07 Hüdavendigâr had a population of 1.69 million (about 8 percent of the entire Ottoman population). The only province more populous was Aydın, with 8.2 percent. For detailed population statistics for 1906–07, see Kemal Karpat, *Ottoman Population, 1830–1914: Demographic and Social Characteristics* (Madison: University of Wisconsin Press, 1985), 168–169.

could only have discussed by traveling abroad were now debated openly.[11] Young radicals displaced an older generation and gained influence in key institutions. The DP founder most closely engaged in this aspect of the period was Köprülüzade Mehmet Fuat, the descendent of a wealthy Ottoman family that had dominated imperial politics in the late 1600s and continued to offer up its members for posts in government.[12]

Born in 1890, Fuat entered the imperial School of Law in 1907, but his interests lay elsewhere. Within a year of starting university, he was publishing poetry and literary essays; in another two years, he would leave without a degree. Making use of his family's extensive library, he became his own teacher while working as an instructor at prominent high schools in Istanbul. Initially, he was an enthusiast of *divan* poetry and the collage of Turkish, Persian, and Arabic words it drew on. At a time when advocating for a "national" language was increasingly popular among educated youth, Fuat and his peers advocated for the mixture of cultures. As late as 1911, when he began joining organizations like the "Turkish Society," he was still writing that strictly "national" literature was impossible in the twentieth century.[13]

The Greek capture of Salonika in 1912 forced the Unionists to relocate to Istanbul and deeply affected Fuat's intellectual development. He now formed close acquaintances with the advocates of Turkish nationalism whom he had so recently challenged. He was particularly influenced by men like Ziya Gökalp, who argued for an essential Turkish culture that persisted regardless of the civilizational structures and technology that had developed around it. Fuat now joined nationalist organizations like Turkish Hearth (*Türk Ocağı*) and co-edited magazines like the *Milli Tetebbular Mecmuası* (National Research Journal). In 1913, at the age of

[11] The period of press and political freedom was relatively short-lived. As Levi-Aksu describes, the mass gatherings celebrating the restoration of the constitution in 1908 soon became a source of concern for the Unionists. After the 1909 countercoup, the Unionist government restricted political freedoms. According to Brummett, by 1911, when war with Italy began, press freedom had largely come to an end (Palmira Brummett, *Image and Imperialism in the Ottoman Revolutionary Press, 1908–1911* [Albany: State University of New York Press, 2000], 9; Noemi Levy-Aksu, "Freedom versus Security: Regulating and Managing Public Gatherings after the Young Turk Revolution," in *The Young Turks and the Ottoman Empire: The Aftermath of the 1908 Revolution*, ed. Noemi Levy-Aksu and François Georgeon [London: I. B. Tauris, 2016], 212–233).

[12] Abdülkerim Asılsoy, "Mehmet Fuat Köprülü'nün İlmi Hayatı ve Eserlerinde İzlediği Metot Üzerine," in *Tarihimizden Portreler: Osmanlı Kimliği: Prof. Dr. Cevdet Küçük Armağanı*, ed. Zekeriya Kurşun, Haydar Çoruh, 213–244 (Istanbul: Ordaf Yayınları, 2013), 213.

[13] Yalın Alpay, "Fuat Köprülü," in *Modern Türkiye'de Siyasi Düşünce V: Muhafazakarlık*, ed. Tanıl Bora and Murat Gültekingil (Istanbul: İletişim Yayınları), 137; Masami Arai, *Turkish Nationalism in the Young Turk Era* (Leiden: Brill, 1992), 40–44.

twenty-three, without even a degree, he was made a professor of Turkish Literature at Istanbul University (*Darülfünun*), the only such faculty in the country.[14] The appointment of a young man with so few formal qualifications illustrates the extent of Unionist influence.[15]

If Fuat's rise was rapid, a more typical experience was that of Bekir Refik. Born the same year as Fuat to an elite (but less prestigious) family in the province of Sivas, Refik also entered the School of Law in Istanbul. When Unionists forced the sultan to restore the constitution in 1908, Refik recalled being among the students who marched on the seat of government (*Bâb-ı Âlî*) in support.[16] He was appointed as an assistant prosecutor in Bursa after graduation. As a young and, perhaps, ambitious public official, he joined the local Unionist organization and came into contact with the provincial leader, Mahmut Celal.[17]

In coastal provinces such as Hüdavendigâr, officials were faced with the task of settling thousands of Muslim refugees from the Balkans. And, just as the arrival of Unionist leaders in Istanbul had strengthened the nationalist sentiment of academics like Fuat, the loss of territory led to widespread hostility toward those Ottoman subjects (like Greeks) who were seen as connected with other nation-states. As we have seen, local Unionist organizations mobilized their members to boycott and threaten Greeks. When he was moved from Hüdavendigâr to İzmir in 1913, Celal became involved in efforts to force out non-Muslim merchants. In his position as local party secretary, Celal helped create a labor union and Works Bureau to encourage Turkish employment. He pressed the Regie tobacco monopoly to do likewise and had non-Muslim railroad workers removed from their jobs.[18]

The province of Aydın (which included İzmir) was an enticing target for policymakers who hoped to a establish a "national economy" dominated by Muslims. Its 1.6 million people accounted for 9 percent of the total imperial population in 1914. Greek and Armenian Orthodox Christians made up 18 percent and 2 percent of the population, respectively (higher than their combined 15 percent of the empire as a whole). In the 211,000-person population of İzmir itself, the combination of Orthodox Greeks (35 percent), Jews (11 percent), and Armenian

[14] Markus Dressler, *Writing Religion: The Making of Turkish Alevi Islam* (Oxford: Oxford University Press, 2013), 154–161.

[15] During the war, Fuat Köprülü looked into securing a nomination for parliament but was discouraged by Interior Minister Talat (Baban, *Politika Galerisi*, 342–343).

[16] Yüksel, *Milli Mücadele'den*, 11–12.

[17] İbrahim Aslanoğlu, *Sivas Meşhurları*, vol. II (Sivas: Valiliği İl Kültür ve Turizm Müdürlüğü, 2006), 49–50.

[18] Şenşekerci, *Türk Devriminde*, 39–49.

Orthodox (5 percent) outnumbered Muslims. It was, in other words, a province and a city where Muslim businessmen stood to gain significantly from preferential treatment.[19] Also, as the numbers suggest, it was the removal of Greeks more than the removal of Armenians that transformed the province's demographics – in fact, as deportations of Armenians began in April 1915, Armenians in İzmir were generally exempted. This was not the case elsewhere in the empire during World War I: in the central and eastern provinces, the situation was quite different. There, the Armenian population was uprooted and deported, massacred, and left without means of survival. The historian Ronald Suny puts the number of murdered "conservatively" between 600,000 and one million.[20]

Despite some territorial gains in the Caucasus after the Russian withdrawal from the war in 1917, the Ottoman armies lost extensive territory in Syria, Mesopotamia, and Arabia. Their European allies were utterly defeated. When the empire had to sign an armistice in October 1918, the Unionist leadership fled the country. Celal and other members dissolved the organization and briefly relaunched it as the "Renewal Party" (*Teceddüt Fırkası*). Celal administered the İzmir branch under the direction of the city's wartime governor, Evrenoszade Rahmi. During the coming months, however, the victorious Entente forces consolidated their influence in coastal cities like Istanbul and İzmir. Rahmi was arrested and sent to Malta. On May 5, 1919, the Renewal Party was closed, and the new İzmir governor was ordered to arrest Celal, who now went into hiding.[21] The Greek army landed in İzmir on May 15.[22]

Celal spent much of May working with Ottoman army officers and gendarme commanders to organize local irregulars. In the coming months, he fought and commanded paramilitary units around Aydın,

[19] Karpat, *Ottoman Population*, 174–175, 188–189.

[20] Ronald Grigor Suny, *"They Can Live in the Desert but Nowhere Else": A History of the Armenian Genocide* (Princeton: Princeton University Press, 2015), 321, 347.

[21] Tarık Zafer Tunaya, *Türkiye'de Siyasal Partiler 2: Mütareke Dönemi, 1918–1922* (Hürriyet Vakfı Yayınları, 1986), 101–102; Şenşekerci, *Türk Devriminde*, 51–52. As Erik Zürcher describes, the İzmir branch of the Renewal Party made little effort to differentiate itself from the İTC. The words "Union and Progress" (in the original name, *İttihat ve Terakki Cemiyeti*) were barely painted over on its sign. When asked whether the words should be better obscured, Celal recalls saying, "Things that are covered by the times can one day also be uncovered by the times. That's life. Let's just wait and see" (Zürcher, *The Unionist Factor: The Role of the Committee for Union and Progress in the Nationalist Movement, 1905–1926* [Leiden: Brill, 1984], 75).

[22] For an overview of the Independence War, see Hasan Kayalı, "The Struggle for Independence," in *The Cambridge History of Turkey*, ed. Reşat Kasaba, 112–146 (Cambridge: Cambridge University Press, 2008).

using the nom de guerre "Galip Hoca."[23] At year's end, he was elected to the Ottoman parliament as a representative for Saruhan (Manisa) province. He was one of many resistance leaders in the new parliament. Gathering in Istanbul in January 1920, they endorsed the program of the Ankara-based resistance movement headed by former Ottoman general Mustafa Kemal. The endorsement provoked the Entente powers to formally occupy Istanbul in March and pressure the sultan to suspend parliament in April. Celal and many other legislators fled to Ankara to join Mustafa Kemal and his "nationalist" resistance organization. Once there, Celal served as an important intermediary between the regime in Ankara and autonomously operating militias in western Anatolia. By August 1920, he had become minister of the economy with responsibility for crucial operations like levying taxes to fund the resistance movement and increasing coal production to keep the railroads operating.[24]

The struggle against European occupation, subsequently commemorated as the "Independence War" (*Kurtuluş Savaşı*), was a transformative moment in the lives of all the DP founders. The Ottoman defeat led many of their superiors to flee. Others were imprisoned. In any case, the task of organizing resistance to foreign occupation now fell on these young officials and on local elites throughout the empire. In 1918, Celal was thirty-five and an important provincial official – but, nonetheless, a *provincial* official; within two years, he was a member of the self-declared "national" government in Ankara, overseeing a key ministry. Köprülüzade Mehmet Fuat and Bekir Refik, both twenty-eight, likewise occupied important positions at the end of World War I. Fuat was a professor at the country's premier university, just beginning to publish some of his most influential works of historical scholarship. Refik had recently been appointed chief of security for the province of Trabzon with a mandate to prevent uprisings among the province's ethnic Greeks

23 According to Başak Özoral, Bayar named himself after one of his middle school teachers whom he had admired ("The Turkish Transformation and Celal Bayar" [Master's thesis, McGill University, Montreal, 2004], 13).

24 Şenşekerci, *Türk Devriminde*, 101–107. Bayar also served as an important intermediary between Mustafa Kemal and various Unionist officials. In April 1920, for example, he facilitated a meeting between Kemal and a pair of Unionists, "Blind" Ali İhsan (İloğlu) and Memduh Şevket (Esendal), who had been important members of the Istanbul Businessmen Society (*Esnaf Cemiyeti*), which had linked the Unionists and small businessmen, and played a key role in their wartime efforts to create a "national economy" (Selim İlkin and İlhan Tekeli, "[Kör] Ali İhsan [İloğlu] Bey ve Temsili-Mesleki Programı," in *Atatürk Döneminin Ekonomik ve Toplumsal Tarihiyle İlgili Sorunlar Sempozyumu, 14–16 Ocak 1977* [Istanbul: İstanbul Yüksek İktisat ve Ticaret Mektebi Mezunları Derneği Yayını, 1977], 305–306).

subjects.[25] Both emerged from the independence struggle even closer to the center of power.

In contrast to these older men, eighteen-year-old Ali Adnan was a good example of how the resistance movement forged relationships between rural landlords and Mustafa Kemal's emerging regime. Adnan was an orphan who had inherited his large estate in rural Aydın through his maternal grandfather. During World War I, he had been sent to fight on the Syrian front but had caught malaria on the way. He was reposted to İzmir, where he promptly came down with typhoid. When the Ottoman army was ordered to demobilize after the 1918 armistice, he returned to his estate at Çakırbeyli. When the Entente forces occupied the region in 1919, the Greek and Italian armies split the province along the Menderes River, with the north controlled by the Greek forces and the south (including Adnan's estate) under Italian control. Adnan and his childhood friend İbrahim Ethem formed a militia and conducted attacks on the Greeks in coordination with Mustafa Kemal's forces.[26]

Fuat, living in occupied Istanbul, also looked for ways of contributing to the resistance movement. He toyed with involvement in the city's main underground resistance organization, *Karakol* (Guardpost). More concretely, he joined with several other Unionists to funnel money and discuss forming an organization of their own. When their group was discovered, he was briefly jailed. The experience encouraged him to focus on academic matters until the republic was declared in 1923.[27]

Bekir Refik was also in Istanbul following the armistice. In Trabzon, as chief of security, he had helped establish one of the many "Defense of Rights" organizations that were springing up around the country to protest the terms of the armistice.[28] In response, the Ottoman government in Istanbul removed him. Back in the capital, he spent a month or two trying to establish a law practice, before leaving for Konya. Not only had he previously worked in Karaman, a district connected to Konya, from 1915 to 1918, but he also had family in the region who had fled from Sivas during World War I in fear of the Russian advance. Once there, he joined the nationalist resistance movement.[29] Like Celal, he was elected as a representative and made his way Ankara to join the recently

[25] Refik Koraltan, *Tek Parti Devrinden 27 Mayıs İhtilali'ne Demokratlar: DP'nin Kurucusu Anlatıyor*, ed. Kamil Maman (Istanbul: Timaş Yayınları, 2013), 21.

[26] Demir, *Türk Siyasi*, 17–25.

[27] Dressler, *Writing Religion*, 169 n. 28. The other members of Fuat Köprülü's would-be secret organization were Zekeriya Sertel, Hasan Ali Yücel, and Ahmet Ferit Tek.

[28] Hasan Kayalı, *Imperial Resilience: The Great War's End, Ottoman Longevity, and Incidental Nations* (Berkeley: University of California Press, 2021), 89–90.

[29] Yüksel, *Milli Mücadele'den*, 26.

reconstituted parliament. As the body's youngest member, he was appointed secretary to the president of parliament's council (*başkan divanı*).[30] While Celal, drawing on his experience in the banking sector, was involved with financial issues, Refik made use of his legal knowledge and served as a judge for the Independence Courts (ad hoc tribunals that enforced the Ankara-based government's legal authority rather than that of the imperial government in Istanbul).[31] Refik also served as a member of the "official" Communist Party, crafted by Mustafa Kemal in late 1920 when the Ankara regime's future was uncertain and Soviet representatives were looking for possible alternatives. This "official" Communist Party, which served as a means of undercutting the Moscow-backed Turkish Communist Party based in Baku, was dissolved in 1921, after the Baku leadership had been assassinated.[32] The violent elimination of the Communist Party leadership at this early point in Mustafa Kemal's regime helped nip in the bud much further organizational development during the early years of the republic.

By 1922, the regime in Ankara had successfully reoccupied all of Ottoman Anatolia – albeit at the cost of accepting French and British control of predominantely Arab and Kurdish regions south of the October 1918 armistice line. The parliamentary regime in Ankara had also positioned itself as the legitimate national government by voting to dissolve the sultanate (and, thus, the Ottoman Empire) in advance of negotiations with the Entente powers in Lausanne. After the completion of the Lausanne Treaty and national elections in summer 1923, Mustafa Kemal declared that all the Defense of Rights organizations around the country

30 Sabahattin Özel, *Milli Mücadelede Trabzon* (Ankara: Türk Tarih Kurumu Basımevi, 1991), 28, 62; Ahmet Avanas, *Milli Mücadele'de Konya* (Ankara: Atatürk Araştırma Merkezi, 1998), 95–96; *TBMM Albümü, 1920–2010: II. Cilt: 1950_1980* (Ankara: TBMM Basın ve Halkla İlişkiler Müdürlüğü Bakanlıklar, 2010), 538.

31 The Independence Courts were initially concerned with revolts against Ankara's authority and military desertions, which were a serious problem during the Independence War. The tribunals were reconstituted on several occasions, both during the war and after, in response to uprisings and plots against the Ankara government. Refik Koraltan served as president of the 5th Independence Court, with oversight of the Yozgat region after September 8, 1921. In addition to desertions, it prosecuted participants of the 1921 Koçgiri uprising of Alevi Kurds in the region of Sivas (Ergün Aybars, *İstiklal Mahkemeleri*, 2nd ed. [Istanbul: Doğan Kitap, 2018 (1975)], 175–180; Elise Massicard, "The Repression of the Koçgiri Rebellion, 1920–1921," Sciences Po, Paris, France, September 29, 2009, available: www.sciencespo.fr/mass-violence-war-massacre-resistance/fr/document/repression-koa-giri-rebellion-1920-1921.

32 Salahi Sonyel, "Mustafa Kemal and Enver in Conflict, 1919–22," *Middle Eastern Studies* 25, no. 4 (1989): 511–512; Mete Tunçay, *Türkiye'de Sol Akımlar, 1908–1925* (Istanbul: İletişim Yayınları, 2009), 308–315.

would henceforth be part of his "People's Party" (CHP). On October 29, 1923, parliament declared the state to be a republic, not an empire.

Like Celal, Refik, and Fuat, Mustafa Kemal had been a Unionist. The events of World War I and the Independence War had not ended the era of Unionist rule so much as they had discredited a generation of its leaders and shifted power from one faction within the organization to another. The presence of middle-class figures like Celal, notables like Fuat and Refik, and landowners like Ali Adnan in this revised postwar order reveals that the new republic drew together diverse segments of the population. Even so, there is truth to the long-standing characterization of the early republic as a "military-bureaucratic" regime.[33] Whereas Istanbul-based governments prior to World War I and during the occupation had been in frequent contact with the city's powerful merchant community, the Ankara government was at a physical (if not an ideological) remove.[34] This distance did not mean that Kemal and his allies ignored the concerns of the business community, but rather that their attempts to stimulate economic growth tended to be imposed from the top down instead of through consultation.[35]

The İzmir Economic Congress held in February 1923 was an early example of this tendency. Its announcement and organization followed a declaration three months earlier by the National Turkish Commercial Union (*Milli Türk Ticaret Birliği*) that it would hold a congress in Istanbul. The event was canceled at the request of the Ankara government so that a government-supervised version could be held in İzmir. Mustafa Kemal opened the congress with a speech calling for economic growth aided by foreign investment but not beholden to it. Going

[33] See Ergun Özbudun, "Established Revolution vs. Unfinished Revolution: Contrasting Patterns of Democratization in Mexico and Turkey," in *Authoritarian Politics in Modern Society: The Dynamics of Established One-Party Systems*, ed. Samuel Huntington and Clement Moore (New York: Basic Books, 1970), 22–23; Keyder, "The Political Economy," 11; Berk Esen, "Political Mobilization and the Institutional Origins of National Developmentalist States: The Cases of Turkey, Mexico, Argentina, and Egypt" (PhD diss., Cornell University, Ithaca, 2015), 76–77.

[34] Unionist leaders' economic policies had been influenced by their proximity to local merchant communities, first by the religiously cosmopolitan merchants of Salonika, then by the predominantly Muslim, reformist merchants of Istanbul (Zafer Toprak, *Milli İktisat-Milli Burjuvazi* [Istanbul: Tarih Vakfi Yurt Yayınları, 1995], 5).

[35] Semih Gökatalay shows that the number of corporations established during the early years of the republic was not substantially different from the late years of the Ottoman Empire – 265 in 1908–19 as compared with 261 in 1919–29. Many of these were established by political figures and Celal Bayar's İş Bankası. The most striking difference is that no corporation in the years 1923–29 was established solely by a non-Muslim (Gökatalay, "The Political Economy of Corporations in the Late Ottoman Empire and Early Turkish Republic, 1908–1929" [Master's thesis, Middle Eastern Technical University, Ankara, 2015], 22–24, 31, 42).

forward, foreign capital would be welcome and "given the necessary security under conditions connected with our laws," but the result would "not be as before," when "foreign capital held a dominant position in the country."[36] Soon after the speech, he returned to Ankara in order to deal with diplomatic issues related to the peace negotiations still ongoing in Lausanne. Celal, likewise, did not attend the conference, as he was in Lausanne as part of a delegation led by Mustafa Kemal's close ally, the former general Mustafa İsmet (İnönü).

With Mustafa Kemal absent, the congress itself was overseen by another military figure, Musa Kazım (Karabekir), who favored liberal economics. The congress's final recommendations included the elimination of the agricultural tax (*aşar*) and the creation of a commercial bank to support merchants. Musa Kazım, however, lacked much influence in Ankara policymaking circles. Instead, according to historian Michael Finefrock, Mustafa Kemal gave "an entirely free hand" in crafting economic policy to his ally İsmet.[37] Ultimately, the congress served less as a means of empowering merchants and shaping policy than as a way of positioning merchants as but one interest group under the authority of Mustafa Kemal's regime. Policymaking formulated in the national interest but without much input from the nation would be a hallmark of the early republic. Celal, Fuat, and Refik would play central roles in crafting these policies.

Democrats as Republicans, 1923–1931

The declaration of the republic was followed by a period of institutional formation and reformation. During their first six years in power, Mustafa Kemal and his CHP eliminated the caliphate, took control of religious properties, closed Sufi orders, wrote a new constitution, mandated new dress codes, crafted a new civil code, and introduced a new alphabet. In many cases, reforms like a new alphabet had been matters of elite discussion for years; in other cases (such as the new civil code), something similar had actually been accomplished by the wartime Ottoman government.[38] Yet promoting secularism (*laiklik*), in particular,

[36] Atatürk Araştırma Merkezi, *Atatürk'ün Söylev ve Demeçleri II* (Ankara: Türk Tarih Kurumu Basımevi, 1997), 113.

[37] Michael Finefrock, "Laissez-Faire, the 1923 Izmir Economic Congress and Early Turkish Developmental Policy in Political Perspective," *Middle Eastern Studies* 17, no. 3 (1981): 383–384.

[38] On continuity between late Ottoman and early republican reforms, see Hale Yılmaz, *Becoming Turkish: Nationalist Reforms and Cultural Negotiations in Early Republican Turkey, 1923–1945* (Syracuse: Syracuse University Press, 2013).

strengthened the new regime by eliminating competing centers of legal and moral authority. Presenting themselves as the agents of reform helped justify Kemal and his allies' consolidation of power.

One group that was not challenged by the new republican government was the established class of Muslim landlords. Their property was not redistributed following the Independence War, in part because the resistance had been so reliant on these rural elites, in part because there was limited popular pressure. The annihilation and expulsion of the empire's Christian population enabled the republican government to supply extensive property to local elites and newly arrived refugees.[39] That said, there were cases of land seizures: during the war, peasants occupied nearly 90 precent of Ali Adnan's 35–40,000-dönüm (around 9,000-acre) estate. Rather than attempt to reclaim the land, Adnan settled for around 4,000 dönüm (988 acres) of the best land.[40] Like many landlords during the early years of the republic, he focused on improving his land rather than directly involving himself in national politics.

In contrast with Adnan, the other DP founders we have discussed – Celal, Fuat, and Refik – were all deeply involved in forging the regime during the 1920s. Following the declaration of the republic in 1923, Fuat was invited by Mustafa Kemal to serve as an advisor to the ministry of education and develop an Institute for Turkology. During the following year, he worked on various committees in Ankara alongside his old mentor Ziya Gökalp and other leading nationalist thinkers like Ahmet Agayef (Ağaoğlu) (to whom we will return in Chapter 2). Once the institute was up and running in late 1924, Fuat resigned from the ministry and focused on running it. He would spend the next four years either in Istanbul or abroad, being feted at various international conferences.[41] He also accumulated important titles: dean of the Istanbul University Literature Faculty in 1923, dean of the Divinity Faculty in 1927, and president of the Turkish Historical Society the same year.[42]

Celal, meanwhile, remained in Ankara for much of the 1920s, becoming general director of İş Bankası (Business Bank). The bank was established as part of an effort to reform Turkey's economic order after the war: it would supply merchants with credit to finance their transactions;

[39] Uğur Ümit Üngör and Mehmet Polatel, *Confiscation and Destruction: The Young Turk Seizure of Armenian Property* (London: Continuum, 2011), 66–74; Ümit Kurt, "Revisiting the Legal Infrastructure for the Confiscation of Armenian and Greek Wealth: An Analysis of the CUP Years and the Early Modern Republic," *Middle Eastern Studies* 53, no. 5 (2017): 704–705.

[40] Karpat, "Actors and Issues," 121. [41] Alpay, "Fuat Köprülü," 142–143.

[42] Erdem Sönmez, "A Past to Be Forgotten? Writing Ottoman History in Early Republican Turkey," *British Journal of Middle Eastern Studies* 48, no. 4 (2021): 762.

it would provide insurance to encourage commercial activity; and it would finance and manage large-scale enterprises in industries like mining and manufacturing, which required more capital investment than could be accessed by private individuals. In its first several years, İş Bankası financed (either on its own or in partnership) a pair of mining operations in Zonguldak and sugar refineries in Kırklareli, Eskişehir, and Tokat. It also established both an insurance and a reinsurance company.[43]

Prior to his appointment, Celal had been jumping from position to position in Ankara. During the war and its immediate aftermath, he had served as interim minister of finance, attended the Lausanne Conference as an advisor, and, finally, overseen the forcible exchange of "Turkish" and "Greek" populations that followed the war.[44] In contrast to this frequent movement, Celal remained at the bank for eight years, a sufficient time to develop close relationships with the country's business and financial community. During his time as general director, Celal continued to serve as a member of parliament (and as a board member of Fuat's own Istanbul University).

Bekir Refik also served in parliament during the 1920s, holding various important posts. During his second term in parliament (1923–27), he again served as secretary to the president of the parliament's council and on the Istanbul Independence Court. The tribunal oversaw prosecutions of journalists who criticized the elimination of the caliphate.[45] It also investigated a plot to assassinate Mustafa Kemal. While the evidence in this case was rather scanty, a more serious plot emerged in İzmir in 1926 and was heard by the Ankara Independence Court. The trial served as an opportunity for arresting many of Mustafa Kemal's rivals.[46] The Ankara Court also issued punishments for violations of the 1925 "Hat Law," which required officials to wear hats and forbade them to wear

[43] *The Development of National Banking in Turkey* (Ankara: Press Department of the Ministry of Interior, 1938), 76–83. According to this state-produced history, another reason for establishing İş Bankası was to compete with the high rates offered by foreign banks and, thus, drive those rates down. For a general account, see Uygur Kocabaşoğlu (ed.), *Türkiye İş Bankası Tarihi* (Istanbul: Türkiye İş Bankası Kültür Yayınları, 2001).

[44] For the purposes of the population exchange, "Turkish" or "Greek" were effectively synonyms for Muslim and Christian. Turkish-speaking, Anatolia-dwelling Orthodox Christians ("Karamanlids") were included in the exchange (Emine Yeşim Bedlek, *Imagined Communities in Greece and Turkey: Trauma and the Population Exchanges under Atatürk* [London: I. B. Tauris, 2016], 27–33; Bruce Clark, *Twice a Stranger: The Mass Expulsions That Forged Modern Greece and Turkey* [Cambridge, MA: Harvard University Press, 2006], 103–105).

[45] Aybars, *İstiklal Mahkemeleri*, 245–277; Mete Tunçay, *Türkiye Cumhuriyeti'nde Tek-Parti Yönetimi'nin Kurulması* (Ankara: Yurt Yayınları, 1981), 78–84.

[46] Zürcher, *The Unionist Factor*, 160.

fezes.[47] Though Refik did not serve on the Ankara Court, it was he who had introduced and defended the Hat Law in parliament. Nor was that his only contribution to the new regime's attempts to remove symbols and institutions associated with the Ottoman era: five days after introducing the Hat Law, he also introduced a bill to close all Sufi lodges and saints' tombs to the public.[48]

While Independence Courts might help suppress resistance to reforms like the Hat Law or the closure of Sufi lodges, they were inadequate to address the discontent engendered by the 1929 depression. The fall in global demand hit those western areas of Turkey that were most dependent on international trade. Whereas Turkey exported TL174 million in goods in 1928, the value fell to TL151 million in 1930 and would drop to TL92 million by 1934.[49] This decline in trade was particularly painful, given the centrality of agricultural exports in Turkey's efforts to earn foreign exchange.[50] Loss of agricultural income could not be easily offset. During the six years between the declaration of the republic and the beginning of the depression, the government's efforts to stimulate industrial growth had had limited success – and, as labor historian Ahmet Makal points out, much of the growth that *did* occur was just recovery from the war years.[51]

Amidst this economic uncertainty, Mustafa Kemal moved to divert popular frustration by opening up the political system. He encouraged the creation of a loyal opposition party, the Free Republican Party (SCF), led by a close ally, former prime minister Ali Fethi. But the initiative proved *too* successful. In western provinces, large crowds turned out to meet Fethi. His promises to increase credit to farmers

47 Zeynep Kezer, *Building Modern Turkey: State, Space, and Ideology in the Early Republic* (Pittsburgh: University of Pittsburgh Press, 2015), 102–110.

48 Aybars, *İstiklal Mahkemeleri*, 430–434; Tunçay, *Türkiye Cumhuriyeti'nde*, 149–152; Proceedings of the Turkish Grand National Assembly (*Türkiye Büyük Millet Meclisi Tutanakları*, hereafter TBMM), November 25, 1925, 220–229; TBMM, November 30, 1925, 282–289.

49 Selim İlkin and İlhan Tekeli, *Uygulamaya Geçerken Türkiye'de Devletçiliğin Oluşumu* (Istanbul: Bilge Kültür Sanat, 2009 [1982]), 34.

50 In 1928, agricultural exports accounted for 77.7 percent of all exports, which was lower than the average of 83.4 percent from 1924 to 1927; this percentage would rise to 81.4 percent and 82.2 percent in 1929 and 1930 respectively (Şevket Raşit Hatipoğlu, *Dış Ticaretimizde Ziraatın Payı* [Ankara: Yüksek Ziraat Enstitüsü, 1936], 7).

51 In 1927, the government passed a Law for the Encouragement of Industry (*Teşvik-i Sanayi Kanunu*), which gave businesses access to state land tax-free. It also offered a variety of tax incentives for raw materials and transportation. Despite these inducements, the historian Ahmet Makal observes that industrial growth of 8.5 percent was less than the average GNP growth of 10.5 percent and, thus, "insufficient" given the level of encouragement (Avcıoğlu, *Türkiye'nin Düzeni*, 381–384; Ahmet Makal, *Türkiye'de Tek Partili Dönemde Çalışma İlişkileri, 1920–1946* [Istanbul: İmge Yayınları, 1999], 218–222).

and revise the bankruptcy law were immensely appealing to a population dependent on agriculture and facing a global economic depression.[52] Worried that the SCF would do well in the October 1930 local elections, officials from the ruling CHP suppressed the vote. Afterwards, Fethi was encouraged to "voluntarily" dissolve his new party. Even thereafter, pressure on critics of the government did not let up. In December, when a religious protest in the Aegean town of Menemen resulted in the particularly grisly murder of a young soldier, CHP members accused supporters of the SCF of being linked to religious reactionaries.[53]

This was a mischaracterization of the party. Its program and campaign rhetoric centered on excessive taxation, misallocation of public investment, and the need for the government to increase its support of merchants. Rather than pursue autarkic economic policies, as many European states were doing, the SCF called for a reorientation of trade to neighboring Balkan countries that were similarly affected by the slump in global trade.[54] Such liberal economic policies died along with the brief experiment in multiparty elections. Moreover, the conditions for moving toward greater autarky were especially inviting at this moment: under the Treaty of Lausanne, the government had been prohibited from adjusting tariffs until 1929. Thereafter, the government was once more in possession of the policymaking tools to protect domestic industry. As early as February 1930, parliament moved to take control of foreign exchange rates.[55] More interventions soon followed.

Most of the men who would go on to found the DP remained loyal followers of Kemal and the CHP during the brief lifespan of the SCF. But there was one crucial exception: Ali Adnan. In the six years following the Greek defeat, Adnan had focused on developing his estate

[52] Ömer Karakaş, "Balıkesir'de Serbest Cumhuriyet Fırkası'nın Teşkilatlanması ve Belediye Seçimleri (1930)," *Turkish Studies* 8, no. 5 (2013): 363.

[53] For accounts of the SCF, see Walter Weiker, *Political Tutelage and Democracy in Turkey: The Free Party and Its Aftermath* (Leiden: Brill, 1973) and Cem Emrence, *99 Günlük Muhalefet: Serbest Cumhuriyet Fırkası* (Istanbul: İletişim Yayınları, 2006). For discussion of the "Menemen Incident," see Murat Belge, "Menemen Olayı," in *Cumhuriyet Dönemi Türkiye Ansiklopedisi 2*, ed. Murat Belge (Istanbul: İletişim Yayınları, 1983), 573.

[54] Emrence, *99 Günlük*, 78–81.

[55] As Yahya Sezai Tezel describes, the Great Depression created a glut of manufactured goods, lowering prices of European and US exports to Turkey. As a consequence, the cost of imports to Turkey fell 44 percent during the years 1929–33. This opportunity encouraged Turkish importers to make purchases, but it had the effect of sapping Turkey's reserves of foreign exchange, since the value of Turkish goods abroad was also declining, making it difficult to earn foreign exchange (Tezel, *Cumhuriyet Döneminin İktisadi Tarihi, 1923–1950* [Istanbul: Türkiye İş Bankası Kültür Yayınları, 1982], 199–204).

in Aydın.[56] Beginning in 1928, he changed his focus from cultivating crops to cultivating a political career. He married Berrin Evliyazade, part of a well-connected İzmir family and the niece of Turkey's foreign minister, Tevfik Rüştü (Aras). Two years later, he took an active role in the SCF. He was introduced to Fethi by a mutual acquaintance, the former mayor of Aydın. Adnan established a local SCF branch and recruited around the region until the party was closed. During this period Adnan made a name for himself. Of the 502 races in which the SCF competed, it won 31; of these, 8 were in Aydın.[57]

Immediately after the SCF was closed, a CHP delegation visited to take stock of the local situation. It was led by important figures from the region, including Celal and Hüseyin Vasıf, a former minister of education and former teacher of Adnan's. The delegation asked Adnan to become president of the CHP organization in Aydın. Always careful to surround himself with loyalists, he accepted on the condition that his allies be brought with him into the local party leadership, displacing a rival faction. Seven months later, Mustafa Kemal toured the country's western coastal provinces as part of an effort to reestablish his connection with "the people" in general and the local elites like Adnan in particular. This was the men's first encounter. The early minutes of their talk were awkward. Kemal refused offers of cigarettes and coffee. Then and later, however, Adnan would prove himself to be skillful in the art of charming important people. He launched into a discussion of local conditions that gripped Kemal's attention. By the time the president departed, he had drunk four cups of coffee and smoked a full pack.[58] Not long after their meeting, Adnan was nominated for a seat in parliament – though, Celal would note in later years, this appointment was probably due to the recommendation of Adnan's uncle-in-law rather than the impression made on Kemal.[59]

While Adnan was entering national politics with links to the SCF, the differences between the parties were far from insurmountable. The SCF leaders championed liberal economic policies insofar as they called for freer trade and limits on government intervention in people's lives, but they also called for government action to encourage trade and limited

[56] Adnan also busied himself during the 1920s by having an affair with the daughter of his estate steward, leading the girl's brother to murder her in "defense" of her honor (Demir, *Türk Siyasi*, 28 n. 55).

[57] Ibid., 40.

[58] Ibid., 42–43; Mehmet Birand, Bülent Çaplı, and Can Dündar, *Demirkırat: Bir Demokrasinin Doğuşu* (Istanbul: Milliyet Yayınları, 1991), 18–19.

[59] Bayar, *Başvekilim Adnan*, 27.

their membership to citizens who had "accepted Turkish culture."[60] And though they eschewed talk of "national economy" favored by many Unionists (and nationalists more generally), SCF leaders accepted the notion that a culturally defined sense of belonging should undergird attempts to promote domestic economic activity. To the extent that Adnan (or the other DP founders) were sympathetic to the SCF's arguments, they were subscribing to a fairly limited notion of liberalism.

Likewise, Celal's two decades in politics had brought him into close relations with the banking establishment, but this did not necessarily mean that he was a champion of free enterprise and limited state intervention. To the contrary, as head of İş Bankası, he was a leader of the major state-sponsored efforts to establish new domestic industries. To the extent that debate emerged in the 1930s over economic intervention, it was often focused on whether the essential industries being created should remain in state hands for perpetuity, or whether the state should function in a temporary, tutelary capacity toward the private sector. Such a debate could have formed the basis for multiparty competition, but with opposition parties no longer allowed, policy debates became factional struggles *within* the CHP's single-party state over the nature of the regime.

Democrats as Kemalists, 1931–1938

The eight years following the closure of the SCF – the last years of Mustafa Kemal's life – were a period of "High Kemalism" during which the regime sought to deepen its connection with society through the institutions of a single-party state.[61] In order to achieve this goal, the government closed civil society organizations such the Women's Union (*Kadın Birliği*), the Masons, and the nationalist Turkish Hearths organization.[62] The CHP's Third Congress in 1931 laid the groundwork for replacing these institutions with "People's Houses," party-run cultural centers. In addition, the party's official ideology was defined as

[60] Emrence, *99 Günlük*, 84–85. *Hars*, the term used for culture in the SCF program, was popularized by the Turkish nationalist intellectual Ziya Gökalp (Ziya Gökalp, *Turkish Nationalism and Western Civilization: Selected Essays of Ziya Gökalp*, ed. Niyazi Berkes [New York: Columbia University Press, 1959], 316 n. 14).

[61] I borrow this term from Soner Çağaptay's book *Islam, Secularism and Nationalism in Modern Turkey: Who Is a Turk?* (London: Routledge, 2006). Çağaptay himself appears to be playing with the concept of "High Modernism" used in James Scott's *Seeing Like a State: How Certain Schemes to Improve the Human Condition Have Failed* (New Haven, CT: Yale University Press, 1999), 4–5.

[62] The Turkish Hearths had become associated with the SCF and liberal opposition in general (A. Hollie Shissler, *Between Two Empires: Ahmet Agaoglu and the New Turkey* [New York: I. B. Taurus, 2002], 195).

including six principles: Republicanism, Nationalism, Populism, Statism, Secularism, and Revolutionism.

Four of these principles dated from programs produced at previous conventions, but "Revolutionism" and "Statism" were new. The former was not a commitment to perpetual revolution but rather a commitment to "stay faithful and defend the principles born and developed from the revolutions for which our nation has sacrificed so much."[63] As for Statism (*Devletçilik*), the program declared:

> While maintaining the foundations of individual effort and action, in order to achieve national welfare and prosperity in as short a time as possible in affairs necessary for the nation's general and highest benefit – especially in the economic field – the state is, de facto, involved.[64]

The coming years witnessed ongoing efforts to involve the state in people's lives. In addition to developing and articulating a definable revolutionary ideology, party leaders worked to enforce the language and dress reforms already enacted. There were campaigns such as "Citizen, Speak Turkish," as well as attacks on citizens, like Jews, who were seen as not fully embracing Turkish culture.[65] All citizens were required to adopt surnames.[66] Mustafa Kemal assumed the name Atatürk, meaning "Father of the Turks." Mustafa İsmet, who served as prime minister for much of Atatürk's time as president, took the name "İnönü," after a crucial battle he had won in 1921 in a town of that name. Some people with prestigious lineages Turkified their Persianate family names – thus, Köprülüzade Mehmet Fuat became "Mehmet Fuat Köprülü." Others picked names that evoked their region of the country – thus, Ali Adnan, after initially choosing "Ertekin," settled on "Menderes" as his surname, in reference to the nearby Menderes River. (His friend from the war years, İbrahim Ethem, who would go on to serve key roles in DP governments, also picked the last name "Menderes," which can cause confusion for contemporary readers.) Those at the highest levels of government were often given

[63] Tunçay, *Türkiye Cumhuriyeti'nde*, 449. [64] Ibid., 448.

[65] See Avner Levi, *Türkiye Cumhuriyeti'nde Yahudiler: Hukuki ve Siyasi Durumları* (Istanbul: İletişim Yayınları 1996), 100–130; Ayhan Aktar, *Varlık Vergisi ve "Türkleştirme" Politikaları* (Istanbul: İletişim Yayınları, 2000), 71–99. Attacks on Jews in western Turkey in 1934, while tacitly supported by the national government, were generally organized at the local level. Kurdish-speaking Alevi Muslims in the province of Dersim experienced violence meted out directly by the state in 1937, when they resisted central government authority (David McDowall, *A Modern History of the Kurds*, 3rd ed. [London: I. B. Tauris, 2004], 207–210).

[66] See Emine Gürsoy-Naskali, *Cumhuriyet Tarihi Soyadı Hikayeleri* (Istanbul: Doğan Kitap, 2013); Meltem Türköz, *Naming and Nation-Building in Turkey: The 1934 Surname Law* (London: Palgrave Macmillan, 2018).

names by Atatürk directly. Mahmut Celal, for example, received the name "Bayar," meaning "eminent."[67]

There was also an effort to craft a new "national" history that looked to the region's Turkic heritage rather than its more recent Ottoman influences. In part, this effort involved funding archaeological excavations of Hittite and other civilizations; in part, it involved creating new institutions like the Turkish History Institute under Atatürk's direct patronage.[68] Even more ambitious was the effort to craft a new "Turkish History Thesis" that posited the Turks as the founders of multiple Anatolian civilizations – and, therefore, the true possessors of the land. Initially, Köprülü was a critic of these and other efforts to marginalize the country's Ottoman heritage.[69] He opposed moves to replace Ottoman script with Latin script. In a bid for the presidency of Istanbul University, he blasted an opponent's support for Turkish History Thesis-like ideas, saying such a man could not "represent the scientific personality of Istanbul University."[70]

Unfortunately for Köprülü, his adversary, law professor Yusuf Ziya (Özer), was among those academics who had Atatürk's ear. Not only did Köprülü lose the university presidential election, but he now found himself on the wrong side of increasingly influential academics. When the Turkish Hearth organization (with which Köprülü had been involved for nearly twenty years) established a "Society for the Investigation of History" in 1930, he was not included. The following year, he was demoted on account of not possessing a doctorate.[71] He was also removed from his position as dean of his faculty. Yusuf Ziya's star, meanwhile, was rising. In 1930, he was part of a group selected by Atatürk to produce a new Turkish history book that could be used in schools and serve to "liberate Turks from faulty thoughts."[72]

[67] Süleyman Yeşilyurt, *Bayar Gerçeği* (Ankara: Stratejik Araştırma ve Kültür Yayınları, 1997), 80–81.

[68] Tuğba Tanyeri-Erdemir, "Archaeology as a Source of National Pride in the Early Years of the Turkish Republic," *Journal of Field Archaeology* 31, no. 4 (2006): 383–384.

[69] According to Erdem Sönmez, scholarly claims that Ottoman studies were marginalized in the 1930s are overblown. One of the four textbooks designed to disseminate the "Turkish History Thesis" was devoted to the Ottomans, which "means that a considerable part of high school history education in 1930s Turkey was allocated to the teaching of Ottoman history alone." Rather than denigrate the empire as a whole, Mustafa Kemal and his allies emphasized its decline over time, necessitating their intervention (Sönmez, "A Past to Be Forgotten?," 757).

[70] Murat Ergin, *"Is the Turk a White Man?": Race and Modernity in the Making of Turkish Identity* (Leiden: Brill, 2006), 134.

[71] Ömer Faruk Akün, "Mehmed Fuad Köprülü," in *Türkiye Diyanet Vakfı Islam Ansiklopedisi*, vol. XXVI (Istanbul: Türkiye Diyanet Vakfı, 2002), 478.

[72] Çiğdem Atakuman, "Anatolia and Archaeology in the Early Years of the Turkish Republic, 1923–1938," *Journal of Social Archaeology* 8, no. 2 (2008): 221.

The book's mass publication in 1931 was followed in 1932 by a Turkish History Congress, at which Yusuf Ziya and others presented their new national history to schoolteachers. At the congress, Köprülü spoke out – albeit politely now – against Atatürk's adopted daughter Afet (İnan), who served as something of a figurehead for the history reform movement. Köprülü pointed out that while her arguments might be true, there was not sufficient evidence to be sure. His concerns were met with scorn from Afet and others at the congress who accused him of having old notions. Compared with other dissenting voices, however, he got off easy: another professor from Istanbul University, Zeki Velidi (Togan), was accused of betraying his ethnic brethren at points in his career and browbeaten into resigning his position and leaving the country.[73] Köprülü got the message. Later that year, at the Turkish Language Congress, he joined in the criticism of a dissenter.[74] The following year, he was elevated to the position of "distinguished professor" and again made dean. In 1935, he was made a member of parliament and began splitting his time between Istanbul and Ankara.

Adnan Menderes was beginning his second term in parliament in 1935. His first term had been uneventful – a biographer describes him as rather "quiet and indistinct."[75] Though he served on various committees, he did not even speak in the assembly itself until 1933. One cause of this silence may be that he was focused elsewhere: from 1932 to 1935 he was attending law school, earning a college degree. Though Bayar and Köprülü's ascents demonstrate that a university degree was not essential for a political career, it certainly helped, especially for a younger politician like Menderes. In his second term, degree in hand, he began to take more important roles. He served as the head of the Turkish Sports Association and traveled the country as a party inspector, reporting on the activities of local People's Houses and the popular mood.[76] During Bayar's brief time as prime minister, prior to Atatürk's death, Menderes was recommended by his uncle-in-law for the post of minister of agriculture, but nothing came of it.[77] Menderes's failure to observe the norms of political culture in the early republic may have slowed his rise; though he

[73] Ergin, *"Is the Turk,"* 136–138; Büşra Ersanlı, *İktidar ve Tarih: Türkiye'de "Resmî Tarih" Tezinin Oluşumu, 1929–1937* (Istanbul: İletişim Yayınları, 2003), 167–174.

[74] At the Turkish Language Congress, Hüseyin Cahit Yalçın cautioned against moving too fast to purify the language of Persian and Arabic words. He was roundly criticized (Cemil Koçak, "Hüseyin Cahit Yalçın ve *Fikir Hareketleri* Dergisi, 1933–1940," in *Modern Türkiye'de Siyasi Düşünce VII: Liberalizm*, ed. Tanıl Bora and Murat Gültekingil [Istanbul: İletişim Yayınları, 2005], 248; Yılmaz Çolak, "Language Policy and Official Ideology in Early Republican Turkey," *Middle Eastern Studies* 40, no. 6 [2004]: 76).

[75] Demir, *Türk Siyasi*, 48.

[76] See Ergun, *CHPli Menderes, 1931–1945*.

[77] Demir, *Türk Siyasi*, 52–53.

brought his wife, Berrin, to Ankara, he would not bring her to social events, as Atatürk expected of officials.[78]

Köprülü was more careful in this regard. Once in parliament, he remained active in cultural affairs. In Istanbul, he had overseen the official magazine of the Eminönü People's House; in Ankara, he became editor of the most influential People's House magazine, *Ülkü* (Ideal), one of the primary sources of CHP propaganda during the mid 1930s.[79] For his efforts, he became a regular guest at Atatürk's late-night dinner parties. The group of friends and advisors who met at these gatherings formed something akin to a shadow cabinet – certainly in the mind of Prime Minister İnönü, who saw his own authority being undermined.

One of many differences between İnönü and Atatürk was over the extent to which the state should intervene in the economy. Allies of İnönü during the 1930s tended to be more expansive in their visions of the state's role. İnönü himself even lent his imprimatur to some of the more radical statist arguments by penning an essay in the journal *Kadro* (Cadre) defending the essential role of statism. He argued that statism was necessary to achieve the aims that individuals and private enterprise could not. The essential duty of statism was "defense," but not only "from a conservative point of view but also an expansionist policy of development and progress."[80] Under İnönü's administration, during the height of the Great Depression, the government moved from shielding domestic manufactures (1929–32) to practicing what the economic historian Yahya Tezel defines as "state capitalism" – capitalist in the sense that the government did not seek to eliminate private enterprises, but rather to aid them by manufacturing those primary consumer products which Turkey would otherwise have had to import on terms that left it at a perpetual disadvantage.[81]

With the renewed ability to set customs duties in 1929 (and the creation of a Central Bank in 1930), the government was able to exercise greater control over foreign exchange and the money supply to promote domestic industry. Following the SCF's closure and Atatürk's tour of the country, however, the government moved in the direction of greater support for both farmers and consumers. In 1932, Ziraat Bankası began

[78] Pınar Melis Yelsalı Parmazsız, *Türkiye'nin Modernleşmesinde Kadınlar: 1839'den Günümüze* (Istanbul: İmge Kitabevi Yayınları, 2017), 99.

[79] Akün, "Mehmed Fuad Köprülü," 478; Arzu Öztürkmen, *Türkiye'de Folklor ve Milliyetçilik* (Istanbul: İletişim Yayınları, 1998), 60–61; Ertan Aydın, "Peculiarities of Turkish Revolutionary Ideology in the 1930s: The Ülkü Version of Kemalism, 1933–1936," *Middle Eastern Studies* 40, no. 5 (2004): 64.

[80] İsmet (İnönü), "Fırkamızın Devletçilik Vasfı," *Kadro* 22 (1933): 4–6.

[81] Tezel, *Cumhuriyet Döneminin*, 349.

purchasing a portion of the annual grain harvest in order to prop up otherwise falling prices.[82] Sanayi Kredi Bankası (Industrial Credit Bank) was created the same year, but the legislation infuriated industrialists, since it also ended their duty-free access to raw material imports. Economy Minister Mustafa Şeref (Özkan) and his allies were seen as high-handed in their attempts to exercise control over industry. Mustafa Şeref made additional enemies with the State Industry Office Law (July 1932), which empowered the ministry's general director of industry and labor to approve business licenses. When the official promptly used his authority to block the establishment of an İş Bankası–controlled paper mill, Atatürk had İnönü remove Mustafa Şeref and replace him with Celal Bayar, thus nipping in the bud Mustafa Şeref's "techno-bureaucratic fantasy."[83] In his new position, Bayar's role was not to halt the development of statist economic policies but rather – in the words of economic historian Korkut Boratav – to "smooth the sharp edges off the 1932 laws."[84]

Under Bayar, private enterprises' machinery imports were again given duty-free status on the condition that they not compete with domestic products. In 1933, the Industrial Credit Bank and Industry Office were replaced by a new institution, Sümerbank.[85] Sümerbank was given the task of overseeing a five-year plan by establishing factories both on its own and in partnership with shareholders. By 1938, four cotton textile factories had been established, as well as one for Merino wool. Factories were also built for vegetable oil, semicoke, and sulfur, with a paper mill and additional cotton mill on the horizon. İş Bankası, now overseen by one of Bayar's allies, established such enterprises as a glass factory on Istanbul's Asian side.[86] There were also efforts to coordinate and reduce competition in existing industries: the country's four main cement producers, for example, were united in a sales association that divvied up the national market among them.[87]

During the early 1930s, when the direction of state policy was still under discussion, İnönü's government solicited advice from both the USSR and the US. Each country sent advisors. Whereas the US experts

82 Şevket Pamuk, "Intervention during the Great Depression: Another Look at Turkish Experience," in *The Mediterranean Response to Globalization before 1950*, ed. Şevket Pamuk and Jeffrey Williamson (London: Routledge, 2000), 334.

83 Tezel, *Cumhuriyet Döneminin*, 350–351.

84 Korkut Boratav, *Türkiye İktisat Tarihi, 1908–2009* (Istanbul: İmge Kitabevi, 2015), 68.

85 Z. Y. Hershlag, *Turkey: An Economy in Transition* (The Hague: Uitgeverij van Keulen NV, 1958), 97–98.

86 *The Development of National Banking*, 47–51; Avcıoğlu, *Türkiye'nin Düzeni*, 460; Tezel, *Cumhuriyet Döneminin*, 365.

87 Yıldız Sey, *Türkiye Çimento Tarihi* (Istanbul: Türkiye Çimento Müstahsilleri Birliği, 2003), 41–42.

emphasized agricultural development, the Soviets argued in favor of industrialization – and, perhaps decisively, they offered an $8 million loan repayable over twenty years at just 3 percent interest. Increased Soviet involvement worried other countries and encouraged their leaders to offer Turkey credit on good terms.[88] The UK, for example, provided loans to build Turkey's first steel works. Yet, for all the concern, the risk of the USSR coming to dominate Turkey's economy was minimal: its share of Turkey's imports and exports only rose from an average of 4 percent and 3 percent in 1924–29 to an average of 4 percent and 5 percent in 1930–39. Germany's share of Turkish exports, by contrast, rose from 15 percent in 1932 to 37 percent in 1939. Its share of Turkey's imports rose from 25 percent to 51 percent.[89]

German dominance was achieved through bilateral trade deals with Turkey during the 1930s. Germany willingly purchased Turkish agricultural products at above-market rates, encouraging Turkey to buy German manufactured goods in return. The trade was conducted using a credit system that avoided the need for foreign exchange, which neither country wished to use if they could avoid it. But since the terms of trade tended to favor Germany, Turkey was left in debt, with little choice but to continue dealing with Germany and seeking favorable new credit agreements. In this manner, Germany secured preferential access to Turkish chromite, which was necessary for producing stainless steel.[90] As economic historian Yahya Tezel observes, "the golden age of statism was bound up with a degree of dependence on an imperial power never seen in another period of Turkish history."[91] The point is worth emphasizing: even during the years of "High Kemalism," the years remembered as exemplifying Turkey's autarkic development and independence, the government was at the mercy of its powerful trading partner.

Turkey's leaders were cognizant of their poor strategic position, and, even as Soviet aid was underwriting industrialization, Turkish leaders remained suspicious. In 1935, İnönü requested that Refik Koraltan resign from parliament and serve once again as governor in the province of Çoruh (Artvin) along the potentially sensitive border with the USSR.

[88] Tezel, *Cumhuriyet Döneminin*, 352–353; Eral Tellal, "SSCB'yle İlişkiler," in *Türk Dış Politikası, Cilt I: 1919–1980*, ed. Baskın Oran (Istanbul: İletişim Yayınları, 2001), 321–323; Samuel Hirst, *Against the Liberal Order: The Soviet Union, Turkey, and Statist Internationalism, 1919–1939* (Oxford: Oxford University Press, 2024), 147–150.

[89] Tezel, *Cumhuriyet Döneminin*, 198.

[90] Yücel Güçlü, "Turkish–German Relations on the Eve of World War Two," *Turkish Studies* 1, no. 2 (2000): 73–94; Stefan Ihrig, *Atatürk in the Nazi Imagination* (Cambridge, MA: Harvard University Press, 2014), 213–214.

[91] Tezel, *Cumhuriyet Döneminin*, 211.

Once there, Koraltan pushed for increased funding for agricultural development in the region. After Çoruh, he was assigned to the neighboring province of Trabzon, where he had previously served as police chief. Beginning in 1936, his role as governor meant that he also served as head of the provincial CHP organization. This linkage of party and state structures was part of the ongoing effort to extend the regime's influence throughout society. At the 1935 CHP Congress, the party's general secretary had emphasized the need for "a tighter convergence."[92] In June 1936 this desire was formalized when Prime Minister İnönü declared that interior ministers would henceforth serve as CHP general secretaries, governors as provincial CHP presidents, and party inspectors as inspectors of state institutions as well.

Following Atatürk's death and İnönü's assumption of the presidency in 1938, this system was ended. State institutions again became formally independent of party structures. Furthermore, İnönü allowed old opponents of Atatürk to return to political life. He removed regime stalwarts like Interior Minister Şükrü Kaya and Foreign Minister Tevfik Rüştü Aras from government and oversaw the establishment of an "independent group" of legislators within the parliament.[93] Such moves seemed to signal a break with less savory aspects of the Unionist and single-party periods. Yet these were limited reforms and should not obscure the fact

[92] Çetin Yetkin, *Türkiye'de Tek Parti Yönetimi,1930–1945* (Istanbul: Altın Kitaplar Yayınevi, 1983), 128.

[93] Politicians allowed to reenter parliament via a December 31, 1939 by-election included Kazım Karabekir (a famous general and a leader of the Progressive Republican Party [*Terakkiperver Cumhuriyet Fırkası*] opposition in 1924–25), Fethi Okyar (a former prime minister, head of the SCF, and ambassador to the UK), and Hüseyin Cahit Yalçın (an influential Unionist and journalist). Zeki Kuneralp, whose father, Ali Kemal, had served as interior minister during the final Ottoman government, was also allowed back; he joined the diplomatic corps. Rauf Orbay (a former prime minister) and Halide Edib Adıvar (an author and activist) were allowed to return, but did not reenter parliament immediately (Cemil Koçak, *Türkiye'de Milli Şef Dönemi, 1938–1945*, vol. I [Istanbul: İletişim Yayınları 1996 (1986)], 179–180; Vanderlippe, *The Politics of Turkish Democracy*, 34–35). As for the ministers who were excluded from cabinets in the İnönü era: the long-serving interior minister, Şükrü Kaya, had been a leading figure in the Ottoman Directorate for Settlement of Tribes and Immigrants, which oversaw the removal of Armenian Christians and the settlement of Muslims during World War I. Kaya's ouster was punishment for his efforts (along with Foreign Minister Aras) to block İnönü's path to the presidency. For Kaya, see Reuben Silverman, *Turkey's Ever Present Past: Stories from Turkish Republican History* (Istanbul: Libra Yayınevi, 2015), 41–54. For discussions of the "Independent Group" in parliament, see Osman Akandere, "1939–1946 Yılları Arasında Türkiye Büyük Millet Meclisinde Bir Denetleme ve Kontrol Organı Olarak Müstakil Grup'un Yapısı ve İşlevi," *Selçuk Üniversitesi Türkiyat Araştırmaları Dergisi* 7 (2000): 305–326; Volkan Payaslı, "Tek Parti İktidarı'ndan Doğmuş Bir Denetim Organı: Müstakil Grup (1939–1946)," *Çağdaş Türkiye Tarihi Araştırmaları Dergisi* 14, no. 28 (spring 2014): 175–197.

that it was İnönü himself who had been head of government for all but one year since the establishment of the republic. Like the founders of the DP, he was a creator of the political order, not an opponent.

İnönü and his allies could also be brutal in their consolidation of power. On October 25, 1937, İnönü had been temporarily forced out of government by Atatürk and replaced with Bayar. During his year as prime minister, Bayar was unable to sufficiently expand his support within parliament and the military. As a result, following Atatürk's death on November 10, 1938, military figures and parliamentarians were quick to line up behind İnönü, who was elected president on November 11. Bayar remained as prime minister – but only briefly. By late December, Minister of Finance Şakir Kesebir (a long-time ally of Bayar's) had been forced out and replaced with an ally of İnönü's. On January 24, 1939, police conducted searches of the Istanbul offices of Denizbank's Technology Bureau and the offices of İmpeks, an import-export firm whose owner's brother was the manager of the Technology Bureau and whose founders included Bayar's son, Refii. Bayar resigned the following day. Denizbank officials were accused of various improper sales and purchases. The prosecutions dragged on for three years and ultimately ended in acquittal. In 1940, however, long before this result, Bayar's son committed suicide.[94]

As for Bayar, following his resignation, he kept his distance from politics. He stood for reelection in 1939 and 1943, but mainly worked on his memoirs. He also made visits to his home province of Bursa, where he struck up good relations with its newly appointed governor, Refik Koraltan. In his position as enforcer of central government dictates, Koraltan was aware (and concerned) that the new prime minister had placed Bayar under surveillance.[95] He was also personally frustrated that various policy recommendations he made to the government were being ignored.[96] Nonetheless, Koraltan, always a loyal official, continued in his post until the eve of the next election in 1943, when he arranged his return to parliament. It was during the 1943–46 session that political activity would move from internal party struggles to multiparty politics.

Democrats as Internal Opposition, 1939–1945

DP leaders would later make a distinction between Mustafa Kemal Atatürk's regime and that of İsmet İnönü. As they explained it, under

[94] Koçak, *Türkiye'de Milli Şef Dönemi, 1938–1945*, vol. I, 189–192, 210–228.

[95] Koraltan, *Tek Parti*, 32.

[96] Metin Toker, *Tek Partiden Çok Partiye, 1944–1950: Demokrasimizin İsmet Paşa'lı Yılları*, 3rd ed. (Istanbul: Bilgi Yayınevi, 1990), 50.

İnönü, the worst tendencies of single-party rule were given free rein, placing the interests of the state far above those of the citizenry. Given the authoritarian methods of the preceding fifteen years (and considering the slight opening of İnönü's first year), such narratives were clearly self-serving. On the other hand, faced with the specter of World War II, İnönü's regime did rely on heavy-handed, invasive policies to keep the army fully mobilized for the duration of the conflict. Sustaining such an operation while also providing for people's daily needs led to shortages, rationing, and a growing black market. To address these challenges, İnönü's regime crafted laws that gave the state sweeping powers to set prices, force people to work, and extract extraordinary levels of taxation from them. The most widely resented of these wartime laws, the National Protection Law, empowered the government to coerce labor in strategic industries like mines. In addition, the law required the sale of grain to the state and permitted the seizure of livestock, which set many farmers in opposition to the government.[97]

The most controversial law, the Wealth Tax, levied extraordinary taxes, disproportionately on Turkey's minority populations. Nonpayment was often punished with imprisonment and hard labor. The ease with which the government was able to target private property unsettled powerful commercial interests and alienated non-Muslim minorities, who felt excluded from the equal protections of citizenship. The law passed without dissenting votes, but seventy-six legislators absented themselves from the vote. Bayar was among them. (Menderes, Koraltan, and Köprülü supported the bill.)[98] This method of signaling opposition to a bill was common during the single-party era. As late as 1945, for example, Köprülü and Bayar both absented themselves from a vote to "Turkify" the language of the constitution by removing words of Arabic and Persian origin.[99]

That said, this indirect method of opposition had begun to change, and Bayar was among the first to voice his dissent on important matters. In 1944, he broke single-party–era norms by voting against the budget. His act carried symbolic weight; his speech expressing his concerns was his first in parliament since resigning as prime minister five years earlier.

[97] See Şevket Pamuk, "War, State Economic Policies and Resistance by Agricultural Producers in Turkey 1939–1945," in *Peasants and Politics in the Modern Middle East*, ed. Farhad Kazemi and John Waterbury (University Presses of Florida, 1991), 125–142.

[98] Şenşekerci, *Türk Devriminde*, 174; TBMM, November 11, 1942, 33. Menderes, Köprülü, and Koraltan also supported the government when, two years later, Bayar cast the sole vote against the government's 1944–45 budget (TBMM, May 29, 1944, 420–422).

[99] TBMM, January 10, 1945; Cemil Koçak, *İkinci Parti*, 58–59.

In criticizing the government's wartime financial policies, he argued that the Central Bank was printing money at a rate far greater than the growth in Turkey's productive capacity.[100] This imbalance was causing inflation. The weak lira would lead to an outflow of foreign exchange and gold reserves when peace returned and trade resumed. Inflation was also increasing the cost of living for government officials on fixed incomes.[101] Yet while bureaucrats, along with farmers and merchants from minority communities, might have been frustrated with the government, it was not until the end of World War II was in sight that their discontent became incorporated into a political movement. And, even for this movement to develop, the CHP leadership had to anger the most powerful component of the post-Ottoman political order: landlords.

On May 14, 1945, the government introduced a bill to break up large estates by distributing land to sharecroppers and other workers, leaving landlords with no more than 50 dönüm (12.4 acres). According to the historian Asım Karaömerlioğlu, the bill was a way of shifting blame for Turkey's economic backwardness onto landowners and, perhaps, "a test of the power of the emerging opposition."[102] In the latter case, it was a resounding success. The bill elicited strong reactions from members of parliament, including Menderes, who owned around 4,000 dönüm (988 acres).[103] According to Menderes, the bill was simply unnecessary as "the management of our lands with respect to the population distribution" was a far more important cause of the low productivity that kept Turkey's farmers poor. Taking land from landowners was misguided when, "in some of our regions, vast and productive lands lie without people or farmers."[104]

The following weekend was Youth and Sports Day (May 19), which marked both Atatürk's birthday and the day in 1919 when a thirty-eight-year-old Mustafa Kemal had arrived in the city of Samsun to begin leading the national liberation struggle. To commemorate the day,

100 The value of banknotes in circulation rose from TL194 million in 1938 to TL961 million in 1944 (Haluk Cillov, *Türkiye Ekonomisi* [Istanbul: Sermet Matbaası, 1965], 406).

101 TBMM, May 22, 1944, 146–151; Toker, *Tek Partiden Çok Partiye*, 29–30. Bayar's vote against the budget was the first negative vote a budget had received since İnönü became president (TBMM, May 30, 1939; TBMM, May 29, 1940; TBMM, May 29, 1941; TBMM, May 27, 1942; TBMM, May 27, 1943).

102 Asım Karaömerlioğlu, "Turkey's 'Return' to Multi-Party Politics: A Social Interpretation," *Eastern European Quarterly* 40 (2006): 90–97.

103 Menderes, with his large estate, is listed in parliamentary records as a "farmer" (*çiftçi*). This is a vague term – especially when translated into English – and obscures the distinction between peasants and magnates.

104 TBMM, May 16, 1945, 112.

President İnönü gave a speech acknowledging that Turkey had passed through the stresses of World War II and assuring that now, "in the political and intellectual life of the nation, the principles of democracy will reign ever more widely."[105] Two days later, as if giving an opportunity to test İnönü's words, the government offered up *another* contentious bill: the annual budget. It too received criticism from Menderes and others. Menderes argued that the budget directed money to an expanded bureaucracy at a time when other priorities were more important. With World War II ending, he explained, it was likely that global agriculture prices would fall. The government would need to protect farmers while bringing Turkey's prices in line with the world market. Spending on officials should be subordinated to these measures and to economic development.[106] When the vote was held on May 29, only 5 of the 373 representatives opposed it. These five were Bayar, Koraltan, Köprülü, Menderes and Emin Sazak (another influential landlord looking for ways to vent his frustrations with the government).

Following this challenge to his authority, the prime minister called for a vote of confidence. Two more members joined the five.[107] On June 7, Bayar, Menderes, Koraltan, and Köprülü presented a proposal to the CHP parliamentary group. They declared:

> Around the world, the movements of freedom and democracy have won a great victory. Now, the principles of democratic freedom are secured by international guarantees. In our country too, it cannot be doubted, from the president to the smallest [among us], that the whole nation carries the same democratic ideals.[108]

In light of these developments, and in keeping with the goals of Atatürk and İnönü, they called for greater parliamentary oversight, individual freedom, and intraparty democracy in accordance with the constitution. Historian Cemil Koçak argues that this proposal was not an attempt to break with the single-party regime. Rather it "should be interpreted as a demand for a change of administration within both the CHP and the political system," perhaps resulting in the four signatories receiving cabinet posts.[109] With the budget debate just concluded and the fate of the Land Reform Bill still undecided, the proposal could have led to

[105] Cemil Koçak, *Türkiye'de Milli Şef Dönemi, 1938–1945*, vol. II, 3rd ed. (Istanbul: İletişim Yayınları, 2007 [1986]), 553.

[106] TBMM, May 21, 1945, 228–230.

[107] TBMM, May 29, 1945, 506, 508. The two additional members to vote against the government were Hikmet Bayur, who had been critical of the Land Reform Bill, and Recep Peker, an avid supporter of single-party rule who likely hoped to position himself as a credible candidate for prime minister, should the government fall (Koçak, *Türkiye'de Milli Şef Dönemi, 1938–1945*, vol. II, 553–555).

[108] Koçak, *İkinci Parti*, 315.

[109] Ibid., 314–316, quotation on 327.

major changes within the party. Yet this was not to be. On June 11, the Land Reform Bill was passed with 345 votes and 104 abstentions, including Bayar, Menderes, Koraltan, and Köprülü. The following day, the parliamentary group rejected the four men's proposal, thereby signaling that a political opening would not come from within the party.

During the summer, talks between the four men intensified. Koraltan met with Ahmet Hamdi Başar, a long-time proponent of state intervention in the service of developing a "national" (i.e., Turkish) economy. Together, they began drawing up the program for a potential opposition party. The program they proposed, however, was opposed by Menderes and Köprülü, who favored a less intrusive role for the state. Bayar sided with Menderes and Köprülü, leading Koraltan to back away from the program.[110] As a result, the economic program that emerged was largely shaped by Menderes and Köprülü. Come mid September, the two men were ready to challenge the CHP more openly by publishing articles in the liberal paper *Vatan* (Homeland). As punishment for their public criticism, they were expelled from the party on September 21. Bayar resigned from parliament on September 28, and Koraltan, who defended the actions of Menderes and Köprülü, was expelled on October 2. At the November 1 opening of the parliamentary term, President İnönü identified the lack of an opposition party as "our sole deficiency" in relation to "democratic nations," thus signaling his support for such a development.

[110] Cemil Koçak, *İktidar ve Demokratlar: Türkiye'de İki Partili Siyasi Sistemin Kuruluş Yılları, 1945–1950*, vol. II (Istanbul: İletişim Yayınları, 2012), 19–20. Ahmet Hamdi Başar (1897–1971) was an important figure in Turkey's early economic debates – albeit seldom victorious. Born to an elite family (his father was a royal tutor, his mother was from the powerful Karaosmanoğlu family), he studied at the Istanbul University Faculty of Literature and joined organizations like Turkish Hearth, where he would likely have met cultural nationalists such as Fuat Köprülü. With his brother-in-law, he published *Ticaret-i Umumiye Mecmuası* (Journal of Public Commerce), which called for "raising Turkish merchants." During the Entente-occupation of Istanbul, he taught in high schools while funneling money to the Ankara government and publishing *Türkiye İktisat Mecmuası* (Turkey Economic Journal). At the war's end he was involved with organizing the İzmir Economic Congress, sat on the board of important state enterprises, and was appointed manager of the Port Authority (*Liman Şirketi*). Following the closure of the SCF, Başar and other economic experts joined Mustafa Kemal's tour of the countryside. Subsequently, they proposed reforms. Başar pushed for reducing taxes on agricultural production and shifting the burden to consumption (i.e., urban areas), but both İnönü and Atatürk disliked these suggestions and grew weary of his repeated attempts to get their attention. He lost his job with the Port Authority in 1934. Thereafter, he involved himself in private business and carried on debates with other gadflies like Ahmet Ağaoğlu. Başar became a member of the DP and served in parliament from 1950 to 1954, leaving the party in 1953 and eventually joining the opposition Freedom Party (HP) (Murat Koraltürk, "Ahmet Hamdi Başar Kimdir?," in *Ahmet Hamdi Başar'ın Hatıraları, Cilt I: "Gazi Bana Çok Kızmış ...,"* ed. Murat Koraltürk [Istanbul: Bilgi Üniversitesi Yayınları, 2007], 1–39).

At the same time, the speech served as a demand for party dissidents to reveal themselves. He declared:

> This we know: In a political institution, both in principle and in practice, it is better for those who are not supporters of their friends to take a public stand for their convictions and their programs rather than carrying on their work in a factional manner. It is the better path for the development of our political life and the more constructive behavior for political maturity and the national interest.[111]

Though he promised to revise the Press Law and the Associations Law (which regulated political parties), he did not specify when these changes would be made. He was telling his intraparty opponents to reveal themselves without guaranteeing their safety.[112]

On December 1, despite lacking clearly defined legal protections, Bayar, Koraltan, Köprülü, and Menderes announced their intention to establish a new party. Bayar then formally resigned from the CHP. On December 4, the opposition received a clear warning that the boundaries of anti-government activity would be violently enforced. Three Istanbul publishing houses associated with Bayar and other opposition figures were attacked and burned by a mob.[113] The publishers targeted, Sabiha and Zekeriya Sertel, Sabahattin Ali, and Cami Baykurt, were left-wing critics of the government and frequently accused of pro-Soviet sympathies. The attacks followed the Sertels' announcement of a new magazine named *Görüşler* (Views), which would be produced by their publishing house, *Tan* (Dawn), and contain contributions from Menderes and others.[114] According to the historian Kemal Karpat, a university student at the time and witness to the attacks, the vandalism would have been extended to liberal critics of the government like *Vatan* but was directed toward left-wing publishers at "the last moment in order to give the manifestation an anti-communist only and not an anti-opposition feature."[115]

The anti-communist aspect of the attacks is a reminder that the DP was formed at a moment of acute international tension. Turkey had

111 TBMM, November 1, 1945, 7, 9. For discussion, see Karpat, *Turkey's Politics*, 144–147; Eroğul, *Demokrat Parti*, 13–15.

112 Koçak, *İkinci Parti*, 740–745.

113 For a discussion of the "Tan Incident" from multiple perspectives, see James Ryan, "Republic of Others: Opponents of Kemalism in Turkey's Single-Party Era" (PhD diss., University of Pennsylvania, Philadelphia, 2017), 155–211.

114 Writing years later, Sabiha Sertel would recall being skeptical of Bayar, whom she viewed as a representative of the "commercial bourgeoisie" and who, when she pressed him on issues like unions and land reform, had given her evasive answers, such as "Our program isn't prepared yet" (*Roman Gibi*, 2nd ed. [Istanbul: Belge Yayınları, 1987 (1969)], 271).

115 Karpat, *Turkey's Politics*, 150 n. 39.

declared war on Germany on February 23, 1945, in time to receive an invitation to the San Francisco Conference, where the UN would be organized. On March 19, 1945, the USSR had informed the Turkish government that it would be letting the 1925 Friendship Treaty between the two countries expire pending renegotiation. The announcement was both an opportunity for the Soviet government to assert its influence in Turkey and a way of punishing Turkey for the four years of war during which Turkey's leaders had withheld meaningful support. In coordination with these diplomatic moves, the Soviet press began criticizing Turkey and calling into question Turkey's right to the north-eastern provinces of Kars, Artvin, and Ardahan, which had at one point been under Russian imperial control.[116]

Though land reform had been a long-standing ambition of the CHP leadership, the introduction of the bill, combined with İnönü's calls for greater democracy in May, cannot be divorced from these surrounding events. Not only did the moves position Turkey as part of a postwar community of democracies, but they helped defuse the sort of rural unrest that the Soviets might seek to foment. Meanwhile, by encouraging anti-communist politicians like Bayar, İnönü was able to sideline other opponents with potentially pro-Soviet inclinations.[117]

On June 7, 1945, the same day that the four men submitted their reform proposal to the CHP parliamentary group, Soviet Foreign Minister Molotov reiterated to his Turkish counterpart that the USSR wished to renegotiate Soviet access through the Bosporus Straits and the status of Turkey's northeast provinces. While the British supported Turkey by demanding that any negotiations be multilateral, US officials refused to lend any support for the time being. A decision on the issue was avoided at the Potsdam Conference (July 17–August 2) and tensions persisted. Four days after the conference ended, the United States

[116] Jamil Hasanlı, *Stalin and the Turkish Crisis of the Cold War, 1945–1953* (Lanham: Lexington Books, 2011), 11; "Review of Events in Turkey, 1945," February 1, 1946, FO 371/59297.

[117] It would not have been difficult for İnönü to accuse the DP of pro-Soviet tendencies. The founders were closely associated with İnönü's long-time opponent, Tevfik Rüştü Aras, and Aras was widely seen as friendly with the USSR. In addition to arguing for warmer relations with the USSR in publications like *Tan*, Aras was reported to frequent the Soviet embassy. In later years, these actions led İnönü allies such as Asım Us and Faik Ahmet Barutçu to accuse him of sinister designs. The British embassy also viewed him with suspicion. Still, it should be noted that his 1945 book, *Görüşlerim* (My Views), does not advocate for alliance with the Soviets alone but rather for alliance with *all* powers, avoiding commitment to one particular bloc (Tevfik Rüştü Aras, *Görüşlerim* [Istanbul: Semih Lütfi Kitabevi, 1945], 17; "Review of Events in Turkey, 1945," February 1, 1946, FO 371/59297; "Leading Personalities in Turkey," November 13, 1950, FO 371/87924; Koçak, *Türkiye'de Milli Şef Dönemi, 1938–1945*, vol. II, 360, 552).

dropped a nuclear bomb on the Japanese city of Hiroshima. Nagasaki was bombed three days later, bringing World War II to an end on August 15, the same day Turkey signed the UN Charter. The British cruiser HMS *Ajax* arrived in Istanbul in early September and, on November 2, the United States also proposed multilateral discussions regarding commercial transit through the straits, thereby undermining the Soviet position and favoring Turkey. İnönü backed the US proposal on December 5, one day after the attacks on socialist publishers in Istanbul.[118]

The DP was formed amid this flurry of international and domestic activity. The end of the war had weakened the position of politicians with pro-German sympathies, but it was not yet clear how the postwar settlement would affect Turkey or be turned to the benefit of one domestic faction or another. Throughout 1945, the Turkish government was faced with concrete threats from a Soviet regime now occupying Bulgaria and Iran (not to mention the Armenian, Georgian, and Azerbaijani Soviets that it had controlled since the 1920s). Under these circumstances, the need to seek British and American support was of paramount importance to Turkey's leaders. After an initial flirtation with pro-Soviet figures like former Foreign Minister Tevfik Rüştü Aras and the Sertels, the DP founders distanced themselves and began associating with journalists who voiced liberal and anti-communist positions such as Ahmet Emin Yalman (editor of *Vatan*) and Cihad Baban (editor of *Tasvir*). Baban would stand for parliament in 1946 as an "independent" candidate for Istanbul, backed by the DP. He formally joined the party for the 1950 election, which it would win, bringing Baban and the four party founders to power.

Conclusion: The Unionist Factor in Turkish Democratization

When the DP was formally established on January 6, 1946, its program was little different from that of the CHP. As historian Cemil Koçak observes, how could it be otherwise? The DP program declared loyalty to the constitution and, since 1937, the constitution had incorporated the main principles of the CHP.[119] Moreover, as I have shown throughout this chapter, we should not expect dramatic differences: the men who established the DP had been involved in the country's politics since before there was a Republic of Turkey. They began their careers in the

[118] "Review of Events in Turkey, 1945," February 1, 1946, FO 371/59297.
[119] Koçak, *İktidar ve Demokratlar*, 59.

İTC, seeking to preserve the Ottoman Empire. Even Adnan Menderes, the youngest of the four, did not take up arms against foreign occupiers with the intention of creating a new state but rather to defend an existing one. Nonetheless, by the time he joined the national struggle, it was also clear that the "nation" he was fighting for was primarily a Muslim one. This concern with protecting the empire's Muslim population and developing opportunities for Muslim merchants (particularly the Turkish-speaking ones) had linked men like Bayar, Köprülü, and Koraltan even before World War I began. The genocide of Armenians during the war and the population exchanges after the war reinforced this association of religion and nation.[120]

In order to achieve their goal of a strong imperial (and, later, republican) state, these men were not opposed to using violent, nondemocratic means. They formed secret societies, organized boycotts, purged rivals, moved populations, constrained civil society, and made use of state security services. They believed the results justified the means. By the mid 1920s, Turkey was free of foreign control, while other states carved out of the Ottoman Empire were ruled by France and the UK – or, in the case of the Arabian Peninsula, contested by rival tribal chieftaincies. Over the next two decades, as other post-Ottoman states remained under colonial rule and newly created Central and Eastern European states were caught up in World War II, Turkey remained independent. In other words, the founders of the DP might have believed in the utility of democratic politics, but they had seen the potential benefits of authoritarian systems.

The frustrations these four men had developed with the single-party regime during İsmet İnönü's seven years of rule were not unique to them. While İnönü's assumption of power was hardly a break with Atatürk's policies, it led to a reordering of power within the single party. İnönü did not secure his position by going to the countryside and rallying public support; instead, he based his claim on preeminence within the single party. While the party, as formed by Atatürk and his allies in the early 1920s, may have had extensive links to the society, under İnönü, it narrowed. In other words, even if we generously imagine that the CHP of the 1920s claimed the support of 70 percent of the population, then İnönü's dominance depended on – again, generously – 70 percent of that original 70 percent, which is to say 49 percent of the population. The

[120] For a discussion of Gagauz (or "Christian Turks"), see Gözde Emen-Gökatalay and Semih Gökatalay, "Was There Room for Christian Turks in Early Republican Turkey? Debates on the Migration and Turkishness of the Gagauz," *Middle Eastern Studies* 59, no. 2 (2022): 199–220.

opportunity was now open for İnönü's opponents within the party to reach out to the majority of the population and outflank him. Moreover, all four of the DP founders could appeal to portions of the CHP coalition (landlords, businessmen, academics, and members of the security apparatus). They could offer the reassurance of continuity while calling for change.

Political leaders who are part of an authoritarian system but willing to break with it are often crucial to democratic transitions. Their experiences before they break with the system are important in understanding the choices they make during and after the transition. That said, the DP grew rapidly beyond these four men. In 1945, it was little more than a discontented faction of the CHP; by 1950, it was the most popular political party in the country. To the extent that it came to differ from the CHP over the following five years, it was by positioning itself as the representative of individuals and "the people" against the state. The next chapter looks beyond the four founders and considers the ways in which various party activists struggled to shape the DP in its early years.

2 Children of the Revolution: Defining the Democrat Party, 1946–1950

Before he announced the formation of the DP on January 7, 1946, Celal Bayar visited President İsmet İnönü at his official residence atop Ankara's Çankaya Hill. According to İnönü's son-in-law, the men had a pleasant conversation, joking about the party pins that Bayar had brought with him. When Bayar presented the DP program, İnönü asked three questions. First: "Is there a clause [as in the program of an earlier opposition party] that says … 'we are deferential to religious faith?'" Second: "Will you meddle with the [policy of expanding education with] Village Institutes and the primary school campaign?" Third: "Is there any dissent [in terms of] foreign policy?" Bayar promised to maintain the CHP regime's stances on education, secularism, and foreign policy, and İnönü gave his approval.[1] Critics of the DP argue that, in power, the party went back on these promises, closing the Village Institute schools, allowing excessive religious expression in public life, and subordinating the country to foreign interests.

Whatever the merits of these accusations, the overall criticism misses something crucial: the DP was little more than a name in early 1946. Over fourteen years, it would grow and change. The ambiguous nature of the party at the outset led activists to promote their own agendas. Whereas the previous chapter showed how the lives of the DP founders, taken together, reveal significant continuities between the late imperial, early republican, and multiparty party eras, this chapter considers the experiences of other important party activists at the national and provincial levels. While some were, like the four DP founders, involved in the creation of the republican system, many are better understood as *products* of that system. As Samet Ağaoğlu, one of the more articulate members of this cohort, wrote:

> These were [young people who] emerged from the law faculties in Istanbul and Ankara believing in things they'd heard from their professors: the principles of

[1] Toker, *Tek Partiden Çok Partiye*, 80–81.

freedom, national sovereignty, public administration, and respect for human dignity and honor. From reading one or two translated books about the French Revolution they'd become devotees of the Dantons, Robespierres, Saint-Justs, Camille Desmoulinses, and Mirabeaus … [Adnan] Menderes represented the Democrat Party's young idealists.[2]

As we will see, the quotation is rather self-serving in the way it smooths over the pettiness and ambition that also motivated a politician like Ağaoğlu. Nonetheless, this hopefulness is important to recall at the outset. Democrats like Menderes and Bayar did not attract vast crowds of enthusiastic citizens to their rallies merely thanks to a shared sense of spite or, later, the promise of material benefits through networks of patronage and clientelism. Rather, they combined a critique of the single-party era with an optimistic vision of a better future. The nature of this critique and the means for achieving that future, moreover, were contested and changing. They led to splits in the party as early as 1948 and shifts in emphasis when faced with new economic conditions.

In this chapter, we will consider some of the people and conditions shaping the DP during its years in opposition – not only Ağaoğlu, but also some of his peers from more provincial backgrounds. In particular, we will consider the contrasting provinces of Malatya and Balıkesir to see how local elites established and developed the DP in diverse regions of the country. Though Bayar and Menderes may have drawn the largest crowds, these other party leaders played an important role in shaping the party's program and giving voice to the frustrations of voters. Sometimes their concerns were abstract, focused on ideas of freedom and praising the liberal ideals of the postwar era, but often they were more material, focused on economic hardships brought about by Turkey's integration into the emerging American-led economic order.

Fathers, Sons, and Daughters: Traditions of Liberal Opposition in Turkey

Samet Ağaoğlu was one of the DP's most prominent ideologues. Born in 1908, he was typical of the men who would serve in DP governments during the 1950s: too young to have fought in the Independence War but old enough to have extensive experience working for the state in the single-party era. In the 1920s and 1930s, when the four DP founders were crafting the republic's institutions, Ağaoğlu was in school, preparing to serve in those institutions. By the time the ruling party fractured in

[2] Ağaoğlu, *Arkadaşım Menderes*, 20.

1945, he had risen to a high post in the bureaucracy despite his misgivings about the regime he served. This position of being critical-but-complicit was common to many DP elites. What set Ağaoğlu somewhat apart (and connected him to the DP founders) was his pedigree: his father, Ahmet, was a revolutionary émigré from Russian Azerbaijan. He had been a supporter of the Unionists and, later, Mustafa Kemal's nationalist government in Ankara, where he edited the movement's main newspaper, played an active role in Turkish nationalist cultural associations, served in parliament, and helped draft the 1924 constitution.[3]

Ahmet became both a dependable supporter of Mustafa Kemal and a leading advocate of liberalism, both in terms of abstract, spiritual freedom (*hürriyet*) and a more contractual, economic freedom (*serberstiyet*).[4] Balancing these commitments was difficult, since neither form of freedom was a consistent priority for the leaders of the early republic. While many followers of Kemal hoped to use the state to liberate people from traditional forms of social control – feudal, religious, and patriarchal – they also sought to replace these with a sense of national belonging. Along these lines, some of Ahmet's nationalist allies argued for a version of the "nation" in which individuals were subordinate to the interests of the larger Turkish collective. When members of the "liberal" opposition parties argued that such large-scale state interventions impinged on people's freedom of conscience and called for a degree of religious toleration, many followers of Mustafa Kemal derided their views as religious "reaction" (*irtica*). Despite the risks, Ahmet too opposed these more radical nationalist visions, arguing that individuals were essential parts of the nation and that the most successful nations in Europe were those composed of strong individuals. As he saw it, the legacy of the Independence War should not be to subordinate citizens to the will of the state but rather to free them from foreign exploitation.[5]

Ahmet's principled stands earned him the respect of Mustafa Kemal and others in the government, but his unwillingness to shift with the political winds eventually cost him their support. In 1930, Kemal personally asked him to join the opposition SCF. Ahmet gave the new party his full commitment. When it met persecution from the government and

[3] Ahmet Ağaoğlu's colorful life has been the subject of numerous monographs, including Shissler, *Between Two Worlds* and H. Ozan Özavcı, *Intellectual Origins of the Republic: Ahmet Ağaoğlu and the Genealogy of Liberalism in Turkey* (Leiden: Brill, 2015). For an account of Turkic émigrés from the Russian Empire, see James Meyer, *Turks across Empires: Marketing Muslim Identity in the Russian–Ottoman Borderlands, 1856–1914* (Oxford: Oxford University Press, 2015).

[4] Ahmet İnsel, "Türkiye'de Liberalizm Kavramının Soyçizgisi," in *Modern Türkiye'de Siyasi Düşünce VII: Liberalizm*, ed. Tanıl Bora and Murat Gültekingil (Istanbul: İletişim Yayınları, 2005), 41–42; Turnaoğlu, *The Formation of Turkish Republicanism*, 126–128.

[5] Özavcı, *Intellectual Origins*, 185–186.

was forced to close, he did not rejoin the CHP and the Ankara social scene. Instead, he returned to Istanbul to teach. After a short hiatus from journalism, he began publishing critical pieces about the government in the paper *Akın* (Torrent). One column especially incensed Mustafa Kemal, who confronted Ahmet at an evening gathering, reading the text and demanding an explanation. "It wasn't right," the president argued, "for a guy [*zat*] to both teach at the university and criticize the government." He reminded Ahmet of his status as an undesired dependent (*sığıntı*) in the country.[6] Fuat Köprülü, who was also present, supported Kemal's arguments. Ahmet did not back down, replying that "with those words you are plunging a sword into the heart of Turks." Mustafa Kemal apologized, but Ahmet soon stopped publishing *Akın*.[7] While the editor of the major daily paper *Cumhuriyet* (Republic) gave him a job as a columnist, his overall loss of income and his poor relations with the government came at the same time as the death of his wife. The succession of setbacks left Ahmet deeply embittered toward the regime during the last six years of his life.

Ahmet's treatment made a strong impression on his children – Samet and his sister Süreyya both describe it in their memoirs – but it did not discourage them from active engagement with the regime's state-building project. All five Ağaoğlu siblings became highly accomplished members of the republican elite. Of the three eldest, Süreyya was the first women to earn a law degree and pass the bar in Turkey; Tezer (Taşkıran) was a philosopher and, by the 1940s, the head of the prestigious Ankara Girls School; and Abdurrahman was a representative for Siemens and its Turkish partner, Koç. The youngest sister, Gültekin, was a pediatrician.[8] Samet, under pressure from his father, followed his sister's path into law school. Though his interest lay in literature, he earned a degree from Ankara Law School in 1932 and then enrolled at the University of Strasbourg for an advanced degree. Samet's time in France was cut short when his father's financial difficulties mounted, necessitating his return to Ankara in 1934. His father used his remaining connections to secure Samet a post in Celal Bayar's Ministry of Economy. There, by 1944, he worked his way up to general director of domestic commerce. He also married Neriman Babaoğlu, the daughter of an appeals court judge.[9]

[6] Gülay Sarıçoban, "Demokrat Partiden Bir Siyasi Portre: Samet Ağaoğlu," *Cumhuriyet Tarihi Araştırmaları Dergisi* 9, no. 17 (2013): 83.

[7] Süreyya Ağaoğlu, *Bir Ömür Böyle Geçti* (Istanbul: Ağaoğlu Yayınevi, 1975), 65.

[8] Ibid., 121; Günseli Naymansoy, *Türk Felsefesinin Öncülerinden Tezer Taşkıran* (Ankara: Atatürk Kültür Merkezi, 2013), 2–15.

[9] Muzaffer Çandır, *Manisa Milletvekili: Yazar Samet Ağaoğlu: Hayatı, Sanatı, Eserleri* (Manisa: Manisa İl Özel İdaresi, 2013), 25–26. Celal Bayar rented a house on the Ağaoğlu property during the mid 1920s (Ağaoğlu, *Bir Ömür*, 37).

Samet's rise through the state economic bureaucracy occurred as World War II was placing that bureaucracy under strain. Wartime mobilization led to rationing, encouraging hoarding and black-market activity, which Samet's office was meant to control. In January 1940, parliament passed a National Protection Law, granting the state broad powers to set prices. In 1942 a ration card system was developed. As the historian Murat Metinsoy describes, these laws and regulations served to alienate people from the government, which they viewed as protecting the large war profiteers while inspectors like Samet harassed small merchants.[10] For his part, Samet recalled the era as one in which the ineptness of the state and its political leadership in economic matters caused consternation among citizens and actually provoked shortages and high prices.[11] The criticism suggests less of an opposition to state intervention than to the methods of those overseeing it.

The Ağaoğlu siblings became involved in party politics after their father's death in 1939. Samet's initial experience is particularly illustrative of how the CHP integrated the country's elite into its political organization. In 1943, he was invited by Recep Peker to join a slate of candidates for the coming elections. Peker was a former CHP general secretary, currently on bad terms with President İnönü and antagonistic toward the new general secretary, Memduh Şevket Esendal, who was in the process of drawing up his own electoral list. It was through these lists that party leaders like Peker and Esendal developed personal political factions, often drawing on talented young officials. In this way, a successful bureaucrat like Samet might be rewarded with a place in parliament.

Since Samet was familiar but unimpressed with Esendal and the religiously infused conception of Turkish nationalism that he promoted, he agreed to be considered for Peker's list.[12] Yet his nomination was blocked by Esendal, who nominated Samet's sister Tezer instead. (Apparently, in her role as a school administrator, she had gained the confidence of President İnönü.) Samet was left to fume.[13] In what would become a pattern, he quickly began criticizing any organization that would not have him as a member. In 1944, he published *The Spirit of the National Forces*, a book that recounted the early successes of the

[10] Murat Metinsoy, *İkinci Dünya Savaşında Türkiye Gündelik Yaşam Devlet ve Toplum* (Istanbul: Türkiye İş Bankası Kültür Yayınları, 2017), 87–102.

[11] Samet Ağaoğlu, "Memur meselesi," *Demokrat İzmir*, February 16, 1949, 1, 4.

[12] Metin Çınar, *Anadoluculuk ve Tek Parti CHP'de Sağ Kanat* (Istanbul: İletişim Yayınları, 2013), 245–247; İlker Aytürk, "Nationalism and Islam in Cold War Turkey, 1944–69," *Middle Eastern Studies* 50, no. 5 (2014): 695–696.

[13] Ağaoğlu, *Bir Ömür*, 85; Naymansoy, *Türk Felsefesinin*, 16–22; Samet Ağaoğlu, *Siyasi Günlük: DP'nin Kuruluşu*, ed. Cemil Koçak (Istanbul: İletişim Yayınları, 1992), 29.

parliament, before it became dominated by a single party and, implicitly, went astray.[14]

Petty as he could be, Samet's distaste for the ruling CHP was not only a reaction to his father's poor treatment or his own exclusion from the candidate list. His (and his siblings') unease with heavy-handed state intervention also stemmed from their experience as Russian émigrés. The Ağaoğlu family had lost its lands in Azerbaijan after the Soviet takeover in the 1920s. Oppression and dispossession helped make émigrés advocates of Turkish nationalism and skeptical toward socialism and statist methods more broadly. Whereas these sentiments would draw Samet into domestic politics, his sister Süreyya would become active in an array of postwar international liberal organizations. In fact, in 1942, even before the war ended, she was meeting with such leaders as Wendell Willkie, the 1940 Republican Party candidate for the US presidency. Wilkie was visiting Turkey as part of a global "goodwill" tour, touting his vision of liberalism in which the state encouraged open markets and free enterprise rather than paternalistically shielding people (or the markets themselves) from foreign competition.[15]

In her memoirs, Süreyya praised leaders such as Wilkie while presenting Turkish politicians in a negative light. President İnönü, in particular, exemplified the high-handedness of state officials, but other examples abounded. A focal point in her account of the 1940s is the Wealth Tax, which funded neutral Turkey's wartime mobilization by extracting onerous sums, particularly from the country's religious minorities. One of her clients, a Turkish Jew, was targeted by the law and sent off to the infamous Aşkale labor camp. His health never fully recovered. Reflecting on this injustice and the government's general unwillingness to admit Jewish refugees, she concludes, "Had the Germans won the war, I'm saying it's likely that our Government would have done some procedures parallel with Hitler. In fact, the Wealth Tax was such an example."[16]

Depicting the government's heavy-handed, ethnically targeted policies as "German" was an effective means of discrediting it once the tide of battle turned against the Nazi government in 1942–43. But where then should Turkish liberals look to for a model? Prior to the Nazis' rise to power, Germany had offered a model of liberal government, but now, no more. The USSR was no champion of liberal values either – and, geographically, too close for comfort. France was under German occupation

[14] See Samet Ağaoğlu, *Kuva-yı Millîye Ruhu* (Istanbul: Yapı Kredi Yayınları, 2011 [1944]).

[15] David Levering Lewis, *The Improbable Wendell Willkie* (New York: Liveright, 2018), 225–265.

[16] Ağaoğlu, *Bir Ömür*, 84.

(and, even before the war, was seen as a state in decline). The British were as menacing as the Soviets: since 1941 the UK had invaded and occupied Iraq and Syria; jointly occupied Iran with the USSR and forced the shah of Iran to abdicate; and deposed the king of Egypt. Only the United States was well-positioned to serve as a model. Its combination of free markets and "freedom from fear and want" that liberal internationalists such as Willkie and Franklin Roosevelt championed had great appeal to educated professionals like the Ağaoğlu siblings.

When opposition became organized in 1945, Samet was not among the founders or leadership, which often came from Bayar's allies in the financial sector.[17] Since childhood, however, he had been familiar with Bayar and Köprülü. Eager to join the DP organization, he wrote Bayar in late December 1945 and received a favorable response. In the summer of 1946, with the country heading toward early elections – a CHP maneuver to catch the DP off guard – Samet was formally invited to join the party. He accepted and ostentatiously resigned his post in state service (as was required of all candidates, save for university professors).[18] In an election marred by widespread voter fraud carried out by CHP officials, he was among the candidates who failed to win a seat. Without a job, he turned to private law practice and partisan journalism. These incomes were supplemented with a position as a DP party inspector, in which he traveled western Turkey, giving speeches to local organizations. By January 1947, he was elected to the party's executive committee.[19] Süreyya was less eager to join. Although she had frosty relations with

[17] Cemil Koçak points to the role of former İş Bankası officials like Yusuf Ziya Öniş in organizing the party in 1946. Öniş had been the general director of DenizBank (Maritime Bank) when Bayar was prime minister (1938–39), but he had been removed once Bayar lost power. Koçak describes how Öniş encouraged the DP's first Istanbul provincial president, Kenan Öner, to bring several rich businessmen onto his leadership team. Interestingly, Öniş was also one of several leading DP figures with extensive connections in the world of sport. He had been president of Galatasaray FC and the first president of the Turkish Football Federation. Similarly, Zeki Rıza Sporel, an owner of the official DP paper, *Zafer*, had played for Fenerbahçe FC and the national team during the 1920s and 1930s (Koçak, *İktidar ve Demokratlar*, 132–133, quoting extensively from Kenan Öner, *Siyasi Hatıralarım ve Bizde Demokrasi* [Istanbul: Osmanbey Matbaası, 1948], 11–12).

[18] Ağaoğlu publicly explained his decision to resign and run as a DP candidate by publishing an announcement in the pro-DP paper *Vatan* on July 1, 1946 (Ağaoğlu, *Siyasi Günlük*, 36).

[19] According to its 1946 rules, the DP was organized around party congresses. These congresses were to be held once every two years and would elect a party president, an executive committee (which included the president), and discipline committee. The executive committee had the power to create and inspect provincial organizations. Delegates to the congress included the party president, the executive committee, and representatives from the provinces, allocated according to the size of a province's membership. Until the party held its First Congress on January 7–10, 1947, the

President İnönü and positive feelings toward Bayar, she was distrustful of Köprülü, remembering his role in berating her father at Atatürk's dinner table. During the coming years, she would focus on her legal career and contributions to charities and liberal organizations such as the Society for the Spread of Free Ideas (*Hür Fikirleri Yayma Cemiyeti*), which included many DP members, as well as prominent party supporters such as journalist Ahmet Emin Yalman.[20]

Like the DP founders, Yalman had been intimately involved in the Unionist regime, writing for its official paper and coming to know such leading ideologues as Ziya Gökalp while at Istanbul University. Subsequently, their paths diverged. After the establishment of the republic, he had taken a critical stance toward the regime – even more so than Ahmet Ağaoğlu. For his efforts, he had been repeatedly prosecuted and banned from publishing.[21] Throughout the late 1940s, he was an avid supporter of the DP – according to one DP leader, he even coined the party's name.[22] But Yalman's support was contingent upon the party's defense of liberal values, especially journalistic freedom and economic liberalism.[23] Its failures in these regards would eventually lead him to break with the party.

Keeping to the Program: Early Struggles to Define the Democrat Party

From the outset, the DP was united less by ideology than by its members' opposition to the CHP and the overbearing control that CHP leaders exercised over their own party organization. When they had still been

founders exercised effective control. Beginning with the First Congress, this control grew more difficult. The election of a presiding officer at the First Congress, for example, revealed splits between Istanbul and Aegean (i.e., İzmir) factions of the party (Koçak, *İkinci Parti*, 65–69; Cemil Koçak, *Rejim Krizi: Türkiye'de İki Partili Siyasi Sistemin Kuruluş Yılları, 1945–1950*, vol. III [Istanbul: İletişim Yayınları, 2013], 261–304).

20 Reuben Silverman, "Süreyya Ağaoğlu and the Emerging Liberal Order in Early Cold War Turkey," *Middle Eastern Studies* 60, no. 2 (2023): 328–330. Shortly after the DP's 1950 victory, Süreyya told an official from the US consulate in Istanbul that Bayar had asked her to run in the election, but she could earn more money in private practice and preferred having the freedom to criticize the government if she desired (Baldwin to US embassy Ankara, May 24, 1950, RG 84, Box 57, UD 3288, NND 842831 [hereafter RG 84, Box 57]).

21 Aliyar Demirci, "Ahmet Emin Yalman," in *Modern Türkiye'de Siyasi Düşünce VII: Liberalizm*, ed. Tanıl Bora and Murat Gültekingil (Istanbul: İletişim Yayınları, 2005), 473–479.

22 Sarol, *Bilinmeyen Menderes*, vol. I, 179.

23 In addition to running the newspaper *Vatan*, Yalman was also involved with his family business, Tatko, which was the distributor in Turkey for Goodyear tires, Dodge automobiles, and Caterpillar tractors.

CHP members, the DP founders had focused their calls for reform on internal party democracy and freedom of speech. What they hoped to advocate for with that speech was less clear. This vagueness offered liberals like Yalman and Ağaoğlu, as well as more radical critics of the single-party regime, an opportunity to define the DP's public image.

The DP program, hashed out during 1945 and announced in early 1946, was "pragmatic" rather than revolutionary in its proposals.[24] It stated broad principles that distinguished the new party from the CHP by emphasizing the party's commitment to "democracy" and the "national will," as well as its subordination to the "human dignity and basic human rights" enunciated in the UN Charter.[25] Despite these calls for limits and restraints on the power of the state, the program was equally an argument for state power being directed to new purposes. The call for increased state intervention was clearest in the program's support for additional loans to farmers, as well as the provision of tools and spare parts. The program also called for a major expansion of road and water systems across the country while simultaneously lowering taxes. To pay for these new expenditures, the program suggested seeking foreign loans.[26] To those who might question such large increases in spending, the program explained, "Our party believes that fiscal affairs should be carried out with an understanding, appropriate to our economic and social principles, that does not see the interests of the Treasury as separate from or superior to the public interest."[27]

Alongside these calls for increased spending, there was an emphasis on "private enterprise and capital." Especially when discussing plans for industry, the program argued that the government should only involve itself in matters where private enterprise and capital had not entered owing to a lack of likely profits. Where possible, enterprises that had been established by the state, but which could be managed by private initiative, should be handed off. More generally, the private sector would benefit from "stability and trust," which could be best achieved by a "general long-term plan." At the provincial and municipal level, planning was identified as crucial.[28]

The phrasing of these positions left considerable room for interpretation. In its discussion of statism (*devletçilik*), for example, the program declared:

[24] Koçak, *İktidar ve Demokratlar*, 19.
[25] See DP program clauses 3, 4, and 8, contained in ibid., 48.
[26] See DP program clauses 56, 57, 63, 72–73, 75, 78, and 84, contained in ibid., 54–56.
[27] See DP program clause 76, contained in ibid., 56.
[28] See DP program clauses 21, 42–44, and 47, contained in ibid., 50–53.

> To raise citizens' standard of living and level of welfare by expanding the amount of economic activity in order to fill the vacuum that has persisted in the economic field, we take the meaning of statism as *the duty to develop private enterprise and capital in the shape and means most suited for the general welfare, either through the state's direct involvement in economic activity or through means of organization, encouragement, and aid.* The organization of private enterprise and capital activity and investment by the state comes from the need to guarantee and protect the interests of private enterprise and the general interest. [Italics mine.][29]

This was ambiguous and not discernably different from the CHP's official understanding of statism. Consequently, advocates of more liberal policies found it necessary to impose their preferred definitions onto the DP program. Writing for a foreign audience in early 1947, seeking to shape its understanding of what the DP represented, Ahmet Emin Yalman declared, "The essential point of opposition to the [CHP] lay in the Democrats' understanding of *etatism*," which might seem the same "in theory" but was, "in practice," different. And, in any event:

> The significance of the Democratic Party did not consist in the wording of its program, but in the fact that its aims and ideals had emerged from the government's failure to apply various principles which were embodied in the constitution.[30]

In mid 1947, Samet, writing for a Turkish-speaking audience, attempted a similar imposition of his views by means of his book *The Differences between the Two Parties*. According to Samet, under DP rule, the state would only enter into "economic activities to assure economic development and raise its countrymen's welfare and standard of living; for any other reason or excuse, it does not enter."[31] While not wholly misrepresenting the party's policies, his depiction gave the impression of an organization that had committed itself more firmly to nonintervention than its program suggested. Other spokesmen for the party were more circumspect. Burhan Belge, a supporter of the DP who had once been a strong advocate of economic planning, simply suggested that any plan that was formulated should not be autarkic.[32] Muhlis Ete, an economics

29 See DP program clause 17, contained in ibid., 49.

30 Ahmet Emin Yalman, "The Struggle for Multi-Party Government in Turkey," *Middle East Journal* 1, no. 1 (1947): 55.

31 Samet Ağaoğlu, *İki Parti Arasındaki Farklar* (Ankara: Arbas Matbaası, 1947), 65.

32 Burhan Asaf Belge, "İktisadi işlerimiz," *Demokrat İzmir*, May 18, 1947, 1, 4. Belge had once been part of the Kadro group, whose members advocated for extensive state intervention in the economy. During the years 1945–60, he moved from criticism of the CHP to participation in the DP; from criticism of the DP to a position on the CHP electoral list in 1950; and from renewed support for the DP to representing the party in parliament after 1957. For a detailed biography, see Aytaç Yıldız, *Üç Dönem Bir Aydın: Burhan Asaf Belge, 1899–1967* (Istanbul: İletişim Yayınları, 2011).

professor who would go on to serve as minister of economy and trade (1950–52), looking at the same party program as Samet, declared that it "showed [the DP] to still be attached to statism," but, he added, "it does not carry a socialist character."[33]

Elsewhere in his book, Samet also suggested a vision of Turkish society that differed from that in the party's founding documents. Whereas the initial platform had championed various forms of unity and social justice as a means of countering the competition "that naturally results from the division of labor," Samet emphasized the impermanence of these divisions, arguing that the party saw "individual initiative and ability" as the central differences between people. Society was not divided into immutable economic classes enforced by law; rather, people could move between them.[34] Given this fluidity, democratic societies should not have "farmers" and "workers" parties that represented particular interests but, instead, broad-based parties that sought the benefit of the whole society.[35]

Samet's emphasis on the individual in opposition to collectivities led him to vacillate on the issue of workers' rights. In regard to unions, he argued in early 1946 that, given the size of Turkey's population and the limited number of factories, they should develop "stage by stage," so as to avoid a profusion of competing organizations.[36] Neither he nor the DP program was opposed to the creation of unions, which became legal, starting in 1946, but their number and their freedom of action were left an open matter.[37] His book was silent on the issue. Speaking in August 1947 before a crowd of workers at a DP branch in the town of Umurbey, Samet praised their desire to have "a standard of living equal to the assistance they have done for the war of production in this country; to be healthy, to have a healthy house and a healthy workplace."[38] He did not elaborate on how the DP would help them realize these desires.

While there was no acknowledgement of the right to strike in 1947, the party grew more favorable to the idea over the following year. By September 1948, Samet was drawing a connection between countries

[33] Muhlis Ete, "Demokrat Parti ...," *Tasvir*, February 8, 1946, 3.

[34] Ağaoğlu, *İki Parti Arasındaki*, 8; also see DP program clause 6, contained in Koçak, *İktidar ve Demokratlar*, 48.

[35] Ağaoğlu, *İki Parti Arasındaki*, 11. Elsewhere, Ağaoğlu argued that class conflicts did not exist in Turkey, because the Independence War had established "nationalism and a sovereignty of the people" ("Yeni sosyal ...," *Tasvir*, January 4, 1946, 3).

[36] "Yeni sosyal ...," *Tasvir*, January 5, 1946, 2.

[37] The CHP government established a ministry of labor (RG, June 27, 1945); ended the ban on "class-based" organizations (RG, June 10, 1946); and passed a bill regulating labor unions (RG February 26, 1947) (Makal, *Türkiye'de Tek Partili*, 477–482).

[38] "Samed Ağaoğlu'nun ...," *Demokrat İzmir*, August 11, 1947, 1.

that allowed strikes and countries with a high level of industrial production, while still cautioning that strikes were not a political matter but "a technical matter, a matter of production."[39] At the party's Second Congress in June 1949, support for the right to strike was added to the party program ("with the condition that [strikes] remained without political influence or intents").[40] Henceforth, Samet not only touted the party's support for the right to strike but connected it with a larger argument about the ruling CHP's preference for excessive state intervention. The government, he explained, saw workers as a group needing paternalistic "protection," while the DP recognized the issue as one of "rights."[41]

Opposition to "protection" (*himaye*) was a persistent theme in Samet's writings. He pointed to President İnönü's conflation of state involvement in the economy with "national defense" as evidence that the CHP government saw its sphere of action as potentially "limitless."[42] Yet, he argued, state involvement was detrimental: monopolies prohibited the development of private enterprise, and protection of private enterprise made businesses uncompetitive.[43] It also fostered a dangerous dependence on the state. "Industrialists forget," he reminded, "that the government which today appears to be protecting them for one reason or another may tomorrow try for this or that reason to make merchants happy and remove those protections."[44]

The fickleness of officials was part of more general critique Samet leveled against high-ranking government administrators. They were caught up in displays of power and, thus, capricious. He recalled his own time as a bureaucrat in the ministry of economy and trade, recounting how the minister would call him with complaints about spelling in reports

39 Samet Ağaoğlu, "Grev hürriyeti meselesi," *Demokrat İzmir*, September 1, 1948, 1, 6.

40 Ahmet Makal, *Ameleden İşçiye: Erken Cumhuriyet Dönemi Emek Tarihi Çalışmaları* (Istanbul: İletişim Yayınları, 2007), 277. The DP's Second Congress elected a new executive committee on June 24, 1949 with votes as follows: Celal Bayar (901 votes), Refik Koraltan (803), Adnan Menderes (797), Fevzi Lütfi Karaosmanoğlu (755), Fuat Köprülü (743), Refik Şevket İnce (635), Samet Ağaoğlu (615), Sıtkı Yırcalı (575), Hulusi Köymen (499), İhsan Şerif Özgen (473), Üzeyir Avunduk (451), Nuri Özsan (448), Celal Ramazanoğlu (423), Kamil Gündeş (386), and Kemal Özçoban (301) (*Tasvir*, June 25, 1949, 1).

41 Samet Ağaoğlu, "İşçilerin himayesi mi? …," *Demokrat İzmir*, September 29, 1949, 1, 2. On the other hand, he caveated his support for strikes by saying that precautions must be taken to prevent strikes being "exploited" ("Çalışma Bakanının …," *Demokrat İzmir*, October 5, 1949).

42 Samet Ağaoğlu, "Himayeci devlet!" *Demokrat İzmir*, December 23, 1949, 1.

43 Samet Ağaoğlu, "Hususi teşebbüsün himayesi," *Demokrat İzmir*, December 19, 1949, 1.

44 Samet Ağaoğlu, "Sanayiin himayesi," *Demokrat İzmir*, December 24, 1949, 1.

rather than the contents themselves.[45] The focus on style over substance was most apparent at the top: President İnönü was given overly reverential treatment in his public appearances, and officials, including the prime minister, lavished praise on him.[46] Also worrying to Samet was the extensive power given to appointed governors over municipal affairs.[47] From the presidency on down, self-regard and hunger for power dictated government action, leading officials to seek domination for its own sake.

Other pro-DP writers made similar arguments about the excessive power of officials, but the focus on the Nietzschean will to power was particular to Samet. In addition to his political writing, he also wrote numerous short stories, publishing one collection, *Zürriyet* (Progeny), in 1950 and another two collections during his decade in government. His stories frequently centered on men caught in the grip of depression or panic.[48] The concern with individual psychology also informed his political analysis. When discussing the moral compromises that state officials were forced to make during the single-party era, he could be quite perceptive – especially when the empathy served to forgive his allies or himself. Reflecting on the resignation of a long-serving CHP member of parliament, he depicted the man's political career as a "clash of sense and sensibility, a perpetual battleground between his demon and angel."[49]

Psychological analysis extended to economics as well. While Samet and other DP members offered numerous explanations for Turkey's economic difficulties, Samet tended to emphasize unquantifiable factors like "trust." The capriciousness of officials led to a loss of "the nation's confidence" and, thus, a lack of investment. To increase this confidence, Samet argued, the government must pass laws that give investors "security." Only then would foreign and domestic investment increase.[50] Similarly, while the intrigues of profiteers were an important cause of high prices, the "psychologic" factors, such as people's fear of scarcity, mattered as well.[51] The Keynesianism implicit in Samet's analysis was in keeping with the liberal economic thought of the time and yet, much as Keynes himself struggled with whether he was "a liberal," so too did Samet. In *The Differences between the Two Parties*, he did not describe the

45 Samet Ağaoğlu, "Memur meselesi," *Demokrat İzmir*, February 16, 1949, 1, 4.

46 Samet Ağaoğlu, "İ. İnönü halk …," *Demokrat İzmir*, August 8, 1949; Samet Ağaoğlu, "Sağol!" *Demokrat İzmir*, May 21, 1949, 1.

47 Samet Ağaoğlu, "İller Kanunu," *Zafer*, June 2, 1949; Samet Ağaoğlu, "Vali devletin …," *Demokrat İzmir*, June 8, 1949, 1, 6.

48 See Samet Ağaoğlu, *Bütün Öyküleri* (Istanbul: Yapı Kredi Yayınları, 2013).

49 Samet Ağaoğlu, "Behçet Kemal Çağlar," *Tasvir*, February 2, 1949, 2.

50 Samet Ağaoğlu, "İktisadi kalkınmamızın ana şartları," *Demokrat İzmir*, January 31, 1949, 1, 3–4.

51 Samet Ağaoğlu, "Cehaletle mücadele," *Demokrat İzmir*, May 27, 1949, 1, 6.

DP as a "liberal" party; instead, he talked of it as a party of "revolution," focused on achieving the promise of the republic, when sovereignty become vested in a legislature and, thus, the people. The DP would "guide the Turkish revolution into a new phase" and "open the country to a new age of true democracy, free people and free citizens." It would serve as a "representative of a social order based on mutual rights and duties between the individual and the state," as was the norm in "Anglo-Saxon" countries.[52]

Ağaoğlu finished the book in May 1947, not long before July 12, a key moment in Turkey's "transition to democracy." Two events of long-term significance occurred on this date. First, the Turkish government signed an aid agreement with the United States. The agreement enabled Turkey to access part of a $400 million congressional appropriation that President Truman had requested in March, following news that the UK would no longer provide aid to Turkey or Greece. Although the lion's share of the money connected with this "Truman Doctrine" would go to the Greek government, which was actively engaged in a civil war with a domestic communist movement, Turkey received $100 million by the end of the year.[53] Much of this aid was in the form of advanced military equipment such as torpedoes, anti-aircraft guns, artillery, and aircraft, while another portion of the funds contributed to building all-weather roads and airfields.[54]

Second, President İnönü positioned himself above partisan politics by announcing that he would, henceforth, adjudicate disputes between the parties despite still being the leader of one of them. His conciliatory move undercut the efforts of Prime Minister Recep Peker, whom İnönü had appointed following the contentious 1946 election, to paint the DP as acting outside the bounds of acceptable politics. Radical DP members perceived İnönü's move as an obvious attempt to sustain his position and called for the party to maintain a hostile stance. Bayar, however, chose to treat İnönü's statements as sincere. By eschewing a wholly antagonistic stance, Bayar kept the DP in the president's good graces while the governing CHP began to tear itself apart. A split quickly emerged

[52] Ağaoğlu, *İki Parti Arasındaki*, 21.

[53] David Brewer, *Greece, the Decade at War: Occupation, Resistance and Civil War* (London: I. B. Tauris, 2016), 221–240; Andre Gerolymatos, *An International Civil War: Greece, 1943–1949* (New Haven, CT: Yale University Press, 2016), 256–264.

[54] Joseph Satterthwaite, "The Truman Doctrine: Turkey," *The Annals of the American Academy of Political and Social Science* 401, no. 1 (1972): 80–83; Melvyn Leffler, "Strategy, Diplomacy, and the Cold War: The United States, Turkey, and NATO, 1945–1952," *The Journal of American History* 71, no. 4 (1985): 817–818. As parliament was in recess, the agreement was not approved until September 1, 1947.

between defenders of single-party rule, such as Peker, and more reformist members. The struggle culminated after several weeks with Peker's resignation. His successors were more tolerant of the two-party system and accepted President İnönü's self-proclaimed role as mediator between the parties.

By showing a willingness to work with İnönü, Bayar shielded his party from accusations that it was seeking to undermine the political system and, thus, the threat of closure. Convincing party activists that this was the right course was not always easy, however – especially in the face of continued pressure from the government. In the provinces and districts, the DP's efforts to organize were often met with official resistance. Governors refused permits to hold events, landlords were afraid to rent office space, and pro-DP newspapers were prosecuted for "slander." In mid 1947, multiple papers and journalists, including Samet, were prosecuted for reprinting a speech of Menderes's. At the trial, Süreyya successfully argued for her brother's acquittal.[55]

As creators of the single-party state, the founders of the DP may have been able to keep such repression in perspective. Party members who lacked experience in national politics were less forgiving. Bayar's cooperative strategy prompted a split in the party between its more conciliatory and its more confrontational members. The DP's stance toward İnönü and his status as "National Chief" became a fundamental division in the party, but there were smaller issues as well, ones that would prove to be endemic to the DP organization for years to come. Sometimes the line between these fundamental disputes and the more quotidian ones was hard to distinguish: for example, Istanbul Provincial President Kenan Öner led the opposition to Bayar's accommodation with İnönü while also clashing with moderates like Köprülü and Menderes, who both sought to fill his Istanbul organization with their allies. Köprülü tried to place his son Orhan in a leadership position, while Menderes tried to bring in an ally from İzmir, Mükerrem Sarol.[56] (Even once the struggle with Öner was settled, the rivalry between Sarol and the Köprülü family would continue to unsettle the Istanbul organization for years to come.)

The months of late 1947 and early 1948 were filled with intrigues. Bayar and others traveled to provincial party congresses, trying to limit the influence of Öner and his radicals. Though Bayar, Menderes, Köprülü, and Koraltan did not exercise full control over the party's

[55] "Sekiz gazeteci dün beraat etti," *Demokrat İzmir*, August 10, 1947, 1, 4; Ağaoğlu, *Bir Ömür*, 103–104.
[56] Koçak, *İktidar ve Demokratlar*, 136.

parliamentary group, they *did* control the executive committee and the disciplinary committee in combination with another five allies (including Ağaoğlu). This advantage allowed them to strip their opponents of party membership before the Second DP Congress, at which it would have been possible for Öner's faction to change the leadership structure.[57] This ouster reduced the sixty-one-member DP parliamentary group by one-third but left the party founders firmly in control.

Öner and the other expelled radicals would go on to establish the Nation Party (*Millet Partisi*, MP) in mid 1948. The party was explicit in its rejection of the political and social order that the CHP had created during the previous twenty-five years. In its platform, it declared itself "bound to ideals of republicanism, justice, and liberalism, and fundamentally nationalism."[58] Whereas the remaining DP leaders such as Ağaoğlu moderated their language and positions according to political circumstances, Nation Party members were far more confrontational. Their removal gave moderates like Ağaoğlu even more influence in shaping the DP's message.

Democrats in the Provinces: Balıkesir and Malatya

Within two years of its establishment, the DP had become a nationwide political organization, meaning that its internal power struggles were hardly limited to the major cities of Istanbul, Ankara, and İzmir. They could be found across the country as various local elites competed for influence against their rivals. Often, the factions dominating a provincial branch of the DP were associated with local leaders who had lost out in earlier struggles during the single-party period. Yet, despite these setbacks, they remained influential elites, not a peripheral class wholly marginalized from the politics of the republic.[59] Here and in the next chapter, examples from two provinces – Balıkesir and Malatya – give a sense of these nationwide dynamics. The first is representative of the provinces where the DP would prove successful throughout the 1950s; the second gives us an understanding of the provinces where the DP made few inroads.

The distinctions between the two provinces go beyond electoral outcomes. Located in western Turkey, with access to both the Sea of

[57] Karpat, *Turkey's Politics*, 211–222; Toker, *Tek Partiden Çok Partiye*, 212–231; Cemil Koçak, *Uzlaşma: Türkiye'de İki Partili Siyasi Sistemin Kuruluş Yılları, 1945–1950*, vol. V (Istanbul: İletişim Yayınları, 2016), 400–464.

[58] Koçak, *Uzlaşma*, 480. Also see Karpat, *Turkey's Politics*, 431–435; Burçak, *Türkiye'de Demokrasiye Geçiş*, 157–158.

[59] Koçak, *İktidar ve Demokratlar*, 103–134.

Marmara and the Aegean, Balıkesir had a long history of integration with European markets. In addition to fruits, vegetables, lumber, tobacco, cotton, and minerals such as lignite coal and boracite, Balıkesir produced one-quarter of Turkey's olives in the mid 1950s.[60] Its powerful landowners were involved in international commerce to a far greater degree than their peers in eastern provinces like Malatya, which had been, historically, tied to the internal Ottoman market and the city of Aleppo. These ties had been disrupted by war and the creation of a border.[61]

While both provinces had been affected by the genocidal exterminations and expulsions of the war years, their postwar demographics were distinct. After expelling Greek Christians, who made up 23 percent of the provincial population in 1914, Balıkesir became largely Sunni Muslim and Turkish-speaking.[62] Malatya, even following the removal and annihilation of Armenian Christians (9.8 percent of the population), remained heterogenous, with large numbers of Kurdish-speaking and/or Alevi Muslims.[63] In material terms, as in other parts of the empire, the removal of Christians and redistribution of their lands allowed local elites to accumulate more wealth. In more psychological terms, the violent elimination of neighbors drew together those who remained in a shared complicity.

Power in both provinces rested with individuals (and families) that had been actively involved in the Independence War and consolidated power during the 1920s. In Malatya, for example, a Defense of Rights organization was established on March 12, 1919.[64] The leadership of the

[60] "Economic Report No. 11 for the Month of November 1954," British Embassy Ankara, December 9, 1954, FO 371/112934; Mustafa Salman (ed.), *Balıkesir İktisat Kılavuz* (Balıkesir: 1957), 50–51; "Foreign Agriculture Circular," US Department of Agriculture (November 1961), 10, available: https://hdl.handle.net/2027/osu.32435031407281.

[61] According to Mevlüt Oğuz, Malatya remained oriented toward Aleppo in the 1950s. For example, though people liked to smoke, the Turkish government limited legal access to rolling papers, generally produced in Syria. Faced with shortages, local people either smuggled in paper from Aleppo or made do by smoking waterpipes – often mixing tobacco with tree fungus for flavor, or just substituting locally grown marijuana (Oğuz, *Malatya Tarihi ve Sosyoekonomik Durumu* [Istanbul: Kurtiş Mabaatcılık, 2000], 503).

[62] In 1914, Balıkesir had a population of 466,000, around 106,000 of whom were Christian. By 1923, there were fewer than 200,000 Christians *in all of Turkey* (Karpat, *Ottoman Population*, 186; Clark, *Twice a Stranger*, 195).

[63] The combined population of Akçadağ, Arapkir, Besni, Hasanmansur (Adıyaman), Kahta, Malatya, and Pütürge was 271,923 in 1914. There were 23,848 Armenians (8.8 percent of the population) out of a total 26,771 Christians (Karpat, *Ottoman Population*, 182).

[64] The boundaries of Malatya changed frequently as new administrative divisions were drawn up. When referring to "Malatya" for the period 1900–26, I am referring to the subprovinces of Akçadağ, Arapkir, Besni, Hasanmansur (Adıyaman), Kahta, Malatya, and Pütürge, which were part of the province of Mamuret-ül-Aziz. When Malatya was

committee included men who held important positions in the community as landlords, tribal chiefs, religious leaders, and merchants. Many served in the national parliament and local government.[65] Rather than signal a break with traditional political arrangements in the region, the uncertainty of 1918–19 actually served to *strengthen* local elites' position as the representatives of their people at a moment when Ottoman leaders seemed unreliable. Over the coming years, it was elites of this sort whom Mustafa Kemal would organize into a political base from which he could effectively challenge the Entente forces and Ottoman government. Many would go on to form the basis of Kemal's CHP in Malatya.

One such individual was Hacı Bedir Ağa. As leader of the Kurdish Risvan tribe (*aşiret*), he led 400 infantry and 500 cavalry fighters into battle against French forces in Antep, Urfa, and Maraş. He was elected to the nationalist movement's parliament in Ankara in 1920. Among the representatives from Malatya who joined him was Mustafa Fevzi Effendi, the local *mufti* (scholar of religious law) and a member of the local governing council.[66] Both men represented different elements of the local leadership drawn into Mustafa Kemal's coalition. Yet they were also the sort of men who would ultimately be sidelined. Following an uprising of Kurdish elites in 1925 (the "Shaykh Sait Uprising"), the government exiled Kurdish notables from their lands. Hacı Bedir was sent to the coastal province of İçel (Mersin) in 1926 and given a small parcel of farmland to oversee during the final two years of his life.[67]

Exiling notables served the government's goal of minimizing resistance, but it did little for the population at large: landlords were often allowed to maintain ownership of their lands from a distance, which meant that the rents they extracted did not even recirculate in the region.[68] At the same time, little in the way of government spending made its way east. Malatya was rare in the 1930s in that it was one of two eastern provinces where a factory was built as part of the government

created in 1926, Besni was attached to the province of Gaziantep. It was attached to Malatya in 1933 along with the subprovince of Darende.

65 Mehmet Serkan Şahin, *Erken Cumhuriyet Dönemi'nde CHP'nin Malatya Teşkilatı, 1923–1950* (Istanbul: Libra Yayınevi, 2016), 29–32.

66 Ahmet Demirel, *İlk Meclisin Vekilleri: Milli Mücadele Döneminde Seçimler* (Istanbul: İletişim Yayınları, 2010), 91–92; Hamdi Doğan, *Birinci Mecliste Malatya Milletvekilleri ve Siyasi Faaliyetleri, 1920–1923* (Ankara: Akçağ Yayınları, 2011), 133–134.

67 "Atatürk Fırat'ın dedesi için kanun değiştirdi," *Radikal*, July 28, 2014, available: www.radikal.com.tr/turkiye/ataturk-firatin-dedesi-icin-kanun-degistirdi-1204197/.

68 McDowall, *A Modern History of the Kurds*, 399. Hacı Bedir Ağa's brother, Zeynel (Turanlı), was allowed to remain in Malatya and oversee the several dozen villages he controlled (Hüdai Sayın, "Malatya'da Siyasal Seçkinler" [Master's thesis, İnönü Üniversitesi, Malatya, 1996], 177).

industrialization drive. The Sümerbank textile factory, built in 1939, not only served as a primary employer in the provincial center but also doubled as a meeting space for public events.

While funds for economic development were limited, the national government spent heavily on security in the region. To suppress the Kurdish revolt in 1925, the government sent 50,000 soldiers to eastern Turkey and devoted around one-third of the year's budget to funding military operations.[69] In the aftermath, the government ended any effort to establish political organizations in eastern provinces and relied instead on centrally appointed governors and inspectors for administration.[70] Once again, Malatya remained something of an outlier in the region: the national government's success there was achieved with the support of local elites who then went on to lead the CHP political organization. Hacı Abdizade Hasan, for example, was a powerful landowner who served as mayor from 1924 to 1928. He helped defeat the 1925 revolt and served as the head of the local CHP party organization. By 1930, however, he had fallen out with other factions in the provincial CHP and was leading the opposition SCF in the region. Although the SCF put up fifty-four candidates in the province's local elections, thirty dropped out, claiming pressure from CHP officials.[71]

While the SCF challenge did not shift the political arrangements in Malatya, its popularity in the western provinces frightened the national government and encouraged the regime to deepen its connections to the society and state. As discussed in Chapter 1, distinctions between the party and the state were erased, and provincial governors now doubled as provincial party heads. Moreover, CHP leaders worked to connect the party with the people. Local People's Houses served as a primary institution for spreading the party's influence. In Malatya and around the country, these buildings were established in the provincial center and were intended as sites where the CHP might disseminate its cultural vision to the public. Especially in smaller urban areas, the local People's House would often be the most prominent building (and, therefore, a focus of ire for opponents of the regime).[72]

[69] Veli Yadirgi, *The Political Economy of the Kurds of Turkey: From the Ottoman Empire to the Turkish Republic* (Cambridge: Cambridge University Press, 2011), 168–169.

[70] Murat Turan, *CHP'nin Doğu'da Teşkilatlanması, 1923–1950* (Istanbul: Libra Yayınevi, 2011), 271.

[71] Şahin, *Erken Cumhuriyet Dönemi'nde*, 71–74.

[72] Reuben Silverman, "Republican People's Party People: Partisan Polarization in the Republic of Turkey, 1950–1953," *The Middle East Journal* 73, no. 1 (spring 2019): 85–88.

Infrastructure and industrial projects were another local manifestation of the regime's presence in society. They also created an opportunity for leaders to present themselves to the public as a source of largesse. Mustafa Kemal's first presidential visit to Malatya, for example, came in 1931. It was part of his general effort to connect with local leaders and "the people" following the SCF challenge, but the official reason for his visit was to inaugurate a new rail line to Fevzipaşa. His second visit, six years later, was in connection with the new Iran–Turkey–Iraq line. That Kemal's visits were all connected with new rail lines suggests the close association that he and his regime drew between infrastructure and national political organization. A textile factory completed in 1939, after Kemal's death, likewise served to tether Malatya to a national economy, rather than a regional or transnational one.

Throughout these years of state formation in eastern Turkey, the larger grouping of families involved in local politics did not change dramatically. Following the 1934 law requiring all citizens to adopt surnames, members of Hacı Bedir Ağa's tribe took the last names of "Fırat" and "Turanlı."[73] Mustafa Fevzi Effendi's family now went by "Bilgili." And Hacı Abdizade Hasan and his descendants took the name "Derinkök." These would be leading names in local politics during the 1950s. While many leaders from the 1920s passed away during the single-party era, the 1946 and 1950 elections would be contested by their sons.

The same was true in Balıkesir, albeit with some local differences. Whereas landlords and tribal leaders in Malatya had contributed to the Independence War by leading irregular forces off to combat, Balıkesir itself had been a theater of battle, pitting leading figures in the Muslim community against the Greek army and their own neighbors, linking them to the government in Ankara. Consider the example of Yırcalızade Ahmed Şükrü. Born in 1881 (the same year as Atatürk and only a few years earlier than İnönü and Bayar), he pursued a career more focused on local concerns than those famous figures of his generation had. He studied at local schools, worked as a dry goods merchant, and married into a family of local notables. His wife gave birth to their first child, İbrahim Sıtkı, in 1908. That same year, Ahmed Şükrü joined the İTC and served on the municipal education commission and city council (even becoming mayor briefly in 1916). When news of the Greek

[73] Because "Fırat" is the Turkish name for the Euphrates River, it is a popular name among Malatya notables. In addition to the pro-DP descendants of Hacı Bedir Ağa, the pro-CHP descendants of Haşim Efendi, who dominated provincial politics in the interwar years, also took the surname (Mehmet Serkan Şahin, "Cumhuriyet Halk Partisi'nin Malatya Teşkilatı, 1923–1950" [Master's thesis, Dokuz Eylül Üniversitesi, İzmir, 2008], 2 n. 8).

invasion reached Balıkesir on May 16, 1919, he was among those who gathered to issue a declaration of resistance and raise a militia. During the following year, he was involved in important battles.[74]

In the aftermath, he returned his focus to business and municipal politics under the umbrella of Mustafa Kemal's CHP. In 1930, however, he switched his allegiance to the opposition SCF and became one of its provincial leaders. The SCF appealed to local frustrations with the central government and its representatives: heavy taxes on olive trees were eating into profits, and the rates offered by the state tobacco monopoly were worse than those offered by foreign merchants.[75] Though the SCF did well in the province, winning three districts in the September 1930 municipal elections, the party was soon pressured to close. Opponents in the CHP accused SCF leaders of stirring up religious sentiment. The father of SCF General Secretary İbrahim Sururi was said to have proselytized to local women. Sururi himself was said to have served meals to occupying Greek officers during the war. When a religious protest in the Aegean district of Menemen culminated in the decapitation of a soldier, the government increased its repression of local elites associated with the SCF: Sururi was sentenced to six months in jail for encouraging "reaction" and Yırcalızade Ahmed Şükrü was detained in Istanbul for a year.[76]

Ahmed Şükrü passed away in 1938, but his sons continued his political activities. Sıtkı Yırcalı, thirty by the time of his father's death, attended law school in Istanbul and then traveled to Paris for additional education. On his return, he worked as an inspector for the ministry of finance. His brother Sırrı, ten years his junior, also attended law school in Istanbul and joined the ministry of economy and trade as a price inspector before returning to Balıkesir to work in the private sector. Sırrı married into the family of Muharrem Hasbi Koray, the owner of a cotton and a flour factory. Following the creation of the DP in 1945, Celal Bayar wrote to Koray, asking him to join. Though Koray demurred, he recommended his son-in-law's brother, Sıtkı, and several other young men. In April 1946, Sıtkı established the province's DP organization along with Esat Budakoğlu, another Istanbul University Law School graduate. Sıtkı

74 Aydın Ayhan, "İzmir'in İşgali Sırasında Balıkesir," in *Milli Mücadele'de Balıkesir* (Istanbul: Kent Basımevi, 1986), 34–42; Zekeriya Özdemir, *Balıkesir Bölgesinde Milli Mücadele Önderleri* (Balıkesir: Balıkesir Belediyesi, 1998), 149–150; Kerim Kani Akpınarlı, *Balıkesir Şehir ve Belediye Tarihi* (Balıkesir: Balıkesir Belediye Yayınları, 2009), 96–102.

75 Murat Metinsoy, *Power of the People: Everyday Resistance and Dissent in the Making of Modern Turkey, 1923–38* (Cambridge: Cambridge University Press, 2021), 29.

76 Karakaş, "Balıkesir'de Serbest Cumhuriyet," 370–371; TBMM, November 15, 1930, 33–34; Sıtkı Şeremetli, *Balıkesir'de Demokrat Parti Hareketi, 1946–1960: İktidardan-İhtilale* (Balıkesir: Liva Yayınevi, 2006), 52.

became the president of the organization. Along with Budakoğlu, he wrote for its newspaper, *Balıkesir Postası*.[77]

Like the SCF in 1930, the new opposition party faced intense pressure from government officials in the province as the 1946 election approached. After an initial attempt to coopt the local DP leadership by offering them jobs, CHP officials worked to undermine them. Property owners were discouraged from renting office space to Democrats.[78] DP leaders argued that the local results were manipulated in favor of the ruling CHP.[79] During the following four years, Yırcalı, Budakoğlu, and another young leader, İbrahim İlşekerci, campaigned and organized around the province. Yırcalı was brought to court on multiple occasions for speeches criticizing high prices and accusing CHP of fraud in the İzmir elections.[80] Yet the organizational efforts paid off: in the 1950 election, the DP won 58.6 percent of the vote in Balıkesir, and Yırcalı and Budakoğlu were elected to parliament.[81] Another local lawyer, Mücteba Iştın, whose father had also been a local leader during the Independence War, replaced Yircalı as head of the provincial party organization, and Yırcalı's brother Sırrı became president of the chamber of commerce (*ticaret odası*) with İlşekerci as his second-in-command. At municipal assembly elections on September 3, 1950, the party won 70.5 percent. Its highest vote-getter, Tevfik Yoldemir, was elected mayor ten days later.[82]

In coastal provinces like Balıkesir, the early DP organizations were established by close allies of the party founders, as well as by people who

77 Alparslan Ayral, *Balıkesir'in Kültür Hayatı* (Sivas: Dilek Ofset Matbaası, 1995), 97–98; Şeremetli, *Balıkesir'de Demokrat Parti*, 21–26, 52; Aydın, "Demokrat Parti İktidarı," 21–23.

78 Şeremetli, *Balıkesir'de Demokrat Parti*, 50–51, 98–99.

79 Aydın, "Demokrat Parti İktidarı," 23–24. For a less flattering account of the local DP's rise to power, see Şeref Laçın Akgün's *Balıkesir Demokrat Parti İçyüzü* (Balıkesir: Türkdili Matbaası, 1950), in which the former member criticizes the lack of internal party democracy. The local CHP published his account.

80 Şeremetli, *Balıkesir'de Demokrat Parti*, 50–51. İbrahim İlşekerci was also from one of the notable families in the province (as the name suggests, they were involved in the sugar trade). Like other young leaders of the DP, his father, Seyit, had been a member of the SCF and had been prosecuted for his involvement (119).

81 The defeated CHP candidate list in Balıkesir consisted of sitting representatives (Muzaffer Akpınar, Esat Altan, Süreyya Örgeevren, Abdi Ağabeyoğlu, and Hasan Cemil Çambel), local doctors (Muammer Yasa and Esat Baykal), local mayors (Necat Sarlıcalı and Mustafa Çakıroğlu), a forestry official (Niyazi Gürer), a lawyer (Sami Duyum), and a banker (Cemil Topçu) (*Ateş*, April 28, 1950, 1).

82 Şeremetli, *Balıkesir'de Demokrat Parti*, 119–123. Tevfik Yoldemir (1908–54) was from a family of Bulgarian immigrants who worked in the fruit-and-vegetable wholesale trade. He studied engineering at Yıldız Technical University in Istanbul and worked briefly for the state railways before returning to Balıkesir to run his own business (177).

were known to be antagonistic to the government.[83] In areas of the country such as Malatya, where the DP founders had less familiarity, party organizations tended to rely on the opponents of whichever local faction ruled in concert with the national CHP organization. Malatya was not so different: the DP organized in the summer of 1946, just before the elections and too late to prepare a slate of local candidates.[84] Therefore, the provincial leaders threw their support to a group of independents, including Hüseyin Doğan and Ali Gebeş, both of whom had tried and failed to win a place on that year's CHP candidate list.[85] Doğan, a leading Alevi shaykh, was thought to have between 30,000 and 40,000 votes that he could deliver come election time.[86]

The CHP won the 1946 elections in Malatya, but hardly through fair means. The party repeatedly blocked independent candidates' efforts to print ballots for their supporters to use on election day.[87] During the four years that followed, local notables chose sides and local organizations competed to attract young, popular candidates to their respective sides. The CHP convinced Nuvit Yetkin to become editor of the party paper, *Gayret* (Endeavor), even though Yetkin's uncle was a leader in the local DP.[88] Hüseyin Doğan was also added to the CHP candidate list in the 1950 election.[89] The DP managed to attract Hamit Fendoğlu (better known as "Hamido"), a member of the Kurdish İzol tribe on his father's

[83] For a discussion of early DP party-organizing efforts, see Koçak, *İktidar ve Demokratlar*, 102–161.

[84] According to Koçak, a DP branch was opened in Arapkir, Malatya on June 8, 1946, but Fikret Avcı suggests that the provincial organization was not announced until the early weeks of July (Koçak, *İktidar ve Demokratlar*, 112; Avcı, "Demokrat Parti [DP] İktidarı," 23 n. 45).

[85] In an interview in 1996, Kemal Özmumcu, one of the founders of the provincial DP organization, recalled the names and occupations of eight of his ten cofounders. These included engineers (Bedri Ener and Enver Gürsel), dentists (Cevdet Güray and someone he refers to as "Kaya Bey"), two merchants (Kamil Güzel and Kerim Ağır), and two bakers (Kemal Akmete and Arif Buğdaycı) (Sayın, "Malatya'da Siyasal Seçkinler," 211).

[86] Şahin, *Erken Cumhuriyet Dönemi'nde*, 113–115; Murat Gözel, *İz Bırakanlar: Malatyalı 44 Şahsiyet* (Istanbul: Malatya Kent Konseyi Yayınları, 2013), 171–173.

[87] Şahin, "Cumhuriyet Halk Partisi'nin," 83–84.

[88] Nüvit Yetkin (1916–2007) was born in Malatya. He was the grandson of Lütfi Bey (Evliyaoğlu), who was an ally of Mustafa Kemal and had briefly served in parliament. His maternal uncle, Kemal Evliyaoğlu, was a leader in the provincial DP (Sayın, "Malatya'da Siyasal Seçkinler," 154).

[89] In 1950, in addition to Doğan on the CHP list, both the CHP and DP placed several shaykhs on their electoral lists, including Kasım Küfrevi (DP, Ağrı), Selahattin İnan (CHP, Bitlis), and Hacı Ömer Cevheri (DP, Urfa). The CHP also maintained friendly relations in the late 1940s with the Ticani order. This should not be seen as a new phenomenon connected with democratization: İbrahim Arvas, who represented Van from 1923 to 1950, came from a family closely associated with the Nakşibendî order (Pınar, "Van'da Demokrat Parti," 35; Kadir Dede, "İnönü'den Bayar'a Gericilik: Çok

and Risvan tribe on his mother's side. He had previously made a splash in local politics by leading protests against the erection of a statue of President İnönü (who had family ties to the region) in front of the city hall.[90] The DP also attracted middle-aged local elites such as Mustafa Saltoğlu, who owned the anti-CHP paper *Fırat* (Euphrates) despite his father having been involved in the CHP since its establishment.

The inclusion of Hamido and other Kurdish notables in the DP does not mean that the DP in 1950 was the "pro-Kurdish" party. It was, rather, a party that promised to reorder the balance of power in the provinces, giving local elites greater influence in decision-making. Speaking to the public at rallies in southeastern cities like Diyarbakır, Bayar framed the DP message around economic rather than cultural issues. He pointed out that the region remained "backward" in matters of education and health, and promised to rectify the situation.[91] That said, party leaders did not shy away from courting ethnic communities. The author Musa Anter recalls Bayar, Mükerrem Sarol, and the journalist Cihad Baban (himself descended from a family of Kurdish notables) attending a Newroz festival organized for Istanbul's Kurdish community in March 1950. When Anter received news during the event that his wife had given birth to a son, he even recited a celebratory couplet from a Kurdish-language poem in front of the audience, including the DP leaders.[92]

Partili Hayata Geçiş," in *Resmi Tarih Tartışmaları 7*, ed. Fikret Başkaya [Ankara: Özgür Üniversite Yayınları, 2009], 107–108).

90 Şahin, *Erken Cumhuriyet Dönemi'nde*, 123; Raşit Kısacık, *Malatya'da Toplumsal Olaylar* (Istanbul: Ozan Yayıncılık, 2012), 124–125. Hamit Fendoğlu, also known as "Hamido," was born in 1919 in Bulgurlu, Malatya. His father was part of the Kurdish İzol tribe, and his mother was from the Risvan tribe. He studied in the provincial center and secured a job in the Physical Education Regional Inspectorate. While in school, he had become a fervent Turkish nationalist. When his father was hit with a TL2,800 fine under the World War II–era Wealth Tax, he became a harsh critic of the CHP. In 1946 he joined the DP and became a leader in its provincial organization. After the 1950 election, he was given a job in Ankara as assistant director of coal distribution facilities. After the 1960 coup, he was jailed for three years and six months. He joined the Justice Party (AP) and was elected as a representative for Malatya in 1965 but was later expelled from the party after a feud with Hüseyin Doğan. He was elected mayor of Malatya in 1977 but was killed with a parcel bomb on April 17, 1978. Following his death, there were pogroms against the Alevi community, which nationalists associated with leftist politics (Gözel, *İz Bırakanlar*, 200–202; Kısacık, *Malatya'da Toplumsal Olaylar*, 220–221; Massicard, *Türkiye'den Avrupa'ya*, 62; Ahmet Dinç, *Hamido: Meclis'in Son Kabadayısı İlk Faili Meçhulü!* [Istanbul: Hayykitap, 2015]).

91 "Diyarbakırda demokratların ...," *Cumhuriyet*, June 28, 1948, 3.

92 Musa Anter, *Hatıralarım, 1–2* (Avesta Yayınları, 1999), 58–59. While Anter (probably correctly) supposes that Bayar would not have understood his words, Bayar was far from a stranger to policies relating to Kurds. While minister of the economy in 1936, he produced a report on the conditions of the Kurdish-majority provinces (Celal Bayar, *Şark Raporu* [Istanbul: Kaynak Yayınları, 2006]).

In April 1950, the Malatya DP determined its nine-man candidate list.[93] Four were lawyers, two were farmers, and there was also a doctor, a dentist, and a merchant who had previously worked as a teacher. Yet these titles do very little to help us understand the composition of the party, since they do not exclude the possibility of other identities like "landowner" or "tribal leader." For example, the party's leading candidate, Hüseyin Fırat, was mentioned simply as "a lawyer," but he was also the son of Hacı Bedir Ağa.[94] At the same time, it is hard to argue that the candidates represented the voices of those excluded from the single-party regime's state-building project: of the nine, at least four (and likely more) received degrees at universities in Istanbul or Ankara and worked for the state in various capacities before entering provincial politics.[95]

As this discussion illustrates, making a clear distinction between the DP and CHP in Malatya (or elsewhere) based on class categories like landlord, professional, or bureaucrat leads to a false impression of the DP as representing a break with the established political order in the region. A better differentiation is that the DP at the local and national level was a coalition based largely on personal frustrations with the ruling CHP. People joined because they had lost out in some intraparty dispute or because their families had suffered at the hands of the government. Whatever the merits of these grievances, they would come to play themselves out in petty, vindictive behavior once the DP gained control of the national government.

High Hopes, High Prices: The Democrat Party on the Eve of Power

The strength of the DP lay in its ability to draw on the enthusiasm of national and provincial elites, but the party's emergence and survival were closely connected with (if not wholly dependent on) international

[93] The DP candidate list for Malatya in 1950 included Hüseyin Fırat; Reşat Emek, Sait Ağar; Kemal Özmumcu; Sabri Özbek; Kemal Evliyaoğlu; Sait Bilginer; Mustafa Saltoğlu; and Rıfkı Garipoğlu (*Yeni Malatya*, April 20, 1950).

[94] After his father had been exiled to the coastal province of İçel (Mersin), Hüseyin Fırat attended law school in Istanbul and worked in such provinces as Adana and Hatay. In 1950, he was placed on both the Malatya and İçel DP electoral lists. He won only in İçel, but visited Malatya frequently in the coming years, acting like a local party boss. He gives an account of his life and political activities in his written statement of defense from the 1960–61 Yassıada trials, which followed the 1960 coup (Prime Ministerial Republican Archives [hereafter BCA] 010.09.00.00 45 134 6).

[95] *Yeni Malatya*, April 20, 1950; *Yeni Malatya*, April 27, 1950; *Yeni Malatya*, May 2, 1950; *Yeni Malatya*, May 3, 1950; *Yeni Malatya*, May 5, 1950; *Yeni Malatya*, May 9, 1950; *Yeni Malatya*, May 11, 1950; Sayın, "Malatya'da Siyasal Seçkinler," 152–154, 214.

developments. Soviet threats in 1945 had encouraged leaders of the single-party regime to allow multiparty democracy so that Turkey might be seen as a country worth defending. The US willingness to support Turkey against Soviet pressure in late 1945 and the United States' financial largesse in 1947 seemed to validate this strategy, but they also made repressing the DP more difficult. Unlike the opposition in a country such as Japan or Italy, where left-wing movements were strong and the United States was willing to tolerate (or encourage) their marginalization, the DP was quick to repudiate any potential associations with socialists, let alone communists. By presenting itself as a moderate, liberal party in the US style, the DP denied the CHP regime a potential line of attack.[96]

Turkey's increasing involvement with the United States and its postwar institutions helped protect the DP, but the resulting entanglement created an economic crisis that the DP leaders had to carefully navigate in order to secure electoral advantage. The crisis stemmed from the nature of the economic order devised by US and British officials in the early months of 1944 and approved at an international conference held in Bretton Woods, New Hampshire. The ambition of the new system was to end the autarkic economic order of the 1930s, in which countries had hoarded gold and conducted trade with other countries largely through bilateral agreements, thereby slowing the pace of economic activity. To move away from the economic arrangements of the interwar years, planners at Bretton Woods envisioned a system of currencies pegged at fixed rates to both gold and to one another such that one currency could be converted to another with ease while retaining the possibility of government intervention if the need arose. Countries hoping to benefit from the new institutions undergirding this system – the IMF and the International Bank for Reconstruction and Development (IBRD) – committed to fix their currencies by 1947 and then eventually return to full convertibility. Though the USSR signed the initial agreements, it never ratified them in a binding treaty. As a result, the new international payments system contributed to the postwar consolidation of a bipolar economic order.[97]

[96] Reporter Dana Adams Schmidt astutely described Turkey's political situation as more a "conflict between the 'ins' and the 'outs' than of social and ideological differences between the two parties. This makes them more like American parties" ("Democratization in Turkey …," *New York Times*, August 5, 1947, 19).

[97] Eric Helleiner, *States and the Reemergence of Global Finance from Bretton Woods to the 1990s* (Ithaca: Cornell University Press, 1994), 33–48; Micheal Bordo, "The Bretton Woods International Monetary System: A Historical Overview," in *A Retrospective on the Bretton Woods System: Lessons for International Monetary Reform*, ed. Micheal Bordo and Barry Eichengreen (Chicago: University of Chicago Press, 2003), 30–37; Filippo Cesarano, *Monetary Theory and Bretton Woods: The Construction of an International Monetary Order* (Cambridge: Cambridge University Press, 2009), 159–169.

For Turkey's leaders, still under pressure from the USSR, the Bretton Woods system was an opportunity to access credit and affirm ties with the United States and the UK. On September 7, 1946, well in advance of the deadline, Turkey fixed its currency at TL2.80 to the dollar, reducing the lira's value by more than half. The new currency rate encouraged foreign firms to buy goods from Turkey, but the sudden devaluation disrupted Turkish people's consumption patterns. While citizens felt the pinch of higher prices, the government accomplished its larger goal of linking the national economy to the emerging US-led postwar order. In the coming months, military links were added to these economic ones. As the UK reduced its military commitments in the region, US military planners moved in the opposite direction. As diplomatic historian Melvyn Leffler puts it, US leaders were coming to believe that, in the event of a war, Turkey could "provide a cushion, absorbing the initial Soviet blow and deterring Soviet advances, while the United States prepared to undertake the counteroffensive, particularly from the Cairo–Suez area."[98]

Turkish and US strategic interests converged in March 1947, with the announcement of the Truman Doctrine, discussed earlier in this chapter. Turkey's ties with the United States were further strengthened in the coming months as a consequence of economic instability in Europe. Whereas Turkey had set its exchange rates low and passed the pains of devaluation on to the public, European governments had set theirs so high that they could not secure the dollars necessary to purchase the products they needed. In response to this crisis, the Truman administration proposed a program that would provide European countries with the dollars necessary to stabilize their economies. This fund – the "Marshall Plan" – would take shape in the $17 billion Economic Cooperation Law passed by the US Congress in April 1948. Turkey was included among the eligible countries, and Republicans in the US House of Representatives earmarked $275 million in military aid for Turkey and Greece as part of the bill.[99]

In addition to developing Turkey's ability to slow a Soviet military offensive, US strategists had another ambition: they hoped to increase Turkey's agricultural capacity. The US policy of economically isolating the USSR relied on finding substitutes for the Central and Eastern European countries that had once traded with Western Europe.[100]

98 Leffler, "Strategy, Diplomacy, and the Cold War," 814.

99 Benn Steil, *The Marshall Plan: The Dawn of the Cold War* (New York: Simon and Shuster, 2018), 529.

100 According to Richard Overy, grain exports from Central Europe to Western Europe had been declining during the 1920s, falling from 50 percent of Western Europe's imports in 1914 to 6 percent in 1929, the United States supplying the rest. Still, specific countries like Norway and Austria were more reliant on the east–west trade. After

Though Turkey's leaders were not interested in giving up their industrial ambitions, US officials pushed for Turkey to invest in agriculture rather than heavy industry.[101] They also criticized Turkey's reliance on rail transport and advocated for more roads, which they saw as preferable for both military and commercial reasons. Roads could reach mountainous areas of the country, which rail could not. And roads, US advisors believed, would create a more united national market and culture. As the political scientist Begüm Adalet explains, US officials believed highways would "accommodate flexible schedules for volitional travel through a national space increasingly organized around the figure of the individual consumer."[102] Roads, in this understanding, would transform Turks into Americans.

Nationalist politicians were not eager to become Americans. The erstwhile members of the DP who had formed the Nation Party criticized high prices and military weakness in the face of Soviet aggression, but they did not see the Truman Doctrine funds or the Marshall Plan as a solution. The CHP government had failed to develop the economy as a "national economic regime" and had now "remedied the situation [by allowing] foreign capital to penetrate the nation."[103] The only solution was to replace the CHP regime. Unfortunately, they argued, the DP offered no solution, since it was nothing more than a "faction" (*hizip*) of the CHP, lacking a real social base or raison d'être.[104]

Unsurprisingly, the DP leaders did not share this analysis of the situation. In parliament in March 1949, Fuat Köprülü declared, "Today the world is divided into two fronts. It is a fact that one is a front of peace and democracy, the other a front of imperialist aggression." Given these stakes, he mocked those who criticized a close relationship with the United States. "Are we selling Turkey for $100 million? Is that our value?" To suggest such a thing was "a perfect statement of betrayal, of treachery."[105] Pro-DP papers likewise criticized the Nation Party for

World War II, the United States pushed its allies in Europe to reduce their trade with the east but had limited success. According to Jacqueline McGlade, by 1951 20 percent of Western Europe's 7 million tons of imported livestock feed grain came from the USSR and 8 percent of its 13 million metric tons of bread grain imports. Robert Wood argues that replacing Eastern European markets also depended on reviving European colonial markets in places like Indonesia and Indochina (Overy, *The Interwar Crisis, 1919–1939,* 2nd ed. [London: Pearson, 2007], 27; McGlade, "More a Plowshare than a Sword: The Legacy of US Cold War Agricultural Diplomacy," *Agricultural History* 83, no. 1 [2009]: 87; Wood, *From Marshall Plan to Debt Crisis: Foreign Aid and Development Choices in the World Economy* [Berkeley: University of California Press, 1986], 31–52).

101 Avcıoğlu, *Türkiye'nin Düzeni 1*, 557–561. 102 Adalet, *Hotels and Highways*, 126.

103 Nureddin Ardıçoğlu, "İktisadi uçurum kenarında," *Kudret*, September 17, 1948, 1, 4.

104 Nureddin Ardıçoğlu, "Partinin doktrin ve sınıfı," *Kudret*, October 3, 1948, 1.

105 "D. P. nin görüşü," *Tasvir*, March 17, 1949, 1, 5; TBMM, March 16, 1949, 33–35.

its opposition to NATO membership and preference for a nonaggression pact with the USSR, comparing these stances to promoting "communist propaganda.[106] If anything, the DP's support for foreign money and American advice was often more full-throated than that of the government itself. The party called for more foreign investment and rapid integration into security pacts like NATO. In *Zafer*, the official DP paper, head writer Mümtaz Faik Fenik argued that Turkey was receiving less from the Marshall Plan than other European countries, even though Turkey was on the frontlines.[107] "While we keep our manpower under arms, other countries' manpower is mostly used in production, on account of which they can sell their products to us at high prices."[108]

Complaints aside, integration into an US-led military and economic order brought significant rewards. In addition to the $100 million in aid connected with the Truman Doctrine in the 1947–48 fiscal year, Turkey received $49 million in 1948–49, and $132 million in 1949–50 through a combination of Truman funds and Marshall funds.[109] Put in perspective, $49 million amounted to TL137 million, or 7 percent of the amount allocated for public expenditures in the 1948 budget; $132 million was equal to 15 percent of the total public expenditures for 1950.[110] Much of this money was in the form of privileged access to US products and materials, whether for military or civilian use. To purchase these goods, Turkish importers deposited lira at the Central Bank in exchange for the dollars they needed. These lira accumulated at the bank as "counterpart funds," which were then used for development projects in Turkey with

106 Mithat Perin, "Türkiye ve tarafsızlık politikası," *Demokrat İzmir*, March 30, 1949, 1, 6.

107 Mümtaz Faik Fenik was born in Istanbul in 1905. He studied law in Istanbul and economics in Brussels. He returned to Turkey after 1934 and spent the next fifteen years working for various newspapers and radio programs, including the CHP's official paper, *Ulus*. As a supporter of the DP, he was fired from *Ulus* in 1946 and began working at Ahmet Emin Yalman's *Vatan*. In 1949, he helped start the DP's official paper, *Zafer*. He was imprisoned briefly in early 1950 for a "press offense." He served as a member of parliament for Ankara from 1950 to 1957. Though he continued to write for *Zafer*, overall control was given to a party-appointed committee in 1952. After losing reelection in 1957, he became editor of *Havadis*, another DP-controlled paper. Until the 1960 coup he worked for both publications. After his release from prison in 1963, he wrote for *Havadis*. He died in 1974 (James Bowker to Selwyn Lloyd, "Leading Personalities in Turkey," July 2, 1958, FO 371/136451; Alemdar, *İletişim ve Tarih*, 137–138).

108 Mümtaz Faik Fenik, "Amerikan yardım ...," *Zafer*, June 9, 1949, 1.

109 *Marshall Plan in Turkey 24*, The Organization for International Economic Cooperation, Ministry for Foreign Affairs (1955).

110 Memduh Yasa (ed.), *Cumhuriyet Dönemi Türkiye Ekonomisi, 1923–1978* (Istanbul: Akbank Kültür Yayını, 1980), 580.

the consent of a US-appointed administrator.[111] The system cycled lira back into the domestic economy while simultaneously tying Turkish merchants to the US market. By giving Turkey easy access to dollars, it also discouraged Turkey's policymakers from further devaluing the lira.

Aid, combined with bond issues, helped close the budget deficits that grew after 1947. Even so, economic problems persisted. State-owned enterprises were also covering their loses by issuing treasury-guaranteed bonds, which the Central Bank bought up with little pressure to repay. Meanwhile, the Bank's hard currency reserves were being drained by trade imbalances as merchants imported both crucial necessities and luxuries. Demand for these products drove up prices. During 1948, there was a particularly sharp rise in prices, bringing the issue to the forefront of public discussion.[112] By mid 1948, the DP was making high prices a central issue. Writers at various pro-DP national dailies declared that the CHP and its bureaucrats were at fault. In *Zafer*, Mümtaz Faik Fenik argued that the government lacked credibility when it claimed that prices would not increase. Voters remembered how previous governments had promised to hold the line only to suddenly announce price hikes. In *Vatan*, Muhlis Ete suggested that government monopolies were themselves at fault since, by their very nature, they limited price competition.[113]

The issue of high costs was an effective line of attack for DP leaders. In May 1949, the DP held a rally in Istanbul to protest high prices. Before the large crowd, DP activist Nazlı Tlabar lamented that, "With all materials in our hands in this bountifully endowed land, we can't even cook and eat sweets." She identified two culprits: one was taxes, which she argued had risen rapidly since İnönü had come to power; the other was Turkey's free-riding allies in Europe. Turkey's misery was due to the greater sacrifices it was making. By revaluing the currency in 1946, the government had begun the transition to a "liberal" economic system, but the "liberal countries" had maintained their restrictive trade regimes.[114]

Her complaint reflected a frustration among DP leaders with the ways ostensible allies were manipulating the emerging economic order. Mümtaz Faik Fenik voiced a similar hostility toward devaluation in the

[111] Alan Milward, *The Reconstruction of Western Europe, 1945–51* (London: Routledge, 2006), 107.

[112] According to the International Cooperation Administration, the cost of living during the period 1947–51 was actually "relatively stable." In Ankara, prices rose 2 percent in 1946–47, 1 percent in 1947–48, 8 percent in 1948–49, and fell 7 percent in 1949–50 (Council for Economic and Industry Research, Inc., "Evaluation of Industrial Development: Turkey," International Cooperation Administration [1957], 58–59).

[113] Muhlis Ete, "Tekel politikamız," *Vatan*, May 10, 1948, 2; Mümtaz Faik Fenik, "Şeker darlığı …," *Vatan*, May 15, 1948, 1, 5.

[114] "Hayat pahalılığını protesto için," *Tasvir*, May 9, 1949, 1, 5.

context of the developing system of international trade. He pointed to West Germany, which had devalued and been able to sell its goods more easily. Turkey, by contrast, did not produce enough industrial goods for its own needs, let alone for sale abroad.[115] If anything, a devaluation would make purchasing foreign industrial products even more costly. The DP's opposition to devaluation was reiterated in the fall of 1949 when the UK devalued its own currency, leading other countries to follow suit.[116] Turkey was among the few that did not. Under the DP, it would not until 1958.

One particularly popular DP organizer who harped on the issue of high costs and poor government management was Sıtkı Yırcalı. In his columns in *Balıkesir Postası*, he decried price increases by the state monopolies and limitations on livestock sales that made it difficult for farmers to earn a living. He criticized the government's reliance on loans to fund imports as well as its introduction of a luxury tax. He complained that the tax was too broadly focused. Instead, it should target real luxuries like cars and "fancy dogs."[117] On account of his diatribes against the government and President İnönü, Yırcalı faced multiple prosecutions in the late 1940s. And though he remained with the DP throughout its existence, he caused no end of difficulties for his fellow party leaders. Among the earliest of these came at the party's Second Congress in 1949 when, as acting presiding officer, he helped push through a declaration justifying civil unrest in the face of state despotism.[118] Dubbed the "National Enmity Declaration" (*Milli Husumet Andı*) by the DP's opponents in the CHP, the resolution undermined the efforts of Bayar and others to present themselves as defenders of order and progress, occupying a middle ground between extremes – the radicalism of the Nation Party and complete accommodation with the government; the statism of the CHP and a state of unbridled capitalism. In recent months, for example, Cihad Baban, editor of the pro-DP paper *Tasvir*, had argued that the DP did not advocate either "laissez-faire" or a form of "socialism … that would bring about state capitalism."[119] Bayar had echoed this

115 Mümtaz Faik Fenik, "İktisaden istikrarsız tek devlet Türkiye," *Zafer*, July 6, 1949, 1.

116 Mümtaz Faik Fenik, "İngiliz lirası ve Türk parası," *Zafer*, September 22, 1949, 1.

117 Sıtkı Yırcalı, "Son günlerin," *Balıkesir Postası*, September 30, 1948, 1; Sıtkı Yırcalı, "Lüks Vergisi," *Balıkesir Postası*, November 30, 1948, 1.

118 Toker, *Tek Partiden Çok Partiye*, 233–235; Koçak, *Uzlaşma*, 535–538.

119 Cihad Baban, "Demokrat Partinin iktisadi anlayışı," *Tasvir*, March 10, 1949, 1, 5. Baban (1911–84) was the descendent of a Kurdish notable family, the Babanzade. His father, İsmail Hakkı, had been a journalist and Unionist in the 1910s, serving briefly as minister of education. Cihad was a graduate of Galatasaray Lycée and Istanbul University's Law School. He had briefly worked in the justice ministry before turning to journalism, where he took liberal, anti-communist positions. He was a critic

formulation by telling crowds, "We are not socialist. But we don't agree with Adam Smith's 'Manchester School' either."[120] At the Second Party Congress in 1949, he told delegates, "There's no need to speak of extreme leftism or rightism. There is no one among us who approves of extreme leftism."[121] It must be noted: he did not say the same of "rightism."

Distinguishing themselves from more radical critics was important for DP leaders, since the government continued to repress socialists and communists. In January 1949, for example, newspapers officially reported the murder of Sabahattin Ali, one of the country's most famous left-wing authors. Though his publishing house had been among those attacked in 1945, he had continued to print criticisms of the government regardless of closures, prosecutions, and jail sentences. He had gone missing in early 1948, after he had been released from jail. Initially, it was assumed he had fled the country, but he had, in fact, been killed near the border by the man whom he had hired to guide him to safety.

Like the earlier attacks on *Tan* and other publishing houses, the murder of Sabahattin Ali had a chilling effect on left-wing activists in Turkey. It was reflective of a larger crackdown on the left among members of the emerging US-led alliance. In countries as disparate as the Philippines and France, the Allied victory in World War II had weakened domestic right-wing movements and emboldened left-wing groups. Concerned that communist parties would use this opportunity to gain influence, the US government and its allies moved toward a consistent policy of "containing" communism in 1947–50. Activists found their room to maneuver subjected to increasing limitations. In Turkey, for example, the left-wing owners of *Tan*, Sabiha and Zekeriya Sertel opted to flee the country.[122]

On the opposite end of the political spectrum, deaths of a less premeditated sort also left the Nation Party in disarray on the eve of the elections. Kenan Öner, the Istanbul party leader, died in 1949, and the party's honorary president Fevzi Çakmak died in April 1950. Çakmak had been the commander of the armed forces from 1924 to 1944, and was seen as a champion of religious and nationalist causes. His funeral was an opportunity for conservatives to gather en masse in Istanbul, but their sadness did not translate to increased support for the party. When the election

of the CHP and served in parliament as an independent in 1946–50, before being reelected in 1950 and 1954 as a member of the DP (Baban, *Politika Galerisi*, 9–12).

120 "Bayar diyor ki …," *Demokrat İzmir*, March 26, 1949, 1.

121 "Celal Bayar'ın …," *Vatan*, June 24, 1949, 1–2, 4.

122 Sertel, *Roman Gibi*, 384–385. After six months of waiting for their passports and finally writing directly to Adnan Menderes, the Sertels left Turkey on September 9, 1950.

was held a month later, the Nation Party won only 4.6 percent of the vote. Even without the support of these former allies, the DP won 55.2 percent of the vote and, with that, the election.

Ankara Palas Intrigues: Forming the First DP Cabinet

During its four and a half years in opposition, the DP held together, united by its shared opposition to the CHP. With victory not fully imaginable prior to May 14, 1950, it was easy to delay firm decisions regarding the shape of a government. Following the election, however, power actually had to be allocated. Koraltan was elected president of parliament with the support of the DP parliamentary group. Then came the more significant decision: choosing the president of the republic. After initially suggesting that they might name an elder, relatively non-partisan figure, the party leadership decided to nominate Bayar instead. In turn, Bayar named Adnan Menderes as his prime minister rather than party leaders like Fuat Köprülü or Fevzi Lütfi Karaosmanoğlu, both of whom were older than Menderes. Köprülü was given the prestigious post of foreign minister, but Karaosmanoğlu, left with nothing, was bitter.

As a member of the party executive committee, Karaosmanoğlu had expected a position in government that reflected his high status in the party – and perhaps in society as well: like Menderes, he was a wealthy landowner from the Aegean region and, like Köprülü, he was from a family that had been prominent for centuries. He had worked as a journalist in the 1920s and been prosecuted for his criticism of the CHP. Thereafter, he had focused on his estates. Following the establishment of the DP in 1946, he joined and became a leading member. Therefore, he was further surprised when he *also* lost out to Menderes in the elections for the presidency of the DP's executive committee. According to some accounts, he was so magnanimous (or overconfident) that he cast his own vote for Menderes – only to lose by a single vote.[123]

Menderes's first cabinet contained several leading figures in the party. In addition to Köprülü, two other executive committee members received posts: Refik Şevket İnce became minister of defense, and Nuri Özsan became minister of customs. Several ministers, however, were elderly or technocratic figures who had little support in the party.[124]

[123] Noel Charles to Foreign Office, November 1, 1950, FO 371/87940; Baban, *Politika Galerisi*, 359–369; Karpat, "Actors and Issues," 129–130.

[124] Sixty men served in DP governments. When the party came to power in 1950, their average age was forty-seven. Yet this is slightly misleading, since, of the nine who were already sixty or older in 1950, *five* served during the years 1950–52. If these five are

Within six months, four had resigned. They would not serve in government again.[125] The most prominent figures in the party left out of the cabinet were Karaosmanoğlu, Samet Ağaoğlu, and Sıtkı Yırcalı. Samet, who had high expectations, did not hide his bitterness. He spent much of the following two weeks at the Ankara Palas hotel, directly across from the parliament building, complaining to fellow legislators about his shoddy treatment until Menderes finally brought him into the government as a "state minister" on June 5.[126] Karaosmanoğlu was brought in as well a month later.

excluded, the average age falls to forty-five. Thus, average cabinet ministers in the DP would have been born in 1905 and begun their careers around 1928, just as the first slate of republican reforms were coming to an end, and just as the SCF experiment was being launched. Their professional lives would have coincided with the intensification of single-party rule.

125 Minister of Education Hüseyin Avni Başman resigned on August 2, 1950; Minister of Health and Social Assistance Minister Nihat Reşat Belger on September 19; Minister of Public Works Fahri Belen on October 28; and Minister of Finance Halil Ayan on December 14. According to UK reports, Başman was frustrated by questioning in parliament. Belger resigned after his attempts to impose his will on doctors were blocked by Menderes. Belen was angry at not being made minister of defense; he was opposed to the budget cuts Menderes required him to make; and he was annoyed at being sent on a visit to Mersin to inspect ports. Ayan was forced out after he opposed Menderes's budget priorities (see Ankara to Foreign Office, August 3, 1950; Noel Charles to Foreign Office, September 21, 1950; Noel Charles to Foreign Office, November 1, 1950; Noel Charles to Foreign Office, December 19, 1950, all in FO 371/87940).

126 Samet was but one member of his family in the parliament. His sister Tezer Taşkıran had been reelected as a CHP representative for the province of Kars. She remained in parliament for the 1950–54 term, but she resigned from the CHP on December 30, 1950, just a few months after her the election. According to journalist Cüneyt Arcayürek, she felt that her peers in the CHP parliamentary group were treating her as though she were a "spy" for her brother. Tezer was one of only three women in the Ninth Parliament (1950–54), the other two being Halide Edip Adıvar and Nazlı Tlabar. The former was a famous writer and political activist who had spent much of the 1930s in exile for her opposition to Mustafa Kemal. She ran for office as an independent on the DP list. Tlabar had been a DP stalwart since 1946. That women accounted for only 0.6 percent of parliamentarians in 1950 was a step backward in terms of representation, but the previous higher percentages had been engineered by the CHP leadership. Women became eligible to serve in parliament in advance of the 1935 elections. In the 1935, 1939, and 1943 elections, the regime was able to shape electoral lists to reflect its goal of greater female visibility in public life. As a result, female representatives numbered eighteen (4.5 percent of all representatives), sixteen (3.7 percent), and sixteen (3.5 percent) respectively in the abovementioned elections. When the party allowed provincial organizations to exercise more control over crafting party lists starting in 1946, the number of women fell to nine (1.9 percent). In the Tenth Parliament (1954–57), there were four female representatives (0.7 percent): Nazlı Tlabar, Aliye Timuçin Coşkun (a botany teacher and school administrator), Nuriye Pınar (a geologist), and Edibe Sayar (a judge and journalist). In the Eleventh Parliament (1957–60), there were eight (1.3 percent): Tlabar, Pınar, Ayşe Günel (a member of the Red Crescent board, Tobacco Bank board, and several provincial councils; also the sister of leading DP figure Emin Kalafat), Necla Tekinel (a

Menderes presented his government's program to parliament on May 29. Referring to the French Revolution, he promised to avoid "the sinister inclination toward creating an *ancien regime*" (*devr-i sabık*) – in other words, persecuting the former government. Yet his speech began with a thorough denunciation of his predecessors' policies.[127] "Lacking national or political oversight over many years [had] opened the way to many mistakes, improprieties, extravagances, and excesses." Over time, "an interventionalist, capitalist, bureaucratic, and monopolistic type of state had emerged," which used "every type of customs barrier" to protect unproductive and expensive products. Rather than keep interest rates low to encourage investment in local industries, the government had made borrowing difficult. As a result, sectors such as agriculture remained uncompetitive, and Turkey was unable to sell enough of its products abroad to pay for its imports. In only a few years, the country's gold reserves had fallen by 39 percent.[128]

To address these challenges, Menderes promised to direct state investment "only toward production"; to take measures "that provide private enterprise with the feeling of both *de jure* and *de facto* security"; to facilitate "the flow of capital currently in the country toward production"; to solicit "the capital and techniques of foreign enterprises"; to set aside money in the budget for investments "by considering our country's natural conditions"; and to "free productive life from the state's damaging interventions and various bureaucratic impediments." This would be accomplished through: turning over state enterprises, when possible, to private hands; reforming the tax code; and improving the conditions of the agricultural sector. He emphasized this last point, declaring, "The greatest difference in perspective between the new government and the [CHP] manifests itself in the field of agricultural affairs."[129]

The previous government had filled its 1950 budget deficit through a combination of TL19 million ($6.8 million) in borrowing and TL155

lawyer and local politician in the Istanbul municipality of Sarıyer), Hilal Ülman (a history teacher), Piraye Levent (a teacher and pharmacist), and Perihan Arıburun (a lawyer and judge, married to Turkish air force commander Tahsin Arıburun). The sole CHP representative was Ubeyde Elli (a member of various charitable organizations and leader of the CHP Women's Arm). To give some comparison: in the United States, women in the House of Representatives won 3 percent of seats (1944), 2 percent (1950), 4 percent (1954), and 4 percent (1958) (Bedia Turgay Ahmad and Feroz Ahmad, *Türkiye'de Çok Partili Politikanın Açıklamalı Kronolojisi, 1945–1971* [Istanbul: Bilgi Yayınevi, 1976], 78; Cüneyt Arcayürek, *Yeni İktidar Yeni Dönem, 1951–1954* [Ankara: Bilgi Yayınevi, 1985], 154; Filiz Çolak, "Demokrat Parti Dönemi'nde TBMM'deki Kadın Milletvekilleri ve Meclisteki Faaliyetleri, 1950–1960," *Tarih Okulu Dergisi* 10, no. 32 (2017): 115–158; Gülşah Kurt Güveloğlu, *Demokrat Partinin Kadın Milletvekilleri* (Istanbul: Kriter Yayınları, 2018), 15–26.

[127] TBMM, May 29, 1950, 30. [128] Ibid., 25. [129] Ibid., 26–28.

million ($55.4 million) in Marshal Plan funds. Menderes implied the new government would support itself rather than depend on others. With his final words, he thanked "our great friend the United States" for its military support and hoped his government could now achieve "a broader scale and more rapid benefits."[130] What Menderes could not have anticipated was the outbreak of the Korean War only a month later, which increased the flow of funds from the United States and the global demand for Turkish grain. These new sources of revenue for development projects would alter the *political* calculations and ambitions of Menderes and his governments.

As for Samet, his first official speech in parliament came on June 21, in response to a question about removing officials for corruption and other misconduct. Samet emphasized the government's commitment to removing bad officials, since "[o]ne of the conditions for functioning state governance is governance with a smiling face and sweet words."[131] As we will see in the coming chapters, this concern with removing "bad" officials would become a particular concern of the DP leaders at the national and provincial levels.

Conclusion: Girondins or Montagnards?

Despite the increase in US influence during the late 1940s, DP leaders remained fond of allusions to the French Revolution and French politics more generally. We see this in their memoirs: Ağaoğlu wrote of the impression revolutionary figures made on young professionals like himself, while the journalist (and, for a time, DP legislator) Cihad Baban explained the relations between Menderes and Karaosmanoğlu through reference to Robespierre and Saint-Just.[132] But we also see this from their statements at the time: once in power, Menderes himself was concerned with how to deal with the *ancien régime* of single-party rule. And members of the DP's own internal opposition would come to refer to themselves as *yaylacılar*. *Yayla* were the mountain meadows where pastoralists moved in the summertime, and the term meant something like "uplanders," a reference to the seats they occupied in the elevated back of the parliamentary group's meeting chamber. It was a clear allusion was to the "Montagnards," who occupied the same position in the French Revolution's National Assembly.[133]

[130] Ibid., 31–32. [131] TBMM, June 21, 1950, 217.

[132] Baban, *Politika Galerisi*, 361.

[133] Samet attributes the term *yaylacılar* to Sıtkı Yırcalı and says that Yırcalı's reference to the French Revolution was intentional. Şevket Süreyya Aydemir dates the group's

DP leaders and legislators imagined themselves to be following in historic footsteps. One wonders how they would have placed themselves in relation to sociologist Theda Skocpol's characterization of these revolutionaries. According to Skocpol, the historical Montagnards were "from the administrative centers that formed the base of the absolutist monarchy, whereas the Girondins [their rivals] were heavily recruited from commercial port cities that had historically existed in some dissociation from, and tension with, the monarchical state."[134] Turkey was not France, but versions of the various cleavages she describes were certainly present. Many of the DP's older founders, for example, had been integrated into the Ottoman political system through institutions of higher education or state service. Nazlı Tlabar, the only woman in the DP parliamentary group from 1950 to 1954, was the granddaughter of the Ottoman Empire's last grand vizier (*sadrazam*) on one side and an Ottoman interior minister on the other. Cihad Baban was the descendent of a once-powerful Kurdish notable family that had become supportive of the Ottoman state; his father had been a Unionist member of parliament. While not old enough to have such deep connections to the Ottoman Empire, Samet Ağaoğlu was thoroughly integrated into the republican order by the time he was an adult. The same was true of Sıtkı Yırcalı in Balıkesir. These were not isolated examples.

The point is *not* that elite origins and experiences make people so complicit in one political system that they are unable to play constructive roles in a new one. Rather, the point is that old ideologies, assumptions, and interests coexisted with new ones. The DP was a party formed by dissatisfied CHP elites hoping to appeal to a general frustration with the single-party regime. They promised to improve the regime, not remake it. And even in this narrow sense, the DP program was vague. Some of this ambiguity may have been due to censorship – to fully reject statism was dangerous, since it was part of the constitution and rejecting it could open critics to charges of subversion. But the fact that DP leaders never called for radical alteration in the system, and never enacted any,

origins to 1951, which makes sense, given that Fahri Belen, one of its leading figures, had been pushed out of Menderes's first cabinet around that time. In 1960, Belen published a memoir recounting the DP's failings, in which he accused Menderes (among other things) of deciding to return the call to prayer to Arabic during an alcohol-filled dinner and, moreover, doing so in order to quash suggestions that he was a Mason (Belen, *Demokrasiden Diktatörlüğe* [Istanbul: İstanbul Matbaası, 1960], 64; Ağaoğlu, *Arkadaşım Menderes*, 109; Aydemir, *Menderes'in Dramı?*, 269; Metin Toker, *DP Yokuş Aşağı 1954–1957: Demokrasimizin İsmet Paşa'lı Yılları*, 2nd ed. (Istanbul: Bilgi Yayınevi, 1991 [1966]), 166–169).

134 Theda Skocpol, *States and Social Revolutions: A Comparative Analysis of France, Russia, and China* (Cambridge: Cambridge University Press, 1979), 167.

suggests that their initial ambiguity stemmed from the limited nature of the changes they truly desired to make. Even those activists like Ağaoğlu who desired major reforms eventually moderated their aims and focused on holding power.

In looking at the period of "transition to democracy," this chapter has shown that it was a moment when DP elites were struggling not only for power but also over what ideas could unite the diverse interests driving the opposition movement. Young members of the party like Ağaoğlu or Yırcalı were educated professionals who found fault with the high-handed methods of the single-party regime, but they also opposed the disruptions to rational management that might come with union activism or other radical policies. In their writings, they opposed unwarranted state intervention, but felt that *they* should be the ones to determine what situations qualified as unwarranted.

Moving beyond the four founders, we see that the DP national leadership was full of Samet Ağaoğlus: well-educated officials in their late thirties and early forties who were ready to have a greater say in the political system. Put in terms they would have appreciated: they were "Montagnards," supporters of the system, hoping to have a greater say, rather than "Girondins," outside the regime, looking in. Yet this categorization – admittedly, a bit tongue-in-cheek – raises the question of what they would do once they were in office and had the opportunity to exercise power. That is the subject of the next chapter.

3 The Costs of Success: The Democrat Party in Power, 1950–1954

Military officers contemplated overthrowing the DP even before it entered office. As the May 14, 1950, election results were coming in, revealing the scale of the CHP's loss, top military leaders met with President İnönü and promised to back him if he decided to reject the results. İnönü declined. Menderes and Bayar replaced the military leadership within weeks of taking office, but the threat of military intervention never fully receded.[1] According to one officer who participated in the 1960 coup, his peers were already grumbling within a month of the DP taking power. The focus of their anger was the DP government's decision to allow the call to prayer to be sung in Arabic rather than Turkish.[2] Though this was a policy change that the CHP had set in motion before the elections, it was the DP that passed it into law, and the DP that associated itself with the change.[3] This was not the last time during the decade of DP rule that continuity would be perceived as rupture.

An enduring question of the DP era is whether 1950 marked an important change in the nature of the republic. On the one hand, hundreds of leading politicians were swept from power at the national and

1 William Hale, *Turkish Politics and the Military* (London: Routledge, 1994), 92–93; Pelt, *Military Intervention*, 179. The DP leaders were not without allies in the military. Several factions of officers had formed after 1946 with the aim of preventing the CHP from manipulating elections again. The figurehead of one faction, General Fahri Belen, retired and ran as a DP candidate in 1950 (Abdi İpekçi and Ömer Sami Coşar, "İhtilâlin İçyüzü," *Milliyet*, May 27, 1962, 5).

2 Cemal Madanoğlu, *Anılar, 1919–1953* (Istanbul: Evrim Yayınevi, 1982), 336; Birand et al., *Demirkırat*, 112–113.

3 The expansion of religious training schools (*imam hatip*) is another example of a policy initiated under the CHP but accelerated under the DP. Faced with a shortage of qualified religious officials, the CHP introduced *imam hatip* "courses" in 1949. That same year, it also added weekly religious courses as an elective to the national school curriculum. Under the DP, religious classes became mandatory (unless parents signed a waiver), and *imam hatip* courses were replaced with schools. Under DP rule, according to İren Özgür, these schools increased from seven to nineteen, and enrollment grew from 876 to 3,625 (Özgür, *Islamic Schools in Modern Turkey: Faith, Politics, and Education* [Cambridge: Cambridge University Press, 2012], 40).

local level, and citizens participated in elections at a rate that would not be surpassed until after voting became mandatory in 1982. People saw that their vote could contribute to at least some degree of political change. Even if the DP and CHP were little more than two factions of an established political class, it was now the case that the support of citizens had become key to resolving disputes between these factions. On the other hand, as the example of the Arabic call to prayer illustrates, many of the changes brought about by the DP reflected a bipartisan, elite consensus. This included joining NATO and liberalizing trade. Moreover, many of the crucial events that occurred in the 1950s would have profoundly affected the republic even in the absence of democratic elections. The Korean War, a large influx of refugees from Bulgaria, revolutions in neighboring countries, and unexpected variations in harvests all presented challenges that would reshape the country regardless of who was in charge.

If DP leaders had one constant goal, it was to develop Turkey so that it reached the "level of advanced nations." On the eve of the election, DP candidates promised to achieve this through tax reform, an apolitical bureaucracy, more investment in agriculture, and a less overbearing state that supported "private property," "private enterprise," and "individual economic freedoms."[4] In office, the party translated some of these broad principles into policy: state investments and loans to farmers increased; the gendarmerie acted with more restraint in the countryside; and religious expression in the public sphere was policed less aggressively. In many cases, however, the principles remained largely rhetorical, and party leaders fell back on familiar policies: the state remained central to the economy (in fact, the number of state-owned enterprises *increased*); the party backed away from supporting the right to strike; and repression of intellectuals and religious movements continued. A liberal Press Law, a general amnesty, and reduced sentences (including that of left-wing cause célèbre Nâzım Hikmet) soon gave way to crackdowns on communists and restrictions on journalists and publishers.

Although even critics of the DP acknowledge that the early years of its rule were "golden," these years were also contentious.[5] Turkish citizens traveled across the globe to fight on the Korean peninsula, polarization between the parties increased, and the economy grew dramatically, improving many people's lives but disrupting those of many others.

[4] "Partilerin radyo konuşmaları," *Zafer*, May 6, 1950, 1–2 (see also "D. Parti seçim …," *Zafer*, May 9, 1950, 1, 2, 8; "Vatandaş, reyini …," *Zafer*, May 10, 1950, 1, 6).

[5] For example: Metin Toker, *DP'nin Altın Yılları, 1950–1954: Demokrasimizin İsmet Paşa'lı Yılları*, 2nd ed. (Istanbul: Bilgi Yayınevi, 1991 [1990]).

This chapter considers that complexity by looking at the efforts of DP leaders, amidst this ferment, to consolidate their control at the national and provincial level while also bringing Turkey into a profitable relationship with the US government and institutions such as NATO. To give some shape to these initial years of DP rule, this chapter looks first at the lives of several important figures in the DP, including an architect of its foreign policy, Fatin Rüştü Zorlu, and of its domestic economic policy, Hasan Polatkan – both of whom would be executed following the 1960 coup. Thereafter, the chapter returns to Malatya and Balıkesir to consider how the early years of DP rule were experienced in distinct regions of the country. The two provinces are especially notable in these years, as both were the site of violence that rocked national politics. Finally, we will consider how the favorable economic conditions during the DP's first term in office (1950–54) helped the party please voters and secure reelection, even as the contradictions in its policies were beginning to emerge.

Dollars and Diplomacy in the Early Years of DP Rule

Hasan Polatkan resembled other men who filled Menderes's cabinets: a well-educated product of the provincial elite. His father had arrived in the Ottoman province of Eskişehir as a child, sent by his family in Crimea to live with a wealthy cousin who had already settled there and, thereby, escape the oppression of the Russian Empire. Those family members that remained were killed. He became a merchant and integrated into the local elite. All his children, including Hasan, would marry into the families of local factory owners. According to the recollections of his children, he was a strong supporter of Mustafa Kemal and supplied horses to the nationalist forces. This patriotism was mixed with an understandably strong anti-Russian sentiment.[6]

Polatkan attended the Mülkiye, Turkey's elite civil service university, and then secured a job in Ziraat Bankası, where he worked for the following decade, traveling around Eskişehir and making a name for himself. In 1946, he was recommended to Bayar and Menderes by the provincial governor and invited to help organize the provincial DP along with Kemal Zeytinoğlu, the scion of a wealthy family from nearby Kütahya that was expanding its influence in Eskişehir.[7] The province proved to be a stronghold for the DP; in addition to having a governor

[6] Emiroğlu, *Hasan Polatkan*, 7–9.

[7] Ibid., 15–16; Mustafa Sönmez, *Türkiye'de Holdingler: Kırk Haramiler* (Ankara: Arkadaş Yayınevi, 1988), 285–286.

who was willing to assist the DP leaders, one of its leading politicians was the powerful landowner Emin Sazak, who had joined with the DP founders in their early challenges to the CHP and its attempts to redistribute land. Sure enough, under these favorable conditions, the DP's organizational efforts were successful: the party won the province in 1946. Now a member of parliament, Polatkan proposed to his future wife, the daughter of a wealthy local manufacturer, whose other sons-in-law included a doctor (later to become a DP member of parliament) and a businessman specializing in cars and tractors.[8]

During his five years as a member of the opposition, Polatkan was a regular participant in parliamentary debates. His questions and speeches tended to focus on the management of state-owned enterprises and labor issues, such as salaries (often one and the same, given that state firms employed around one-third of the nonagricultural workforce).[9] He also argued that government budgets allotted insufficient funds to agricultural credit.[10] Given these areas of interest, his appointment as minister of labor in Menderes's first government was unremarkable – except, perhaps, for the fact that the thirty-five-year-old Polatkan was the youngest member of the cabinet.

As discussed in Chapter 2, the first DP cabinet was unrepresentative of the party as a whole: it was composed of older, moderate politicians, lacking the fervor of those party activists who had struggled against the CHP and its officials since 1946.[11] While appointing moderates helped party leaders like Menderes and Bayar smooth the DP's transition into power, it frustrated DP members of parliament. It also led to disagreements within the cabinet. Minister of Finance Halil Ayan, for example, favored a restrained spending policy to avoid large outflows of gold. He also hoped to reduce the deficit by delaying tax cuts for civil servants. These stances created immediate problems during the annual budgetary process (which typically ran from December through February of each

[8] Hasan Polatkan's father-in-law, Kurt Seyit (Çiftkurt), had five children; his daughter Mutahhare was married to Polatkan; his daughter Şaziye was married to Dr. Ali Harputlu; and his daughter Meryem was married to businessman Yusuf Soyugenç, a major donor to the DP. Kurt Seyit's business partner was Mahmut Başkurt, who would become a representative for Eskişehir and serve three terms. Their company also donated to the DP ("Acı bir ölüm," *Milliyet*, June 1, 1958, 2; BCA 010.09.00.00 364 1113 2).

[9] TBMM, December 28, 1946, 742–743. In 1950, according to Ahmet Makal, 455,793 people were employed as workers or managers in state firms out of a total national workforce of 9,454,269; if we assume that around 85 percent of this workforce was employed in agriculture, then these state employees accounted for some 32 percent of all other workers (*Türkiye'de Tek Partili*, 246, 465).

[10] TBMM, December 27, 1946, 610–613; TBMM, February 27, 1949, 853.

[11] Sarol, *Bilinmeyen Menderes*, vol. I, 125.

year). Ayan's obstinacy drew criticism from advocates of increased spending like Polatkan, who replaced Ayan when he resigned in late December.[12] Polatkan would remain in the position for all but one year over the next decade. With the exceptions of Prime Minister Menderes and Nedim Ökmen, the long-serving minister of agriculture, no other DP member remained in the same office for so long.

Defending the party's first annual spending bill on the floor of parliament, Polatkan expressed sadness that the DP had not achieved all it desired. In terms of size, the annual budget was not substantially different from its CHP-authored predecessor. At TL1.5 billion, it was only a 6 percent increase on the previous year, roughly in line with inflation.[13] Polatkan justified the modest nature of the budget by emphasizing that the party had inherited a dire situation. "It would be closing one's eyes to the truth," he explained, "to expect that the first budget of a new government – which follows a series of budgets that reduced constructive possibilities to a degree of insignificance and extended their effects for years to come – would be freed from the heavy pressure and influences of the past."[14] Among the chief evils of past budgets was a belief that the state was the source of economic dynamism; consequently, "the real economic activities and the real production taking place outside the state sector never even came to mind."[15]

Aside from blaming the former ruling party for the DP government's difficulties, Polatkan pointed to another significant challenge affecting the government's budgeting: the Korean War. The DP government's announcement on July 25, 1950, less than two months after taking power, that it would send soldiers to fight in Korea was among the most consequential decisions that it made in the coming decade. By participating in the conflict, the DP government demonstrated Turkey's willingness to support the Cold War aims of the United States, thereby strengthening its efforts to join NATO and requests for financial aid. Henceforth, when US diplomats observed that Turkey received far more than needy countries like India, Turkish diplomats could justify the difference by pointing to their country's military sacrifices.[16] Domestically, involvement in the war

[12] Cahit Kayra, *'38 Kuşağı: Anılar* (Istanbul: Türkiye İş Bankası Kültür Yayınları, 2002), 149–153.

[13] Hershlag, *Turkey*, 201; Morris Singer, *The Economic Advance of Turkey, 1938–1960* (Ankara: Ayyıldız Matbaası, 1977), 334. According to Haluk Cillov, the Soil Products Office (TMO) paid farmers 25 percent more than the crop was worth in the United States (30 kuruş rather than 24); by 1957, the TMO was paying 87 percent more (45 kuruş rather than 24) (Cillov, *Türkiye Ekonomisi*, 209.)

[14] TBMM, February 19, 1951, 203. [15] Ibid., 204.

[16] Drawing on several sources, Gavin Brockett calculates that around 14,936 Turkish citizens served in the Korean War. Dead and wounded were 721 and 2,147

created a shared national experience that transcended local interests. During the first, most violent year of the war, papers across the country followed events in Korea closely. Provincial papers published poetry extolling the virtues and sacrifices of Turkish soldiers. Politically, the government's decision to commit soldiers without seeking parliamentary approval handed a ready-made issue to both the CHP and the intraparty opposition. At the same time, the apparent public support for the action made opposition criticism seem somewhat petty, obscuring the government's willingness to flout procedural – and, perhaps, constitutional – requirements.

Participation in the Korean War also strengthened anti-communists within the DP. While party leaders had hardly been favorable to communists or left-wing intellectuals following a brief, initial outreach to publishers like the Sertels in 1945, there had been some degree of tolerance. As late as June 1950, influential DP-supporters were advocating successfully for the release of the poet Nâzım Hikmet.[17] The war foreclosed further tolerance. A letter protesting Turkey's involvement in Korea, published on July 29 by the Peace Lovers Society (*Barışseverler Cemiyeti*), received a quick response: its leaders were arrested that day. They were eventually sentenced to fifteen months in prison.[18] Starting in January 1951 and continuing for months, the government began

respectively, with 234 prisoners of war and 175 missing. By comparison, 5.7 million Americans served, 36,574 died, and 103,284 were wounded. Though these numbers are obviously vastly different in scale, they show that while the odds of death for Turkish soldiers was 1:20 (and 1:7 for being wounded), for American soldiers it was 1:156 and 1:55 (Brockett, "The Legend of 'The Turk' in Korea: Popular Perceptions of the Korean War and Their Importance to a Turkish National Identity," *War & Society* 22, no. 2 [2004]: 116; David A. Blum and Nese F. DeBruyne, "American War and Military Operations Casualties: Lists and Statistics," Congressional Research Service, January 29, 2020, 2, available: https://sgp.fas.org/crs/natsec/RL32492.pdf).

17 Though Hikmet's imprisonment was an ongoing concern for socialist activists, by 1947 it had also become an issue for such liberals as *Vatan* publisher Ahmet Emin Yalman and his newspaper's lawyer, Mehmet Ali Sebük. Yalman would lose faith in the DP soon after it gained power, but Sebük would serve as a representative for İzmir from 1954 to 1957. Though he did not serve another term, he remained a defender of the DP legacy (if not all its methods). He translated from French the Ali Fuad Başgil book *27 Mayıs İhtilali ve Sebepleri* (The May 27th Revolution and Its Reasons), which criticized the excesses of the coup, and stood as an AP candidate for an Istanbul senate seat in 1966 (Meyer, *Red Star over the Black Sea: Nâzım Hikmet and His Generation* [Oxford: Oxford University Press, 2023], 246–249; "Aday adayı …," *Cumhuriyet*, April 15, 1966, 1).

18 "Moskovanın ağzile …," *Cumhuriyet*, July 29, 1950, 1, 3. The Peace Lovers Society was led by Behice Boran, one of several recently removed Ankara University professors who had close connections to Turkey's underground Communist Party (Gökhan Atılgan, *Behice Boran: Öğretim Üyesi, Siyasetçi, Kuramcı* [Istanbul: Yordam Kitap, 2007], 58–62, 154–158).

arresting and prosecuting alleged communists. Nâzım Hikmet chose to escape the country in June. By November, the leadership of the underground Turkish Communist Party had been arrested.[19] In parliament, hardline members of the DP such as the wealthy landowner Şevket Mocan transformed from gadflies into prominent figures able to push legislation. In Mocan's case, this included revisions to the criminal code that made leadership of a revolutionary organization an offense punishable by death.[20] And while Mocan never made his way into the government, right-wing politicians like Tevfik İleri did. In his first speech to the DP parliamentary group after being appointed minister of education, İleri acknowledged the "reality" of "communist teachers in every level of education" and promised to "clean" them from the system.[21]

The willingness of DP leaders to participate in Korea and root out domestic communists demonstrated to their US peers that Turkey was committed to the anti-communist bloc. But it also demonstrated that stance to Soviet leaders and *their* allies. On August 10, just two weeks after the DP government announced its decision to send soldiers to Korea, the communist-led government of Bulgaria demanded that Turkey accept 250,000 Turkish emigrants. During the next three months, until Turkey temporarily closed the border, more than 15,000 people crossed from Bulgaria into Turkey. In the month of December, when the border reopened, another 20,000 people arrived.[22] Within a

19 The trials, which concluded in 1954, prosecuted 184 people and sentenced 131 to as much as ten years in prison ("Dün 184 kömünist ...," *Cumhuriyet*, October 8, 1954, 1, 6; "120 kızıl mahkum ...," *Dünya*, October 8, 1954, 1, 7).

20 RG, December 11, 1951; Eroğul, *Demokrat Parti*, 95 n. 10. Mocan's insistence on the death penalty for leading communists was rather personal. Mocan had once been married to Sara (Okçu), the aunt of Nâzım Hikmet. In the fall of 1950, against Mocan's wishes, their daughter, Ayşe, eloped with Dündar Baştımar. Dündar had been jailed in 1945 for his communist connections, and his brother, Zeki, was the leading figure in the party in 1951 ("Komünist Partisi ...," *Vatan*, November 4, 1951, 1, 4; "Nâzım'ın teyzesi Sara," *Cumhuriyet*, October 17, 1989, 18).

21 *TBMM Demokrat Parti Meclis Grubu Müzakere Zabıtları* (DPMGMZ), November 14, 1950, 87. Tevfik İleri served as education minister in 1950–53, 1957, and 1959–60, as well as in other important posts. As a leader of the National Turkish Student Union (*Milli Türk Talebe Birliği*, MTTB) from 1929 to 1933, he was prosecuted for organizing an unauthorized protest outside the Bulgarian embassy following the desecration of a Turkish graveyard in the city of Razgrad. İleri and his associates were pardoned, but the organization was closed in 1936 for its continued, unsanctioned protests. It was opened again in 1946 (M. Çağatay Okutan, *Bozkurt'tan Kur'an'a Millî Türk Talebe Birliği [MTTB] 1916–1980* [Istanbul: Bilgi Üniversitesi, 2004], 27–29; Bozkurt, *Tevfik İleri*, 32–36).

22 Turkish Ministry of Agriculture to Oren McJunkins, February 12, 1951, RG 84, Box 61, UD 3288, NND 842831 (hereafter RG 84, Box 61). Mary Neuberger notes that the term "expulsions," which is often used to characterize the departure of Turks from Bulgaria in 1950–51, does not fully capture the situation. Many emigrants willingly left

year, over 150,000 had come; half were settled in provinces around the Sea of Marmara, and the rest were placed throughout the country (southeastern Kurdish-majority provinces largely excepted).[23] Although the US Secretary of State Acheson told his officials in Turkey "that primary responsibility in solving refugee problem rests with the Turks," more than TL7 million ($2.5 million) of available counterpart funds was directed to the costs of resettlement in 1950–51.[24]

Despite firm language, US officials understood that pressure on Turkish finances in domestic matters could affect military spending and readiness. In negotiations, DP leaders played up the linkage between military spending and other areas of their budget. The man most associated with this tight linkage was Menderes's chief foreign policy advisor, Fatin Rüştü Zorlu. Though he never served so long in a single position as Polatkan did, Zorlu was another policymaker whose influence persisted throughout the DP's decade in party. Moreover, whereas Polatkan spent several years as an opposition member of parliament before gaining power, Zorlu was never out of power. In fact, by 1950, he was already a high-ranking official in the ministry of foreign affairs. It is likely that he would have played an important role in 1950s diplomacy even if the DP had not come to power.

The ministry of foreign affairs was one of the last bastions of the Ottoman ruling class. The linguistic skills, etiquette, and familiarity with world affairs that diplomacy required was hard to replace. Consequently, many diplomats successfully managed the transition from empire to republic with their careers intact.[25] For much of Mustafa Kemal's time in power, the MFA was overseen by Tevfik Rüştü Aras, an acquaintance

to avoid the collectivization push underway (Neuberger, *The Orient Within: Muslim Minorities and the Negotiation of Nationhood in Modern Bulgaria* [Ithaca: Cornell University Press, 2004], 187–190).

[23] See Huey Louis Kostanick, "Turkish Resettlement of Refugees from Bulgaria, 1950–1953," *Middle East Journal* 9, no. 1 (1955): 53. The government had originally planned to settle Bulgarians in the southeast, especially around Van, Bitlis, and Bingöl, but later ruled this out owing to lack of transportation and concerns over potential clashes with the local Kurdish population ("Report on Reception and Care of Turkish Refugees from Bulgaria," Special Mission of the International Refugee Organization, 8, and Clifford Wilson, "A Settlement Plan for Turkey," Economic Cooperation Administration, October 1951, 8, both in RG 84, Box 61).

[24] "Doc. 744: Secretary of State to Embassy in Turkey," November 30, 1950, *Foreign Relations of the United States (FRUS), 1950*, vol. V: *The Near East and Africa*. In Turkey, the influx of Bulgarian immigrants and shocking military setbacks in late 1950, resulting from China's entry into the Korean War, were followed by a year of crackdowns on left-wing and communist organizations. The arrests and prosecutions decimated the left in Turkey for much of the 1950s.

[25] Yücel Güçlü, *The Life and Career of a Turkish Diplomat: Cevat Açıkalın* (Ankara: Ministry of Foreign Affairs, 2002), 26; "Marshall Aid Funds," RG 84, Box 61. During the 1930s,

of Kemal's since the early 1900s, when the two men had been members of the Unionist organization in Salonika.[26] As discussed in Chapter 1, Aras was pushed out of government following Kemal's death as punishment for his attempts to block İsmet İnönü's presidential bid.[27] The gambit failed, and Aras was removed from the cabinet, excluded from the CHP's 1939 electoral list, and appointed ambassador to the UK, where he served until retiring in 1943. Upon returning to Istanbul, he wrote newspaper columns for the socialist newspaper *Tan* and remained involved in politics behind the scenes. No doubt, this continued to include promoting the career of Menderes, his nephew-in-law, and Zorlu, his son-in-law.

Zorlu came from an elite Ottoman family. His father was a major general under Abdulhamid II and his mother came from another high-ranking military family. He attended Istanbul's prestigious Galatasaray Lycée before traveling to Paris and Geneva for higher education. Returning to Turkey in 1932, he entered the foreign service. Within a year, he had caught the eye of Aras's wife, Makbule, who arranged his marriage to her daughter Emel (a cousin of Adnan Menderes's wife, Berrin). The union was approved not only by the respective families but also by Mustafa Kemal, who allowed them to hold the wedding in Dolmabahçe Palace, on the shore of the Bosporus. Thereafter, Zorlu was periodically invited to Atatürk's all-night gatherings at the presidential residence in Çankaya. In the following four years, he participated in key diplomatic initiatives like the Montreux Conference and negotiations with France over the southern border province of Hatay.

Despite his father-in-law's exile to London in 1939 and his own lack of connection with President İnönü, Zorlu continued to be posted to important diplomatic missions, including Bern and Paris, where he served as first secretary of the legation during the initial year of the German occupation.[28] In 1942, he became the chargé d'affaires in the Soviet wartime administrative capital of Kuibyshev. Finally, in 1943, he received his first ambassadorship with a posting to the newly declared

as the threat of Italian expansion in the Mediterranean dominated the regime's strategic thinking and European diplomacy became vital, members of the *ancien régime* consolidated their positions in the bureaucracy (Doğan Gürpınar, "The Reinvention of Kemalism: Between Elitism, Anti-Elitism and Anti- Intellectualism," *Middle Eastern Studies* 49, no. 3 [2013]: 461–462).

[26] Melih Tınal, "Bir Siyasal Kişilik Portresi Olarak Tevfik Rüştü Aras" (PhD diss., Dokuz Eylül Üniversitesi, İzmir, 2001), 8–22.

[27] Koçak, *Türkiye'de Milli Şef Dönemi, 1938–1945*, vol. I, 131.

[28] According to one biographer, his rapid rise slowed in 1938, following Aras's removal (Koç, *İdam Sehpasındaki*, 32).

Republic of Lebanon. Returning to Ankara in 1946, Zorlu was appointed head of the MFA's office of trade. While many Turkish diplomats were focused on the immediate threat of Soviet territorial demands, Zorlu found himself in the equally momentous position of shaping Turkey's long-term relationship to the world economy. In the immediate aftermath of World War II, a new set of US-led economic institutions were being established that would shape the Cold War order. Zorlu was present at their creation.[29]

After 1947, as the likelihood of an immediate Soviet attack faded, the centrality of economic issues came into focus. The United States sought to revive the economies of countries in Western Europe so that they could buy US goods and be a credible threat to the USSR. The failure of the UK to return its currency to full convertibility and the inability of Western European states to buy the materials necessary to rebuild their economies convinced US policymakers that they would have to take the lead in reviving trade. The Marshall Plan was one aspect of this new US initiative; the European Payments Union (EPU) was another. In both cases (and, soon, with NATO as well), US geostrategic goals for Western Europe were being achieved by committees of men in boardrooms rather than on battlefields. And Zorlu was one of those men. Starting in 1948, as director general for economic affairs, Zorlu dealt with the United States on issues relating to Marshall Plan funds. On the eve of the May 1950 elections, he was promoted to the rank of undersecretary.[30] His position during these crucial years, combined with his family links to Menderes, made him ideally suited to craft DP foreign policy in the years to come.[31]

Zorlu dominated foreign policymaking – especially its economic aspects – through much of the 1950s, but it was not until 1955 that he finally secured the post of foreign minister.[32] For the first half of the

[29] Zorlu was a part of the Turkish delegation to the UN Conference in Havana that crafted the (ultimately unsuccessful) International Trade Organization (ibid., 36–37).

[30] Noel Charles to Ernest Bevin, March 27, 1959, FO 371/87958; Mehmet Halis Özer, "The Effects of the Marshall Plan Aids to the Development of the Agricultural Sector in Turkey, the 1948–1953 Period," *International Journal of Economics and Financial Issues* 4, no. 2 (2014): 427–439.

[31] While both Zorlu and Menderes's rise through politics was facilitated by their marriages, neither man was a loyal husband. Menderes, famously, pursued a rather public relationship with the opera singer Ayhan Aydan. Zorlu too was relatively open in his relationship with Vesamet Kutlu, the wife of a subordinate in the MFA (Emin Çölaşan, *Unutulmayan Söyleşiler: Tarihe Düşülen Notlar* [Istanbul: Doğan Kitapçılık, 2006], 111–143).

[32] As early as July 1951, the British commercial counselor was reporting that Zorlu was "in charge of all economic matters" at the MFA (Noel Charles to Foreign Office, July 23, 1951, FO 371/95290).

decade, the position remained occupied by Fuat Köprülü. Though Köprülü, with his glorious family lineage, seemed to be a perfect fit for the MFA, his rivals dismissed him as a man of letters, unprepared for politics. Menderes, for example, liked to refer to Köprülü by the overly familiar term *hoca* (teacher) and took pleasure in tormenting him with barbs like, "Have you ever seen a statesman emerge from the university? Politics is innate, not a matter of study, a matter of intuition, like an art!"[33] The reality was more complicated. As we have seen, Köprülü had a lengthy involvement in politics and a commitment to Turkish nationalist ideology.[34] He also had political ambitions for himself and his family. Zorlu, by contrast, was ambitious within the confines of the diplomatic bureaucracy. He seldom challenged Menderes and contented himself with the role of preeminent advisor.

In the early years of DP rule, Fevzi Lütfi Karaosmanoğlu posed the most serious threat to Menderes's dominance of the party. When he was finally brought into Menderes's first cabinet in late 1950, he was appointed minister of state. His responsibility was to deal with the Economic Cooperation Administration (ECA) and the Marshall Plan monies it administered (a particularly important role during the first year of DP rule, as the party established its working relationships with US officials). The presence of Menderes and Karaosmanoğlu in the leadership of the party, vying for influence in Ankara as well as the Aegean region, must have made it difficult for US officials to see the DP as anything but a party of wealthy landlords. And self-interested ones as well: in a January 1951 meeting with US officials, they pushed for the release of additional counterpart funds to fill the budget deficit created by the Korean War. The meeting followed a month of back-and-forth discussions over whether Turkey would provide fresh soldiers for the war effort. Although Menderes had promised more troops would be forthcoming, "he felt the Turkish people must first realize that the US appreciates the Turkish sacrifices and that the Americans are making similar sacrifices."[35] When the US ambassador suggested that the government raise taxes on large landowners and businessmen, Karaosmanoğlu reportedly replied that "[r]eneging on [electoral] promises would produce opposite results, and public opinion would turn against the government. Consequently, increased taxes are not considered advisable at this time." When the

33 Karpat, "Actors and Issues," 137; Baban, *Politika Galerisi*, 339.

34 Olivier Bouquet, "Old Elites in a New Republic: The Reconversion of Ottoman Bureaucratic Families in Turkey (1909–1939)," *Comparative Studies of South Asia and the Middle East* 31, no. 3 (2011): 599.

35 "Doc. 752: Memorandum by JAMMAT," December 28, 1950, *FRUS, 1950*, vol. V: *The Near East, South Asia, and Africa.*

ambassador noted that the United States was asking its wealthy citizens (himself included) to pay more in the national interest, Menderes "replied that Turkey was in a special position today, that America's democracy was established many years ago, but that Turkey was still trying to set their democracy on firm footing." He ended the meeting by hoping that they were close to a deal on TL80 million ($29 million) – a hope which was ultimately realized.[36]

By the time the money arrived in the spring of 1951, Karaosmanoğlu had been pushed out of the cabinet. In addition to the competition of their factions, Menderes and Karaosmanoğlu disagreed over whether the United States should control counterpart funds. Whereas Menderes argued that US oversight limited Turkey's sovereignty, Karaosmanoğlu believed that humoring the United States would ensure a steady stream of support over a longer period. According to British diplomats, this tension came "to a head" when Menderes rejected a deal to purchase tractors that Karaosmanoğlu and the minister of economy and trade had negotiated.[37] When Menderes dissolved his first cabinet and announced a second government in March 1951, he again left out Karaosmanoğlu – only to bring him back within months, first to oversee the resettlement of Bulgarian migrants, then to serve as interior minister.[38]

In these positions, Karaosmanoğlu continued to rankle at Menderes's efforts to limit his authority. Moreover, according to one DP representative-turned-memoirist, he was frequently in conflict with Samet Ağaoğlu due to the two men's "opposite characters."[39] By April 1952, Karaosmanoğlu was out of government again. At the time of his resignation as interior minister, there were also rumors that Menderes was frustrated by the insufficiently hard line he was taking against "subversive" activity, but this is just as likely to have a been a smear campaign to force out a popular politician.[40]

[36] CD Rhymes Memo, January 5, 1951, RG 84, Box 58, UD 3288, NND 842831 (hereafter RG 84, Box 58); "Doc. 653: Acting Administrator for Economic Cooperation (Bissell) to the ECA Mission in Turkey," April 12, 1951, *FRUS, 1951*, vol. V: *The Near East and Africa*.

[37] Noel Charles to Herbert Morrison, March 13, 1951, FO 371/95272.

[38] Karaosmanoğlu replaced Interior Minister Halil Özyörük after opposition newspapers reported that Özyörük was using official vehicles to transport his wife ("Devlet otomobilleri …," *Ulus*, October 18, 1951, 1, 4).

[39] Emrullah Nutku, *Demokrat Parti Neden Çöktü ve Politika'da Yitirdiğim Yıllar, 1946–1958* (Istanbul: Fakülteler Matbaası, 1972), 203.

[40] Telegram from Embassy to State Department, April 8, 1952, RG 84, Box 57. Banking was another area in which DP leaders sought to extend their influence. US State Department officials discussed attempts by the "Bayar Group," as well as DP legislator (and founder of Yapı ve Kredi Bankası) Kazım Taşkent, to pack the board of the Türkiye Sınaî Kalkınma Bankası (Turkey Industrial Development Bank) (see a variety of

The disputes between Menderes and Karaosmanoğlu in these early years were typically administrative turf battles rather than ideological conflicts. There was very little at stake in terms of principles. In later years, as we will see, Karaosmanoğlu would break from the DP and present himself as a champion of "freedom," but during the party's first years in office, he was a supporter of its high-handed policies toward the CHP. In August 1951, for example, he supported a bill to seize control of the People's Houses, a network of cultural centers around the country, which the CHP had administered since 1931, when the government had seized and repurposed the facilities of the Turkish Hearth Organization.[41] While it may have made administrative sense in the single-party era to have the ruling party organization oversee these institutions and their project of spreading the regime's high-modernist ideology, the CHP's continuing control after 1946 – and even after defeat in 1950 – infuriated the DP rank and file. Likewise, in December 1953, with just months to go before the elections, Karaosmanoğlu would vote with the party to seize the CHP's property, on the grounds that it was the illegitimate result of the single-party era. The seizure, he told his fellow legislators, was a "duty that is impossible to escape."[42]

Samet Ağaoğlu also supported these moves against the opposition, dismissing the dire effects that property seizures would have on the opposition so near an election as merely "a political question."[43] Like Karaosmanoğlu, he was a vocal champion of "liberty" who found justifications for the government's illiberal acts when the need arose. During Ağaoğlu's first year in office, for example, he oversaw a controversial policy: the distribution of official announcements to newspapers, which received payment for printing these notifications. Under the CHP, pro-government papers had received a share that was disproportionate to their circulation. Rather than end the practice, the DP opted to shift the distribution in favor of their preferred papers, placing the authority for determining distribution in the hands of the cabinet, with Ağaoğlu the state minister responsible from 1951 to 1952.[44]

documents in RG 84, Box 60, UD 3288, NND 842831 [hereafter RG 84, Box 60], including George McGhee to Secretary of State, March 31, 1951, and Lewis to Secretary of State, April 3, 1951).

41 Kemal Karpat, "The People's Houses in Turkey: Establishment and Growth," *Middle East Journal* 17, no. 1/2 (1963): 58.

42 TBMM, December 14, 1953, 203.

43 DPMGMZ, December 8, 1953, 5.

44 RG, August 1, 195; Ayşe Elif Emre Kaya, "Demokrat Parti Politikalarının Cumhuriyet Gazetesinde Ele Alınış Biçimleri, 1950–1960" (PhD diss., Ankara Üniversitesi, Ankara, 2009), 95–96. In parliament, in response to a question from the opposition, Ağaoğlu reported that in the first half of 1950 (i.e., prior to the election) the CHP paper *Ulus* and the DP paper *Zafer* had received TL185,219 ($66,150) and TL33,647 ($12,017),

These moves against the CHP infuriated its supporters and stoked partisan tensions, but they did not in change the US attitude toward the DP government. The Korean War had altered the US government's strategy in southern Europe and the Middle East. Now President Truman was concerned that the USSR might take control of strategic oil fields in the region. Whereas NATO leaders had turned down membership requests by both the CHP-led government (in 1949) and the DP-led government (as soon as it came to power in May 1950), US diplomats took a renewed Turkish request in August 1950 very seriously.[45] At the time of this request, Turkey had a standing army of 330,000 with an estimated mobilization potential of over 500,000. By comparison, the potential of Egypt, Iraq, Syria, Saudi Arabia, Ethiopia, Israel, Lebanon, Jordan, and Iran *combined* was 548,000.[46] The head of the US military aid mission argued in 1951 that the United States should guarantee Turkey's security as it developed "a limited offensive capability" sufficient to "hold Russia at bay until we complete the arming of Western Europe."[47] Though some NATO members were skeptical, Turkey and Greece were given "associate status" at a September 1950 meeting.[48] The United States, the UK, and other countries debated over the next six months whether to offer full membership, until May 1951, when the UK finally accepted the idea, provided that Turkey support its efforts to create a NATO-style security organization in the Middle East that would protect British interests. Turkey and Greece formally joined in February 1952.[49]

In addition to the security of NATO membership, money, in one form or another, continued to flow into Turkey. ECA aid fell from $100.7 million in 1950–51 to $70.6 million in 1951–52 and $67.8 million in 1952–53, but military aid to Turkey rose from $104.3 million to

respectively. In the latter half of the year, after the elections, *Zafer*'s revenue rose to TL264,544 ($94,480) while *Ulus*'s revenue stayed the same at TL185,631 ($66,297) (TBMM, February 7, 1951, 60).

45 United Kingdom Delegation New York to Foreign Office, April 22, 1949, FO 371/78667; Behçet Kemal Yeşilbursa, "Turkey's Participation in the Middle East Command and Its Admission to NATO, 1950–52," *Middle Eastern Studies* 35, no. 4 (1999): 73–76.

46 "Form at a Glance," March 10, 1950, FO 371/87982. By 1955, Turkey's mobilization potential had risen to 550,000. The actual size of the armed forces, however, was reduced to 280,000 soldiers, now supplied with advanced American equipment ("Form at a Glance," March 24, 1955, FO 371/123999).

47 William Arnold, February 6, 1951, RG 59, Lot 58, Box 1, D610, NND 917365 (hereafter RG 59, Lot 58, Box 1).

48 "Doc. 730: Memorandum by the Joint Chiefs of Staff to the Secretary of Defense (Johnson)," September 9, 1950, *FRUS, 1951*, vol. V: *The Near East and Africa*.

49 Şuhnaz Yılmaz, "Turkey's Quest for NATO Membership: The Institutionalization of the Turkish–American Alliance," *Southeast European and Black Sea Studies* 12, no. 4 (2012): 489–491.

$159.9 million to $225.3 million over the same three fiscal years.[50] This support enabled DP leaders to increase social spending and industrial investment alongside military spending while also cutting taxes. The total amount of loans issued by Ziraat Bankası and local cooperatives reached TL1.1 billion ($393 million) during 1951, a 39 percent increase on the previous year. The rate paid to farmers for their crops via the Soil Products Office (TMO) also rose during 1951, increasing the office's annual debt by 34 percent from the previous year.[51] In the primary budget, ECA aid and treasury bond issues helped cover the deficit. As for the deficits of state-owned enterprises (which had a separate budget from the annual bill debated in parliament each February), these losses were covered with Central Bank bonds whose repayment was never demanded. Such methods sustained entities like the TMO, which purchased grain from farmers at above-market prices.

Marketing tobacco, cotton, raisins, grain, and other agricultural commodities abroad was Turkey's primary means of earning foreign exchange to finance imports. But dependence on these exports complicated the DP's efforts to both develop the country and satisfy citizens' consumption demands. With limited industrial production, the economy moved in seasonal cycles: the harvest began in late summer of each year and marketing began in earnest in the fall and into the winter. Ideally, early in the year, exports would near or exceed imports and help balance out payments during the rest of the year. Yet, even in good years, foreign exchange grew scarce as the summer approached. By mid 1951, for example, Turkey was running such a large trade deficit with European countries that the DP government requested additional credit from the EPU. The request was denied, leading the government to try a different tact: defaulting on debt payments to the UK, which had provided Turkey with nearly £40 million in armaments, loans, and credits on the eve of World War II as part of an effort to secure Turkey's loyalty in the conflict.

With interest payments of around £1.5 million (TL11.8 million) due at the end of June 1951, Turkey presented the UK with an aide-mémoire requesting a cancellation of the debt in consideration of Turkey's ongoing contributions to the common defense. In addition, the mémoire noted that Turkey's balance of trade with the sterling area was in serious deficit, making repayment of pound sterling debts especially difficult. The observation indicated a point of tension between the two countries: since the DP government had further liberalized trade in 1950, allowing importers

[50] "Fact Book Prepared for the Visit of Secretary Dulles to Ankara May 26–27, 1955," RG 84, Box 3, UD 3289, NND 842832 (hereafter RG 84, Box 3).

[51] Singer, *The Economic Advance*, 201, 223.

to buy freely from the UK and other European countries, UK merchants had not reciprocated.[52] While Turkey's trade with most Organization for European Economic Cooperation (OEEC) states was in balance, it had a $35 million (TL98 million) deficit with the UK.[53] When the payment came due, no money was forthcoming from Turkey. The British embassy's commercial counselor met with Zorlu to ask if this nonpayment should be understood as a default, and Zorlu apologized, claiming Turkey had little choice, given the various difficulties it was facing.[54]

British officials had little way of forcing Turkey to pay. In the first place, the UK had little leverage: Britain's share of Turkey's exports was indeed falling – in fact, the British government was intentionally directing trade away from Turkey, which (as Turkish officials argued) had little British currency in reserve, and toward the United States, with which the UK had trade deals.[55] Second, the UK's subordinate position in the US-led Cold War order diminished the authority of British diplomats; as they lamented, Turkey's arguments "will undoubtedly find a sympathetic hearing among the other Allies, and particularly with the Americans," who would rather not see their aid to Turkey be used to pay interest on twelve-year-old debts to the UK.[56] British officials also acknowledged to one another that the armaments given in 1938–39 were "very poor stuff" and agreed to avoid antagonizing Turkey over the debts while they were also trying to encourage Turkish leaders to support their Middle East defense organization.[57] (That said, when the defense initiative came to naught, the British attempted to put pressure on Turkey by temporarily delaying loans for the Seyhan dam project in Adana.)[58]

[52] After removing some quantitative limitations on imports in 1946–47 (i.e., liberalizing trade), the CHP government had reimposed restrictions in 1947, following a sterling convertibility crisis in the UK. In September 1950, the DP government liberalized the trade regime again. In April 1951, the government's representative attended the Toquay Conference and signed the necessary protocols for joining the General Agreement on Trade and Tariffs; these went into effect on October 1, 1951 (RG, August 15, 1950; RG, September 1, 1950; RG, October 1, 1951; Hershlag, *Turkey*, 245–249; Cillov, *Türkiye Ekonomisi*, 469).

[53] RG, October 4, 1950; Ankara to Foreign Office, May 19, 1951, and Turkish Ministry of Foreign Affairs, "Aide-Mémoire," July 18, 1951, both in FO 371/95290.

[54] Noel Charles to Foreign Office, July 23, 1951, FO 371/95290.

[55] N. J. A. Cheetham to Noel Charles, February 3, 1951, FO 371/95290.

[56] H. H. Eggers to N. J. A. Cheetham, November 1, 1951, FO 371/95292.

[57] "Minutes of Meeting held on Monday, 16 July, 1951," FO 371/95290. The dispute would not be resolved until August 1953, when Turkey agreed to pay back £7.5 million – but in lira, and based on the overvalued official rate – provided that the UK used the lira it earned to buy Turkish products (FO 371/107565; RG, March 13, 1954).

[58] "No. 464: Memorandum of Conversation, by the Ambassador in Turkey (McGhee) aboard the Turkish President's Train, May 6–8, 1952," May 6–8, 1952, *FRUS, 1952–1954*, vol. VIII: *Eastern Europe; Soviet Union; Eastern Mediterranean.*

During the DP's first year and a half in office, however, these diplomatic maneuvers and growing economic concerns occurred far from public view. For most people, this period was marked by news of heroic accomplishments on battlefields abroad and vigorous government action at home. Policies started under the CHP, such as tractor imports and a general liberalization of trade, were amplified under the DP. In the case of tractors, the number in Turkey jumped from 10,000 at the beginning of 1950 to 24,000 by the end of 1951.[59] With this new equipment, the area under cultivation grew by 37 percent from 1948 to 1953.[60] Wheat exports soared from 20,000 tons in 1950 to 600,000 tons in 1953.[61] Foreign exchange earnings rose by 57 percent between the periods 1946–50 and 1951–53.[62] In provinces like Adana, heavy investment in cotton production led to a boom, with the harvest 27 percent larger in 1951 than a year before.[63] Money flowed into Adana such that, by January 1952, a visiting US diplomat was reporting seeing more Cadillacs, Buicks, Chryslers per capita "than in any other city in Turkey."[64]

Presenting the DP's 1952–53 budget to parliament in February of 1952, Polatkan emphasized the positive effects that the party's investments were having.[65] This new spending bill proposed an increase of 11 percent on the previous year, much of it directed at irrigation projects, roads, and the military. Once again, revenues did not fully fund the spending and left a TL190 million deficit to be covered by loans and credits. Not only were increased taxes on landlords off the table, but the DP also abolished or reduced several existing taxes that targeted peasants. These included the Road Tax, which required local governments to annually assess a labor (or payment) requirement from all working-age men. Not only was forced labor unpopular, but even those with the

59 Singer, *The Economic Advance*, 200. The number of tractors in Turkey surged from 1,750 in 1948 to around 40,000 in 1953 (it leveled off thereafter). Government agricultural credit offered through Ziraat Bankası and the TMO rose from TL437 million ($336 million) in 1946 to TL1.8 billion in 1953 ($643 million) ("Position of Turkey: Report by the Chairman of the Council," Organization for European Economic Cooperation, March 29, 1954, FO 371/111288).

60 Edwin Cohn, *Turkish Economic, Social, and Political Change: The Development of a More Prosperous and Open Society* (New York: Praeger Publishers, 1970), 18.

61 Cillov, *Türkiye Ekonomisi*, 185.

62 Feridun Cemil Özcan, "Ellili Yıllarda Türkiye Ekonomisi," in *Türkiye'nin 1950'li Yılları*, ed. Mete Kaan Kaynar (Istanbul: İletişim Yayınları, 2015), 45.

63 Nadir Yurtoğlu, "Demokrat Parti (DP) Dönemi'nde Pamuk Politikaları ve Dokuma Sanayisine Etkileri, 1950–1960," *Atatürk Araştırma Merkezi Dergisi* 37, no. 103 (2021): 304.

64 Embassy to Dept of State, March 6, 1952, RG 84, Box 57.

65 When CHP legislators suggested that good weather rather than DP policies was the cause of the successes in 1951, Polatkan asked them sarcastically if it "had never rained" during the single-party era (TBMM, February 21, 1952, 469).

means to pay the tax disliked the fact that their money was often diverted to projects other than roads.[66] Ending these unpopular taxes pleased voters. The roughly $70 million (TL196 million) in aid provided by the United States helped the DP government avoid import restrictions, budget cuts, or tax hikes to cover the projected deficit.

By the time the annual budget was passed in late February 1952, however, potential weaknesses in the government's policy were becoming clear. Whereas Turkey had at least achieved a small surplus with its European trading partners in the early months of 1951 (before going into serious deficit), the country was already in deficit in the first months of 1952.[67] In parliament, Polatkan acknowledged the situation, but blamed it on the failures of the CHP regime. "The primary reason for this," he lamented, "was that until the time we came to power, our production was always stuck at the same low level," sometimes necessitating that Turkey import grain for bread "despite being an agricultural country." In the short term, he explained, the only solutions open to the government were reducing imports to the level of export earnings, or "the road that our government is following": investing in the country's productive capacity so that it could rapidly increase its export earnings.[68] Yet these were long-term aims. As the 1952 marketing season ended and the summer approached, reserves of foreign currency continued to fall, leaving the government with little choice but to implement unpopular measures like credit restrictions or a currency devaluation.

Consolidation and Polarization in the Provinces: Balıkesir and Malatya

In defending the 1952–53 budget, Prime Minister Adnan Menderes had presented it as evidence that "our citizens living in the furthest corners of our land [can] find a frank and honest reflection of their troubles and needs" in the parliament.[69] This depiction of the party as addressing the needs of citizens throughout the country rather than seeking to remold them according to some a priori modernist vision was central to DP leaders' presentation of their party. It also captured the way they described politics operating: bottom up rather than top down.

[66] RG, February 29, 1952; Nuray Özdemir, "Cumhuriyet Döneminde Türkiye'de Yol Vergisi," *Tarih Araştırmaları Dergisi* 32 (2013): 222–224. In July 1951, the government also reduced the scope of the Animal Tax (*ağnam*) (Ali Rıza Gönüllü, "Milli Mücadele ve Cumhuriyet Döneminde Hayvanlar Vergisi, 1920–1962," *Selçuk Üniversitesi Türkiyat Araştırmaları Dergisi* 1, no. 38 [2015]: 83–84).

[67] "Turkey: Economic Report No. 4 Period April 1952," May 4, 1952, FO 371/101866.

[68] TBMM, February 20, 1952, 355.

[69] TBMM, February 29, 1952, 1297.

In practice, the relationship between the DP and the people was more complicated. As the political scientist Ergun Özbudun argues, the 1950 DP victory was "a provincializing election," in the sense that it transferred power to elites with regional (i.e., provincial) bases of support.[70]

As we saw in Chapter 2, the provincial notables were already deeply involved in the regime prior to 1950, but the elections that year brought them into the national leadership. The most obvious example of this shift might be Adnan Menderes himself, who was brought into the CHP in the 1930s as part of an effort to improve relations with restive provincial notables. While it is possible that he might have eventually received a cabinet post, such as minister of agriculture, in a CHP administration, the fact of the matter is that he did not enter government until 1950. Other important figures in the DP, like Hasan Polatkan, Fevzi Lütfi Karaosmanoğlu, Sıtkı Yırcalı, and Hüseyin Fırat, had similarly strong political bases in the provinces. The goal, then, for many of these leaders was to consolidate their power in Ankara while also maintaining their base of support at the provincial level.

The demands that emerged from provincial party organizations in the early years of DP rule were often far more combative than the DP leadership would have liked. There was a strong desire among many in the DP for a thorough rooting out of the *ancien régime*, and while CHP partisans liked to point out signs of religious "reaction" at DP provincial congresses, the more common occurrence was demands for harsh measures against the CHP itself.[71] Yet while it was one thing to purge communists from institutions (which DP governments were quite ready to do), it was another to purge members of the former regime. Not only did CHP supporters bring a wealth of experience to their positions, they also had the ear of US officials. Moving too quickly against them in the initial years of DP rule could stoke resentment, slow down government policies, and undermine the image that the DP hoped to project as it sought membership in organizations like NATO and aid via the Marshall

[70] Özbudun, *Social Change*, 47–49.

[71] On March 15, 1951, Ahmet Emin Yalman's *Vatan* reported that a DP congress in the Konya district of Kadınhan had called for Quran courses in schools, Friday as a weekend instead of Sunday, head coverings for women, and other religious demands. The news came only three weeks after a man in the nearby province of Kırşehir had attacked a bust of Atatürk and local student groups had responded with large pro-Atatürk demonstrations. The DP disputed *Vatan*'s claims, and student groups in Konya held protests as well. The journalist Altan Öymen recalls a rather mixed crowd in Konya: at least one speaker accused demonstrators of "Idolizing Atatürk, which Islam does not allow" ("D.P. Konya ...," *Zafer*, March 15, 1951; 1–2; Toker, *DP'nin Altın Yılları*, 118–122; Altan Öymen, *Öfkeli Yıllar* [Istanbul: Doğan Kitap, 2009], 173).

Plan. Consequently, as we will see, repression of the opposition moved in fits and starts, a series of measures, confrontations, and moving of the electoral goalposts rather than a single, decisive blow.

In a province like Balıkesir, where the DP was dominant, successfully managing expectations, expressing just enough radicalism to fend off internal party challenges, promised significant political rewards. Money for new projects flowed into the province, and local leaders like Sıtkı Yırcalı quickly became important national figures. Yet this is not to say that the balancing act was easy: factional struggles were fierce, and the province cycled through four governors and, effectively, three mayors in less than two years.

In the early months of DP rule, this contentiousness was less apparent, and Sıtkı Yırcalı and his paper *Balıkesir Postası* had much to brag about to the public. By August 1950, Yırcalı could approvingly point to the amnesty law, a reduction in the term of military service, lower taxes on sugar and wheat, the reinstatement of the Arabic call to prayer, an "expansion" of Marshall Plan aid, and the decision to send soldiers to Korea.[72] The arrival of a new governor in September provided opportunities to highlight the failures and the wastefulness of the CHP era. The new governor moved to a smaller residence, saving the province as much as TL20,000 a year. The following year, the provincial council voted to lower members' salaries by 15 percent.[73] And these purported savings came alongside promises to increase the housing supply, credit, and investment in water, sewer, and electrical systems.

In general, the DP was able to follow through on those of its promises which were simplest to achieve. With a huge majority in parliament, removing taxes and increasing credit were easy. Promises that required outside help were more difficult to honor. Selling off state enterprises required willing buyers, and increasing foreign investment depended on international firms. The Law to Encourage Foreign Investment of 1951 was not particularly enticing, since it only allowed foreign firms to repatriate up to 10 percent of the capital they invested. In the next four years, only $6 million in private capital would be invested in Turkish enterprises.[74] Balıkesir was exceptional, since its rich mineral resources did interest foreign firms. In 1951, the province earned TL381,313 ($136,000) from just the fees associated with exploration licenses.[75] And any company hoping to do business in the region would likely

[72] Sıtkı Yırcalı, "Hemşehri reyini," *Balıkesir Postası*, August 29, 1950, 1.
[73] "Valimizin örnek," *Balıkesir Postası*, September 2, 1950, 1; "İl Genel Meclisi," *Balıkesir Postası*, January 18, 1951, 1.
[74] Hershlag, *Turkey*, 208. [75] "Vilayetimizde," *Balıkesir Postası*, August 1, 1952, 1.

find itself dealing with the Yırcalı family, which owned many mines of its own.[76]

The family's growing national power helped the province. Following the 1950 election, Sıtkı was chosen as one of the deputy presidents of the parliament. By December 1951, he secured a post in the cabinet, first as minister of customs and monopolies, nine months later as minister of operations (i.e., state-owned enterprises). In November 1952, Enver Güreli, another Balıkesir representative, became minister of economy and trade. In other words, within two years of coming to power, leaders of the local DP gained key posts in the national government, and they were not shy to make use of these positions. In late 1952, a new cloth and canvas factory was announced, and the Balıkesir municipality of Susurluk was declared as the site of a new sugar factory, which it achieved despite President Bayar's preference for its establishment in his own neighboring province of Bursa.[77]

While the provincial and local governments moved ahead on these fronts, they also faced unexpected challenges. Accommodating the arrival of some 9,000 Bulgarian refugees required significant coordination; only three provinces (Istanbul, Tekirdağ, and Bursa) resettled a larger number of people.[78] More particular to Balıkesir was a fire in August 1950 that destroyed the city's main marketplace. All told, some 488 stalls were destroyed and another 185 damaged, leaving hundreds of livelihoods in ashes.[79] President Bayar rushed to visit the site, and in the coming days various central government figures promised that relief and increased bank credit would be made available. Mayor Yoldemir made multiple trips to Ankara to discuss further plans, and Sıtkı Yırcalı's paper *Balıkesir Postası* found a "point of consolation" in that "we remember with thankfulness the energetic intervention of our friend Sıtkı Yırcalı."[80]

Sıtkı's self-promotion was a sign of things to come. In the coming year, other powerful local figures were pushed aside. DP Provincial President Mücteba Iştın stepped down in January 1951 and was replaced in April by Sıtkı's brother Sırrı.[81] In November 1950, the recently appointed governor resigned under murky circumstances. There were rumors that he had done an unsatisfactory job of securing relief funds, but there was

76 Nimet Arzık, *Menderes'i İpe Götürenler* (Ankara: Kurtuluş Matbaası, 1966), 112–113.

77 "Şeker ...," *Balıkesir Postası*, March 4, 1952, 1; "Ticaret ...," *Balıkesir Postası*, August 29, 1952, 1–2; "İplik ...," *Balıkesir Postası*, November 5, 1952, 1; Şeremetli, *Balıkesir'de Demokrat Parti*, 125–128.

78 Kostanick, "Turkish Resettlement," 53.

79 "Balıkesir Çarşısı ...," *Balıkesir Postası*, August 5, 1950, 1, 4.

80 M. Tüncer, "Balıkesir'in uğradığı ...," *Balıkesir Postası*, August 8, 1950, 1.

81 "Aslı olmayan ...," *Balıkesir Postası*, January 17, 1951, 1.

also the fact that his brother was a CHP member of parliament and that he himself had run for parliament as a CHP candidate in the province of Bursa. His list had lost, and the winning DP list had included his new superior, the current interior minister.[82] For eleven months the post was filled by an acting governor – and when a new governor was appointed, he was replaced after three months.[83] Without a stable governor, the province's most prominent links with the national government became representatives like Sıtkı, as well as the various mayors who periodically visited Ankara. Yet local government was not stable either: in October 1951, Mayor Yoldemir (a rival of Sıtkı's) was accused by the city council of multiple misdeeds, including misusing funds.[84]

The provincial center was not the only municipality experiencing trouble. In Sındırgı, the mayor was forced out by his council over frustrations with his purchase of an expensive and faulty generator.[85] In Ayvalık, disputes were between the two parties rather than internal to the DP. The local CHP filed formal complaints that the mayor had been appointed despite having been barred from running for office owing to a criminal record.[86] This accusation did not succeed in removing the mayor, but it certainly helped increase local tensions. As early as March 1951, there were fights between party members and attacks on businesses owned by CHP members. In July, an investigation was started into Ayvalık's former CHP mayor.[87] The most dramatic development came in September 1952, when the DP mayor (a gun on his hip) and a group of supporters threatened a CHP rally. Nothing came of their threats, but hostility to the former ruling party was fierce in the province. Complaints about CHP-allied officials and village headmen were a common refrain at DP congresses. In the district of Burhaniye, there were reports of local DP members vandalizing CHP buildings. Yet there was also a sense that attacks on the CHP were proportional responses, not just for past wrongs but for present ones. *Balıkesir Postası*, for example, reported vandalism of a DP automobile and signs in Malatya.[88]

82 "S. Tümerkan'ın …," *Türk Dili*, November 12, 1950, 1; "Eski Valinin …," *Balıkesir Postası*, November 13, 1950, 1; "Vali niçin …," *Balıkesir Postası*, November 18, 1950, 1.

83 A plan in July 1951 to assign the governor of Samsun to Balıkesir was stopped when complaints emerged that he had suppressed DP votes while serving as governor of Bursa during the 1946 election ("Haşim İşçan'ın …," *Balıkesir Postası*, July 16, 1951, 1).

84 "Dün …," *Balıkesir Postası*, October 3, 1951, 1.

85 "D.P. li başkana …," *Türk Dili*, February 1, 1951, 2; "Sındırgı …," *Türk Dili*, March 1, 1951, 1.

86 "Ayvalık …," *Türk Dili*, January 11, 1952, 1.

87 "Altınova …," *Türk Dili*, March 13, 1951, 2; "Eski …," *Balıkesir Postası*, July 14, 1951, 1.

88 "D.P. Merkez …," *Balıkesir Postası*, February 28, 1951, 1; "C.H.P. lilerin Malatya'daki …," *Balıkesir Postası*, June 9, 1951, 1; "D.P. Genel Kongresinde,"

In Malatya, where the DP had lost the 1950 elections, these early years were also contentious. Malatya was, in fact, one of the few provinces where the CHP won. Since President İnönü was a candidate on the provincial list, the victory assured him a seat in parliament. Rather than retire, İnönü chose to remain active, both in parliament and as leader of the CHP. His ability to retain his preeminent position was helped by the electoral defeat, which left many of the party's major figures outside parliament. The result – a CHP parliamentary group composed of relatively unknown political figures from eastern and Black Sea provinces – left İnönü with a free hand but also led to tensions over who *really* spoke for the party, these elected unknowns or the unelected party grandees. Amid this uncertainty, the scale of the CHP loss emboldened voters and notables to shift their support to the DP. In Malatya's village headman elections on August 13, the DP and independents made gains. The CHP managed to win the provincial council elections on September 3, but suffered another blow ten days later when the influential religious leader Hüseyin Doğan resigned from the party and declared that he would henceforth be "independent." Within six months, he had joined the DP.[89]

Despite such setbacks, CHP elites sought to make the most out of their presence in Malatya. Echoing CHP media in Ankara, party-linked papers moved swiftly from congratulating the newly elected DP and promising to hold it to its campaign pledges to criticizing its initiatives. The pro-CHP paper *Gayret* argued, for example, that a national amnesty bill would "butter the bread" of traitors like communist poet Nâzım Hikmet. After the amnesty had passed, the paper highlighted news items in which beneficiaries of the amnesty reoffended.[90] Meanwhile, the CHP itself emphasized the seriousness with which it took the province. Returning in July from a meeting with İnönü in Ankara, the mayor announced plans to pave more roads, expand the electrical grid, and order a new garbage truck from England.[91] The local party touted its ability to extract benefits in the capital, but the reverse seemed closer to the truth: politicians in the capital dictated policy in the province. After the provincial elections, the mayor (a local) was replaced with Muzaffer Akalın, a former CHP parliamentarian who had lost his seat in the 1950 election and had little connection with Malatya.

Balıkesir Postası, October 22, 1951, 1; "Bu utanmazlar …," *Türk Dili*, January 20, 1952, 1; "D.P. kongresinde …," *Türk Dili*, May 15, 1952, 1.

89 "Malatya C.H.P. milletvekili Hüseyin Doğan istifa etti," *Zafer*, September 19, 1950, 1; "Hüseyin Doğan D.P.'ye girdi," *Yeni Malatya*, April 6, 1951, 1.

90 Savcıoğlu, "İktidar ve muhalefet," *Gayret*, May 23, 1950; Savcıoğlu, "Af Kanunu hakkında," *Gayret*, May 31, 1950; "Aftan istifade …," *Gayret*, July 22, 1950.

91 "Belediye başkanımız …," *Gayret*, July 10, 1950.

The CHP was not the only political party looking for sinecures for its losing candidates. In late September, the DP government appointed a new governor for the province, Turgut Babaoğlu. Though the claim (repeated frequently by CHP leaders in the months to come) that governors were supposed to be impartial figures was something of an invented norm, Babaoğlu was a provocative choice. Not only had he run unsuccessfully for parliament in 1950 as a DP candidate in the province of Kars, but he was also the brother-in-law of DP leader Samet Ağaoğlu.[92] Clearly, he had been appointed to impose DP policies on the opposition-controlled province.

The first clash came quickly. Babaoğlu demanded that the city government remove a picture of İnönü that was hanging on the wall of the mayor's chambers. It was part of a more thoroughgoing effort by the DP to remove images of İnönü from state spaces and materials (like stamps). Akalın refused, on the grounds that İnönü was a local boy made good and, regardless, the relevant law did not stipulate removal, only that an image of President Bayar must be hung as well.[93] When the governor sent three of his staff to remove it, the mayor resisted, and the provincial council supported him. On October 14, 1950, Babaoğlu sent officers from the gendarmerie to remove the picture, leading to scuffles with CHP partisans. The CHP provincial president, Nüvit Yetkin, criticized the governor and was removed from his paid posts as the province's lawyer and the supervisor of its stud farm. He was also sued for TL100,000. On October 16, Governor Babaoğlu removed Mayor Akalın from his post and replaced him not with Yetkin (who also held the post of deputy mayor) but rather with the province's director of health and social assistance. Akalın appealed to the national administrative courts, and the case dragged on until March 1952, at which point the national government dissolved the municipal council and called fresh elections.[94]

While the DP-led national government put political pressure on the CHP-led provincial government via a friendly governor, provincial papers linked to the DP developed a critique of the CHP, which associated the party with all the troubles of the province. Prior to the 1950 elections, these papers connected the region's underdevelopment to a

[92] The province of Kars was won by a slate of CHP candidates that, ironically, included the Ağaoğlu sibling Tezer Taşkıran.

[93] Local DP journalists rejected the idea that İnönü was a "child of the country," arguing that the former president was really from the region of Bitlis and had only added himself to the CHP election list for Malatya after "realizing he had lost his electoral ability in Ankara" (M. Oğut Yazman, "Kimdirler? …," *Yeni Malatya*, October 19, 1950, 1).

[94] Şahin, "Cumhuriyet Halk Partisi'nin," 113–118; Kısacık, *Malatya'da Toplumsal Olaylar*, 130–134; "Fesih kararı," *Gayret*, March 3, 1951, 1.

local leadership who "only thought of getting their monthly salaries."[95] The list of local needs was long, including an expanded electrical and water grid, a library (and improved literacy), more roads, and more sports facilities. But there was also a suggestion in these newspapers that a DP victory could stimulate a general change in the local culture. *Yeni Malatya* (New Malatya), for example, called for local businessmen to be taught better sales methods, observing that while Jewish merchants succeeded around the world by "inviting customers with sweet language," Malatya merchants just screamed.[96] Similarly, in the case of brothels, hourly hotels, and vendors loudly hawking baked goods in the early morning, the paper hoped the city government would take a firm hand.[97]

In general, the DP critique of governance in Malatya was not posed as a call for *less* state intervention in daily life but rather as a condemnation of those who currently held power. While local CHP officials were criticized, Governor Babaoğlu was presented in DP papers as the conduit to government largesse. Governors had never been neutral officials: they represented the state. Under the single-party regime, this meant that they represented the party as well. In the provinces, following its election, the DP limited the power of the state in people's lives by restraining the gendarmerie – in 1952, the government ended emergency rule in the eastern provinces – but it did little to reform the system by which executive authority in a province was bound up with control of the national government.[98] As a result, as parties multiplied and the distinction between state and party became meaningful, coercive power became more explicitly partisan.

On his return from trips to Ankara, Babaoğlu would give speeches promising new roads, schools, irrigation projects, and agricultural credit. (As for electrification, it would be sorted out "after the mayoral election.")[99] The most immediate challenge facing the governor, however, was overseeing the settlement of refugees from Bulgaria. About 1,500 Bulgarian migrants were settled in Malatya, primarily around the village

95 "Hekimhan Belediyesinin çalışmaları," *Yeni Malatya*, July 7, 1949, 1.
96 M. Oğuz, "Malatya Ne Şekilde ...," *Yeni Malatya*, February 28, 1950, 1, 4.
97 Isırgan, "Malatya Belediyesi ...," *Yeni Malatya*, January 27, 1950, 1; Lütfi Beydağı, "Fuhuşla Mücadele," *Yeni Malatya*, July 7, 1949, 1.
98 A system of regional inspectorates to oversee the eastern provinces was created in 1927. These officials, answerable to the president, superseded civilian and military officials. Parliament abolished these in 1952 (RG, July 16, 1927; TBMM, June 19, 1952; RG, November 29, 1952; Cemil Koçak, *Umûmî Müfettişlikler, 1927–1952*, 2nd ed. [Istanbul: İletişim Yayınları, 2010 (2003)]; Senem Aslan, *Nation-Building in Turkey and Morocco: Governing Kurdish and Berber Dissent* [Cambridge: Cambridge University Press, 2015], 48).
99 "Valimiz Ankara'dan döndü," *Fırat*, February 5, 1951, 1.

of Dilek. The national government devoted TL30 million ($10.7 million) in Marshal Plan counterpart funds to the refugee resettlement program, but provincial-level fundraising also helped smooth the transition: an "Aid for Migrants Committee" was established in Malatya and raised more than TL12,500 ($4,400) by February 1951.[100]

Pro-DP papers praised the government for its "embrace" of these refugees in contrast, they suggested, to the CHP.[101] Reporters interviewing migrants contrasted the warm welcome they received in Turkey with the conditions they had faced in Bulgaria, where studying the Quran was reported to be a crime.[102] Such accounts reinforced a commonly held anti-communist sentiment. By drawing on ethnic and religious concerns that were familiar to Turkish citizens, these reports helped build support for the government's deepening participation in the United States' anti-Soviet alliance.[103] According to pro-DP authors, the USSR was constantly working to destabilize the region in order to extend its influence as far as the Mediterranean. This influence could come in many forms. In neighboring Iran, the Soviets were "trying to fire up" Kurds with nationalist sentiments, but Soviet propaganda might just as easily come under the guise of a "green [religious] turban."[104] In other words, religious appeals should be as suspect as nationalist ones.

The key concepts linking events around the world were "stability" and "peace."[105] The Soviets sought to undermine both, and a loss of either might enable a communist takeover. Turkey was, therefore, committed to defending both, at home and abroad. It was for this reason, pro-DP columnists argued, that the government had joined the fighting in Korea. And it was for this reason that domestic organizations like the "Peace Lovers Society," which called for neutrality in the Korean conflict, were committing "TREASON."[106] Likewise, an editorial in *Yeni Malatya*

[100] "Vali Dr. Turgut Babaoğlu ...," *Fırat*, February 27, 1951, 1; "Sayın Valimiz ...," *Demokrat Malatya*, February 27, 1951, 1; Alexander Knox Helm to Foreign Office, March 21, 1952, FO 371/101868.

[101] "Eşen düşer," *Demokrat Malatya*, November 6, 1951, 1.

[102] Nihat Alparsalan, "Bulgaristan'dan şehrimize ...," *Fırat*, January 16, 1951, 1.

[103] For a discussion of anti-communist sentiment in the Turkish press, see Brockett, *How Happy to Call Oneself a Turk*, 144–172.

[104] "İrandaki Kürt meselesi," *Yeni Malatya*, February 3, 1950, 1; "Mitink niçin ...," *Yeni Malatya*, August 2, 1950, 1.

[105] In defending the cabinet's decision to send soldiers to Korea, Foreign Minister Köprülü explained that Turkey's essential foreign policy was to support the security, independence, and territorial integrity of all nations. He added, "It is a requirement of those essentials, our close collaboration with the US, and our current union with England and France to provide clear, unambiguous, and honest service to the stability of peace on the face of the earth" (TBMM, June 30, 1950, 312).

[106] Sabri Özbek, "Politikada ahlak," *Yeni Malatya*, August 26, 1950, 2.

accused Turkish citizens who participated in the Communist Party of wanting Turkey to become "a satellite state, even going further, a part of the USSR like Armenia," and concluded, "On this soil, there is no need now for those who are just citizens on paper."[107] To be a Turkish citizen and a communist was presented as an impossibility.

The USSR was not the only country that Turkey, under the DP leadership, would avoid becoming. Pro-DP papers in Malatya also invoked neighboring states like Iran and former Ottoman Arab dominions as cautionary tales. By attempting to maintain its independence from Western powers and nationalizing its oil industry in 1951, Iran's government risked "losing its independence" to the USSR.[108] "Doubtless," concluded the paper *Fırat*, the strikes and the organizations supporting the Iranian government showed signs of Soviet influence.[109] Yet, if the Iranian government had gone too far by permitting popular mobilization, then countries like Egypt and Syria had not gone far enough. By failing to provide for the needs of their people, regimes in those countries had created a fertile environment for communist infiltration.[110]

Perhaps surprisingly, there was little talk of becoming like the United States. Instead, there was an emphasis on shared goals and, in some instances, even a critique of US weakness. According to *Demokrat Malatya*, Turkey should be part of NATO because the organization was "an ideologic pact" of countries opposed to "red imperialism," and Turkey could be an important contributor.[111] Turkey was no beggar: the sizeable aid packages offered by the United States were on account of the United States' own failures. The "endless good will" Roosevelt had shown Stalin had enabled the present global tensions. The money was, thus, "a type of weapon" to be used against the communist threat that the United States had allowed to grow in the first place.[112]

107 "Komünist kırıntılarına," *Yeni Malatya*, November 9, 1951, 1.
108 "İran petrolleri …," *Demokrat Malatya*, June 8, 1951, 1, 4.
109 H. S., "İrandaki karışıklık," *Fırat*, March 19, 1951, 1. Though the DP had supported the right to strike during the 1950 campaign in order "to win the favor and votes of a mass [of people]," the paper *Fırat* concluded that "we are of the opinion that it was mistaken," at least until statism had been done away with (H. S., "Bizde iş …," *Fırat*, April 28, 1951, 1).
110 "Taşkınlık, şaşkınlık," *Yeni Malatya*, November 5, 1951.
111 Yüksel Sezel, "Atlantik Paktı …," *Demokrat Malatya*, May 12, 1951, 1.
112 "Hata'yı tamir …," *Yeni Malatya*, October 27, 1951, 1. Even the money and advisors provided by the United States revealed American weakness as much as strength. In one case, *Fırat* reported that an American road engineer staying at a Malatya hotel had shot up his room and injured his translator after drinking an entire bottle of wine and becoming convinced that a "woman residing in the hotel" had stolen TL100 ($36) from him ("Malatya Palas hadisesi," *Fırat*, September 1, 1950, 1).

The United States was not invoked as an ideal against which the single-party regime's economic policies and authoritarian methods might be criticized; instead, writers focused their comparisons closer to home and drew parallels between the CHP and Ottoman failures. The Turkish state remained "slow" due to "numerous formalities remaining from imperial times and continuing until today."[113]Although the DP and the CHP both had their roots in the late imperial era, only the DP had taken to heart the notion "First country and nation, then party."[114] This was contrasted with İnönü and the clique that surrounded him. During Atatürk's lifetime, İnönü had been among those who sought to "put a break on the democratic republic he hoped for."[115] Following Atatürk's death, the CHP under İnönü had governed the country with a "totalitarian mentality."[116]

The frequency of verbal attacks on the local CHP government increased during the five months between March 1951 (when the municipal council was dissolved) and July (when new elections were held). During these months, a series of important figures passed through the province. The most important was Hüseyin Fırat, who, despite losing his Malatya race, had won a seat in İçel (Mersin) and continued to make frequent visits to the region, where his family was based. Speaking at a local cinema, he emphasized the DP's connections to the "worker" and "peasant" classes, and recounted how the DP had heroically rejected the CHP's demand that it avoid organizing in eastern provinces like Malatya.[117] Samet Ağaoğlu also toured the province and, speaking at the textile factory, talked abstractly of how "freedom" was spreading through the country and, more concretely, of how the budget for agriculture would rise from TL39 million to TL100 million in the coming year.[118]

Yet none of this political star power helped turn the vote in the DP's favor. On election day (July 22), the CHP won 10,268 votes to the DP's 4,689.[119] Faced with this rebuke, the DP appealed the results on the grounds that election lists and registers did not match. Once again, the CHP named Nüvit Yetkin mayor and, once again, the interior minister refused to recognize Yetkin on the grounds that he had insulted

[113] "DP Merkez İlçe ...," *Yeni Malatya*, March 7, 1951, 2, 3.
[114] Reşat Onur, "İttihat ve Terakki," *Demokrat Malatya*, March 1, 1951, 1.
[115] Dalya, "Atatürk İsmet ...," *Yeni Malatya*, November 30, 1951, 1.
[116] Necmettin Bilgili, "14 Mayısın ...," *Demokrat Malatya*, May 16, 1951, 1.
[117] "D.P. 17.7.951 salı günü ...," *Demokrat Malatya*, July 16, 1951, extra edition; "Parti müfettisimiz...," *Yeni Malatya*, July 17, 1951, 1, 4.
[118] "Ağaoğlu'nun dünkü ...," *Fırat*, April 20, 1951, 1, 3.
[119] "İlimiz Belediye ...," *Yeni Malatya*, July 23, 1951, 1. Mustafa Albayrak, citing *Ulus*, gives slightly different numbers: 11,706 for CHP and 4,809 for DP (*Türk Siyasi Tarihinde*, 221).

Governor Babaoğlu.[120] To some extent, however, the issue was moot: Babaoğlu had been recalled to Ankara in late March and replaced with a new governor in May. The matter was finally settled in September when Nurettin Aykurt was named mayor. The resolution of the standoff did little to calm political resentments. Pro-DP papers were soon accusing Aykurt of canceling municipal contracts for printing and construction that would otherwise have gone to local DP members.[121]

While images of former president İnönü inflamed partisan tensions in Malatya and nationwide, DP leaders approached images of Atatürk with reverence. Though the DP contained many members for whom Mustafa Kemal was synonymous with the detested single-party regime, the party's political strategy – probably heartfelt by leaders like Bayar – was to associate themselves with Atatürk and attribute all faults to İnönü. Thus, following a series of attacks on statues of Atatürk during the first half of 1951 – mostly attributed to the Ticani religious order – the DP leadership pushed through parliament a bill criminalizing such acts. Though many DP members publicly questioned the constitutionality of passing legislation aimed at a particular individual, the bill passed on July 25.[122]

In August 1951, the DP-controlled parliament launched its most direct attack on the CHP thus far by expropriating the CHP's nationwide network of People's Houses. DP partisans depicted these buildings as "a hotel for [CHP] party inspectors, a gathering place for naughty kids and out-of-work youths," where acolytes of the single party "pass by great portraits of İnönü and worship them like an idol."[123] By seizing these properties from the CHP and closing them, the DP removed an important location for the opposition to organize, but it also eliminated an important venue for cultural activities in provincial centers. Moreover, the move did not sufficiently satisfy critics of the CHP, who wanted to see the party stripped of all its possessions. Papers questioned where the CHP's money was *now* coming from. Pressure began building again for further action, and bills were introduced to parliament proposing to seize CHP property.[124]

120 "D. Parti Belediye ...," *Demokrat Malatya*, July 23, 1951, 1; "Nüvit Yetkin'in ...," *Yeni Malatya*, August 30, 1951, 1.

121 "Tecrübesiz belediye ...," *Demokrat Malatya*, September 10, 1951, 1; "Ters tarfından bravo!," *Demokrat Malatya*, March 8, 1952, 1.

122 TBMM, July 25, 1951, 324; Selçuk Koca, "Atatürk'ü Koruma Kanunu," in *Türkiye'nin 1950'li Yılları*, ed. Mete Kaan Kaynar (Istanbul: İletişim Yayınları, 2015), 321–330; Temür, *Demokrat Parti'de*, 273–275.

123 Üç Yıldız, "Isparta lisesi ...," *Yeni Malatya*, October 4, 1951, 1.

124 Mekki Sait Esen, "Hazineye intikali ...," *Cumhuriyet*, June 5, 1952, 1, 5; "C.H.P. nin Parası," *Yeni Malatya*, June 19, 1952, 1.

In the fall of 1952, CHP leader İsmet İnönü toured Turkey's western provinces, including a planned stop in Balıkesir. The tour produced a war of words between Menderes and İnönü as well as scuffles between their supporters in cities such as Manisa. The day of İnönü's arrival, *Balıkesir Postası* ran the headline "If İnönü repeats the lie-and-slander-filled speeches he gave in İzmir and Manisa in our city ... Democrats will protest." According to the paper, İnönü's words were creating "an environment of unrest and insecurity in the country."[125] The local DP, meanwhile, requested to hold a rally in the same location that the CHP had already announced its rally. The main speaker was to be the stridently anti-İnönü legislator Mükerrem Sarol. The governor approved both events, and the pro-CHP paper *Ateş* (Flame) hoped that Sarol's words would not lead listeners to "excess."[126] On October 8, supporters of both parties started pouring into the center of the city at 10 am. Fights broke out after 3 pm, resulting in three stabbings – two CHP supporters and a police officer attempting to break up scuffles. Several more people were sent to the hospital with injuries. The CHP called off İnönü's speech and left. DP leaders gave triumphal speeches thereafter.[127]

Initially, DP leaders claimed to feel pride in what had occurred. Provincial Party President Sırrı Yırcalı argued İnönü's recent speeches had been "offensive and provocative," requiring a response.[128] A column by Istanbul publisher (and DP supporter) Selim Ragıp Emeç was run in *Balıkesir Postası* praising "Lion Balıkesir" for its bravery.[129] Only toward the end of the month did a more conciliatory tone creep into the pro-DP press coverage of the events – though, even then, editors argued that "Until today, [CHP] governments have caused this division to be apparent among us, [the people] of Balıkesir. They have wanted to play us off against each other. The traces of this bad mentality remain apparent."[130] To lower tensions, Menderes held meetings with a group of leading journalists. According to their spokesman, Ahmet Emin Yalman, the prime minister promised them that he would replace Ağaoğlu as minister responsible for distributing official announcements. Moreover, going forward, there would be less support for low-circulation pro-government papers, and he would consider appointing known moderates (or even

[125] "İnönü İzmir ve Manisadaki ...," *Balıkesir Postası*, October 8, 1952, 1, 4.
[126] "Mükerrem ...," *Ateş*, October 8, 1952, 1.
[127] "İsmet İnönü dün ...," *Balıkesir Postası*, October 9, 1952, 1; "Kanuna ...," *Türk Dili*, October 9, 1952, 1, 2; "Nerede ...," *Ateş*, October 9, 1952, 1; Ankara Embassy to Department of State, October 21, 1952, RG 84, Box 57.
[128] "Son ...," *Balıkesir Postası*, October 19, 1952, 1, 4.
[129] Selim Ragıp Emeç, "Aslan ...," *Balıkesir Postası*, October 13, 1952, 1.
[130] "Balıkesir ...," *Balıkesir Postası*, October 24, 1952, 1.

members of the opposition) to posts at the Anadolu Agency, the state news office.[131]

Despite the national DP leadership's moves to reduce tensions following the events in Balıkesir, hostility toward the CHP persisted. Demands at local party conventions for seizure of CHP properties reflected the ongoing struggle within the DP. As described in Chapter 2, these differences had led to splits in the party as early as 1947. Yet those departures had not enabled the national leadership to craft a more ideologically coherent party by the early 1950s. This tension was evident in local party organizations and was reflected in the pro-DP papers. *Demokrat Malatya*, for example, was run by a leader of the local DP, Kemal Özmumcu, and remained fairly restrained in its tone. *Yeni Malatya*, on the other hand, was run by local DP members, but not leaders; it printed far harsher critiques of the CHP and allotted space to representatives of nationalist organizations like the Turkish Nationalists Association (*Türk Milliyetçiler Derneği*).[132] *Fırat*, another paper managed by DP members, gave space to the general secretary of the Islamist political organization Great East Society (*Büyük Doğu Cemiyeti*).[133]

During 1950–52, nationalist and the Islamist movements were becoming more organized around the country. Part of this success came from government support. Under Education Minister Tevfik İleri, who had first entered politics as a nationalist student leader in the late 1920s, conservatives gained influence, and there was a concerted effort to cleanse the education ministry of left-wing influence.[134] Nationalists were convinced that under İnönü's regime the ministry had become a haven for communists.[135] Like the People's Houses, Village Institutes became a focus of intense concern. Nationalists saw these small teacher training schools as communist incubators and, under İleri, they were closed. İleri also threw his support behind the Turkish Nationalists Association. In Malatya the group met frequently to hear poetry, music,

131 Rountree to State Dept, October 30, 1952, RG 84, Box 57.

132 "Lutfi Baydağı ...," *Yeni Malatya*, November 16, 1951, 1.

133 "Büyük Doğu ...," *Fırat*, December 22, 1950, 1–2.

134 Karpat, "Actors and Issues," 139–140; Bernard Burrows to Selwyn Lloyd, "Leading Personalities in Turkey," August 18, 1959, FO 144740.

135 In matters of education, the bête noire for nationalists was Hasan Ali Yücel, education minister from 1938 to 1946. In the late 1940s, Yücel was involved in a libel suit against the DP's Istanbul provincial president, Kenan Öner, who had accused Yücel of communist ties. Even six years after Yücel left office, Malatya journalist Nevzat Bulun was still referring to him as "godless" and "immoral." One reason for this dislike was the fact that Yücel had presided over purges of right-wing nationalists in 1944 – which was still described as "cruelty" (*mezalim*) at nationalist meetings (Nevzat Bulun, "Kızıl 'Profesör,'" *Gayret*, July 10, 1952, 1; "Türk Milliyetçiler ...," *Yeni Malatya*, March 3, 1952; Koçak, *Rejim Krizi*, 321–362).

short plays, and speeches. Topics included "Communism and War" and "Nation and Nationality."[136] Its provincial president, Lütfi Baydağı, and other speakers were writers for pro-DP newspapers. Baydağı gave speeches emphasizing the importance of "God, Homeland, morality, religion, family, history, tradition, and language" and railing against famous left-wing artists like Nazım Hikmet and Sabahattin Ali.[137]

According to the pro-DP press, the CHP-dominated provincial and municipal governments were not capable of exercising moral leadership. But which faction of the local DP *was*? In the aftermath of the 1951 municipal election loss, the provincial DP president and founder of *Demokrat Malatya*, Kemal Özmumcu, resigned in favor of Kamil Çomoğlu. The change was reflective of power struggles within the party organization. Usually, intimations of intra-DP divisions were only printed in the CHP-run press, but by October 1951 even *Demokrat Malatya* was talking of "apparent conflict" in the party.[138] At the municipal party congress in April 1952, Özmumcu argued with Çomoğlu and his supporters. Fights broke out. When voting for posts finally occurred, critics of Özmumcu gained key posts. Hamid "Hamido" Fendoğlu, a young, impolitic firebrand, was elected vice president of the congress.[139] Until the beginning of the year, Fendoğlu had been working as the regional director of physical fitness. Since then, he had been using his own paper, *Son Söz*, to accuse the DP-appointed governor of oppressing locals when he was a district official in the mid 1940s. Other DP papers printed lengthy denunciations of Fendoğlu's tactics and responses from the governor himself.[140]

The local party was, in short, riven by internal conflicts when Prime Minister Menderes arrived in November 1952 to attend the provincial

[136] "Türk Milliyetçiler …," *Gayret*, January 23, 1952, 1; "Türk Milliyetçiler …," *Yeni Malatya*, February 19, 1952, 1.

[137] "Türk Milliyetçiler …," *Yeni Malatya*, May 22, 1952; "Türk Milliyetçiler …," *Yeni Malatya*, May 23, 1952.

[138] "Demokrat Parti …," *Demokrat Malatya*, October 12, 1951, 1.

[139] "Demokrat Parti …," *Yeni Malatya*, April 30, 1952, 1.

[140] "Sayın Valimiz …," *Gayret*, January 30, 1952, 1; "Vali Şefik San'ın," *Yeni Malatya*, January 30, 1952, 1; "Sonsöz," *Fırat*, March 10, 1952, 1; Zülfikar İnanç, "Bizim şehir …," *Gayret*, March 27, 1952, 1. Fendoğlu would briefly break with the DP in the run-up to the 1954 election and campaign for the Peasant Party of Turkey (*Türkiye Köylü Partisi*). In discussing the government's Cyprus policies, he accused Prime Minister Menderes and Foreign Minister Köprülü of bending to the will of Christians – allegedly saying they were being un-Muslim. For his statements, he was charged with slander and arrested. According to Hüdai Sayın, he was only released when his brother İbrahim promised they would rejoin the DP (BCA 030.01.0.0 55 338 9; BCA 030.01.0.0 41 244 4; Sayın, "Malatya'da Siyasal Seçkinler," 181 n. 61).

congress.[141] But if Menderes had hoped to achieve good publicity in the province by making an appearance, he was to be disappointed. On the night of November 22, following Menderes's speech, the journalist Ahmet Emin Yalman was shot and wounded outside the central post office. As we saw in Chapter 2, Yalman had been supportive of the DP in the late 1940s, but he had grown more critical once the party gained power. As editor of *Vatan*, he was unyielding in his attacks on what he deemed to be religious reaction and the DP's failure to discourage it. As an avid liberal and champion of American culture, Yalman promoted events like beauty pageants that incensed religious conservatives. He was frequently criticized by the Great East Association and its leader, Necip Fazıl Kısakürek, who emphasized that Yalman was part of the Dönme community, Muslims who had converted from a millenarian Jewish sect in the 1600s. Such rhetoric inspired the radical religious nationalists, who tried to kill Yalman.[142]

141 The local DP was able to coordinate when partisan advantage necessitated. In November 1951, for example, when CHP candidates won elections for Malatya's chamber of commerce, the result was dismissed after the DP called the voter rolls into question. According to pro-CHP journalists, in advance of the election rerun in July 1952, the governor packed the chamber's election committee with DP partisans and pressured electors to ensure a DP victory. Hasan Çuhaçı, a DP leader, became president ("İlimiz Ticaret …," *Demokrat Malatya*, November 6, 1951, 1; "Seçim Değil …," *Malatya Postası*, July 15, 1952, 1, 3).

142 Hüseyin Üzmez, *Malatya Suikastı* (Istanbul: Timaş Yayınları, 2004), 22. The "Dönme factor" in the history of the DP is too important to be ignored. While discussing it risks falling into conspiracy theories, works that do not mention it are ignoring an important aspect of the party's history. The millenarian Jewish movement from which the Dönme community originated was primarily located in Salonika and İzmir. The former city was the headquarters of the Committee of Union and Progress. During the Union's time in power, prominent leaders like Finance Minister Mehmed Cavit came from the Dönme community. According to historian Cengiz Şişman, Hüseyin Cahit Yalçın, the editor of the main Unionist paper, *Tanin*, was "possibly" from the Dönme community. The fact that even sympathetic historians like Şişman and Marc Baer have trouble establishing whether leading figures from Ottoman and Turkish history were part of the "Dönme" community leaves the door open for wild speculations. The most prominent speculator is Soner Yalçın. His 2004 book, *Efendi: Beyaz Türklerin Büyük Sırrı* (Master: The Great Secret of the White Turks), argues that the Dönme community secretly controls Turkey. As historian Rıfat Bali points out, this line of argumentation is particularly appealing to nationalist and Islamist political movements that seek to delegitimize Mustafa Kemal's regime by portraying it as inauthentically Muslim or Turkish. The genealogies and social connections in Yalçın's book seem especially compelling if one chooses to forget the religious and ethnic diversity of the Ottoman Empire. Once we accept this diversity, the presence of Jews, Armenians, Dönme, and others in the Young Turk movement becomes less surprising – as does the fact that a young Mustafa Kemal, growing up in Salonika, would have attended a middle school run by the Dönme community. All that said, the fact that Atatürk's long-serving foreign minister, Tevfik Rüştü Aras, was from the Dönme community, that his daughter was married to DP foreign minister Fatin Rüştü Zorlu, that Adnan Menderes's wife Berrin was Aras' niece, and that Ahmet Emin Yalman's pro-DP newspaper was backed by a consortium of

The attempt on Yalman's life – remembered as "the Malatya Assassination" – had important implications for national politics. Initially, *Demokrat Malatya* suggested that the attackers could have been anyone – perhaps members of the Great East Association, but also possibly the CHP. It soon emerged that the assassin and his allies were members of the Turkish Nationalists Association and acolytes of the Great East Association.[143] The Turkish Nationalists Association was closed within weeks of the incident, and its leaders were prosecuted. Its president, a DP parliamentarian named Sait Bilgiç, was temporarily expelled from the party.[144] The minister of education, Tevfik İleri, resigned his post in April 1953. Nationwide, the historian Gavin Brockett argues, the shooting had a chilling effect on public debates about the role of religion in Turkish civic life. The perceived threat of nationalist and religious publications stirring up violent sentiment encouraged the DP to place limits on the press that would soon be extended to a broader range of journalism.[145]

While the extent to which the assassination attempt influenced local politics is difficult to gauge from the newspapers, the provincial congress

investors from the Dönme community can feel like an overwhelming number of coincidences to one looking to be overwhelmed. Yet, while there were many Dönme community members in Turkish politics during these years, their political programs did not always cohere. Another famous member of the community, Sabiha Sertel, was a harsh critic of the single-party regime and the DP – not a sensible stance if she were secretly controlling it. As for the fact that she (like other writers) does not talk about the community in her autobiography, we should remember that discussing one's Greek, Armenian, Kurdish, or other non-Turkish roots was not common in the Republic of Turkey until recent decades (see Sertel, *Roman Gibi*; Rıfat Bali, *A Scapegoat for All Seasons: The Dönmes or Crypto-Jews of Turkey* [Istanbul: The ISIS Press, 2008], 320; Marc Baer, *The Dönme: Jewish Converts, Muslim Revolutionaries, and Secular Turks* [Stanford: Stanford University Press, 2010]; Cengiz Şişman, *The Burden of Silence: Sabbatai Sevi and the Evolution of the Ottoman-Turkish Dönmes* [Oxford: Oxford University Press, 2017], 273).

143 "Müessif hadisenin ...," *Demokrat Malatya*, December 26, 1952, 1. The would-be assassin, Hüseyin Üzmez, was born in 1931. He had attended school at Malatya Lycée until early 1952, when he was expelled for threatening the principal, accusing him of communist sympathies. For his murder attempt, Üzmez was sentenced to twenty years in jail, of which he served ten. After release, he earned a law degree at Ankara University and worked as a columnist for pious newspapers like *Vakit*. In 2009, he was sentenced to thirteen years in prison for "sexual abuse" of a minor. He died in 2014 ("Yalmana yapılan ...," *Malatya Postası*, November 27, 1952, 1; Nail Kahraman, Erdoğan Paçin, and Hüseyin Tüccar, "Hüseyin Üzmez'e ...," *Radikal*, September 16, 2009, available: www.radikal.com.tr/turkiye/huseyin-uzmeze-13–yil-hapis-cezasi-954761/).

144 "Milliyetçiler Derneği ...," *Zafer*, January 23, 1953, 1, 3; Murat Kılıç, *"Allah, Vatan, Soy, Milli Mukaddesat": Türk Milliyetçiler Derneği, 1951–1953* (Istanbul: İletişim Yayınları, 2016), 198–224.

145 Brockett, *How Happy to Call Oneself a Turk*, 219–221.

did result in a victory for the less confrontational members of the local party – as opposed to those, like Hamid Fendoğlu, who had criticized the governor and other officials. Fendoğlu was not elected to the provincial executive council, whereas his rival (and former local party leader) Kemal Özmumcu was. The executive council, in turn, selected Ali Fırat as the new provincial president. Fırat was the son of Hacı Bedir Ağa; his brother Hüseyin Fırat was a DP representative for İçel. For the moment, more traditional figures had reestablished control.

Spoils of Victory, Spoiled by Victory: The Benefits of Democrat Rule

The assassination attempt on Ahmet Emin Yalman in Malatya, coming a year after the spate of attacks on statues of Atatürk, led the DP government in Ankara to constrain the activities of religious and nationalist movements across the country. These measures followed years of state repression against communist and socialist parties. Over the course of 1953, however, the DP began taking action against opposition parties that were more "mainstream," insofar as they had been founded by influential politicians from the single-party era.

The Nation Party was first major party to be closed. Started in 1948 by more radical members of the DP, it had performed poorly in 1950, following the sudden deaths of its most popular leaders. Thereafter, it had been led by Osman Bölükbaşı, another former DP member who had worked with Samet Ağaoğlu as a DP organizer in the party's early years. Not only was he the party leader, he was its only elected member in parliament, representing the province of Kırşehir, where he was born and his family held large estates.[146] Like the leaders of the DP, Bölükbaşı had trouble restraining his party's rank-and-file members, many of whom sought to upend the political order in more profound ways than he was arguing for. At the Nation Party's June 1953 congress, delegates voted down resolutions expressing the party's commitment to Atatürk and his revolution. Bölükbaşı and other leaders resigned, accusing the party of becoming a haven for those in favor of returning to Arabic script and ending the equality of women.[147]

Within days of the congress, *Zafer* writer Mümtaz Faik Fenik was accusing Nation Party members of "sticking out their tongues at Atatürk," and wondering whether an organization so riven by division

[146] Adem Çaylak, *Osman Bölükbaşı ve Siyasal Hareketi* (Ankara: Atatürk Araştırma Merkezi, 2010), 34.

[147] "İrticaın maskesi düştü," *İstanbul Ekspres*, June 30, 1953, 1, 2.

could even be called "a party."[148] Over the next week, the Ankara prosecutor's office opened an investigation into the party leadership and accusations that its members were in league with the recently closed Turkish Nationalists Association and groups attempting to replace the civil code with Islamic laws.[149] The party was closed on July 8 by court order. Announcing its closure, Fenik declared in his headline that it was "Not a Party, [but rather] a Vile Gang of Rebellion!"[150]

The rapid closure of the only other major opposition party worried CHP members.[151] The national leadership issued a statement, carefully worded to emphasize that the CHP's "main principle" was defending "the Republic and the revolutions" it had brought about, but adding that the sudden closure of the Nation Party was a point of concern and suggesting that the Association Law did not sufficiently protect political parties.[152] One Balıkesir CHP leader declared that "Multiparty politics means the clash of ideas. Perhaps the Democrat Party wants all parties silenced and ideas covered up such that only its voice is heard."[153] Between July and December 1953, relations between the parties grew worse. Rumors spread that the CHP was considering an alliance with Bölükbaşı, and Menderes declared that, if members of the CHP did not steer their leadership away from its current aggressive style, "The DP government knows … to take the necessary measures."[154]

In November, the DP moved ahead with a bill to strip the CHP of its "unjust acquisitions" – in other words, all the property the party organization had accumulated during its decades in power: in particular, buildings and newspapers. Rather than move the legislation through a standing (and bipartisan) parliamentary committee, the DP created a special committee composed entirely of DP representatives to draw up the legislation. Within days, the bill was introduced and quickly pushed through parliament, leading the entire CHP to march out of the chamber.[155] In the coming days, the CHP moved into new offices and began

148 Mümtaz Faik Fenik, "Buna hala parti diyecekmiyiz?" *Zafer*, July 2, 1953, 1, 3.
149 "Savcılık …," *Milliyet*, July 2, 1953, 2, 7.
150 Mümtaz Faik Fenik, "Millet Partisindeki gizli dosya!" *Zafer*, July 4, 1953, 1, 3; Mümtaz Faik Fenik, "Hilafetçiler! Mecelleciler!" *Zafer*, July 4, 1953, 1, 3; Mümtaz Faik Fenik, "Parti değil …," *Zafer*, July 9, 1953, 1, 3.
151 Many parties had been closed prior to 1953, but none with representation in parliament. These included parties like the Islamic Democrat Party, closed as recently as March 3, 1952 (Ahmad and Ahmad, *Türkiye'de Çok Partili Politikanın*, 94).
152 Toker, *DP'nin Altın Yılları*, 242–243.
153 Cevat Demiraray, "D. Partideki sinirlilik," *Türk Dili*, July 18, 1953, 1.
154 Toker, *DP'nin Altın Yılları*, 252.
155 TBMM, December 14, 1953, 169–170; Toker, *DP'nin Altın Yılları*, 253–257; Öymen, *Öfkeli Yıllar*, 412–420.

receiving donations from supporters. Its official paper, *Ulus* (Nation), was now published as *Yeni Ulus* (New Nation) under the ownership of a member rather than the party itself.

The seizure of property is remembered as a "turning point" by CHP members.[156] Many of the party's future leaders recall it as a moment that deepened their commitment to the party and spurred them to activism.[157] For most people in Turkey, however, the DP government's strong-arm tactics do not seem to have shifted sympathies. The party would go on to win a larger electoral victory in May 1954 than in 1950 (58.4 percent, up from 55.2 percent). The CHP would do even worse, falling from 39.6 percent of the vote to 35.1 percent. If sympathy shifted in any direction, it was to Osman Bölükbaşı's new party, the Republican Nation Party (*Cumhuriyetçi Millet Partisi*, CMP), which improved on the performance of the Nation Party (5.3 percent, up from 4.6 percent).

Not only did the DP's share of the overall vote increase nationally, but it increased significantly in provinces that the party had lost in 1950. In eastern provinces like Van, Bitlis, and Hakkari, as well as in the southern border province of Hatay, voters (and local power brokers) in 1950 had preferred to support the ruling party rather than take a risk on the opposition.[158] Four years later, the same logic worked in the DP's favor. Given the fact that most of a province's seats were allotted to the

156 Öymen, *Öfkeli Yıllar*, 412.

157 Alptekin Gündüz, *En Sevdiği Güneşti: Dr. Suphi Baykam'ın Fırtınalı Yaşamı* (Istanbul: Piramid Yayıncılık, 2004), 112; Ahmet İsvan, *Başkent Gölgesinde İstanbul* (Istanbul: İletişim Yayınları, 2002), 4.

158 The province of Van provides a good example of how the DP expanded on its 1950 gains in the 1954 election. In 1946 and 1950, the CHP held on to the province. In 1946, the DP had established an organization in the province too late and opted to support several "independent" candidates. In 1950, the DP's candidates were two retired military officers with connections in the region and Hamit Kartal, a leading member of the Burukan tribe. Yet the party had experienced splits during the period 1946–50, with at least one of its founders leaving and joining the Nation Party; with 41 percent of the vote, it received only one seat in parliament. The CHP won 50.5 percent of the provincial vote and secured two seats: one for Ferit Melen, a former official in the finance department, and one for Kazım Özalp, a former military officer and a long-serving member of parliament, who had fought in Van during World War I and even had a town in the province (re)named after him. The remaining 8.5 percent of the vote went to independent candidates, including İbrahim Arvas, whose family had strong ties with the Qadiriyya Sufi order. For thirty years prior to 1950, Arvas had been a CHP member, representing either Van or the neighboring province of Hakkari. Only that year did his conservative religious views lead him to break with the CHP. By 1954, the DP had created more connections with tribal leaders; not only was Hamit Kartal a candidate again, but he was joined by Muslih Görentaş, a member of the Görentaş tribe. The local party was also aided by the government's attention to the province. Several ministers visited during the DP's first years in power, and the ministry of economy and commerce even developed an investment plan for the province. In the election, turnout rose, and the DP won 64.1 percent of the vote; the CHP, with 35.3

victor, DP's victories in these provinces turned its 55.2 percent of the vote into 93 percent of the seats in parliament.

An important factor in determining these results was the visible improvement in people's lives under DP rule. The central elements of DP economic policy remained in place: credit expanded by 12 percent over 1953, and 19 percent over 1954.[159] Investment, meanwhile, rose from 17.6 percent of expenditure in the 1950–51 budget to 25.8 percent of the 1954–55 budget. These expenditures underwrote projects like roads, airfields, ports, dams, and electrical power stations. All could be framed as essential for military preparedness, which qualified them for US economic and military aid. Furthermore, all were highly visible, meaning that their construction served as a constant reminder of government activity. Road spending grew from TL53 million ($19 million) in the 1950–51 budget to TL153 million ($55 million) in the 1953–54 budget.[160] Progress on roads and other projects was a primary focus of pro-DP newspapers. Coverage of the planning and discussion phases highlighted the activity of local leaders; the work of securing allocations from the national budget drew attention to intermediaries like mayors and governors; and groundbreaking and completion ceremonies provided national leaders with a reason to visit provinces and give speeches.

In Balıkesir, the mixture of development and propaganda was particularly apparent. This was due, in part, to the location of the province and, in part, to the skill of local political leaders in securing money from the national budget. There were projects to extend transportation, electrical, and drinking-water grids; establish additional hospital facilities and schools; and build new factories.[161] By the end of 1952, in addition to the announcement of a sugar factory and a cloth and canvas factory, there were rumors of a cement factory in the near future.

The textile, sugar, and cement factories each illustrated a means by which economic development was achieved under DP rule. Like so many of Turkey's industrial enterprises, the textile factory was underwritten by

percent, received no seats (Pınar, "Van'da Demokrat Parti," 35–47; Şerif Demir, "Van'da Siyasi Hayat 1945–1960," *Van Yüzüncü Yıl Üniversitesi Sosyal Bilimler Enstitüsü Dergisi* [2021]: 140–146; Fırat Ayhan, "Demokrat Parti ve Demokrat Parti Van milletvekilleri" [Master's thesis, Necmettin Erbakan Üniversitesi, Konya, 2023], 61–63).

159 Singer, *The Economic Advance*, 201.

160 "Memleketimize yeniden …," *Balıkesir Postası*, February 11, 1953, 1; "Turkey's Economy," March 31, 1955, 3–5, sent by Thomas Brimelow to D. M. O'Brien on April 2, 1955, FO 371/117727.

161 Unexpected projects became necessary as well. The city had to rebuild the central market after the 1950 fire and create additional housing following a serious earthquake in March 1953 that killed thirty-five people.

a consortium of banks and state enterprises – in this case, Sümerbank, İş Bankası, and Ziraat Bankası. As semi-autonomous institutions, all of these operated independently of the primary government budget. In addition to these institutions, 25 percent of the initial investment was raised from local investors. The start of construction in September 1953 was a festive event, timed to coincide with the anniversary of Balıkesir's liberation from Greek occupation, and with Prime Minister Menderes in attendance.[162]

The cement factory was one of twenty tenders issued by Turkey Cement Industry Inc. (ÇİSAN), which was created by parliament in October 1953 with TL50 million in capital from Sümerbank, Emlak Bankası (Property Bank), and İş Bankası. The new factories enabled Turkey to move from an importer of cement to an exporter during the course of the decade. Whereas production had risen from 24,000 tons a year in 1924 to 396,000 tons a year in 1950 (a growth of 14,000 tons each year), production reached 2 million tons in 1960 (a growth of 160,000 tons each year).[163] The sugar factory was part of a similar state-led initiative to substitute domestic products for foreign imports. In 1951–52, Turkey's four sugar factories produced a total of 186,000 tons. By 1956, eleven new factories had been built. Production had risen to 643,000 tons in the 1960–61 season.[164]

Running large industrial facilities – especially sugar production, which required high-temperature processes – demanded large amounts of electricity, and this too was a focus of the DP. In 1950, the country's power stations produced 789.5 million kwh, 96.2 percent of which was produced from thermal sources (i.e., coal). By 1960, Turkey was producing 2.8 billion kwh. Owing to the government's focus on dam-building, 35.6 percent now came from hydroelectric sources. Balıkesir was not the site of a major power-station project in the 1950s, but it did receive electricity from the newly built coal-fueled Soma power station in the neighboring

162 "Yeni fabrikamız," *Balıkesir Postası*, January 22, 1953, 1; "Yeni fabrikamız," *Balıkesir Postası*, May 1, 1953, 1; "Dokuma fabrikamız," *Balıkesir Postası*, August 19, 1953, 1; "Fabrikamız ...," *Balıkesir Postası*, September 7, 1953, 1.

163 "Çimento ...," *Balıkesir Postası*, October 9, 1953, 1; Sey, *Türkiye Çimento Tarihi*, 68–71; Nadir Yurtoğlu, "Kalkınmanın Önemli Bir Unsuru, Kuruluşundan 50. Yılına Türkiye'de Çimento Sanayi (1910–1960)," *Atatürk Araştırma Merkezi Dergisi* 31, no. 92 (2015): 113–164.

164 A. Cevdet Eyüpoğlu, "Şeker Fabrikasyonun Tarihçesi ve Türkiye'de Şeker Sanayii," *Kimya Mühendisliği* 2, no. 23 (1967): 18. The new sugar factories were built by German and French firms. Of the eleven new factories, five were "private" in the sense of being underwritten by banks (Adapazarı, Amasya ve Kütahya) or private investors (Konya and Kayseri). Nonetheless, all were run by the Turkish Sugar Corporation (Sedat Avcı, "Türk Şeker Sanayiinin Kuruluş ve Gelişmesinde Devletin Etkisi," *Coğrafya Dergisi* 4 [1996], 293–294).

province of Manisa after 1958.[165] Until then, the various city centers of Balıkesir depended on smaller generators, which – at least to judge from newspaper coverage – frequently broke down, leading to recriminations over how such subpar machines had been purchased in the first place.[166]

In the lead-up to the May 1954 elections, the opposition focused less on interruptions in service than on the "single-party mentality" of the DP.[167] The pro-CHP paper *Türk Dili* printed letters from former DP members who had grown frustrated with the party. It reported that local DP leaders were pressuring workers to join and noted that the national DP was directing TL10,000 into the provincial election.[168] When the names of primary candidates for the DP list were announced, the opposition paper *Ateş* congratulated the editor of *Balıkesir Postası* on his inclusion. With, perhaps, some sarcasm, *Ateş* expressed its hope that his positions in the regional physical education directorate, Anatolian News Agency, and provincial council would all be filled by people as qualified as him in the future.[169] This list of multiple local posts occupied by a single individual suggests the degree to which the DP had monopolized power in the province on the eve of the elections. Yet, for all that, the editor was not among the final nominees. Of the three new additions, one was a sitting member of parliament who had served in a different province in 1950–54; another was from the district of Sındırgı, where the provincial DP was weak; and the third was Sıtkı Yırcalı's brother Sırrı.

Sırrı's inclusion on the list was an indication of Balıkesir notables' continuing influence in national politics. At the same time, the province was something of an outlier: in 1954, Balıkesir gained an extra seat in parliament, bringing its total to fourteen – the same as Bursa. Only major provinces like Istanbul (30), Ankara (21), İzmir (19), and Konya (19) had more. Of these fourteen, the local DP organization picked twelve and the national party organization nominated two, roughly 15 percent of the total.[170] This was slightly less than in 1950, when the national leadership

[165] "Belediyemizin …," *Balıkesir Postası*, January 1, 1953, 1; Nadir Yurtoğlu, "Cumhuriyet Türkiyesinde Elektrik Enerjisi Üretimi ve Enerji Politikaları, 1923–1960," *Atatürk Araştırma Merkezi Dergisi* 34, no. 98 (2018): 237–265.

[166] "D.P. li başkana …," *Türk Dili*, February 1, 1951, 2; "Elektrik …," *Balıkesir Postası*, January 29, 1952, 1; "Elektrik …," *Balıkesir Postası*, October 24, 1952, 1; "Belediye Meclis …," *Ateş*, February 15, 1953, 1.

[167] For example, "D.P. den istifa …," *Türk Dili*, February 4, 1954, 1–2.

[168] "D.P. den istifa …," *Türk Dili*, February 4, 1954, 1; "D.P. ye alınmak …," *Türk Dili*, March 10, 1954, 2; "Balıkesir D.P. teşkilatı …," *Türk Dili*, March 11, 1954, 1.

[169] "D.P. adaylarından Münir Yenal," *Ateş*, March 18, 1954, 1.

[170] The national DP leadership added Mekki Sait Esen (a journalist) and Haluk Timurtaş (a bureaucrat) to the Balıkesir candidate list. In addition to Sırrı Yırcalı, two other new candidates were added by the local party: Ahmet Karagür (a doctor from the town of

appointed 20 percent of the candidates. While local leaders in Balıkesir were consolidating their influence, the trend was moving in the opposite direction elsewhere.[171] In many provinces, the national DP leadership rejected a large proportion of local lists and, in some cases, rejected the provincial lists entirely.[172] Overall, half of the members elected in 1950 were not renomin-

Sındırgı) and Halil İmre (a banker from the town of Bandırma who had severed as a representative for Sivas in the previous parliament). The remaining nine candidates had served as Balıkesir representatives from 1950 to 1954. They were: Vacit Asena (lawyer), Ali Enver Güreli (bureaucrat), Esat Budakoğlu (lawyer), Mücteba Iştın (lawyer), Arif Kalıpsızoğlu (farmer), Ahmet Kocabıyıkoğlu (farmer), Yahya Pelvan (teacher), Muharrem Esir Tunçay (doctor), and Sıtkı Yırcalı (bureaucrat/lawyer). Four representatives failed to win renomination: Salahattin Baskan (teacher), Mufit Erkuyumcu (lawyer), Muzaffer Emiroğlu (farmer), and Ali Fahri İşeri (merchant). İşeri's absence was not surprising, since he had fallen out with the party and resigned in February 1953 to preempt formal expulsion. Erkuyumcu was placed on the Bursa candidate list. Emiroğlu would be renominated in advance of the 1957 elections. Salahattin Baskan's failure to be renominated is the least explicable (by me), since he had been a founder of the provincial party and was the former owner of *Balıkesir Postası*.

Though I list the professions of these politicians, it bears repeating that these can be very misleading: the presence of powerful landowners like the Yırcalı brothers illustrates that such a person could also be a "bureaucrat" or a "lawyer." Nonetheless, all those caveats aside, it is notable that of the forty-two candidates for the party-list primary, titles included: lawyers or judges (11); teachers (6); doctors (4); farmers (4); businessmen (4); and journalists (3). The remaining eleven had a variety of jobs. Only one had a job that might be categorized as "engineering" – interesting, when one considers the status of engineers in a developing country like Turkey and the fact that center-right politics in Turkey from 1965 to at least 1980 would be dominated by dam engineer Süleyman Demirel ("İhraç …," *Balıkesir Postası*, February 27, 1953, 1; "D.P. nin aday listesi," *Ateş*, March 21, 1954; "D. P. mebus …," *Balıkesir Postası*, March 29, 1954, 1; "D. P. Balıkesir mebusları …," *Ateş*, May 4, 1954, 1).

171 Erzurum representative Rıfkı Salim Burçak's description of how the 1954 electoral list was crafted in his province may be taken as typical. Sixty-nine people, including the currently serving ten representatives, applied to be candidates. A vote by the local party narrowed these applicants down to ten. In the process, seven of the current representatives were left off; four of these were placed on lists in other provinces, and one (Bahadır Dülger) was retained at the request of the national party. The national party also wanted to veto half of the ten nominees. Burçak argued for one of the five, but the national government got its way with four vetoes, as well as its standard two nominations. As a result, half of Erzurum's candidates were named by the national party rather than the provincial party (Burçak, *On Yılın Anıları*, 197–199).

172 In Istanbul, the national party rejected the candidate list so that it could install its own preferred candidates. To facilitate this heavy-handed move, Menderes encouraged various nominees to withdraw "voluntarily." Most were placed on lists in other provinces. *Zafer* reported these resignations as "a very beautiful example of democracy," and Menderes ally Mükerrem Sarol argued in an editorial that the entire process was necessary so that "local judgements" did not overshadow the needs of the nation ("Çok güzel …," *Zafer*, March 30, 1954, 1; Mükerrem Sarol, "Asil bir …," *Türk Sesi*, March 30, 1954, 1; Toker, *DP'nin Altın Yılları*, 283–284; Albayrak, *Türk Siyasi Tarihinde*, 255).

ated, skewing the composition of the parliamentary group toward the national party leaders' desires.[173]

The months leading up to the elections in Balıkesir were marked by multiple rallies. The first was organized in early April by the local party. A crowd of 20,000 gathered – bussed in for free from surrounding villages, the opposition papers grumbled.[174] It was festive: local leaders gave speeches, poems were read, and decorated camels were on display. Sıtkı Yırcalı criticized the CHP, while Enver Güreli made a more nuanced argument, acknowledging that the DP had made some errors since it had come to power, but that "The Democrat Party is still a sapling. All of us are cultivating it and all of us will eat the fruit."[175]

President Bayar visited toward the end of the month to attend the groundbreaking of the Susurluk sugar factory. Two days later, on April 21, İnönü finally visited Balıkesir to give a speech. It was part of a national tour during which he criticized the government's recent law to encourage foreign investment. According to İnönü, the law would return the country to the Ottoman era, when the sultan had signed "capitulations" with foreign powers, giving them special privileges.[176] *Balıkesir Postası* mocked İnönü for criticizing the government when his own governments had failed to develop Turkey's resources. Sıtkı Yırcalı echoed these sentiments and went further, arguing, "Talking in such a way demonstrates a mentality that is betraying the government which he turned over [to the DP in 1950]. Today, [that mentality] is on the way to betraying the duty of opposition." As for why the DP was succeeding where the CHP had failed, he pointed to the legitimacy derived from the people. The measures the DP was enacting "could [only] be carried out by manly governments, whose identity rests in their determination to carry out their ideas ... supported by the national will."[177]

Talk of the "national will" was not mere hyperbole. In 1950 and 1954, the DP could rely on large numbers of voters to turn out on election day. When DP politicians organized rallies, they could likewise expect a large turnout – albeit, as critics noted, one inflated through free transportation. Yet, besides these spectacles, the DP lacked ready means of mobilizing citizens directly. In many regions of the country, get-out-the-vote efforts depended on powerful local elites, and how that vote was cast depended

[173] Ahmad, *The Turkish Experiment*, 87; Beril Yaşar, "Demokrat Parti'de Parti İçi Demokrasi, 1946–1960," *Tarih Okulu Dergisi* 7, no. 18 (2014): 519–520.
[174] "Bol para ile ...," *Türk Dili*, April 6, 1954, 1, 2.
[175] "D.P. miting ...," *Ateş*, April 6, 1954, 1, 2.
[176] "Yabancı sermayenin ...," *Türk Dili*, April 25, 1954, 1.
[177] "Petrol ...," *Balıkesir Postası*, April 21, 1954, 1, 2; "Balıkesir nutku," *Balıkesir Postası*, April 22, 1954, 1, 3.

on family pressure. The importance of these factors can be seen in news reports of party switches, which often included multiple members of a family lineage.[178] One new development on the eve of the 1954 election, therefore, was the attempt by the DP to develop its political organization through the creation of a "Youth Arm."

The DP was responding to the CHP, which had begun developing its own youth organization after the government had closed its previous means of connecting with the public, the People's Houses.[179] On January 7, 1954 an "Organization of Young Democrats" was established in Ankara.[180] In the following months, multiple DP "youth locals" were established around Balıkesir and the country.[181] In the short term, these organizations contributed little to the elections besides an excuse to hold an event and to rally supporters on the eve of the elections. In the long term, however, the effort to organize "youth" foreshadowed more thoroughgoing attempts to make various social groups politically conscious – and, more importantly, associated with the DP.

Following the election, these mobilization efforts would taper off again. In Balıkesir, the DP's victory had been overwhelming.[182] In the aftermath, the main concern was to send the victorious candidates off to Ankara and rearrange local party posts. In provinces where the DP lost, however, the next steps were more dramatic. Malatya was split in half, creating a new province called Adıyaman, which contained the districts where the DP had been successful. Similarly, the province of Kırşehir, which Osman Bölükbaşı's Republican Nation Party (CMP) had won, was stripped of its provincial status altogether.

178 As the election neared, the number of people reported to be switching parties swelled to the hundreds. In one notable instance, *Demokrat Malatya* reported that 3,095 CHP members in the district of Kahta had switched. When the numbers were this large, village names were included rather than family names (i.e., "Koçar 200, Narin 390 ...," etc.) ("Aday...," *Demokrat Malatya*, March 31, 1954, 1–2).

179 Asıl Kaya, "Türk Siyasi Tarihi'nde CHP'nin Gençlik Kolları" (Master's thesis, Dokuz Eylül Üniversitesi, İzmir, 2010), 61–74.

180 Akkuş, "Demokrat Parti Aydın Milletvekilleri," 82.

181 "D.P. nin şehrimizde ...," *Balıkesir Postası*, January 17, 1954, 1; "D.P. Karabey ...," *Balıkesir Postası*, January 28, 1954, 1; "Edremitte ...," *Balıkesir Postası*, February 16, 1954, 1; "D. P. gençlik ...," *Balıkesir Postası*, April 1, 1954, 1.

182 In the 1954 election, the DP's percentage of the vote increased in nearly every Balıkesir district, including Sındırgı, the only district it lost to the CHP. There were gains in Ayvalık (from 58% in 1950 to 62% in 1954), Edremit (60% to 61%), Gönen (56% to 58%), Manyas (66% to 63%), Erdek (54% to 59%), Bigadiç (52% to 56%), Burhaniye (43% to 54%), İvrindi (55% to 64%), Susurluk (61% to 66%), and Sındırgı (31% to 41%). Even a major decline in Bandırma (from 75% to 66%) was still a sizeable victory ("Kazanan ...," *Ateş*, May 16, 1950, 1; "Balıkesir'de ...," *Balıkesir Postası*, May 5, 1954, 1).

Conclusion: Seasonal Adjustments

During the DP's first four years in power, party leaders oversaw an economic boom, ensured Turkey's security by gaining membership in NATO, and increased investment in infrastructure and social services. Under their leadership, Turkey become a symbol of what was possible for "non-Western" countries that allied with the United States. These accomplishments were facilitated by high global demand stimulated in part by the Korean War and aided by bumper harvests. The imperatives of the Korean conflict and uncertainty of the early Cold War years increased Turkey's importance in the eyes of US policymakers and made it easier for DP leaders to secure aid. Yet, as we have seen, even under these favorable conditions, DP leaders felt pressure from the party rank and file, the electorate, and their Western allies. Moreover, the government's economic policies of liberal trade, increased agricultural subsidies, and low taxes were already proving unsustainable.

At first the government's difficulties were somewhat obscured. Businessmen and merchants felt the pinch before the public at large. Trade deficits had grown large enough by mid 1952 that the existing liberal trade regime could not be maintained. The effort to stabilize these deficits began in earnest after Balıkesir representative Enver Güreli become minister of economy and trade in July 1952. On September 22, 1952, his ministry officially informed banks that all future applications for credit must be passed on to the Central Bank, which would then pass them on to his ministry for final approval.[183] A month followed during which the government halted further allocations while a new, ad hoc system was being organized.[184] The decrees ended the free-trade regime that had prevailed for the previous three years. In September 1953, a new system took formal shape with the creation of a new licensing and quota system for imports and a special fund to subsidize exports.[185]

US and international financial institutions also began to pressure the DP government. On October 1, 1952, the head of the Mutual Security Agency in Turkey (which oversaw US aid) informed Polatkan that the

183 Informally, the ministry of finance requested that banks raise the initial deposit that merchants must make to secure foreign exchange from 20 percent up to 35–50 percent of the total amount (J. Svoboda to M. Leon Dayton, September 22, 1952, RG 84, Box 60).

184 "Turkey: Economic Report No. 8," September 8, 1952; "Turkey: Economic Report No. 9," October 7, 1952; "Turkey: Economic Report No. 10," November 5, 1952, FO 371/101866.

185 RG, September 3, 1953; RG, September 12, 1953. Announcing this new system, *Zafer* explained that it was a necessary response, given other countries' protectionist policies ("Yeni dış ...," *Zafer*, September 3, 1953, 1, 3).

United States would provide $45 million in nonmilitary assistance for the coming year – but probably no more. He recommended that Turkey revise its liberal trade regime and sell wheat at reduced prices on the international market in order to stimulate demand. According to US Ambassador George McGhee, Polatkan did not take these suggestions in a "statesman-like" fashion.[186] For his part, the ambassador told Foreign Minister Köprülü that Turkey would not be able to use US aid to cover its debts to the EPU and repeated the suggestion that the DP government tax agricultural wealth. As in previous meetings, Köprülü dismissed the idea on the grounds that it would discourage production and assured McGhee that the shortage of funds was merely "seasonal."[187]

The tone of US officials was becoming harsher as the Korean War was winding down and a new administration was set to take power in the United States. Eisenhower and his policymakers were no less committed to waging the Cold War than their peers in the Truman administration, but they were hoping to do so more cheaply. Faced with a penny-pinching US administration, DP leaders still had means for ingratiating themselves: on November 10, 1952, a week after the US election, Bayar invited McGhee to the presidential residence to meet with Menderes, Köprülü, and himself. They informed McGhee, a Texas oilman prior to entering government service, that Turkey was now ready to develop its oil industry with the aid of US firms.[188] Needless to say, McGhee was pleased.

This mix of pleasing and frustrating Americans and other allies would be crucial to the DP during the mid 1950s as economic conditions grew worse.

[186] BCA 030.01.0.0 88 551 4; "No. 468: Memorandum of Conversation, by the Ambassador in Turkey (McGhee)," October 24, 1952, *FRUS, 1952–1954*, vol. VIII.
[187] Embassy to Dept of State, October 15, 1952, RG 84, Box 57.
[188] Memorandum of Conversation, November 13, 1952, RG 84, Box 57.

4 De-democratization and Discontent: Backing away from Economic Liberalism, 1954–1955

With only five weeks to go before the 1954 national elections, Mükerrem Sarol, a DP representative for Istanbul, launched a new paper called *Türk Sesi* (The Turkish Voice). Sarol was a close ally of Adnan Menderes and had played a key role in organizing the party in the prime minister's home province of Aydın during its early years. By the end of the 1940s, he had resettled in Istanbul, where he continued to represent Menderes's interests. In his first column, Sarol explained that the paper would bear "firm witness to the realization of an age of happiness and welfare" that was occurring under DP rule.[1] In Istanbul, *Türk Sesi* performed the same function as the provincial papers we encountered in Chapters 2 and 3. Its positive coverage was aided by amendments to the Press Law (enacted just a week before the paper's launch), which mandated one to six years in jail and sizeable fines for releasing material that, through false reporting, aimed "to shake the financial or political credibility of the state or cause general panic and excitement."[2]

The only excitement *Türk Sesi* was interested in was excitement *for* the DP. The paper emphasized the scale and scope of industrial and infrastructural development during the previous four years. It reported on "collapses" in opposition parties' local organizations. It even declared in one column that "If Atatürk had remained healthy, he would doubtlessly have entered the Democrat Party."[3] Its confident tone would not have misled its readers as to the result of the elections on May 2, 1954. The DP's share of the vote rose to 58.4 percent. No party in the subsequent history of the Republic of Turkey has secured such a resounding victory.[4] As a reward for his loyalty, Sarol was made a state minister in the new

[1] Mükerrem Sarol, "Yeni devirlerin ...," *Türk Sesi*, March 25, 1954, 1, 8.

[2] RG, March 17, 1954, 8653; Nuran Yıldız, "Demokrat Parti İktidarı (1950–1960) ve Basın," *Ankara Üniversitesi SBF Dergisi* 51, no. 1 (1996): 492.

[3] Muvaffak Garan, "Atatürk ...," *Türk Sesi*, April 10, 1954, 2.

[4] Türkiye İstatistik Kurumu Başkanlığı (TÜİK), *Milletvekili Genel Seçimleri, 1923–2011* (Türkiye İstatistik Kurumu: Ankara, 2012), 1, 25, available: www.tuik.gov.tr/IcerikGetir.do?istab_id=152.

cabinet with the responsibility of overseeing newspapers. This was a role that Samet Ağaoğlu had filled during much of the DP's first term, and in which he had antagonized journalists by distributing government advertising to pro-DP papers. Now Sarol too would become a bête noire for the national press.

During the DP's second term in power (1954–57), there would be much for the press to criticize. Over these three and a half years, the country's economic condition would deteriorate, and the issue of economic management, which had previously favored the Democrats, would become a political liability. The DP's own policies were often to blame; even as conflict ended on the Korean peninsula, decreasing demand for Turkey's agricultural products and lowering global market prices in general, the government continued to provide loans to farmers and purchase their goods at above-market prices. Credits to businessmen and merchants also continued, albeit at a reduced rate. These expansionary monetary policies doubled the amount of currency in circulation between 1950 and 1955.[5] Inflation accelerated. The real value of the lira fell, and commercial debt to international creditors grew.

Domestically, the risks inherent in many of the government's policies were becoming more apparent than the rewards. National income rose 7.6 percent and 6.2 percent in 1954–55 and 1955–56 respectively, but remained behind inflation of 8.3 percent and 16.8 percent.[6] Prices for basic commodities were rising at rates that citizens could not afford. During this time, urban populations also grew rapidly, driving up rents. Between 1927 and 1950, Turkey's level of urbanization had remained flat, with around 25 percent of the population living in towns and cities; now the proportion rose to 29 percent in the brief period of 1950–55. It would reach 32 percent by 1960.[7] This sudden acceleration in urbanization was stimulated by the government's simultaneous policies of agriculture mechanization and industrialization, which left rural peasants jobless while creating new opportunities in the cities.[8] These new arrivals

[5] Orhan Morgil, "The Social Structure and Economic Development of Turkey, 1950–1960" (PhD diss., University of California, Riverside, 1972), 103. Currency in circulation rose from TL900 million in 1950 to TL1.8 billion in 1955. When bank deposits are included, the stock of money rises from TL1.59 billion to TL4.21 billion (Singer, *The Economic Advance*, 335).

[6] Cillov, *Türkiye Ekonomisi*, 116; Cohn, *Turkish Economic*, 21; Morgil, "The Social Structure," 124.

[7] Dale Lightfoot and Halil Taş, "Gecekondu Settlements in Turkey: Rural–Urban Migration in the Developing European Periphery," *Journal of Geography* 104, no. 6 (2005): 266–267.

[8] Studying villages with an eye to the effects of mechanization was a popular pastime among sociologists and other researchers in the 1950s. According to Singer, the number of

settled on unregistered plots of state land on the outskirts of major cities. And they were not alone in relying on "unofficial" means of securing their livelihood: urban professionals and businesses were turning to the black market to procure consumer products, raw materials, and food.

Fighting black marketeers and attempting to ameliorate the pain of industrialization led DP governments to intervene in the economy to a degree reminiscent of their CHP predecessors and not easily squared with their liberal, anti-statist rhetoric. One important example of this government intervention went wholly unmentioned in the premiere edition of *Türk Sesi*: just a day earlier, on March 24, 1954, new legislation had gone into effect empowering officials to set prices at the local level and to cap profit margins for importers, wholesalers, and retailers at the national level.[9] The new regulations were issued under the authority of the National Protection Law (*Milli Korunma Kanunu*), which had been frequently (and controversially) employed during World War II. The March regulations were limited in their effect, but they set the stage for much more comprehensive legislation in the months and years to come.

As previous chapters have shown, DP leaders were anything but novices at crafting statist, authoritarian policies. Nonetheless, reliance on price controls, credit limits, and inspections constituted a shift in the DP's methods of governing. During the party's early years in power, government policies had benefited from favorable global economic conditions and ample US aid. DP governments could please large numbers of citizens by building factories and roads, cutting taxes, and allowing the unrestricted import of consumer goods. By the mid 1950s, however, government policies were creating losers as well as winners. Facing criticism, DP governments sought to reimpose constraints on the political system, limiting the bounds of public dissent in schools, the media,

tractors in Turkey rose from under 1,756 in 1948 to 42,136 in 1960. A single tractor could do the work of ten farmers. Even accounting for the jobs created by expanded cultivation (and the fact that a lack of spare parts rendered many of these tractors useless), this rapid mechanization served to displace large numbers of workers and concentrate capital in the hands of those wealthy villagers who could afford to invest in expensive equipment (Richard Robinson, "Tractors in the Village: A Study in Turkey," *Journal of Farm Economics* 34, no. 4 [1952]: 451–462; John Hiltner, "Land Accumulation in the Turkish Cukurova," *Journal of Farm Economics* 42, no. 3 [1960]: 615–628; Kemal Karpat, "Social Effects of Farm Mechanization in Turkish Villages," *Social Research* [1960]: 83–103; Singer, *The Economic Advance*, 199).

[9] RG, March 24, 1954. The new price limits were reported in *Zafer* ("Yeni …," *Zafer*, March 25, 1954, 1, 2). The authority for setting prices was given to several different, sometimes overlapping, ministries. For example, prices for domestically produced industrial and mineral products were set by both the ministry of economy and trade and the ministry of operations. Not surprisingly, turf wars between ministries resulted.

and political organizations. As this and the next chapter show, DP governments pursued policies of de-democratization, undermining the institutions needed to ensure democratic competition in order to maintain the party's hold on power.

This chapter focuses on the period beginning with the party's May 1954 electoral triumph and ending with its November 1955 parliamentary group crisis in which the government nearly fell. Within the space of nineteen months, the scale of the economic challenges facing the country came into view. Prime Minister Menderes and his allies, however, resisted calls from economic liberals in their own party (as well as US officials) to devalue the lira, increase taxes, and develop a long-term economic plan. The resulting tensions fractured the DP, leading to the departure of many of its most liberal members.

Making Do with Less in the Mid 1950s

DP governments depended on US aid to underwrite their development programs, but the conclusion of fighting in Korea made Turkey's utility less self-evident to cost-conscious US policymakers in the Eisenhower administration. Leading diplomats like Fatin Rüştü Zorlu continued to emphasize Turkey's importance while simultaneously seeking foreign capital and holding off creditors. Yet, without a single, clear means of demonstrating Turkey's value to US leaders, DP governments pushed on a variety of fronts. In foreign policy, they participated in regional anti-Soviet initiatives, including the Balkan Pact and Baghdad Pact.[10] In their domestic policies, DP leaders muddled through with a mix of price controls, agricultural subsidies, salary hikes, and credit limits. As we saw in the previous chapter, ministers like Enver Güreli attempted to address Turkey's structural trade imbalances as early as 1952. Nonetheless, the government came under pressure from institutions like the IBRD to address Turkey's foreign debt and inflation. Menderes and his officials argued that the IBRD recommendations constituted excessive meddling in Turkey's affairs.[11]

President Bayar's two-month-long US tour in early 1954 led to an especially nasty spat. Outwardly, the visit – the first by a Turkish head of state to the United States – symbolized a high-point in the two countries' relations. Mayors and governors met Bayar as he disembarked from trains; Vice President Nixon greeted him on his arrival in Washington,

[10] For a discussion of the Balkan Pact, see David Stone, "The Balkan Pact and American Policy," *East European Quarterly* 28, no. 3 (1994): 393–407.

[11] Welles Hangen, "World Bank …," *New York Times*, March 21, 1954, 1, 27.

DC; President Eisenhower held a state dinner for him at the White House; and both houses of congress convened to hear him give an address. In New York, Chicago, and Los Angeles, he was feted with musical performances and parades. He was flown over the Hoover Dam; given tours of foundries, oil fields, and cigarette factories; taken to Universal Studios to watch a western being filmed; and presented with the keys to the city of Washington, an honorary law degree from Columbia University, and a complimentary crate of cranberries from a large agricultural corporation with a note explaining that "Turkey and cranberries are a great American tradition – as traditional as the long-standing friendship between your country and ours."[12]

Throughout his travels, Bayar remained focused on his goal of securing increased aid from the US government and increased investment from US firms.[13] In his speeches to gatherings of American notables, he emphasized that there was no distinction between Turkey's economic and military needs. More US aid was necessary if his country were to stand as a bulwark against communist aggression. "Your economic aid," he explained to the US Congress, "has constituted a valuable factor in supporting our efforts to strengthen our economic structure, so that we may maintain a strong army."[14] Three days later, at New York's Waldorf Astoria hotel, he was less optimistic. "Unfortunately," he lamented, "my country is not possessed of such an economic structure as to enable her to carry single-handedly, without going under, the whole burden of a large army."[15]

Though Bayar emphasized in public that his trip was a "goodwill visit" in response to an invitation from Eisenhower, newspapers reported in advance of his arrival that he planned to push for as much as $76 million in additional aid.[16] To strengthen his case, Bayar ensured that his trip

[12] Clay Gowran, "Turkey's Chief Pledges ...," *Chicago Daily Tribune*, February 5, 1954, 14. The film Bayar watched appears to have been *Dawn at Socorro* (Cecil Smith, "Turkish President Greeted Royally," *Los Angeles Times*, February 10, 1954, 1).

[13] Each city on Bayar's US tour was selected with an eye to investment objectives. In Los Angeles and Dallas, Bayar met with oil companies and engineering firms, one of which was in the process of building Turkey's first refinery. In Chicago, he visited the International Harvester tractor plant. Turkey had already imported tens of thousands of tractors from the company and, in addition to posing amiably for photographers atop one model, Bayar complained to the firm's president that sufficient spare parts were not reaching Turkey (Cecil Smith, "Turkish President Departs ...," *Los Angeles Times*, February 11, 1954, A1, 7; Gowran, "Turkey's Chief Pledges ...," *Chicago Daily Tribune*, February 5, 1954, 14).

[14] "Address of His Excellency Celal Bayar, President of Turkey," *Congressional Record* 83, no. 2 (January 29, 1954): 1034–1035.

[15] "Text of Speech ...," *New York Times*, February 2, 1954, 6.

[16] Peter Kihss, "President of Turkey ...," *New York Times*, January 27, 1954, 1.

coincided with the approval of two key bills in Turkey's parliament. One was a new Foreign Capital Investment Law, which allowed foreign firms to repatriate an increased share of the profits they made in Turkey. The other was a defense treaty between Turkey and Pakistan, which laid the groundwork for the Baghdad Pact, an alliance of anti-communist states along the USSR's southern border.[17] Both measures bolstered Bayar's argument that Turkey was an open market to US business and a key partner in achieving the Eisenhower administration's strategy of encircling the USSR with hostile security alliances.

The choice to frame Turkey's problems as the United States' problems paid off. Bayar returned home having secured an additional $30 million in aid for the fiscal year ending on June 30, 1954.[18] Nonetheless, he did not get all that he wanted: when Bayar broached the possibility of a $25 million loan to Eugene Black, the president of the IBRD, he was told that Turkey's generous credit to farmers should first be reconsidered. Bayar replied that Turkey would determine its own economic policies. Upon Bayar's return, Menderes demanded the removal of the IBRD's representative in Turkey and the closure of its offices.[19] In the following months, Menderes continued to attack the bank, threatening to forbid Turkey's representative from attending its meetings and instructing Turkey's UN ambassador to denounce the organization. In the latter case, the US State Department informed Turkey that such an action would make it impossible to hold the next year's IBRD and IMF meetings in Istanbul, as currently planned.[20]

The IBRD was not the only international institution pressing Menderes and his governments. Turkey was deeply enmeshed in the economic system of the US-led Cold War order, a recipient of Marshall Plan funds from the OEEC, credits from the EPU, and loans from the IMF. The flows of capital into Turkey and the government's own expansionist monetary policies led to a far higher rate of inflation than in the countries with which Turkey was trading. The imbalance caused the lira's real value to fall relative to these other countries' currencies. Yet the insistence of DP-led governments on maintaining

[17] The Foreign Capital Investment Law was passed on January 18, 1954, the day Bayar left Turkey on his trip; the treaty with Pakistan was signed on January 26, the day he arrived in the United States. After his return, a new Petrol Law was passed, on March 7 (TBMM, March 7, 1954).

[18] "Bayar Visit Adds …," *New York Times*, March 18, 1954, 5.

[19] Welles Hangen, "World Bank Staff Ousted by Turkey," *New York Times*, March 21, 1954, 1.

[20] John Foster Dulles to US Embassy, Ankara, September 24, 1954, and State Department to US Embassy, Ankara, April 16, 1954, both in RG 84, Box 66, UD 3288, NND 842831 (hereafter RG 84, Box 66).

the peg of TL2.80/$ meant that the cost in lira of Turkish-made goods was far higher than any sensible foreign importer would want to pay. Turkish products became uncompetitive abroad. At the same time, the overvalued exchange rate encouraged Turkish importers to make purchases. The result of DP policies was a growing trade deficit.

By the middle of the 1950s, this situation seemed to be nearing a crisis. Even in 1953, the best year for Turkey's international trade, export earnings of $396 million had not surpassed import costs of $533 million. Even with regulations and reduced credit, the underlying problem hardly improved. Imports averaged $410 million throughout the decade.[21] This ongoing balance of payments deficit meant that Turkey's reserves of gold and foreign currency were routinely insufficient to pay for the foreign products that its producers and consumers desired. The inability to meet demand led to shortages, high prices, and a growing black market for goods obtained through smuggling, hoarding, and inside-dealing. The inability to secure the raw materials needed to operate factories also led to layoffs and the specter of social unrest.[22]

As the demand for Turkish goods abroad diminished in the mid 1950s, the government increasingly resorted to bilateral deals with Western European countries and appeals for assistance like those Bayar made on his US tour. Trying to leverage Turkey's strategic value was a risky economic strategy, but it was a calculated risk in the context of the US Cold War security system. Turkey was a crucial ally in the region, and both its leaders and Western officials understood this strategic reality.

Fighting the Bureaucracy, Profiteers, and Each Other

In presenting his program in May 1954, following the DP's electoral triumph, Menderes emphasized economic accomplishment rather than impending economic crisis. He continued to oppose measures that might constrain the party's economic policies, rejecting suggestions that Turkey should devalue its currency or reduce payments to farmers. He argued that doing so would reduce the foreign exchange earnings of Turkish exports and increase the costs of imported materials for domestic industry. It would, in short, "do nothing other than halt the construction and

[21] William Hale, *The Political and Economic Development of Modern Turkey* (London: Croom Helm, 1981), 105.

[22] Taking 1952 as an example, 45.3 percent of imports consisted of such items as iron, steel, and technical instruments; 10.6 percent consisted of rubber and petroleum products; 35 percent of wool, cotton, and other fabrics; and 15 percent of "luxury goods," including watches, cars, silk, cameras, and film ("Position of Turkey: Report by the Chairman of the Council," OEEC, March 29, 1954, FO 371/111288).

development phase of our national economy and national development drive [*kalkınma hamlesi*]."[23]

He recalled all that had been accomplished since 1950. The Democrats had inherited a country in which "[domestic] security was gone, foreign security was gone, the state's entire reputation had fallen to zero" and transformed it. The DP's first term had been an "age of transition," but the meaning of the 1954 elections was different. The *ancien régime* had campaigned in the election "as if nothing had happened" during the previous four years, but his new government "would not allow the continuation of political struggles based on lies and slander." Such tactics were not in keeping with democracy, which he defined as "a regime of manners, courtesy, and toleration." Yet, "if the administrative, legal, and all State institutions [could] be adjusted according to this view, then a moral climate of democracy would be created." The role of state officials in achieving this "climate" was essential, even if many of them had developed their skills during the single-party era, "according to the needs and demands of a totalitarian administration."[24]

All this talk was subtle in comparison with the goals elaborated ten days earlier in the DP's official paper, *Zafer*. There, former Defense Minister Seyfi Kurtbek had written that, "Before all else, it is necessary to expel the previous fascist regime, remove the institutions of the dictatorship, its traces and influences." The time for the "second leap" had come, and it required "all State organizations to be reformed from A to Z."[25] A day after Menderes's speech, *Zafer* editor Mümtaz Faik Fenik brought together the ideas of both Kurtbek and the prime minister by arguing that "Those considered to be deceivers can never be used in key positions in officialdom."[26] Clearly, the groundwork was being laid for a purge of the bureaucracy and, Menderes hinted, the judiciary as well. Yet while the government did work to remove judges and other officials over the coming months, it was economic conditions, rather than a hostile bureaucracy, that soon became the government's primary challenge.

23 TBMM, May 24, 1954, 27. 24 TBMM, May 24, 1954, 22–25.

25 Seyfi Kurtbek, "İkinci hamle," *Zafer*, May 14, 1954, 2.

26 Mümtaz Faik Fenik, "Kilit ...," *Zafer*, May 26, 1954, 1, 7. According to the journalist Metin Toker and DP executive committee member Rıfkı Salim Burçak, after the election President Bayar gathered the party leadership at the presidential mansion on Çankaya Hill in Ankara and railed against those members of the bureaucracy who had sought office on the CHP list and now expected their positions back (as per the Election Law). According to Toker, Bayar declared that the party's resounding victory meant that the country desired "A break from polite [*ince*] democracy" (Toker, *DP Yokuş Aşağı*, 25–26; Burçak, *On Yılın Anıları*, 223).

During the first months of its new term, however, the government may have still had grounds for optimism. Menderes's US visit in June 1954 focused on securing US aid and was more successful than Bayar's had been.[27] Prior to Menderes's visit, the Eisenhower administration had been considering reducing military aid to Turkey from the $200 million given in the 1953–54 fiscal year down to $87 million in 1954–55.[28] Rather than just fight to maintain the previous year's funding level, Menderes and Zorlu upped their requests and talked up the idea of an $800 million aid package. The US Foreign Operations Administration (FOA) representative to Turkey humored them, but the US ambassador opposed it. The ambassador, along with President Eisenhower and FOA Director Harold Stassen, gave Menderes and Zorlu a stern talk about Turkey's economic situation.[29] Faced with calls for reform, Menderes and Zorlu promised to draw up an economic plan by November. They emerged from meetings having secured promises of $200 million for the US fiscal year starting in July and the payment of nearly $500 million in military aid that had been promised earlier but delayed owing to other US commitments in Indochina and the Korean peninsula.[30]

Upon Menderes's return to Turkey on June 6, the DP legislators turned their attention to penalizing the opposition and consolidating the party's control. Each week brought new legislation. On June 14, Democrats in parliament approved a bill to split the province of Malatya in two, uniting its pro-DP districts into the new province of Adıyaman.[31] A week later, they altered the retirement law to force out

[27] "Visit of Prime Minister of Turkey," Dept of State for the Press, May 25, 1954; British Embassy (Washington) to Foreign Office, June 3, 1954, FO 371/111288. In advance of Menderes's arrival in Washington, the US Department of State announced that the prime minister would be visiting "primarily for the purpose of discussing … certain economic and financial matters of mutual interest." Worried that this phrasing presented Turkey as a supplicant, the Turkish government requested that subsequent statements include mentions of "broader" issues like security.

[28] Hugh Ellis-Rees, "Record of a Conversation with Mr. Webster Todd of FOA Paris, on His Return from Washington [March 15, 1954]," March 16, 1954, FO 371/111287; James Bowker to Anthony Eden, June 12, 1954, FO 371/112936.

[29] "IBRD–IMF," Edmund Hall-Patch to Edward W. Playfair, June 14, 1954; Washington to Foreign Office, June 16, 1954, FO 371/111288. During his visit, Menderes avoided meeting Eugene Black, the president of the IBRD. The two men remained on bad terms after Menderes had demanded the removal of the bank's representative in Turkey a month earlier.

[30] Owen Jones, "Economic Review, Turkey: April–June 1954," August 16, 1954, RG 84, Box 65, UD 3288, NND 842831 (hereafter RG 84, Box 65); James Bowker to Anthony Eden, June 12, 1954, and James Bowker to Geoffrey Harrison, June 18, 1954, FO 371/112936.

[31] On the same day that parliament voted to split the province of Malatya along partisan lines – albeit with the justification that there were "historical" and "geographical" divides

officials who had either served twenty-five years or who were over sixty-five.[32] On June 30, parliament passed a bill removing the provincial status of Kırşehir (the only province won by the small Republican Nation Party) and creating a new province out of those districts that had backed the Democrats. It also passed amendments to the Election Law, which "freed the radio from being used as a tool in electoral struggles" – in other words, denying opposition parties access to the radio while allowing cabinet ministers the ability to tout the DP government's accomplishments.[33]

Finally, on July 5, before parliament took its summer recess, a bill was passed that empowered the government to place officials on leave at reduced salary for six months and fire them if they had not found a different position by that point. The bill passed 309–25, but with 201 abstentions. Among these absent votes were Samet Ağaoğlu and Fevzi Lütfi Karaosmanoğlu, both of whom had once again been left out of the cabinet following the election, and both of whom had subsequently developed significant concerns with the government's "anti-democratic" legislation.[34] At least in Ağaoğlu's case, the concern would not last. In December, he was brought back into government as minister of operations, responsible for overseeing state-owned enterprises. He replaced Fethi Çelikbaş, a former professor of economics and advocate of liberal economic policies. Çelikbaş had angered Prime Minister Menderes by publicly admitting that the country was facing an imminent coal shortage and, privately, advocating that Turkey import coal to make up for the shortfall. Out of government, Çelikbaş joined Karaosmanoğlu in defending democratic principles.[35]

As the coal shortage indicates, amid intraparty squabbles, economic conditions were growing worse. By the time parliament entered its summer recess, it was apparent that the fall harvest would not meet

as well – it also voted to split the province of Kocaeli in two. This change, however, merely created two pro-DP provinces (TBMM, June 14, 1954).

32 TBMM, June 21, 1954.

33 TBMM, June 30, 1954, 6. Amendments to the Electoral Law also prohibited people who ran and lost in party primaries from subsequently running as independents. Changing the electoral law unilaterally in this manner presaged more dramatic amendments. But, on this occasion, the DP was addressing a rather specific intraparty issue: Press and Publications Director Halim Alyot had won in the party's Çanakkale primary but been excluded from the party list. His subsequent campaign as an independent won only 0.8 percent of the vote but still annoyed Menderes (Toker, *DP Yokuş Aşağı*, 35–36).

34 TBMM, July 6, 1954, 476; "Demokrasi," *Akis*, July 3, 1954, 4–5; James Bowker to Anthony Eden, July 16, 1954, FO 371/112924.

35 UK Embassy Ankara to Foreign Office, December 7, 1954, FO 371/112924; "S. Ağaoğlu …," *Akşam*, December 7, 1954, 1, 2; "Kabine," *Akis*, December 11, 1954, 4–5.

expectations, meaning that foreign exchange earnings would be less than predicted and debt higher. In addition, the lira's value was slipping. Despite the steady official rate of TL2.80 to the dollar, the lira's real rate had fallen from TL5.63 in January to TL6.42 by June.[36] The continuing overvaluation of the lira encouraged merchants in Turkey to apply for cheap dollar credit with their liras and import more in the short term, thereby using up the country's available foreign exchange reserves and leading to shortages and debt in the long term.

Regardless of Menderes's confident rhetoric, his governments began taking measures to halt rising prices, shortages, and black-market activity. These policies affected large segments of the population and reminded citizens of the state's coercive power rather than its generosity. To defend their policy shift, DP leaders and their publications also shifted their rhetoric. Reports of ongoing economic hardships were either dismissed as an attempt by opposition journalists to frighten the public or, when acknowledged, explained away as the result of hoarding by "profiteers" and "speculators."[37]

These groups and their activities were to be thwarted using a strengthened version of the Monetary Value Protection Act (*Türk Parası Kıymetini Koruma Kararı*) and stepped-up inspections. New amendments to the act required banks that loaned out money to merchants to turn over all repayments to the Central Bank within a week of receipt. The regulation prevented banks from using this money as the basis for additional loans, which would increase the money supply and drive inflation. Additional new regulations limited the number of import licenses that merchants could apply for in a given period of time. Applications now required a down payment of 10 percent, and, once issued, the validity of licenses was reduced to four months. These new rules were intended to conserve limited foreign exchange reserves and discourage merchants from submitting multiple, speculative applications.[38]

In the short term, inspections of businesses and warehouses pressured merchants to sell their stocks rather than wait for prices to rise. As necessities like sugar reappeared in stores, Fenik declared in *Zafer*

36 "Economic Report No. 1 for the Month of January 1954," British Embassy Ankara, February 8, 1954, and "Economic Report No. 6 for the Month of June 1954," British Embassy Ankara, July 15, 1954, FO 371/112934.

37 "Vurgunculara ...," *Türk Sesi*, June 16, 1954, 1; Mümtaz Faik Fenik, "Vurgunculara ...," *Zafer*, July 8, 1954, 1; "İhtikarla ...," *Zafer*, June 18, 1954, 1, 5; Mümtaz Faik Fenik, "Şekerimiz ...," *Zafer*, November 18, 1954.

38 RG, July 8, 1954, 9843; RG, July 21, 1954, 9919; "Economic Report No. 7 for the Month of July 1954," British Embassy Ankara, August 14, 1954, and "Economic Report No. 9 for the Month of September 1954," British Embassy Ankara, October 14, 1954, FO 371/112934.

that any merchants still withholding their wares "were not Turkish citizens; they were traitors, degenerates. In commerce, they have set morality aside."[39] Yet, just two days later, he pointed to a wholly different cause of shortages: wealth. According to Fenik, the "economic leap" fostered by the Democrats had stimulated a level of consumption that domestic production and foreign exchange reserves had not caught up with.[40] The variety of causes Fenik pointed to suggests that the government and its supporters still had the freedom to choose between either divisive or optimistic narratives to explain the growing economic crisis. In parliament, for example, Minister of Economy and Trade Sıtkı Yırcalı chose the latter, framing present difficulties as the side effect of success.[41]

In the months to come, Fenik and other pro-DP writers would continue to vacillate between explanations of Turkey's economic woes, but an emphasis on morality would persist. *Türk Sesi* explained that the essence of the new legislation lay not in its price fixes but rather in the opportunity it provided for merchants to police their peers and prove "whether merchants [as Atatürk once said] are the trustees of the country, or not. Whether [assuring] the level of dignity and morality in national business life was their essential attribute, or wasn't."[42] One *Zafer* columnist answered the question himself by arguing that merchants were at fault because they lacked "commercial morality," a failing with its roots in the "era of sultans."[43] Another writer likewise argued that those engaged in black-market activity were lacking in higher values: while most people were motivated by "thoughts, principles, and ideals," for some "everything is connected to their stomachs."[44]

By late July, *Zafer* writers were combining these calls for moral commerce with the larger DP project of remaking the bureaucracy, arguing that "honest officials" were needed to prevent profiteering by greedy merchants.[45] The paper praised the upright officials assigned to inspection teams and even sent one journalist to ride along with an Ankara team as it made its rounds. The reporter dramatically described how, "As our automobile sped through the dark streets, [the inspector] explained … 'Our principal is not to penalize the merchants but rather to assure compliance with the laws.'"[46] In *Türk Sesi*, the nobility and effectiveness of these officials were contrasted with the potential among some other

[39] Mümtaz Faik Fenik, "Darlığı …," *Zafer*, June 26, 1954, 1, 7.
[40] Mümtaz Faik Fenik, "Döviz sıkıntısı," *Zafer*, September 28, 1954, 1.
[41] TBMM, July 2, 1954, 390. [42] "Bir döviz …," *Türk Sesi*, July 19, 1954, 1, 7.
[43] Orhan Seyfi Orhon, "Ticaret ahlakı!" *Zafer*, July 6, 1954, 2.
[44] Muazzez Aruoba, "Karaborsa …," *Zafer*, July 27, 1954, 2.
[45] "Karapazar …," *Zafer*, July 21, 1954, 1.
[46] Attila Onuk, "Esnaf …," *Zafer*, October 2, 1954, 3.

officials to be "inefficient" and for this inefficiency to alienate citizens from the government.[47]

Papers (pro-government and otherwise) provided daily reports on the results of inspections: the number of businesses visited; the number of warnings and citations given; the number of merchants sent to court. Among the numerous examples of economic criminality reported in newspapers, the role attributed to foreign actors stands out. Multiple instances of merchants flouting price controls were listed in a given day, but these were often vaguely described as involving "street sellers," "drivers," and so on. More specificity, by contrast, was given to crimes committed by foreigners and citizens from ethnic minorities. Here, names were often stated directly in the paper.[48] Beyond Turkey's borders, foreigners were also depicted as undermining Turkey's economy and the value of its currency. A *Zafer* column in July 1954 argued that lira and Turkish products were being smuggled across the Syrian border but reassured readers that the finance ministry was taking "measures" to address the outflow.[49] In such stories, the press did little to encourage readers that contact with the outside world was to the benefit of the population.

The DP leaders and their allies in the media were presenting a vision of Turkey's economic development in which national self-sufficiency was the ultimate objective. Foreign trade and foreign investment played a role in realizing the government's development goals, but that role was wholly functional, not part of some larger commitment to the free flow of capital.[50] The goal was to build factories that could provide for basic needs in the short term and industrial needs in the long term. To this end, the government continued building new sugar, cement, and fertilizer plants, as well as dams and power plants to supply electricity. In most cases, the state partnered with foreign firms during the construction process. French and German firms, for example, divvied up tenders for twenty new cement factories in January 1954. By May, talks were

[47] Vakur Versan, "Bürokrasi ...," *Türk Sesi*, August 21, 1954, 2.

[48] For example, contrast "Belediyenin kontrolleri" (The Municipality's Inspections), *Zafer*, July 6, 1954, 3, which talks in general terms with "450 bin dolarlık büyük bir döviz kaçakçılığı" (a big forex smuggling of $450,000), *Zafer*, July 15, 1954, 1, 7, which specifically names the Bank of Salonica official caught smuggling foreign exchange. The most eye-catching example (at least from my perspective!) is the case of a merchant named Ruben Asa, which dragged on for over a year in 1956–57.

[49] Mümtaz Faik Fenik, "Cenup ...," *Zafer*, July 31, 1954, 1, 3.

[50] To those who argued that the government was repeating the mistakes of the Ottomans by opening the economy up to foreign capital, Mümtaz Faik Fenik observed that the United States too had once been dependent on the investment of foreign nations ("Yabancı ...," *Zafer*, May 15, 1954, 1, 7).

underway with the US firm Minneapolis-Moline to build a tractor factory.[51] Yet these deals should not be overstated; the actual level of foreign investment during the DP's decade of rule was inconsistent, especially when contrasted with the steady increase in public expenditure.[52] Nonetheless, the impression of large-scale foreign investment was encouraged in part by the media, which reported any rumor of possible investment, thereby giving the sense of ceaseless activity.

Many reports of foreign investment came and went with little investigation or follow-up. A notable exception was Migros, a Swiss grocery chain. Its owner, the businessman and politician Gottlieb Duttweiler, visited Istanbul in January 1954 to advise municipal officials on how to deal with rising food prices. His recommendation for a fleet of trucks, moving around the city, offering standardized prices that would force down the rates that local merchants could charge was received with enthusiasm by the ministry of economy and trade. Duttweiler was invited back a month later, this time to discuss the possibility of establishing his firm in Istanbul, with 70 percent of its TL7 million initial capital provided by the Central Bank and with President Bayar's son Turgut overseeing the organization.[53] Until the first Migros trucks began making their rounds in late 1955, the progress of the deal was a frequent topic in newspapers.

Turkey also signed a credit deal with the Federal Republic of Germany (FRG, i.e., "West Germany") in December 1954. Menderes had laid the groundwork two months earlier by traveling to Bonn and meeting with West German officials. To endear himself in advance, he authorized the repayment of $25 million of Turkey's $40 million in outstanding commercial debt to West Germany. The meetings ended with a joint

[51] Yasa (ed.), *Cumhuriyet Dönemi Türkiye Ekonomisi*, 62–63; Sey, *Türkiye Çimento Tarihi*, 68–71.

[52] According to Hamdi Kara and Nuri Yavan in "Türkiye'de Doğrudan Yabancı Yatırımları ve Bölgesel Dağılışı," *Coğrafi Bilimler Dergisi* 1, no. 1 (2003), foreign direct investment in 1954 was $2.2 million, followed by $1.2 million (1955), $3.4 million (1956), $1.3 million (1957), $1.1 million (1958), $3.4 million (1959), and $1.9 million (1960) (29). These numbers can be compared with the private/public state investments for these years: TL1.2 billion/TL925 million ($428 million/$330 million) in 1954; TL1.3 billion/TL925 million ($464 million/$330 million) in 1955; TL1.1 billion/TL940 million ($393 million/$336 million) in 1956; TL1.1 billion/TL1 billion ($393 million/$357 million) in 1957; TL1.2 billion/TL905 million ($428 million/$323 million) in 1958; TL1.2 billion/TL1 billion in 1959 ($133 million/$111 million); TL1.2 billion/TL1.2 billion (both $133 million) in 1960. Though these domestic investment numbers are similar from year to year, it should be noted that from August 1958 onward, the lira effectively fell from TL2.80/$ to TL9/$ (Yasa [ed.], *Cumhuriyet Dönemi Türkiye Ekonomisi*, 74–75).

[53] İhsan Tekeli, *Cumhuriyetin Belediyecilik Öyküsü, 1923–1990* (Istanbul: Tarih Vakfi Yurt Yayınları, 2009), 165–167.

communiqué promising increased investment in Turkey. This plan, hashed out in December, promised 225 marks ($53 million) of credit through the middle of 1955 to purchase West German exports.[54] The deal constituted more of a stopgap measure than a long-term solution, allowing Menderes's government to avoid changing course. Turkey's overall trade deficit grew by 29 percent over 1955, reaching $185 million. Meanwhile, the lira lost another 27 percent of its value against the dollar as the government insisted on maintaining the peg of TL2.80 to the dollar (rather than TL8.40).[55] The growing divergence in value encouraged smuggling and stimulated black-market activity, since anyone in possession of dollars would be foolish to turn them in to a bank in return for lira at the official rate.

In budget debates during the early months of 1955, DP leaders maintained that the economic situation was under control in the face of growing criticisms from within the party. In late January, members of the budget committee issued a report criticizing the outflow of foreign exchange and rising prices. In response, Minister of Economy and Trade Sıtkı Yırcalı reminded the committee of the government's accomplishments and promised that recent trade deals would ease the situation.[56] Addressing foreign audiences in the French magazine *La Revue Française*, Yırcalı assured readers that the government was still committed to the DP's liberal program of 1950. The country had "opened a new age in its economic life … supportive of the Turkish nation's individual enterprise," wherein the state "played the role of intellectual organizer" for private enterprise and worked to increase the value of the people's collective efforts so that they would be successful in their contact with the world market.[57] In the budget committee, Yırcalı was stalling for time. In foreign publications, he was depicting a set of policies with little connection to the reality that many citizens in Turkey were experiencing.

[54] "Müşterek …," *Zafer*, December 22, 1954, 1, 7; "Economic Report No. 10 for the Month of October 1954," November 16, 1954, FO 371/112934.

[55] "European Payments Union: The Economic Situation of Turkey," OEEC, May 3, 1958, 21, FO 134424. The exchange rate of the lira to the dollar was $1 = TL6.60 in October 1954; by November 1955, it had fallen to TL8.40 ("Economic Report No. 12 for the Month of November 1954," 12/9/54, FO 371/112934 Economic Reports 1954; Ankara to FO, 10/17, FO 371/117730).

[56] "İktisadi …," *Zafer*, January 21, 1955, 1, 7; *Akis*, January 29, 1955, 11. Among the critical members of the budget committee were Feridun Ergin, Ekrem Cenani, Haluk Timurtaş, and Kenan Akmanlar. Despite their criticisms, all but Ergin remained with the party and were reelected in 1957.

[57] Translation of a February 1, 1955 column, reprinted as "Türkiye'nin iktisadi hamlesi," in *Zafer*, February 11, 1955.

The 1955–56 budget, passed on February 28, did not signal an effort to restrain spending. It totaled TL2.9 billion – 26 percent larger than the previous year's budget – with a deficit of TL151 million. This deficit did not include the budgets of state-owned enterprises, which were approved separately and operated at a loss.[58] Moreover, members of parliament both rejected an income tax *and* increased their own monthly salaries from TL1,500 to TL2,800 – a fairly substantial amount, considering that the average monthly salary of a male worker in Ankara was around TL300.[59] Nonetheless, the successful passage of a budget and the opening of the long-touted Minneapolis-Moline tractor factory four days later gave Menderes and other party leaders an opportunity to remind voters of their accomplishments.[60]

As late as May 1955, government officials maintained their hope that additional US aid might help them through their difficulties. *Türk Sesi* explained that Turkey devoted "a large portion of our budget" to improving military readiness for the benefit of NATO and reiterated the argument that Turkey, being a "less developed" country, should not be expected to bear such burdens alone.[61] Fatin Rüştü Zorlu made this same argument during his June visit to the United States, yet he emerged from talks empty-handed. The Eisenhower administration and US-dominated institutions such as the IBRD doubted whether the DP government had a plan to deal with credit, inflation, and state enterprise debt.[62]

This critique was not merely a foreign one. The lack of explicit economic planning had become a rallying cry for both CHP politicians and opponents of Menderes within the DP. *Zafer* pushed back against critics, arguing that, for all their talk of "plans," they offered no specifics. Perhaps this meant they were thinking of the "totalitarian" planning

[58] RG, March 1, 1955; Cillov, *Türkiye Ekonomisi*, 530. According to the OEEC, state-owned enterprises' costs were covered by a combination of budgetary allocations, money from state pension funds and insurance funds, and the amortization fund into which commercial banks placed their minimum reserve requirements ("European Payments Union: The Economic Situation of Turkey," OEEC, May 3, 1958, 13, FO 371/134424).

[59] Eric Wendelin to Department of State, June 8, 1955, RG 84, Box 72, UD 3288, NND 959265 (hereafter RG 84, Box 72). The average daily salary of an Ankara worker in 1955 was TL9.25 (TL277.50/month). By 1957, it had risen to TL10.81 (TL324.30/month); a janitor made a monthly salary of TL150–300, a chauffeur TL350–600, and the general manager of a state factory TL1,200–2,000. Foreign language skills could raise salaries by one-third ("Labor Report, Turkey – January 1958 through June 1958," August 13, 1958, RG 84, Box 79, UD 3288, NND 959265 [hereafter RG 84, Box 79]).

[60] "İlk traktör ...," *Zafer*, March 5, 1955, 1, 7.

[61] Zeynel Besim Sun, "Amerikalı ...," *Türk Sesi*, April, April 29, 1955, 1, 5; Zeynel Besim Sun, "Türkiye-Amerika," *Türk Sesi*, May 7, 1955, 1, 5.

[62] Chancery (Ankara) to Foreign Office, June 11, 1955, FO 117730.

models of the interwar years rather than New Deal–style ones.[63] In *Türk Sesi*, a DP legislator wrote confidently that "Our American friends will not delay in repairing the miserliness shown to our country, which holds the key to security in the East, and thus common sense will yet triumph."[64] The government issued a statement accusing the opposition of using the lack of additional US aid to spark panic for its own political gain, declaring, "We are facing an economic and financial assassination attempt. There is no doubt of the desire to shake our political stability by these means."[65] DP leaders like Samet Ağaoğlu took to the radio to report on the progress of their ministries and reiterate the government's accusations. Ağaoğlu emphasized his desire to counter a "sneaky propaganda operation, which tries to achieve through secretive efforts a means of creating a general economic crisis."[66]

But, for all their talk of imminent support, the summer was approaching. During these months, with the harvest still to come and little to market abroad, Turkey's foreign exchange reserves typically fell to their lowest levels. The government found itself left with little choice but to raise the price of state-produced consumer goods like tea and cigarettes, constrict credit, and discourage all but essential imports.[67] Enforcing these policies necessitated a reassertion of state power over private enterprise.

The legislation passed in 1952–54 had laid the groundwork for extending state authority, but as economic conditions grew worse, calls for action intensified. As we have seen, despite the statements of ministers in favor of private enterprise and liberal economics, suspicion of merchants and commerce persisted. One *Türk Sesi* columnist argued that wealthy citizens should spend their money on social welfare rather than frivolities.[68] Turkey, he argued, "like any nation on the road of development ... must enter a period of troubles ... in order to live, we must sacrifice."[69] If necessary, luxury goods should be banned, since that would be preferable to fully adopting a system of statism.[70] In a column titled "The Era of Precautionary Measures," *Zafer* asserted that other NATO countries like Canada and Greece were also facing the challenge of "profiteers" and reiterated that "Turkey is in a developmental leap.

63 "Plan ...," *Zafer*, June 21, 1955.
64 Hüseyin Hüsnü Yaman (a DP representative for Kırklareli), "Amerikan ...," *Türk Sesi*, June 17, 1955, 1, 5.
65 "Muhalefetin meş'um ...," *Zafer*, July 4, 1955, 1, 3.
66 "İşletmeler Vekili ...," *Zafer*, July 6, 1955.
67 Avra Warren to Department of State, June 29, 1955, RG 84, Box 72.
68 Zeynel Besim Sun, "Varlıklı vatandaşlar," *Türk Sesi*, January 13, 1955, 2.
69 Zeynel Besim Sun, "Hayat ...," *Türk Sesi*, January 23, 1955, 1, 3.
70 Zeynel Besim Sun, "Yatırımlar ...," *Türk Sesi*, January 21, 1955, 1, 3.

As a final phase of the great Turkish revolution, protective measures appear more necessary than ever."[71] Far from Ankara, a columnist for *Demokrat Malatya* took a less restrained view, arguing that "More modern than the atom bomb, sharper than a sword, we have THE NATIONAL PROTECTION LAW."[72]

The DP government also saw the National Protection Law as an essential tool for addressing inflation and shortages of key products. New legislation came on July 11, 1955. Some of it had been in the works for months. *Zafer* had already reported that businesses might soon be required to post prices in order to prevent price gouging, and that the distribution of essential materials might soon be overseen by the provincial governor in consultation with local governments.[73] Now these measures became a reality. They were followed by a new decree increasing penalties for hoarding and overcharging to as much as TL10,000 in fines and over three years in jail. Businesses were given two days to provide lists of their stocks of essential goods, including tin, tires, sacks, nails, iron and steel, rubber, aluminum, and fertilizer. In explaining the new measures on the radio, Sıtkı Yırcalı and Samet Ağaoğlu both suggested that new punishments were in store for any news outlets that stirred up the public with rumors of shortages.[74] In the days that followed, pro-government papers reported on the diligence of inspection teams, the successful measures against cross-border smuggling, the establishment of coordinating bodies at the local level, and the reappearance of products on store shelves.[75] All this positive coverage was buttressed by the press law, which prohibited any news that might be construed as causing "general panic and excitement."

Outfoxing Allies: Debt and Trade Negotiations

Exercising control over the domestic economy and media was only one strategy the DP pursued. Equally important were DP governments' ongoing efforts to secure aid from the United States and other allies. As we have seen, Bayar and Menderes often asked directly for aid, but

[71] "Tedbirler devri," *Zafer*, July 6, 1955, 1, 7.
[72] Doğan Toros, "Karaborsalar," *Demokrat Malatya*, March 4, 1955, 1.
[73] "Kar …," *Zafer*, March 31, 1955, 1; "Bazı …," *Zafer*, May 4, 1955, 1, 7.
[74] "Muhtekir …," *Türk Sesi*, July 9, 1955, 1, 2; "Muhtekirlere …" and "S. Ağaoğlu …," *Zafer*, July 9, 1955, 1, 7; RG, July 11, 1955, 1; Thomas Brimelow to O'Brien, July 21, 1955, FO 117728.
[75] "Müsbet …," *Zafer*, July 11, 1955, 1, 7; "Piyasa …," *Zafer*, July 11, 1955, 3; "Kaçakçılara …," *Zafer*, July 12, 1955, 1, 7; "Muhtekirlerle …," *Zafer*, July 13, 1955, 1, 7; "Hükümetin …," *Türk Sesi*, July 18, 1955, 1.

the project of securing funds involved many diplomats as well – Zorlu chief among them, but also ambassadors and representatives to international institutions like the OEEC. Delaying old payments while soliciting new ones was difficult and risked antagonizing creditors. Given the size of Turkey's debts, these officials had to perform a delicate balancing act, emphasizing the reliability and centrality of Turkey to the Cold War struggle but also the seriousness of its financial need. Throughout the mid 1950s, Zorlu and other diplomats found themselves fending off efforts to make Turkey pay up.

One means by which foreign creditors might pressure the Turkish government was the EPU and the council of the OEEC, which administered it. The EPU existed to increase trade between Western European countries by making all currencies in the union interchangeable, convertible to credits that could be paid back in dollars and gold. Member countries were required to reduce trade barriers with one another, but could maintain them with non-EPU countries. Were a country like Turkey to use up its credits, it would be referred to the OEEC, which would then give it "advice," lest it lose access to the EPU and its benefits.[76] This was precisely the point that Turkey had reached by early 1954. Yet, despite Turkey having reached the point at which profligate economic policies would seem to have made it vulnerable to the terms of its creditors, Turkish officials were able to play their Western allies against each other, thereby avoiding immediate concessions or acknowledgement of economic mismanagement. The image of the DP as competent stewards of the economy helped secure the party a victory in the May 1954 elections.

Turkey's creditor countries understood that Turkey was too important to fail. Consequently, although each country's diplomats claimed they were committed to collectively pressuring Turkey to implement economic reforms, their economic officials were busily negotiating separate, bilateral deals.[77] In August 1953, for example, Turkey signed a repayment agreement with the UK and a credit deal with West Germany.[78] In both cases, Turkey prioritized repayment debts to these two countries

[76] Barry Eichengreen, "The European Payments Union: An Efficient Mechanism for Rebuilding Europe's Trade?," in *Europe's Post-War Recovery*, ed. Barry Eichengreen (Cambridge: Cambridge University Press, 1995), 169–173.

[77] Turkey's continued use of bilateral deals as a means of resisting the pressures exerted by institutions of the liberal order was not new: as Samuel Hirst argues, this was also a strategy of the interwar years (*Against the Liberal Order*, 34–54).

[78] For the UK deal, see Chapter 3, n. 57. In the case of West Germany, Turkey promised agricultural exports in return for industrial goods such as pharmaceuticals and trucks ("Economic Report No. 8 for the Month of August 1953," September 7, 1953, 4, FO 371/107559).

rather than others. This lack of unity among Western European creditors was, in turn, pointed to by US officials as a reason for not fully backing the demands those countries placed on Turkey. In March 1954, the US FOA, which oversaw military development in countries like Turkey, explicitly told British economic officials that the United States "could not be sympathetic" to OEEC attempts to make Turkey devote its resources to paying back its debt within three years if, as rumor had it, West Germany was offering a seven-year deal. At the same time, US officials emphasized:

> [U]nless some help was given to Turkey in return for a programme of internal measures, exporters [in the United States and Western Europe] would take the law into their own hands and Turkish imports would be reduced. Those countries that were interested in Turkey, militarily and politically, would have to take this into account.[79]

In other words, Turkish officials and businessman were operating with a safety net.

Rather than serving as a tool for forcing Turkish officials to alter their domestic economic agenda, the council of the OEEC's reports and recommendations in 1954 became, at best, a means of making the Turkish government provide a full accounting of the country's commercial debt. Yet even forming a clear picture of the Turkish financial situation was difficult, because Turkey's representative to the OEEC, Mehmet Ali Tiney, delayed providing information. When he finally did, he used a categorization scheme that ignored nearly $100 million of potential debt.[80] Though he accepted the dire findings of the OEEC report when it was presented to him in March 1954, he asked that it not be released until after the May 2 election. The council president replied that the council was "more or less reconciled to the impossibility or the undesirability of making all the recommendations they would like to make until the elections were over and a new Government was established."[81] Tiney's request and the OEEC's willingness to delay had a circular logic: the DP government was asking the institution to delay publicizing the problems occurring under DP rule lest the news influence

[79] Hugh Ellis-Rees, "Record of a Conversation with Mr. Webster Todd of FOA Paris, on His Return from Washington [March 15, 1954]," March 16, 1954, FO 371/111287.

[80] "Note by the Chairman of the Council: Coordination of Work in Regard to Turkish Affairs: Arrears of Payment," January 18, 1954, FO 371/111287. Turkish officials only wanted to count imports for which importers had already secured licenses and customs visas. This calculation left out purchases for which orders had been placed but were not yet in hand – a substantial amount of trade at any given moment.

[81] Hugh Ellis-Rees, "Record of Conversation with M. Tiney, Turkish Delegate, on 16th March, 1954," March 17, 1954, FO 371/111288.

people's decision in the upcoming referendum on DP rule. Though Tiney himself was a nonpartisan official – he remained in his post after the 1960 coup – he and other diplomats were following instructions that served the interests of the DP more than any national interest.

In addition to asking the OEEC itself for special consideration, Turkish officials focused on addressing the particularistic concerns of OEEC member states. West German Chancellor Konrad Adenauer visited in late March 1954 and signaled his willingness to find a solution to the issue of Turkish arrears to his country. Though he gave lip-service to the EPU (and though West German diplomats maintained that they were committed to a multilateral approach), Adenauer had other interests. He sought to appease German exporters who wanted quick payment and to maintain a German presence in the Turkish market against competitors like the French and British, as well as secure Turkish support for his policy of West German integration into NATO. When pushed to defend their retreat from multilateralism, German officials argued that the British-chaired council of the OEEC had not "shown energy" in its dealings with Turkey.[82]

By late May 1954, Turkish officials were securing bilateral deals with both Switzerland and France, and Menderes was preparing for his post-election trip to the United States. Prior to Menderes's departure, Melih Esenbel, the foreign ministry undersecretary responsible for economic affairs, visited the UK embassy in Ankara and made it clear that Turkey was open to a bilateral deal with Britain as well.[83] British officials replied that they could not make such deals, on account of their commitment to multilateralism and their inability to pressure Britain's domestic merchants. Among themselves, however, these officials were in discussions about how to make precisely such a deal. As matters stood, Turkey owed the UK around $30 million, second only to Germany, which was owed $40 million.[84]

In the final days before Menderes's departure to Washington, he and Zorlu met repeatedly with the UK ambassador to push the idea of a

[82] British Embassy (Ankara) to Foreign Office, March 27, 1954; John Leckie to John Coulson, May 11, 1954; F. Hoyer Millar to Foreign Office, May 12, 1954; and F. Hoyer Millar to Foreign Office, May 18, 1954, all in FO 371/112938.

[83] James M. Walsh to Nicolas Cheetham, May 26, 1954, FO 371/111288.

[84] Hugh Ellis-Rees to Foreign Office, May 26, 1954, FO 371/111288. Another reason that British officials were hesitant to cut a deal was their concern that such a move would anger members of the Commonwealth such as Australia (which had just been turned down for a loan) and economic dependants like Brazil (which had also been pressured in recent months) (W. W. Wilson, "Turkey and OEEC," June 8, 1954, FO 371/111288).

bilateral deal so that the UK would not end up with worse terms than other countries. When, on May 29, the UK ambassador reiterated the need for adopting OEEC recommendations, Zorlu declared that such "multilateral" suggestions were unacceptable, because they required Turkey to reduce its agricultural subsidies when the *real* problem was that Western European countries were not buying sufficient amounts from Turkey. What Turkey needed, he argued, were "bilateral solutions."[85] It was hardly incidental that these deals would enable Turkish diplomats to negotiate with creditors individually rather than as a united front. The following day, Turkey signed such an agreement with West Germany. It provided Turkey with additional credit from the EPU in return for sales of Turkish grain.[86]

Returning from Washington, Menderes, Zorlu, and the diplomatic corps resumed their efforts to cut separate deals with Western European trading partners. At the OEEC, with the election over, Representative Tiney now rejected the Council's official findings and recommendations, reiterating his superiors' argument that bilateral deals were necessary.[87] In pursuit of such a deal, Menderes traveled to West Germany in October 1954 to negotiate limited debt payments in return for additional short-term credit. These successful negotiations undercut any effort at placing collective pressure on Turkey.

Turkish officials further strengthened their bargaining position by solving another problem that might be used as leverage against Turkey in negotiations: food shortages. In November, following another dismal harvest, Turkey secured 500,000 tons of grain from the United States. The terms were favorable. Instead of using dollars, Turkey would be able to exchange chrome ore for the first 100,000 tons of grain; the rest could be purchased with a combination of Turkish lira, which the United States would then use to improve Turkey's military and pay off its own commercial debts to Turkey, and US dollars that had already been earmarked

[85] James Bowker to Foreign Office, May 31, 1954, FO 371/111288.

[86] Charles Johnston to Foreign Office, June 3, 1954, FO 371/111288. As part of the 1954 deal with West Germany, Turkey accepted that some grain would be re-exported to Israel. Given Turkey's general opposition to re-exportation, this was an important concession. Turkish diplomats in the 1950s often stipulated in commercial treaties that Turkish goods not be re-exported, because they understood that established firms in Western Europe could market Turkish products such as tobacco, cotton, and grain with greater ease than Turkish merchants could – and, by doing so, they reduced Turkey's direct access to those markets and, thus, foreign exchange (Raymond Mikesell, *Foreign Exchange in the Postwar World* [Maryland: The Twentieth Century Fund, 1954], 301–303).

[87] Hugh Ellis-Rees to Foreign Office, June 24, 1954, FO 371/111288.

for Turkey via the FOA.[88] The deal bought Turkish officials time to continue negotiations with the country's trading partners, but it underlined Turkey's dependence on American largesse, even in an area like agriculture, where the country was supposed to be strong.[89] Even the editors at *Türk Sesi* acknowledged the uncomfortable reality that "although we are an agricultural country, we find it necessary to import grain," before going on to attribute the situation to the "lazy mentality which dominated the previous regime."[90]

US officials in Ankara also felt that the grain deal had reduced their ability to exert pressure on the Turkish government.[91] The US commercial counselor in Ankara complained to his British counterpart that Zorlu believed "the Turks need not bestir themselves unduly as they can, in the last resort, always rely on the US to extricate them from their economic difficulties ... [and the grain deal] would no doubt confirm him in his wrong-headedness."[92] Given that Turkey's mixture of stonewalling multilateral institutions, cutting bilateral deals, and using funds intended for security purposes to shore up its economy had been largely successful, it is difficult to see where Zorlu and his officials were "wrong-headed" in their calculations. The only setback was that the Turkish government would have preferred that the deal not be made public – a request that their US counterparts claimed was impossible.[93]

The unwillingness of US diplomats to bend on the issue of publicity may have reflected frustration with their Turkish peers. In early January 1955, the FOA representative complained to British diplomats of Turkey's reliance on "secret" deals and its leaders' belief that the

[88] Francis Lincoln to William Baxter, March 4, 1955, RG 59, Lot 58, Box 2, D610, NND 917365 (hereafter RG 59, Lot 58, Box 2). FOA funds were allowed to cover 100,000 tons; lira could cover 300,000.

[89] State Department Press Release, November 16, 1954, FO 371/112940.

[90] Burhan Apaydın, "Türk iktisadi ...," *Türk Sesi*, August 22, 1954, 1, 7.

[91] Grain sales to Turkey were a source of interdepartmental tension in the US government. The agriculture department (and some members of congress) questioned why Turkey should receive any grain so long as it continued to sell certain varieties to secure foreign exchange. The US government also received complaints from Turkey: as the State Department was pushing the deal through, Undersecretary Melih Esenbel complained to US diplomats in Ankara that the terms were too harsh (Memorandum of Conversation, November 9, 1954, RG 59, Lot 58, Box 2).

[92] State Department Press Release, November 16, 1954; Thomas Brimelow to O'Brien (BOT), November 20, 1954; David Scott Fox to William H. Young, November 29, 1954, FO 371/112940.

[93] Ronald Bailey to D. M. O'Brien, January 6, 1955, FO 117730. Even as the grain deal was going through in November 1954, US embassy officials were reporting that the DP government "was not decisively implementing its stabilization process" (Owen Jones, "Economic Review, Turkey: July–September, 1954," November 26, 1954, Economic Matters General, 1953–54 File, RG 84, Box 65).

United States would "bail them out." He referred to Menderes and Zorlu as "unscrupulous foxes."[94] Yet their methods were having results. Western European countries, unable to pressure Turkey, now raced to secure priority over their fellow creditor nations. On January 17, 1955, the UK signed a bilateral deal by which Turkey would repay £12 million ($33 million) in arrears. Ten days later, the Italians followed suit.

With several of Turkey's major European trading partners now tied to bilateral deals, Turkish diplomats again began wooing both the United States and the OEEC for more aid. They were met with more resistance than before. Undersecretary Melih Esenbel visited Washington in March 1955 to ask for additional grain purchases using lira rather than dollars, but made little headway.[95] He was only able to secure a modest deal – Turkish manganese in return for American wool; Turkish lira in return for cottonseed oil.[96]

Despite their meager results, Esenbel's efforts in Washington were a major success compared with Zorlu's simultaneous dealings in Ankara. During March, he met with the US ambassador, Avra Warren, and Leon Dayton, the director of the FOA in Turkey, to discuss the possibility of a $300 million loan for the 1955–56 year. These meetings went poorly. Zorlu emphasized that Turkey was strategically placed "at [the] junction of capitalist and communist economic systems," and yet the standard of living was lower than in countries like Poland or Bulgaria.[97] The US officials were unmoved by these arguments and suggested that Turkey should do more to rein in imports. Reports of these demands were leaked

[94] "Discussion with Mr. Dayton," included in James Bowker to William Young, January 10, 1955, FO 371/117730.

[95] Malcolm Gale to G. G. Simpson, March 5, 1955, FO 371/117730.

[96] One reason for the US unwillingness to receive more lira was the DP's exchange-rate policy. The DP government continued to resist a devaluation. From the US government's perspective, this intransigence created negative incentives for US soldiers in Turkey. If they traded in their dollars on the base and bought lira at the official rate of TL2.80, they would receive far less than they would on the black market. Consequently, many soldiers refused to buy from the US government's stock of lira and simply sold their dollars on the black market, where the rate was more than TL6 to the dollar. Lacking a means of disposal, the official US supply of lira continued to grow – as did the discontent of the US officials. US diplomats in Ankara found themselves under pressure from both the military and their own staff to press the Turkish government for a better rate, but the State Department in Washington felt that pushing Turkey to establish multiple rates would be interpreted by the Turkish government as an attempt to force a devaluation. After all, if the Turkish government admitted that its declared rate was not good enough for the US, how could it justify that rate as good enough for its other trading partners? (British Embassy [Ankara] to Foreign Office, October 17, 1955, FO 371/117730; "Cost of Living in Turkey," February 15, 1955, RG 59, Lot 58, Box 1.)

[97] Avra Warren to State, March 8, 1955, RG 84, Box 72.

to the opposition paper *Dünya* (World), which employed the wife of Aydın Yalçın, an academic and occasional writer for *The Economist*, whom the US embassy had been employing to develop its in-house analysis of Turkey's economic policies. Furious, Menderes accused Yalçın of being part of a "small group, mainly journalists with communist connections … [who were] attempting to undermine [the Turkish] government and Turco-American relations."[98]

At the following meeting on March 21, Dayton pressed Zorlu on touchy subjects such as whether the government would include the debts from state-owned enterprises in the general budget and whether the government had accounted for spare parts when allocating foreign exchange to import tractors and other equipment. These questions, Dayton emphasized, had been raised by the "working group" in Washington on account of the "small staff" in Ankara – in other words, he implied, they did not come from Yalçın. According to the US account of the meeting, the discussion then grew acrimonious:

> [Zorlu] retorted … with considerable vehemence. He said that if there is a working group on this problem in Washington, they should come here to discuss it with the Turks … what the Turks need is a prompt decision on the part of the United States … The Turkish credit deficit is largely a result of the "trade liberalization program" which the United States encouraged.

Further, Zorlu dismissed Dayton's questions as "theoretical discussions." When the ambassador tried to ease tensions by suggesting that a high-level State Department delegation be sent, Zorlu replied that:

> The Turkish problem is a simple one. He could not believe that the Turks would be expected to slow up their investment program and cut consumption and the standard of living of a people who even now were on minimum standards … If the United States does not give help, the Turkish Government will simply have to say so to the Turkish people and to explain that their difficulties are due to American unwillingness to help.

Dayton replied that "no reasonable United States official has ever advised" the Turks to "cut the investment rate beyond their capacity to pay." Rather than let the issue rest, Zorlu observed that Dayton "was a fine specimen of an economist; but he could only offer advice within the material means he gets." Dayton pointed out that "he was no economist, but he was a businessman" and "wondered if Mr. Zorlu had ever applied

[98] James Bowker to W. H. Young, August 6, 1954, FO 371/112931; quote from Avra Warren to State Department, March 21, 1955, RG 84, Box 72.

to a bank for a loan." The meeting ended on this note, though the men agreed to continue such consultations in the future.[99]

The following week, the Turkish government tried a different tack. The OEEC deputy general secretary, John Cahan, was flown to Ankara, put up in the bridal suite of the Ankara Palas hotel, and given a pair of Cadillacs for the duration of his stay. In meetings, Zorlu even went so far as to admit that a reduction in spending might be necessary, provided it fell on cities rather than the countryside. Though Cahan told British diplomats he would lobby the OEEC on Turkey's behalf if the government implemented reforms, he was not encouraged by his conversations with Zorlu.[100]

The Afro-Asian (or "Bandung") Conference, held in April 1955, just weeks after this series of unsuccessful meetings, provided Zorlu with an important opportunity to remind Turkey's allies of the country's value. US officials worried that the meeting of newly independent countries, including India, Indonesia, and Egypt, would condemn defensive alliances like NATO and the Southeast Asian Treaty Organization (SEATO) as detrimental to world peace. Such a rejection would leave US allies like Iraq, Iran, Pakistan, the Philippines, and Turkey isolated in their regions, looking like Western puppets, on account of their participation in such organizations. It was important, therefore, that any effort to oppose these alliances be defeated. In addition, US officials wanted any formal denunciation of colonialism to implicate Soviet domination in Eastern Europe and Chinese rule over Turkic peoples. In his speeches and committee meetings, Zorlu made the arguments that US officials hoped to hear. He defended alliances like NATO and drew attention to the neo-imperialism of communist regimes.[101]

Zorlu's willingness to support defensive alliances included Turkey's own regional alliance with Iraq, Iran, Pakistan, and the UK (the Baghdad Pact). The inspiration for the pact was rooted in the British desire for a "Middle Eastern Command" that would protect UK interests in the Middle East and Eastern Mediterranean. These included airfields, oil fields, naval bases, and the Suez Canal, all of which British leaders

[99] The meeting transcript is included in Avra Warren to State Department, March 23, 1955, RG 84, Box 72.

[100] Thomas Brimelow to G. G. Simpson, March 30, 1955, FO 371/117727.

[101] In addition to a speech defending defensive alliances like NATO, Zorlu also criticized the wisdom of nonalignment. During a discussion on nuclear disarmament, Zorlu suggested that Indian prime minister Jawaharlal Nehru's attempts to find a middle path in the Cold War would lead him to a fate similar to that of deposed Czechoslovakian leader Edward Benes ("Fatin Rüştü Zorlu'nun ...," *Zafer*, April 22, 1955; Zeki Kuneralp, *Sadece Diplomat* [Istanbul: İstanbul Matbaası, 1981], 108–112).

perceived as vital for holding together what remained of the empire. In the years since the command's conception the British position had weakened. The UK had withdrawn from Palestine and incited protests in Iraq in 1948; Iran had tried to nationalize the British-controlled oil industry in 1951; the pro-British Egyptian monarchy had been expelled in 1952; and Greek Cypriots had launched an anti-colonial guerrilla campaign in 1954. All these events suggested the unpopularity of the UK and the governments it supported. Joining the Baghdad Pact helped regimes secure more military aid, but it was a difficult commitment for many of its prospective members to justify to their publics. Within the DP government, there was also hesitation. According to US diplomats, Foreign Minister Köprülü was skeptical that Turkey should enter closer formal relations with states in the region.[102] In this regard, a regional security alliance was, perhaps, a larger step than he preferred to take. On April 15, the day that a defensive treaty between Turkey and Iraq went into effect, Köprülü's reassignment as minister of state was also announced.[103]

On the heels of his performance at Bandung and with his influence in foreign policymaking strengthened, Zorlu prepared for a new trip to Washington, to attend a NATO meeting and press again for a $300 million loan. In the meantime, Turkish newspapers complained that the US government's refusal to acknowledge Turkey's importance by providing more money showed a "lack of political maturity."[104] The attacks led US diplomats to contact Zorlu and tell him to restrain his allies.[105] If Zorlu had hoped that diatribes in the press would help his case by putting pressure on US officials, he was mistaken. He arrived in Washington on May 19 and was promptly informed that Turkey would not be receiving a $300 million loan. Zorlu and Esenbel promised "Draconian" measures to restrain inflation and debt. They proposed that the government would maintain import licensing, include indebted state enterprises in the budget, and stimulate exports with premia in order to earn more foreign exchange.[106] US officials assured Zorlu that the annual $200 million in military aid and $70 million in economic aid would still be

[102] Foy Kohler to Department of State, June 21, 1956, RG 84, Box 78, UD 3288, NND 959265 (hereafter RG 84, Box 78).

[103] TBMM, April 15, 1955, 341; "Bir devin sonu," *Akis*, April 23, 1955, 5–6.

[104] British Embassy (Ankara) to Foreign Office, May 3, 1955, FO 371/117730.

[105] Secretary of State John Foster Dulles suggested that if Turkish leaders claimed that they lacked the power to control the press, then US officials should prompt Menderes to make a formal statement to the press reaffirming the strong relations between the two countries (Dulles to State, April 29, 1955, RG 84, Box 72).

[106] Department of State to US Embassy, Ankara, May 21, 1955, and John Foster Dulles to US Embassy, Ankara, May 28, 1955, both in RG 84, Box 72.

forthcoming, but they denied his additional request. By late June, Turkey could secure no more than an extra $30 million to buy spare vehicle parts and industrial inputs such as tin plate and chemicals.[107]

Zorlu was named minister of foreign affairs in July 1955, and the blame for his failed effort was placed elsewhere. President Bayar argued that a "lower level of officials" in Washington had imposed themselves between Zorlu and the "highest level American Government."[108] Turkey's US ambassador, Feridun Cemal Erkin, was blamed for not laying the groundwork and was soon sent off to Spain. He was replaced with Haydar Görk, a Paris-educated diplomat with years of experience in the foreign ministry's economic affairs division. Upon taking his post, Görk suggested that Turkey hire Thomas Dewey to act as its primary lobbyist in Washington. Dewey held a great deal of political clout. He was the former governor of New York and twice the Republican nominee for president. With the Republican administration of President Eisenhower headed into an election year, Dewey was the sort of power broker whom the administration would need to satisfy. Turkey paid him $150,000 for his services and brought him to the country for a tour.[109]

The timing of the trip was not ideal. Dewey visited Turkey to meet with his new employers on September 28, just weeks after anti-Greek pogroms rocked Turkey's major cities. These pogroms heightened the discontent with Menderes's government that was already growing within the DP. Tensions came to a head in late November, when Menderes faced the most significant intraparty challenge to his leadership, and the DP reached a turning point in its history.

The Fracturing of the Democrat Party

The DP had come to power with support from journalists and intellectuals. Leading figures in the party either owned or wrote for newspapers, and newspapers remained a main means of influencing and contesting policy. Even loyal papers like Sarol's *Türk Sesi* or Mithat Perin's *İstanbul Ekspres* might complain about prices or shortages in order to spur

107 Department of State for the Press, April 28, 1955; James Bowker to John G. Ward, May 25, 1955; Thomas Brimelow to D. M. O'Brien, July 1, 1955, all in FO 371/117730.

108 Avra Warren to Department of State, June 14, 1955, RG 84, Box 72.

109 British Embassy (Ankara) to Foreign Office, October 10, 1955, FO 371/117730. Whether Dewey's involvement helped is unclear from the archives, but as late as January 1958, employees of his law firm were still dropping in at the State Department to receive updates on the situation in Turkey (Memorandum for the Files, January 24, 1958, RG 59, Lot 58 Box 2).

government action. Policy-minded intellectuals – which is to say, faculty at Turkey's elite universities – also used the press as a forum for their ideas, but they were less attached to the governing party. This was a change from a generation earlier, when intellectuals would have passed into the bureaucracy and the CHP. Since the mid 1940s, however, they were less tightly affiliated with a particular party. Many had supported the DP in its early years but moved away from it once it achieved power. Others remained supportive for longer, but kept their distance from party activity, taking advantage of the new opportunities for study abroad available in the early 1950s. In any case, by 1955, consistently supporting the DP was difficult for many academics.

The parliamentarian Turan Güneş exemplified the growing disillusionment with the DP among intellectuals. Güneş was born into a well-connected family in the town of Kandıra (in Kocaeli province, about 100 miles east of Istanbul). The town's other notables were from the Erim family – one of its scions, Nihat, would go on to be a leading figure in the CHP in the mid 1940s. As befitted notables with more tenuous connections to the central government, the Güneş family backed the SCF in 1930. Turan himself was too young at the time for political activity, but, after finishing law school in 1946, he threw himself into building the local DP organization in Kandıra. His older brother was the provincial president. Though the party did not win there in 1946, it did in 1950.

Güneş did not stand for office in 1950, preferring to spend much of the late 1940s and early 1950s in France. As a university student in Turkey, he had studied alongside up-and-coming peers like Turhan Feyzioğlu. As a graduate student in Paris, he mixed with exiled left-wing academics. Returning to Turkey, he agreed to stand for parliament in the May 1954 elections on the DP list. Even before he entered parliament, however, it was clear that he was not likely to toe the party line. Since April 1954, he and a number of other intellectuals (including Turhan Feyzioğlu) had been publishing a magazine called *Forum*, which was, from the outset, critical of the DP and its lack of long-term economic planning.[110] Following the publication of a critical essay, Feyzioğlu and another editor (both professors in the Ankara University Department of Political Science) were called in by the minister of education and given a tongue-lashing. When another *Forum* regular, Osman Okyar, the son of

[110] Yüksel Taşkın, "Turan Güneş," in *Modern Türkiye'de Siyasi Düşünce II: Kemalizm*, ed. Tanıl Bora and Murat Gültekingil (Istanbul: İletişim Yayınları, 2009), 452–455; Cemal Fedayi, *Kandıralı Profesör Turan Güneş: Hayatı, Düşüncesi, Kişiliği* (Ankara: Kadim Yayınları, 2012), 10–29.

SCF founder Fethi Okyar and head of economic research at the Industrial Development Bank, penned a critical column in the paper *Cumhuriyet*, he was fired.[111]

The desire of these intellectuals to freely debate policy intersected with a separate effort by journalists to exercise their "right of proof" when prosecuted under the Press Law. In these instances, journalists argued, they should be allowed to offer the evidence on which their reports were based. Even more than economic planning or academic freedom, the "right of proof" became the issue around which the DP's internal opposition now rallied. In early May 1955, Güneş was among a group of eleven parliamentarians who called for the right of proof to be added to the criminal code.[112] This opposition gained force in July, when Fevzi Lütfi Karaosmanoğlu, one of the leading figures in the DP, gave his support to the movement. What might seem to be an issue of principle appeared more personal to Menderes: the cases in which journalists sought to exercise their "right to proof" tended to involve Menderes's allies. A main target was *Türk Sesi* owner Mükerrem Sarol, who was accused of a variety of corrupt activities, including pressuring government ministries to subscribe to his paper and misusing his position in a housing development cooperative to buy and sell essential material such as iron for his own benefit.[113] At a time of rationing and shortages, a connection to such corruption could be damaging to Menderes.

While parliament was in August recess – and prior to the DP's planned party congress in October 1955 – Menderes moved against his internal party critics. Feridun Ergin (one of the budget committee members who had criticized the government's policies in January) was expelled on

[111] Thomas Brimelow to O'Brien, July 13, 1955, FO 371/117727. Aydın Yalçın, another *Forum*-editing professor who gained the government's enmity, was denied a promotion in 1956. In response to the heavy-handed treatment of Yalçın, Feyzioğlu (now dean of their department) criticized the government in his speech beginning the 1956–57 academic year. Soon after, he resigned (Albayrak, *Türk Siyasi Tarihinde*, 382; Kadir Dede, "Forum Dergisi," in *Türkiye'nin 1950'li Yılları*, ed. Mete Kaan Kaynar [Istanbul: İletişim Yayınları, 2015], 460).

[112] The eleven MPs calling for the "right of proof" were Fethi Çelikbaş, Enver Güreli, Kasım Küfrevi, Muhlis Bayramoğlu, Şeref Kamil Mengü, Seyfi Kurtbek, Ekrem Alican, Turan Güneş, İbrahim Öktem, Raif Aybar, and Mustafa Ekinci. Although Kurtbek withdrew his support, they were joined by nine more: Fevzi Lütfi Karaosmanoğlu, Ekrem Hayri Üstündağ, Sabahattin Çıracıoğlu, Behçet Kayaalp, Safaeddin Karanakçı, İsmail Hakkı Akyüz, Ragıp Karaosmanoğlu, Muzaffer Timur, and Ziyad Ebüzziya (Burak Özçetin, "Democracy and Opposition in Turkey: Locating the Freedom Party" [Master's thesis, Middle East Technical University, Ankara, 2004], 67 n. 304; Bülent Bal, "Aydın Siyaset İlişkisi Bağlamında Hürriyet Partisi" [PhD diss., Marmara Üniversitesi, Istanbul, 2017], 82 n. 293).

[113] Tekin Erer, *On Yılın Mücadelesi* (Istanbul: Ticaret Postası Matbaası, 1963), 265–271; Bal, "Aydın Siyaset İlişkisi Bağlamında," 83–84.

August 14 for criticizing the government in the pages of *Cumhuriyet*.[114] On the same day, newspapers reported that a court in Istanbul had ordered the arrest of CHP Secretary General Kasım Gülek for questioning the legitimacy of the government as he set out on a tour of Black Sea provinces.[115] While these exemplary punishments might have been sufficient to keep the DP's internal and external critics in line, circumstances soon gave opponents of Menderes's government a new reason to sense weakness. Three weeks later, on the night of September 6, urban centers experienced the worst anti-Greek pogroms in the history of the republic.

Most immediately, the pogroms were a response to news that a bomb had been thrown into the courtyard of Atatürk's childhood home in the (now Greek) city of Thessaloniki. Yet several details suggested that the pogroms were far from spontaneous. In the first place, the bomb attack occurred as Turkish officials were in London with Greek officials, discussing the future status of Cyprus.[116] Whether the island remained a British possession, became independent, or merged with Greece was a highly contentious issue. In Turkey, calling for the protection of the island's Turkish population had become a central preoccupation of nationalist organizations, particularly student movements. Both opposition and pro-government papers vied to present their party as being the more concerned with the condition of Turkish Cypriots.

In addition to this political context, the details of the attack and the pogroms implicated the government. As historian Dilek Güven describes, soon after the bombing at Atatürk's childhood home, the Greek government arrested and prosecuted a Turkish exchange student and a security guard who worked at the site. During their trial, a Turkish diplomat was also accused of smuggling explosive material into the

114 In the column, Ergin suggested that the government had created a "political atmosphere" in which the opposition's recent decision to boycott local elections was understandable ("Siyasi hava," *Cumhuriyet*, August 11, 1955, 1, 3).

115 "Gülek tevkif edildi," *Ulus*, August 14, 1955, 1, 7; "Kasım Gülek dün …," *Zafer*, August 14, 1955, 1, 7; Toker, *DP Yokuş Aşağı*, 132–140.

116 By late 1955, the UK had decided to include Turkish diplomats in the Cyprus negotiations in the hope that Turkish claims would conflict with Greek ones and lead to a state of diplomatic chaos. Amid this uncertainty, the UK could present continued British sovereignty as the only viable option. The more aggressive the Turkish diplomats were, the better for the UK. Though British officials did not explain their overall strategy to their Turkish peers, they did encourage Turkish leaders to argue their position firmly. Privately, British officials suggested to each other that "a few riots in Ankara would do us nicely" in uniting public opinion in Turkey. As British diplomats hoped, Foreign Minister Zorlu took a hard line at the conference in late August, arguing that Cyprus was historically part of Anatolia and its population "Turkish." The bombing and the riots followed quickly (Robert Holland, *Britain and the Revolt in Cyprus, 1954–1959* [Oxford: Oxford University Press, 1998], 68–73, the British official's quotation is from 69 n. 54).

country. Under pressure from the Turkish government, the suspects were released. The student was given a job in the Istanbul municipality. As for the bombing, news of its occurrence spread quickly because, following the initial radio report, the pro-DP paper *İstanbul Ekspres* published and distributed a special evening edition. This publication coincided with a rally in Istanbul called by the Cyprus Is Turkish Society (*Kıbrıs Türktür Cemiyeti*). The group had already organized protests with encouragement and organizational support from DP leaders, nationalist student organizations, and the national security service (*millî emniyet hizmeti*). This protest drew large, angry crowds. During the night of September 6, hundreds of Greek-owned businesses throughout Istanbul were ransacked, between forty and sixty women reported sexual assaults to the authorities, and around a dozen people were killed. The violence led many Greek-speakers living in Turkey to emigrate. Between 1955 and 1960, their numbers fell from 79,691 to 65,139, an 18 percent decline.[117]

First and foremost, the pogroms were a humanitarian disaster. But they were also a public relations disaster, coming less than a week before the IBRD and IMF's tenth annual meeting was scheduled to begin in Istanbul. By the time the sessions commenced, the government had reasserted authority over major cities. The pogroms were blamed on "communists," martial law was declared, and the cabinet was reshuffled.[118] The new political balance left Menderes in an uncertain position: on the one hand, he replaced his ally at the interior ministry with an even closer ally; on the other, he gave the post of defense minister to party cofounder Fuat Köprülü. The appointment was a significant concession: in recent months, the two men had been feuding, leading Menderes to remove Köprülü as foreign minister. Now Köprülü was back, and his son Orhan was allowed to remain the party's Istanbul provincial president. The Köprülü family's local rival, *Türk Sesi* owner Mükerrem Sarol, resigned from the cabinet.

[117] Dilek Güven, *Cumhuriyet Dönemi Azınlık Politikaları ve Stratejileri Bağlamında 6–7 Eylül Olayları* (Istanbul: İletişim Yayınları, 2006), 54–55, 82, 92–95, 178.

[118] Arthur Richards, the US consul general in Istanbul, found the accusation that communists had organized the pogroms "incredible" and the government account "distorted." The conclusion of US Ambassador Avra Warren was that "the riots during their anti-Greek state were organized," but "for many reasons" the embassy did not believe that senior government officials allowed the riots; rather, "they did not keep themselves fully enough informed," given that "they admit unofficially" to knowing about the planning (Arthur Richards to William Baxter, September 13, 1955, RG 84, Box 2, UD 3297, NND 959261 [hereafter RG 84, Box 2]; Avra Warren, "The Istanbul–Izmir Disturbances of September 6, 1955," December 1, 1955, RG 84, Box 71, UD 3288, NND 959265 [hereafter RG 84, Box 71]).

For the moment, Köprülü remained supportive of Menderes and helped the prime minister fend off his internal party opponents. At the final session of the DP's executive committee before the October convention, Köprülü served as chair. The committee demanded that Karaosmanoğlu and others withdraw their support for the "right of proof." When the dissidents refused, they were expelled from the party. Another ten members of parliament (including Güneş) resigned from the party before they could be expelled. Two days later, at the national DP congress, a new executive committee was elected without the "right of proof" supporters.[119] Following the congress, the executive committee dispatched leading party figures to the provinces to reform local organizations where "factionalism" had raised its head.[120] But opposition was present in Ankara as well: in late October, the DP parliamentary group rejected Menderes's preferred candidate for group president by a vote of 208 to 136, and President of Parliament Refik Koraltan held off a challenge by the relatively narrow margin of 198 to 147.[121]

All this activity was in advance of the November 15 municipal elections. As the examples of Güneş and Karaosmanoğlu suggest, the expelled politicians were often leading figures in their local organizations, capable of crippling the national party at the provincial and local level.[122] Splits within the local DP organizations helped the opposition. Although

[119] The new DP executive committee was elected by 1,284 delegates at the Fourth DP Congress on October 16, 1955. Vote totals were as follows: Adnan Menderes (1,247), Fuat Köprülü (1,004), Refik Koraltan (986), Samet Ağaoğlu (967), Sıtkı Yırcalı (935), Tevfik İleri (852), Emin Kalafat (845), Rıfkı Burçak (809), Kamil Gündeş (631), Atıf Benderlioğlu (624), Remzi Birand (569), Osman Çiçekdağ (556), Cemal Ramazanoğlu (408), Mükerrem Sarol (399), and Rauf Onursal (391). As a point of comparison, consider the votes for the previous executive committee, elected at the Third Congress on October 19, 1951: Adnan Menderes (827), Fevzi Lütfi Karaosmanoğlu (767), Fuat Köprülü (734), Refik Koraltan (687), Cemal Ramazanoğlu (669), Samet Ağaoğlu (589), Sıtkı Yırcalı (571), Refik Şevket İnce (369), Fethi Çelikbaş (338), Atıf Benderlioğlu (331), Emin Kalafat (321), Kamil Gündeş (247), Tevfik İleri (236), Rıfkı Burçak (226), and Mustafa Zeren (223) (*Zafer*, October 21, 1951, 1; *Akşam*, October 17, 1955, 1).

[120] "D.P. hizipleşme ...," *Akşam*, October 23, 1955, 1, 2.

[121] Menderes's candidate for parliamentary group president was Tevfik İleri, who served as minister of transport, education, and public works during the 1950s; he was defeated by Burhanettin Onat, a comparatively unknown politician from Antalya, whom the opponents of Menderes coalesced around. Koraltan's challenger, Fahri Belen, had served in the first Menderes cabinet (1950–51), but resigned after four months. He managed to garner 142 votes to Refik Koraltan's 198 ("Burhanettin Onat," *Akis*, November 5, 1955, 10; Eroğul, *Demokrat Parti*, 170–175; Yaşar, "Demokrat Parti'de," 518).

[122] Several of the expelled representatives from the eastern provinces were particularly influential: Mustafa Ekinci could deliver votes around Lice and Seydan, while Kasım Küfrevi was a shaykh with a substantial following in Ağrı. According to Kemal Bağlum, President Bayar was once so overshadowed by Küfrevi during a visit to the province that

the CHP was protesting the DP's repressive policies and did not formally participate in the elections, CHP candidates ran as "independents" and succeeded in winning eight provinces.[123] *Türk Sesi* dismissed losses in provinces like Adana, attributing them to "a number of parasites" in the local organization, but the losses were significant enough to cause concern within the DP.[124] Less than a week after the elections, Karaosmanoğlu and his allies announced they would be establishing a new party, called the Freedom Party (the HP). As the "right of proof" issue had become associated with these expelled opponents of Menderes, critics who remained within the DP now refocused their attacks on the economic management of the prime minister and his allies.

On November 22, at the DP's first parliamentary group meeting following the announcement of the HP, several representatives made lengthy speeches criticizing the government's economic policies. One legislator, Refet Aksoy, declared that "Today, a wind of antipathy to our government blows through the nation's public opinion." In particular, he directed his criticisms at Minister of Economy and Trade Sıtkı Yırcalı, explaining that Yırcalı's management was "leading down a broken road." A sudden shortage of tin was held up as a prime example of Yırcalı's incompetence. Another legislator pointed to the recent elections and suggested that the nation believed "us to be on the edge of a precipice."[125] Any conclusive discussion was postponed for a week until Menderes returned from a trip abroad.

A week's reprieve did not strengthen either Menderes or his cabinet's position. At the meeting on November 29, legislators raised additional issues. The most damning was the allocation of foreign exchange to a firm owned by Finance Minister Hasan Polatkan's brother-in-law. The money had been used to import low-quality East German trucks. Yırcalı, who sat on the foreign exchange committee, attempted to defend himself but was forced to offer his resignation in the face of catcalls. He was followed by Foreign Minister Zorlu, who was also on the committee. Zorlu resigned after his attempt to address criticisms was also met with heckling. Even Menderes, when he stood, was greeted with harsh language. One attendee recalls the representative beside him screaming,

he vowed never to visit again (Kemal Bağlum, *Anıpolitik, 1945–1960* [Istanbul: Bilgi Yayınevi, 1991], 185; Yadirgi, *The Political Economy of the Kurds of Turkey*, 195–197).

123 Ali Eşref Turan, *Türkiye'de Yerel Seçimler* (Istanbul: Bilgi Üniversitesi Yayınları, 2008), 97.

124 "Seçim neticeleri," *Türk Sesi*, November 16, 1955, 1.

125 "22.11.1955 tarihli DP Meclis Grubu müzakerelerine ait tutanak," BCA 010.09.00.00 72 215 2, 11–12, 39.

"Get off our backs, pervert!"[126] Rattled and seeking to emphasize his subservience to the group, Menderes declared, "It's not Menderes's [authority, but rather] your authority that has no bound ... You could bring back the sultanate, the caliphate." Such a suggestion did nothing to calm tensions.[127] During a break, with a vote of no confidence looming, Menderes met with Sarol and his other advisors to craft a new strategy. When the session restarted, Menderes declared that his entire cabinet was resigning except for himself. He then called for a vote of confidence and won.[128] In effect, the crisis strengthened Menderes by positioning him as the only essential leader in the party. All others could be tossed aside when necessary. Even Sarol, who had devised Menderes's vote-of-confidence gambit, was offered no support in the following two weeks as his rival Fuat Köprülü engineered his expulsion from the party for a full year.[129]

Conclusion: Announcements and Silences

Since 1950, Menderes had been the most prominent figure in the DP (aside from President Bayar, who kept some distance from public politicking), but he had always had powerful rivals within the party. The defection of liberal members like Karaosmanoğlu to the HP left the DP with no obvious alternative to Menderes. And though it would take him time to fully reassert his authority after the parliamentary group crisis, his efforts were eased by the absence of a formidable intraparty opponent. In consolidating power from 1955 onwards, however, Menderes ran the same risks that İnönü had after Atatürk's death in 1938: he was centralizing power over the party rather than broadening his appeal across the country. Even if Menderes could count on the loyalty of a vast majority of people who voted for the DP – some 58.4 percent of the electorate in 1954 – that still implied that more than half of voters disliked him.

In announcing his new government on December 14, 1955, Menderes sought to deflect the economic critiques leveled against him. He appointed several technocrats to his new cabinet rather than his closest loyalists. He declared that the new government's program

[126] Nutku, *Demokrat Parti*, 295.

[127] "29.11.1955 tarihli DP Meclis Grubu müzakerelerine ait tutanak," BCA 010.09.00.00 72 215 3, 98.

[128] "29.11.1955 tarihli DP Meclis Grubu müzakerelerine ait tutanak," BCA 010.09.00.00 72 215 3, 170–175. According to Nazlı Tlabar, the vote was close – 180–171 – but other sources do not give such precise numbers (Outgoing Telegram #897, November 30, 1955, RG 84, Box 72).

[129] "D.P. istenen kelle," *Akis*, December 10, 1955, 9–10; "Dr. Sarol ...," *Cumhuriyet*, December 16, 1955, 1, 5; Burçak, *On Yılın Anıları*, 373–376.

continued the fundamental goals of expanding agricultural production and supporting industry, but it also signaled "the transition into a new phase." The program would address both the difficulties resulting from the government's ongoing "development drive" and "[advance] that drive in proportion to what resources allow." To this end, Menderes proposed a new ministry of industry and mining to aid the development of individual enterprises as well as a separate ministry to deal with energy production. Both these measures were meant to bring "rationalization."[130] His statements were sufficient to encourage US diplomats, who now recommended that the United States "sympathetically" consider any request for additional loans and delay debt service payments due on December 31.[131]

At the same time, Menderes's speech lacked any mention of "planning" or "devaluation," which suggested that he felt little need to make meaningful policy concessions to his intraparty opponents or critics in academia and the media. In the year and a half since his reelection, despite a worsening economic situation Menderes had managed to maintain his control of the party and government. Even so, the HP was a potential threat. Five of its thirty founders had been cabinet ministers, and many of its members were the sort of young intellectuals and journalists who had once propelled the DP to power.[132] Silencing their criticisms long enough to rebalance the economy would be a primary focus of government activity during the next two years. Assuring future Democrat victories would require a number of anti-democratic measures.

130 TBMM, December 14, 1955, 253–254.

131 Avra Warren to State (#1047), December 23, 1955, and Avra Warren to State, December 23, 1955 (#1052), RG 84, Box 71.

132 Diren Çakmak, "Türk Siyasal Yaşamında Bir Muhalefet Partisi Örneği: Hürriyet Partisi (1955–1958)," *Akademik Bakış* 2, no. 3 (winter 2008): 155.

5 Democratic Deficits: Moving toward Political Illiberalism, 1955–1958

British diplomats hoped that the announcement of a new DP government in December 1955 signaled the waning influence of policymakers like Fatin Rüştü Zorlu, who consistently linked support for their priorities to Turkey's own demands for financial aid. Not only had Zorlu been forced to resign his cabinet position but, by early January, he was also under parliamentary investigation for misallocating foreign exchange.[1] His post as foreign minister was again filled by its long-time occupant, Fuat Köprülü. Under these circumstances, the British anticipated a new willingness to compromise from the DP government. They were soon disappointed. Neither were they helped by the mixed signals coming from Washington.

In late January, President Eisenhower's advisor, Clarence Randall, arrived in Ankara to assess the economic situation.[2] In a sign of the administration's renewed solicitude toward Turkey, he declined to press Menderes on devaluation. He also suggested that OEEC countries should revise their bilateral deals with Turkey as part of a broader aid package.[3] The visit led the British ambassador to conclude, "Menderes is being supported [by the United States] primarily for political reasons," which would strengthen Zorlu, since he had "always argued that the United States could not afford to let down the present regime." There was further evidence to support the ambassador's assessment: a week before Randall's arrival, Zorlu had been placed on the parliamentary

[1] TBMM, January 11, 1956, 30.

[2] Clarence Randall (1890–1967) was an executive at Inland Steel in 1952 when President Truman nationalized the industry. He became the spokesman for the campaign against the nationalization policy. When Republicans retook the White House in 1953, the Eisenhower administration appointed Randall head of the commission on foreign economic policy. In this position, he pushed for lower tariffs, less foreign aid, and more private foreign investment ("Clarence Belden Randall," *Washington Post Times Herald*, August 9, 1967, A20; Robert Bowie and Richard Immerman, *Waging Peace: How Eisenhower Shaped an Enduring Cold War Strategy* [Oxford: Oxford University Press, 1998], 211).

[3] James Bowker to Foreign Office, February 7, 1956, FO 371/124024.

budget committee. Furthermore, though Foreign Minister Fuat Köprülü refused to include Zorlu in discussions during Randall's visit, Turkey's US ambassador urged Randall to meet with Zorlu directly, which suggested his continuing influence within the foreign ministry and Köprülü's comparative weakness.[4] At a moment when Menderes and his expansionary economic policies were receiving intense domestic criticism, this visit bought the government time.

The three-year period covered in this chapter marked a crucial turning point in the nature of DP rule and democratization in Turkey. During these years, the DP went from winning a majority of the vote to losing a majority of the vote, in large part owing to voters' dissatisfaction with the economic situation. Unlike the DP's early years in power, when international economic conditions were favorable and there had been little need for DP-led governments to demand much in the way of sacrifice, the mid and late 1950s were unfavorable, forcing DP leaders to start privileging some groups in their coalition to the detriment of others. The party had come to power by appealing to rural voters, who composed a large majority of the electorate; it was unlikely to forsake them now. Consequently, the burden of the DP's economic policies fell on urban areas. Rather than reducing agricultural subsidies as a means of slowing inflation, the government focused on price controls. The failure of the National Protection Law to achieve its ends was felt acutely by urban voters and contributed to the DP's losses in the 1957 election.

The narrow electoral victory emphasized to DP leaders the difficulty – perhaps impossibility – of maintaining democratic institutions if they were to both continue their program of rapid industrialization and maintain a grip on power. Cement production may have risen 80 percent between 1954 and 1957 – and then another 62 percent in the following three years – but, for many people, the only numbers that mattered were 50 percent and 45 percent, the increases in the wholesale price index during those same periods.[5] If prices were rising, citizens were unlikely to stick with the DP out of pure affection. If the DP was to retain power, it would have to placate these voters – or find a means of silencing them. Either way, it would need support from Turkey's allies. This chapter looks at the illiberal tactics Menderes and his allies in the DP used to

[4] James Bowker to William Young, February 14, 1956, FO 371/124024.

[5] In 1954–57 and 1957–60, sugar production rose 79 percent and 101 percent, and energy production 47 percent and 37 percent (Ömer Alp, *Ortak Pazar Ülkeleri ve Türkiye Şeker Endüstrileri* [Ankara: Yeni Desen Matbaası, 1963], 222, 430; Cohn, *Turkish Economic*, 21).

maintain power while they continued, with increasing desperation, to seek aid from the United States and other allies.

Waging the "Second War of Independence"

Prime Minister Menderes spent much of 1956 asserting his control over the government and his own party. The new cabinet – his fourth since 1950 – was certainly not devoid of loyalists, but allies like Zorlu, Mükerrem Sarol, and long-serving Finance Minister Hasan Polatkan were absent. The key economic posts of finance, monopolies, and economy and trade were now overseen by a trio composed of bureaucrats, less prominent Menderes allies, and even a rival. Of these, the ministry of economy and trade was the most crucial, since it dealt directly with merchants and took the lead in shaping trade through the allocation of foreign exchange.[6] It was a thankless job, and Menderes had difficulty filling it – Samet Ağaoğlu and sixteen others allegedly turned it down.[7] During the first months of the new cabinet, the ministry was overseen by Fahrettin Ulaş, who had served until the 1954 election as head of the Central Bank's Istanbul branch. He was less of a politician than a technocrat, with a hawkish attitude toward deficits. Perhaps, as a consequence, he was also the shortest-lived of the new ministers: by April 1956, he was gone.[8]

Ulaş's five months in office were spent considering new economic control measures and attempting to convince US officials that the

[6] According to British officials, the ministry of economy and trade was the most corrupt ministry *because* it was the most exposed to businessmen and their foreign exchange demands. That said, DP leaders also took advantage of their privileged access to foreign exchange. For example, British officials reported £1,000 (equivalent to £21,000 in 2025) given to the minister of labor for one day of shopping in London (Michael Stewart to Selwyn Lloyd, September 25, 1956, FO 371/124001).

[7] In addition to telling US embassy officials about Menderes's difficulties in filling cabinet posts, Nazlı Tlabar claimed that the confidence vote on Menderes and the politicking surrounding it had disgusted her to the point of resignation, which she had to be talked out of by her fellow Istanbul representatives (Outgoing Telegram #897, November 30, 1955, and Outgoing Telegram #910, November 30, 1955, both in RG 84, Box 72).

[8] "Şayia ...," *Cumhuriyet*, December 8, 1955, 1. Menderes allies in key positions included Ethem Menderes as defense minister and Samet Ağaoğlu as minister of state enterprises. As for the other economic ministries: finance was helmed by Nedim Ökmen (minister of agricultural since 1951, but, prior to entering parliament, the chief inspector at the ministry of finance; he was seen as an ally of Bayar and potential rival to Menderes); monopolies by Hadi Hüsman (a former official in the ministries of finance and monopolies; he had served in parliament since 1950 as a member of the budget committee and was known to be loyal to Menderes); and economy and trade by Fahrettin Ulaş. (James Bowker to Selwyn Lloyd, "Leading Personalities in Turkey," July 2, 1958, FO 371/136451; Toker, *DP Yokuş Aşağı 1954–1957*, 184–188).

government was taking serious action to stabilize the economy. Potential measures included regulations on the distribution of essential goods, price reductions on state-manufactured products like cigarettes, sugar, and coal, and increased penalties for profiteering.[9] These proposals worried merchants. At the January 1956 meeting of the Istanbul chamber of commerce, members cautioned against excessive punishments.[10] Though *Türk Sesi* dismissed these concerns, saying that merchants who "work honestly and consider national interest alongside personal benefit have nothing to worry about from these laws," the fact that the paper was reporting their statements suggests the seriousness of such complaints.[11]

The new regulations remained undetermined by late February, when the annual budget was passed. Despite being under investigation, Zorlu used his position on the budget committee to influence the final bill, which offered few concessions to critics of his and Menderes's policies. At TL3.27 billion, it was a 10 percent increase on the previous year – a smaller increase than the previous year's 26 percent, but still an indication that advocates of tight fiscal policy like Ulaş and Finance Minister Nedim Ökmen had only limited influence.[12] Frustrated with the prime minister's unwillingness to compromise, Ulaş resigned, claiming illness. His replacement, Zeyyat Mandalinci, was a close associate of Zorlu's, having served on the foreign affairs committee in parliament and as a representative to the Council of Europe.[13]

The limited influence of Ulaş, Köprülü, and others was not simply a result of Zorlu's behind-the-scenes intrigues; they were also undermined by Menderes. In March, for example, the prime minister backed away from a promise to invite an IMF mission to visit and inspect the progress of reforms. When questioned about Menderes's backtracking, Foreign Ministry Undersecretary Esenbel defended the prime minister's move, arguing to US officials that bilateral deals had stabilized the situation and that IMF prescriptions were inappropriate for Turkey, given that so little American aid was on offer. When reminded of the grain supplies Turkey

9 "Karaborsayı ve ihtikarı ...," *Türk Sesi*, January 3, 1956, 1; "Devlet mamullerinde ...," *Türk Sesi*, January 4, 1956, 1.

10 "Milli Korunma ...," *Türk Sesi*, January 20, 1956, 1; Mustafa Demircioğlu, "İst. tacirleri ...," *Türk Sesi*, January 20, 1956, 3; "İhtikar nasıl önlenebilir?" *İstanbul Ekspres*, January 20, 1956, 1, 2.

11 Atıf Sakar, "Yersiz telaş," *Türk Sesi*, January 21, 1956, 1, 3.

12 In comparison with a 1956–57 national budget of TL3.27 billion ($1.2 billion), the IMF put overall debt at $1.21 billion in April 1956; this was composed of $509 million (public debt), $257 million (import credits), $179 million (commercial arrears), $151 million of debts to foreign banks, and $25 million (credits issued in bilateral deals) (Michael Stewart to Selwyn Lloyd, October 15, 1956, FO 371/124024).

13 James Bowker to Foreign Office, May 9, 1956, FO 371/124001.

might still need, Esenbel complained that Turkey had received a bad deal compared with countries like Brazil, Egypt, and Yugoslavia, which had done far less to advance US interests.[14] The following week, he conveyed the message that Menderes was frustrated that the aid for the 1956–57 fiscal year looked to be the same as the previous year, even though Turkey was in a "more perilous" situation.[15]

This assertive behavior was not limited to meetings in Ankara. Turkey also engaged in a campaign of public diplomacy. Two female legislators from the DP were sent on trips to the United States in April and June. Nazlı Tlabar's trip was the more transparently diplomatic one in the sense that her activities were mainly in Washington. Nuriye Pınar, on the other hand, ostensibly came to attend a scientific conference in Berkeley, California. Pınar, Turkey's leading scholar on the geology of earthquakes, presented to an audience of 300 male peers. As the lone woman, she served as a reminder of Turkey's progressive character.[16] When passing through Washington, she also had a direct message for US officials: America risked being hated in Turkey for the paltry level of aid it was providing. She also criticized the tendency of embassy officials and the American press to second-guess Turkey, saying, "What the French do [in Algeria] is alright, but you are ready enough with your criticism of my own people."[17]

Yet it was not only US officials who DP leaders felt were questioning their policies. During the month-long interregnum between Ulaş's resignation and Mandalinci's appointment, the Istanbul chamber of commerce issued a report recommending a slew of reforms. These included cutting consumer goods imports, taxing agricultural earnings, including the deficits of state-owned enterprises in the official budget, narrowing the gap between the official and real exchange rate, and systematizing credit allocation.[18] The recommendations were similar to those being made by members of the HP.[19] With the business community sounding increasingly like the opposition, the government went on

[14] Memorandum of Conversation, March 15, 1956, RG 84, Box 78.

[15] Memorandum of Conversation, March 19, 1956, RG 84, Box 78.

[16] "Turkish Women's Status Told," *Los Angeles Times*, June 22, 1956, B1; Elizabeth Shelton, "'Quakes Her Special Interest," *Washington Post*, June 28, 1956, 36.

[17] Fay Kohler to State, June 28, 1956, RG 84, Box 74, UD 3288, NND 959265 (hereafter RG 84, Box 74). This quotation is the paraphrase of a US diplomatic source. Given that Nimet Arzık describes Nuriye Pınar as being the most "foul-mouthed" (*küfürbaz*) of the female DP representatives, I like to imagine that her *actual* language in Washington was more direct (Arzık, *Menderes'i İpe Götürenler*, 119).

[18] Semih Benli, "Türkiye'nin ekonomik ...," *Akşam*, April 23, 1956, 1, 3.

[19] Speaking for the HP, Feridun Ergin argued that penalties would not help and that inspections needed to be strengthened (TBMM, May 7, 1956, 490–493).

the offensive. Menderes toured southern provinces during April 1956, declaring that, "Even the communist papers published in France don't criticize the government in this language. Even the communist parliamentarians in France don't talk in the style of those in our parliament."[20]

These critiques of the political opposition were followed by attacks on figures within the party and bureaucracy who might still oppose Menderes and his allies. In May, three judges on the appeals court (*Yargıtay*) and another thirteen lower-court judges were retired. Though Menderes's allies defended the move as fully in keeping with existing laws, it served as a rallying cry for intraparty opponents in much the same way that the "right of proof" had done a year earlier.[21] At the subsequent meeting of the DP parliamentary group, Fuat Köprülü's cousin, Cemal, questioned the basis for the retirements and followed up with a motion criticizing Menderes's attacks on the opposition, the government's economic policies, and its anti-democratic measures. Within days, Cemal had been referred to the party disciplinary committee and expelled. In Istanbul, Köprülü's son, Orhan, briefly resigned as local party president, under pressure owing to his own criticisms of the DP leadership. What was bad for the Köprülü family was good for its opponents. Rumors swirled that an investigation of Mükerrem Sarol was coming to an end and that Köprülü was being sidelined by Menderes.[22]

Amid these tensions, parliament discussed potential amendments to the National Protection Law. A proposal by several DP legislators that the death penalty be applied in profiteering cases received heavy coverage in the press.[23] Parliament ultimately rejected the proposal, but amendments passed on June 6 expanded the authority of the state in people's lives. Businesses were required to post prices (and these prices were to be determined by governors and municipal governments); customers could now demand receipts for any transaction over TL2.50; importers could no longer double as wholesalers or retailers without explicit government approval, and the profit margins of each group were fixed at 20 percent, 10 percent, and 25 percent, respectively. The profit margin for state-manufactured goods was set at 2 percent. Violations of these new

[20] "Millet büyük davalar peşindedir," *Zafer*, April 10, 1956, 1, 4.

[21] "Emekliye ayrılan hakimler," *Zafer*, May 4, 1956, 1, 4.

[22] "Fuat Köprülü-Adnan Menderes ...," *Cumhuriyet*, May 12, 1956, 1, 5; Kayhan Sağlamer, "Orhan Köprülü ...," *Cumhuriyet*, 1, 5; "Cemal Köprülü'nün ...," *Cumhuriyet*, May 21, 1956, 1, 3; "Dr. Sarol hakkındaki ...," *Cumhuriyet*, May 25, 1956, 1; Ankara to Foreign Office, May 23, 1956, FO 371/124001. Orhan Köprülü returned as Istanbul party president after two weeks ("O. Köprülü ...," *Cumhuriyet*, May 25, 1956, 1, 5).

[23] TBMM, May 9, 1956, 316. The amendment to include the death penalty was rejected 202–117 ("Muhtekirlere idam ...," *Akşam*, June 5, 1956, 1).

regulations could be punished with three years and three months in prison and a TL50,000 fine.[24] In the days following the law's passage, the national government created a ministerial coordination committee and appointed special judges to deal with violations in major cities; municipalities issued lists of official prices; and the government announced that inspectors would be paid salaries of at least TL1,500 a month – enough, in theory, to keep them honest.[25]

The new regulations had immediate results. Both opposition and pro-government papers reported that the prices of consumer goods were falling as much as 50 percent during June and July 1956.[26] According to reports by British officials, however, these measures lost their luster on closer inspection. The price of essential goods (which had already been regulated) was only slightly affected, while the significant fall in the price of consumer goods was due to so many merchants simultaneously offering their merchandise. The same process that had occurred in the summer of 1954 was happening again: items like washing machines and vacuum cleaners, which merchants would previously have kept in storage pending a rise in prices, were now made available in order to avoid charges of hoarding. This momentary glut lowered prices. In major cities, the value of gold fell as people converted their savings to lira to buy radios, refrigerators, and the like. After being sold at official prices, these products were resold on the black market.[27]

Newspapers during the summer months were filled with stories of merchants arrested for overcharging customers. Many of these violations were minor (e.g., a stationery store owner charging TL2 for leather book coverings that should have been TL1.25, or a button-maker selling TL0.21 buttons at TL0.24), but some were more significant (e.g., a merchant selling automobile transmissions for TL463 above the official price). Regardless of the scale of the offense, the citations and prosecutions were meant to be exemplary: the auto parts dealer was sentenced to thirty-nine months in prison and a TL6,000 fine, while prosecutors initially demanded a ten-year sentence for the stationery store owner, followed by a fifteen-year ban from trade and a fine of up to TL20,000.[28]

[24] RG, June 11, 1956; Thomas Brimelow to O'Brien, June 20, 1956, FO 371/124024.

[25] "Fiatler süratle ...," *Akşam*, June 13, 1956, 1, 2; "Toplu Milli ...," *Cumhuriyet*, June 29, 1956, 1.

[26] "Eşya satış ...," *Zafer*, June 13, 1956, 1, 4. The newspaper *Akşam* reported that high-end shoes had fallen from TL130 to TL60–70, and stoves from TL300 to TL130–150 ("Yerli ve ithal ...," *Akşam*, June 15, 1956, 1, 2).

[27] Philip Broad to James Bowker, July 12, 1956, and Thomas Brimelow to O'Brien, July 16, 1956, FO 371/124024; "Gıda maddelerine ...," *Akşam*, July 28, 1956, 1, 2.

[28] "İstanbul ve Ankara ...," *İstanbul Ekspres*, June 14, 1956, 1, 2; "Kağıt tüccarının ...," *İstanbul Ekspres*, June 14, 1956, 1, 2; "Eşya satış ...," *Zafer*, June 16, 1956, 1, 4; "Belediye

Less common in the reporting was any criticism of the government or its officials. This was, in large part, because parliament passed new amendments to the Press Law that expanded the grounds for which reporters and publishers could be prosecuted. These included the publication of articles that "cause the public worry or excitement."[29] The legislation's passage in parliament on June 8 followed the new economic controls, but its formal publication (and, thus, implementation) actually *preceded* publication of the controls by three days, thereby ensuring that the new commercial regime would be carried out under conditions of intense press censorship.

More than just silencing coverage of economic policy, the new press restrictions served to silence reporting on the efforts of Menderes and his allies to protect their own interests. The investigations of Zorlu, Yırcalı, Polatkan, and Sarol were still ongoing, but the outcome was hardly in doubt. From the start, it had been clear that their political careers were far from over: as early as January, Polatkan and Yırcalı had received posts on the foreign affairs committee, and Zorlu (as mentioned above) had been placed on the budget committee. During the February budget debates, Menderes had often answered questions in parliament instead of his new cabinet ministers – or, in some instances, even deferred to Zorlu.[30] By May 1956, the investigations were winding down, and the tensions were rising between supporters of Menderes and Köprülü, who was one of the few remaining DP leaders with sufficient stature to challenge Menderes.

An election for DP parliamentary group president in early June served as a trial of strength between Menderes's allies and his opponents. Namık Gedik, who had been removed as interior minister following the anti-Greek pogroms, ran as Menderes's preferred candidate and won,

yıldırım ...," *İstanbul Ekspres*, June 28, 1956, 1, 2; "Milli Korunma ...," *Zafer*, July 4, 1956, 1, 4.

29 RG, June 8, 1956, 14505. The Press Law revisions provoked arguments in the DP parliamentary group, culminating in the resignation of Group President Burhanettin Onat on May 29. He was replaced on June 5 by Namık Gedik, an ally of Menderes's and advocate of harsh measures against the opposition. Once the group had approved the bill, arguments moved to the floor of parliament. Fighting broke out. In one instance, while İnönü was talking about the important role played by an opposition in politics, DP representative Muhlis Erdener shouted that İnönü had called the DP "sons of donkeys" at a rally. In response, Arslan Bora, a CHP representative, yelled back, "You're the son of a donkey," and threw his briefcase at Erdener. During the fight that predictably followed, a gun fell out of the briefcase of the HP representative Mustafa Ekinci, causing a stir in the chamber. Ekinci admitted the briefcase in question was his, but maintained the gun belonged to his son (TBMM, June 6, 1956, 101, 125; Yaşar, "Demokrat Parti'de," 527 n. 88).

30 Michael Stewart to Foreign Office, March 6, 1956, FO 371/124001.

demonstrating that Menderes still commanded support.[31] The victory was followed by another move against his internal opponents: on June 16, a committee report cleared Sarol of wrongdoing. Köprülü resigned from his post as foreign minister three days later – just one day before Polatkan, Yırcalı, and Zorlu were also cleared of all charges. Although Zorlu would not officially return to the foreign ministry for another year, his hardline tactics were again dominant.[32] Operating under the new press restrictions, journalists could do little more than reprint the initial charges and make note of the heated reactions to the acquittals in parliament.

In case media censorship was insufficient for restraining public protest, the government also passed a bill amending the Public Meetings and Demonstrations Law on June 27. Except during election campaigns, political parties would now have to meet indoors. Any outdoor rally would have to be approved two days in advance by the district's highest-ranking civil official. Most controversially, public gatherings that violated the law could be dispersed by authorities using firearms (albeit only after issuing verbal warnings and then firing in the air).[33] The law did nothing to ban the de facto rallies held by government ministers every time they appeared at ribbon-cutting ceremonies.

Following on the heels of the amended Press Law, these new restrictions were a step too far for the opposition. On June 26, the final day of debate, all of the opposition parties marched out of the chamber.[34]

[31] There were three candidates for parliamentary group president: 1) Namık Gedik (1911–60), who had entered parliament in 1950 as the representative for Menderes's home province of Aydın. He had previously worked as a specialist in tuberculosis in Istanbul's Haydarpaşa hospital. He received 152 votes. 2) Rüknettin Nasuhioğlu (1891–1973), who had been an official in the ministry of the interior prior to joining the DP. He had served as governor in several provinces and as the general director for local governance (*Mahalli İdareler Umum Müdürü*). According to British reports, he was believed by many in the DP to have helped rig the 1946 elections in Samsun in favor of the ruling CHP. He served as interior minister in Menderes's first (and most independent) cabinet in 1950–51. He received ninety votes. 3) Osman Kapani (1915–81), who had been a state minister responsible for land and refugee resettlement issues from 1954 to 1955. He received eighteen votes. Gedik would serve until December, when he was reappointed as interior minister. His successor, Hayrettin Erkmen, was another Menderes ally ("[D.P.] Grupu dün ...," *Cumhuriyet*, June 6, 1956, 1, 5; James Bowker to Selwyn Lloyd, "Leading Personalities in Turkey," July 2, 1958, FO 371/136451; Gök, "Demokrat Parti Döneminin Önemli Bir Siması").

[32] In talks with US officials, the deputy director general of the Türkiye Sınaî Kalkınma Bankası, Bülent Yazıcı, suggested that Zorlu was not the only member of Menderes's inner circle pushing for bilateral deals rather than devaluation: Sarol too, he argued, represented the interests of Istanbul merchants, who preferred the steady income guaranteed by bilateral trade agreements (Owen Jones, August 1, 1956, RG 84, Box 78).

[33] RG, June 30, 1956, 14716.

[34] TBMM, June 27, 1956, 528.

The CHP only returned on July 11 in order to express its opposition to yet another move by the government to undercut opposition-party political organizing – in this case, a bill to delay by-elections for a year.[35] The government argued that even if the opposition won all fourteen open seats, it would have no effect on the balance of power in parliament, where the DP held 85 percent of the seats. This argument obscured the fact that these by-elections would have offered the opposition one of the few legal opportunities to tour the countryside under the revised Public Meetings and Demonstrations Law.[36]

Parliament went into recess as the country headed into the summer months – the last months before the harvest and, thus, the ones in which foreign exchange reserves were lowest. During this period, devaluation would continue to take a back seat to ad hoc measures like import restrictions and price controls. Merchant organizations complained that the government was not consulting them before announcing new prices and profit margin limits. They called for increased credit for imports and premia for exports.[37] Speaking for the government, Economy and Trade Minister Mandalinci argued that export premia were "not the issue" and emphasized that Turkey would try to reduce import costs by opening offices in the United States and West Germany to regulate costs at source.[38]

Despite potential legal liability, criticism crept back into press coverage as fall approached. In addition to the complaints of merchants, there were reports that manufacturers were halting production, given the low profit margins. Retailers in Anatolia were sending items back to wholesalers, asking for cheaper products. Factories were laying off employees.[39] In an attempt to head off discontent, Mandalinci met with representatives from organizations such as the chamber of commerce,

35 The CHP was also present at the following session when parliament approved a major revision of the tax code, which replaced the existing Transaction Tax (*Muamele Vergisi*) with a new "Expenditure Tax" (*Gider Vergisi*), which consolidated several different taxes on primary material production, services, tobacco, sugar, and alcohol. More crucially, it continued a trend in DP tax policy of exempting large groups – in this case small manufacturers ("Muamele Vergisi kalktı," *Akşam*, July 14, 1956, 1, 2; RG, July 23, 1956).

36 TBMM, July 11, 1956.

37 Many merchants also hoped for a bill lowering rents to a level in keeping with their diminished profits ("Milli Korunma …," *İstanbul Ekspres*, July 7, 1956, 3).

38 "Milli Korunma …," *Akşam*, July 24, 1956, 1, 2; "İthalat borçlarımızı …," *Akşam*, July 25, 1956, 1, 2.

39 "Esnaf yüzde 10 …," *Akşam*, July 29, 1956, 1; "Piyasa neden durgun," *Akşam*, August 9, 1956, 1, 2; "Kararımızı bir kaç …," *Akşam*, August 13, 1956, 1, 2; "Toptancı tüccarlar …" and "Bir mensucat fabrikası …," *Akşam*, August 17, 1956, 1–3.

and the government began to talk of revising profit margins.[40] At the İzmir Trade Fair in late August, Mandalinci praised merchants as being "in possession of an honorable duty linked directly with the fate and ... wealth of the nation," emphasizing that the National Protection Law was only intended to ensure that "our national commercial life develops within legitimate bounds."[41] The speech suggested that the government was giving in to pressure from commercial interests, which likely led to the resignation of Finance Minister Nedim Ökmen a day later. In early September, a bill was passed adjusting profit margins on some items and providing additional credit.[42]

The concessions were not enough to satisfy the merchants. According to state intelligence reports from September 1956, importers, wholesalers, and retailers were secretly selling to one another in order to avoid adhering to the margins specified by the National Protection Law. Other merchants, meanwhile, were developing code words to avoid providing receipts: "with a necktie" if customers wanted a transaction to be official, "without a necktie" if they wanted to conduct business under the table.[43] More generally there was a sense, as fall began, that the law's effects were "fading." People were again turning to the black market for basic commodities like eggs and milk, or stockpiling gasoline, which was mostly imported and, therefore, always at risk of a foreign exchange crisis.[44]

Mandalinci and Menderes promised additional measures to address merchant complaints and free up foreign exchange.[45] These included a new "tourist exchange rate" in early October that applied to both foreigners and nationals traveling abroad, providing a rate of around TL5.50 per dollar rather than the official TL2.80.[46] Though it was an improvement on the previous rate, which discouraged foreigners from bringing hard currency into Turkey and encouraged Turkish citizens to compete for access to undervalued foreign exchange, the new rate was still less than the black-market rate of TL9.90, which had held through

40 "Perakendeci karı ...," *Akşam*, August 19, 1956, 1, 2.

41 "Ticaret Vekili ...," *Zafer*, August 21, 1956, 1, 4.

42 "Maliye Bakanı ...," *Akşam*, August 23, 1956, 1, 2; "Hükümet," *Akis*, September 1, 1956, 5; "Yeni kar hadleri," *Akşam*, September 2, 1956, 3; RG, September 3, 1956; "Tüccarlara kredi hacmi," *Akşam*, September 11, 1956, 3.

43 "Muhtelif konularda istihbarat raporu," September 26, 1956, BCA 030.01.00.00 68 426 5.

44 "Çeşitli konularda istihbarat raporu," October 27, 1956, and November 5, 1956, BCA 030.01.00.00 68 427 2.

45 "Esnafla belediye ...," *Akşam*, September 12, 1956, 3; "Yeni bazı...," *İstanbul Ekspres*, September 17, 1956, 3.

46 "Turist dövizinin ...," *Akşam*, October 9, 1956, 1, 2; RG, October 8, 1956, and RG, December 29, 1956; "Turkey Establishes New Exchange Rate," *New York Times*, October 9, 1956, 66.

most of 1956.[47] Moreover, by early October, it was clear that that the fall wheat harvest would be less than the previous year. Yet again Turkey would be paying for grain imports rather than exporting its own in return for desperately needed foreign exchange.

News of a poor harvest and consequent purchases of foreign grain was the headline on the premiere edition of *Havadis*, a new pro-government paper launched by Bahadır Dülger.[48] Dülger had been a DP member of parliament for Erzurum since 1950, as well as being an editor at both *Zafer* (in its early years) and the state-run Anadolu Agency (briefly in 1952). Like other Istanbul-based DP newspapers, *Havadis* defended the party in general, but it also offered frank accounts of economic woes. In an early column, for example, Dülger complained that the cost of onions and potatoes had nearly doubled in Istanbul after the municipality had allowed the prices to float.[49] He argued that such rising costs called the municipality's authority into question, "leaving the impression [that it was] a scrawny wrestler, easily thrown."[50]

Pro-government papers fell into lock step with Menderes, however, as he launched a new rhetorical offensive during the October parliamentary recess. At the beginning of the month, he attended the openings of sugar factories in both Erzurum and Malatya. In Erzurum, he mocked those in the opposition who said a lack of foreign exchange would leave the Democrats' industrial projects little more than unfinished "piles of dirt."[51] By the time he arrived in Balıkesir at the end of the month for the opening of a new cotton mill, his speeches had grown more dramatic. According to Menderes, the nation was in the midst of a "struggle

47 Heathcote-Smith to O'Brien, October 9, 1956, and Michael Stewart to Selwyn Lloyd, October 15, FO 124024.

48 "Amerikadan 600 bin …," *Havadis*, October 18, 1956, 1, 5.

49 Bahadır Dülger, "Yeni fiat artışları," *Havadis*, October 28, 1956, 1. Bahadır Dülger (1911–68) was born in Istanbul. He was educated at Galatasaray Lycée and Ankara Law School before beginning a career in journalism. He represented Erzurum and Gaziantep from 1950 to 1960. Similar examples from pro-DP papers in this period can be seen in *Son Posta*, which was owned by Selim Ragıp Emeç (1899–1970), like Dülger a graduate of Galatasaray Lycée, and a DP parliamentarian for Bursa and İzmir from 1950 to 1960. Emeç's newspaper attributed rising prices not to government policies or market forces but rather "some opportunists" ("Satış fiatını …," *Son Posta*, October 26, 1956, 2; James Bowker to Selwyn Lloyd, "Leading Personalities in Turkey," July 2, 1958, FO 371/136451).

50 Bahadır Dülger, "Bir otorite meselesi," *Havadis*, October 20, 1956, 1.

51 "Başvekilin nutku," *Zafer*, October 1, 1956, 1, 4. The *Zafer* reporter covering Menderes's Malatya trip remarked that the provincial market was the "least affected by the new national protection regime" of any in the country. In other words, the CHP-controlled municipal government was shirking its responsibilities (İlhan Tarus, "Malatyayı dolaşırken," *Zafer*, October 3, 1956, 3).

[*mücadele*] of national independence."[52] In the face of such a challenge, Turkey could not depend on others for products like iron, coal, cement, and cotton. Just as the nation had become self-sufficient in sugar production, so too must it become self-sufficient in these other industries. Discussing the Balıkesir speech in *Havadis*, Dülger echoed Menderes's talk of struggle, but opted for the more modern vocabulary of "war" (*şavaş*).[53] He observed that even after achieving political independence in 1923, Turkey remained economically dependent. In *Zafer*, a columnist elaborated on Dülger's argument by explaining that the DP government was following Atatürk's command that 'The New Turkey would be an economic state'" – one that could "remove the semi-colonial economy that had resulted from foreign exploitation."[54]

Though their confident statements obfuscated Turkey's – or, at least, the DP's – dependence on US financial support, they were right that Turkey was not simply a beggar on the international stage. In meetings with US officials during the summer, for example, Undersecretary Esenbel could still reject suggestions that Turkey devalue its currency and assert that regulations were achieving their aims.[55] And while his American interlocutors might be skeptical, they cautioned their superiors in Washington against letting Turkey "stew in her own juices," given "what her failure to loyally cooperate with us would mean in men and dollars."[56]

Southern Discomforts: The Challenge of Arab Nationalism

Menderes's Balıkesir speech came less than a week before the opening of the new parliamentary session on November 1, 1956. In his opening address, President Bayar touted ongoing successes in the fields of infrastructure, medical care, and education. His main request of parliament was that it further "modernize" the tax code during the next year. He touched on economic difficulties only briefly in the middle of his remarks, emphasizing the need for tight controls to "defend the price stability of necessary materials" and dismissing the notion of "anything like devaluing our currency." In fact, in his account, a main cause of Turkey's economic hardship seemed to emerge from the Syrian border

52 "İktisadi İstiklal Savaşı," *Zafer*, October 26, 1956, 1, 4.
53 Bahadır Dülger, "İktisadi istiklal," *Havadis*, October 27, 1956, 1.
54 Zühtü Velibeşe, "Yeni Türk Devleti," *Zafer*, October 29, 1956, 6, 10.
55 Memorandum of Conversation, August 20, 1956, RG 59, Lot 58, Box 2.
56 Fletcher Warren to Herbert Hoover, Jr. July 28, 1956, and Herbert Hoover, Jr. to Fletcher Warren, August 24, 1956, RG 59, Lot 58, Box 2.

region where, Bayar noted, "the professional smuggling that has chronically shaken economic stability and commercial morality continues."[57]

As Bayar's speech suggested, Syria was a prime source of concern. Since 1955, the country had refused to join the Baghdad Pact with Turkey, Pakistan, Iran, Iraq, and the UK. Though the United States was not a direct participant, the alliance was part of a larger anti-communist strategy to ring the USSR with pro-Western countries bound by defensive treaties such as NATO and SEATO. From the perspective of radical leaders in the region who sought to uproot the vestiges of European imperialism, the Baghdad Pact appeared to perpetuate Western influence. The Egyptian leader, Gamal Abdel Nasser, opposed the pact and pressured other regimes to abstain as well. Not only was Nasser particularly influential in Syria, but the USSR also seemed to be gaining a foothold there over the course of 1955–56.[58] Rather than helping encircle the USSR, Turkish leaders now feared encirclement by pro-Soviet states and expressed concerns to the British about Soviet flyovers in September 1956.[59] Bayar's mention of Syria, therefore, was reflective of a growing unease among DP leaders regarding events on Turkey's southern border.

Unmentioned in Bayar's November 1 speech was any comment on the Israeli offensive that had begun in the Sinai Peninsula on the night of October 29, or the landings by British and French forces the following day. These moves constituted the beginning of the "Suez Crisis," in which Israel, France, and the UK sought to punish Nasser for his nationalization of the Suez Canal (and support for Arab nationalist movements in the region). Yet the effort backfired. It reminded as yet nonaligned governments in the region how potentially dangerous Britain was to their security and, thus, undermined the Baghdad Pact. Rather than cut Nasser down to size, the crisis raised his profile and increased the luster of his military-led model of national independence. By contrast, countries allied with the UK and the United States, such as Lebanon, Iraq, and Iran, were either monarchies or republics run by a mix of lawyers and businessmen that resembled the DP coalition. To avoid seeming like puppets of the British in the aftermath of the Suez Crisis, DP leaders needed to establish some diplomatic distance. Turkey withdrew its ambassador from Israel – an act that *Havadis* praised

[57] TBMM, November 1, 1956, 4, 8–10.

[58] The USSR had begun offering aid to Syria in mid 1955; by August, a military attaché was resident in Damascus; an embassy was established in November (Patrick Seale, *The Struggle for Syria: A Study of Post-War Arab Politics 1945–1958*, 2nd ed. [London: Tauris, 1986 (1965)], 255).

[59] James Bowker, "Turkey: Annual Review for 1956," January 31, 1957, FO 371/130174.

as showing Arab states that "communists" were not the only ones willing to stand up to Israel.[60] But breaking off relations with the British was a step too far: the DP government continued to allow the British military access to Turkish airspace and insisted that the UK be allowed to remain in the Baghdad Pact.[61]

Trying to play the role of intermediary between post-Ottoman states and the US-led Cold War alliance was a difficult balancing act, but one which offered DP leaders potential financial rewards. Following the Suez Crisis, the Eisenhower administration sought to cultivate allies in the region who might otherwise look to the USSR for support. By late December the Turkish press was reporting that the US president was preparing to request a large aid package from the US Congress.[62] This "Eisenhower Doctrine," announced on January 5, 1957, called for an additional $200 million to be spent in the region during the coming year in order to counter the expansion of "International Communism." The amount was equal to the total aid Turkey had received in 1955–56, meaning that even securing a portion of these new funds would be significant.[63]

Ultimately, leaders in Turkey, Iran, Iraq, and elsewhere were able to gain access to considerable sums of money by emphasizing the threat of communism. By June 1957, the United States committed $12.5 million to joint projects in the region. (Though, since the United States was not officially a signatory to the Baghdad Pact, all the funds went directly to pact members.) Projects included an improved radio communications infrastructure between the various capital cities ($8.37 million), new roads linking Turkey to Iran and Iraq (an initial $2 million), and a rail line connecting Turkey and Iran (an initial $1 million).[64] Not to be outdone, British officials scrambled to offer a package of £1.73 million ($4.8 million) as well, so that leaders in the region did not – in the words of the UK ambassador – "acquire the habit of turning automatically to

60 Bahadır Dülger, "Türkiye'nin İsrail …," *Havadis*, November 27, 1956, 1.

61 James Bowker to Foreign Office, February 4, 1958, FO 371/136450; Abou El-Fadl, *Foreign Policy as Nation Making*, 238–240.

62 "Yeni Amerikan yardımı," *Akşam*, December 29, 1956, 1.

63 "Text of the Address …," *New York Times*, January 6, 1957, 34; Michael Cohen, *Strategy and Politics in the Middle East, 1954–1960: Defending the Northern Tier* (London: Frank Cass, 2005), 179–182. To give some perspective: total US aid to Turkey for 1956–57 was reported as $176 million; total Turkish budget expenditures for the year were set at TL3.27 billion ($1.2 billion at official exchange rates); thus, US aid had been equal to 15 percent of government expenditures (*Marshall Plan in Turkey 40*. The Organization for International Economic Cooperation, Turkish Ministry for Foreign Affairs, 1959]; Cillov, *Türkiye Ekonomisi*, 547).

64 Behçet Kemal Yeşilbursa, *The Baghdad Pact: Anglo-American Defence Policies in the Middle East, 1950–59* (London: Frank Cass, 2005), 190–194.

the Americans."[65] This money was separate from the $280 million of direct military aid and defense support provided to Turkey by the United States for the 1957–58 fiscal year. Such a level of support enabled Menderes's government to devote a comparatively small portion of that year's budget to defense (about 28 percent) and devote more to development projects and agricultural credit.[66]

This budget was overseen by a reshuffled cabinet. Mandalinci resigned as minister of economy and trade on November 28 and was replaced with Abdullah Aker, a Menderes ally with close ties to İzmir merchants.[67] Three days later, the empty post of finance minister was filled by Menderes ally Hasan Polatkan. Finally, as if to drive home the message that his confidants would remain influential regardless of their errors, Menderes reappointed Namık Gedik as interior minister on December 24, despite his association with the anti-Greek pogroms. Whereas the previous year had ended with Menderes momentarily isolated, supported by his fellow legislators but shorn of his closest allies, he was ending 1956 surrounded again by loyalists.[68] The prime minister was now leading his most loyal cabinet to date, but he entered the new year with economic conditions growing worse, opposition parties gaining strength, and tensions with Egypt and Syria rising.

If the Soviet threat from the north had preoccupied Turkey's leaders in the decade after World War II, the mix of anti-colonialism, Arab nationalism, and socialism that constituted "Nasserism" to the south was becoming the preeminent concern by the mid 1950s. Relations with Egypt had fluctuated over the previous five years. When Egypt's monarchy was initially overthrown in 1952, pro-DP papers like *Zafer* generally took Nasser and his fellow coup leaders at their word, casting

[65] James Bowker to Foreign Office, May 2, 1957, FO 371/127844.

[66] James Bowker to Foreign Office, February 4, 1958, FO 371/136450; Cillov, *Türkiye Ekonomisi*, 530. At 28 percent of total spending, Turkey's defense budget in 1957–58 was the smallest in the history of the republic. According to Yahya Tezel's statistics, only during the depression years of 1929–33 had the percentage been as low (29 percent–32 percent). Expenditures for defense of only TL1.13 billion ($400 million at the official lira rate) in a budget of TL4 billion ($1.4 billion) did not go unremarked on by US Congressmen. During Senate appropriations hearings on July 19, 1957, Senator Allen Ellender (D-LA) asked whether "in Istanbul much money is being spent beautifying streets which will not improve the economy one iota" (Tezel, *Cumhuriyet Döneminin*, 540; "Mutual Security Appropriations for 1958," Committee on Appropriations [Washington, DC: US Government Printing Office, 1957], 306).

[67] Abdullah Aker (1905–77) worked for many years in the ministry of education and the ministry of economy and trade before entering parliament in 1954. He was a founder of the İzmir chamber of commerce. The immediate cause of Mandalinci's resignation is unclear.

[68] On November 3, 1956, journalist and İzmir representative Cihad Baban switched to the HP ("Cihat Baban D. P. den istifa etti," *Akşam*, November 4, 1956, 2).

their moves against various political parties as a much needed "cleaning," even if the methods could at times appear "fascist."[69] By May 1954, however, the paper was declaring that the "great hope" the world had felt following the king's deposition had come to naught but factional infighting "from which red agents had benefited."[70] When, four months later, an assassination attempt on Nasser was attributed to the Muslim Brotherhood, *Türk Sesi* suggested the incident was *really* attributable to Egypt's "hesitant" stance toward Turkey and the West.[71] Hoping to win Egyptian support for the Baghdad Pact in late 1954, the DP briefly took a more flattering line: *Zafer*'s main writer, Mümtaz Faik Fenik, declared that Turkey and Egypt should work together for the "perpetuation of free nations" and was sent on a junket to Egypt, during which he produced columns praising the various projects of Egypt's "dynamic administration."[72] But when these blandishments failed to achieve their aim, rhetoric again turned harsh: in March 1955, Fenik wrote that there was "not the slightest difference between the policies [of pan-Arab unity that] Egypt wants to pursue today and Hitler's policies of Lebensraum and racism implemented for a time in Europe."[73]

The Hitler comparisons were also lobbed at Syria. As early as 1953, *Zafer* was arguing that Syrian demands for the return of Hatay province were reminiscent of the imperialist claims of both Hitler and Stalin.[74] This border province had been administered by France as "the Sanjak of Alexandretta," an autonomous district within the Syrian mandate from World War I until the late 1930s. On the eve of World War II, Turkish leaders had seized the opportunity provided by negotiations between the French government and Syrian nationalist leaders to assert their own claims over the territory.[75] It had formally joined with Turkey in 1939, but its status remained a point of contention – at least from the Syrian perspective. Nor was it the only source of tension between the two governments: although the border stretching eastwards from Hatay toward Iraq was not in dispute, the lack of enforcement was. According to Turkish officials, Syrian smugglers moved with ease across the

[69] Mümtaz Faik Fenik, "Misirdaki temizliğin mânası," *Zafer*, September 10, 1952, 1, 3.
[70] Mümtaz Faik Fenik, "Ortadoğu barışı …," *Zafer*, May 2, 1954, 1, 4.
[71] Burhan Apaydın, "Mısır hadiseleri," *Türk Sesi*, September 15, 1954, 1, 7.
[72] Mümtaz Faik Fenik, "Türkiye ve Mısır," *Zafer*, October 1, 1954, 1, 7; Mümtaz Faik Fenik, "Mısır dönüşü," *Zafer*, December 29, 1954, 1, 7.
[73] Mümtaz Faik Fenik, "Suriye'nin istiklali tehlikede!," *Zafer*, March 11, 1955, 1, 3.
[74] Mümtaz Faik Fenik, "Şu şımarık komşuya …," *Zafer*, September 6, 1953, 1, 3.
[75] Philip Khoury, *Syria and the French Mandate: The Politics of Arab Nationalism 1920–1945* (Princeton: Princeton University Press), 494–514; Sarah Shields, *Fezzes in the River: Identity Politics and European Diplomacy in the Middle East on the Eve of World War II* (New York: Oxford University Press, 2011).

boundary. *Zafer* asserted that Syria had established an entire "industry" across the border, making products that could be smuggled into Turkey and sold for a higher value than in Syria.[76] Likewise, livestock and overvalued lira were said to be flowing out of Turkey and into Syria. Since, by the mid 1950s, the DP's economic policy depended on maintaining Turkey as a sealed-off monetary unit, the leakage occurring along the border was a significant threat. And, even more threatening, the Syrian government was said to be conducting unapproved flights through Turkish airspace, leading one *Türk Sesi* columnist to wonder, "If we don't bow to this terror demonstration of Syria's, will Damascus's planes be bombing Ankara?"[77]

Speaking to the US ambassador in January 1957, Bayar repeated many of these accusations – emphasizing, for example, that Syrian smuggling "seriously affects our balance of payments" and that Soviet influence was growing. As for Nasser, despite the DP government's public efforts at rapprochement, Bayar described him as an opportunist in comparison with the "civilized, cultured" leaders in Iraq and Lebanon. Working with the Arab world, he declared, Turkey and the United States "can break Nasser's back." And this would be a positive development, since, "if the Egyptians could get rid of Nasser and live normally, they would know what prosperous life means." As for Syria, which had grown more hostile to members of the Baghdad Pact and more solicitous of Soviet aid and expertise, he deemed it "hopeless."[78] Turkey began encouraging neighboring regimes in Iraq, Jordan, Lebanon, and Saudi Arabia to take action. As the political scientist Reem Abou El-Fadl describes, the goal of Bayar's efforts was to "emphasise the utility of the Turkish role" in mobilizing Middle Eastern regimes to deal with the spread of communism.[79] Such "utility," DP leaders hoped, would be rewarded by the United States and UK.

Turkey's diplomatic efforts, as well as a build-up of 50,000 soldiers on the southern border by September 1957, did not push neighboring governments to intervene in Syria. They did, however, draw threats of intervention from the USSR, which, in turn, led the United States to align itself with Turkey to a degree it had not formally done before.[80] Under the terms of NATO, Turkey could expect support in the event of

[76] Mümtaz Faik Fenik, "Suriye'de kaçakçılık endüstrisi," *Zafer*, March 31, 1955, 1, 4.
[77] Zeynel Besim Sun, "Suriye'nin küstahlığı," *Türk Sesi*, March 30, 1955, 1, 5.
[78] Fletcher Warren to State, January 24, 1957, RG 84, Box 73, UD 3288, NND 959265 (hereafter RG 84, Box 73).
[79] Abou El-Fadl, *Foreign Policy as Nation Making*, 245.
[80] David Lesch, *Syria and the United States: Eisenhower's Cold War in the Middle East* (Boulder: Westview Press, 1992), 156.

an invasion. Now it seemed as if the DP government might expect support in the event of a conflict that *it* initiated. US officials offered strong words of support even as they pressured DP leaders to reduce troop levels and tone down their own belligerent talk. Rhetoric and provocative actions aside, it is unclear whether DP leaders actually intended to attack Syria; rather, they may have sought to draw the United States further into the situation in order to extract additional security and economic guarantees. As the historian Salim Yaqub observes, "Throughout the Syrian crisis, Turkish officials had lobbied Washington for increased economic and military aid, arguing that events in Syria were forcing Turkey to divert precious resources to its defense."[81]

Whether DP leaders were really prepared to invade a country like Syria to check communist influence remains a matter of conjecture. Given that Syria joined with Egypt to form the "United Arab Republic" just months later, in February 1958, Turkish efforts to check Syrian radicalism were certainly ineffective. Yet by making an aggressive display, DP leaders made it easier for US and British officials to justify continued financial support – and difficult, politically, to deny such support. It was necessary to provide frequent reminders to the United States of Turkey's anti-communist bona fides, because the US diplomats with whom Zorlu and others dealt were incredibly touchy and suspicious. In August 1957, for example, just prior to the outbreak of tensions on the Syrian border, US Ambassador Fletcher Warren had signed off on a memo to his superiors that suggested Turkish support for the United States might be softening. He listed a series of events (dancers from Soviet Uzbekistan being issued visas and Menderes being "too tired" to attend a commemoration of the Truman Doctrine's tenth anniversary) as evidence of a concerted campaign by Turkey to signal to the United States that "it is not impossible for Turkey to find elsewhere its political and economic requirements." This diplomatic stratagem was attributed to Zorlu, who Fletcher noted was "part

[81] Salim Yaqub, *Containing Arab Nationalism: The Eisenhower Doctrine and the Middle East* (Chapel Hill, NC: University of North Carolina Press, 2004), 172. Ayşegül Sever makes a similar argument in "The Compliant Ally? Turkey and the West in the Middle East 1954–58," *Middle Eastern Studies* 34, no. 2 (1998): 81–86. A glance at the pro-DP press during the 1957 Syrian Crisis suggests that the government was not particularly serious in its threats. With the election due in October, coverage of Syria was limited. To the extent that coverage continued, it tended to emphasize the centrality of DP leaders in diplomacy, with such headlines as "Our Prime Minister's Answer to Bulganin" and "Important Foreign Meetings Are Being Held in Ankara" – or, alternatively, headlines that overstated the government's American support by stating "If Turkey Is Attacked, America Will Be at Its Side" and "American State Department: 'We Are in Agreement with Menderes'" ("Başvekilimizin Bulganin'e cevabı," *Zafer*, October 5, 1957, 1; "Ankara'da çok mühim …," *Havadis*, October 9, 1957, 1; "Türkiye tecavüze …," *Zafer*, October 12, 1957, 1; "Amerika Harciyesi …,'" *Havadis*, October 12, 1957, 1).

Russian" genetically and whose "father [in-law]" had been foreign minister during years in which Turkey and the USSR were close.[82] In other words, Turkish diplomats were dealing with American peers capable of jumping to dramatic conclusions based on limited evidence. Whether or not Zorlu was a diplomatic genius, he was certainly a virtuoso at playing on American anxieties.

Scholars critical of Turkey's participation in the US-led Cold War order have argued that during the 1950s the DP leaders overstated the Soviet threat. The political scientist Baskın Oran, for example, argues that this hyperbole was "an economically bankrupt regime's strategy of securing foreign aid and foreign loans by continually exaggerating this communist threat." Commitment to this exaggeration led DP leaders to ignore Soviet efforts to improve relations.[83] Yet, such depictions of DP errors say as much about a scholar's own assessment of the USSR in the 1950s as they do about DP leaders' judgement. While DP governments certainly leveraged US anxieties to their benefit, these leaders also had anxieties of their own. DP leaders were not radicals seeking to upend the social order, as were their peers in Egypt or, increasingly, Syria. They were creators and products of the existing social order. Like their peers in countries such as Iraq and Lebanon, they sought to maintain it.

Winner Take All: The Election of 1957

Not only did DP leaders appeal to American fears of communist expansion, but they also played on Western European fears of losing access to Turkey's markets. British firms pressured their government to support their Turkish ventures in order to prevent West German firms from displacing them. Similarly, leaders in Western Europe believed that it was necessary to provide support for their firms in Turkey in order to prevent commercial gains by Eastern European firms, whose communist system ostensibly allowed them to underbid on contracts.[84] Thus, while

[82] Fletcher Warren to State, August 2, 1957, RG 84, Box 74.

[83] Baskın Oran, "Dönemin Bilançosu," in *Türk Dış Politikası, Cilt I: 1919–1980*, ed. Baskın Oran (Istanbul: İletişim Yayınları, 2001), 497. Oran's evaluation, although made in 2001, reflects a line of argument dating back at least to the 1960s, when Oran was himself a student and efforts to rethink the origins of the Cold War were becoming common. Yet the notion that the DP was willfully inattentive to the diminishing seriousness of the Soviet threat continues to be made by a new generation of scholars such as Reem Abou El-Fadl, who argues that the DP leaders' foreign policy was not strictly "realist" (i.e., reacting to objective threats), but rather focused on more abstract concerns like "the making and projecting of the meaning of the 'nation,'" which they defined as anti-communist (El-Fadl, *Foreign Policy as Nation Making*, 7, 17).

[84] Clifford Heathcote-Smith to D. M. O'Brien, November 10, 1956, FO 371/124024.

the various bilateral deals signed in 1954–55 had committed Western European countries to purchase from Turkish producers so that Turkey could pay off its backlog of commercial debts, the Turkish government was able to play on inter-European rivalries in order to attract new business and investment as well.[85]

Skillful as these diplomatic and commercial maneuvers were, they did not solve Turkey's underlying problems. The tight credit policies imposed in 1956 meant that Turkey's trade deficit was smaller in 1957 than it had been in nearly a decade; nonetheless, it was still $31 million by the end of the year. Total debt amounted to $1.1 billion (only a slight decline from a year earlier), and annual debt payment obligations had risen to $238 million, around 70 percent of Turkey's entire "prospective" earnings from exports in 1958.[86]

Faced with these challenges, DP leaders had no clear short-term solutions. Government officials argued that a devaluation would not stimulate exports, since the problem was insufficient production, and this could only be solved by continued investment.[87] Likewise, despite talk of curbing inflation, the policymakers remained reluctant to take measures that might slow the government's economic development drive or provoke public discontent. They resisted capping bank credit or further increasing the prices of goods produced by state-owned enterprises, which currently financed their large deficits by borrowing. With an election scheduled for 1958, there was an incentive to maintain subsidies.

Sensing the DP was vulnerable and likely to grow more unpopular in the year to come, the opposition parties began negotiations in early 1957 over how they might coordinate in the coming election. Hoping

[85] Though Turkey continued to seek new business with Western Europe, the DP government was encouraging businesses to shift their trade away from countries in the EPU in order to avoid accumulating more debts. While countries in the EPU had provided 69 percent of Turkey's imports and bought 59 percent of its exports in 1951, by 1957 these volumes had fallen to 41 percent and 48 percent, respectively ("European Payments Union: The Economic Situation of Turkey," OEEC, May 3, 1958, 19, FO 371/134424).

[86] Ibid., 20.

[87] "Turkish Ambassador's Speech before the New York Board of Trade," January 16, 1958, RG 59, Lot 61, Box 16, D48, NND 897232 (hereafter RG 59, Lot 61, Box 16). One rare concession was the announcement of a "tourist" exchange rate that applied to foreigners. US officials hoped that this acceptance of multiple rates would help transition to a complete devaluation following the October 1957 election. In the near term, however, the "tourist" rate was a source of diplomatic headaches, since it was not always recognized by the Turkish banks that tourists patronized. These occasions led to recriminations between diplomatic officials and promises from Turkey's directorate of exchange control in May 1957 that it would be more consistent in enforcing the rate (RG, December 29, 1956, 16077; Foreign Service Dispatch, June 4, 1957, The Exchange Rate File 1955–56, RG 59, Lot 58, Box 2).

to preempt a united opposition, the DP moved up the elections to October 1957.[88] There would be no reduction in spending before then. In fact, according to the economist (and government critic) Osman Okyar, 1957 saw the government's expansionary monetary policy reach its "highest tempo. Bank notes in circulation and Central Bank credits both increased by 27 percent. Commercial bank credits rose by 33 percent and bank deposits by 23 percent." In contrast, agricultural and industrial output only rose 6 percent.[89] The gap between money in circulation and items actually available to purchase spurred inflation.

As in recent years, a large portion of Central Bank credit went to cover the debts of the TMO and agricultural cooperatives, both of which racked up substantial losses by buying and selling agricultural products at prices set far above market rates. The TMO's debt of TL346 million in early 1957 was about one-third of all state-owned enterprise debt. Yet other indebted enterprises also illustrate the problems the government was facing. Sugar factories were TL188 million in debt and Etibank, which underwrote many of the large electrical projects, was TL225 million in the red.[90] While some degree of debt was inevitable when building factories, dams, and power stations, the main problem lay in the increasing difficulty of importing raw materials *combined with* price controls that limited what enterprises like the Etibank-managed coal mines could charge.[91] Attempts to raise prices were met with criticism from opposition parties and the public more generally. An attempt to raise Istanbul bus fares in early January 1957 was quickly scuttled at Menderes's request.[92]

It was unclear how much longer the government could sustain its economic policies. People in urban areas were experiencing shortages of farm products like meat and bread. Nationwide, people were unable to reliably procure staple imports like coffee. During periods of acute dearth, President Bayar began demanding that his guests make do with tea. His symbolic measure was reflective of a common necessity.[93] In order to stretch limited resources, merchants were mixing coffee with ground-up chickpeas, barley, and hazelnuts, prompting the Istanbul city

88 Toker, *DP Yokuş Aşağı*, 194–196.
89 Osman Okyar, "Inflation in a Mixed Economy," in *Capital Formation and Investment in Industry* (Istanbul: İstanbul Matbaası, 1963), 363.
90 "European Payments Union: The Economic Situation of Turkey," May 3, 1958, FO 371/134424.
91 Okyar, "Inflation in a Mixed Economy," 360.
92 "Zamların kaldırılması," *Akşam*, January 5, 1957, 1.
93 Arzık, *Menderes'i İpe Götürenler*, 48. Mehmet Alkan observes that during the 1957 campaign, the CHP printed posters declaring, "Coffee Is Gone, But Justice Survives" (Alkan, "Kahve-Kahvaltı ve Çay Tiryakiliği," in *Türkiye'nin 1950'li Yılları*, ed. Mete Kaan Kaynar [Istanbul: İletişim Yayınları, 2015], 620).

government to issue warnings that such concoctions were "outside the regulations."[94]

Regulations had, in fact, become both omnipresent and insufficient. The National Protection Law's ambit ranged from fixing the price of basic items like eggs, milk, and cheese to rationing gasoline, from briefly halting sales of sugar and other items to dictating the size and print runs of newspapers.[95] In this sense, the law was a consideration that had to be accounted for in people's everyday lives. At the same time, people often considered it in order to avoid it. Newspapers might decry black-market activity, but they also reported the unofficial prices of items. In her *Zafer* column, the novelist Mükerrem Kamil Su argued that acceptance of the black market was undermining social cohesion. Recalling how "we" sought out black-market items regardless of laws, she concluded: "There's still a hypocrisy within us ... confronted with an occurrence contrary to individuals and society, we've learned to shrug our shoulders and say, 'Who am I to fix the world?'"[96] Rather than maintain order, the National Protection Law had led many to lose faith in the government.

Whereas pro-government newspapers emphasized the positive steps taken to fix the law, those critical of the government, like the Istanbul daily *Akşam* (Evening), focused on the struggles over crafting these fixes. Merchants, it reported, were particularly eager to end the separation of importing, wholesaling, and retail so that they could operate in multiple sectors. These demands did not fall on deaf ears. The president of the Union of Chambers of Commerce, Industry, and Exchanges, Üzeyir Avunduk, was not only a businessman himself but also general director of İş Bankası, a close friend of President Bayar, and a leader of the DP. During the union's May 1957 meeting, Avunduk argued that the "necessary organization had not been established" to achieve the law's objectives.[97] The chamber of commerce added specificity to these criticisms by preparing its own report calling for a system of export premiums (tantamount to a devaluation), a strict and clearly budgeted system of foreign exchange allocation, and improved price controls.[98] Parliament discussed revisions over the course of the spring, but without any result, leaving merchants disgruntled.[99]

94 Orhan Tahsin, "Kahve yerine ...," *Akşam*, July 11, 1956, 3; "Çekirdek kahvenin kilosu ...," *Akşam*, January 22, 1957, 3.
95 Mustafa Albayrak, "Demokrat Parti Döneminde Milli Korunma Kanunu Uygulamaları, 1955–1960," *Atatürk Araştırma Merkezi Dergisi* 23 (2007): 239–241.
96 Mükerrem Kamil Su, "İstifçilik," *Zafer*, November 22, 1956, 3.
97 "Tüccar ve sanayici ...," *Akşam*, May 31, 1957, 1, 2.
98 "Dış ticaret ...," *Akşam*, May 27, 1957, 1; "İhracatımızın ...," *Akşam*, June 8, 1957, 1, 4.
99 "Tacirler Milli Korunma ...," *Cumhuriyet*, June 9, 1957, 1, 5.

Other legislation, meanwhile, intensified interparty tensions. Kırşehir, the electoral base of popular opposition parliamentarian Osman Bölükbaşı, had been reduced to the status of a district following the 1954 election. Now, the DP restored its provincial status while simultaneously detaching two of its districts to create a new pro-DP province. As a result, Kırşehir lost one of its five seats in parliament.[100] During the parliamentary debate, Bölükbaşı pointed to President Bayar himself as the "vindictive man" responsible for penalizing the province.[101] In response to this accusation, DP legislators voted to strip Bölükbaşı of his legal immunity. On July 2, he was arrested for "slander" on the orders of the Ankara investigating magistrate's office.[102] He found himself sharing a cell with İnönü's son-in-law, the journalist Metin Toker, who had recently been jailed for libel after alleging that Mükerrem Sarol had not divested himself of ownership in *Türk Sesi* upon becoming a minister.[103]

Menderes was not present for the vote on Bölükbaşı's immunity, which was held on the last day of the session before a two-month recess. The prime minister was busy preparing for a tour of the country. His trip marked the beginning of an intense four months of campaigning. As with the 1954 election campaign, the DP's 1957 effort combined rallies and factory openings. In late June, Menderes and Bayar attended the groundbreaking of a cigarette factory. In July, they attended the groundbreaking for Atatürk University in Erzurum.[104] In August, Menderes was in Kastamonu to open a sugar factory and Zonguldak to open new port facilities. This pattern was interrupted in early September when parliament briefly reconvened. For a moment, headlines shifted focus from factory openings to promises of up to TL102 million in "additional" budget appropriations for road and water projects.[105] Thereafter, DP

[100] In order to keep up with population growth, the number of seats in parliament increased from 541 (in 1954–57) to 610 (in 1957–60); consequently, most provinces gained seats irrespective of party affiliation. Only four provinces lost seats: Kırşehir (which, as discussed above, lost a seat to the newly created neighboring province of Nevşehir); Malatya (which lost three seats on account of its pro-DP districts being reorganized as the five-seat province of Adıyaman); Niğde (which voted for the DP in 1954, but had some of its more pro-DP districts added to Nevşehir); and the pro-DP province of Kocaeli, which lost six seats owing to the creation of the eight-seat Sakarya province (effectively creating two *additional* DP seats).

[101] TBMM, June 12, 1957, 163.

[102] TBMM, June 24, 1957; "Osman ...," *İstanbul Ekspres*, July 3, 1957, 1, 5.

[103] Toker, *DP Yokuş Aşağı*, 106, 225–245; Erer, *On Yılın Mücadelesi*, 284–285; Cüneyt Arcayürek, *Bir İktidar Bir İhtilal, 1955–1960* (Ankara: Bilgi Yayınevi, 1984), 155–160.

[104] Richard Garlitz, "Land-Grant Education in Turkey: Atatürk University and American Technical Assistance, 1954–68," in *Turkey in the Cold War Ideology and Culture*, ed. Cangül Örnek and Çağdaş Üngör (London: Palgrave Macmillan, 2013), 177–197.

[105] "Köylerin ...," *Zafer*, September 8, 1957, 1, 4.

politicians dispersed to their provinces and pro-DP media again turned its attention to factory openings, only now with greater intensity.[106]

In speeches around the country, DP leaders emphasized how much Turkey had developed under their stewardship. Development was treated as a form of battle, thus justifying the hardships that citizens were enduring in the present. Samet Ağaoğlu, now serving as minister of operations (i.e., state-owned enterprises), toured the country, pointing to rises in production and income.[107] At a rally in Istanbul, he declared, "This is one of the grand struggles that fill the great eras of history." The country was witnessing a battle between "those who want to hold the Turkish Nation back and those who want to bring it forward." The former wanted "nothing other than anarchy" because they feared what stability might bring. It was, after all, easier to rule over the weak and poor, "More difficult is governing a nation that has reached a high level of material and spiritual life, a national economic order, and taken a side in the world of economic relations."[108]

President Bayar's speeches relied less on rhetorical flourishes. Instead, he emphasized the accomplishments of the party and the improved material conditions of citizens, sometimes even adding a joke. He pointed to the three-fold expansion of credit, the increased production of industrial materials, land distribution, roads, and oil exploration – all coupled with the removal of "damaging" taxes and the "stick in the hand of [their] collector."[109] As for worries over inflation, the balding president promised crowds in Konya, "Believe this: I am a person who pulls his hair out over such matters."[110]

This folksy style was even more common to Menderes's speeches, many of which were framed as an imagined argument with İnönü. The opposition leader, Menderes explained to crowds in İzmir, was accusing

106 In the six weeks before the October 27, 1957 election, official events that doubled as campaign events included: a groundbreaking for worker housing in Ankara on September 23; the opening of a pasteurized milk factory on September 30; a groundbreaking of a new building for the general directorate of statistics on October 3; a groundbreaking for a new cement factory in Niğde on October 5; the opening of a munitions factory on October 7; a groundbreaking for a jute and canvas sack factory in Mudanya on October 8; and the opening of a cement factory in Afyon on October 11 ("Blok ...," *Zafer*, September 24, 1957, 1, 4; "Pastörize ...," *Zafer*, October 1, 1957, 1; "İstatistik ...," *Zafer*, October 4, 1957, 1; "Türkiye'nin ...," *Zafer*, October 6, 1957, 1; "Gazi ...," *Zafer*, October 8, 1957, 1; "Jüt ...," *Zafer*, October 9, 1957, 1; "Türkiye ...," *İstanbul Ekspres*, October 12, 1957, 1).

107 "Politika Hasbihalı ...," *Zafer*, August 24, 1957, 1.

108 "Her anarşiden ...," *Havadis*, October 21, 1957, 1.

109 "Reisicumhurun ...," *Zafer*, October 13, 1957, 1,3, 5; "Reisicumhur ...," *Zafer*, October 19, 1957, 1–2.

110 "Bayar ...," *Zafer*, October 20, 1957, 1, 3.

the DP of "wastefulness" and of moving ahead with excessive speed. Yet, the prime minister explained, "we have no patience for waiting five years for what can be done in one month." What had İnönü and his CHP accomplished in their twenty-seven years in power? "A few factories and railroads. That's it." The DP's efforts had brought people a higher standard of living. Shortages reflected this. Production of eggs, milk, and other food was up, and yet these were hard to find. "Did we export these? Did we toss them into the ocean? No," Menderes explained, these shortages were a result of people being able to increase their consumption for the first time as a result of their growing wealth.[111]

The opposition, he told crowds in Samsun, was out to trick voters. The DP came to the nation with "a shovel in one hand and scissors in the other," the first to bring welfare, the second to cut the ribbon on all its new projects. The opposition, by contrast, had a "fist full of spinach [in one hand] and a broom or cup of coffee in the other." When the DP opened a new port, the opposition would talk of spinach prices; when the DP showed off a new factory, the opposition would draw attention to the expensive broom and coffee. Yet the CHP had no actual plan. Its main proposal was to revise the constitution in league with the other opposition parties, implement a system of proportional representation, and then hold new elections. According to Menderes, these changes would ignore the will of the voters and turn Turkey into an unstable country like France, where communist "satellite parties" held sway.[112]

These references to French political instability were Menderes's way of justifying the measures that the DP had taken to stymie any coordination between opposition parties. As late as September 1957, the CHP and HP had planned to formally coordinate their candidate lists. Assuming that the DP did worse in the coming election than it had in 1954, such coordination could deny the DP victories in large provinces like Adana (where it had previously won with 49.2 percent) and Sivas (where its 52.7 percent victory might not withstand bad economic conditions). Although the leaders of the HP lacked Menderes's common touch and the financial resources of the DP's organization, the party's very existence served as a reminder that the governing party had lost its reformist zeal. Not only had the DP lost academics like Turan Güneş and Osman Okyar, but it had also alienated important activists. For example, the head of the DP's

[111] "Başvekilimizin ...," *Havadis*, October 21, 1957, 4.

[112] "İnönü ...," *Zafer*, October 17, 1957, 1, 4. The CHP's concern with the high cost of brooms was not merely fanciful phrasing on Menderes's part. During a rally in Malatya featuring Interior Minister Namık Gedik, CHP members hung a broom from a balcony overlooking the plaza with a sign reading, "In 1950, 75 kuruş; in 1957, 495 kuruş" ("Malatya ...," *Akşam*, October 17, 1957, 3).

Youth Arm, a young lawyer named Hüsamettin Cindoruk, had quit the party in response to the leadership's high-handed tactics at the 1955 congress. In notifying the party of his departure, he declared, "I am resigning from the un-democratic Democrat Party." Within months he was organizing an HP Youth Arm.[113]

The most potentially damaging resignations from the DP came only months before the election. In July 1957, Sarol's faction of the Istanbul DP finally succeeded in ousting Orhan Köprülü as provincial president. Orhan promptly quit the DP entirely and joined the HP. On September 6, he was named president of the party's Istanbul branch. The following day Fuat Köprülü resigned from the DP with the announcement that the party's recent actions had "entirely repudiated the fundamental ideas that brought it to power."[114] As a party founder, Köprülü's accusations could not be easily dismissed. Even if he lacked popular appeal, he was a symbol of the party's struggle for democracy against the single-party regime. In order to ensure that he could not be added to the HP list, the DP spent the final day of the parliamentary session amending the Election Law. The new version prohibited parties from coordinating and barred candidates who resigned from one party from standing as a candidate for another party within a six-month period.[115]

Newspapers echoed Menderes in justifying these measures. *Havadis* described interparty coordination as a form of "vote-smuggling" and wondered how, "[since] we prohibit heroin smuggling, can we not prevent this political smuggling intended to deceive the popular will?"[116] In addition to smuggling and theft as preferred metaphors, papers followed Menderes's lead in comparing opposition coordination to French precedents. At *İstanbul Ekspres*, a columnist wrote that when French politics became dominated by shifting factions in the 1930s, the Communist Party gained influence and the state halted construction on the Maginot Line defenses protecting the country from invasion by Nazi Germany.[117] On October 25, with less than two days to go before the elections and a ban on further domestic political coverage in effect, *Havadis* ran an editorial titled "Unstable Governments in France," which lamented that parties were seeking their own interests rather than the interest of the nation, which benefited the communists.[118] It was not hard to see the allusions to domestic politics.

113 "Hürriyet ...," *Milliyet*, December 26, 1955, 7; Bal, "Aydın Siyaset İlişkisi Bağlamında," 269.
114 "Kurucu ...," *Cumhuriyet*, September 8, 1957, 1, 5.
115 TBMM, September 11, 1957, 715–716.
116 "Rey ...," *Havadis*, August 23, 1957, 1, 5.
117 Cevdet Perin, "İşbirliği ...," *İstanbul Ekspres*, August 17, 1957, 1, 5.
118 "Fransa'da ...," *Havadis*, October 25, 1957, 1, 5.

The ouster of Orhan Köprülü by Sarol and other Menderes allies in Istanbul was part of a larger move by the national DP leadership to exert control over the provinces. During the 1954 election, the DP's executive committee had overruled numerous provincial party organizations by imposing its preferred candidates on their lists; in 1957, these interventions grew more numerous. Out of sixty-seven provinces, the executive committee determined the list without a local primary in twenty-eight.[119] When the candidate lists were announced on October 7, around a quarter of the DP representatives had been replaced. Menderes allies – even those who, like *Havadis* editor Bahadır Dülger had lost their primaries – remained on the list.[120]

The remainder of October was devoted to speeches and events. Although this was the election campaign in which Bayar famously declared to a rally in Istanbul that Turkey would someday become "a little America," the United States itself was seldom explicitly at the forefront of the campaign. Even that reference to "a little America" was part of a larger speech based on familiar campaign themes of fewer taxes and more projects.[121] "America" was symbolic of a larger ambition to, in the words of a *Zafer* editorial, "raise a country underdeveloped for centuries to the level of today's advanced nations." The editorial went on to sum up the DP's justification for its repressive policies:

> Turkey today is not under normal living conditions. It is in the midst of a deep, wide, and extensive social and spiritual revolution. This revolution will follow a course that changes social conditions at the root, whether we want it or not. In this as yet unstable situation, in order to prevent dangerous trends, it is the state's duty to pay attention to some rights being misused.[122]

This "social and spiritual revolution," which necessitated careful attention to how "some rights" were used, was manifested through construction projects. During September and October, *Zafer* ran a series of articles covering "What the Provinces Have Gained beyond the Grand Main Facilities of the Great Development Battle." It listed in minute detail the projects that each province had received.[123] For many readers,

119 "40 ilin ...," *Milliyet*, October 1, 1957, 1; Burçak, *On Yılın Anıları*, 479–480.

120 "D.P. yoklamaları ...," *Milliyet*, October 3, 1957, 1, 5. "Demokrat Parti ...," *Milliyet*, October 8, 1957, 5.

121 "Milletimizin ...," *Havadis*, October 21, 1957, 1, 5.

122 "Kalkınma ve demokrasi ...," *Zafer*, September 3, 1957, 1, 4.

123 In the case of Malatya, *Zafer* stated that the province had received TL4.28 million for roads over the previous seven years. Two middle and seventy-three primary schools had been built, with another twenty-four in the tendering stage. Some TL888,000 had been spent on bringing drinking water to thirty-nine villages, though the degree of success was not specified ("Malatya," *Zafer*, October 9, 1957, 3).

the most obvious example would have been the DP's urban renewal projects in Istanbul. Beginning in 1956, Menderes had pushed ahead with a refashioning of the city that included multilane thoroughfares cutting through old neighborhoods – and through the city's ancient walls.[124] The construction program, with its seizure of property under eminent domain laws, was merely the most dramatic example of a process that had already been occurring in provincial centers likes Balıkesir. As in those other cases, redundant property seizures compensated at market rates were a source of controversy. Some people were unhappy to part with their homes and places of business. Others were all too happy, since they could use connections with the municipality to secure an inflated valuation of their property. The latter possibility was at the heart of a scandal that emerged in September, when it was reported that a group of Istanbul city councilmen and contractors had conspired to defraud the municipality. All the politicians were DP members. One was a district president.[125]

This scandal, like others before it, did not cost the DP the election in either Istanbul or the country at large, but it likely contributed to a general decline in enthusiasm for the party. Nationwide, the party's share of the vote fell from the 58.4 percent it had won in 1954 down to 48.6 percent. The CHP, on the other hand, improved on its performance in the previous two elections by wining 41.4 percent of the vote (up from 35.1 percent). The party even succeeded in winning back key provinces like Ankara and Adana. In the capital province, with its high proportion of government workers on fixed incomes, the DP's inability to tame inflation and stabilize the economy was likely an important factor. In Adana, a province where the DP was particularly riven by factionalism, the CHP was able to gain the support of disaffected local power brokers.[126] In Malatya, where the DP-voting provinces had been separated to create the province of Adıyaman after the previous election, the

[124] Murat Gül, *The Emergence of Modern Istanbul: Transformation and Modernisation of a City* (London: I. B. Tauris, 2009), 140–171; Murat Gül, *Architecture and the Turkish City: An Urban History of Istanbul since the Ottomans* (London: I. B. Tauris, 2017), 87–116.

[125] "İstimlak ...," *Akşam*, September 3, 1957, 1; "İstimlak ...," *Cumhuriyet*, September 4, 1957, 1, 5.

[126] Béatrice Garapon attributes the DP's loss in Adana to dissatisfaction among small merchants, who joined with some of the large landowners that had remained loyal to the CHP (like CHP General Secretary Kasım Gülek). The DP retained the support of industrialists, many of whom had come to Adana from Kayseri in the 1920s. Karataş emphasizes dissatisfaction within the provincial DP regarding the electoral list, which did not include representatives from key districts and which include candidates imposed by the national party (Karataş, "Demokrat Parti Döneminde," 100–112; Garapon, "Aux origines de la Turquie conservatrice", 460–461).

CHP was predictably dominant.[127] On the eve of the election, the CHP had controlled only 6 percent of seats in parliament, fewer than the breakaway HP. Now it held 29 percent of the seats. As can be seen in the graph reproduced here (Figure 5.1), however, the gap between representation in parliament and actual share of the vote reflected the continuing advantage the DP derived from the winner-take-all electoral system, which the CHP itself had created (and which the DP adjusted to its own benefit). According to calculations by the newspaper *Akşam*, had the opposition parties been allowed to coordinate in the election, the DP would have been defeated in an additional twenty-one provinces and lost control of parliament.[128]

The opposition parties argued that the DP had won reelection only through legislative trickery. Yet the ability of opposition leaders to convince their voters to back each other party's list was never tested during the 1957 election. When such coordination was attempted in subsequent years, it led to mass defections from the HP back to the DP. Moreover, a close look at the numbers suggests that the opposition did little to expand its base of support. Between 1954 and 1957, the registered number of voters grew by 18 percent, and yet the actual number of people voting for the CHP increased only 19 percent, hardly evidence of a groundswell of support. Then again, at least the party leadership could take pleasure in having *maintained* its level of support among voters. The DP, by contrast, attracted 15 percent fewer individual voters than in 1954 – and *25 percent fewer* if we factor in population growth. Rather than switch party loyalty, however, many of these voters seem to have simply abstained. Turnout, which had been 89.3 percent and 88.6 percent in the previous two elections, fell to 76.6 percent in 1957. Over the next six decades, there would be elections with lower participation, but never such a sizeable decline.[129] After seven years and three elections, the DP remained in

[127] The CHP's share of the vote in Malatya rose from 54.3 percent (1954) to 65.3 percent (1957). In Adıyaman, the DP won a plurality with 49.8 percent, against 37.7 percent for the CHP and 12.2 percent for the HP. If Malatya and Adıyaman in 1957 are analyzed as a single province, however, then the CHP vote total is 54.3 percent, unchanged from the previous election (TÜİK, *Milletvekili Genel Seçimleri*, 27, 69).

[128] "İşbirliği ...," *Akşam*, October 28, 1957, 1.

[129] TÜİK, *Milletvekili Genel Seçimleri*, 25. The verdict of voters was especially hard on the HP, which secured only 3.5 percent of the national vote and won only the province of Burdur, which gave it four seats in parliament. Burdur was the home of Fethi Çelikbaş, one of the party's leading figures. Like many HP leaders, Çelikbaş was an influential landowner (which accounted for some of his success), but even in Burdur the HP only won 35.7 percent, as against the DP's 33.4 percent. In Manisa, the home province of party leader Fevzi Lütfi Karaosmanoğlu, the HP received only 7.5 percent of the vote (TÜİK, *Milletvekili Genel Seçimleri*, 25, 40, 70).

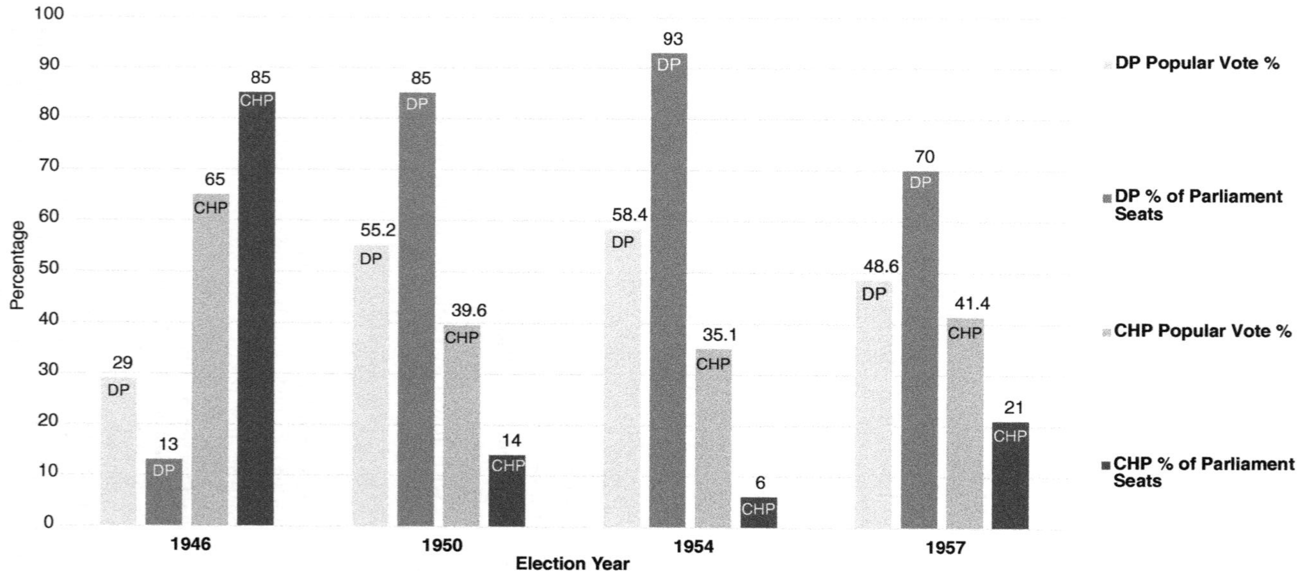

Figure 5.1 Popular vote share in Turkish general elections compared with share of seats in parliament, 1946–57.

power, but it had lost support among the majority of citizens who cast their ballots, as well as those too uninspired to even bother voting.

Bailout

The DP's underwhelming performance in the 1957 elections discouraged its leaders from taking dramatic (and unpopular) steps to balance the economy. From the perspective of Menderes and Zorlu (who was reappointed foreign minister following the election), any reform on the scale of a devaluation would be unpopular. It would require sizeable financial commitments from the United States and other Western countries. But these same countries had been expecting DP leaders to enact reforms following the election. Within eight months, the US government would finally lose patience with the DP's delaying tactics.

In a meeting with the US ambassador, Fletcher Warren, on December 10, 1957, Zorlu emphasized the economic element of Turkey's problems, announcing that stocks of key goods were "exhausted." Menderes, also present, connected the DP's political difficulties with US interests by asserting that "Recent elections have clearly shown that Communist pressures [have] become heavier on Turkey, encouraging any and every kind of opposition. This is becoming increasingly harmful for Turkey's political stability."[130] Faced with these challenges, the DP moved to further constrain institutional checks on its actions by limiting parliamentary oversight. During the last week of December, the DP passed legislation that limited debate, reducing the time set aside for questioning ministers, allowing ministers more leeway to not respond to questions, and making it easier to temporarily expel and fine representatives.[131] These bills were well-timed: Turkey had already been failing to make bilateral debt payments since September; at the end of December, it defaulted on payments to several petroleum firms.[132]

With political leaders' nerves already on edge, a military conspiracy was discovered on December 27, 1957, when a junior officer reported it to the owner of the pro-DP paper *İstanbul Ekspres*. Arrests quickly followed, and reporting on the event was censored in the press. Several members of the conspiracy had close ties to the CHP, and, in meetings with US officials, Zorlu implied that there might be a link between the CHP and the USSR. Whether or not Zorlu believed in the connection,

130 Fletcher Warren to State, December 11, 1957, Economic Aid Turkey General 1956–1957 File, RG 84, Box 78.

131 Eroğul, *Demokrat Parti*, 207. For the legislation and debate, see TBMM, December 25 and 27, 1957.

132 Colin Brant, "The Turkish Economic Situation," January 22, 1958, FO 371/136470.

Ambassador Warren was certainly skeptical. Hearing from Zorlu that İnönü had recently met with the Soviet ambassador – and, perhaps, sensing where such implications might lead – Warren emphasized İnönü's "prestige both inside and outside Turkey" and hoped that the "investigation would not produce any info which would involve İnönü."[133]

The incident increased pressure on both DP leaders and the US government to prevent the continuation of economic conditions that might lead to social unrest and favor other would-be coup plotters. Already, the United States was promising $70 million in defense aid for 1958–59, $46.8 million in cheap grain, and $4.5 million in technical assistance, but Turkish diplomats deemed these insufficient. Suat Hayri Ürgüplü, Turkey's US ambassador, noted that the United States was giving as much or more to countries with "Communist leanings" than it gave to Turkey.[134] Speaking at a dinner given by the New York board of trade, Ürgüplü expanded on this critique, arguing that "Friends and allies should be treated on a different basis from foes and uncommitted countries." He observed that Turkey received less money per capita than other members of NATO, despite providing 28 percent of its ground forces. It was unjust to overlook Turkey's outsized contribution, given its comparative underdevelopment. Appealing to shared values, he argued, "[A] free society is not an economic machine. There are various other points, political points, social points, strategic points and others that have to be considered."

In case his moral argument for better treatment did not appeal to the assembled businessmen, Ürgüplü also made a more economistic argument as well: Turkish soldiers were paid only $0.16 a month, meaning that "the annual maintenance cost of one Turkish soldier amounted to one hundred thirty six dollars, as against some five thousand five hundred dollars for one United States service man." In light of such savings, it was wrong for the United States to be so stingy or to ask a nation of poor peasants to tighten their belts – "Most of them," he observed, "have no belts." Certainly, he acknowledged, "we may have made some mistakes … [but] the responsibility is not ours alone. It is shared with you, and it is our duty to work together to correct them."[135]

[133] Fletcher Warren to Secretary of State, January 16, 1958, Turkey 1958 File, RG 84, Box 77, UD 3288, NND 959265 (hereafter RG 84, Box 77); Metin Toker, *Demokrasiden Darbeye 1957–1960: Demokrasimizin İsmet Paşa'lı Yılları* (Istanbul: Bilgi Yayınevi, 1991 [1966]), 44–55; Hale, *Turkish Politics and the Military*, 100–104.

[134] "Your Forthcoming Trip to Ankara," January 14, 1958, RG 59, Lot 58, Box 2; Memorandum of Conversation, January 10, 1958, RG 59, Lot 58, Box 3, D610, NND 917365 (hereafter RG 59, Lot 58, Box 3).

[135] "Turkish Ambassador's Speech before the New York Board of Trade," January 16, 1958, RG 59, Lot 61, Box 16. In fiscal year 1955, the United States' NATO expenditures "excluding Turkey" were $1.7 billion, while Turkey received $200

With its mix of lofty sentiments and frank calculation, Ürgüplü's speech encapsulated the range of ways in which DP diplomats had been pushing for access to US aid over the previous seven and a half years. Now, with the domestic economic situation worsening, all the arguments were being made at once. The question was not whether a deal was necessary (all the parties involved understood that it was), but what the terms and timing would be. Zorlu still hoped to obtain a clear US commitment before agreeing to any deal with the IMF or OEEC, but US diplomats remained evasive, and their West German peers continued to emphasize the need for currency "reevaluation."[136] Merchants and financiers were not blind to the imminent devaluation. Turkish exporters were facing difficulties marketing the recent tobacco crop while buyers held out for lower prices. During March and April 1958, the price of gold rose 24 percent in Turkey as confidence in the long-term value of the lira plummeted.[137]

In May and early June, Turkish officials maneuvered to improve their bargaining position. Bayar made an official visit to West Germany, with Zorlu in tow, from May 7 to 15. Though West German officials had no illusions about receiving full repayment of the arrears owed German merchants, and even shared the Turkish view that devaluation would be "politically impossible" without financial aid, they maintained a less generous stance in meetings.[138] Zorlu pushed hard on his German peers, reiterating Ürgüplü's points. He complained about German credits to Egypt and pushed for a bilateral deal. When told that the credits to Egypt were "a political decision" made to counter Soviet influence, he replied that Turkey should likewise be evaluated "on political grounds," and added cryptically that there was "another group" ready to help Turkey.[139] Faced with such threats, the West German officials replied that "Germany had more confidence in the future of the Egyptian economy."[140] Zorlu was again told that aid would be multilateral and

million, or about 10 percent of the total, if the two amounts are added together. For 1957, the estimated expenditures were $1.3 billion and $400,000, or 23 percent, which was approaching the percentage that Ürgüplü cited ("10. Draft Memorandum Prepared for the National Security Council," November 28, 1955, *FRUS, 1955–1957*, vol. X: *Foreign Aid and Economic Defense Policy*).

136 Fletcher Warren to State, February 26, 1958, RG 84, Box 78.

137 Clifford Heathcote-Smith to Lambert (Treasury), April 30, 1958, FO 371/136471; Fletcher Warren to State, May 24, 1958, RG 84, Box 78.

138 James Bowker to Foreign Office, May 21, 1958, FO 371/134424.

139 James Bowker to Foreign Office, May 26, 1958, FO 371/134424; Warren to State, June 7, 1958, Economic Aid Turkey General 1956–1957 File, RG 84, Box 78.

140 Memorandum of Conversation, June 4, 1958, Turkey Stabilization-Implementation File, RG 59, Lot 61, Box 17, D96, NND 897232 (hereafter RG 59, Lot 61, Box 17).

dependent on a clear program of reform. When he argued that such reforms were for Menderes to approve and suggested that the prime minister arrange a visit, the West Germans declined to make such an invitation. The whole trip, West German diplomats told their British peers, caused "grave embarrassment."[141]

With West German support unlikely, Bayar wrote "personally" to President Eisenhower on June 3. He reminded his US counterpart that Turkey's dire economic situation was due, in part, to the amount of resources it devoted to military rather than social needs. "Turkey," he cautioned, "is able to bear this heavy burden only through the patriotism and unlimited willingness of sacrifice of the Turkish Nation." He observed that West Germany was committed to finding a solution via the IMF and OEEC but worried that these organizations' "structural composition" leads them to:

> [e]xamine questions from a technical angle rather than attributing enough importance to their political consideration and exigencies. But I have no doubt that Your Excellency would also agree with me that the economic problems of countries cannot be considered apart from their political impacts.[142]

The official response from Eisenhower on June 13 stated that "notwithstanding the progressive increase in the amount of aid rendered to Turkey," the economic situation was worsening, suggesting that solutions "do not lie solely in the amount of aid ... but rather ... in measures of economic stabilization which, I am pleased to learn, are being considered by your government."[143] American forbearance seemed to have run out.

On June 20, Menderes's government proposed a reform package to the IMF. Without formally devaluing the currency, Turkey would introduce a series of export premia that effectively cheapened the cost of Turkish goods and encouraged the inflow of foreign exchange. In return, Turkish officials hoped for a moratorium on debt payments.[144] Though US and British representatives at the IMF were skeptical of the statistics Turkish representatives were providing and frustrated with the vagueness of the

[141] James Bowker to Foreign Office, June 4, 1958, FO 371/134424.
[142] Celal Bayar to Dwight Eisenhower, June 3, 1958, Economic Letter from President Bayar to President Eisenhower and reply File, RG 59, Lot 62, Box 1, D35, NND 959393 (hereafter RG 59, Lot 62, Box 1).
[143] Dwight Eisenhower to Celal Bayar, June 13, 1958, RG 59, Box 1, Lot 62, D35, NND 959393. An earlier draft of Eisenhower's letter ended with the lines: "Please accept, Mr. President, renewed assurances of my highest regard and esteem." These were crossed out and removed before the final draft (William Rountree to the Secretary, June 11, 1958, RG 59, Lot 62, Box 1).
[144] James Bowker to Foreign Office, June 27, 1958, FO 371/136475.

"plan" being offered, there was only so far that they felt comfortable pushing the issue, given that West Germany and several other countries now seemed willing to provide money "for political reasons ... even if a truly solid stabilization program is not developed."[145] By June 28, there was agreement on the program of export premia, coupled with tight bank credit, in return for several hundred million US dollars in aid.[146]

Turkish officials were eager to conclude negotiations before the OEEC took its summer recess at the end of July (and before Turkey's seasonal foreign exchange shortage reached its nadir). They asked US officials to put pressure on the organization to expedite the process. As late as July 11, the United States was not visibly concerned with the speed. Rather, officials at the US embassy in Ankara were preoccupied with the question of why Kemal Aygün, who had just been elected governor/mayor of Istanbul that day, was being sent, along with Bayar's personal physician, on a trip to Moscow.[147] As with other Turkish government maneuvers, it seemed calculated to excite US suspicion. Was the USSR the "other" group Zorlu had been referring to in his attempts to gain West German support? Regardless, five days later, by July 16, Aygün had been pulled from the delegation, and US Secretary of State John Foster Dulles had written to UK Foreign Minister Selwyn Lloyd asking him for "help in our efforts to implement quickly a broad program of assistance to Turkey and to prevent further economic and political deterioration in this key ally of ours at this critical time in the Middle East."[148] What accounted for the rapid change?

In the space of those five days, the government of Iraq had been overthrown in a military coup. The king, his uncle, and their powerful political advisor, Nuri al-Said, had all been executed. In one blow, the strongest opponents of Egypt in the Baghdad Pact had been killed and US policy in the region had been thrown into disarray. Fearing this to be part of a multipronged push to overthrow allies in the region, the United States invoked the Eisenhower Doctrine as grounds for sending 15,000 military personnel to Lebanon over the following month. Britain

[145] Robert Bee, Memorandum of Conversation, June 24, 1958, RG 84, Box 78.

[146] Fletcher Warren to State, July 11, 1958, RG 84, Box 78. By early July, the final outlines of the deal were clear: $100 million from the United States (supplemented by money already appropriated to the Development Loan Fund and other accounting gimmicks to give the impression of a $250 million commitment); $25 million from the IMF; and perhaps $75 million via the OEEC.

[147] Fletcher Warren to State, July 11, 1958, RG 84, Box 74.

[148] John Foster Dulles to Selwyn Lloyd, July 15, 1958, FO 371/136475; Hall to State, July 16, 1958, RG 84, Box 74. In addition to removing Aygün, the Turkish government also canceled a previously approved Soviet art show on the grounds that it contained propaganda, such as Nâzım Hikmet's poetry.

dispatched two brigades of paratroopers to Jordan. Amid such a crisis, the particulars of loan discussions were subordinated to the need to buttress the stability of allies in the region.[149]

Under pressure from the United States, the OEEC moved quickly. Turkey submitted its proposed reforms on July 17; a report on Turkey was reviewed and approved on July 18; and on July 29, the OEEC council in Paris voted to approve $100 million in credit via the EPU.[150] The headline in *Zafer* the next day read, "Largescale Economic Aid to Turkey."[151] Within days, the Turkish government presented the general outlines of the deal. New premia for imports effectively lowered the value of the lira from TL2.80 to TL9.00 to the dollar. A moratorium was placed on arrears pending a renegotiation of payments.[152] By combining both newly promised aid and already promised aid, the government increased the values reported to the public from $235 million to $359 million, a far more impressive amount.[153]

Conclusion: Zero-Sum Negotiations?

Toward the end of August, Zorlu threw a "stag dinner" for Ambassador Warren and two dozen other US officials as a means of thanking them for their help in recent months. Partway into the night, Zorlu rose and gave an "exceptionally warm" toast to the Americans, saying:

149 For a general discussion of these events with a focus on Lebanon, see Irene Gendzier, *Notes from the Minefield: United States Intervention in Lebanon and the Middle East, 1945–1958* (New York: Columbia University Press, 1997), 295–337; Yaqub, *Containing Arab Nationalism*, 205–236. For Jordan, see Uriel Dann, *King Hussein and the Challenge of Arab Radicalism: Jordan 1955–1967* (Oxford: Oxford University Press, 1989), 86–95. For Iraq, see Hanna Batatu, *The Old Social Classes and the Revolutionary Movements of Iraq* (Princeton: Princeton University Press, 1978), 764–807.

150 Hugh Ellis-Rees to Foreign Office, July 29, 1958, FO 371/136475. On July 20, Zorlu gave his thanks to US officials for their efforts in pressuring Western European officials on Turkey's behalf (Warren to State, July 20, 1958, RG 84, Box 78).

151 "Türkiye'ye büyük …," *Zafer*, July 30, 1958, 1. In the announcement, Zorlu shared the headline with Finance Minister Hasan Polatkan. According to Nimet Arzık, this would have frustrated Zorlu, who frequently got angry when his picture was not prominently featured on the paper's front pages (Arzık, *Menderes'i İpe Götürenler*, 30).

152 James Bowker to Foreign Office, August 5, 1958, FO 371/136475.

153 From the United States, Turkey would receive $100 million ($25 million in "Special Aid"; $37.5 million from the Development Loan Fund; and $37.5 million from the Export-Import Bank); $75 million in defense support and $15 million in agricultural surplus from the PL 480 program that would have come regardless; and the equivalent of $44 million from postponement of Marshal Loan repayments. The OEEC provided $100 million ($50 million in credit from Germany; $10 million from the UK; $25 million from the EPU more generally; and $15 million from various OEEC members). The IMF provided $25 million (Ankara Embassy to Foreign Office, August 8, 1958, FO 371/136475).

bers of these professions are being organised into professional hierarchies headed by a member of their own profession. This has happened particularly since the reorganisation of the National Health Service in 1974.

Nurses are almost universally organised in hierarchies under the management of a senior nurse but they are also 'subject to the treatment-prescribing authority' of the doctors (Rowbottom *et al.*, 1973). The main problem, they say, is to discuss exactly what internal structure is required in the nursing hierarchy for each situation, as three kinds of role are likely to be needed: managerial, staff, and supervisory roles, They also suggest that the hospital ward is probably a 'natural' managerial unit, as the senior nurse in charge of the ward is not just the leader of a team of people caring for patients but also a manager of all the operational services which bear on the patients within the ward unit.

WHAT IS AN ORGANISATION?

In spite of the great deal that has been written about complex organisations, writers have been somewhat casual about clearly defining what they are.

Even March and Simon (1958), in their very comprehensive review of the literature, offer no definition whilst others such as Etzioni (1964) dismiss the definition with a few words. 'Organisations', in Etzioni's view, 'are social units (or human groupings) deliberately constructed and reconstructed to seek specific goals'. Other writers seldom agree on the priority of organisational characteristics. A review of the literature tends to indicate that, where a definition is suggested, it points on the whole to the characteristics which interest and concern the particular author.

It is not possible to describe *the* organisation, as each organisation is uique. Even the organisations of the hospital and community care services are uniquely and significantly different during the two periods 8 am to 8 pm to 8 am.

Nevertheless, using organisational models helps to describe and assist in the understanding of complex organisations and provides frameworks within which experiments can be conducted. Models also help the investigator to see new relationships and help in making predictions when experimentation is impossible, provided that they do not encourage overgeneralisation and divert useful

The following table gives the number of days lost through industrial action in the National Health Service from 1974 to 1978. (*Source:* Written parliamentary reply from Sir George Young to Mr Laurie Pavitt, MP, on 30th October, 1979.)

Year	*Number of days lost*
1974	23 000
1975	20 000
1976	15 000
1977	8 000
1978	15 000

Increasing numbers of nurses and other health care workers are member of TUC affiliated trade unions such as the Confederation of Health Service Employees (COHSE), National Association of Local Government Officers (NALGO), Nation Union of Public Employees (NUPE) and the Health Visitors Association (HVA).

'Membership of COHSE and NUPE alone has arisen from 190 000 in 1970 to 360 000 in 1974— an increase of nearly 90 per cent in four years' (Armour and Torrington, 1975). They further point out that until very recently industrial action in the health services 'was directed at influencing national negotiations' but now appears to be increasingly 'directed at altering local working arrangements'.

The little known HVA has a long-standing tradition as a trade union with an exclusive membership of nurses who are health visitors. According to a letter from the HVA's general secretary, published in the *Nursing Times* on 31st July 1975, the membership stood at 8000; a not insignificant number for such a specialist group of nurses. By October 1979, the HVA membership, according to an HVA spokesman, was just under 13 000.

This increasing support of nurses for trade unions forced the chairman of the Royal College of Nursing to concede at the annual meeting held in Bournemouth 1975 that if the college withdrew from its membership of the International Council of Nurses (ICN) it may be possible for 'any other organisation in this country with nurses in membership' to represent United Kingdom nurses on the International Council. The chairman's comments encouraged the meeting to reconsider a decision to withdraw from ICN membership made by the Royal College of Nursing membership at an extraordinary general meeting held in April 1975 (Nursing Standard No. 45). It is interesting to note that in October 1979 the Royal College of Nursing membership was 151 000, compared with

114 000 in October 1978. By the end of 1980, the College's membership was approximately 175 000.

The organisational disorder caused by trade union activity in the health services in the 1970s has a ring of irony about it and, as Armour and Torrington stress, 'can prove a hollow victory for the trade union members themselves'. Organised labour depends for its effectiveness on management being organised to meet it, confront the issues in dispute and produce jointly acceptable solutions. In the health services, however, this essential effectiveness is lacking due, in the view of Armour and Torrington, to the lack of clear guidance and policies on joint consultations and representative procedures, grievance and disciplinary arrangements. This was particularly noticeable in the first few months of 1979, when the NHS was reduced to chaos by industrial action throughout the United Kingdom, initiated chiefly by NUPE and COHSE. Ancillary workers and large numbers of nursing staff withdrew their services completely from time to time.

It is perhaps not insignificant that COHSE, on 19th October 1979, issued new 'binding' notes on guidance on industrial action to its members. These were to be incorporated into COHSE's rule book in 1980. The notes on guidance stress that 'when operating restrictive measures, a reasonable standard of patient care will be maintained and the respect of human dignity, which is of course a normal feature of COHSE membership, will be observed'.

In the first few months of 1979, the total number of working days lost through industrial action in the United Kingdom was 5 915 000, compared with 1 830 000 during the same period in 1978. The NHS chaos caused by industrial action in 1979 was therefore a microcosm of the national chaos. According to a DHSS spokesman 621 000 working days were lost in the NHS due to industrial action in 1979.

'The discrepancy between the health service and sophisticated practice in private industry is illustrated by the fact that the Whitley Council handbook devotes thirty-five pages to the single substantive issue of leave and only four pages to set out arrangements for settling differences.'

Trade unions have other less militant means of influencing the British health care systems by virtue of their members who are nominated and appointed to regional and area health authorities and community health councils. This involves them to some great extent in the allocation of health care resources. And increasingly, trade union local officials (stewards) are being closely involved with management on local joint consultative committees.

Trade union influence is therefore potentially great. Fear of this influence, which is occasionally demonstrated by managers, is usually a misguided fear based on ignorance. There is no greater fear than the fear of the unknown.

Trade unions in perspective

The danger of considering trade unions in an historical perspective is stressed by Victor Feather, then general secretary of the Trades Union Congress (TUC) who points out in *The 1970 E.W. Hancock Paper* that: 'Historians can seek to discover the laws of past historical development but their discoveries do not help much in an actual contemporary situation.' Understanding how the 1920 dock strike was dealt with by Ernest Bevin does not help in a productivity bargain in an oil refinery (or in the health services, for that matter) in the 1970s, he argues.

'To understand either a dock strike in 1920 or a productivity bargain in 1970 one needs to know the circumstances and relative factors of the specific case in the context of the time and place at which it happened. Once can take time to research and analyse the past event but one has to make decisions about a current situation without any certainty that all the facts are taken into account or even known.'

Considerable changes in industry and industrial relations took place in the 1960s and in Feather's view the changes were significantly different to any that had taken place in previous decades. This he holds sets the 1960s apart, for historians at least, from previous periods of change in which the organisations and institutions concerned with industrial relations, being young and malleable, were still to be moulded by future events.

'Today we recognise, at least in trade unions, that we need to plan more consciously and act more deliberately if we are to adapt successfully our ideas and institutions, moulded by past periods of changes, to the needs of the future much more rapidly, and to meet far-reaching changes.' These words suggest that the trade union movement is now beginning to reflect the ideas and attitudes of the society of which it is part.

In discussing the fundamentals of trade unionism, Feather defines a trade union as 'an association of workpeople possessing common interests based especially on their particular occupation or employment'.

The important characteristic, he holds is the existence of common interests which may take the form of having a common employer, working in a common industry or having common skills. On this analysis it is not difficult to see how unionisation can so easily spread through large-scale health care organisations.

But no matter what the form of the common interests, the chief aim of trade union organisation is to regulate the terms and conditions of its members' employment. In the first edition of this book I wrote that it was interesting to note that non-union professional organisations of health care workers such as the Royal College of Nursing and the British Medical Association are increasingly involving more of their resources in the regulation of the terms and conditions of their members' employment, which suggests that the differences between trade unions and professional associations might be more philosophical than real. As it turned out, within two years of its publication, the Royal College of Nursing, the Association of Nurse Administrators, the Royal College of Midwives and the British Medical Association had all become certificated trade unions.

'A trade union, in the British context, is independent of the employer and the state. Moreover, it is an organisation that is essentially democratic. Its democracy is a basic characteristic in that in the ultimate the power of the membership is decisive.'

It is clear then that trade unions are not primarily concerned with increasing productivity except in so far as this contributes to the achievement of the aims of trade unions which, Feather stresses, should be borne in mind when criteria for assessing the effectiveness and efficiency of trade unions are being established.

Trade unions and social progress

History records that the trade union movement has contributed significantly to social progress, even though trade unions operate in a radically different economic, industrial and social environment today from that of the nineteenth century in which they were constantly struggling to establish themselves.

'It was unions that insisted that industrial change must be matched by social advance . . . society no longer tolerates the gross abuses of human dignity that characterised industrial developments in the nineteenth century . . . it was the workers' own organisations that were the real vehicles of social change.'

This argument is difficult to challenge when it is recognised that from the beginning, trade unions did not confine their activities to improving wages and conditions of work but also 'with the needs of society as a whole, with the protection of children and those who are too old to work, of the sick and the disabled.' 'It was compassion', Feather argues, 'not self interest, that drove them to protest and that inscribed on their banners the maxims of social progress.'

Trade unions therefore have to deal with a dynamic process of change, not with a series of static states and solutions and Feather further argues that if solutions can be devised at all, they 'have to deal with a continuum of change, not be suited just to a moment of history'.

The role of the Trades Union Congress

The TUC, at its annual meetings, lays down the broad policy for the trade union movement. Between the meetings the policy is interpreted by the General Council of the TUC working through its various committees. The General Council membership is representative of all trade unions in membership with the TUC. 'The TUC stands in relation to its unions as individual unions do to their members.'

Although the TUC has gradually decreasing opportunities for initiating policy, it can represent to each union the interests of the trade union movement as a whole and can defend and advance the trade union movement in relationships with government, employers and other bodies. 'Its job is to provide leadership but its leadership depends on its ability to persuade unions and to win their consent.' The Health Visitors Association has a long association of membership with the TUC. But so far, the Association of Nurse Administrators and the Royal College of Midwives have rejected the idea of TUC affiliation. At its annual general meeting on 7th November 1979, the Royal College of Nursing also rejected a proposal that it should affiliate to the TUC.

Conclusion

In this chapter, the concept of organisation has been discussed together with the implications of political, ideological and financial influences on organisations: organisational change was perceived to be an evolutionary process. It was suggested that when people in the organisation are involved in the process of change they are more likely to be committed to the consequences of change: the contributions of good communications and effective education were not underestimated.

Finally, the impact of modern-day trade unions on organisations was considered. All of this might lead the reader to agree with the cynicism of Sackur (1974) when he says:

'More and more insistently, managers are being asked what they are doing about "organisation development". More often than not the answer comes in a prepackaged form . . . It is scientism which turns useful and interesting speculation into full-blown theories, and leads to a whole industry of packaged solutions and techniques of management . . . It is often alarming to planners used to clear-cut systems and the belief in objectivity that the eventual outcome of a development process may be obscure at the outset . . . Change is no more and no less than a learning process.'

REFERENCES

Argyris, C. (1956) *Diagnosing Human Relations in Organisations. A Case Study of a Hospital.* Yale University.

Armour, W. & Torrington, D. (1975) Industrial relations in hospitals. *Health and Social Service Journal,* 28th June.

Baly, M. (1973) *Nursing and Social Change.* London: Heinemann.

Bendall, E.R.D. (1973) Education for change. *Nursing Mirror,* 14th September.

Clay, T. (1976) *The Role of Nursing and Midwifery Advisory Committees in the Reorganised NHS.* Uxbridge: Brunel University.

Davis, F. (ed.) (1966) *The Nursing Profession: Five Sociological Essays.* New York: Wiley.

Etzioni, A. (1964) *Modern Organisations.* New Jersey: Prentice Hall.

Feather, V. (1970) *Trade Unions in Perspective (The 1970 E.W. Hancock Paper).* The Institution of Production Engineers, 12th September.

Likert, R. (1967) *The Human Organisation.* New York: McGraw Hill.

March, J.G. & Simon, H. (1958) *Organisations.* New York: Wiley.

Maxwell, R. (1974) *Health Care—The Growing Dilemma.* New York: McKinsey.

Merton, R.M. (1957) *Social Theory and Social Structure.* Glencoe, Illinois: Free Press.

Michels, R. (1965) *First Lectures in Political Sociology.* New York: Harper & Row.

Revans, R.W. (1964) *Standards for Moral: Cause and Effect in Hospitals.* Oxford University Press.

Rowbottom, R. *et al.* (1973) *Hospital Organisation.* London: Heinemann.

Sackur, J. (1974) How to diagnose organisations. *Management To-day,* May.

Scott Wright, M (1969) Implementation of change in nursing. *Nursing Times* occasional paper, 13th February.

Scott Wright, M. (1974) Nursing: present perspectives and future prospects. *Nursing Mirror*, 31st October, 53–60.
Smith, J.P (1963) A Russian polyclinic. *Nursing Times,* 1st February.
Smith, J.P (1967) Services for mothers and children in Scandinavia. *Nursing Mirror,* 28th July.
Smith, J.P. (1968) Care of the mentally subnormal in Scandinavia. *Nursing Mirror,* 12th July.
Smith, J.P. (1968) Psychiatric care in the community. Report of a Royal Society of Health conference. *Nursing Mirror*, 27th December.
Smith, J.P. (1979) The role of the nurse in an integrated National Health Service. *Journal of Advanced Nursing*, **4,** 439–452.
Taylor, F.W. (1947) *Scientific Management.* New York: Harper.
Weber, M. (1946) *From Max Weber: Essay in Sociology*. Translated by H.H. Gerth & C. Wright Mills, Oxford University Press.
Wickings, I. *et al.* (1975) *Evaluating Management Information presented to Clinically Accountable Teams.* London: Health Information Unit, Brent Health District.
Report of the Committee on the Internal Administration of Hospitals (HMSO, London, 1954)
Experimental nurse training at Glasgow Royal Infirmary (HMSO, Edinburgh, 1963)
Report of the Committee on Senior Nursing Staff Structure (HMSO, London, 1966)
Report of the Working Party on Management Structure in the Local Authority Nursing Services (DHSS, London, 1969)
Draft guide to planning in the National Health Service (DHSS March 1975)
Flexibility in the use of financial resources (DHSS letter, 9th July, 1975)
The study of psychiatric nursing in the community——progress report (Queen's Nursing Institute Council Meeting 15th July 1975—paper to support agenda item 11)
Nursing Standard (No. 43, Royal College of Nursing, July/August 1975)

Population characteristics
Sources of population data
Fertility
Birth rate
Death rate
Infant mortality
Expectation of life
Migration
Application of demography to nursing

8

Demography

Demography is the study of human populations, or more specifically, the statistical description and analysis of human populations. The people who practise demography are known as demographers. They concern themselves with questions about the size of the population and its rates of growth and decline. More importantly, the reasons for growth and decline are sought and an assessment made on the effects of changes in population caused by the numbers of births, deaths and migrants. The skills of the demographer and the data he collects make up the core of population study.

Demography aims at ascertaining the numbers and distribution of people in a certain area such as a city, a village or country. Analyses are also made of changes in these numbers and populations in time, particularly the changes brought about by fluctuating birth, death and migration rates in the population. Birth, death and migration rates are the three main components of population change and as these three variables affect population size constantly, the demographer considers the three ongoing processes of fertility, mortality and migration to be the three basic demographic processes.

The demographer is not the only worker in population studies. Indeed, when answers are sought for why certain demographic processes take place, such as the high birth rate in developing countries, a number of social scientists become involved. These include economists, geographers, historians, sociologists and psychologists, all of whom make use of data assembled by demographers.

POPULATION CHARACTERISTICS

Knowledge of absolute numbers of people in an area, whilst interesting, is not very useful without information about the characteristics of that population. It is also necessary to consider the different groups and other categories of people that make up that society. For purposes of analysis of British Society, the social class index (Table 8.1) is often used which is based on occupation; but

Table 8.1 Social class

Social class	*Description of occupation*	*Percentage of workers*
I. Upper and middle	Higher professional, e.g. doctors, engineers, lawyers and scientists, large employers and directors of businesses	3.5
II. Intermediate	Lower professional, e.g. teachers, nurses, pharmacists, social workers and farmers, owners of small businesses and managers	14.5
III. Skilled and clerical workers	Artisans, clerks, foremen and supervisors	53.0
IV. Intermediate	Semi-skilled workers, e.g. factory operatives and agricultural workers	16.0
V. Unskilled workers	Labourers, domestic servants and casual workers	13.0
	Total:	*100.0*

Source: Markham & Smith (1975)

populations have other attributes which can be measured such as age, sex, marital status, race, place of residence, and income.

Age and sex are directly related to fertility and mortality and are therefore very important population characteristics. As only women produce children and within a relatively short span of their lives, the age-sex composition considerably affects the numbers of births and deaths in the population.

The vast majority of children in most societies is borne by married women and therefore marital status is another very important population characteristic, as trends in the numbers of marriages in the population are closely related to trends in the numbers of births.

The other characteristics noted above are also related in some way to fertility, mortality and migration and a study of these characteristics can produce a great deal of useful sociological and economical information about society. Occupational groups, for example, usually differ with respect to fertility and mortality and 'life chances'. And information gleaned from occupational distribution in a population can indicate a great deal about the population's socioeconomic structure.

Sources of population data

A most important source of population data is the national census, which is conducted on a prearranged day every ten years in the United Kingdom and was first introduced in 1801. The census, which is conducted by the government, is in fact a ten-yearly head count which also seeks information from respondents about age, sex, country of origin and about earnings and social conditions such as housing.

Another primary source of population data are the national vital statistics produced in reports by the Registrar General and Chief Medical Officer of Health at three-monthly and yearly intervals. These are supported by other government publications such as *Social Trends* and *Health Trends*.

The census gives a static cross-sectional description on a particular day of the effects of births, deaths and migration in the previous decade, which provides an opportunity for making inferences about population trends.

The census, however, is a very costly and major undertaking and therefore the Registrar General's reports on the population's vital statistics are essential for keeping track on population trends between censuses.

Present-day population size can be assessed by adding to the census numbers the numbers of births and immigrants. A fairly accurate assessment of population rests on the accuracy of these vital statistics. In England and Wales, registration of births and deaths has been compulsory since 1874 but there are no very accurate records of immigrants and emigrants. This is conceded by the British Government in its white paper on *Immigration from the Commonwealth* (1965) wherein it is only possible to give estimates because 'Until 1962 every Commonwealth citizen was entitled to enter the United Kingdom at will. This right had been freely exercised for many years . . . During the period from 1st January 1955 to 30th June 1962 the net intake (that is, the total number entering during the year less the total number leaving during the year) is estimated to have been . . .'

Subsequently some control in the form of entry vouchers has been introduced but there still seem to be numerous ways of avoiding official entry routes to the United Kingdom. In any case, Wrong (1965) warns of the dangers of putting too much faith in any vital statistics: 'Even in the highly industrialised countries, the registration of births and deaths is often less than 95 per cent complete in some areas, and in non-industrial countries the recorded statistics should be viewed with considerable caution.'

A great wealth of information about population statistics, trends and analyses is also contained in the *Report of the Royal Commission on Population* (1949), and perusal of this document will illustrate the fascinating, socially useful data provided by demographers.

For comparative purposes the demographer requires relative rather than absolute measures of population and therefore relates numbers of births, deaths and migration to numbers in the population to obtain rates.

Fertility

Fertility is a measure of the actual reproductive performance of a society. It is socially controlled in most populations to some extent, not only by birth control methods, but also by voluntary celibacy and childlessness and certain proscriptions against childbearing outside marriage. There is also a biological control in so far as women are normally only capable of bearing children during the ages of 15 and 44 years. Even so, the maximum biological capacity (fecundity) is never reached as it is unknown in any society for all women capable of child bearing to produce their full potential number of children, which could be up to 20 for any one woman.

'The fertility of a population depends', Wrong holds, 'on the balance between those parts of its culture and social system that favour reproduction and those that hinder it. Study of the motivations and social determinants underlying fertility variations is inescapably a task for the sociologist.'

Birth rate

The crude birth rate is the most commonly used measure of fertility. It is the annual number of births per 1000 of the total population.

Table 8.2 indicates how the crude birth rate has fluctuated in

Table 8.2 Crude birth rates for England and Wales

Year	1956	1961	1966	1971	1972	1973	1977
Crude birth rate	15.7	17.6	17.8	16.0	14.8	13.7	11.6

England and Wales since 1956 and how it has been falling gradually since 1966.

A number of factors can affect birth rates, such as the age-sex composition: in 1973 there were approximately 106 male births for every 100 female births and the age-sex structure of the English population can be seen in Table 8.3.

Table 8.3 Age and sex structure in England at mid-1973

Age (years)	Males (%)	Females (%)	Totals (%)
0–14	24.9	22.4	23.6
15–44	40.5	33.3	38.9
45–64	23.7	23.9	23.8
65 and over	10.9	16.4	13.7
Table %	100.0	100.0	100.0
Total numbers	22 582 300	23 843 000	46 425 300

Source: Chief Medical Officer (1974)

The recent fall in the annual number of births is the most striking demographic feature of modern years and started in 1964. Previously the numbers had been rising since the mid-1950s.

The previous lowest crude birth rate was 14.4 in 1933. However, the general fertility rate was considerably higher in 1973 than in

1933, being 72 births per 1000 women aged 15 to 44 in 1973 compared with 59 in 1933, and about the same as the average for the period 1951 to 1953, according to the chief medical officer of the Department of Health and Social Security (1974).

Some significant changes in the pattern of age-specific fertility rates within the reproductive age span have also occurred (Table 8.4). The rates for each five-year group of women have fallen

Table 8.4 Total live births per 1000 female population by age of mother at birth in England and Wales

	Age of mother at birth					
Period	15–19	20–24	25–29	30–34	35–39	40–44
1951–55	22	132	138	87	45	13
1961–65	41	177	181	104	49	13
1971	51	154	154	78	33	8
1972	48	142	143	70	29	7
1973	44	131	134	63	24	6
1977	30	105	119	59	18	4

consistently from 1971 to 1973. However, compared with averages for the early 1950s, the 1973 rate for women aged 15 to 19 was higher, about the same for the 20 to 24 and 25 to 29 age groups but much lower in the age groups over 30.

There is also some evidence that postponement of first births for those recently married has contributed to the recent fall in births. For example, in 1964, 74 per cent of women aged 20 to 24 were still childless one year after being married. In 1971 this phenomenon had increased to 81 per cent.

The chief medical officer, however, argued in 1974 that: 'It should be borne in mind that annual or short-run changes in the number of births and birth rates cannot in themselves be taken to indicate long term trends.'

Some group differences

The birth rate and fertility estimates of a country are clearly averages for the whole population and conceal the fertility differences which exist between different social groups in the population.

Fertility tends to vary with the degree of urbanisation. It is lower in urban than rural communities and Wrong (1965) claims that rapid urbanisation since the industrial revolution has been one of the major factors bringing about lower fertility. This appears to be an international phenomenon. 'Family limitation by contraceptive means originated in the cities.'

There are also social class differences and lower social classes everywhere tend to demonstrate higher fertility rates. Farmers and agricultural workers are usually the most fertile. Among people of similar social class and occupational background there is a tendency for those with the largest incomes to have more children than those with smaller incomes.

The diffusion of birth control is another most important factor influencing birth rate. Its effectiveness does not only depend on availability but a desire to use it and there is some indication in the literature that there are social class differences.

'Furthermore the decisions of couples to have or not to have a child at a particular point of time are likely to be influenced by prevailing social and economic conditions and, given the improvements in family planning and the enhanced ability of couples to plan the timing of births and size of families, it is likely that family formation may well be more closely related to the current social and economic circumstances than in the past.'

Death rate

Crude death rate is the annual number of deaths per 1000 of the total population. In conjunction with the crude birth rate, it is a necessary measure for estimating the natural increase of the population. But there are serious difficulties in comparing the death rates of any two countries' populations, without taking into account the difference in the age compositions of the two populations.

Populations with a high proportion of young adults will have a lower death rate than populations with a high proportion of ageing adults, as people over 40 years old die in greater numbers. Therefore, countries with a young adult population such as Jamaica tend to have a lower crude death rate than countries with an ageing adult population such as the United Kingdom. It is nothing to do with different standards of health and hygiene.

Comparisons between the crude death rate of two countries are made by comparing the age-specific death rates between the two countries.

The standardised mortality ratio (SMR) takes changes in the age structure of the populations into account; the base year of

1968 = 100. In the United Kingdom this ratio was 96 in 1971, 100 in 1972 and 96 in 1973. The crude death rate was 11.7 average for the decade 1963 to 1972, 12.0 for 1972 and 11.9 in 1973. The SMR varies in the different social classes (Table 8.5). 'The two factors

Table 8.5 Male standardised mortality rates by social class: England and Wales

Social Class	1970–72 (age 15–64)
I Professional occupations	77
II Managerial and lower professional occupations	81
III Skilled occupations	104
IV Partly skilled occupations	113
V Unskilled occupations	137

Source: Report of the Royal Commission on the NHS

which contribute most to variations in total mortality are weather and influenza' in the United Kingdom.

There is little change from year to year in the pattern of causes of death. Fifty per cent of all deaths in the United Kingdom are caused by circulatory diseases. Twenty-one per cent of deaths are caused by the various forms of cancer. About fifteen per cent of deaths are caused by respiratory conditions. These are the chief causes of death and a full list of the principal causes of mortality are listed in each annual report of the chief medical officer of health.

Infant mortality

Mortality is heavier in the first year of life and because of this death rates of children are computed for that year. This rate is called the infant mortality rate which is the number of infant deaths related to the total number of live births in any year. It is the most sensitive index of the standards of social welfare and state of health of a country and is a truer measure than crude death rate, as the infant mortality rate is not affected by age composition of the population. Another rate which is computed for children is the perinatal death rate (the number of still births and deaths within the first week of life per 1000 total live births *and* still births). Both infant and perinatal mortality rates have dropped over the years in the United Kingdom. However, there are regional variations. For example, in 1971 the perinatal mortality rates in two adjoining London boroughs of Brent and Harrow were 25.0 and 18.5 respectively.

International variations are even more dramatic. In 1971, perinatal mortality rates ranged from 15.6 (Sweden) to 37.2 (Portugal). England and Wales had a rate of 22.3, Northern Ireland 27.2 and Scotland 24.5. In 1972 infant mortality rates ranged from 11.1 (Sweden) to 49.8 (Portugal). The rate in England and Wales was 17.2, Northern Ireland 20.5 and Scotland 18.8.

Other rates which are computed are neonatal mortality rate (deaths under four weeks per 1000 total live births), early neonatal mortality rate (deaths under one week per 1000 total births), legitimate infant mortality rate per 1000 legitimate live births and illegitimate infant death rate per 1000 illegitimate live births. Other rates closely associated with infant mortality are the maternal mortality rate which measures death of mothers associated with childbirth, abortion (per 1000 total live and still births), and the stillbirth rate (per 1000 total live and still births).

The stillbirth rate in 1973 (11.5) was the lowest ever recorded in England and Wales and the infant mortality rate (16.86) showed a big improvement over previous years. By 1977, the infant mortality rate was down to 13.8. For several years the statistics have indicated that the reduction in infant mortality are proportionately equal in the first week in life and in the remainder of the year. There have also been substantial improvements in the perinatal mortality rates. In 1972, this improvement was 'wholly due to a reduction in stillbirths, but in 1973 the contribution to improvement in the perinatal mortality rate was because survival in the first week is greater than from stillbirths although the rate of reduction of the latter is maintained', according to the chief medical officer (1974). In 1977, the perinatal mortality rate was 17.0 for England and Wales (in 1948, it was 38.5). Regional variations in the different mortality rates for the UK are illustrated in Table 8.6.

Expectation of life

In England and Wales the expectation of life at the age of 1 year for males is 2.5 years less than the best figure of 71.7 years (Sweden), whereas for females it is 1.4 years short of the best figure of 76.6 years (Netherlands). The figures of life expectancy at 1 year in England and Wales, Scotland and Northern Ireland are given in Table 8.7. Richard M. Titmuss (1968), commenting on increased

Table 8.6 Regional differences in infant and perinatal mortality rates: UK 1977

	Infant mortality rate	Perinatal mortality rate
ENGLAND	13.7	16.9
Northern	14.9	19.1
Yorkshire	15.5	18.1
Trent	13.9	16.7
East Anglia	11.2	13.0
NW Thames	11.8	14.8
NE Thames	14.0	16.1
SE Thames	13.1	16.8
SW Thames	11.6	14.6
Wessex	13.1	15.5
Oxford	12.7	15.0
South Western	12.5	16.2
West Midlands	15.0	19.4
Mersey	14.4	18.8
North Western	14.8	18.5
WALES	13.5	17.9
SCOTLAND	16.1	18.3
N IRELAND	17.2	21.1

Source: Office of Population Censuses and Surveys.

life expectancy, notes that women have gained most and argues that 'the steadily widening differential between the sexes—especially after the age of 75—has important implications for social policy. For one thing, it means more widows and longer periods of widowhood. One of the interesting demographic facts today is that among women the chance of having a husband by them is nearly as great when they are aged 15 to 24 as when they are aged 65 and over.' But he concedes the difficulties inherent in predicting demographic trends, noting that: 'Death rates among the elderly have not fallen as much as the 1952 estimates implied.' (See Tables 8.7 and 8.8.)

Table 8.7 Life expectancy at age 1 year: UK 1950–1977

	Sex	1950–52	1961–63	1973–75	1975–77
England and Wales	M	67.7	68.6	69.8	70.0
	F	72.4	74.3	75.7	76.0
Scotland	M	66.2	66.7	67.9	68.2
	F	69.9	72.5	74.2	74.4
N Ireland	M	67.5	69.0	67.6	67.9
	F	70.3	74.1	71.1	74.1

Source: Office of Population Censuses and Surveys.

Table 8.8 Mortality rates: England and Wales 1948–1977

		1948	1977	% Change 1948–1977
Perinatal mortality		38.5	17.0	55.84
Infant mortality		34.0	13.8	59.41
Mortality[1]				
Age 35–44	M	3.15	2.01	36.19
	F	2.45	1.41	42.45
Age 45–54	M	8.24	6.81	17.35
	F	5.33	4.09	23.26
Age 55–64	M	21.60	18.77	13.10
	F	12.20	9.87	19.10

Source: Office of Population Censuses and Surveys.

Migration

Migration is a term which designates a permanent change of residence. If the change involves a move over an international boundary, such as movement from Geat Britain to France, this is called external migration. Movement out is known as emigration and movement in is known as immigration.

In 1978, the estimated number of emigrants from the UK fell for the fourth successive year and was 16 000 less than in 1977. The number of immigrants, however, increased by 24 000 to 187 000 (see Table 8.9).

Table 8.9 International migration: UK

thousands

	1971	1972	1973	1974	1975	1976	1977	1978
Immigrants	199.7	221.9	195.7	183.8	197.2	191.3	162.6	187.0
UK citizens	92.0	111.2	82.6	78.9	85.3	86.6	73.1	73.5
Non-UK citizens	107.6	110.7	113.2	104.8	111.9	104.7	89.5	113.5
Emigrants	240.0	233.2	245.8	269.0	238.3	210.4	208.7	192.4
UK citizens	170.6	159.9	175.7	198.8	169.4	137.3	143.7	126.5
Non-UK citizens	69.4	73.3	70.1	70.2	68.9	73.1	65.0	66.0
Balance	−40.4	−11.4	−50.1	−85.3	−41.2	−19.1	−46.1	−5.5

Source: Office of Population Censuses and Surveys.

APPLICATION OF DEMOGRAPHY TO NURSING

Nurses in the United Kingdom have important advisory and executive roles in the National Health Service and therefore their advice to regional and other health authorities and in the managerial decisions at district management team level must be based on the actual needs of the community. The use of vital statistics is therefore invaluable as they enable nurses to assess present and predict future health care and nursing needs. An ageing population needs health care and nursing resources for the aged. A young adult population needs resources for midwifery and child health services (providing they are fertile), as well as resources to deal with high numbers of industrial and road accidents. If birth rates are falling this indicates a gradually reducing demand for paediatric inpatient services and school health services.

Infant and perinatal mortality rates serve as indices for monitoring purposes, as do other death rates. Presumably, if more resources are allocated to child health care services in a district that has a high infant mortality rate, the district nursing officer would rightly review the rate annually and not unnaturally expect it to drop and/or approach the national rate. Tables 8.10 and 8.11 give some indication of the priority of needs of the lower social classes and illegitimate infants.

Table 8.10 Deaths in infants (legitimate) by Social class: England and Wales 1975–1976

	Social Class				
	I	II	III	IV	V
Stillbirth rate	7	8	10	11	14
Perinatal mortality rate	13	15	18	20	26
Neonatal mortality rate	7	8	9	11	14
Infant mortality rate	10	11	13	16	23

Source: Office of Population Censuses and Surveys.

Table 8.11 Comparison of deaths in infants in England and Wales 1975–1976

	Legitimate	Illegitimate
Stillbirth rate	10	13
Perinatal mortality rate	18	25
Neonatal mortality rate	10	15
Infant mortality rate	14	22

Source: Office of Population Censuses and Surveys.

In each of the health districts in this country, health care planning teams have been established in which nurses play a most important role. At least one community (primary care) nurse and one hospital (specialist) nurse join other professional colleagues to draw up health care plans for the district, for services to the elderly, children, mentally handicapped and so on. The reports prepared by these teams play a most important role in influencing the decisions made by district management teams and health authorities who will expect recommendations to be based on objective fact and explicit criteria. Nurses therefore need to be aware of the sources of vital statistics, be able to cite them knowingly and to analyse them scientifically and with care, and ensure that the recommendations and advice they submit at all levels in the National Health Service are based on valid assessements of present-day nursing and health needs. Only then can predictions of both short-term and long-term health needs of the community they serve be made with some confidence. The resources poured into health care increase annually, and as the source of support for these resources derives from taxes it is obviously self-limiting. Reviews of expenditure are essential therefore. Dr Jack Hall (1972), director of medical education at the Methodist Hospital of Indiana, made the point effectively

Table 8.12 International comparisons of life expectancy at 1 year, perinatal mortality and maternal mortality

Country	Life expectancy at age 1 M	F	Perinatal mortality (per 1000 live births)	Maternal mortatlity (per 100 000 births)
Australia	68.5	75.4	22.4	11.3
Canada	69.7	77.0	17.7	10.8
Finland	66.8	75.5	17.1	10.6
France	69.5	77.1	18.8	24.0
Italy	70.0	76.0	29.6	42.4
Japan	70.8	76.0	18.0	38.3
Netherlands	71.2	76.9	16.4	10.3
Norway	71.4	77.7	16.8	3.3
Sweden	72.0	77.4	14.1	2.7
USA	68.0	75.6	24.8	15.2
W Germany	68.6	74.9	23.2	45.9
England and Wales	69.5	75.6	21.3	13.0
Scotland	67.7	74.0	22.7	21.5
N Ireland	67.0	73.6	25.9	17.1

Source: Report of the Royal Commission on the NHS.

when he said that in spite of escalating health costs: 'Since 1957, the life expectancy of Americans has not increased by one month.'

In the past, nurses have made valuable contributions to health care with their hands and their hearts. In the future their hands and hearts will continue to be of great importance, but their heads will also play an extremely important role and those heads must be capable of generating sound thoughts, ideas and concepts of care. It is always easy to make a case for more nursing and health care resources, based on the emotions of the heart. But it may be necessary in the future to be able to make a rational case for *less*. That kind of recommendation will need to be well supported by facts and will be intellectually demanding. An understanding of demography is therefore an essential tool for nurses working in present-day health care organisations. Table 8.12 gives some international information.

REFERENCES

Department of Health and Social Security (1974) *On the State of the Public Health*. The annual report of the chief medical officer of health. London: HMSO.

Hall, J. (1972) *Patients' concerns and responsibilities* (cited in First International Education Conference on Health Sciences by J.P. Smith). *Nursing Mirror*, 1st December.

Markham, J. & Smith, J.P. (1975) *Community Care*. London: Heinemann.

Titmuss, R.M. (1968) *Commitment to Welfare*. London: Allen & Unwin.

Wrong, D.H. (1965) *Population and Society*. New York: Random House.

Report of the Royal Commission on Population (HMSO, 1949).

Immigration from the Commonwealth (White Paper, HMSO, August 1965).

The Prevention of Perinatal Mortality and Morbidity (WHO, Geneva, 1970).

Setting up a research programme
Research tools
Common research errors
Statistics
Ethical principles
Research as a basis for the practice of nursing

9 Research and nursing

The purpose of this chapter is not to teach the reader how to become a researcher but to afford some insights into the methods of research and the problems of the researcher. Research is not something which should be approached lightly: it needs rigorous preparation and supervision because if garbage is put into the exercise then garbage will certainly come out of it.

Quite obviously many major decisions have to be made by workers in health care organisations and, as large amounts of resources are often involved, it is important to base those decisions on the best available information. Sometimes this information may not be 'scientific', but any information is better than none at all. However, the research process enables the investigator to systematically observe and describe a situation or event, such as how the accident and emergency department actually functions; it enables relationships to be established between two or more variables such as high deviancy rate in immigrants by controlling in an experimental fashion those factors which could account for the apparent relationship, e.g. subconscious selective prosecution by the police force. As indicated in the early pages of this book, introducing controls is a particularly difficult factor in social research as people cannot be controlled and manipulated in the same way that inanimate objects can. But, even with these reservations, some attempts at experimentation have been done in health care, particularly in studying the effects of health education and preoperative counselling of patients, as well as studies on the effects of certain drugs.

In a nutshell, the objectives of sociological research are to describe and explain social situations or events, to make predictions about society and, quite often, to explode certain myths about society. Research creates knowledge, the documentation of which develops a body of knowledge which is crucially important to any profession and is still somewhat lacking in the nursing profession.

SETTING UP A RESEARCH PROGRAMME

Whichever objective the researcher has in mind will influence the research method he uses so that the data obtained will be relevant to the investigation being carried out. But whatever the purpose of the investigation or the methods used, a number of steps are common to all research programmes:

1. Define the objectives of the investigation
2. Review the relevant literature
3. Select and plan the methods of investigation
4. Carry out pilot studies to test the proposed research methods
5. Collect the data
6. Analyse the data
7. Write the research report.

These are more or less the steps commonly associated with the scientific method, but they can also be applied to all kinds of problem-solving activities, particularly in the context of the nursing process and managerial decision making.

From the outset, it must be stressed that sociological researchers are also social beings, as social research is difficult to carry out in isolation. It requires constant contact and good rapport with colleagues and experts for consultation and discussion.

The steps outlined above will now be discussed in a little more detail.

Define the objectives of the investigation

Observation is the keynote and at this stage one need not be afraid of verbalising hunches or intuitions. Nurses practising in clinical areas often have these, and as a result certain practices such as

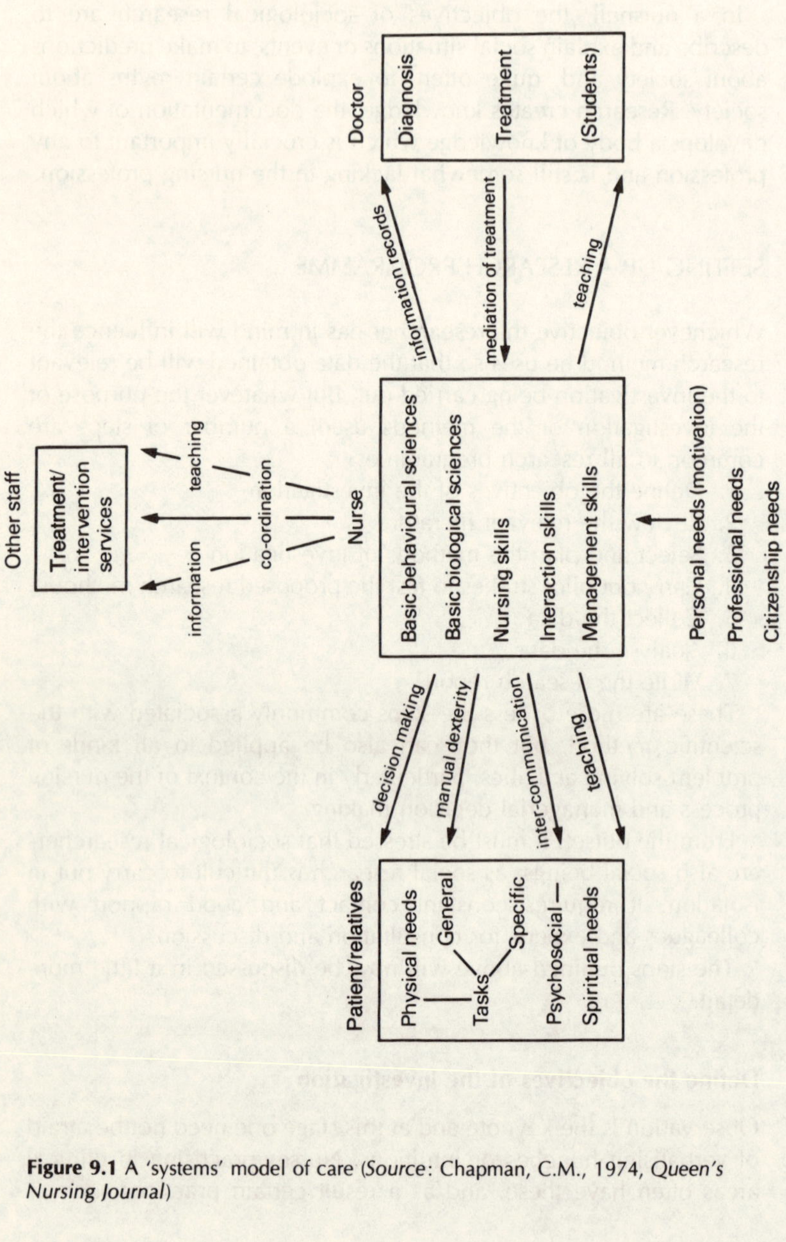

Figure 9.1 A 'systems' model of care (*Source*: Chapman, C.M., 1974, *Queen's Nursing Journal*)

starving patients for long periods before operation have been successfully challenged.

This period of observation is sometimes called the 'playing the field period'. The researcher goes into the field with an open mind to look, to listen and to learn about any facet of the topic to be investigated. After this period, it is essential to write down clearly and concisely the problems for investigation (accepting that the study might only offer sufficient insight to enable you to cope with the problem, rather than solve it) and the questions that need to be asked about the problem. The null hypotheses that need to be tested should be stated.

Precise definition of objectives is essential, albeit difficult, but if due care and attention is given to the exercise less difficulties are likely to arise during the subsequent research steps.

Indeed, if financial backing is sought for an investigation, clear written details are essential, otherwise the research project might well progress no further.

Review the relevant literature

Reports of other similar studies should be perused with care and a thorough search made of the literature dealing with methods and tools of social investigation. This gives the researcher an invaluable appreciation of the essential background knowledge for the proposed research. It might also demonstrate that the proposed questions have already been answered or that the proposed hypotheses have already been tested and thereby foster a somewhat different approach.

If similar investigations are discovered, this might stimulate replication for comparative purposes. Unfortunately, as yet, replication has not been too common in health care and nursing investigations, probably due to the poverty of the professional body of knowledge. It should be stressed, however, that repeats of similar investigations are replications, a perfectly genuine scientific process, not duplications in any sense.

After reviewing the literature, a number of researchers not surprisingly find it necessary to redefine their objectives.

Select and plan the methods of investigation

This stage involves careful and detailed consideration of the complete investigation.

Decisions have to be made about the most appropriate method of enquiry, about the data, about the kind of sample to be used and about the techniques to be used for collection of the data.

It is particularly important to consider how the data will be analysed, especially if machines or computers are to be used. Appropriate statistical significance levels must be determined at which hypotheses will be accepted or rejected.

Before embarking any further, it is important to prepare the research participants carefully. Permissions must be sought and obtained from all significant authorities and persons (including patients). Confidentiality must be guaranteed and ethics of social investigation must be strictly adhered to. If the investigation is to be conducted in health care agencies it will also be necessary to submit the research programme to a local ethics committee for approval before starting the study.

A time-table should now be prepared and the cost estimated.

Carry out pilot studies to test the proposed research methods

It is always wise to carry out at least one pilot study; sometimes many pilot runs will be necessary but the number tends to be limited by the lack of time and money. Occasionally, it might be necessary to proceed without any pilot studies at all if sufficient time or money are totally lacking, but this is not to be recommended.

During this stage a small sample, as similar as possible to the kind of sample chosen for the major study, is used to test out the research method or tool. It can be a most illuminating and sobering experience, especially if the questionnaire that has been designed after many hours of sweat and toil proves to be useless. But it is better to discover it at this stage, rather than to attempt to conduct a major, but meaningless, research project.

Collect the data

As soon as the pilot studies are completed satisfactorily, full scale data collection should start. It is wise to start quite soon after completing the pilots to prevent undue bias resulting from pilot study subjects discussing their involvement too widely.

Data are collected either by the researcher or a specially trained team of research assistants.

Research subjects should normally be asked to participate and thanked afterwards. Incidentally, if a postal questionnaire is used, the chances of its being returned are greater if a stamped addressed envelope is enclosed. The stamp must be stuck on, not franked: the latter does not appear to be very effective!

Analyse the data

For many researchers, this is a time of near despondency. The data must be counted, grouped, classified and coded according to a prearranged system, followed by rigorous analysis with the aid of statistical techniques and the help of a statistician.

Technology can be very useful at this stage, and there are a variety of card puncher, card sorter, tabulator, calculator and computer systems available to help—if the researcher can afford them.

After the analysis, follows the testing of the hypotheses and drawing conclusions.

Write the research report

Quite obviously, the researcher needs scientific skills for the research but he also needs literary skills for the report writing. There is little point in possessing exciting and novel knowledge if it cannot be communicated to others.

The report should critically discuss the methodology as well as the findings. Copies and details of all research tools should also be included. References and bibliographies should be appended and an acknowledgement of all source material made. It is important to be aware of copyright laws if inserting quotations in the report from other sources. Normally, if the quotation is longer than one page, permission to quote must be sought from the publishers and/or author.

RESEARCH TOOLS

A great variety of tools are used by social researchers and it would be impossible to give details about all of them as there are whole textbooks devoted to each of them. But some tools and techniques commonly used by sociologists are discussed below.

Models

Biology students are quite used to using models and almost everyone has seen a model of an atom. Sociologists also create models sometimes. These models are based on simplifications of the real world. A 'systems' model of care is shown in Figure 9.1. Systems models are very popular among social scientists and have been used to illustrate the dynamics of nursing (Chapman, 1974) and of the hospital ward organisation (Melia, 1979), and as a suggested alternative model to the problem-solving approach to the nursing process (Altschul, 1977).

'Not only has the nurse to meet the patients' (and relatives') needs, but she must be able to work with the doctor, relaying information regarding the patient and his condition and carrying out treatment; to alert, where necessary, paramedical and other staff and co-ordinate their function and maintain records of ever increasing complexity; . . . concern herself with teaching . . . and find time to evaluate the effect of these activities' (Chapman).

Melia used the systems approach in a sociological fashion to analyse nursing work. She drew an interesting analogy between work organisation in the coal mining industry and the work of hospital ward nurses: 'The systems approach has the advantages of embracing the different aspects of the work organisation whilst recognising their separate properties and of seeking to understand the relationship between them. A system is a set of inter-related parts, each of which is related to every other part.' Support for the systems approach comes also from Altschul as part of the search for a more rational approach to nursing practice, for a more scientific approach to nursing research and for a more appropriate and convincing approach to the teaching of nursing.

Even though models are not 'real', they provide a useful step towards producing theories and hypotheses. They cannot be claimed to be 'true' or 'false' in the sense that hypotheses can, only more or less useful on a continuum ranging from 'no use' to 'very useful' in helping one to derive hypotheses and theories. But the models need to be constructed with a view to constructing theories and hypotheses one wants to construct.

An appropriate question might be: 'Why not just use theories?' Well, there may be no theories and even if there are theories, a model might enable calculations to be made which would be impossible with theories. And models make deliberate assumptions which might afford insights into theory normally difficult to grasp.

There are other advantages in using models. They help describe and help us understand complex systems and events which have been useful for teaching complex finance and warfare skills, for example.

They help the researcher see new relationships and help decide when experiment is impossible. Using models has been very useful in engineering designs, as well as in developing nursing care equipment. And last, but not least, they are amusing.

It would be naive to underestimate the dangers inherent in using models, the greatest of which is the danger of reification or mistaking the model for reality, which it is not. They also tend to encourage overgeneralisations and entice one into committing the fallacy of confirming the obvious without seeking independent evidence. An obvious hazard to scientific enquiry. Too often models are not validated and may divert useful energy into non-productive activity.

But models can be useful if a start is made with a simple model which is gradually modified, extended and built upon and if the model builder always seeks a philosophical justification for his activity.

Interviews

An interview should be considered a conversation with a purpose. It strikes at the heart of social investigation because conversation is the basis of human interaction, differentiating humans from animals.

The interview technique is commonly used to obtain data in sociological investigations. Nurses and doctors use the interview regularly to help them assess nursing needs and make a diagnosis respectively. Valuable data can be gleaned if the interview is conducted with care.

To maximise the forces of communication during the interview, it is important to pay particular attention to questioning technique, personal behaviour and reactions and dress as these can all affect the kind of responses obtained. Care must be taken to direct and control the communications process to the specific objectives of the investigation.

The interviewer should be kind and considerate to the interviewee. Sometimes one might argue with or bully the interviewee during depth interviews. But this requires particular skills and is not to be recommended to novices.

Establishing good rapport is important, but it can be overdone and may detract from the aims of the interview. There is a need sometimes in the interview situation to teach the respondent to be a respondent. This is most important in social research, especially with children who are often so curious that they attempt to switch roles. There is some evidence that too much rapport can reduce the amount of information obtained during an interview. At the end of the interview, the respondent should be left feeling emotionally satisfied and, at the very least, should feel no worse off than before the interview started.

The interview can take a number of forms, from being completely standardised using a written questionnaire and yes/no/disagree type of answers to one that is completely free and non-directed, as the psychoanalytical or eavesdropping variety. The standardised interview is useful when a simple collection of information is required such as 'Should nurses prescribe medicines?' The open-ended interview is most useful for dealing with difficult and sensitive areas such as assessing attitudes on birth control and abortion.

The open interview creates a number of difficulties for the interviewer. The technique requires better training and the recording and analysis of data is more problematical then in the closed interview. Psychoanalytical mechanisms can influence the interview situation and it is difficult to do in homes because of the possible and often frequent interference from other relatives and friends who often are very anxious to join in. I remember one particular open interview I was conducting which was ruined by the invasion of a large Alsatian dog who decided to urinate on the side of the armchair in which I was sitting!

There are a number of possible variations on the standardised interview technique by using probes such as 'I see', 'I understand', 'ahah!, 'Yes?'; by pausing (for up to 30 seconds): by seeking more information—'How do you mean?'; by echoing the respondent's words: by summarising for the respondent: and, by seeking clarification from him.

Would-be interviewers need a lot of practice before going out into the field.

Field techniques

This is a global term used to cover the method of observation of people as they go about their normal daily lives. People are discovered as they really are. The researcher usually goes to live or work among the society or group to be studied and stays in a role acceptable to the group and one which permits observations and reporting. The researcher, as a result, becomes involved in a web of social interaction which has to be observed, analysed and reported.

Field techniques are not really a research method, but rather a research style which includes using information obtained from observation, informant interviewing, document analysis, respondent analysis, participant observation, self analysis, case studies and life histories.

There are two basic problems with this method. First, the problem of establishing and maintaining good working relationships with the research subjects in the field. And second, the problem of maintaining a balance between involvement in investigation and detachment from it.

It would appear that this is a method that might be more easily used by nurses, as it is fairly easy for them to become part of a group in the institution of the hospital as a hospital nurse or part of society by taking on the role of community nurse. The opportunities could be tremendous. In fact, hospital and community nurses have helped with a number of investigations as research assistants but this has presented problems, particularly in the kinds of responses received.

Before entering the group to be studied a good 'social map' of the formal and informal groupings should be obtained if possible. Introductions can be helpful. One of the greatest problems in this kind of research is the 'calculated opinion leader' whose identity is often difficult to establish and can usually only be discovered after going into the field.

There is also a problem associated with the dual or multiple interview. For example, if doctors and nurses have to be interviewed in a hospital study and one group is interviewed before the other, the second group interviewed in a hospital might perceive the researcher to be on the 'other side' and this might influence how the second group perceive their status. This could lead to distorted and biased responses.

Establishing a role acceptable to the group can also be problematical. This role can mean being a complete participant, and some researchers, for example, have taken on roles of 'tuberculosis patient' (Roth), 'mental patient' (Caudill), 'jazz musician' (Becker).

And somewhere in the United Kingdom there are researchers working as student and auxiliary nurses.

Where the researcher is a participant observer and is known by the group his role must be known. It is often sufficient to say: 'I am writing a book' (Whyte). Otherwise a role will be allotted. Many anthropologists have been considered to be 'missionaries'! There seem to be some advantages in being a foreigner (Sweig).

The closer the participation, the better the results of the study tend to be. Complete participation is of course easier in Western societies than in primitive societies where the effects of different colour, speech and dress would affect the situation.

There are other problems of complete participation. The researcher cannot interact uniformly with all members of the group. Once in the role of participant, the researcher cannot step out of the role and too many questions cannot be asked as in an interview. Another problem which can be quite acute is that occasionally the researcher has to chose sides and thus run the risk of becoming identified with a clique.

It might also be impossible as a participant observer to make contact with isolates and this will give a distorted view of the society being observed. Contact with members of the group considered to have 'highest' or 'lower' status might be seen as a threat by one or other group.

This, for example, could be a difficulty if a hierarchal profession like nursing was being observed in a hospital. In that situation, the greater the participation with one group the greater the isolation from the other, and as a result certain critical features may be missed.

There are also problems associated with not being able to record on the spot: memory is fallible, problems of role conflict, problems caused by the strain of living with a group, problems of losing objectivity as time passes—'going native' as it is sometimes called resulting in over-identification with the group or society being studied.

The presence of the investigator is bound to influence the behaviour of those he meets. But there is no doubt that field methods enable the investigator to explore social processes more efficiently than any other method of social enquiry. It can be particularly valuable if it provides rich details of the society and verbatim quotations.

The main disadvantage of health workers investigating health problems with this method in agencies they know well is that field techniques tend to be more effective when the investigator knows very little about the field investigated. But provided that the nurse has the personality to cope, fitted by temperament, time and physical energy, there is no reason why that last sentence should not prove to be an appropriate challenge in the future.

Systematic observation

This method is a more commonly used alternative to participant observation. It is a systematic observation and recording of events and their consequences as they actually occur: a method that has recently been used in a number of nursing care studies conducted from the research unit of the Royal College of Nursing.

This method enables the investigator to study also non-verbal behaviour such as facial expressions and body movements. It is especially useful in studies of children, and in most psychological assessment units there is usually an observer behind an invisible screen. The Tavistock Clinic films on the effects of hospitalisation on children were made by taking film shots at 3 minute intervals.

The subjects can be studied in the actual situation and groups can also be set up experimentally. A great deal of the maternal deprivation theories have been derived from systematic observation on experimentally set up groups of monkeys.

The observers need carefully supervised training to avoid the dangers of observer bias.

Certain problems are associated with this method. Reactivity between observer and observed exists but it has been argued that it is easier to alter verbal behaviour at an interview than to alter actual behaviour when observed. The producers of the Tavistock films mentioned above confirmed this, for they noted that the children quickly became familiar with the cameras and then ignored them. Of course the observer can be concealed but that raises certain ethical problems.

Some behaviour such as sexual, voting and defaecating behaviour cannot be observed, of course, and this can only be ascertained by questions.

Finally, systematic observation, like all field methods tends to be expensive in time and money and in these days of mounting economic depression that will remain a major problem.

Triangulation

This is methodological concept derived from the growing realisation that using a variety of methods of social investigation is the source of greatest strength for sociology and the other social sciences.

The concept was developed initially by a philosopher and a psychologist. Its proponents argue that investigators should use multiple methods and, as far as possible, apply different theories in their investigations and that the greater the degree of triangulation, the greater is the confidence in research findings.

Another argument in favour of triangulation is that any one proposition should be tested by two or more methods because every method has its limitations and any proposition verified by two or more methods therefore diminishes the uncertainty of the proposition.

COMMON RESEARCH ERRORS

Social research by its very nature inevitably gives rise to a number of possible errors which are discussed below.

1. *Observer error*. This is caused by the investigator's subconscious bias to produce research findings or to interpret research findings in the way he wants them . This error has been commonly noted in psychiatric clinical studies.

2. *Recording errors*. Numerous studies have demonstrated high levels of recording errors. Analyses of these errors suggest that observers tend to err in the direction most favourable to their own attitudes or that the errors tend to favour the experimental hypothesis. 'Rounding up' figures can also bias results.

3. *Interpretation errors*. There is some indication in a number of experiments that the investigator's own perception of a situation can cause errors of interpretation. The anthropologists Fortune and Mead, for example, described the Arapesh tribe in significantly different terms. In Mead's, but not Fortune's, view the Arapesh were a placid domestic people.

This error can also creep in at the sampling stage and studies have demonstrated that there is a tendency to choose a sample that ensures that unwanted data do not appear. This criticism has been directed at studies of American institutions for the white middle-class aged which demonstrated no deprivations!

4. Errors associated with biosocial attributes. There is a fair amount of evidence that the sex, race, age, religion and social class of the investigator and subject can all cause some error in research findings.

STATISTICS

Any investigator will at some time or other need to use the science of statistics during his research process.

Statistics is a science, based upon mathematics, to assist decision-making under uncertainty.

The basic statistical problem involves obtaining a sample from a large body of data called a population. A population is any arbitrarily designated group, for example all babies born in the maternity ward on Tuesday. A sample is a selection of the members of the population, such as every fourth baby born in the maternity ward on Tuesday.

From information contained in this sample of babies an inference about the characteristics of the population of babies can be obtained.

Populations in the statistical concept of the word need not be concerned with people. The characteristics of general practitioners' prescriptions could well be of interest to some health service decision makers. An inference about the types of drugs prescribed can be obtained from the information obtained in a sample from this population.

There are four main elements in the solution of a statistical problem: quantification, design, analysis, and inference.

The sample used to draw the inference about a population contains a quantity of information which, in statistics, is quantified. Therefore the necessary first element in statistics is to decide upon the information required and the method of quantification. This is often obviously in terms of people, costs and the like, but sometimes methods of measurement and quantification may have to be devised by the investigator.

The next element involves deciding on the most economical procedure for obtaining a specified quantity of information. The statistician asks the questions how are the data going to be obtained and how much is required? The sample procedure and experimental design are decided at this stage.

Thereafter the data are extracted from the sample, the objective being to extract the maximum amount of information. The analysis of the data follows, from which an inference is made about the population from which the sample was drawn. But since the information has been derived from data obtained from the sample it is only partial information about the population and any inferences made will therefore be subject to error. Although some inferences made can be very accurate, others can be inaccurate.

It is therefore necessary to clearly define a measure of reliability regarding such inferences to be able to assess their practical value in the decision-making process.

The science of statistics therefore can be seen to assist the decision maker to make inferences about populations of interest to him. And a measure of reliability is added to the inference which can be open to error due to the fact that the inference is based on a sample which may not reflect the true characteristics of the population.

A null hypothesis is an hypothesis set up to be statistically tested and states that no difference exists between a sample statistic and a hypothetical population value. If the statistic is 'significant' the null hypothesis is rejected. This means that the view that any difference between the sample statistic and population value is due to chance fluctuations in sampling. The level of significance at which the null hypothesis is rejected is a measure of the degree of probability of rejecting the null hypothesis when it is true.

ETHICAL PRINCIPLES

The social researcher, during his research pursuits, should remember at all times that he has a responsibility to safeguard the proper interests of his research subjects, as well as maintaining his own professional integrity.

Work should not be undertaken unless the investigator is qualified to carry it out; boundaries of professional competence must be recognised.

Limitations on detachment and involvement in the area of study should also be recognised.

Guarantees of confidentiality should not be given unless they can be fulfilled.

Observation of subjects without their knowledge should, where possible, be avoided and, if used, the anonymity of the subjects should be completely safeguarded.

Caution should be exercised in communications with the press, radio and television as their standards and interests in the areas or subjects being studied are not necessarily the same as the sociologist's.

The investigator should always try to avoid raising his subject's hopes which he cannot satisfy and try to avoid causing anxieties which he may be unable to allay.

Contributions from other research assistants and authors should be acknowledged and names should not be cited without first seeking permission to do so.

And, finally, the investigator should be aware of his particular responsibility with regard to any use to which his published research results may be put.

In an attempt to give further specific guidance to nurses involved in research the Royal College of Nursing, in 1977, published the guide *Ethics related to research in nursing*. This document was drawn up by members of the College's Research Society and endorsed by the Council of the College. Guidance is directed to nurses undertaking research, nurses in positions of authority where research is to be carried out, and nurses practicing in places where research is being carried out. For, as the document states in the introduction, 'The ethics of nursing research must be consistent with the ethics of nursing practice.'

RESEARCH AS A BASIS FOR THE PRACTICE OF NURSING

It was the *Report of the Committee on Nursing* (Briggs Report, Her Majesty's Stationery Office, 1972) which stated that nursing should become a research-based profession. 'Research' means a systematic investigation towards the sum of knowledge, and the word 'base' means that on which a thing rests. What the Briggs Report really meant then was that the practice of nursing should rest on the body of knowledge based on systematic investigation.

Florence Nightingale, the founder of modern professional nursing, based her reforms of the nursing profession firmly on meticulous investigation and she examined every set of plans with great care and enquiry. Modern professional nursing therefore had its origins in Miss Nightingale's pioneering research. She was also a passionate statistician and a positive genius for marshalling knowledge. There can be no doubt that her pioneering philosophical and scientific spirit of enquiry dramatically changed the practice of nursing from caretaker activity of a very poor quality to that of administering nursing care of a very high quality indeed. Unfortunately, as Simpson (1971) has pointed out, Miss Nightingale's 'research approach to problems was . . . never transmitted as part of the Nightingale tradition'. This was partly due to Miss Nightingale's particular kind of charismatic leadership, for what was considered good for herself was not considered particularly good for her subordinates. But it was also due to the ethos of the Victorian society in which Miss Nightingale lived and in which nurses were expected to be unquestioningly obedient to doctors, keeping their own critical faculties entirely in the background.

In the United Kingdom, nursing research activity was virtually non-existent until after the 1939–1946 World War. But a tradition of nursing research was fostered in North America long before that time, influenced, no doubt, by the fact that American nurses had developed nursing education programmes within the institutions of higher education from the end of the 19th Century. As long ago as 1899, a course in hospital economics for qualified nurses was inaugurated at the Teachers College of Columbia University in the USA. And the first university-controlled school of nursing was established at the University of Minnesota, USA, in 1909 (Davis, 1966).

One of the chief aims of universities is to create the knowledge that is taught. It therefore follows that teachers of nursing in these institutions must, as part of their brief, create nursing knowledge; and that requires research activity. In addition, facilities for training in research skills are also more likely to be available in institutions of higher education than in hospital schools of nursing.

Although much of the nursing research which has been carried out in North America could be described as pure research, there has recently been a marked change in emphasis in nursing dissertations and there appears to be a move away from pure research to research applied to nursing (Smith, 1974). Nursing research has long been an accepted activity of nurses working in North America.

British nurses did not start to exploit the facilities provided by centres of higher education for professional nursing education until the 1950s. Even as recently as 1971, Marjorie Simpson, then research nursing officer in the Department of Health and Social

Security, London, had to conclude that 'the idea of the nurse using research methods to examine nursing problems is alien, even today, to many people in our society, to nurses, doctors, to the public . . .'

At about the same time as Miss Simpson was making these comments in the United Kingdom, the chief executive officer of the Royal Australian Nurses Federation, Mary Patten (1972), stated in a paper discussing the future development of nursing in Australia that there was a desperate need for activity 'particularly in the area of nursing research'.

Nevertheless, in recent years and in particular during the 1970s a great deal of nursing research activity has been going on in the United Kingdom. And yet, while research studies of poverty have produced numerous doctorates and masters degrees, they have not done anything dramatic to relieve the burden of those suffering the poverty, and it remains difficult to demonstrate any large-scale benefit to patient care as a result of the recent proliferation of nursing research activity in the United Kingdom. But Clark and Hockey (1979) are more optimistic. 'Because of, or perhaps in spite of, research', they argue, 'there is, happily, a growing tendency among nurses to challenge the accepted conventions and traditions of their profession.'

There does indeed seem to be a growing international interest among nurses in nursing research and in extending the body of knowledge of nursing. For example, in the first two years of the existence of the *Journal of Advanced Nursing*, launched in 1976, over 78 per cent of authors were nurses. By the end of the third year, it was read in 57 countries. During the 1970s the Research Society of the Royal College of Nursing was firmly established. This had been pioneered by a research discussion group originally founded as a self-help group by the few nurses who were involving themselves in research in the United Kingdom during the 1950s. And recently, throughout the United Kingdom, research interest groups have proliferated, and in many towns and cities nurses meet at regular intervals to share their research interests and activities and discuss findings.

This explosion of interest in nursing research and in extending the body of nursing knowledge is very heartening, but it is important that this new interest is accompanied by action. In a great deal of British nursing research there has been a preoccupation with studies of nurses rather than nursing. The reason for this may be that nurses are such a highly disciplined group of people that they willingly answer questionnaires or offer themselves as subjects for research investigations. This is a most fortuitious position from the researcher's point of view because the greater the response rate, the greater the significance of the result. But studies of nurses will not necessarily help to provide a scientific base for the practice of nursing. Although there have been a large number of studies related to nurses, it is not possible to generalise with too much confidence from any of the findings.

In a review of over 60 studies on withdrawal of British nursing students from training, MacGuire (1969) concluded that the attempt to demonstrate a relationship between the large variety of factors studied and withdrawal of nursing students 'has not been particularly successful'. Cynics who read MacGuire's publication could be excused for not being particularly surprised that nursing students withdrew from training, rather they may well be amazed that any of them decided to stay and complete their training.

A more recent comprehensive review of the literature on absence and wastage in trained nurses (Redfern, 1978), shows that there is 'very little valid and reliable evidence to indicate the nature of the relationship between any kind of withdrawal and personal, organisational and external factors in qualified British nurses.'

It is worth noting that in spite (or because) of all this work on nurses who leave the profession before or after qualifying, very little is known about those who stay and work in the nursing profession after qualification.

Additionally, a great deal of activity in the United Kingdom has been devoted to patient-nurse dependency studies. These too have been rigorously appraised (Wilson-Barnett, 1978). In a review of numerous studies conducted during the previous 12 years, she had to conclude that 'no one study design, at present, serves to give the answer for calculating deployment or establishment figures . . . at present there is no easy way to calculate a staff norm'. She warns that it would be a great mistake to implement any inadequate method.

Focus on nursing

It is reassuring that since the 1960s there has been an increasing emphasis on research studies of nursing care, sponsored by the Department of Health and Social Security in conjunction with the Royal College of Nursing of the United Kingdom. A number of nurses were appointed within the College's Institute of Advanced Nursing Education specifically to conduct nursing care investigation. The reports of these studies and a number of studies conducted elsewhere have been published as monographs.

The Royal College of Nursing studies of nursing care have undoubtedly added to the body of knowledge of nursing, but it must be stressed that most of them were descriptive and small-scale studies. Of course, this does not detract from their usefulness, only from their predictive power. Nevertheless, the College's nursing care studies have provided some very interesting and useful information which if considered seriously could influence nursing practice. For example, it is now known that there is an odd lack of attention by nurses to the nutritional needs of unconscious patients (Jones, 1975), that unpopular patients in general hospital wards can be socially isolated by nurses (Stockwell, 1972) and that an informed talk to patients before operations can significantly affect their experience of postoperative pain (Hayward, 1975).

There is also some indication that current American nursing research activities are contributing to nursing care in America. Three American nurses (Gortner, Bloch and Phillips, 1976), after a rigorous assessment of ongoing nursing research activity, indicate that contributions of nursing research to nursing practice are increasing rapidly in the following four major areas: The science of nursing practice, the artistry of nursing practice, the structures needed for optimal delivery of care, and the methodologies needed for measurement and evaluation of nursing care. They cite illustrative studies in each of these four areas and conclude with a plea for implementation of research findings.

What may be necessary now is to establish some experimental wards in which to test the conclusions of researchers. There is hope on the horizon in this respect. In 1979, the first national nursing practice research unit was established in the United Kingdom. It is based at Northwick Park Hospital, Middlesex, and is under the direction of a nurse, Dr Rosemary Crow. There is also an urgent need for replication of studies. Even though this, too, is a respectable research activity, if has not been widely used in nursing studies in the United Kingdom or elsewhere.

IMPLEMENTING RESEARCH FINDINGS

'Enthusiasm for nursing can be greatly enhanced by enthusiasm for research' (Clark and Hockey, 1979). They believe that there is a great deal of apathy in the nursing profession regarding the promotion of knowledge and that this is one of the most important hindrances to research fulfilling its potential as a change agent. Certainly, in my view, it is the professional responsibility of all professional nurses to be well-acquainted with current research activity and research reports, and to seriously consider the implications of these.

Research into nursing can be justified on several grounds, claims Nancy Roper (1977), a former research nursing officer at the Scottish Home and Health Department, Edinburgh. Original studies are needed to increase the nursing profession's body of knowledge and replication should provide credance to findings of the original studies. Justification can also be made on economic and legal grounds, she argues. Ignorance of well-known nursing research, for example, would probably not be defensible in a Court of Law trying a case of negligence.

Other justifications for research into nursing are economy of effort for nurses as well as patients, economical use of material resources, and improvement in nursing curricula and manpower planning. 'The objective of all nursing research is directly or indirectly to improve the quality of nursing', Roper argues, even though this quality may be difficult to measure.

But it is up to members of the nursing profession to decide whether they wish to implement the findings of any nursing investigation, particularly those nurses directly concerned with patient care, be it in hospitals, in general practices, in schools, prisons, factories or other settings.

Nursing research findings should be considered critically and discussed with great care. Surely there must be at least one finding in most nursing research reports that could be implemented without too much difficulty in one or two wards or units in many hospitals or in non-institutional settings so that practising nurses themselves could assess the effects on the care given to their own patients or clients? Certainly, teachers of nursing should make use of published research studies, otherwise their teaching will lack reality.

'We are quite sure that nursing needs research but it should not be forgotten that research also needs nursing. Without practical application in the important and realistic settings like the hospital or community health centre the usefulness of the researcher's contribution will be limited' (Clark and Hockey, 1979).

Difficulties

A working group of the European Office of the World Health Organisation was set up in 1977 to evaluate current inpatient nursing practice. In addition to many other difficulties inherent in research of nursing practice, the working group found that evaluation presented particular problems, as the work of nurses was often still relatively ill-defined. (A study conducted in the nursing research unit of the University of Edinburgh on the role of nursing auxiliaries in the National Health Service (Hardie and Hockey, 1978) demonstrated that throughout the United Kindom there are numerous nursing auxiliaries practising most of the procedures taught in the basic nursing programmes and that most of them have received no training at all). The WHO working group therefore concluded that 'little or no emphasis has been placed on the need to define objectives and measure outcomes in terms of the patient's progress . . . evaluation of the outcomes of nursing interventions is rarely done in a planned and systematic manner'.

Nurses really must take the matter into their own hands. Nursing is their profession and it is therefore up to them to define nursing and to evaluate their own nursing care and nursing education programmes. As Hockey (1978) so pertinently pointed out, there is also still 'a need for research into all stages of the process of nursing and most particularly into the sequence of the stages which constitute the process'. She urges that the first task of nurses must be to identify situations where the process of nursing is used. This may be followed by comparative studies at a variety of levels or by prospective studies in areas where the process of nursing is about to be introduced, retrospective studies or, ideally, a combination of these. There is also room, she contends, for almost any known research technique to be used during this fundamental research activity in nursing.

Another rich source of research ideas is the Australian nurse Mary Patten (1972). Although she was referring to Australia, the topics she discussed are, I believe, international problems: 'a questioning of the dehumanisation of the health services', 'rumours that the nurse is forcing herself out of existence', 'under-utilisation of skill', 'What are sufficient numbers?', 'the intangible element in quality of service which is less easily identifiable', and 'Community expectations must be built into any index of quality of care'. The above suggestions are sufficient to keep nurses involved and interested in nursing research for decades to come.

Nursing education

If the nursing profession is to become truly research-based, nursing students must be encouraged to become interested in research from the very outset of their training. 'Research-mindedness' is 'the readiness to look analytically at all events or working methods with which we are concerned, a willingness to encourage scientific study or experimentation, and an ability to accept the proven conclusion and act accordingly' (Dame Muriel Powell in the 9th *Nursing Mirror Lecture*, University of Edinburgh, 1967). A nursing education research unit has been established in the University of London directed by a nurse, Mrs Caroline Cox.

The attitudes of teachers of nursing are crucial, for they are in a position to emphasise from the beginning of training that no knowledge is finite, that no one method of practice is correct for all time, and that the most important attribute of learning is to know how and where to find more knowledge and how to profess nursing (Altschul, 1977). Teachers can also encourage students to question assumptions and ask for evidence, to argue and synthesise, and to acquire the capacity for self-criticism without loss of self-respect and self-confidence.

This puts heavy responsibilities on teachers of nursing who in the past, according to a WHO consultant (Allen, 1977), have confined their efforts to the teaching of knowledge and skills—'the mere pre-requisites to nursing'. Allen argues that learning to nurse is a complex problem-solving process. Teachers of nursing must therefore seek to provide conditions in which nursing students can learn to solve problems.

There can be no doubt that 'research-mindedness' will be enhanced by stressing the 'process of nursing' in the approach to patient care. This entails observation of the patient in his total environment, assessment of his needs, planning care, giving the care and evaluating the effectiveness and suitability of that care. Those simple steps are also simple basic research steps. This approach will do much to make nursing rational, systematic and research-based.

REFERENCES

Allen, M. (1977) *Evaluation of Education Programmes in Nursing*. Geneva: WHO.

Altschul, A. (1977) *Professing Nursing*. Inaugural Lecture No. 62, University of Edinburgh.

Altschul, A. (1978) A systems approach to the nursing process. *Journal of Advanced Nursing,* **3,** 33–340.

Chapman, C.M. (1974) Nursing education—curriculum content. *Queen's Nursing Journal,* **17,** 149–152.

Clark, J.M. & Hockey, L. (1979) *Research for Nursing*. Aylesbury: H M & M.

Davis, F. (1966) *The Nursing Profession: Five Sociological Essays*. New York: Wileyk.

Gortner, S.R., Bloch, D. & Phillips, T.P. (1976) Contributions of nursing research to patient care. *Journal of Advanced Nursing,* **1,** 507–518.

Hardie, M. & Hockey, L. (1978) *Nursing Auxiliaries in Health Care*. London: Groom Helm.

Hayward, J.C. (1975) *Information—A Prescription Against Pain*. London: Royal College of Nursing.

Her Majesty's Stationery Office (1972) *Report of the Committee on Nursing*. London: HMSO.

Hockey, L. (1978) *Research and the Process of Nursing: Research Methods* (paper read at the Research Society Annual Conference). London: Royal College of Nursing.

Jones, D. (1975) *Food for Thought*. London: Royal College of Nursing.

MacGuire, J. (1969) *Threshold to Nursing*. London: Bell.

Melia, K.M. (1979) A sociological approach to the analysis of nursing work. *Journal of Advanced Nursing,* **4,** 57–67.

Patten, M.E. (1972) The future development of nursing in Australia. *National Hospital,* **16** (10), 19–22.

Powell, M.B. (1967) The challenge of nursing education. *Nursing Mirror*, 24th March, 581–584.

Redfern, S. (1978) Absence and wastage in trained nurses: a selective review of the literature. *Journal of Advanced Nursing,* **3,** 231–250.

Roper, N. (1977) Justification and use of research. *Journal of Advanced Nursing,* **2,** 365–371.

Royal College of Nursing (1977) *Ethics Related to Research in Nursing*. London: RCN.

Simpson, M. (1971) Research in nursing—the first step. *Nursing Mirror*, 12th March, 22–27.

Smith, J.P. (1974) Nursing in North America. *Nursing Mirror*, 28th November, 53–56.

Stockwell, P. (1972) *The Unpopular Patient*. London: Royal College of Nursing.

Wilson-Barnett, J. (1978) *A Review of Patient-Nurse Dependency Studies*. London: DHSS.

World Health Organisation (1977) *Summary Report of a Working Group on the Evaluation of Inpatient Nursing Practice*. Copenhagen: WHO.

10

The British Welfare State

Numerous definitions of the 'Welfare State' can be found, but the most appropriate definition, in my view, is derived from Titmuss (1968) who describes it as a society which accepts the responsibility of providing services to satisfy social needs, which enables society to survive as an organic whole, and to satisfy individual needs, which assists in the survival of the individual in society.

It is not really possible, however, to conceive social and individual needs as being separate, for one type of need tends to shade into the other as societies progress and change. The situation in which different needs arise and are recognised as needs has changed throughout the present and previous centuries and will continue to do so in the future, as a result of the barrage of ideological, psychological, sociological and technological influences which continually and persistently impinge on any individual in society.

The concept of community care has been called the 'everlasting cottage trailer' of the welfare state and the precise social origins of the term community care are difficult to determine. However, it is safe to assume that the concept of community care has naturally evolved from the idea of the welfare state.

In British society at least, it is now generally accepted that the state should provide numerous health, social and welfare services for its citizens according to their needs. Increasingly it is recognised that these services are 'rights', even though there are still large gaps in the quantity and quality of services available. Voluntary organisations play an important part in the provision of community care services and often provide specialist services for the blind and deaf and those who suffer from physical and mental handicaps.

THE ORIGINS OF THE BRITISH WELFARE STATE

If origins can be detected at all, the origins of the British Welfare State probably can be claimed to be in the provisions for relief of the destitute poor contained in the Elizabethan Poor Law of 1589. This law distinguished between the different causes of poverty among the old and sick, among children and able-bodied adults and prescribed different treatments. The law was benevolent and vested the responsibility for looking after the poor in the *parish*. The cost of looking after the poor was met by monies raised through parish rates (poor rates). This legislation was set up against a background of economic unrest, mobile agricultural labour and increased mobility of vagrants. As each parish had to look after its own poor, they were sometimes returned to the parishes they had moved from. There was no control by the central government.

The 1589 Law and other associated legislation were codified into the Elizabethan Poor Relief Act of 1601 which influenced society right through to the twentieth century. During this time the relief of the poor moved gradually from an organisational framework that was repressive to an organisational framework that placed some emphasis on prevention.

The Elizabethan Poor Law aimed to deter the able-bodied ('underserving') pauper whose poverty was considered to be due to his own moral weakness. The 'deserving poor' were recognised to be the old and the sick paupers, and although it is true that these groups of poor were always given some concessions, they inevitably became stigmatised by the system.

By the end of the eighteenth century the Poor Law had become totally inadequate in Great Britain which had been rapidly industrialised. There were many more mobile poor and the parish as a unit of organisation was no longer a viable reality. Nevertheless, the central government still felt it had no obligations to interfere.

The initiative was taken by a parish in Berkshire in the last decade of the eighteenth century which devised its own 'Speenhamland' system of relief. This recognised that standards of living vary according to changes in the economic situation, and relief was paid to the poor on a scale which varied according to the wage rate and the price of bread. Unfortunately, this system did not fully consider the implications for the contributors to the poor rates. Inevitably, the rates were increased. This placed a heavy burden on property owners and also offended the pervading principle of 'economy and efficiency'.

By the beginning of the nineteenth century, change was thought to be needed and the newly reformed parliament was faced with a great deal of dissatisfaction arising from the administration of the Poor Law. As prices had continued to rise since the Napoleonic War, there had been massive increases in the costs of the Poor Law. The burden of supporting the poor also fell unevenly throughout the country as each parish was responsible for its own poor. Often, the parishes containing the greatest numbers of poor were those least able to cope with the inevitably heavy poor rates.

Enclosure of common lands in agricultural areas had also caused much distress and the payments made under the Speenhamland system had tended to keep wages permanently depressed. Corruption was rife in the administration of poor relief and distribution of relief throughout the country was uneven.

Following an enquiry by the *Commission on Conditions of the Labouring Poor*, directed by Edwin Chadwick, the *Poor Law Amendment Act* was passed in 1834. A central government organisation was formed and Boards of Guardians were appointed by the government to oversee the relief of the poor in each 'union'. From the 1300 parishes, 568 unions were formed.

Administration was improved, but outdoor relief was abolished and the aim of the legislation was to deter people from seeking relief. A *workhouse* was established in each union to which the able-bodied poor were sent. This isolated the poor from the rest of the community and the inmates of workhouses lost the normal rights of citizenship. In order to deter the poor further from seeking relief an attempt was made to make the workhouses as unpleasant as possible, as the able-bodied poor were considered to be poor through their own faults.

The workhouse system of poor relief was also cheaper and reduced the burden of poor rates. It encouraged the 'virtue' of work and because the poor were not visible they could easily be forgotten.

In theory, the sick, old and children who were poor were to be cared for differently but in practice, all the poor ended up in the same institutions. Family units were broken up, men and women were segregated, and young and elderly, sick and healthy all mixed together.

There is no doubt that, viewed from the present, the 1834 law would be considered harsh in the extreme, but the nineteenth century perspective was significantly different and the law can only be fully understood in the context of the society and ethos prevailing at that time. There was a belief in a natural order of society: that leaders were born, that the poor laboured for the rich, that each person should be left to sort out his own affairs without interference from the government. Government's role was considered to be one of *laissez-faire*.

The writings of Malthus on the theory of population and Darwin on the theory of evolution, as well as the writings of nineteenth century political economists reinforced these social attitudes.

The workhouses were also seen as a means of social control of the poor who might prove to be sources of social discontent and cause revolutions as they had done in France. This discontent, it was believed, could be curbed by the workhouse where they were given means of subsistence and isolated from the community.

At the end of the nineteenth century there had been many political and social changes. Changes in attitudes towards the poor were also detectable and there was growing concern about the conditions of people living in British society.

The 1909 Royal Commission on the Poor Laws resulted in two reports—a minority and a majority report which reflected both the consensus and the difference of opinions prevailing. Some wanted the Poor Law, some did not. Both reports agreed that the concept of 'less eligibility' should be sacrificed in the interests of treatment and prevention.

It was recognised in the report that the term 'pauper' included other groups besides the able-bodied poor, namely the elderly, the sick, the widowed and the orphaned. Groups which in fact outnumbered the able-bodied poor. Recommendations were made that a form of unemployment insurance should be linked to relief for the able-bodied poor and the idea of government sponsored labour exchanges was fostered.

Non-statutory relief of poverty

Running parallel to the statutory relief of poverty discussed above were two other movements: the working-class movement of educational and economic improvement through individual and collective efforts and the philanthropic movement, the members of which not only gave material relief to the poor but were also genuinely concerned at the plight of those members of society who were less fortunate than themselves.

The working-class movement of self-help echoed the ethos of a *laissez-faire* government and found expression in the formation of a number of social institutions resulting in the growth of strong and powerful friendly societies, trades unions and cooperative societies.

The success of the friendly societies in the nineteenth century, later attracted a commercial counterpart, Industrial Life Assurance Companies, which were mainly concerned with life and burial insurance.

The trades unions developed the welfare aspects of their work extensively, and the cooperative societies, founded in Rochdale, Lancashire, became involved in manufacture and distribution of goods and were particularly strong in the industrial areas of the north of England before eventually developing on a national scale.

The management of friendly societies and cooperative societies was eventually regulated by statute and hence given official sanction, and working-class thrift was given added impetus by the introduction of statutory savings banks in the middle of the nineteenth century.

The philanthropic movement derived its support mainly from the middle classes and many of them pioneered social reforms that were outside the mainstream of accepted nineteenth century attitudes. A number of outstanding philanthropists exerted great influence on both local and national social reforms. Reform of legislation relating to education, factories and public and mental health owe much to the efforts of Lord Shaftesbury. The Salvation Army, founded by William Booth, succeeded in presenting a form of religion that could meet both physical and spiritual needs. The simple faith and quiet conviction of Dr Barnardo brought practical relief to thousands of homeless children.

The changing status of educated women in the nineteenth century brought them new opportunities for exercising their talents within the philanthropic movement. The names of Josephine Butler,

Elizabeth Fry, Octavia Hill, Florence Nightingale and Elizabeth Webb appear often in the pages of the history of social reform.

Following the 1834 Act, there was a fairly rapid growth of distribution of material relief through a number of charitable societies based on the criteria of 'deserving' or 'underserving' poverty. This was often the only alternative to the workhouse; it also relieved the burden on the rates and was therefore officially approved. But there were some who held that long-term and indiscriminate relief of poverty did not improve the condition but merely perpetuated it. These people only supported relief within the Poor Law terms of reference.

The need to organise charitable relief of poverty was recognised in 1861 when the precursor to the Charity Organisation Society (now known as the Family Welfare Association) was founded. Initially, its aim was to coordinate charitable relief on the principle (as per Poor Law policy) that charity was to be given where it enabled the recipient to become self-dependent. In time this was found to be untenable and as social needs changed, the Charity Organisation Society modified its aims and work, and in many respects helped to pioneer the development of the social work profession.

TWENTIETH CENTURY REFORMS

The *laissez-faire* period came to an end at the beginning of the twentieth century when the Poor Law administration began to disintegrate as a result of rapid population increases and spread of political franchise.

The majority Liberal Government which came to power in 1906 was pledged to a policy of social reform.

Government responsibility began to be assumed for social security payments with the passing of the Old Age Pension Act in 1908. The Insurance Act of 1911 gave some measure of security during periods of unemployment and sickness. Insurance benefits were based on the number of contributions paid and unlike the earlier relief systems were not subject to a means test.

Impetus to statutory responsibility was afforded by the First World War and the post-war period. Although new concepts of social welfare were developed particularly in the fields of health, education and infant and maternal welfare services, much of the extension and development of these services was prevented by the devastating economic depression which lasted throughout the 1920s and 1930s. The demands for relief on the Poor Law unions rendered them bankrupt and in 1928 the Boards of Guardians were abolished. Poor Law administration was then vested in public assistance committees, part of the major local government organisation. But unemployed ex-soldiers bitterly resented applying for public assistance.

To deal with unemployment benefits and the re-establishment of the unemployed, the Unemployment Assistance Board was established in 1934. The functions of this Board were extended at the outbreak of the Second World War in 1939 to include the relief of those in distress as a result of war circumstances. The renamed Assistance Board (1940), now also assumed the responsibilities for granting supplementary pensions to widows and the elderly. The cost and administration was thereby transferred from local to central government.

By the beginning of the Second World War therefore, poverty and distress were relieved by three statutory means: national assistance benefits were available to the elderly, the unemployed, widows and war sufferers, social insurance benefits were available to employees, and some local relief was available through Public Assistance Committees, but this last remnant of Poor Law administration was soon to disappear.

Environmental health services

In evidence to the 1909 Royal Commission on the Poor Law, the weight of medical opinion was heavily in favour of seeking out and treating sickness among the poor instead of waiting for the sick to become paupers and eligible for treatment under the provisions of the Poor Law.

In the nineteenth century there was in fact a ferment of enquiry into health matters, and a number of reports, including Edwin Chadwick's Report on the *Sanitary Conditions of the Labouring Population* in 1842, revealed lack of clean water, drainage and fresh air, bad and overcrowded housing with bad waste disposal facilities, and high death rates. The Public Health Act of 1848 which resulted was in fact largely ineffective. The legislation was permissive and there was no official government minister responsible for health. The Act lapsed in 1854 and in the same year

Chadwick was pensioned off. There was little change until the Local Government Act (1871) reformed local government administration and divided the country into sanitary districts whose authorities were obliged to appoint medical officers of health. Further powers to remedy some of the worst health problems, such as powers of inspection, were afforded the sanitary districts in 1875 with the passing of a Public Health Act.

The Ministry of Health was established in 1919 'for the purpose of promoting the health of the people of England and Wales' and henceforth the division between the sick and the sick pauper no longer existed officially. By the time the 1936 Public Health Act was passed to consolidate existing public health legislation, the crude death rate was 11.4 per 1000 and the infant mortality rate was 58 per 1000, which compared favourably with the respective rates of 18.6 per 1000 and 159 per 1000 which had existed at the turn of the twentieth century.

The general health and welfare of the nation has been continually fostered throughout the twentieth century by legislation concerning the environment. This includes The Clean Air Act, 1956, The Noise Abatement Act, 1960, The Factories Act, 1961, The Offices, Shops and Railway Premises Act, 1963, The Housing Acts, 1936 to 1969, The Rent Act, 1968, The Chronically Sick and Disabled Persons Act, 1970, and the Health and Safety at Work Act, 1974.

A team of environmental health officers is today employed by the local authority to look after the environmental health services for the community and such things as adequate shelter and clothing, congenial and safe work, leisure facilities, domestic security and an environment free from noise and pollution are all readily accepted as essential ingredients of health.

THE BRITISH NATIONAL HEALTH SERVICE

The National Health Service is a comprehensive service providing health care in institutions and in patients' homes which embraces diagnostic, curative and preventive concepts of care.

The British National Health Service evolved throughout the nineteenth and early twentieth centuries and can be traced in the development of voluntary hospitals and, later, public hospitals through the provisions of the Poor Law. Personal health and welfare services developed in the early twentieth century following the attack on the worst aspects of disease in the nineteenth century. Services such as infant welfare services began to appear as a result of enterprising people often working within a voluntary organisation. But there was real cooperation between voluntary and statutory agencies at local level. Although the central government encouraged this partnership at local level, it provided very little direction in the early days. However, the importance of child health assumed new dimensions in 1915 when legislation was passed making the notification of all births compulsory and this was enhanced by the passing of the first Maternity and Child Welfare Act at the end of the First World War. However, the provisions of this Act remained only permissive until the beginning of the National Health Service in 1948.

During the first half of the twentieth century a statutory service for the 'deprived' child was also established. The report of the Royal Commission on the Poor Law in 1909, revealed that 14 000 children under 16 were living in mixed workhouses. Many babies taken to the workhouse were separated from their mothers, the workhouse school was not an educational institute at all and older children were exploited as cheap labour as pauper apprentices or by being traded out to commercial and industrial concerns.

In spite of some improvements, dissatisfaction with the inadequacy of the child care services grew after the Second World War and culminated in the scandal of the dramatic death in 1945 of a foster child, which forced the government to set up The Care of Children Committee under Dame Myra Curtis. This committee subsequently recommended that children's departments be established under the direction of a children's officer. The Curtis Report indicated that some of the conditions in which children under care were living were very similar to those commonly found in the nineteenth century workhouses. The Report's recommendations were embraced in the Children's Act, 1948, and thereafter the newly established children's departments took over the responsibility for all children deprived of a normal home life.

The National Health Service was legally established by the passing of the National Health Service Act in 1946, which began to operate from July 1948.

The Service established at that date had three main branches: hospital services, family practitioner services and local health authority services.

In the administration of the hospital services there were three tiers: the Ministry of Health, the regional hospital boards and local management committees. Under the general guidance of the Ministry, regional hospital boards planned, coordinated and supervised the development of the hospital services. The hospital management committees were responsible for the day-to-day running of the hospitals for which they were accountable to the regional hospital authorities. In addition to these management committees, there were thirty-six boards of governors who were responsible for the management and control of hospitals which contained medical schools. The total membership of all these bodies ran to over 10 000 unpaid volunteers.

The family practitioner services carried the main brunt of medical care, which included general medical (family doctor) services, pharmaceutical services, general dental services and ophthalmic services. These services were placed under the separate administration of Executive Councils which, in matters of policy, were largely controlled by the Ministry of Health in consultation with the particular professions concerned. Generally, the geographical areas covered by these councils were coterminous with those of the local health authorities. Their membership consisted of about 3500 voluntary members.

The local health authority services, namely maternity and child welfare, domiciliary midwifery, home nursing, home help, health visiting, prevention of illness, care and after-care services and ambulance service administration, were provided as a statutory duty by the major local health authorities. The central government gave the local authorities a grant to assist in the cost of these services.

Reform of the health services

Serious discussions about the need to reform the health services started in July 1968 with the publication of a government green paper which proposed the unification of all the health services under the direction of about fifty area health boards. It was proposed that these boards would take over all the responsibilities of the authorities which, at that time, were responsible for administering the hospital and local health services and family practitioner services. A second green paper appeared in April, 1970. This also fostered the idea of area health boards and suggested that the geographical areas of these boards should be coterminous with those of the (new) local authority boundaries. A single tier administration was recommended but with provisions for non-executive district committees.

Deliberations were also going on around the same time about the future of local authority social services. The Seebohm Committee was set up in 1966 to consider these and in its report, published in 1968, it was recommended that social service departments under the supervision of a director of social services be established by local authorities.

The new departments were to take on responsibility for the services provided by children's departments, welfare services, education welfare services and child guidance services, home help services, mental health social work services, adult training centres, other social work services provided by local health and hospital authorities and housing departments, and day nurseries.

The report stated that these proposed departments were to take on 'responsibilities extending well beyond those of existing local authority departments'.

Legislation for these recommendations was introduced in May 1970.

THE REORGANISED NATIONAL HEALTH SERVICE

The administration of the National Health Service was unified on 1st April 1974 and all existing health authorities ceased to exist on that date.

The functions previously discharged by the former health authorities, together with the functions of local education authorities relating to medical and dental inspection and treatment of schoolchildren, were brought together under the new health authorities who were henceforth to be responsible for the whole field of health care.

Two kinds of health authority were established: regional health authorities and area health authorities.

Fourteen regional health authorities were established in England. Their boundaries roughly corresponded to those of the former regional hospital boards. Ninety area health authorities (16 inside London and 74 outside London) were also established whose boundaries generally matched those of the local authorities. There were a few exceptions, however, mainly in London. Those area health authorities which have special responsibilities for providing facilities in support of medical and dental teaching were designated area health authorities (teaching).

The regional health authorities have some executive responsibilities, including the design and construction of major new building work and employment of medical consultants and senior registrars of non-teaching area health authorities. They are also responsible for coordinating facilities in support of medical and dental teaching and review and monitor the plans and performance of the area health authorities.

The area health authority has both planning and operational responsibilities. It is accountable to the regional health authority and has to work within national and regional policy guidelines and within the resources allocated to it each year. The basic task of the area health authority is to assess the needs in its area and to plan, organise and administer the health services so as to provide balanced and comprehensive health care to the population it serves.

A Family Practitioner Committee has been established in each area health authority and its functions are similar to those of the former Executive Council.

In Scotland and Wales there is no regional tier and the area health authorities carry out some of the duties of the English regional tier, but with some modifications. In Northern Ireland, health and social services are administered by one and the same authority.

Each area health authority is divided into a number of localities called *districts,* which are the basic units of the integrated hospital and community health service. There are some 'one-district' area health authorities. The population served by a health district varies from 100 000 to 400 000. The district's health services are managed by a team of health care professionals and administrators, and normally this team—the district management team—consists of a district administrator, a district community physician, a district finance officer, a district nursing officer, a medical consultant and a general practitioner, but in health districts where a medical school exists, the dean of the medical school is usually a member of the district management team. In each health district a number of health care planning teams have been set up to assess needs of, and to plan appropriate service for, particular groups such as children, the mentally sick and the elderly.

As the delivery of comprehensive health care depends on the

closest possible working relationship with the local authorities who are responsible for the provision of social services, statutory Joint Consultative Committees, consisting of representatives of the local and area health authorities, have been established. These two authorities are required to cooperate with one another in matters affecting the health and welfare of the population they jointly serve (Figure 10.1).

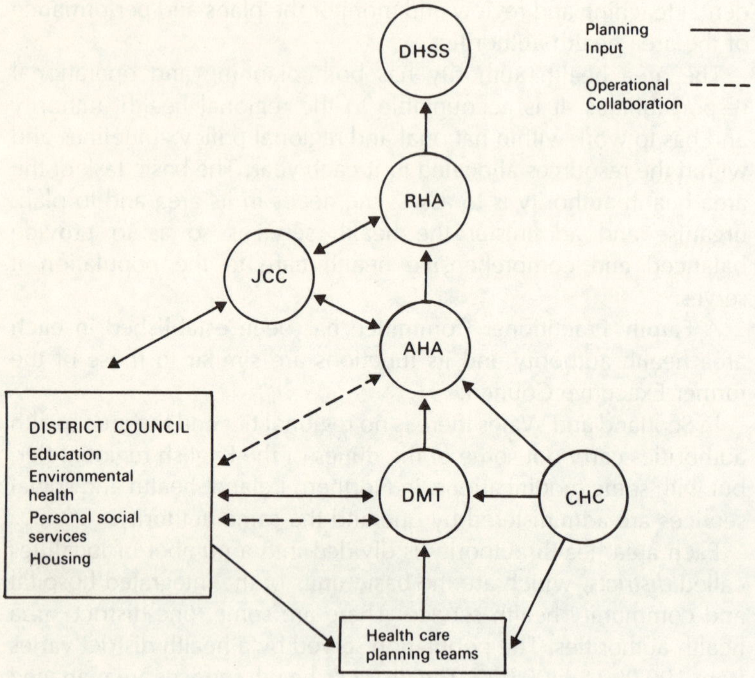

Figure 10.1 Collaboration between the National Health Service and local government

Arrangements have also been made to ensure that at all levels health care professionals have an effective voice in the planning and running of the National Health Service. Professional advisory committees representing doctors, dentists, opticians, pharmacists, and nurses and midwives have been set up at regional and area level to ensure this. The first members of these committees were appointed but subsequently they were elected by their professional peers.

The consumers of health care can also influence the development and management of health care services through the Community Health Councils which consist of representatives of local authorities, local voluntary organisations and other local bodies. These committees are entitled to visit health care establishments and to receive any information from the area health authority which they deem necessary for their work. They are also entitled to receive published replies from the area health authority recording the action taken on issues raised in community health council reports.

THE ROLE OF VOLUNTARY ORGANISATIONS

Since the inception of the reorganised National Health Service the government has actively encouraged area health authorities to foster the participation of voluntary organisations in health care. But this collaboration between statutory and voluntary organisations, as noted above, has developed from the nineteenth century and throughout the twentieth century. Many voluntary agencies in fact pioneered health and welfare services which later became statutory services. Many welfare services, for example the meals on wheels and mental health welfare services, may well have taken much longer to develop if they had not been pioneered by voluntary organisations. Social work and district nurse training were also pioneered by voluntary organisations—the Family Welfare Association and the Queen's Institute of District Nursing respectively.

A large number of voluntary organisations also provided institutions for care, such as Dr Barnardo's children's homes and the Salvation Army hostels for the homeless and vagrants.

By the 1930s, the welfare services were gradually being taken over by the state or by local authorities. However, from the 1940s onwards there has still been a need for voluntary organisations to provide services not statutorily available in order to meet the particular needs of individuals such as spastics or sufferers from multiple sclerosis. Family service units have also been voluntarily established to support families who for one reason or another do not—or will not—use the statutory services.

Voluntary societies recently have tended to concentrate on giving specialist services, which the government cannot afford to provide to minority groups, for example to those individuals deformed by thalidomide. Attempts are also being made to provide a central organisation so that activity can be channelled to areas of greatest need, and about 170 Councils of Social Service have been established in an attempt to coordinate the work of voluntary and statutory social services. There has also been a recent growth in international voluntary organisations such as Oxfam.

Voluntary organisations, however, have both advantages and disadvantages. Their main advantage is that they tap a good deal of manpower and other resources (particularly money) that probably would not otherwise be made available for the health and social services. They also encourage participation, interest and involvement in the services. Voluntary organisations can also pursue controversial goals which, at that time, may not be appropriate for the central or local authorities such as family planning services (which only became statutory services in 1974, presumably because public opinion was then ripe for that change). Voluntary organisations can also act quicker than statutory authorities in times of crises. For example, the Women's Royal Voluntary Service (WRVS) can speedily organise relief and provision of clothes in cases of fire or flooding and the British Red Cross Society (BRCS) can speedily organise relief for an overseas country stricken by civil war or famine.

The main disadvantage is that the voluntary organisation cannot be as impartial in the way its funds are dispensed as statutory authorities can. If a voluntary society has been founded for the deaf—then only the deaf must receive its benefits. Furthermore, services are not given as a right but because someone else (perhaps a committee member) perceives the need. Therefore the resources may not necessarily be directed to the people with greatest need. In Finland, for example, there are three societies for poliomyelitis victims; yet there are hardly any Finns who have suffered severe effects from the disease. The Scunthorpe Spastics Society some years ago built one of the most modern training centres, but only one spastic adult needed this facility.

Sometimes voluntary organisations develop a 'holier-than-thou' attitude and become unduly subjective about their own aims because they do not have the overview of health and social care needs which statutory authorities have to have. It is not unknown for voluntary organisations to plead their particular causes by storming into local District Council meetings or by other kinds of demonstrations.

Standards are difficult to maintain and enforce in voluntary organisations, particularly when a good deal of voluntary labour is used. It is difficult to dismiss an inefficient or senile voluntary worker. There is also a fair amount of wastage of administrative skill and a great deal of overlap of functions. There are, for example, about 200 voluntary organisations to serve the deaf. Voluntary organisations also tend to have a particularly acute shortage of salaried trained staff, which may well become worse as the salaries of officers employed by statutory authorities continue to improve dramatically.

GAPS IN THE WELFARE STATE

Audrey Harvey (1960), a social worker in the East End of London, indicates that in a period of five years she and two colleagues dealt with 20 000 personal enquiries, 'nearly all of which have involved welfare state rights and obligations'. A high proportion of the enquiries were 'working class': the men being mainly dockers, seamen, lorry drivers and factory workers and their wives—if working—were employed as office cleaners, factory hands or canteen workers. Although the community depends on these kinds of workers, Harvey believes that there is a tendency on the part of the more comfortable and privileged people to regard them as 'second class citizens' in every respect. 'This is reflected not only in the quality of the services provided for their welfare, but also in the attitude of many who administer those services.' In a study examining the use of volunteers in the NHS, Skeet (1978) argued that volunteers, if trained and used properly, could make a valuable contribution to health care by fulfilling unmet needs in the community at home or in hospital.

Roughly half the working population in the country, Harvey argues, share a similar plight to the workers she met in London's East End. They are 'still poor in education, living space, opportunity and status . . . very far indeed from being insured against poverty . . . they are largely unprotected by private occupational insurance and welfare schemes'.

Their dilemma is made worse by the fact that, unlike others in society, they have no knowledgeable friends who can be consulted on the telephone. Often, they are unware of their rights and obligations under the Welfare State. Even if printed information exists, it is not always available when needed. In any case, they may often be unable to understand it; some in fact may be unable even to *read* it. No official provision is made, Harvey argues, for these citizens. 'The individual, in the eys of the state, has a bright, trained mind. He also has great stamina and considerable leisure. For he needs both if he is to get this information direct from the fountain-head.'

Improved standards of living, which can be demonstrated in British society, are due to full employment, Harvey argues, and she adds that we have been deluded into thinking that the British Welfare State is second to none. 'The Scandinavian countries are ahead of us in providing better old peoples homes and up-to-date hospitals, New Zealand enables young families to buy their own houses by advancing family allowances . . . Germany gives better insurance coverage in illness . . . On housing we spend a lower proportion of our income than all but three out of fifteen other European countries.'

The problems persist

The problems persist even a decade later.

'One of the myths of our age', Anne Allen (1968) argues, 'is that there are thousands of able-bodied men sitting about keeping their families on supplementary benefits, and somehow managing to buy cars and take foreign holidays on what the kindly (lunatic) state gives them unquestioningly.' The tendency among the poor, she points out with regret, is that they are loath to bother to seek out their rights as they often tend to believe that there must 'be people worse off than I am'.

This contention is given support in *Health and Hardship*, an article published in the same journal in which Allen's paper appears, which argues that about five times 'and possibly higher' the number of prescription charges should be reclaimed because 'it appears that most of those eligible do not claim refunds'.

Inequities still persist in the 1970s and a watchful eye is kept on these by a number of voluntary organisations, not least among them the Child Poverty Action Group (CPAG) which in spring 1974 pointed out the failings in the Welfare State with regard to one-parent families, those caring for elderly or infirm relatives, common-law marriages, and old age pensioners.

Although children of one-parent families account for only ten per cent of the child population, about one third of children in the care of local authorities come from one-parent families. Social policy obviously fails to support these families adequately even though a family 'is still the cheapest way of bringing up children'.

According to the *Journal of Community Nursing* (1979), approximately 1.5 million children in the UK are living in one-parent families and 120 000 children are in care. Of those in care in England and Wales, 40 per cent are in residential care.

In 1977, 3840 abortions were performed on girls under 16 years of age. In 1976, 5097 youngsters under the age of 18 were convicted for drunkenness, and one in three of those children who became regular smokers had started smoking before the age of 9.

There is obviously a need for a concerted effort to prevent illness and promote health education (Smith, 1979).

The CPAG also finds that the lot of looking after an elderly or infirm relative usually falls on single daughters. The fact that most of them are over forty which coupled with the fact that the caring period may last up to 20 years, affects their work prospects. Finding future employment is therefore more difficult and certainly earnings will be less than if careers had been uninterrupted. Weekly insurance contributions cease which also affects her sickness and unemployment benefits after she restarts work.

'A right of occupation for life should be given to the child who has stayed at home, other interests being postponed', the CPAG holds.

In November 1972 over 10 000 single women were receiving supplementary benefit because they were at home caring for elderly or sick relatives.

The CPAG also provides evidence to support the view that men and women living together as 'common-law' husband and wife lose benefits which they would receive were they legally married. In 1971, 4712 claimants for social security benefits had their benefits reduced or withdrawn under 'cohabitation' tules. £887 000 was recovered at a cost of £400 000. A point which the CPAG emphasises is that 'common-law marriages are usually recognised by the couples involved and stable unions are far more numerous than the number of DHSS withdrawals of benefit'.

The losses in benefits therefore last for many years and in purely financial terms the losses of the common-law couple 'far exceed any gain by those alleged to be dodging'.

Reviewing the survey of old age pensioners to find out how they spent the 1973 'Christmas bonus' of £10 it is concluded that 'it was clear that in the majority of cases old people needed the bonus for subsistence, not superfluity'. Many of the pensioners who were already receiving a supplementary pension had to spend part of the bonus on food or clothing which 'suggests that the system of discretionary grants and additions is not working. Pensioners either don't know of them, don't apply or don't succeed in their application'.

In 1978, Oswin claimed that of the one million handicapped people living in England and Wales many did not know or make use of the services available to them as a right.

Furthermore, although about 40 of the 1600 diseases known to be genetically determined can be detected prenatally from samples of amniotic fluid, there are very few facilities for genetic counselling in the UK. On 31st March, 1977, 70 015 children under the age of 16 were registered as physically handicapped in England. During 1977, some 11 380 congenitally deformed live babies were born in England and Wales (Smith, 1979). By 1981, there were about five million people in the UK suffering from some form of handicap, physical, sensory or mental. There are more than 450 million throughout the world.

MALDISTRIBUTED EDUCATIONAL RESOURCES FOR SLOW LEARNERS

A study of *Slow Learners in Secondary Schools* (1971) documents the outcome of a survey conducted in secondary modern and comprehensive schools in 20 local education authorities in England during 1967 and 1968.

The percentages of 'slow learners' needing some measure of specialised help range from 7 to 60 per cent of the schools' rolls. More than one in seven schools estimated that over twenty per cent of their pupils need special education. 'The proportion of these pupils, expressed as a percentage of the total school population of the schools visited was 14.'

But even if the right kind of education were to be available for the slow learners, the report of the survey finds that essential background education, medical and social information about the children is totally inadequate and indeed almost non-existent. 'The prevailing impression gained from this survey is that the information is fragmented, incomplete and often unconstructive.'

The report further finds that the schools tend to have a narrow conception of the educational requirements of these pupils. 'Remedial' was emphasised often at the expense of giving specialised help in acquiring levels of literacy and numeracy. The schools fail to arouse and sustain these pupils' interests for long. As a result indifference develops, manifesting itself in declining school attendance in third and fourth year classes. Achievements of the pupils are limited and teaching methods 'unrefined'.

Only 32 per cent of the schools have a special department to cater for these pupils' needs. The remaining 68 per cent have no special department, but some had 'special classes'. But, considering the proportion of pupils with special needs, the report comments that 'it is hard to resist the conclusion that providing for them receives low priority in many schools'.

Lonely citizens

The household composition tables of the 1971 census (ten per cent sample) indicates that two thirds of people living alone in England and Wales are pensioners.

London and the South East have many more people living alone than any other part of the country. In London, 23.3 per cent of households consist of single persons and in the South East generally, the figure is 19.2 per cent. Humberside, the North West and South West follow closely in the league tables.

From 1961 to 1971, the numbers of people living alone in England and Wales increased from 1 768 000 to 3 008 000.

According to Massam (1975), Dr J. C. Gunn of the Institute of Psychiatry at the Maudsley Hospital, London, has 'warned of the serïous medical consequences of loneliness'. The almost total lack of community psychiatric care facilities will inevitably create even greater numbers of casualties in the Welfare State in future years if the situation is not rectified.

Gaps in health services

Inequalities in the health service still persist, as Peter Townsend (1974) indicates, even though he concedes that inequalities in health care have complex aetiologies.

Britain, he argues, devotes a smaller proportion of her resources to health services than several other advanced countries 'and this proportion is growing less swiftly'. The United Kingdom also has substantially fewer doctors per 100 000 population than many other countries. Medical manpower is also maldistributed, he points out. The South East has substantial advantages over the North East or the Midlands and Scotland has substantial advantages over England and Wales 'in man-power and money'.

Utilisation of health services, according to the latest evidence he can cite, indicates that there is relatively low utilisation under the age of five for social classes IV and V, relatively high utilisation in late middle-age and just under average utilisation over the age of 65. 'But most important of all is the fact that utilisation is not standardised by need . . . at least as expressed by those [measures] of mortality, sickness absence and limiting long-standing illness.'

Townsend, however, recognises that there has been an increase in the number of health centres, home nurses and home helps, that the number of mental hospitals has been reduced and that community services such as sheltered housing and workshops, and day centres for the mentally ill, the mentally handicapped, the elderly and the disabled are gradually being developed and extended. And he gives due credit for these developments.

But, he concludes: 'The right of the sick to free access to health care, irrespective of class or income, remains to be firmly established. The treatment in particular of many of the aged, chronic sick and disabled, mentally ill and mentally handicapped, remains scandalously poor and can in the long run be dramatically

Table 10.1 Persons reporting chronic health problems by sex and socioeconomic group: UK 1977.

	Percentage	
	Males	Females
Professional	49	61
Employers and managers	53	68
Intermediate and junior non-manual	54	67
Skilled manual and own account non-professional	58	71
Semi-skilled manual and personal service	60	75
Unskilled manual	65	79
Total	56	70

Source: Office of Population Censuses and Surveys, The General Household Survey, 1977.

improved only by a redefinition of health and health needs . . . and the establishment of social equality.'

These findings have some support in the conclusions of Buxton and Klein (1975) who examine the distribution of hospital resources in terms of current revenue and hospital beds in different specialities in 49 area health authorities. They find that the differences even in acute specialties are so large between different areas that it is doubtful whether some area health authorities can be offering a comprehensive health service at all.

Perhaps too much attention is focused on the acute services at a time when it is becoming obvious that the needs of the chronically sick are steadily increasing in Western Society. Table 10.1 shows that chronic health problems are also directly related to class.

Health trends

'By 1973 the movement from hospital to community health can be plainly seen' (Harry Orris, 1975).

Occupied hospital beds fell from 403 000 in 1962 to 362 000 in 1972, which represent a drop from 8.88 to 7.38 per 1000 population. Average length of stay in hospital dropped from 33.5 to 23.9 days. Outpatient attendances during the same period rose from 29 939 000 to 34 943 000.

In the same decade, numbers of general practitioners rose by 1300 giving an average of 2174 patients per GP. 'Too many', Orris holds, 'if doctors are to give more time to needy patients, and concealing wide variations in register lists between doctors in the socially attractive and unattractive areas, and between urban and rural areas.'

The number of general dental practitioners increased during the period by 210 only and that of ophthalmic practitioners actually declined by 1000. Hospital doctors increased in number from 20 000 to 26 900 and hospital nurses from 213 000 to 304 800 which represented increases per thousand population from 0.42 to 0.55 for doctors and 4.57 to 6.22 for nurses. Midwifery staff increased from 13 000 to 17 500, an increase per thousand population from 0.27 to 0.36. Professional and technical staff increased from 24 000 to 38 000 in the period 1962 to 1972, representing an increase from 0.52 to 0.79 per 1000 population.

The staffing trends, coupled with the opening of a number of purpose-built hospitals, and extensions and improvements to old hospitals suggest that 'clearly the standards of hospital care must have risen markedly during the ten-year period' of 1962 to 1972.

However, after reviewing the statistical data on sickness Orris is forced to conclude that:

'The overall picture is one of increasing sickness, especially in some categories, of the movement from hospital to community care and of much better staffed hospitals and community services. There is evidence too of increasing society permissiveness as well as greater community concern and care for the individual who is sick, disabled or otherwise in trouble.'

Table 10.2 illustrates regional variations in NHS expenditure in

Table 10.2 Distribution of health expenditure: UK 1976/1977

			£ per capita
	Hospital services expenditure	Community health and family practitioner services expenditure	Total expenditure
ENGLAND	61.76	28.31	104.88
Northern	56.19	28.42	100.13
Yorkshire	56.86	27.42	97.44
Trent	50.49	26.67	93.80
East Anglia	53.83	26.94	95.22
NW Thames	74.91	33.21	122.38
NE Thames	76.35	25.95	117.00
SE Thames	73.61	29.28	118.17
SW Thames	67.00	28.67	112.73
Wessex	52.44	28.15	94.00
Oxford	53.18	28.23	96.09
South Western	57.87	30.50	103.33
West Midlands	52.65	26.96	91.52
Mersey	62.16	27.92	107.16
North Western	57.63	28.88	100.46
WALES	61.50	31.21	107.39
SCOTLAND	78.10	30.00	127.10
N IRELAND	83.07	33.67	138.67
UNITED KINGDOM	63.84	28.76	107.98

Source: Report of the Royal Commission on the NHS.

the UK. The Report of the Royal Commission on the NHS in 1979 documented the strengths, weaknesses and persistent gaps in British health care.

THE FUTURE

There will be changes in the management arrangements of the health services. Ideas were being aired in some circles in 1975 that the regional health authorities should be disbanded and their officers absorbed into the civil service staff of the Department of Health and Social Security. That two-district areas should become one-district areas and that line management relationships should be established between officers at health district level and area health authority level. Indeed the Secretary of State for Social Services, Mrs Barbara Castle, in a speech made at the inaugural meeting of the National Association of Health Authorities in England on 11th July 1975, said that although reduction in health care expenditure would probably be necessary 'we cannot start our cost-cutting exercises with services for patients'.

She further added that: 'I shall be inviting authorities to seek ways of reducing their administrative costs . . . and I shall be seeking their help in identifying and redressing any wasteful duplication of functions between areas and regions, and between areas, regions and my Department.' Views which have been reiterated by her successor! It is worthy of note, however, that the United Kingdom is not the biggest spender in the world on health care (see Table 10.3).

Another much more fundamental and important change from the patient's/client's point of view is the possible amalgamation of health and social services on the pattern of the Northern Ireland administration. Even though desirable this may be delayed because

Table 10.3 International comparison of Health Service resources

	Total *per capita* expenditure on health (US $)
Australia	308
Canada	408
Finland	265
France	352
Italy	191
Japan	166
Netherlands	312
Norway	270
Sweden	416
USA	491
W Germany	336
United Kingdom	212

Source: Report of the Royal Commission on the NHS.

of social workers' recently found professional autonomy following the implementation of the Seebohm Report's recommendations which they, not unnaturally, guard jealously. However, a very experienced director of social services assured me in 1975 that the social workers would probably be ready to accept such an administrative change 'in five years time'. But the *Report of the Royal Commission on the National Health Service* (1979) gave no immediate endorsement to that view. It did, however, suggest a review and change of the NHS organisation, not least to drop one tier of the organisation so as to create the equivalent of single-district areas everywhere in the United Kingdom. Changes were also recommended for FPC organisation. In 1980, the government accepted the proposal to drop the 'area' tier by 1982.

A reform of social policy urged on the government was by its own 'think tank' (Central Policy Review Staff 1975) which called for a more coherent approach to the making and execution of social policy and by implication criticises poor coordination and poor planning of social policy as well as poor information as the basis of forming social policies. The report called for studies on the relationship between housing policy and other social policies, financial aspects of social policy, further development of current work on the disabled and a study of the long-term implications for social policies of population changes. Action is however still awaited.

A slight modification of the membership structure of regional and area health authorities was decided upon by the Secretary of State for Health and Social Security in September 1975. Local authorities were given greater representation on area health authorities. Normally their representatives will be elected members of local authority councils, but not always. In addition to the two doctor members and one nurse member who serve on regional and area health authorities, provision has been made for the other health service workers to be represented by two members on each authority. Community Health Councils will also be represented by a member at area health authority meetings. These changes, it was hoped, would enhance the spirit of democracy in the National Health Service.

Whatever the future holds for the administration of the health and social services, if the concept of a welfare state is to have any meaning at all then its administrative framework must always be a means towards meeting social and individual needs and should not become an end in itself.

REFERENCES AND SELECTED BIBLIOGRAPHY

Allen, A. (1968) The feel of poverty. In *Poverty* No. 6 Spring. Child Poverty Action Group.
Arle, T. (1975) Community medicine. *New Society,* 5 June.
Ashton, T.S. (1948) *The Industrial Revolution 1769—1830*. Oxford University Press.
Baly, M. (1973) *Nursing and Social Change*. London: Heinemann.
Benn, S.I. & Peters, R.S. (1959) *Social Principles and the Democratic State*. London: Allen & Unwin.
Bowman, G. (1967) *The Lamp and the Book*. London: Queen Anne Press.
Bruce, M. (1968) *The Coming of the Welfare State*. London: Batsford.
Buxton, M.J. & Klein, R.E. (1975) Distribution of hospital provision: policy themes and resource variations. *British Medical Journal,* supplement 8 February.
Castle, B. (1975) *Speech to National Association of Health Authorities in England and Wales on 11 July*. DHSS.
Central Policy Review Staff (1975) *A Joint Framework for Social Policies*. London: HMSO.
Child Poverty Action Group (1974) *Poverty*, No. 28 Spring, CPAG.
Crosland, C.A.R. (1964) *The Future of Socialism*. London: Cape.
Department of Education and Science (1971) Slow learners in secondary schools. *Education Survey,* 15. London: HMSO.
Family Welfare Association *Guide to the Social Services*. (FWA, revised annually).
Gilmore, M., Bruce, N. & Hunt, M. (1974) *The Work of the Nursing Team in General Practice*. Council for the Education and Training of Health Visitors.
Harvey, A. (1960) *Casualties of the Welfare State*. London: Fabian Society.
Hawthorn, P.J. (1971) *The Nurse Working with the General Practitioner—An Evaluation of Research and a Review of the Literature*. DHSS.
Jones, K. (1960) *Mental Health and Social Policy 1845–1959*. London: Routledge & Kegan Paul.
Journal of Community Nursing (1979) *Children: the Facts,* **2** (8), 30.
Lees, D.S. (1965) *Health Through Choice (Freedom or Free-for-all)*. London: Institute of Economic Affairs.
Lewis, R.A. (1952) *Edwin Chadwick and the Public Health Movement 1832–54*. London: Longman.
London Council of Social Service (1975) *Family groups*. LCSS.
Low Pay Unit (1975) *Counting Out the Disabled*. London: Child Poverty Action Group.
Markham, J. & Smith, J.P. (1975) *Community Care*. London: Heinemann.
Massam, A. (1975) London is topping the league of loneliness. *Evening Standard,* 21 August.
Maxwell, R. (1974) *Health Care: the growing dilemma*. McKinsey.
Mayhew, H. *Mayhew's Characters*. Ed. by Quennell, P. London: Hamlyn.
National Council of Social Service *Voluntary social services handbook and directory of organisations*. (NCSS, revised regularly).
Office of Health Economics (1970) *Building for Health*. London: OHE.
Office of Health Economics (1974) *The NHS Reorganisation*. London: OHE.
Orris, H. (1975) Statistical health picture. *Health and Social Service Journal,* 9 August.
Oswin, M. (1978) *Holes in the Welfare Net*. Plymouth: Macdonald & Evans.
Parnell, J.W. (1974) *Home for the Weekend—Back on Monday*. Queen's Nursing Institute.
Peacey, B. (1969) *The Red Cross*. London: Muller.
Political Quarterly (1969) Special issue on the future of the social services vol 40, No. 1. Oxford University Press.

Regional Office for Europe (WHO) (1973) *Trends in the Development of Primary Care*. WHO, Copenhagen.
Rodgers, W. *et al.* (1967) *Socialism and Affluence*. London: Fabian Society.
Sampson, A. (1965) *Anatomy of Britain Today*. London: Hodder & Stoughton.
Simpson, J. *et al.* (1968) *Custom and Practice in Medical Care*. Oxford University Press.
Skeet, M. (1974) *Home from Hospital*. London: Macmillan Journals Ltd.
Skeet. M. (1977) *Health Needs Help*. Oxford: Blackwell.
Slack, K.M. (1966) *Social Administration and the Citizen*. London: Michael Joseph.
Smith, B. Abel (1960) *A History of the Nursing Profession*. London: Heinemann.
Smith, B. Abel (1964) *The Hospitals 1800–1948*. London: Heinemann.
Smith J.P. (1979) The challenge of health education for nurses in the 1980s. *Journal of Advanced Nursing,* **4,** 531–543.
Stern, W.M. (1962) *Britain Yesterday and Today*. London: Longmans.
Tawney, R.H. (1964) *Equality*. London: Unwin.
Titmuss, R.M. (1963) *Essays on 'the Welfare State'*. London: Allen & Unwin.
Titmuss, R.M. (1968) *Commitment to Welfare*. London: Allen & Unwin.
Titmuss, R. M. (1970) *The Gift Relationship—From Human Blood to Social Policy*. London: Allen & Unwin.
Townsend, P. (1974) Inequality and the health service. *The Lancet,* 15 June.
Willcocks, J. (1967) *The Creation of the National Health Service*. Library of Social Policy and Administration.
Willmott, P. (1967) *Consumers' Guide to the British Social Services*. Harmondsworth: Penguin.
Wilson, J. Douglas and McLachlan, G. (eds) (1975) *Health Service Prospects—an International Survey*. The Lancet and Nuffield Provincial Hospitals Trust.
Wolfenden, J. (1973) *Lasting Ideals in New Settings*. British Red Cross Society.
Woodward, J. (1974) *To Do the Sick No Harm: a Study of the British Voluntary Hospital System to 1875*. London: Routledge & Kegan Paul.
Woodward, L. (1964) *The Age of Reform 1815–1870*. Oxford University Press.
Report of the Committee on Local Authority and Allied Personal Social Services (1968). London: HMSO.
The Administrative Structure of the Medical and Related Services (1968). Green paper. London: HMSO.
Report of the Royal Commission on Local Government in England (1969). London: HMSO.
The Future Structure of the National Health Service (1970). Green paper. London: HMSO.
National Health Service Reorganisation: England (1972). White paper. London: HMSO.
Management Arrangements for the Re-organised National Health Service (1973). London: HMSO.
Draft Guide to Planning in the National Health Service (1975). March.
Mental Handicap Services (1975). DS 76/75, March.
Management Education and Training in the NHS: Review of Guidelines (1975). HSC (IS) 189, DHSS, September.
Democracy in the National Health Service (1975), HSC (IS) 1942, DHSS, September.
Census 1971 England and Wales: Household (1975) Composition Tables (10 per cent sample). London: HMSO.
Health Trends (quarterly review published by the DHSS).
Report of the Royal Commission on the National Health Service (1979). London: HMSO.

Index

> Turkish-American friendship and cooperation during the last two months have been tested anew, and have gone through this test with remarkable success. I am, of course, referring to recent events in the Middle East and to new development of the Turkish-American cooperation in [the] economic field … [which] have shown to us once again how closely our two countries are tied together.[154]

British officials (not invited to this event) were more cynical than their US peers. One foreign office official complained that "the United States Government, by seeking to achieve a settlement at the end of last month, have raised the Turkish approach to OEEC from the economic to the political plane … the situation subsequently arising in the Middle East has incontestably played into the Turks' hands."[155]

The observation was true insofar as circumstances beyond Turkey's control had ultimately served to expedite a bailout process that would have otherwise taken longer to finalize. Time had not been on the side of the DP government; an extended period of negotiation would have weakened its position and advantaged Turkey's creditors. The possibility of a military coup, however, had been clarifying for Americans and Western Europeans: in the event of a revolution, the repayment on arrears could easily be zero.

The negotiations in 1958 bring the risks and rewards of DP-era diplomacy into stark relief. By 1958, successive DP-led governments had integrated Turkey into the institutions of the US-led Cold War order. In previous chapters, we have seen the benefits that this integration brought. It created conditions in which the DP could win power; it gave leaders access to financial and military resources that supported their economic goals and security needs; and it drew them into mutually dependent relationships with leaders in other countries such that they could exact political favors. In this chapter, we have seen additional examples of these benefits, including the support of US officials like Clarence Randall and the money allocated by the Eisenhower Doctrine. At the same time, we also saw DP leaders run up against the limits of the system. By the summer of 1958, the Americans, West Germans, and other creditor–allies were fed up with Turkey's leaders. And yet, even at this moment, these creditor–allies realized they were too interdependent with their Turkish peers to simply let one another completely lose a negotiation.

Just when tried-and-true strategies seemed to be failing, the Iraqi Revolution gave DP leaders a moment to catch their breath. Going

[154] Warren to State, August 26, 1958, RG 84, Box 74.
[155] Colin Brant, "Minutes," August 8, 1958, FO 371/136475.

forward, they would need to adjust their methods. In the following chapter, we will consider how, in the aftermath of the 1958 coup in Iraq, DP leaders became even less tolerant of opposition. Through new laws, mass public mobilization efforts, and divisive rhetoric, DP leaders pursued an increasingly polarizing political strategy, setting the stage for Turkey's own military coup in 1960.

6 A Front to Democracy: The Democrat Party and the Return to Authoritarian Rule, 1958–1960

The 1958 Iraqi coup came as a shock to Turkey's political elite.[1] *Zafer* columnist Nimet Arzık, whose husband was head of the government-run Anatolian News Agency, recalls the disbelief when the news broke. At the time, she was in the Istanbul suburb of Florya, relaxing at the Municipal Apartments, a summer retreat for ministers' families, mistresses, and hangers-on.[2] Many there had met the assassinated young king of Iraq and his influential minister, Nuri al-Said. Nuri was a frequent visitor to Istanbul and, as a man born and educated in the Ottoman Empire, was conversant in Turkish. His execution by a group of young military officers, unfamiliar to Turkey's elite, presaged a real change in the relationships undergirding regional diplomacy. It raised the question of whether the future belonged to the men in uniform.[3]

Though the initial panic caused by the coup reminded US leaders of Turkey's importance and helped the DP government secure financial aid from the OEEC, the instability that followed added to the government's concerns. The revolution in Iraq upended the post-Ottoman regional order. Iraq had been ruled since the 1920s by the Hashemite family, which depended on traditional sources of authority like merchants, landlords, and religious leaders (as well as an alliance with the UK). A similar

[1] The Iraqi leadership was executed as they prepared to embark on a trip to Istanbul for a Baghdad Pact meeting. Turkish leaders learned of the coup as they waited on the tarmac to receive the king and his entourage. There was immediate discussion of a joint military effort to reinstall the regime. According to Metin Toker, Foreign Minister Zorlu raised the idea of invading Iraq, but the move was opposed by Iran and Pakistan. The United States also gave the suggestion a "red light" (Telegram to State Department, July 15, 1958, RG 84, Box 73; Toker, *Demokrasiden Darbeye*, 125). For an account of the coup, see Marion Farouk-Sluglett and Peter Sluglett, *Iraq since 1958: From Revolution to Dictatorship*, 3rd ed. (London: I. B. Taurus, 2001), 48–50.

[2] Arzık, *Menderes'i İpe Götürenler*, 45–46.

[3] Turkey's political elite was not alone in wondering about the possibility of a coup in Turkey. The US State Department requested reports from the embassy. An August 5, 1958 report concluded the likelihood was "remote and will, we estimate, continue to be so, provided conditions of relative political freedom exist" (John Goodyear, "The Iraqi Coup – Can It Happen in Turkey?" August 5, 1958, RG 84, Box 77).

dynamic was evident in other "conservative" regimes in Lebanon, Jordan, and Saudi Arabia. Even in the Republic of Turkey, Mustafa Kemal's regime had made accommodations with traditional power brokers. In Egypt and Syria, by contrast, young military officers now dominated politics and sought to radically remake the social order.[4] By moving Iraq into this more radical camp, the coup emboldened communists and other groups that had been suppressed by the monarchy. Fighting between Kurdish, Turkish, and Arabic-speaking Iraqi citizens in cities like Kirkuk had the potential to create a refugee crisis on Turkey's southern border.

Amid this uncertainty, ensuring Turkey's stability was a priority for the United States and its allies. Yet it would take nine months for the precise terms of the August 1958 financial stabilization program to be worked out. In the meantime, DP leaders were faced with the challenge of both pursuing the developmental policies that enabled their electoral success and implementing strict economic controls to reassure their US and Western European peers. These measures included a cap on credit and a currency devaluation. In the short term, these policies benefited businessmen and merchants who had the necessary connections to secure credit. Government officials and workers on fixed incomes bore the brunt. Without enough money to appease all sectors, the DP became enmeshed in a new round of inter- and intraparty disputes that threatened to undermine the party's hold on power. In response to these challenges, DP leaders reasserted the authority of the state and the party. They pressured citizens to join the DP, using all the tools of the state at their disposal; they limited the ability of the opposition to meet with citizens; and they restricted the freedom of the press and academia to criticize government policies. In justifying these measures, DP leaders presented the public with sharp binaries in which they embodied the "national will" and their opponents its subversion.

As we have seen, DP politicians and partisans were already portraying the opposition in unfavorable terms well before 1958. Yet the rhetoric and repression increased thereafter, encouraged in part by a larger shift among members of the US-led Cold War order toward restricted democracy. Whereas many accounts of the DP explain the party's increasing authoritarianism in terms of Prime Minister Menderes's inability to bear criticism, this chapter emphasizes the late 1950s Cold War context, in

[4] Following Syria's merger with Egypt in early 1958, Nasser and his allies initiated a policy of land redistribution that, according to *İstanbul Ekspres*, targeted Turkish-speaking landlords in Syria ("Nasır ...," *İstanbul Ekspres*, November 17, 1958, 1).

which such illiberal, authoritarian measures were tolerated.[5] DP elites witnessed and discussed the restriction (or outright elimination) of democratic politics in allied countries like France and Pakistan. DP leaders not only saw their peers in the US-led Cold War coalition employing illiberal methods of rule, they were also convinced that they faced equivalent domestic challenges. To defend against these threats to the nation and maintain their own grip on power, DP leaders altered the rules of political contestation to assure their dominance.

Rather than explaining the origins or causes of the May 1960 coup, this chapter reveals how hollowed out the democratic political order had become by the time military officers finally launched their operation. Many institutions that sustained democracy had already been weakened. Moreover, the rhetoric of freedom and democracy that Democrats once voiced had been replaced by calls for "stability" and praise for the "national will." Such words would be easily repurposed by the coup leaders, idealistic young officers eager to make their move. As mentioned in Chapter 3, grumblings had started as early as 1950. Active plotting had begun by 1954.[6] If the relatively calm conditions of the early decade offered them grounds for launching a coup, then the contentious, increasingly violent conditions of 1960 suggested that action was long overdue.

Weak Economies, Strong Men: The Temptations of Populism

Military coups were common during 1958, but the DP elite's reactions toward them varied greatly. Pro-DP media presented the events in Iraq as a cautionary tale. Whereas coverage of Egypt's 1952 coup had been cautiously optimistic in its early years, coverage of the Iraqi coup was panicked and hostile from the outset. *İstanbul Ekspres* ran an extended series of articles recalling the life and works of Iraq's leading – and now deceased – politician, Nuri al-Said. *Havadis* criticized opposition

[5] Geoffrey Lewis explains that after the 1954 election, "Puffed up by the adulation, Menderes became quite unable to endure the sight of any support given to the opposition." Erik Zürcher, though more attentive to material conditions, agrees that "[Menderes, who] had always found it very hard to accept criticism … now … became positively allergic to it" (Lewis, *Modern Turkey* [New York: Praeger Publishers, 1974], 152; Zürcher, *Turkey: A Modern History*, 3rd ed. [London: I. B. Tauris, 2004], 230).

[6] Dündar Seyhan, *Gölgedeki Adam* (Istanbul: Nurettin Uycan Matbaası, 1966), 42–43. Celal Bayar himself would point to Dündar Seyhan's memoirs as evidence that the events of 1960 were an ex-post facto justification for plotting that was underway regardless (İsmet Bozdağ, *Bir Darbenin Anatomisi: Celal Bayar Anlatıyor*, 3rd ed. [Istanbul: Emre Yayınları, 2006 (1991)], 17).

journalists for reminding readers that Nuri and Iraq's Hashemite monarchs had founded their state by rebelling against the Ottoman Empire. The past was past. What mattered now was the support they had provided to the "community of free nations and ideal of peace" through participation in the Baghdad Pact alongside Iran, Pakistan, the UK, and Turkey.[7] That Iraq might now leave the pact was one concern; the safety of Turkish-speaking minorities was another. *İstanbul Ekspres* emphasized the dangers posed to Turkey's "racial brothers" (*ırkdaş*).[8] The presence in Iraq of a large population of people who spoke Turkish and were Muslim was presented as an "ethnic" and "national" issue that necessitated Turkey's involvement. As in Cyprus, where Turkish and Greek populations jostled for power in advance of British departure, Iraq's Turkish population lived alongside non-Turkish speakers – in this case Kurdish speakers – who might take advantage of the changing balance of power in the region.

Newspapers pointed to Arab nationalists under the sway of Egyptian leader Gamal Abdel Nasser and communists directed by the USSR as the masterminds of the Iraqi coup.[9] *Demokrat Malatya* attributed the coup to "Nasser's marauders" (*çapulcular*), and the official DP paper, *Zafer*, cautioned the coup leaders against following the example of Syrian leaders, who had recently merged their country with Egypt and subsequently lost influence over national affairs.[10] But any advantage Nasser gained from the coup was limited. The United States dispatched marines to Lebanon, and the UK dropped paratroopers into Jordan. Meanwhile, many of the young officers who had toppled the Iraqi monarchy were not eager to turn over power to the Egyptian leader. Perhaps sensing these potential divisions, Turkey, Iran, and Pakistan recognized the new Iraqi government on July 31, just two weeks after the coup. Britain and the United States followed suit over the next two days. The tone of pro-DP papers like *Havadis* softened, now emphasizing that the new Iraqi regime's domestic nationalist roots dated back to the 1940s rather than to links with Nasser.[11]

In Turkey, opposition politicians and their papers sought to link the DP leadership with the deposed Hashemite regime in Iraq. Prime

[7] "Milliyetçilik …," *Havadis*, July 22, 1958, 1, 5. *İstanbul Ekspres*'s multi-part series started on July 18, 1958, with Leyla Yazıcıoğlu's "Nuri Said Pasha, Who Broke the Record for Premierships" ("*Başvekillik Rekorunu Kıran Nuri Sait Paşa*").

[8] "Irak'ta …," *İstanbul Ekspres*, July 18, 1958, 1.

[9] *Havadis* linked Nasser with communism by pointing to his recent meetings with the leaders of Yugoslavia and the USSR ("Nasır'ın …," *Havadis*, July 22, 1958, 1, 5).

[10] Faruk Taşkıran, "Irak …," *Demokrat Malatya*, July 22, 1958, 1–2; Hulki Keymen, "Irak …," *Zafer*, July 30, 1958, 2.

[11] "Irak …," *Havadis*, August 3, 1958, 3.

Minister Menderes was particularly offended when the pro-CHP paper *Ulus* printed graphic photos of the murdered Iraqi leadership.[12] *Zafer* condemned a speech given in Istanbul by CHP General Secretary Kasım Gülek in which he said, "Those who died in Iraq in the recent events were the mentors of our [governing party]. They recommended that our [governing party] do what they were doing in Iraq: you have a problem with a party? Close it. You have an issue with the press? Silence the journalists." According to *Zafer*, these inflammatory comparisons were evidence of the CHP's "craving" for power.[13]

In addition to castigating opposition leaders, *Zafer* also published a column by a former general who had served in parliament as a DP representative since 1957. He emphasized that the military must not become involved in politics, as this was the mark of "backward nations." The military existed to defend the country, provide aid during disasters, assist in foreign missions, and provide security. (He added that thwarting strikes might be acceptable as well under some circumstances.)[14] Such injunctions from a powerful military figure might serve to dissuade other officers from taking inspiration from events in Iraq.

The coup in Iraq was neither the first nor the last of the year, merely the most radical. Military takeovers of civilian governments in France and Pakistan, by contrast, did not threaten the existing Cold War order and were treated differently in the pro-DP press.[15] In France, these papers had already been criticizing the weaknesses of democracy. The inability of politicians to form stable governments was attributed to a

12 Albayrak, *Türk Siyasi Tarihinde*, 519.

13 "İhtiras ...," *Zafer*, August 5, 1958, 1. Also see Onur Çelebi, "14 Temmuz 1958 Irak Darbesinin Türk İç Politikasına Yansımaları," *Electronic Turkish Studies* 12, no. 31 (2017): 48–49.

14 Nurettin Aknoz, "Irak'taki ...," *Zafer*, July 19, 1958, 2. Before entering civilian life, General Aknoz had overseen the martial law regime imposed on Istanbul after the 1955 anti-Greek pogroms. Altan Öymen alleges that Aknoz demanded to see communists (who he claimed were responsible for the anti-Greek pogroms) hanged "in bunches" in public squares. Aknoz was also the military leader whom US diplomats in mid 1956 thought "the most likely" to take power in the event of a coup in Turkey. According to Ömer Aslan, he had already been involved in flouting minor orders in November 1954 (John Goodyear, "Military Interest and Influence in Turkey's Politics," June 15, 1956, RG 84, Box 77; Altan Öymen, *...Ve İhtilal* [Istanbul: Doğan Kitap, 2013], 124; Ömer Aslan, *The United States and Military Coups in Turkey and Pakistan: Between Conspiracy and Reality* [London: Palgrave Macmillan, 2018], 124).

15 For accounts of the military coups in France and Pakistan, see Martin Evans, *Algeria: France's Undeclared War* (Oxford: Oxford University Press, 2012), 232–236, and Ayse Jalal, *The State of Martial Rule: The Origins of Pakistan's Political Economy of Defence* (Lahore: Vanguard Books, 1991), 268–276, and *The Struggle for Pakistan: A Muslim Homeland and Global Politics* (Cambridge, MA: The Belknap Press of Harvard University Press, 2014), 95–100.

flawed electoral system. *Zafer* editors explained that France's method of allocating seats in parliament proportionally led to "the establishment of governments that came and went, lacking majorities or clear characters."[16] The foreign affairs columnist elaborated that these governments were full of people and groups pursuing only their own "personal, narrow interests."[17] According to *Havadis*, this system did not provide France with "the stability, peace, and organized administration that it needs."[18]

The main cause of instability in France in May 1958, however, was the war in Algeria. France had already lost control of its Southeast Asian colonies; now it risked losing its hold on North Africa as well. Though pro-DP papers did not support French efforts to dominate Algeria's majority Muslim population, any criticism of Turkey's NATO ally was restrained. Moreover, writers linked the forces resisting French colonial policies to Nasser, communism, and instability more generally. In France, *Havadis* explained, "Nobody supports giving up Algeria … except the communists."[19] On May 13, 1958, French generals in Algeria, concerned that the national government was seeking an accommodation with the rebels, seized power in Algiers. They declared a "Committee of Public Safety" and demanded that Charles De Gaulle, leader of Free French forces during World War II, be placed in charge of the national government. Though the prime minister initially resisted, by June 1 De Gaulle was standing before parliament, on the verge of being voted into power. In the coming months, he and his allies drew up a new constitution, creating a more powerful presidency. Both *Havadis* and *İstanbul Ekspres* noted that the military leaders who brought Charles De Gaulle to power in 1958 and hoped to maintain a colonial order in Algeria were opposed by the French Communist Party.[20] As in Egypt, Syria, Iraq, and elsewhere, communism was associated with any effort to destabilize the existing order – colonial or otherwise – even if DP leaders were themselves critical of that order.

De Gaulle's consolidation of power in France provided a particularly enticing model of personalistic leadership for Menderes and his allies.[21] De Gaulle had already established a party that sought to draw together voters on the center-right of French politics. The propaganda in favor of his new presidential system (e.g., "Yes to France") linked his political

[16] "Fransa'daki …," *Zafer*, May 18, 1958, 1.
[17] Mücahit Topalak, "Fransa'da …," *Zafer*, December 22, 1958, 3.
[18] "Fransa'da …," *Havadis*, May 17, 1958, 1, 3. [19] Ibid.
[20] "Fransa'da …," *Havadis*, May 28, 1958, 1, 5; "Başvekil …," *İstanbul Ekspres*, May 28, 1958, 1.
[21] Şevket Süreyya Aydemir argued that Menderes hoped to bring about a more Gaullist-style regime in Turkey after 1958 (*Menderes'in Dramı?*, 274–275).

interests with the national interest and helped secure overwhelming approval in a September 1958 referendum. Two rounds of parliamentary elections in November gave his party a plurality – and constituted a clear victory when compared with the performance of his avowed opponents on the left. *İstanbul Ekspres* ran the headline, “Reds Routed in French Elections,” presenting De Gaulle’s presidential system as a victory in the Cold War.[22] A year later, reflecting on the developments in France, a *Zafer* columnist suggested that the era of parliamentary dominance was passing, declaring “democracy in the second half of the twentieth century is a democracy of leaders.”[23]

DP papers and leaders also praised the authoritarian regime of General Ayub Khan in Pakistan. Ayub had seized power from the president in October 1958, only three weeks after the president himself had suspended the constitution, declared martial law, dissolved all political parties, postponed elections, and placed the prime minister under house arrest. Following the president’s initial seizure of power, papers like the pro-DP *Balıkesir* published his announcement in which he explained, “The mentality of political parties has fallen … such that I now believe in helping establish a stable, powerful government that can … put in order the internal confusion [in advance of] the coming elections.”[24]

Ayub’s subsequent military coup was given limited coverage. *İstanbul Ekspres* made it a headline for one day and *Zafer* relegated the news to a small notice on the bottom of the front page.[25] In the coming months, however, papers emphasized the positive steps that his regime was taking. *Havadis* declared that “for the first time” the people of Pakistan were seeing their leaders take concrete actions to improve the country. Special courts were set up to prosecute tax dodgers, strict regulations were implemented to combat the black market, and land was taken from powerful notables and redistributed.[26] This “white revolution” would “create a powerful middle class, opening the way to creating a society able to manage a Democratic regime.”[27] *Zafer* noted that Ayub’s first act in office had been to “set the nation’s affairs in order by tossing out the

22 “Fransız Seçimlerinde…,” *İstanbul Ekspres*, December 1, 1958, 1. See Robert Gildea, *France since 1945* (Oxford: Oxford University Press, 2002), 50–57; Julian Jackson, *A Certain Idea of France: The Life of Charles de Gaulle* (London: Penguin, 2018), 453–508.

23 Cengiz İlhan, “Demokrasi …,” *Zafer*, December 15, 1959, 2, 4.

24 “Pakistan Reisicumhuru …,” *Balıkesir Postası*, October 13, 1958, 3.

25 “Pakistan’da …,” *İstanbul Ekspres*, October 28, 1958, 1; “Bütün …,” *Zafer*, October 28, 1958, 1. The coverage in *Zafer* was literally passive. The notice read: “Full Authority Will Be Given to Ayub Khan.”

26 “Pakistan’daki …,” *Havadis*, March 7, 1959, 3.

27 “Pakistanı …,” *Havadis*, November 18, 1959, 3.

unbeneficial elements that had infiltrated the state structure."[28] When Ayub Khan visited Turkey in November 1959, he was greeted by newspapers featuring his face and columns reiterating this praise. President Bayar emphasized Turkey's appreciation of Pakistan's continued commitment to the Baghdad Pact – now renamed "the Central Treaty Organization" (CENTO) – and to working with Turkey "to establish a just and lasting peace in the world."[29]

Lauding peace and justice might be popular stances, but, in doing so, Bayar and others were focusing less on means than on ends. If achieving these outcomes was the highest good, then allowing people and institutions to – as the DP saw it – undermine them was tantamount to a dereliction of duty. By elevating these ends above all else, the DP began to tie its legitimacy to maintaining peace, justice, development, and stability. Accusations that it was sacrificing political freedom to achieve these were dismissed. *İstanbul Ekspres*, for example, mocked critics of the government who argued that "when freedom is absent, nothing can be accomplished." Assuming they were right, the paper asked, how did they account for the "factories and dams rising in every direction"? Clearly then, there *must* be freedom in Turkey and, even better, all this industrial development indicated triumph in Turkey's "War of Economic Independence."[30]

War metaphors not only linked the DP government's policies back to the "War of National Independence" (1919–23), which had led to the establishment of Turkey, but they also helped justify the economic hardship people were experiencing in the present. Despite some temporary relief following the bailout announcement of August 1958, the overall stabilization program necessitated reduced commercial credit and higher prices for state-produced goods. Until the details of the $225 million loan program were finalized in December and a debt restructuring plan in May 1959, the government was in no position to ignore the demands of its foreign creditors.[31] The DP's limited room to maneuver in these

[28] "Pakistan …," *Zafer*, August 14, 1958, 2.

[29] "Dost …," *Havadis*, November 19, 1959, 1, 5. For a discussion of CENTO, see Behçet Kemal Yeşilbursa, "CENTO: The Forgotten Alliance in the Middle East, 1959–1979," *Middle Eastern Studies* 56, no. 6 (2020): 854–877.

[30] Mithat Perin, "Niçin …," *İstanbul Ekspres*, March 24, 1958, 1.

[31] Major sticking points in debt negotiations included interest rates, whether to include debts to airlines, and whether to announce the debts multilaterally or bilaterally – the latter option being the DP government's preference, since it worried that dealing with European creditors as a group would remind voters of the Ottoman Public Debt Administration. The deal was concluded on May 11, 1959 as a series of bilateral agreements. Turkey promised to repay all debts accrued before August 3, 1958 (and through 1963) by the end of 1969. Interest on the consolidated debts would be set at 3 percent ("Financial Aid for Turkey," December 2, 1958, and Colin Brant, "Turkey:

months made criticisms by the opposition all the more dangerous and increased the party's need to present a united front to the public.

Pro-government journalists were willing to defend tighter credit and a weakened lira. *İstanbul Ekspres* pointed to importers' ongoing willingness to apply for foreign exchange, despite its smaller quantities and higher cost, as evidence that criticisms of the government's policies were unwarranted. These merchants clearly had enough capital on hand – and those who called for expanded credit were simply "bloodsuckers" whose demands would mean "assassinating the nation's finances."[32] Such sentiments were echoed in *Demokrat Malatya*, where a columnist argued that excess credit was harming "commercial morality." Tighter credit would loosen the bonds uniting black marketeers' "union of malevolence," just as it would weaken the union between opposition parties.[33]

Unlike tight credit, however, higher prices remained controversial among pro-government writers. Even before the devaluation, this had been a policy debate in which some were willing to acknowledge the problem, albeit with some apologetics. Throughout the DP's time in office, the cost of living had been rising. Yet, even by that standard, the year following the devaluation was hard to bear. In Ankara, rising prices carried a particular bite for the large number of officials living on fixed incomes. Costs there had risen by a relatively gradual 19 percent between 1950 and 1954, but this growth accelerated from 1954 to 1958, rising another 75 percent. The single largest annual increase in inflation occurred during 1959, as prices rose 24 percent.[34] Trying to keep pace with real prices, the government raised the official price of products like cheese, eggs, butter, and other essentials by around 20 percent in November 1958, prompting the pro-DP *İstanbul Ekspres* to publish an editorial calling for less severe price hikes.[35]

In addition to its own supporters denouncing price increases, the government was confronted by some groups calling for *higher* prices. Some of these demands were rather particular – barbers, for example, complained that they had not raised prices since 1955 – but others were far more threatening to the DP's political future.[36] Farmers faced a

Debt Settlement," December 10, 1958, FO 371/136479; "Agreement on Commercial Debts Owed by Residents of Turkey," May 11, 1959, FO 371/144761).

32 Mithat Perin, "İktisadi …," *İstanbul Ekspres*, October 11, 1958, 1, 5.

33 Doğan Toros, "Ticaret …," *Demokrat Malatya*, November 20, 1958, 1.

34 Cohn, *Turkish Economic*, 21.

35 "Gıda …," *Cumhuriyet*, November 8, 1958, 1; RG, November 8, 1958; "Fiyat …," *İstanbul Ekspres*, November 24, 1958, 1. That same month, the price of state-produced alcohol and cigarettes doubled ("Tekel …," *Akşam*, November 20, 1958, 1).

36 Yılmaz Tunçkol, "6,500 berber …," *Akşam*, November 27, 1958, 2.

potential decline in earnings following the devaluation. One way the government deflected these various demands was by proposing to remove the National Protection Law (even though this remained no more than a proposal during the remainder of the DP's administration).[37] More tangibly, the government directed money to important constituencies: farmers benefited from a 25 percent increase in the purchase price of wheat, as well as higher premia for opium, tobacco, and hazelnuts.[38] State employees on fixed incomes received raises and bonuses. In January 1959, for example, the government announced 100 percent raises for workers and pensioners with the start of the budget year in March. Workers at state economic enterprises likewise received raises and bonuses the following April.[39]

The budget debates in parliament leading to these increases and bonuses were contentious. During one session, CHP legislators accused the DP of pursuing unplanned development, causing waste and mismanagement in both state enterprises and the tendering process. They pointed, for example, to consistent losses at the Minneapolis-Moline tractor factory and outright favoritism in awarding the tender for a paper mill in İzmit. Samet Ağaoğlu, who had been minister of industry at the time, was accused of directing the tender to a German firm that employed the husband of his sister, Süreyya.[40] Even though he was not

[37] The National Protection Law was lifted in September 1960, following the coup and the creation of a new cabinet (RG, September 16, 1960).

[38] "Hububat ...," *Akşam*, June 14, 1959, 1; RG, August 15, 1959. In 1956, the purchase price for wheat was 30 kuruş/kilo; it was raised to 40 kuruş for the harvest season in 1957 and 1958. In 1959, it was raised to 50 kuruş.

[39] "Maaşlar yüzde ...," *Havadis*, January 23, 1959, 1, 5; "Memurlar yarın ...," *Zafer*, March 1, 1959, 1, 4; RG, March 3, 1959; "Devlet teşekkülleri ...," *İstanbul Ekspres*, April 6, 1959, 1, 5; "Gemi adamları ...," *İstanbul Ekspres*, April 8, 1959, 1; RG, April 8, 1959, 1–2. The 1959–60 budget was a record TL5.9 billion ($656 million), which was 31 percent larger in lira terms than the previous year, but far less when considered in terms of the lira's lower value (i.e., TL4.5 billion in 1958–59 had been equivalent to $1.61 billion). Budgets for highways, forestry, state monopolies, and universities were passed separately (RG, March 1, 1958; RG, March 3, 1959).

[40] "Bütçe," *Akis*, February 28, 1959, 19. Süreyya Ağaoğlu's husband, Werner Taschenbrecker, was a frequent target of suspicion. According to Süreyya, she received some criticism for marrying a foreigner in 1952 (though she felt these criticisms were really meant to smear Samet more than her). According to the ostensibly tell-all memoir by Menderes's cousin's son, Mehmet Özdemir Evliyazade, Taschenbrecker had served five years in jail for spying. While the account of Evliyazade, who served in the Turkish intelligence service, contains many wild accusations – for example, he accuses Foreign Minister Fatin Rüştü Zorlu of being involved in the heroin trade – there may be some truth to his suspicions about Taschenbrecker. British diplomats report that he had been "dismissed from the West Berlin Legal Service in June 1951 owing to his Communist connections." During the 1960–61 budget debates, in February 1960, CHP members would again raise the issue of Samet's assistance to Taschenbrecker. On this occasion, a fight would break out in parliament, leaving

currently a cabinet minister, Ağaoğlu remained a close confidant of Prime Minster Menderes and enjoyed the spectacle of parliamentary debate. Coming to the podium to respond, he deflected the charges of nepotism by reiterating his most common criticisms of the opposition: its hypocrisy and failure to acknowledge its own behavior in the past. He observed that the DP minister overseeing the Minneapolis-Moline deal had subsequently quit the DP in order to found the HP and ultimately join the CHP. More sarcastically, he asked, "Are there no merchants among your siblings and relatives?"[41]

Ağaoğlu then moved on to a larger defense of the DP's economic development strategy, dismissing the five- and ten-year plans advocated by the opposition as something "carried out in totalitarian regimes" and adding:

> What is a plan in a country broadly lacking the requirements of a civilized, technological life? A plan is roads. A plan is agricultural lands. A plan is ports and bringing tractors ... A plan is obtaining lighting for a country left in darkness, finding electricity for industry bereft of energy ... These are all plans, my friends. Shall we "give up" one of them?

To those who said the loan agreements were a sign of the government's bankrupt policies, he asked:

> To whom does a banker give credit? He gives it to those people who can pay him back. A man who gets credit is a man who has the ability to repay ... [loans are, therefore] evidence that our hard work and our intelligence have been acknowledged.[42]

He concluded and marched out of the room before the opposition could respond. Where verbal dueling ended, physical scuffles began. The day

legislator İsmail İnan (CHP, Ankara) with a broken nose or black eye, depending on the report (James Bowker to Selwyn Lloyd, "Leading Personalities in Turkey," August 18, 1959, 2–3, FO 371/144740; Mehmet Özdemir Evliyazade, *Onları Anlatıyorum* [Istanbul: Yeni Doğuş Matbaası, 1960], 47, 60–61; Ağaoğlu, *Bir Ömür*, 121; "Deputies Trade Blows ...," *Chicago Daily Tribune*, February 18, 1960, 2; "Tahkikatlar," *Akis*, February 24, 1960, 13).

41 "Bu denk ...," *Zafer*, February 22, 1959, 1, 3. Fethi Çelikbaş, who had served in DP cabinets from 1953 to 1954, was a leader of the HP. Before entering parliament in 1950, he was a government official in the ministry of economy and trade and, from 1940 to 1950, an academic. He taught in the Political Science Faculty of Ankara University, eventually becoming dean. As an expert on economic matters, he often sparred with Samet Ağaoğlu. As Ağaoğlu was giving a defense of DP policies, for example, Çelikbaş yelled out that Samet was being "romantic," which was to say, a fabulist. Samet acknowledged that he was a "romantic" and asked his former colleague, "Why have you lost your romanticism?" (James Bowker to Selwyn Lloyd, "Leading Personalities in Turkey," August 18, 1959, FO 371/144740).

42 "Bu denk ...," *Zafer*, February 22, 1959, 1, 3.

before the budget vote, a fight broke out among legislators that left a CHP representative with scratches on his face.[43]

Pressure from the opposition was not the only difficulty facing the DP leadership. There was also a growing internal opposition. The new regime of premia and import controls went into effect on August 25, 1958, along with legislation that strengthened the authority of Coordination Minister Sebati Ataman, who had been serving in the post since it was created a month earlier.[44] At the time of Ataman's appointment, Balıkesir representative Sıtkı Yırcalı had been moved from the ministry of press and tourism to the important post of minister of industry. The two ministries shared objectives and, therefore, bureaucratic turf. The two men quarreled for two months until a dispute over increased paper prices (which Yırcalı opposed) brought matters to a head in the last week of August. According to one account, Yırcalı, finding himself overruled and unable to get in contact with Menderes, traveled to Ankara and confronted Ataman. Threatening to hit him, Yırcalı grabbed a chair and had to be talked down by the minister of labor, who entered in the nick of time.[45]

Yırcalı was a powerful figure in the party. Given Yırcalı's influence in the important province of Balıkesir and position on the DP executive committee, Menderes had kept him in the cabinet despite his associations with the internal party opposition (the *Yaylacılar*). On September 1, 1958, Yırcalı put in his resignation and headed back home.[46] Faced with disunity within their party (and increasing unity

43 "D.P.nin tokatlı …," *Ateş*, February 28, 1959, 1.

44 RG, August 25, 1958. In 1950, Sebati Ataman was elected as the CHP's sole representative for the closely contested province of Zonguldak after a DP nominee had died on the day of the election. On September 7, 1950, his validity as a representative was rejected by the DP-controlled parliament, and he was denied a seat on the grounds that his opponent had died *after* winning, thus necessitating a by-election in 1951. According to British reports, Ataman resented his CHP colleagues for not supporting his bid more forcefully. Menderes offered him a post as governor of Muğla in 1951. In 1954, he was elected as a DP representative for Zonguldak (TBMM, July 7, 1950, 445–466; James Bowker to Selwyn Lloyd, "Leading Personalities in Turkey," August 18, 1959, FO 371/144740).

45 Bağlum, *Ampolitik*, 102–104.

46 Samet Ağaoğlu also resigned as minister of state, but this move was not formally accepted and announced for two more months. On September 2, Emin Kalafat, another minister of state responsible for economic matters (and overshadowed by Ataman), announced his resignation as well. Before entering parliament in 1950, Kalafat had been an inspector in the ministry of finance. For a time, he had been a critic of Menderes allies like Ağaoğlu, but he had moved closer to the prime minister by the mid 1950s. His sister, Ayşe Günel, was also a member of parliament (James Bowker to Selwyn Lloyd, "Leading Personalities in Turkey," August 18, 1959, FO 371/144740; Ankara Embassy to Foreign Office, September 19, 1958, F0 371/136453).

among their critics), the DP leadership sought to draw clear distinctions between themselves and their opponents. On September 6, Menderes, Bayar, and Refik Koraltan traveled to Balıkesir to attend the opening of a new cement factory. The trip was scheduled to coincide with both the provincial DP congress and the annual celebration of Balıkesir's liberation from Greek occupation in 1922.[47] Speaking at the opening of the congress, Menderes alluded to events in Iraq, accusing opposition papers of publishing photos of "the corpses of those murdered in a neighboring country" because "they want to provoke such militant action in this country." But, he reminded his listeners, the opposition seemed to forget that such plots had been hatched against Atatürk as well. Perhaps they would "remember and take a lesson from the lives lost at the gallows by those who dared [to hatch such plots]."[48]

As Menderes's historical allusion suggested, the conflation of the opposition with treachery was not unique to the DP. Yet Atatürk had presented his enemies as agents of religious reaction, whereas Menderes tended to frame his denunciations using the rhetoric of the Cold War. Two weeks later, at the İzmir provincial party congress, Menderes placed the challenges facing Turkey in the more contemporary context, declaring:

> As the expression goes, foreign policy is the continuation of domestic policy ... We know that the world is separated into two opposing military camps ... Our country is found among the group of countries that are peace-loving and democratic ... What [our opposition] wants is not to increase the ability of the country to resist and defend against the great dangers that exist and surround us from outside [our borders]; [what they want] consists solely of discovering opportunities for coming to power by illegal, non-electoral means, by opening the way ... to every sort of disruptive activity.

He went on to praise De Gaulle as "a Statesman" for confronting "anarchy born from the misuse of liberty" and "tossing it outside the national borders." Compared to De Gaulle, Menderes suggested,

47 The following day, Menderes, Bayar, and Koraltan attended the opening of an electrical plant in the nearby town of Soma, a three-hour train ride from Balıkesir's provincial center. Attending that event enabled the DP leaders to skip the second day of the provincial party congress, which was dominated by the family of internal party critic Sıtkı Yırcalı. While Kemal Bağlum, a reporter close to the DP, suggests that the leaders' visit was intended in part to sooth intraparty tensions, it does not seem to have had this effect. In late October 1958, Yırcalı and other internal critics of the party leadership backed Şemi Ergin for president of parliament against Refik Koraltan. Ergin lost 158–175, with six abstentions, on October 31 ("Soma ...," *Zafer*, September 8, 1958, 1, 6; "Sıtkı ...," *İstanbul Ekspres*, September 2, 1958, 1, 5; "D.P. yeni ...," *Balıkesir*, September 8, 1958, 2; Bağlum, *Anıpolitik*, 113–114; Burçak, *On Yılın Anıları*, 584–585).

48 "Başvekilimizin ...," *Zafer*, September 7, 1958, 1, 4.

opposition leader İsmet İnönü resembled the leader of France's wartime pro-Nazi government, Marshall Pétain.[49] İnönü replied the next day that the prime minister was calling for "a break from democracy."[50]

On October 7, Menderes wrote to local DP organizations, informing them that in light of his recent speeches in Balıkesir and elsewhere, they should be prepared for an influx of citizens joining and rejoining the party.[51] In order to "reform" the party, the local leadership in provinces like Malatya was reorganized.[52] The following week, at the Manisa provincial congress, Menderes moved from predicting a flood of new party members to explicitly inviting them. He declared that, faced with the challenge of economic development, "we, as a government, have entered into this trial by fire" to lead the nation, which was "engaged in the greatest struggle of its history and fate." But, with the opposition parties uniting in a "front of spite and enmity," it fell to "citizens free of politics and ambition … to unite and protect" the great works thus far accomplished in "a homeland front."[53]

The official party paper *Zafer* included "homeland front" in its headline the following day, as did the anti-government paper *Cumhuriyet*. Yet pro-DP papers like *İstanbul Ekspres* and *Balıkesir* did not mention it. Only in the coming weeks would it become apparent that the DP had embarked on an effort to extend party influence throughout society, thereby reviving the possibility of a single-party state.

The Homeland Front: The Democrat Party as Mass Party

In the weeks after Menderes's Manisa speech, the DP organization launched a national effort to register new party members and give the impression of a groundswell of support for the party. Pro-DP newspapers began to print letters and telegraphs from people around the country writing to express their love of Menderes and the DP, their disgust with

[49] "Meş'um …," *Zafer*, September 22, 1958, 1, 4.

[50] "İnönü …," *Cumhuriyet*, September 23, 1958, 1, 5.

[51] Yasemin Doğaner, *Türk Demokrasi Tarihinde Vatan Cephesi* (Ankara: Siyasal Kitabevi, 2013), 97. He would reiterate the need to welcome back erstwhile members in further party circulars (for example, BCA 030.01.00.00 45 269 13).

[52] Malatya's provincial party executive committee had been reorganized in April 1958, following yet another loss in the 1957 national elections. As a result, Hüseyin Doğan again became the head of the local party. In October, it was rearranged yet again. Doğan and Celal Bilgili remained, but the rest of the committee was replaced with a mix of former members (Celal Derinkök, Cevdet Güray, and Lütfi Gebeş) and new additions (Talat Barış, Celal Akın, Bedri Tola, and Sıddık Hoşhanlı) ("D.P. il …," *Demokrat Malatya*, April 30, 1958, 1; "D.P. il …," *Demokrat Malatya*, October 11, 1958, 1).

[53] "Nifak …," *Zafer*, October 13, 1958, 1, 4.

the opposition parties, and their intention to join, rejoin, or intensify their commitment to the ruling party. Throughout the day, radio broadcasters read off lists of citizens who had joined the "Homeland Front" (*Vatan Cephesi*). Homeland Front clubs appeared around the country. According to statistics provided by party officials, around 1 million people joined in the twenty months between October 1958 and May 1960.[54] Published sources and troves of letters stored in state archives give the impression that a major political mobilization was underway.

In reality, the Homeland Front seems to have been less impressive.[55] Memoirs from both DP and CHP partisans tend to describe it in comic terms, recalling how the lists of names were often made up or belonged to dead people.[56] The profusion of clubs were often just existing DP branches with the name "Homeland Front" added to them. Since, in practice, there was no clear distinction between the Front and the DP organization, the entire endeavor appears to have been an exercise in rebranding. Yet for all that – or, perhaps, *because* of all that – the Homeland Front venture reveals important changes in how the DP's leaders understood their relationship to voters and to political contestation.

The Homeland Front mobilization combined a number of political strategies employed by the DP and opposition parties during the previous twelve years of multiparty politics. One of these strategies was to overwhelm the public with numbers, names, and statistics. Two days after

[54] Burçak puts the number of Homeland Front members at 973,170, circa December 1959. As to how many DP members there were *before*, it is hard to find precise numbers. The original party rules stated that every province sent delegates to the national convention, and provinces with more than 2,000 members sent an additional delegate for each *additional* 2,000 members. In 1955, for example, there were 1,500 delegates (once internal critics had been expelled). This number of delegates would imply somewhere around 3 million members (assuming ~67 provinces were represented). In a country of around 24 million people, however, this number seems high – especially since the party received 4.5 million total votes in 1957. As a point of comparison, Josef Szyliowicz, using calculations from Donald Webster, puts membership in the CHP at 1 million c. 1935, when the population was 16 million (Szyliowicz, "Political Participation and Modernization in Turkey," *Western Political Quarterly* 19, no. 2 [1966]: 272; Burçak, *On Yılın Anıları*, 604–606).

[55] For an overview of the Homeland Front, see Doğaner, *Türk Demokrasi Tarihinde Vatan Cephesi*; for an excellent provincial-level study, see Zehra Arslan, "Trabzon'da Vatan Cephesi, 12 Ekim 1958–27 Mayıs 1960," *Karadeniz Araştırmaları* 36 (2013): 129–148.

[56] Pro-CHP memoirs emphasize the fraudulent aspects of Homeland Front propaganda. Yet memoirs by DP members and supporters have little positive to say either. Though Burçak, for example, argues the organization was "an enterprise to strengthen the party through new membership" and lacked any larger goals, he believes that the saturation of radio propaganda "exhausted and wore everybody down" (Toker, *Demokrasiden Darbeye*, 298; Burçak, *On Yılın Anıları*, 601; Birand et al., *Demirkırat*, 151; İsvan, *Başkent Gölgesinde*, 11–12; Öymen, *...Ve İhtilal*, 461–466).

Menderes's Balıkesir speech, for example, *Zafer* ran a story titled "Thousands of citizens have again joined the DP." The article reported:

> Yesterday, [in the central Anatolian province of Yozgat], in the village of Fakılı, in the Fehimli subdistrict of Boğazlıyan district, CHP member Ramazan Özcan, Emin Işık, Şevket İriyarı, Zühtü Uçar, Hasan İbis, Mustafa Öztürk, Kazım Yolcusoy, İbrahim Zararsız and sixty people left the CHP and took their place on the side of the DP. Additionally, Fehimli's Republican Nation Party subdistrict president, Seyit Ali Yılmaz, and the entire executive committee resigned and signed up with the DP.[57]

Articles like this would appear almost daily for months to come. Typically, they would name a leading individual in a community and some larger number of his "friends" or family. The articles would often quote from telegrams sent to the provincial party office praising Prime Minister Menderes and/or decrying "disruptive" opposition tactics.[58] News reports of party switches were not a new phenomenon, but their increased frequency was.

The flow of announcements was complemented by Menderes and his ministers' frequent visits to the provinces to open new facilities and give speeches. In just the month following his Manisa speech on October 13, Menderes spoke before large crowds in at least eight other provinces.[59] As with newspapers reporting shifts in party allegiance, there was nothing new about holding large rallies during the fall parliamentary recess.[60] A distinction, however, was the degree to which parallel tours by the opposition were repressed. As Menderes made his way through the DP's Aegean strongholds, CHP leader İsmet İnönü traveled through central Anatolian provinces where the opposition parties had fared well in the 1957 election. In the town of Zile, the chief district official (*kaymakam*) lined the streets with gendarmes to enforce the Public Meetings and Demonstrations Law. When crowds began to gather in defiance, he had them dispersed with sticks, firehoses, and shots fired in the air.

İnönü's son-in-law, the journalist Metin Toker, was traveling in the entourage and was able to report on the events in Zile for his magazine,

[57] "D.P.ye yeniden ...," *Zafer*, October 15, 1958, 1, 4.

[58] For a sample of telegrams from Balıkesir, see BCA 010.09.00.00 214 663 3; for Malatya, see BCA 010.09.0.0 216 671 2.

[59] Menderes spoke in Antalya (October 14), Isparta (October 17), Afyon (October 19), Uşak (October 20), Kütahya (October 22), Eskisehir (October 24), Yozgat (November 14), and Erzurum (November 17).

[60] During the September–October recess in 1956, Menderes had made two tours, the first to eastern provinces like Malatya and Erzurum to open sugar factories, the second to Aegean provinces like İzmir and Balıkesir. The 1957 parliamentary recess had coincided with the national elections, meaning that it was packed with political rallies.

Akis.[61] The following week, *Akis* was closed for two months by court order. Toker was sentenced to a year in prison on an unrelated charge on October 28. On November 4, the CHP paper, *Ulus*, was also closed for a month.[62] These instances seem like clear examples of the government's campaign to silence journalists. Then again, it was not only the DP utilizing the Press Law. Toker had been accused of libel by a CHP member – it was in *choosing* to give him a stiff sentence that the partisan element seems to have entered into the matter.[63] Similarly, the editor of the DP paper, *Zafer*, was sent to prison in December for insulting the editor of a pro-CHP paper.[64] In other words, the recourse to libel suits was not solely a DP tactic but rather a shared tendency among politicians (albeit one whose effects were often unequally distributed thanks to the DP's control of government). Asked for statistics on prosecutions of journalists in November 1958, the minister of justice reported that 1,161 prosecutions had been initiated in the previous four years, leading to 238 convictions.[65]

The government's ability to sanction the press was complemented by its total control of the radio. Radio was limited in Turkey during the 1950s. The only stations were in Istanbul and Ankara, as well as a weak municipal station in İzmir. Yet the number of radio sets in the country was growing, rising from 187,870 in 1946 to 786,553 by 1953, when the DP allocated funds to develop stations in Erzurum, Adana, and İzmir.[66] When in power, both the CHP and the DP restricted their political opponents' access to the airwaves and gave time to speeches from government ministers that doubled as political stump speeches. But the DP took further steps as well: the nightly news program *Radyo Gazetesi*, for example, began focusing on domestic as well as foreign affairs and framing its coverage in highly partisan terms during the late 1950s.[67]

61 "Meslik tesanüdü," *Akis*, October 25, 1958, 12–14.

62 "Basın …," *Cumhuriyet*, October 28, 1958, 1, 5; "Metin …," *Cumhuriyet*, October 29, 1958, 1, 5; "Ulus …," *Havadis*, November 4, 1958, 1; "Basın," *Akis*, December 28, 1958, 15–17; Onur Öztürk, "Demokrat Parti Dönemi Basın Rejimi ve *Zafer Gazetesi* (1957–1960) *Ulus Gazetesi* ile Karşılaştırmalı Bir İnceleme" (Master's thesis, Ankara Üniversitesi, Ankara, 2004), 83.

63 As Toker himself observes, one of the judges involved in his case would run for the senate three years later. During the campaign, the judge's supporters emphasized that he had helped put Toker, "the national son-in-law," behind bars (Toker, *Demokrasiden Darbeye*, 167–168).

64 "Zafer …," *Havadis*, December 24, 1958, 1, 5.

65 TBMM, November 24, 1958, 275–277.

66 Çağla Kubilay and Mehmet Pehlivan, "Demokrat Parti ve Radyo: Bir Islahat Girişimi, 1954," *İlef Dergisi* 6, no. 1 (2019): 55.

67 Nevra Ersarı, "Ellili Yıllarda Radyo ve Siyaset," in *Türkiye'nin 1950'li Yılları*, ed. Mete Kaan Kaynar (Istanbul: İletişim Yayınları, 2015), 394–407; Kubilay and Pehlivan, "Demokrat Parti ve Radyo," 51.

The Homeland Front exacerbated the partisan character of radio broadcasts. In her memoirs, Jülide Gülizar, one of Turkey's first female news presenters, recalls the frustration she felt doing blatant government propaganda, reading the names of those who had joined the organization night after night. The public, she suggests, shared her frustration. In addition to the letters the station received from citizens who proudly described themselves as "those who've entered the Homeland Front" (*VC'ye girenler*), it also began receiving prank letters from "those who've entered the toilet" (*WC'ye girenler*). Three young Istanbul professionals established a "Society of Those Who Don't Listen to Agency News and Partisan Broadcasts."[68] Within days, the new organization had been closed down by the Istanbul governor.[69]

While the Istanbul governor, like his peers elsewhere, played an unofficial political role, he was not the leading DP figure in the city. Since July 1958, that role had been filled by Mayor Kemal Aygün. In addition to being the nephew of DP leader Refik Koraltan, Aygün had held important government posts, including director general of national security and governor of Ankara before assuming his mayoral position.[70] The post was newly created. Previously, the country's largest city had been administered as though it were a province, run by a governor rather than a mayor named by the local legislature. Since governors remained formally above politics, creating a mayoral position enabled the DP to administer Istanbul in a more brazenly partisan fashion. On January 17, 1959, Aygün officially joined the DP and then, a week later, was named as its Istanbul provincial party president. In this capacity, he would spend the next seventeen months attending the opening of new party branches around the city. His old position as governor of Ankara was taken by Dilaver Argun, a former provincial governor who had briefly served as a DP representative from 1957 to 1958 before stepping down to oversee the capital. Unlike in Istanbul, the DP government did not create a mayoral position chosen by the municipal legislature in Ankara – likely because the CHP had won partial control of the city's legislature in the 1955 local elections.[71]

[68] Jülide Gülizar, *Haberler Bitti Şimdi Oyun Havaları* (Ankara: Ümit Yayıncılık, 1994), 70–78.

[69] "Ajans haberlerini ...," *Cumhuriyet*, December 3, 1958, 1.

[70] James Bowker to Selwyn Lloyd, "Leading Personalities in Turkey," August 18, 1959, 5, FO 371/144740. In his account of drug-trafficking and state-building in Turkey, Ryan Gingeras describes Aygün's relations with US officials in the early 1950s. His assistance to US counter-narcotics officials left them unsatisfied. After the 1960 coup, he was accused of shaking down brothels and casinos (Gingeras, *Heroin, Organized Crime and the Making of Modern Turkey* [Oxford: Oxford University Press, 2014], 153–173).

[71] "Ankarada da ...," *Cumhuriyet*, November 14, 1955, 1, 3.

Mayor Aygün and Governor Argun worked to increase Homeland Front membership in their respective cities.[72] In January, both men began pressuring city employees to join.[73] These efforts were mirrored at the national level in state enterprises, where Minister of Industry Sebati Ataman had lifted the regulation prohibiting employees from joining political organizations.[74] And pressure extended beyond state and municipal enterprises to anyone in a dependent relationship with the state; this ranged from leaders of the drivers union to members of the state ballet and opera.[75] Often, even if people asked for their membership to be recorded discretely or declined altogether, they would still hear their names read out on the radio.[76]

Clearly, coercion was a significant inducement to joining the Homeland Front. Yet the degree to which people struggled with the decision to join is difficult to gauge. Following the May 1960 coup, there were clear benefits to stressing how unwillingly one had joined, and clear dangers in defending the choice. Moreover, in the twenty months that the Homeland Front lasted, there were several reasons people might choose to join. For many, joining was merely a strategic response in light of the government's increasing partisanship. As the elevations of Mayor Aygün and Governor Argun emphasized, the DP government was tightening the link between public services and partisan affiliation. For citizens just trying to make ends meet, the benefits of joining were clear enough, regardless of their interest in party politics.

For more ideologically motivated citizens, there were other reasons to join the Homeland Front. In late November 1958, the CHP and HP declared a "Union of Forces" in which the HP dissolved itself, paving the way for a formal merger in January 1959. While HP leaders may have been willing to forgive and forget their disagreements with the former ruling party, their rank and file were less forgiving. Dislike of the CHP remained strong, and its criticisms of the DP for seeking to stifle democracy rang hollow to many activists who now returned to the DP.[77]

72 "Belediye ...," *İstanbul Ekspres*, April 24, 1959, 1.

73 Zehra Arslan, "Vatan Cephesi Davası (Kararname, Savunmalar ve Karar)," *History Studies: International Journal of History* 4, no. 2 (2012): 12.

74 "Vatan Cephesi Davası: Sebati Ataman ve Samet Ağaoğlu hakkında görevi kötüye kullanmak ...," BCA 010.09.0.0 221 684 3.

75 The prominent tenor Aydın Gün and his wife refused to join; the soprano – and mistress of Adnan Menderes – Ayhan Aydan joined ("V.C. ye geçemediler ...," *Ateş*, November 6, 1959, 1).

76 Arslan, "Vatan Cephesi Davası," 10–14.

77 Rather than join with the CHP and HP, Osman Bölükbaşı joined his Republican Nation Party with the even smaller Turkey Peasants' Party (*Türkiye Köylü Partisi*, KP) to create a "third force" in Turkish politics that might appeal to voters fed up with the two main

Hüsamettin Cindoruk, the leader of the HP's Youth Arm, for example, opposed the merger. When the party voted 175–5 in favor, he was among the five dissenters, arguing that while he trusted the sincerity of CHP leader İsmet İnönü, he did not trust the former ruling party as an organization. "[İnönü] is mortal. We cannot turn over the nation's fate to the Grim Reaper."[78] A year later, he officially rejoined the DP.[79]

The DP was also seeking to recruit new members. There were attempts to reenergize the party's Youth Arm, which had lost much of its energy since 1955, when Cindoruk had broken with the DP and switched to the HP. After setbacks in the 1957 elections, Menderes took a renewed interest in youth participation.[80] This inclination was reflected in local party organizations. In Balıkesir, for example, the party opened a half dozen "youth clubs" (*gençlik lokalları*) in late 1958. The openings of these sites provided local party leaders with frequent opportunities to speak to (legally permitted) indoor audiences about the government's accomplishments. Generally, the emphasis was on economics – in one instance, a youth local even organized an exhibition called "Developing Turkey" to display evidence of recent achievements – but some speakers focused on the oppression under CHP rule, including heavy taxes and the forced labor in the nearby mines during World War II.[81]

The DP Women's Arm also had frequent meetings, albeit without the same level of attention and organization as the male-dominated youth branches. Branches would greet visiting government officials and listen to speakers from the local party organization. Similar to speeches at male-dominated DP Youth Arm events, these emphasized the DP's economic accomplishments and reminded attendees that "the path taken by the opposition [was], alas, not legitimate."[82] Beyond the party

blocs, the Republican Peasants' Nation Party (*Cumhuriyetçi Köylü Millet Partisi*). (Baban, *Politika Galerisi*, 453–455; Toker, *Demokrasiden Darbeye*, 170–173; Çaylak, *Osman Bölükbaşı*, 345–349).

78 "Hürriyet P. dün …," *Cumhuriyet*, November 25, 1958, 1, 5; Çakmak, "Türk Siyasal Yaşamında," 184.

79 "5 Eski H.P. mebusu …," *Cumhuriyet*, February 20, 1960, 1, 5.

80 İsmail Öz, "Demokrat Parti'nin Gençlik Politikaları ve Gençlik Teşkilatı, 1946–1960" (Master's thesis, Fatih Sultan Mehmet Vakıf Üniversitesi, Istanbul [2014], 70–119). In Istanbul, Menderes appointed Cemil Bengü (a former representative from Ordu, who had lost his seat in the 1957 election) as president of the provincial organization. Bengü, in turn, reorganized the party's local Youth Arm. After Bengü's death in a car accident, divisions grew between the young leadership and his successor, Servet Sürenkök. For an account of the Youth Arm in Istanbul, see Ertuğrul Mat, *Demokrasi Yolunda Karınca Misali: İstanbul ve Ankara Günleri* (Ankara: Berikan Yayınevi, 2015), 99–122.

81 "D.P. İlçe heyeti …," *Balıkesir Postası*, November 21, 1958, 1; "Oruçgazi …," *Balıkesir*, December 8, 1958, 1, 4; "İş ve para …," *Balıkesir*, December 15, 1958, 1, 4; "Aygören …," *Balıkesir Postası*, December 20, 1958, 1.

82 Ruhi Yıldırım, "D.P. İl Kadınlar …," *Havadis*, September 8, 1959, 1, 5.

auxiliaries, the DP maintained close connections with national women's organizations. Nazlı Tlabar, the leading woman in the DP, served as the president of the (ostensibly nonpartisan) Women's Union, which generally focused on issues that had cross-party support, such as banning the chador (*çarşaf*).[83]

In addition to targeting appeals in terms of age and gender, the DP also sought to incorporate a relatively new group in Turkish society: the growing number of poor migrants who had settled in cities during the previous decade. These recent arrivals settled in neighborhoods dubbed *gecekondu* ("set overnight") – a reference to the rapidity with which new dwellings appeared. Especially in the early years of settlement, the homes lacked water, electricity, or legal title. By 1960, some 60 percent of Ankara residents and 45 percent of Istanbullus were living in in such precarious situations.[84]

As early as 1948, the CHP government had passed laws to both regulate these new dwellings and encourage settlement in more stable housing. A 1949 law strengthened the government's ability to demolish unregistered properties. In 1953, however, the DP passed a new law that legalized houses built up to that point while authorizing the destruction of unregulated housing, going forward.[85] This vacillation between penalty and amnesty would continue for decades, and, in the late 1950s, there was a new push to issue deeds. In Ankara, for example, Governor Argun spoke frequently about the possibility of large-scale, ex-post facto legalizations, and DP leaders made sure that they were associated with the granting of titles. In October 1959, for example, Ankara municipality issued deeds to over 600 homes. Several members of the DP provincial party leadership attended the granting ceremony, thereby reminding residents whom they should be thanking.[86]

In addition to material and partisan self-interest, attachment to the charismatic figure of Adnan Menderes also motivated people to join the

[83] There seem to have been tensions within the Women's Union during the late 1950s. During the May 1958 congress, the pro-CHP magazine *Akis* notes that some delegates spoke critically of the DP government's economic policies, which were encouraging black markets and making household management difficult. During the April 1959 congress, there was an attempt to discipline several members for allowing "voting irregularities" during the 1958 congress; this move was blocked by the general committee, leading several members of the disciplinary committee to resign ("Sosyal Hayat," *Akis*, May 24, 1959, 27–28; "Kadın Birliği ...," *Akşam*, April 9, 1959, 1, 7; Jale Candan, "Davaya İnanmak Lazımdır," *Akis*, April 18, 1959, 27).

[84] Lightfoot and Taş, "Gecekondu Settlements," 266–267.

[85] Ruşen Keleş, *100 Soruda Türkiye'de Şehirleşme, Konut ve Gecekondu* (Istanbul: Gerçek Yayınları, 1972), 203–206; Tansı Şenyapılı, *"Baraka"dan Gecekonduya: Ankara' da Kentsel Mekanın Dönüşümü, 1923–60* (Istanbul: İletişim Yayınları, 2004), 133–139.

[86] "Aktaş'ta 600 ...," *Zafer*, October 26, 1959, 1.

DP or the amorphous Homeland Front. Not only was he popular, but since becoming prime minister in 1950 Menderes had also been accumulating power and pushing aside rivals. His internal party opponents lacked a leader to rally around, and by continuously postponing any national party congress after 1955 he denied them an opportunity to come together.

The only other center of power in the party was President Bayar. According to Rıfkı Salim Burçak, a member of the DP executive committee, Bayar was closely involved in decision-making, especially regarding the government's attitude toward the opposition. In Burçak's account, Bayar pushed Menderes's government to take a hard line against the opposition. On the night of December 7, 1958, for example, after police in Gaziantep broke up an İnönü rally, Bayar called DP leaders to the presidential residence in Ankara, argued that present measures were insufficient, and emphasized that "proportionally serious [security] measures" were necessary to deal with İnönü's tour of the south. Interior Minister Namik Gedik suggested new laws banning "false publications" (which, in this context, would suggest both statements that İnönü was making at his rallies and reports of the methods being used to break up rallies).[87]

On December 10, the DP parliamentary group announced that it was creating a committee to develop further recommendations for changes to the Press Law and the Associations Law, which regulated political parties. Members included Bahadır Dülger, owner of *Havadis*, and Burhan Belge, who was influential in radio programming. Though the committee was clearly intended as a step toward further restricting the opposition, its purpose became muddled when a member of the internal party opposition proposed that the government pass an amnesty for journalists rather than harsher laws.[88] With the parliamentary group divided, the committee's report was shelved until the middle of 1959.

Though the initiative came to nothing in late 1958, it demonstrated a means by which more restrictive laws might be proposed outside the normal parliamentary committee process. In the absence of new regulations, parliamentary politics in the months of January and February 1959 focused on budget debates. These were touched on in the previous section, but the arguments and corridor scuffles take on deeper meaning when set against this larger context of violence at opposition rallies and

[87] "Halkı dağıtmak ...," *Cumhuriyet*, December 8, 1958, 1; Burçak, *On Yılın Anıları*, 587–589.

[88] "Tedbirler ...," *Cumhuriyet*, December 11, 1958, 1, 5; Toker, *Demokrasiden Darbeye*, 195–198.

attempts by the ruling party to further stifle any criticism. It is difficult to say, however, whether events were heading toward some dramatic climax in early 1959, because the normal rhythms of politics were suddenly, violently, disrupted in February.

Spring Offensives: Growing Partisan Tensions

On February 17, 1959, Prime Minister Menderes was scheduled to arrive in London to conduct final negotiations with Greece and the UK over the status of Cyprus. As his plane arrived, it was redirected to Gatwick airport owing to heavy fog. On its approach, the plane lost contact with the control tower and crashed into woods nearby, killing fourteen of the twenty-four aboard. Among the ten survivors was Menderes. Hauled from the wreckage largely unscathed, Menderes would sign the Cyprus accord from his hospital bed two days later.[89] He remained in England for another week and returned to Istanbul on a Thursday. His timing enabled him to attend Friday prayers at Eyüp Sultan, the first mosque built following the 1453 conquest of the city, as well as the site at which new sultans were invested with authority.[90] The symbolism was not lost on his critics. Nor was the public enthusiasm with which he was greeted. People lined the roadside from the airport to Istanbul's old city walls. Many sacrificed sheep, goats, and camels as Menderes passed by. The scene was repeated on his arrival in Ankara, with a bull now added to the mix.[91]

Menderes's arrival in Ankara was also a moment of possible rapprochement with the opposition. İsmet İnönü was at the train station to greet Menderes, standing on the platform alongside the prime minister's family. President Bayar, however, did not join them. Instead, he remained in the station's waiting room in order to avoid having his picture taken alongside his long-time rival. According to allies of İnönü, this moment was a "lost opportunity." Bayar's unwillingness to acknowledge İnönü's status as both opposition leader *and* former president foreclosed any improvement in relations.[92] Yet the possibility that

[89] "Mr. Menderes ...," *The Times*, February 18, 1959, 10; "Menderes, Hastanede ...," *İstanbul Ekspres*, February 18, 1959, 1, 5.
[90] Ünver Rüstem, *Ottoman Baroque: The Architectural Refashioning of Eighteenth-Century Istanbul* (Princeton: Princeton University Press, 2019), 252.
[91] Toker, *Demokrasiden Darbeye*, 209–213.
[92] Ibid., 210–212; quotation from Öymen, ...*Ve İhtilal*, 479. According to Ahmet Emin Yalman (and repeated by Mükerrem Sarol), after the excitement of Menderes's return to Ankara, Sarol spoke with him and argued that he should go visit İnönü. Showing respect in this manner would improve relations. When President Bayar heard this suggestion, he dismissed the idea (Ahmet Emin Yalman, *Yakın Tarihte Gördüklerim ve Geçirdiklerim 2*

showing İnönü more respect at this junction would have had more than a palliative effect on partisan animosity seems unlikely. Better personal relations might have led party leaders to temporarily restrain their aggressive rank-and-file members, but the incentives of electoral politics were encouraging both the DP and the opposition parties to mobilize their supporters. The 1957 elections had revealed widespread discontent with the DP, and citizens were continuing to experience economic hardship, which made them amenable to opposition parties' appeals. Moreover, even if the CHP were to pause its campaigning around the country, there was no reason to think the DP would reciprocate. More likely, the government would continue sending ministers to the provinces to hold rallies at factory openings and praise the DP's accomplishments.

Menderes's near-death experience strengthened his position as the preeminent leader in the party and inspired new outpourings of public support. During the months of March and April, new Homeland Front branches opened at a steady clip.[93] Telegrams from citizens joining the organization pointed to Menderes's survival as a reason for their decision to join, often using religious language to emphasize its miraculous quality.[94] In addition to letters, DP papers like *Demokrat Malatya* even published poems dedicated to Menderes. (One from a local master weaver declared, "You made dams, you made roads ... You made all hearts worship God/ Would this homeland also turn into a paradise.")[95] Giving the ruling party time to build on such enthusiasm was not in the interest of opposition leaders.

In late April, İnönü began planning a "spring offensive" through the Aegean provinces of Uşak (which the CHP had won back from the DP in 1957) and İzmir (which was a DP stronghold).[96] Much like the DP's "war of economic independence" rhetoric, the CHP was invoking military terms like "offensive" (*taarruz*) to remind citizens of İnönü's role in liberating the region from Greek occupation. Noting this martial language, editorials at *Havadis* argued it exemplified the opposition's

[Istanbul: Pera Turizm, 1997 (1970)], 1675; Mükkerem Sarol, *Bilinmeyen Menderes*, vol. II [Istanbul: İnkılap, 2014 (1983)], 293–295).

93 "Vatan Cephesi ...," *Zafer*, March 8, 1959, 1; "Dün 3 Vatan ...," *İstanbul Ekspres*, March 16, 1959, 3; "Altındağ'da iki ...," *Zafer*, March 23, 1; "Vatan Cephesi ...," *İstanbul Ekspres*, April 20, 1959, 1.

94 "Abudullah kul" from Malatya's Karnak neighborhood wrote that he was joining the Homeland Front along with ten family members. He regretted having long been devoted to İnönü, who he now realized was only "mortal." He reminded Menderes that "Faith is the savior" and that Menderes should heed its commands (Telegraph, March 9, 1959, BCA 010.09.0.0 216 671 2).

95 Ahmet Turan Erkan, "Adnan Menderes," *Demokrat Malatya*, July 3, 1959, 1.

96 "C.H.P.," *Akis*, April 25, 1959, 7.

continuing preference for "destructive" over "constructive criticism."[97] "Democracy," they explained, "is a regime of votes ... after a government has been determined, until the next election, normal life must return. Yet our [CHP] opposition is moving toward the end of this time with an unexpected degree of haste!"[98]

Though the analysis of *Havadis* writers tended to be highly partisan, they were pointing to a real phenomenon. Following the election, "politics" had not receded to the chambers of parliament. Both parties continued to mobilize and polarize supporters. CHP leaders were openly questioning the legitimacy of the DP government; this had not been the case in 1950 or 1954. Nor had the DP rejected the legitimacy of the opposition in such consistently strong terms prior to the late 1950s. Now, however, conflating the opposition with communism and subversion was becoming the norm. Similarly, while the violent confrontations that occurred during İnönü's "spring offensive" were far from the first to occur, they suggested that violence was becoming a routine element of political contestation.

In Uşak, fighting broke out soon after İnönü arrived on April 30, 1959. As the opposition leader and his entourage of representatives and journalists made their way to the CHP's provincial party offices, they passed by the local DP headquarters. According to pro-DP accounts, CHP representatives taunted DP supporters. According to pro-CHP accounts, the DP provincial party president threw a tea glass at İnönü and hit a reporter from the magazine *Akis* on the head. All accounts agree that the CHP then surrounded DP offices (though only the pro-government accounts emphasize that CHP tossed stones and broke windows). Other confrontations followed when İnönü visited the house where a Greek general had officially handed over control of the city in 1922. According to *Havadis*, dispersing the crowd gathered outside the house "required the use of 8–10 canisters of tear gas."[99] The following day, DP supporters arrived on the scene as the CHP entourage was preparing to leave town for Manisa. They yelled slogans at İnönü such as "We don't want to be jailed for a two-lira road tax!" and "No matter what face you [present to us], we don't want you!" In addition to insults, they hurled stones, one of which hit İnönü in the head.[100] In response to complaints from the CHP that the government had not provided sufficient security,

97 "Muhalefetin Bahar ...," *Havadis*, April 20, 1959, 1, 5.

98 "İlkbahar mütearrızları," *Havadis*, April 21, 1959, 1.

99 "İnönü'nün Uşak'ı ...," *Akşam*, May 1, 1959, 1, 3; "C.H.P. liler Uşak'ta ...," *Havadis*, May 1, 1959, 1, 5; "Demokrasi," *Akis*, May 7, 1959, 4–10.

100 "İnönü atılan ...," *Akşam*, May 2, 1959, 1, 5; quotations from "Uşak'taki ...," *Havadis*, May 2, 1959, 1, 5.

Interior Minister Namık Gedik issued a statement accusing the CHP of causing these disturbances by planning their "spring offensive" in contravention of the Public Meetings and Demonstrations Law. In fact, he suggested, causing this unrest may have been the opposition party's "essential purpose."[101]

On May 2, İnönü's group traveled from Manisa to İzmir. On the way, they were momentarily stopped by a district official who tried to enforce the ban on demonstrations. After some tense arguments with the official and the local gendarmerie, the group continued on. They arrived in İzmir early in the evening and headed to the Ada casino for a banquet in İnönü's honor. The following hours were chaotic. Police were dispatched to the casino following reports of a plot to assassinate İnönü. More police were sent to the DP provincial office to investigate a small explosion that appeared to be a blasting cartridge. While the police were busy, DP party officials bussed supporters to the city center, telling them that their offices had been bombed and directing them to attack the offices of the newspaper *Demokrat İzmir*, which had once supported the DP but now vigorously opposed it.[102] For several hours, police stood by while printing machines were damaged and paper stocks destroyed.[103]

Reporting details of the evening's events was prohibited by order of the interior ministry. Opposition newspapers in Istanbul and Ankara left their headlines blank in protest the following day. *Havadis* opted for the headline "The Grand Offensive (!) That İnönü Engaged in to Set the People against Each Other Causes Calamitous Events."[104] Interior Minister Gedik published a statement accusing the CHP leadership of "exploiting the honorable history of our national struggle" and treating "the administration, the government, and citizens not in their party as invading enemies."[105] The İzmir governor declared a strict ban on political rallies, leaving İnönü with little to do besides visit the CHP offices,

[101] "Tertipcilere cevap," *Zafer*, May 2, 1959, 1. *Havadis* wondered why the CHP had chosen May 1 (i.e., "International Workers Day") to stir up trouble ("C.H.P. hadise," *Havadis*, May 2, 1959, 1).

[102] For an overview of *Demokrat İzmir*'s increasingly hostile relationship with the local and national DP, see Fevzi Solak-Çakmak and Aslı Şener, "Türk Basın Tarihi İçinde Muhalif Bir Gazete-Demokrat İzmir," *Belgi Dergisi* 2, no. 20 (2020): 2488–2491.

[103] Aytaç Demirci and Yusuf Rıza Düvenci, *Bir Mücadele Gazetası! Demokrat İzmir* (Istanbul: Yapı Kredi Yayınları, 2018), 224–237.

[104] "İnönü'nün halkı ...," *Havadis*, May 3, 1959, 1.

[105] "Dahiliye Vekili ...," *Zafer*, May 3, 1959, 1. In February 1960, when CHP legislators demanded an investigation of Gedik for his handling of security during the "spring offensive," Gedik argued that attacks on the offices of Demokrat İzmir were similar – in a positive sense – to the attacks against the publishing house *Tan* that had occurred under CHP rule in 1945. He reminded his peers that the owners of *Tan*, Sabiha and Zekeriya Sertel, were now considered to have "betrayed the homeland" and had fled

inspect the damage done to the *Demokrat İzmir* building, and prepare for his return to Istanbul scheduled for May 4. That morning, as İnönü was setting off, papers like *Zafer* and *Havadis* published further statements from Interior Minister Gedik stating that the CHP was planning a rally to welcome İnönü without having formally applied to his ministry for permission. He accused the party of "flouting the law" and compared it to the "Fascists marching on Rome … or the SS." He promised to "remove these activities from the root."[106]

When İnönü arrived in Istanbul that afternoon, local DP leaders organized a protest to greet him as he returned from the airport to the city center – the same route Menderes had triumphantly taken on his return from London ten weeks earlier. The crowd confronted İnönü at Topkapı, near the old city walls. It attacked his car and might have done worse if a detachment of soldiers had not arrived to disperse it. As in İzmir, detailed reporting on these events was prohibited.[107] Reflecting on the previous week's events, editors at *Havadis* argued that the CHP were ignoring the will of the voters with their aggressive campaigning and suggested that "if the opposition established a dictatorship through force … it is not hard to imagine what they would do."[108]

Such an accusation in a major daily paper echoed the generally more strident claims in provincial DP papers. Only a few months earlier, for example, the Malatya paper *Gayret* had suggested that opponents of the government blamed the public for supporting the DP and "mutter, 'If we should come to power [once more], then we know we'd take our revenge on the nation.'" More recently, it had echoed the interior minister, observing that when Hitler was leader of his nation's opposition, he too "promised more freedoms to the German people." *Demokrat Malatya*, meanwhile, declared that opposition "politicians [were] not even hesitating from betraying the country," which made the DP "the only political institution in the country making an effort to sustain the legitimate and democratic system in this country today." Even a paper like *Balıkesir*,

abroad. The implication was that the same fate awaited anti-DP publishers (TBMM, February 15, 1960, 814).

106 "Hükümetin C.H.P. ye …," *Zafer*, May 4, 1959, 1; "Dahiliye Vekili …," *Havadis*, May 4, 1959, 1, 5. Opposition papers like *Akşam* also ran Gedik's statement but paired with a statement from the CHP ("İnönü bugün …," *Akşam*, May 4, 1, 3, 5).

107 Nedret Selçuker, "Topkapı hadisesi," *Milliyet*, June 21, 1960, 4; "Tanıklar Topkapı …," *Milliyet*, December 14, 1960, 1, 5; M. Hakan Koçak, "Ellili Yıllarda Emek Rejimi ve Emek Hareketi," in *Türkiye'nin 1950'li Yılları*, ed. Mete Kaan Kaynar (Istanbul: İletişim Yayınları, 2015), 90.

108 "Vatandaşlar huzur …," *Havadis*, May 8, 1959, 1, 5.

which was generally more restrained, reported on events in early May with the headline "CHP Uses Insurrectionary Methods."[109]

In Ankara, the CHP demanded a formal investigation into events in Uşak, İzmir, and Istanbul, but the DP majority rejected such an investigation. Instead, the DP resumed consideration of its committee report from December 1958, which recommended banning "journalists who habitually published false news" from the profession and placing strict limitations on political campaigning.[110] Though the recommendations were not implemented, the group issued a statement on May 14, 1959, accusing the CHP of "violating national unity and solidarity." The next day, fights erupted between CHP and DP members of parliament.[111] During the following two weeks, party leaders worked to ease tensions.[112]

Though physical confrontations stopped, little more came in the way of conciliatory efforts. Nor were relations between the parties improved by a series of court rulings penalizing pro-CHP publications. On May 16, the official CHP newspaper, *Ulus*, was suspended for two months and *Akis* for one month. *Akis* was closed for a column that "belittled" Menderes. *Ulus* was closed for translating and publishing a series of critical articles by an American journalist.[113] Other papers had also published the articles, and separate prosecutions would lead to the imprisonment of prominent liberal publisher Ahmet Emin Yalman and the temporary closure of his paper, *Vatan*.[114] *Ulus*'s closure was extended

[109] "Demokrasiyi ...," *Gayret*, December 8, 1958, 1; "Demokrat Parti'nin ...," *Demokrat Malatya*, May 2, 1959, 1; "CHP İhtilal ...," *Balıkesir*, May 5, 1959, 1; "Daha çok ...," *Gayret*, May 7, 1960, 1.

[110] "CHP ...," *Akşam*, May 7, 1959, 1, 5. For the original report, see "Demokrat Parti Meclis Grubu Başkanlığına," December 24, 1958, BCA 010.09.0.0 21 59 10.

[111] "D.P. Meclis Grubu ...," *Zafer*, May 15, 1959, 1; "Millet Meclisinde ...," *İstanbul Ekspres*, May 16, 1959, 1, 5.

[112] Osman Bölükbaşı, head of the Republican Peasants' Nation Party, attempted to reduce tensions by mediating between İnönü and Menderes, but had little success. Menderes even used Bölükbaşı's moderation as a hook for encouraging other Republican Peasants' Nation Party members to join the DP (Çaylak, *Osman Bölükbaşı*, 363–369).

[113] Eugene Pulliam, the publisher of the *Indianapolis Star*, traveled with his wife to Turkey in September 1958. Their account of the visit was published on the front page with the headlines "Vain 'Dictator' Bankrupts Turkey: US-Aided Ally Slips back into 'Sick Man' Role" and "Turkey Premier Wastes Funds to Build Power" (*Indianapolis Star*, October 1 and 2, 1958).

[114] "Ulus 2, Akis 1 ...," *Milliyet*, May 17, 1959, 1, 5. *Vatan*'s initial sentence was handed down on May 30, but it was not reaffirmed on appeal until December. Commenting on *Vatan*'s closure, DP parliamentarian and owner of *Havadis* Bahadır Dülger wrote a column in *Zafer* titled "This Is Turkey, Gentlemen," which argued that Pulliam's article was "full, head to toe, with slander." He went on to argue that foreign journalists didn't understand Turkey well enough to voice opinions about it. Lacking knowledge, their views were shaped by their CHP interlocutors who criticized Turkey and functioned as

for another month on May 27 – the same day that the DP paper, *Zafer*, lost its own case on appeal and was forced to close for a month as punishment for its coverage of a CHP member.[115] The day following this ruling against the pro-government paper, there were reports that a press amnesty was in the works. Though nothing ultimately came of it, talk of "amnesty" for various crimes would be a frequent topic of press coverage during the rest of the year. A bill forgiving numerous traffic crimes was approved by the parliament's justice committee. When the new parliamentary year started, DP legislators suggested passing it as a way of celebrating the party's tenth anniversary in power.[116] As a consequence of these proposals, headlines holding out the possibility of forgiveness in the future shared space with reports of more journalists going to prison in the present.

News of shortages was less prominent in the headlines. From June to October – typically, the worst months – there were fewer reports than in previous years. The government announced three sizeable import quotas during 1959, which provided merchants the opportunity to obtain foreign exchange and import raw materials, spare parts, and high-demand goods like coffee. The price of cement, steel, and paper was also lowered in July.[117] The availability of necessities, however, did not lead to widespread public contentment. Food prices rose. In late June, the price of bread in Istanbul was effectively raised by reducing the weight of a standard TL0.60 loaf by about one-third – or, as the pro-government paper *Havadis* optimistically reported, "Grams lowered: price the

a "fifth column in Istanbul and Ankara" ("Burası Türkiye Beyler," *Zafer*, December 28, 1959, 1).

115 "Cihat Baban …," *Milliyet*, February 14, 1959, 1, 5; "Zafer Gazetesi …," *Milliyet*, November 22, 1958, 1, 5; "Zafer ve Yenigün …," *Akşam*, May 28, 1959, 1, 5; "Ulus bir ay …," *Milliyet*, May 28, 1959, 1, 5. *Zafer* was ordered to close in November 1958 (owing to its coverage of CHP member Asım Eren); it appealed. Its editor-in-chief, Cenap Yakar, and writer Zühtü Hilmi Velibeşe (a former DP parliamentarian) were sentenced to ten months in jail. Velibeşe's sentence was reduced by one-sixth on account of age. On the same day, the anti-government paper *Yenigün* lost an appeal and was closed for a month. Its overseers, Mehmet Ali Kışla and Cihad Baban, were sentenced to a year in jail for "belittling" DP member Sever Somuncuoğlu in an article published prior to his death in the February 1959 London plane crash.

116 "Basın için …," *İstanbul Ekspres*, May 29, 1959, 1; "Komisyon düne …," *Akşam*, June 9, 1959, 1; "Bazı D.P. mebusları …," *Havadis*, November 10, 1959, 1. *Havadis* conducted man-in-the-street interviews, asking Istanbullus whether they favored an amnesty. Most respondents were supportive of a general amnesty for journalists and "nonmalicious" crimes; some favored including sex crimes and honor killings. Most emphasized that crimes against the state and membership in a communist organization should not be pardoned – and none argued to the contrary (Mehmet Lütfi Ballısoy, "'Af' haberleri …," *Havadis*, November 11, 1959, 3; Mehmet Lütfi Ballısoy, "Af hakkındaki …," *Havadis*, November 25, 1959, 3).

117 "Çimento …," *Tercüman*, July 4, 1959, 5.

same."[118] A day after the prices went into effect, *Havadis* also reported that a bakery owner ("a CHP guy") had thrown 2,000 loaves into the ocean, possibly because of mold – but also possibly, the paper speculated, to create an artificial shortage.[119] Increases in bread prices were coupled with a roughly 10 percent increase in the price guaranteed to farmers for the coming harvest.[120] In combination, these economic policies were in keeping with the DP government's overall strategy of satisfying rural voters at the risk of angering urban voters on fixed incomes.

Throughout the year, the Eisenhower administration signaled its support for the DP government. In March, Turkey (along with Pakistan and Iran) signed bilateral defense cooperation agreements with the United States. These agreements were part of a larger effort to revive the Baghdad Pact as CENTO following Iraq's exit. They "reaffirmed" the American willingness to provide military and economic support to help Turkey and its peers resist "aggression." During an October meeting of the organization, Menderes and Zorlu agreed to base intermediate-range nuclear missiles in Turkey. In doing so, they increased the likelihood that Turkey would be the target of a Soviet first strike in the event of a war. They returned from the meeting having secured a commitment of $80 million in aid from the United States in the coming year.[121] In December, Eisenhower made his first visit to Turkey. A clear sign of confidence in the government.

International institutions offered more measured support throughout 1959. In late June, the deputy secretary general of the OEEC arrived in Ankara to observe Turkey's progress on implementing economic reforms. His final report balanced an optimistic assessment of the reforms with doubt that Turkey would be in a position to support itself in the near future.[122] An equally ambivalent response came from officials at the newly established European Economic Community (EEC), which included France, West Germany, Italy, Belgium, Luxembourg, and the Netherlands. The EEC had been created by these states to maintain trade restrictions in the face of pressure from larger institutions like the OEEC, which advocated for liberalization.[123] From the perspective of Zorlu and other Turkish leaders, it was important to seek membership in

118 "Ekmek ...," *Havadis*, June 16, 1959, 1; "Ekmeğin ...," *Akşam*, June 17, 1959, 1.
119 "Bir fırın ...," *Havadis*, June 27, 1959, 1, 5.
120 "Hububat ...," *Akşam*, June 14, 1959, 1, 3; Commercial Department to Southern Department, June 18, 1959, 371/144755.
121 Charles Heathcote-Smith to J. S. Sadler, November 6, 1959, FO 371/144759.
122 For Secretary General John Cahan's report, see John Flint Cahan, "Report on a Visit to Turkey," July 6, 1959, FO 371/144762.
123 Paul Pitman, "'A General Named Eisenhower': Atlantic Crisis and the Origins of the European Economic Community," in *Between Empire and Alliance: America and Europe during the Cold War*, ed. Marc Trachtenberg (New York: Roman & Littlefield, 2003),

order to secure preferential deals with member states. With US support, Turkey's application was accepted for consideration, but the EEC leadership remained cool to the possibility of Turkey actually joining.[124]

The sharpest criticism of Turkey's policies came from the UN's Food and Agriculture Organization. A report on Turkey (the Baade Report) circulated in 1959, warning that current agricultural practices were unsustainable. Rather than increasing the yield of a given field through the use of fertilizers, farmers were using their newly purchased tractors to expand the area under cultivation or used for grazing. These methods were exhausting the soil and leading to erosion. The report recommended increased reliance on irrigation and fertilizers.[125] It recommended billions of dollars in investments over the coming decade.[126] Implementing these recommendations was difficult, however. During the summer, Turkish officials were in talks with an Italian firm to develop a large-scale irrigation system in the Konya-Antalya region, but the plan was given up when the Italians balked at the cost – $60 million in the short term and $800 million overall. Additionally, they worried that Turkey's foreign investment laws would not guarantee them the imports they required to complete the project.[127]

Foreign Minister Zorlu had been pushing since the beginning of the year for credits above and beyond those offered in July–August 1958. As the year progressed and Turkey's export earnings remained lower than expected, his requests grew impatient.[128] In late September 1959, Zorlu asked US officials for help in securing $92 million in short-term loans to get Turkey through the next three months. The request surprised the Americans and their peers at the IMF and OEEC with whom Zorlu had recently given a figure of $95 million *for the entire year*. The following week, amid CENTO meetings and discussions of missile placements, Zorlu asked US officials to pressure their allies in West Germany to give Turkey more loans. When US embassy officials in Bonn broached the subject, West German officials observed that

36–42; Martin Dedman, *The Origins and Development of the European Union 1945–2008: A History of European Integration*, 2nd ed. (London: Routledge, 2009), 51–83.

[124] For a discussion of US support for Turkey's inclusion in the EEC, see Armağan Emre Çakır, *The United States and Turkey's Path to Europe: Hands across the Table* (New York: Routledge, 2016).

[125] The report on Turkish agriculture by Fritz Baade is discussed in Bernard Burrows to Selwyn Lloyd, July 10, 1959, FO 371/144755.

[126] Lewis Jones to Undersecretary, September 24, 1959, RG 59, Lot 62, Box 1.

[127] Charles Heathcote-Smith to J. S. Sadler, October 10, 1959, FO 371/144759.

[128] In November 1959, the Turkish government announced that export earnings for the second half of the year were likely to be $105 million, one-third less than predicted (Charles Heathcote-Smith to J. S. Sadler, November 6, 1959, FO 371/144759).

Zorlu's requests were not "factually supported."[129] Nonetheless, Turkish officials submitted a request for $70 million to the board of OEEC-managed European Monetary Agreement. The board unanimously agreed that it could not recommend the request.[130]

Western European governments' limited willingness to give additional aid only seemed to encourage Zorlu in his aggressive tactics. In advance of Eisenhower's December visit to Turkey, Zorlu suggested to the West German ambassador that "other possibilities existed" for Turkey and conspicuously attended a dinner with the Soviet ambassador.[131] Two days after Eisenhower's departure from Turkey, the minister of health was sent off to the USSR on an official visit. By the end of December, British diplomats reported, a deal had been signed under which the USSR would provide Turkey £2.7 million ($7.6 million) in credit to build three textile factories.[132] A trade deal was signed in March 1960. Soon after, Menderes received an invitation to visit Moscow.[133]

Many accounts of the DP suggest that these moves by Menderes's government to improve relations with the USSR were the cause of its downfall (insinuating that the coup of May 1960 was a US-backed effort).[134] Yet this connection is tenuous for several reasons. First, junior officers had been plotting as far back as 1953–54, when relations with the USSR remained hostile.[135] Second, Zorlu broached the idea of the prime minister's visit to Moscow to US officials in January 1960 and received a positive response from the ambassador in early February.[136] And, third, Turkey's warmer relations with the USSR were a step *behind* the United States itself. The British prime minister had visited Moscow in February 1959, and the Soviet premier, Nikita Khrushchev, had visited the United States in September 1959. Only French and West German delaying

[129] Donald Kennedy to Under Secretary, November 12, 1959, RG 59, Lot 62, Box 1.

[130] David Pitblado to Hugh Ellis-Rees, November 20, 1959, FO 371/144763. The European Monetary Agreement was the successor organization to the EPU.

[131] Charles Heathcote-Smith to J. S. Sadler, December 3, 1959, FO 371/144759.

[132] Bernard Burrows to Selwyn Lloyd, January 26, 1960, FO 371/153030.

[133] The trade deal with the USSR was made under the terms of an existing 1937 agreement. It was not passed into law until August 1960 ("Soviet, Turkey in Pact," *Washington Post*, March 15, 1960, A15; RG, August 19, 1960).

[134] In his influential account of modern Turkey, Doğan Avcıoğlu concluded his discussion of the DP by saying: "Menderes … announced he was going to Moscow. This was Menderes's end" (Avcıoğlu, *Türkiye'nin Düzeni*, 585).

[135] Hale, *Turkish Politics and the Military*, 98–104; Aslan, *The United States and Military*, 115–125.

[136] Christopher Gunn, "The 1960 Coup in Turkey: US Intelligence Failure or a Successful Intervention?," *Journal of Cold War Studies* 17, no. 2 (2015): 133–134. Also see Behçet Kemal Yeşilbursa, "The 'Revolution' of 27 May 1960 in Turkey: British Policy towards Turkey," *Middle Eastern Studies* 41, no. 1 (2005): 121–151.

tactics had pushed a major summit in Paris as late as May 1960. Thereafter, Eisenhower was scheduled to tour the USSR in June.[137] Menderes would simply be following in the footsteps of his US and Western European counterparts.[138]

The more interesting question may be why Menderes and his allies continued their conflation of the opposition with communism and subversion as they themselves were seeking warmer relations with the world's leading communist regime. During the 1959 summer recess, Menderes sent a circular to party offices accusing the CHP of practicing "Balkan Komiteciliği," the sort of separatist intrigues that had undermined the Ottoman Empire.[139] The state-controlled program *Radyo Gazetesi* also stepped up its criticism of the opposition, accusing the CHP of starting a "cold war" through its refusal to acknowledge DP accomplishments.[140] Speaking to a DP district congress in Istanbul's Fatih neighborhood on August 23, Samet Ağaoğlu contrasted the peacefulness of the DP era with the violence of the Ottoman, and of the CHP regime. He recalled walking through nearby Beyazit Square as a child, seeing bodies hanging from the gallows, and declared, "There is a freedom [now] without bayonets or gallows … There is now freedom of speech and of the pen in the broadest definition. Swear words and

[137] Eisenhower's visit to the USSR was canceled in the wake of the "U-2 Crisis," in which a US pilot was shot down while violating Soviet airspace and photographing military installations (William Taubman, *Khrushchev: The Man and His Era* [New York: W. W. Norton, 2003], 440–455).

[138] In a private meeting with Burrows, the British ambassador, Zorlu explained (perhaps self-servingly) that *even* the Soviets thought that "Turkey would be the last of the Western Powers to partake in the general détente atmosphere which was now spreading through Western Europe" (Bernard Burrows to John Addis, December 5, 1959. FO/371 144763).

[139] "D.P. teşkilatına …," *Milliyet*, July 9, 1959, 1, 5. While the DP leaders' conflation of their political opponents with communists might be explained away as partisan hyperbole, communist-linked subversion was a real concern for state officials. In Iraq in late July 1959, conflict between Kurdish and Turkmen communities turned deadly in Kirkuk, where Kurds dominated the local Communist Party and the security forces. The killings were denounced by Turkish nationalist politicians in Turkey, which led Kurdish students at Istanbul University to protest in late August. The following month, the writer Musa Anter published a poem ("Kımıl" [Wheat Bug]) in his magazine *İleri Yurt* (Progressive Country), criticizing the treatment of Kurds. Concerned that events in Iraq were encouraging ethnic divisions in Turkey, the DP government arrested and prosecuted Anter and several dozen Kurdish intellectuals ("102 üniversiteli kürtlük …," *Akşam*, August 15, 1959, 1; Batatu, *The Old Social Classes*, 912–921; Arbella Bet-Shlimon, *City of Black Gold: Oil, Ethnicity, and the Making of Modern Kirkuk* [Stanford: Stanford University Press, 2019], 145–154; Béatrice Garapon and Adnan Çelik, "From Tribal Chiefs to Marxist Activists: Kurdistan from 1946 to 1975," in *The Cambridge History of the Kurds*, ed. Hamit Bozarslan, Cengiz Güneş, and Veli Yadirgi [Cambridge: Cambridge University Press, 2021], 235–236).

[140] "C.H.P. nin inkârcı …," *Havadis*, August 1, 1959, 1.

slander are what's forbidden. Entering into the privacy of family matters, attacks on honor and dignity – that's what's forbidden."[141] He did not mention freedom to assemble in public outside of a conference hall like the one in which he spoke. This omission enabled him to gloss over tensions both across the country and within the DP.

The Homeland Front had swelled DP membership. It offered former party dissidents an opportunity to return, and it had coerced many citizens into joining for the first time. The surge in membership had created tensions within local party organizations. As the historian Zehra Arslan describes, in provinces like Trabzon, the return of powerful figures and their supporters led to power struggles in local organizations.[142] The general tumult also accentuated preexisting power struggles. In İzmir, for example, a member of the provincial central committee was expelled. The inciting incident had not originated from the Homeland Front mobilization, but, after the fact, the local party attributed his expulsion to a larger struggle against "factionalism" and warned of CHP efforts to "infiltrate" the party via newly established branches.[143]

Party leaders sought to vet new applicants and maintain their control of local organizations, which led to fights at local congresses between new and old members. Just three weeks before Ağaoğlu spoke in Fatih, for example, he had come to Istanbul with two other representatives to investigate a fight that broke out at the Zeytinburnu district congress. There, local DP leaders had refused entry to a group of would-be attendees, prompting these self-identified party members to pull out guns and begin firing in the air. Police had arrived on the scene and dispersed the crowd by also firing skyward. The café hosting the congress was destroyed in the fighting.[144]

Even more common than violence between DP factions was violence directed against the CHP. In mid July, police fired into the air to disperse the crowd outside a CHP congress in İzmir.[145] In early August, in the Black Sea city of Samsun, police dispersed a crowd gathered on the waterfront to meet the CHP general secretary, Kasım Gülek, as he

141 "Fatih kongresinde …," *Havadis*, August 24, 1959, 1, 5.

142 Arslan, "Trabzon'da Vatan Cephesi," 133–138.

143 "D.P. deki hizipçiler …," *Milliyet*, August 2, 1959, 1, 5. The expelled DP committee member, Osman Kibar, was an influential soap manufacturer in İzmir, who had been active in the party since its creation (Donald Eddy to John Goodyear, November 10, 1958, RG 59, Lot 61, Box 17; "Bir C.H.P.li …," *Milliyet*, November 28, 1959, 3).

144 "D.P.'nin 2 toplantısı …," *Tercüman*, July 27, 1959, 1, 5; "D.P. il teşkilatına …," *Milliyet*, July 28, 1959, 1, 5.

145 "CHP Kongresinde …," *Milliyet*, July 13, 1959, 1, 5.

arrived for a provincial congress. Gülek faced similar problems in early September, when he and his entourage were attacked while touring the coastal province of Çanakkale. When a pair of CHP representatives traveled to the region by boat a week later to conduct an "investigation" into the situation, a local DP representative told them not to come ashore.[146] At nightfall, they made their way to land regardless. When news of their arrival spread, they were approached by threatening crowds and decided to return to Istanbul.

Interior Minister Namık Gedik issued an official statement accusing the CHP representatives of stirring up trouble both in Çanakkale and around the country. He dismissed the notion that they had any authority as "inspectors" and stated:

> There can be no state within a state, no government within a government ... The government will not be your guard, the enabler of your revolutionary agitations or your illegal and illegitimate activities, which you conduct in the name of "liberty of travel," as you go around, wrapped in the armor of parliamentary immunity.[147]

When the representatives arrived in Istanbul on September 24, the crowd that had gathered to greet them was dispersed by the police. Eleven people were arrested. *Radyo Gazetesi* reported on the events, declaring that "It's time to say, 'That's enough' to these political festivities."[148]

During fall 1959, radio announcers got their wish, and the political temperature fell several degrees. One reason was Menderes's absence. The prime minister traveled to the United States for two weeks to attend a CENTO meeting, and, as much as they might disagree, the parties generally offered a united front for the purposes of foreign policy. Consequently, criticism of Menderes remained muted until his return midway into the month. Likewise, Eisenhower's visit in December may have paused partisan disputes. A second factor reducing interparty discord was discord within the CHP itself. On September 27, General Secretary Kasım Gülek resigned, forced out by opponents within the party. Gülek had been a rival of party leader İsmet İnönü, and his departure led to a period of retrenchment in the CHP. İnönü now consolidated his grip on the party and began talking of possible elections in the coming year.[149]

146 According to Metin Toker (no fan of CHP General Secretary Kasım Gülek), the attacks on Gülek in Geyikli, Çanakkale came at a time when Gülek had lost support among the CHP leadership. The inspection was as much to check on Gülek's story as it was to check the situation itself (Toker, *Demokrasiden Darbeye*, 245).

147 "Menderes Gedikle ...," *Cumhuriyet*, September 24, 1959, 1, 5.

148 "Dün geceki ...," *Havadis*, September 26, 1959, 1, 5.

149 "İnönü seçim ...," *Milliyet*, October 12, 1959, 1, 5. By 1959, Gülek had burned numerous bridges with other CHP leaders as well as many members of the HP,

Menderes was also considering calling early elections. His control over the DP was secure, and the economic situation was improving. At the start of the parliamentary year, the internal party opposition led by Sıtkı Yırcalı attempted to replace Refik Koraltan as president of parliament but lost 218–121.[150] As the legislative session started, the DP considered bills to create new (presumably DP-leaning) provinces.[151] A 1960–61 budget of TL7.26 million was proposed on December 1, with a supplemental budget of nearly TL363,000. If passed, it would be a 23 percent increase on the previous year. It was structured as an election year budget with more than one-third devoted to investments like roads, water systems, and village schools.[152] In front of the DP parliamentary group on December 10, just days after President Eisenhower had departed, Menderes broached the possibility of early elections by confidently declaring that "We should have the elections today, my God is the witness, I'm 100 percent sure we would win."[153]

Preparing for Victory: The DP's Final Electoral Campaign

During the final months of DP rule, the government and opposition prepared for elections. Both the DP and CHP mobilized their supporters in the provinces and in national institutions like universities, all the while accusing one another of undermining the democratic order. The CHP accused the DP of appealing to religious groups in a manner inappropriate for a secular republic. The DP accused the CHP of destabilizing the country by means of public rallies and secret plotting. The government's unwillingness to let the opposition organize and the opposition's

which had recently merged with the CHP. In July, the pro-İnönü (and, thus, anti-Gülek) magazine *Akis* printed a letter from Gülek to NATO secretary Colonel Johannes Fens, asking to be invited to a London meeting and questioning the qualifications of the CHP member who had been sent, Malatya representative Nüvit Yetkin. Under pressure for disparaging a fellow party member, Gülek finally resigned in September ("Başbakanın …," *Akis*, July 28, 1959, 11; Toker, *Demokrasiden Darbeye*, 247–254).

150 Burçak, *On Yılın Anıları*, 634. Koraltan's fellow İçel (Mersin) representative, Hüseyin Fırat, supported Yırcalı but recalls that Koraltan held no grudge (despite his reputation as being egotistical). At lunch after the vote, Koraltan declared it was simply "the necessities of political life" and suggested the matter be left there (BCA 010.09.00.00 45 134 6).

151 "Villayet olacak …," *Zafer*, November 9, 1959, 1. The districts under consideration were Merzifon, Kırıkkale, Beypazarı, Iğdır, Ardahan, Kilis, Divriği, İskenderun, Karaman, Akşehir, Konya-Ereğlisi, and Aksaray. Many of these would later become provinces.

152 Bernard Burrows to Selwyn Lloyd, December 8, 1959, FO 371/144758.

153 DPMGZ, December 10, 1959; 259.

unwillingness to obey the restrictive Public Meetings and Demonstrations Law led to a series of confrontations. The DP leadership responded by considering more serious restrictions, including closing the CHP. The move provoked protests in Istanbul and Ankara, plunged the country into a political crisis, and provided would-be revolutionaries in the military with the opportunity they desired.

By early January 1960, Menderes and İnönü were trading barbs: the prime minister broadcasting over the radio, the opposition leader responding in speeches at provincial congresses and press conferences. İnönü called for elections and warned the government of the dangers to follow if it did not relinquish power. He accused Menderes of coordinating with Said Nursi, the leader of a popular Sunni religious order that numbered in the hundreds of thousands. There were grounds for his suspicion: Said Nursi had been an advocate of the DP for some time, and, in 1958, Menderes had visited the small town of Emirdağ, where Nursi lived. In 1959, Nursi made a series of highly publicized visits to Istanbul and Ankara.[154]

Menderes also appealed to other religious groups. In February 1960, he visited the tomb of Hacı Bektaş, a saint important both to Alevi Muslims and Sunni Muslim members of the Bektashi Sufi order. *Zafer* followed up his visit with a column that declared "The order of Saint Hacı Bektaş is a Turkish order particular to Anatolia. The saint's tomb is an Anatolian Karbala" (a reference to the Iraqi city sacred for Shia Muslims).[155] The description emphasized both the nationalist

[154] Said Nursi (1876–1960) applied Islamic principles to such contemporary concerns as modern technology. In 1909, he was accused of conspiring to remove the İTC from power (but was found innocent); he supported the Independence War (but was never close to Mustafa Kemal); and he was exiled to Burdur after the Shaykh Sait Revolt in 1925 (but was never central to the uprising). In the 1930s and 1940s, he wrote and disseminated his religious commentaries and expanded his following. During the 1950s, he received support from members of the DP such as Tahsin Tola (a representative from Isparta, where Nursi had been forced to settle). Tola secured Menderes's support for the Latin-script publication of Nursi's books, as well as the paper allocation necessary for manufacturing it (Şerif Mardin, *Religion and Social Change in Modern Turkey: The Case of Bediuzzaman Said Nursi* [Albany: State University of New York Press, 1989], 42; Umut Azak, *Islam and Secularism in Turkey: Kemalism, Religion and the Nation State* [London: I. B. Tauris, 2010], 115–131).

[155] Ragıp Akyavaş, "İmar ve ihya," *Zafer*, February 14, 1960, 2. Akyavaş was a retired military officer and teacher of legal, religious, and military history at the military academy (*Kara Harp Okulu*) in Ankara. His and Menderes's efforts to reach out to Alevi Muslims and, more generally, include non-Sunni Islamic traditions in a broad "Turkish Islam" represented one side in an ongoing struggle within and between state institutions. According to Ceren Lord, during the 1950s the ministry of education tended to promote the version of Islam that Akyavaş was describing, while the directorate of religious affairs (*Diyanet*) published authors advocating against "esoteric

symbolism of Menderes's visit and the inclusive nature of the nation (and political coalition) he sought to represent. But these symbolic gestures came on top of the radio broadcasts of Koran readings, the restoration of Arabic prayer calls, and the religiously inflected celebrations following Menderes's return from London.[156] Many in Turkey's governing elite who desired a secular state were becoming nervous.

In addition to mobilizing voters by means of religious networks, the DP was still pressing people into the Homeland Front. New branches continued to open. By March 1960, there were 140 in Istanbul alone, and political leaders such as Mayor Aygün and Mükerrem Sarol continued to push state employees to join.[157] Government pressure on merchants also increased. On March 11, Menderes and other cabinet ministers met with businessmen at Istanbul's Park hotel. This and similar meetings, which occurred amid a series of announcements promising more credit and easier import-licensing procedures, were presented in the pro-DP press as efforts to hear the concerns of the business community.[158]

Soon, however, opposition journals like *Forum* were reporting that businessmen were being pressured to join the Homeland Front and give substantial donations to the ruling party.[159] In many cases, the businessmen and other prominent figures simply joined; in other cases, they tried to navigate a middle ground. Just two days after the Park hotel meeting, for example, Turkey's leading industrialist, Vehbi Koç, resigned from the CHP (but without joining the DP).[160] A few members of the business community actively resisted: the day after Koç's announcement, the general secretary of the chamber of commerce resigned from his position,

interpretations" of Islam (Lord, *Religious Politics in Turkey: From the Birth of the Republic to the AKP* [Cambridge: Cambridge University Press, 2018], 138–141).

[156] "Radyo'da Kur'an okunacak, "*Cumhuriyet*, July 6, 1950, 1, 3; Ersarı, "Ellili Yıllarda Radyo ve Siyaset," 411.

[157] "Vatan Cephesi ...," *İstanbul Ekspres*, March 28, 1, 5; Arslan, "Vatan Cephesi Davası," 9–12. In March 1960, in a typical example of pressuring government workers to join the Homeland Front, employees at the cement industry directorate were (allegedly) told to join or lose their jobs. After the coup, when these accusations were being investigated, General Director Selahattin Akyol claimed that he was only enforcing the wishes of Industry Minister Sebati Ataman (BCA 010.09.0.00 220 683 2).

[158] "Milli Korunma ...," *Havadis*, March 11, 1960, 1, 5; "İktisadi Tedbirler ...," *İstanbul Ekspres*, March 11, 1, 5; "İktisadi Tedbirler ...," *Akşam*, March 13, 1960, 1, 3; "Esnafa ...," *İstanbul Ekspres*, March 17, 1, 5.

[159] Betty Carp to State, June 7, 1960, RG 84, Box 121, UD 3296, NNND948832 (hereafter RG 84 Box 121).

[160] "Vehbi Koç ...," *Zafer*, March 13, 1960, 1. For a discussion of Vehbi Koç and how he drew on his connections with the state during the single-party era, see Ayşe Buğra, *State and Business in Modern Turkey: A Comparative Study* (Albany: State University of New York Press, 1994), 77–79.

claiming he was being pressured by other members of the executive committee to join the DP, which he did not view as "appropriate."[161]

While the DP's electoral strategy was to leverage its control of the government to gain the support of state employees and businessmen, the CHP's strategy was to highlight the DP's corruption and its role in organizing the political violence of the previous year. In mid February, CHP members of parliament demanded a series of investigations into various matters, including: the attacks on İnönü in Uşak; the government's partisan use of the radio; loans from Ziraat Bankası to particular firms; management of the Meat and Fish Board (*Et ve Balık Kurumu*); improper seizures of property under eminent-domain law; questionable financial transfers to the DP Youth Arm; and nepotism in the tendering process. The final accusation was a rehash of debates from a year earlier in which CHP representatives had accused Samet Ağaoğlu of awarding the tender for a paper mill to a firm employing the husband of his sister, Süreyya.[162] That year's debate had led to an immediate fistfight; this year, fighting was delayed for a week. All these motions for investigation were rejected by the DP-controlled parliament, which then moved on to discuss the annual budget. During the budget debates, a CHP representative mocked Prime Minister Menderes's general absence from parliamentary debates during the previous year. The vice president of the DP parliamentary group waited in the hallway during recess and then punched him in the face. When the session resumed and CHP representatives tried to bring up the incident, President of Parliament Refik Koraltan wondered, "What's the relevance of an incident that happened outside [the chamber]?"[163] Before the week finished, there was at least one more fight – this time in the chamber.[164]

Political violence was not contained to the parliament building. During March, police in Istanbul dispersed CHP-affiliated women holding a meeting in the neighborhood of Zeytinburnu, as well as students gathered outside the provincial CHP headquarters to greet İnönü, who

[161] "Siyasete zorlanan ...," *Milliyet*, March 14, 1960, 1; A. H. Spire to E. N. Smite, March 25, 1960, FO 371/153049. Following the May 27 coup, the general secretary of the chamber of commerce, Cihat İren, would become minister of trade, serving until August 1960.

[162] See Chapter 6, n. 40.

[163] TBMM, Feburary 24, 1960, 342. Mazlum Kayalar, who punched CHP representative Selim Soley, was a member of Menderes's faction (Burçak, *On Yılın Anıları*, 584–585).

[164] During the Saturday, February 27 session, backbenchers Hasan Erdoğan (CHP, Kars) and Ali Latifoğlu (DP, Isparta) got into a fight after Labor Minister Sebati Ataman replied harshly to a question from a CHP legislator ("Mecliste yine ...," *Milliyet*, February 28, 1960, 1, 5).

was in the city to visit *gecekondu* neighborhoods.[165] Like the DP, CHP leaders were attempting to reach out to voters living in *gecekondu* in advance of the election, and their visits created the potential for new clashes. In Adana, for example, fighting broke out when Kasım Gülek visited a *gecekondu* in the provincial center as part of end-of-Ramadan festivities. As his supporters carried him on their shoulders past the local DP branch, DP partisans yelled, "This is a DP area" and "Men are carried by donkeys, you too are being carried by asses." In the clashes that followed, partisans fought each other with sticks, stones, and shovels. Six DP and four CHP supporters were injured.[166]

The most significant clashes occurred in Yeşilhisar, a town in Kayseri province where the CHP had outperformed the DP in the 1957 elections.[167] Tensions had been building for several months. In mid February 1960 the CHP district president shot and wounded his DP counterpart. The following month, on March 24, the local DP organization lost an election for the town's agricultural cooperative – a crucial institution, given its role in distributing credit, seeds, and machinery to potential voters. DP members attacked the houses of CHP members, leading to clashes and prompting the police to arrest partisans on both sides. The local DP president then intervened to free his allies. CHP supporters protested, and the police opened fire on them, injuring three protesters.[168] A familiar pattern took hold: CHP leaders visited to "investigate" the situation, and the government banned press coverage of events in Yeşilhisar on March 28. That night, *Radyo Gazetesi* declared:

> Since the events in Iraq and the 1957 elections, they [the CHP] have been yearning to reject the regime, the state, its own dear parliament and its laws; to give active demonstrations of their rejection; to make those who are with them momentary, aggressive agents of the same violent policy. In a word, to bring

165 "CHP'li kadınları ...," *Milliyet*, March 7, 1960, 1, 5; "C.H.P.' nin tahrikiyle ...," *Havadis*, March 20, 1960, 1, 5. Pro-CHP papers like *Milliyet* did not emphasize the planned aspect of the student gathering ("31 talebe ...," *Milliyet*, March 30, 1960, 1, 5).

166 "Adana'da DP'li ...," *Milliyet*, April 1, 1960, 1, 5; "Adana'da DP-CHP'liler ...," *Akşam*, April 1, 1960, 1, 5. The pro-DP paper *Havadis* emphasized the provocative aspect of Gülek's visit, explaining that he "had taken sixty to seventy of his supporters to the side of the city with the most DP partisans in order to have his hand be kissed" ("Adana'da müessif ...," *Havadis*, April 1, 1960, 1, 3).

167 Veli Altınkaya, "Demokrasinin idamı ve Yeşilhisar olayları 1," *Kayseri Haber*, May 19, 2015, available: http://kayserihaber.com.tr/mobilYazarlarDetay.aspx?id=3144.

168 "Yeşilhisar'da 10 kişi ...," *Milliyet*, March 26, 1960, 1; *Akis*, March 30, 1960, 7–8; Toker, *Demokrasiden Darbeye*, 304–305; Esma Küçükşahin, "27 Mayıs'a giden yolda 'Yeşilhisar olayları,'" *Anadolu Ajansı*, May 24, 2018, available: www.aa.com.tr/tr/demokrasinin-infazi-27–mayis/27–mayisa-giden-yolda-yesilhisar-olaylari/1155518.

about a state in this country where it is natural to declare an *uprising* [italics added].[169]

İnönü had already been planning to attend the CHP provincial congress in Kayseri on April 3. Though all local political activity was now canceled by the government, İnönü continued with his plans to visit the province. What followed were, according to political scientist Cem Eroğul, "the events that signaled the beginning of the end" for the DP.[170] While this characterization may give insufficient consideration to the military coup plotters, whose plans were already well underway, İnönü's visit was crucial in prompting the DP parliamentary group to consider investigating (and, perhaps, closing) the CHP, thereby setting in motion the cycle of protests, crackdowns, and further protests that served as the pretext for military intervention.

On the way to Kayseri, İnönü's train was halted on orders from the governor.[171] İnönü dismissed the idea that the governor had the authority to limit his movement, and a three-hour standoff ensued before the governor (and the government in Ankara) relented and allowed İnönü to continue. The following day (April 3), İnönü and his entourage attempted to drive back to Ankara along a route that would pass Yeşilhisar. Again, they were blocked, this time by a military barricade – which was particularly significant, since gendarmes rather than soldiers were typically used for enforcing order in the provinces.[172] After a period of argument between CHP parliamentarians in İnönü's entourage and government officials, İnönü stepped out of his car and marched toward the military barricade. As his son-in-law, Metin Toker, reported the event, "He went among the soldiers and ... brushing the shoulders of these brave kids, pushed them aside. The barricade was suddenly opened. Everyone was frozen. The officers stood at attention."[173]

169 "'C.H.P. asiliğin ...,'" *İstanbul Ekspres*, March 28, 1960, 1, 5.

170 Eroğul, *Demokrat Parti*, 227.

171 The Kayseri governor in April 1960 was Ahmet Kınık. His biography provides yet another example of how muddy partisan distinctions remained throughout the period 1945–60. He had previously served as governor in Malatya from 1943 to 1949. During this time, he was accused of manipulating local elections to favor the CHP and wasting public funds on unwanted statutes of President İnönü. He went on to serve as a governor in Eskişehir and Adana. He then returned to Ankara for a year to serve as an advisor to the interior minister before being nominated as a DP candidate for Adana in the 1954 elections. He served one term but was not placed on the candidate list for 1957. Instead, he was appointed governor of Kayseri. Rather than being removed after the May 1960 coup, he retired in August 1960 (Cingöz, "Belediye Başkan ile ...," *Yeni Malatya*, May 31, 1950, 1–2; "Demokrat Parti ...," *Zafer*, October 8, 1957, 1; Kısacık, *Malatya'da Toplumsal*, 123–124).

172 Robinson, *The First Turkish Republic*, 263.

173 *Akis*, April 6, 1960, 10.

İnönü repeated this act of defiance once more with a second line of soldiers. Having made his point, he turned back. His entourage returned to Ankara by an alternative route. Toker's account of the event was published in the April 6 edition of *Akis*. He followed his description of İnönü's Moses-like parting of the soldiers with the following historical allusion:

No one would have had the power to change the direction [İnönü] had chosen. But he lacked the slightest ambition to play the game of Napoleon who, after his departure from Elba and arrival at Golfe-Juan, received an official salute from the detachment sent against him and, with their participation, marched on Paris. [İnönü] had the intention of using only one weapon: free elections.[174]

The day after the magazine (with its implied threat) hit the newsstands, the DP parliamentary group met and voted to form a commitee to prepare for a parliamentary investigation of the CHP. Though the official press release would declare that the decision had been unanimous, it was actually opposed by a number of representatives, including Sıtkı Yırcalı. The committee that was formed included Menderes allies such as Mükerrem Sarol, Bahadır Dülger, and Sait Bilgiç (who had been expelled from the party in 1953–54 for his ties with the Turkish Nationalists Association). On April 12, the committee accused the CHP of misleading the public and politicizing the military. It recommended the creation of a special parliamentary-level "Investigation Commission" (*Tahkikat Komisyonu*) with the power to formally investigate the CHP and halt all political activity in the country for the duration of its investigations. This too was approved by the group. On April 18, the leaders of the parliamentary group formally submitted their accusations to the general assembly.

The DP's accusations brought together a series of attacks that the party leaders and media had been making for months.[175] In addition to those mentioned already, these included charges that the CHP was arming its

[174] *Akis*, April 6, 1960, 10.

[175] Since a *Radyo Gazetesi* broadcast on the night of April 5, 1960, the DP had been accusing the CHP of forming an underground organization. The evidence was a "secret memo" to local CHP organizations sent on March 21. As for the accusations of coordinating with communist radio: according to Burçak, DP leaders like Tevfik Ileri had been complaining about *Bizim Radyo* since at least May 12, 1958. The DP's complaints that the CHP was spreading rumors about Turkish girls being "offered up to Americans" dates back to at least February 12, 1960, when a DP representative used it as a justification for the party's attempt to reduce the length of the electoral campaign season from forty-five to seventeen days in order, he argued, to limit such propaganda ("Propaganda …," *Milliyet*, February, 13, 1960, 1; "Beynelmilel Komünizmin …," *Zafer*, March 7, 1960, 1; "Halk Partisi …," *Zafer*, April 6, 1960, 1, 4; Burçak, *On Yılın Anıları*, 555).

partisans; that it was organizing underground cells; that it was in league with the radio station "Our Radio" (*Bizim Radyo*), which broadcast propaganda in Turkish from behind the Iron Curtain; that the CHP was spreading rumors that the DP traded Turkish women to the Americans for military equipment; and that the CHP sought to destroy "the intellectual and moral foundations of our Republic and young democracy." In launching this investigation, the DP sought to "prevent bloody sibling quarrels."[176]

The session was contentious, marked by shouts and threatening confrontations. At one point, a DP representative from Gaziantep pulled out a gun. İnönü denounced the constitutional legitimacy of the Investigation Commision, which could act as both accuser, prosecutor, and judge. Menderes was absent from the chamber, and Samet Ağaoğlu gave the reply to İnönü. He argued that parliament represented the national will and was endowed with legislative, executive, and judicial authority. It could delegate power to the Investigation Commission, as it saw fit. Moreover, establishing a commission would "save Turkish political life, pulling it back from the precipice off which it is about to fall." He described the troubles the country was facing:

> Domestic political disputes have carried from public squares to village coffee houses, from coffee houses to threshing floors, from party branches to family life, from family life to school yards ... At the head of one segment of the forces creating this [troubled] landscape in the country are people who for many years administered the state and homeland.

When he began listing off the "hundreds, thousands" of guilty and innocent people prosecuted during the single-party era, CHP parliamentarians shouted at him, "Don't you realize you're maligning the institutions of the state?" and "Your father [as a constitutional law professor] taught us many things. How sad that he taught you nothing."

Samet thanked them not to "bring those who are dead into this. They have no tongues and can't speak." But he could not stop himself from saying, "But let me add, if my father were alive and at this podium, he would say many things about your esteemed leader." He went on to read headlines from pro-CHP papers, including *Akis*, which described İnönü's actions in Kayseri as a victory comparable to his campaigns against the Greeks in the War of Independence. Samet suggested that the "mentality" of war perpetually dominated the opposition leaders' thinking and returned to his favorite image of the old regime, recalling how, "When I was a child, 15–16 years old [1924–25] ... here in Ankara's

176 TBMM, April 18, 1960, 191.

Ulus Square, I saw politicians hanging from ropes, twitching horribly. In these times, İsmet Pasha was prime minister."

Samet concluded his speech by offering further examples of İnönü's disingenuousness. He quoted from a sixteen-year-old speech by İnönü, which defended limiting freedom of speech by suggesting that "The Turkish nation must determine some particularities of its democracy according to its structure and character ... Every nation, according to its character, has a degree of speech and words it can tolerate." Clearly, Samet argued, the opposition leader was well aware of this national character and was intentionally pushing the nation toward the limits of its tolerance, toward "anarchy." And, Samet told the chamber, "If you don't pull back the country from the precipice of anarchy, you will have opened the doors to despotism."[177]

In his rebuttal, İnönü made a statement that, in retrospect, seems prophetic in its message. He declared that it was the DP that was pushing Turkey toward despotism:

> If human rights are not implemented, if the rights of citizenship are constrained, if a regime of coercion is established, then an uprising will certainly come ... We will not be found in that uprising, it will be done by those beyond us, with whom we have no connection ... If you continue down this path, I cannot save you.[178]

The Investigation Commission was approved by a voice vote, and the DP moved one step closer to eliminating the CHP, a political party representing over 40 percent of the electorate. That night, on the radio, the commission announced a ban on any reporting of its actions unless explicitly mentioned in the parliamentary record. In addition, all gatherings of a "political nature" were banned while the commission conducted its work.[179] Several hundred CHP supporters gathered to protest the following day in central Ankara, and by the following week, the party leadership was discussing a "Struggle Trip," including visits by İnönü to southern provinces in defiance of the commission's edicts.[180]

177 TBMM, April 18, 1960, 197–206.

178 TBMM, April 18, 1960, 207. That evening, İnönü's son-in-law, Metin Toker, spoke with US Embassy Counselor Robert Barnes and asked him how the United States would respond "to the 'new' government of Turkey." When asked what he meant by "new," Toker pointed to İnönü's speech and argued that the Investigation Commission was effectively a "new" government. Given that İnönü's speech had prophesized an uprising – and in light of the coup a month later – Toker's word games are eyebrow-raising, to say the least (Memorandum of Conversation, April 25, 1960, RG 59, Box 3, NND 959393, NAI 2068455).

179 "Meclis Tahkikat ...," *Zafer*, April 19, 1960, 1.

180 "CHP dun Ankara'da ...," *Havadis*, April 20, 1960, 1; "C.H.P. Milletvekilleri ...," *Akşam*, April 25, 1960, 1.

With "politics" ostensibly on hold for the time being, DP leaders continued their normal routines. Menderes celebrated the April 23 holiday (National Sovereignty and Children's Day) by traveling to Kocaeli province to attend the groundbreaking of Turkey's second refinery, a TL231 million ($26 million) project built in partnership with the US firm CALTEX. According to the pro-opposition paper *Cumhuriyet*, around 40 members of parliament and some 300 special invitees such as the US ambassador were brought by train from Ankara. Crowds of spectators were bussed in or transported by barge to the event for free.[181] The following day in İzmit, Menderes attended the groundbreaking of a state-run pipe factory built in partnership with the West German firm Mannesmann.

In his various speeches, Menderes refrained from harsh attacks on the opposition – just the standard observation that his predecessors had not developed industries like petroleum. His focus was on the industrial accomplishments of his governments and the "important role of Turkish-American collaboration" in the achievement of "peace, stability, and security."[182] Two days later, he was off to Tehran to meet with his CENTO ally – a far more authoritarian US ally – the shah.

Conclusion: Stabilizing Authoritarianism

President Bayar spent April 27, 1960 in Istanbul, hosting Pakistani President Ayub Khan, who was passing through Turkey en route to a meeting of British Commonwealth states. Ayub was greeted by Bayar at the Istanbul airport, and the two then drove into the city via the same route that Menderes had followed on his triumphant return from London – the same route on which İnönü had been attacked by a crowd of DP supporters. That night, at a repurposed Ottoman chalet, Ayub was feted at a banquet alongside President Bayar, the governor of Istanbul, and Mayor Aygün. Menderes and Zorlu were at the Tehran CENTO meeting, but Zorlu's wife (Menderes's cousin-in-law) was in attendance.

In Ankara that same evening, police were busy throwing journalists and CHP representatives out of the parliament building. In the space of three days, with Bayar's encouragement, a bill had been rushed through parliament to expand the authority of the Investigation Commission so that its decisions could not be appealed. During the contentious session, İnönü was expelled for comparing the situation in Turkey to the situation in South Korea, where students were currently protesting their

181 "Petrol rafinerisinin …," *Cumhuriyet*, April 24, 1960, 1, 5.
182 "Menderes son …," *Havadis*, April 25, 1960, 1, 5.

government's repressive, authoritarian actions. In the commotion following İnönü's removal, several other CHP parliamentarians were also expelled. When they refused to leave, the government called in police to remove them.

It would be hard to imagine a juxtaposition that better captured the themes of this chapter. We see Turkey's president greeting his authoritarian peer. The Pakistani president, for his part, is en route to a meeting of an international organization whose members are unconcerned with his anti-democratic methods of rule. Meanwhile, the Turkish prime minister is absent, attending a meeting of the US-backed CENTO security organization in Iran, another country run by an authoritarian leader. At the same time, we see the Turkish government rushing a bill through parliament to give extraordinary powers to a fifteen-member commission of hardliners from the ruling party. These simultaneous events reflect the degree to which members of the US-led Cold War order had come to accept illiberal, authoritarian methods of rule as a matter of course by the late 1950s. Even in South Korea, which İnönü pointed to as a model for resistance to authoritarian rule, a momentarily successful pro-democracy movement would give way to a long-lasting authoritarian regime in less than a year.

In Turkey, too, student protests helped bring down the government – albeit without a democratic interregnum before the military intervention. The DP government's heavy-handed tactics provoked a backlash. As Ayub was departing for the next stop on his trip, students were gathering at Istanbul University to protest.[183] Police fired on the demonstrators, killing a nineteen-year-old from Malatya named Turan Emeksiz. Demonstrations spread to Ankara's School of Political Science on April 29, leading the government to declare martial law in Istanbul and Ankara. Critical newspapers were temporarily closed. Protests continued during the following week, including outside a meeting of NATO ministers held in Istanbul May 2–4, and at a large protest in Ankara on May 5.

In the face of this unrest, some members of the DP pushed for the government to make concessions. Sıtkı Yırcalı and other moderates suggested reshuffling the cabinet. Though they did not name specific ministers, the implication was that Menderes allies such as Interior Minister Gedik should go. According to some accounts, Menderes himself was even willing to resign if it would solve the political impasse, but President Bayar rejected the idea out of hand, declaring, "You can't

[183] For an overview of student organizations under DP rule, see Emin Alper, *Jakobenlerden Devrimcilere: Türkiye'de Öğrenci Hareketlerinin Dinamikleri, 1960–1971* (Istanbul: Tarih Vakfı Yurt Yayınları, 2018), 153–164.

change horses while passing through water" and demanding that protestors be severely punished.[184] For his part, Menderes tried to calm moderates within the party, assuring them that the government had the situation under control. Even after cadets from the War College in Ankara staged a protest, Menderes vehemently rejected calls for concessions from members of both the DP executive committee and the parliamentary group. The final meetings of both (on May 24 and 25) ended in acrimony; the former with Menderes storming off.[185]

In part, Menderes's obstinacy stemmed from the information he was receiving from the upper echelons of the army. Commander of the Armed Forces Rüştü Erdelhun assured him after the cadets' protest that the situation was under control. As the political scientist Tanel Demirel suggests, Erdelhun's promises "were believed and desired to be believed."[186] DP leaders were hearing what they wanted to hear. Or, in some cases, they weren't hearing anything: in early May, General Cemal Gürsel, commander of the army, issued a letter to Defense Minister Ethem Menderes that called for President Bayar's resignation, as well as a variety of other measures, including the release of jailed journalists and an end to the exploitation (*simsarlık*) of religion. Ethem shared the letter with the prime minister, but it went no further. The president, interior minister, and other key officials remained uninformed of it.[187] Menderes, for his part, interpreted it to mean that the military was still on his side, even if no longer on Bayar's.[188] He clearly did not know that, over a year earlier, Gürsel had accepted a proposal from younger officers to be the leader of their planned coup.[189]

During these weeks of protest, seemingly unaware that the coup-plotting was already in motion, both the government and the opposition presented their actions as part of a larger, global struggle either *for* freedom or *against* communism. Opposition papers, which were unable to cover domestic protests owing to censorship, emphasized events in

[184] Aydemir, *Menderes'in Dramı?*, 373, 410; Öymen, ... *Ve İhtilal*, 730–738. Some writers are less convinced that Menderes would have resigned if not for Bayar's opposition. Cihad Baban observes how skillful Menderes was at manipulating Bayar when it served his interest (Baban, *Politika Galerisi*, 58–59).

[185] Burçak, *On Yılın Anıları*, 737–749. Burçak emphasizes the misgivings Sıtkı Yırcalı and (especially) he himself felt about the government's policies. He argues that the parliamentary group would have ultimately found a solution for the political crisis of 1960. Yet the resistance he describes is relatively limited. Again and again, moderates voice concerns and are shouted down by Menderes but take no more concrete actions. When precisely their moment of heroic defiance would have come is unclear.

[186] Demirel, *Türkiye'nin Uzun On Yılı*, 379.

[187] Aydemir, *Menderes'in Dramı?*, 392–393; Albayrak, *Türk Siyasi Tarihinde*, 546.

[188] Yalman, *Yakın Tarihte*, 1684.

[189] Ömer Sami Coşar and Abdi İpekçi, "Ve lider bulunuyor ...," *Milliyet*, June 10, 1962, 5.

South Korea, where the protests had now ousted the president (and prompted the suicide of his son).[190] Pro-DP papers countered with reminders of the communist threat faced by regimes in allied countries. On April 29, the day that martial law was declared, *Zafer* ran a column titled "Iranian Communists Were Defeated," recalling how the shah's regime had excluded communist-affiliated parties from power during the previous seven years. A subsequent column emphasized that Iran's development and stable currency were encouraging foreign investment.[191] Such examples mirrored the arguments Menderes was making on the radio and in public speeches. Following the protests on May 2, he declared in a radio broadcast that the aim of the protesters was to bring about:

> a Turkey without stability, where the government in power isn't dominant, where any uprising, revolt, or disorder may occur. And, as a result, a Turkey that loses its reputation as a trustworthy ally … A Turkey that is not a country where foreign capital can be invested or economic cooperation entered into.

According to Menderes, this crisis was no longer a mere conflict between government and opposition, it was between a "legitimate government that had come to power [by means of the] national will and elections" and an "insurrectionary movement," an opposition party that had become "a center of political reaction."[192]

During the month of May, with all political activity still banned, Menderes continued to travel the country, giving speeches in his capacity as head of the government. In the city of Eskişehir, on May 25, he reminded the assembled crowd, "Our way is the way of elections … But before all else, defending the regime is an absolute necessity" and announced to the press that the Investigation Commission had finished its review of the CHP. The speech and the announcement were reported the next day.[193]

Less than twenty-four hours later, on the morning of May 27, military officers seized control of state institutions and began arresting all DP members of parliament. All political activity in the country was ordered to halt until a new constitution was drawn up and new elections were organized. General Gürsel, now head of the "National Unity Committee," announced that the military had intervened to prevent

190 Öymen, …*Ve İhtilal*, 581–582.

191 "İran Komünistleri mağlup oldu," *Zafer*, April 19, 1969, 2, 4; "İran'ın zenginliği ve komünistler," *Zafer*, May 16, 1960, 2. Both *Zafer* articles state they are translated from an unspecified English language source with the initials "M.O."

192 "Bu tertipler …," *Zafer*, May 3, 1960, 1, 4.

193 "Başvekilimizi 150 bin kişi …," *Zafer*, May 26, 1960, 1, 4.

Turkish politics from becoming a bloody "sibling quarrel."[194] It was a justification that adopted the same language that DP leaders had used to defend their own actions. While they might have been removed from power, their goal of stability and limited political contestation had been momentarily achieved. Yet continuity did little to help supporters of the now-ousted DP. In his first post-coup column, long-time pro-DP journalist Mümtaz Faik Fenik echoed Gürsel's words, writing that "It must be admitted that, until the day the Armed Forces intervened, no opportunity had appeared for preventing the strife that had enveloped the nation and pitted brother against brother."[195] The former DP parliamentarian and columnist for its publications dating back to the late 1940s now urged readers to support the military in its efforts. A week later, he too would be arrested.[196]

The day after the coup, US Ambassador Fletcher Warren met with General Gürsel. According to Warren, who had previously served in Venezuela, Nicaragua, and Paraguay, "I commenced by referring to my service in Latin America and many coups which I had seen there. I said that if I were a military man … I would be pleased and proud of the way it had gone off. It was by far the most precise, most efficient, and most rapid coup d'état I had ever witnessed." He emphasized the importance, however, of a quick return to democracy and no mistreatment of Menderes and other leaders. Gürsel replied, "I assure you that there has been no mistreatment and there will be no mistreatment. I am going to supply each of them with [a] seashore cottage with a bath where he can reside in comfort (with his family if he desires) until matters are cleared up" – which was either unintentionally ironic or slyly misleading.[197] The DP leaders were soon sent off to an island prison in the Sea of Marmara to await prosecution. The party was officially closed down in September 1960.[198] Menderes, Zorlu, and Polatkan were hanged a year later.

194 "Yeni bir …," *Havadis*, May 28, 1960, 1.

195 Mümtaz Faik Fenik, "Bize düşen vazife…," *Havadis*, May 30, 1960, 1, 4.

196 On June 8, 1960, Fenik was taken into custody. He was prosecuted for voting to strip the CHP of its property but was found innocent. His wife (and fellow writer), Adviye, ran as a candidate for the DP's successor, the AP. He was later involved with an effort by Celal Bayar to establish a political organization called Our Home (*Bizim Ev*) in 1967.

197 "Document 365: Telegram from the Embassy in Turkey to the Department of State," May 28, 1960, *FRUS, 1958–1960*, vol. X, part II: *Eastern Europe; Finland; Greece; Turkey*; Reuben Silverman, "Show (and Tell) Trials: Competing Narratives of Turkey's Democrat Party Era," *Turkish Studies* 23, no. 1 (2022): 147.

198 "Demokrat Parti, mahkeme …," *Cumhuriyet*, September 30, 1960, 1, 5.

Conclusion

Did the Democrat Party lay the groundwork for early twenty-first century Turkey? On the one hand, as this book has shown, the answer must certainly be no, or at least no more so than their rivals in the CHP. The DP's founders were too similar in experience and outlook to their rivals to receive sole credit. On the other hand, the party governed Turkey during the years in which the country became integrated into the economic and security orders that persist to this day. In relations with foreign allies, the hard-bargaining style practiced by Zorlu, Menderes, and others has remained a common feature of Turkish diplomacy. Domestically, under DP rule, Turkey's agriculture became more mechanized, its people more urbanized, and its politics more polarized. Though all these trends would continue in later years and under different governments, it was during the decade of DP rule that they began to accelerate.

The DP is also associated with dramatic changes in Turkish society, because its leaders actively identified themselves with these developments. Menderes and others hoped to spur dramatic transformations in society. At the same time, they hoped to maintain stability and their own power without significant compromise. The contradictions in these ambitions ultimately proved to be their undoing. By 1960, the DP leadership had alienated leading figures in the media and academia. Moreover, as the previous chapter argued, DP leaders had privileged "stability" over liberal democracy to such an extent that their own inability to maintain order had delegitimized their administration. The campus protests that erupted in April and May provided coup plotters in the military an opening to move ahead with their plans.

The university campuses, where the end of the DP began, exemplify the era's contradictions. As late as 1958, there were only eleven institutions of higher education in the country.[1] Many of these had a specific

[1] Istanbul Technical University (a reorganized version of military engineering schools dating back to 1773); the Military War College (1834); Istanbul University (a

purpose, such as engineering, fine arts, or agronomy. Five had been established within the previous three years. Higher education, in other words, remained highly selective. Attendance at a university immediately placed students on track for a leading role in national affairs, whether as a politician, doctor, lawyer, artist, bureaucrat, or some combination thereof. Student politics and student protest in this context could not be easily dismissed by political leaders, since unrest in the universities meant unrest among the future administrators of the country. During their decade in power, DP leaders expanded higher education only to find students at the vanguard of their opposition.

As with many social groups, of course, the DP's relationship with students was complicated. In 1950, students and professors had supported the DP and the change it promised. A decade later, students were again longing for change, this time promised by the CHP. The historian Sina Akşin, an Istanbul University student in the late 1950s, recalls that "In those years, I think, the large majority of us supported İsmet İnönü and the CHP. The only Democrat Party [supporter] that I know of was my friend Ertuğrul Mat," the president of Istanbul's Democrat Party Youth Arm.[2]

Though Mat was in the minority on campus, he was representative of the emerging political coalition that would carry on the legacy of the DP. Unlike many of his peers (Akşin included), whose families were closely connected with the state, Mat came from a family with a background in commerce. His father had grown disillusioned with the CHP during its three decades of rule, less owing to its secularism or statism than to the high-handed attitude of its local officials. In his memoirs, Mat describes his father's run-in with Şemsettin Günaltay, a one-time prime minister and important figure in the Istanbul CHP organization, who demanded that his father give two jobs at his bakery to CHP loyalists. When Mat's father refused, the government closed the union with which he was involved. On another occasion, his father was called into a district official's office and made to wait. Upon entering, he was tired, and leaned on the official's desk as they spoke; this was enough to infuriate the official, who grabbed

reorganized version of the Darülfünun established in 1863); the State Academy of Fine Arts (1882); Yıldız Technical University (a reorganized version of the Kondüktor Mektebi Alisi established in 1911); Ankara University (encompassing multiple colleges, amalgamated in 1946); Karadeniz University in Trabzon (1955); Ege University in İzmir (1955); Middle Eastern Technical University in Ankara (1957); Roberts College (re-elevated to "college" status in 1957); Atatürk University in Erzurum (1958).

[2] Yaşar Seyman, *Tarihin Deltasına Yolculuk: Sina Akşin Kitabı* (Istanbul: Türkiye İş Bankası Kültür Yayınları, 2009), 50.

his father's hat and tossed it out the door, humiliating him.[3] These experiences led Mat to dislike excessive bureaucratization and the attitudes it encouraged. At Istanbul University, he was involved in the law faculty student society and the Turkish National Youth Organization (*Türkiye Milli Gençlik Teşkilatı*), becoming general secretary of the latter in 1957. His success that year brought him to the attention of the national DP organization, which was hoping to reenergize supporters following its disappointing performance in the October elections.[4] By the time of the coup, Mat was finished with university and doing his mandatory military service. In 1965, he would stand for office as a member of the Justice Party (AP); in 1969, he would be elected to office.

The AP was one of several parties founded in the aftermath of the coup. Within a few years, it succeeded in reconstituting the DP's electoral coalition. With DP leaders banned from politics, in prison, or executed, the AP depended on a new generation of political leaders to fill its ranks. Whereas the DP had brought to power restless young bureaucrats like Samet Ağaoğlu and Sıtkı Yircalı, the AP brought to power officials and provincial political leaders who had not even had time to grow restless. The most famous of these new figures on the political scene was Süleyman Demirel, an engineer responsible for some of the DP era's great dam projects, who now became leader of the AP. Under Demirel's administration, young, conservative officials were brought into government, including the Özal brothers, Turgut and Korkut. Though both men would eventually enter politics as candidates for the religious National Salvation Party (*Milli Selamet Partisi*), they had been supporters of the DP in their youth. Özal remained the preeminent figure in Turkey's politics until his unexpected death in 1993. Demirel remained actively involved until his term as president ended in 2000. Both these examples and the example of Mat suggest that, while the DP may not have won the hearts and minds of most students during the 1950s – including those who went on to become historians – it directly shaped the country's political leadership for forty years to come.

Many of the DP leaders did not live to see this vindication. In addition to the executions of Menderes, Zorlu, and Polatkan, Namık Gedik, the ousted interior minister, committed suicide within days of the coup. Reportedly, he threw himself out the window of the room in which he was being detained.[5] Tevfik İleri, the long-serving education minister, died in December 1961, within months of his death sentence being

[3] Mat, *Demokrasi Yolunda*, 40–42. [4] Ibid., 100.
[5] "Gedik ...," *Milliyet*, May 31, 1960, 1, 7; "Ağaoğlu ...," *Milliyet*, June 1, 1960, 1.

commuted to life in prison.[6] All told, the special tribunal, held on the island of Yassıada, issued sentences to 464 leading Democrats ranging from two years in prison to death. Ağaoğlu received a life sentence.[7] Fifteen leaders received death sentences, twelve of which were reduced by the military high command. Bayar's sentence was commuted on account of his advanced age.[8] Ironic, given that he would live another two decades, dying in 1986 at the age of 103.

⋆

The leaders of the DP paid a heavy price for their failure to answer a central issue of the Cold War: how to balance the desires of citizens with the economic development goals of state officials. Raising Turkey to "the level of civilized nations" was a frequent refrain of DP elites, but it had been the ambition of many leaders before them as well. Depending on the circumstances, Turkey's leaders pursued different strategies, often adopting and adapting the policies of their peers in other countries.[9] For

[6] Over the sixteen months of detention and trial, six DP members of parliament (Zakar Tarver, Yusuf Salman, Nuri Yamut, Lütfi Kırdar, Gazi Yiğitbaşı, and Kenan Akyüz) and the Istanbul chief of security (Faruk Oktay) died from heart failure and other sicknesses. Cemil Keleşoğlu (the governor of Konya) committed suicide. After the verdicts were issued in 1961, İleri and three other members of parliament died (Necati Topçuoğlu, Muhlis Erdener, and Kamil Tayşi) (Ahmet Gökçen and Ertuğrul Ünal, "27 Mayıs 1960 Tarihinde Yürürlükte Olan Ceza Mevzuatımız ve Evrensel Hukuk Bağlamında Yassıada Yargılamaları," *Marmara Üniversitesi Hukuk Fakültesi Hukuk Araştırmaları Dergisi* 28, no. 1 [2022]: 139–140).

[7] "Komite …," and "Hapse …," *Milliyet*, September 16, 1960, 1, 5; "İdam kararların …," *Hürriyet*, September 16, 1961, 1. In total, 464 Democrats were sentenced, 123 acquitted, and 5 cases dropped. Death sentences were initially given to fifteen high-ranking leaders: President Celal Bayar; Prime Minister Adnan Menderes; Foreign Minister Fatin Rüştü Zorlu; Finance Minister Hasan Polatkan; President of the Parliament Refik Koraltan; Customs and Monopolies Minister Emin Kalafat; Army Chief Rüştü Erdelhun; members of parliament who had served on the Investigation Commission Ahmet Hamdi Sancar, Bahadır Dülger, and Nusret Kirişçioğlu; members of parliament who had helped expedite the bill giving further powers to the investigative committee Agah Erozan, Osman Kavrakoğlu, İbrahim Kirazoğlu, and Zeki Erataman; and DP Parliamentary Group Vice President Baha Akşit. Thirty-one received life sentences; two received twenty-year sentences; five, fifteen years; nineteen, ten years; and the rest, sentences ranging from two to eight.

[8] "15 İdam Kararından …," *Tercüman*, September 16, 1961, 1.

[9] Scholars have shown that leaders in Turkey were not merely mimicking elites in other countries: other leaders often looked to Turkey as a model for resisting colonialism and developing an "underdeveloped" nation (see Ihrig, *Atatürk in the Nazi Imagination*). Kemalist Turkey was also an inspiration for people in regions that had formerly been part of the Ottoman Empire (see, for example, Amit Bein, *Kemalist Turkey and the Middle East: International Relations in the Interwar Period* [Cambridge: Cambridge University Press, 2017], 139–178; and Fabio Giomi, "Domesticating Kemalism: Conflicting Muslim Narratives about Turkey in Interwar Yugoslavia," in *Nostalgia, Loss and Creativity in South-East Europe: Political and Cultural Representations of the Past*, ed. Catharina Raudvere [London: Palgrave Macmillan, 2018]), 151–188).

Turkish leaders like Celal Bayar, Fuat Köprülü, and Refik Koraltan, whose political involvements began in the early 1900s, the countries to learn from were in Western Europe, and the model policies included nationalism, secularism, and liberal positivism. During the interwar years (1922–39), Turkish leaders looked to German and Soviet models of development; after World War II, they looked to the United States.

In power, DP leaders' pursuit of economic development and security led them to deepen and consolidate Turkey's integration into the institutions of the American-led Cold War order. Turkey became a crucial member of security organizations such as NATO and CENTO; it supported US positions at the UN and at high-profile international conferences like Bandung; it also became indebted to its allies, which necessitated frequent negotiations with financial institutions such as the IBRD and the EPU. Yet integration into an order that had the United States at its center was not simply a matter of subordination. As this book has shown, DP leaders sought to turn – and often succeeded in turning – these institutions to their benefit. Again and again, DP leaders pushed the United States to provide more aid and convinced European countries to extend more credit – or, at least, delay calling in outstanding debts.

While these efforts were not always successful, that should not be seen as a fundamental flaw in the DP strategy or evidence that Turkey's leaders lacked any meaningful agency in the Cold War. This was, after all, a US-dominated order, and countries whose leaders pursued their long-term goals by means of alternative strategies (spending less, repressing more, remaining unaligned, or seeking support from the Soviet bloc) seldom avoided economic and political crises of their own. Given the constraints of the increasingly bipolar world system, the DP extracted important concessions and laid the basis for Turkey's future development.

⋆

The overthrow of an elected government and the execution of its popular prime minister provoked remarkably little protest. The fact that the coup was swift and supported by the military leadership helped dull resistance (as did the strong support it received from the media, opposition parties, and such elite institutions as universities). Internal divisions within the DP helped as well. There was no united front against the coup in the early weeks. In Balıkesir, for example, much of the local leadership was hostile to the national leadership. Local party leader Sıtkı Yırcalı had actively opposed the formation and further empowerment of the controversial Investigation Commission. Though he was arrested along with other DP parliamentarians on May 27, 1960, he was released a day later and published a statement in support of the military and its efforts to ensure the success of the nation. He promised the remaining DP organization would help the coup leaders' National Unity Committee. Despite his efforts to please the new regime, however, he was arrested again three days later. He emphasized his innocence throughout the subsequent trials but was ultimately sentenced to four years and two months in prison.[10]

Another development that may have discouraged violent resistance to the coup was the fact that older military officers outmaneuvered their younger, more radical counterparts. Rather than an extended period of rule, this victorious faction pushed for a quick resumption of elections. A new constitution and a new election law were drawn up. Initially, this new system blunted the political power of the DP's electoral coalition. The winner-take-all system was replaced with a proportional allocation of seats, which encouraged a proliferation of smaller parties, dividing the DP vote.[11] Much of the DP was reconstituted under the banner of the AP, but many of the voters who had once supported the DP now gave their vote to other parties.

While the interests that the DP represented remained powerful, their electoral clout was briefly fractured. In Balıkesir, for example, the AP won all four of the seats allocated to the province in the newly created senate and seven out of eleven parliamentary seats, but the CHP received four, breaking the decade-long DP dominance of the province. In Malatya, the CHP experienced a similar setback. The province's ten parliamentary seats under the old system were replaced with six seats in parliament and two in the senate. The CHP won both senate seats and five of the parliamentary seats, but a former member of the local DP was elected as a candidate of the New Turkey Party (*Yeni Türkiye Parti*). The New Turkey Party, however, had limited national appeal; within four years, the AP would be able to reconstitute the DP coalition. In Malatya, it even gained ground, winning two out of six seats. The winners, Hüseyin Doğan and Hamit Fendoğlu, had been leading members of the local DP in the 1950s.[12]

The system that resulted from the 1961 constitution and electoral law is remembered as more democratic insofar as it allowed a wider range of political parties to form and a greater range of political ideas to be

10 "Yırcalı ...," *Milliyet*, May 29, 1960, 8; "Yırcalı'nın ...," *Balıkesir*, May 30, 1960, 1, 4; "Yırcalı ...," *Milliyet*, May 31, 1960, 8; "Yüksek Adalet ...," *Cumhuriyet*, September 16, 1961, 1, 5.

11 For the 1961 Constitution, see RG, August 20, 1961; for the 1961 Election Law, see RG, May 30, 1961.

12 "Kesin sonuç ...," *Milliyet*, October 17, 1961, 1, 5.

expressed. Yet it should also be understood as reflecting the larger Cold War shift toward de-democratization in which DP leaders had sought – and failed – to position themselves. The military retained influence both formally (through the national security council) and informally (through the convention that a general always be named president). A senate, partially appointed by the president, was established to check parliament, and a supreme court was created to check the decisions of the legislature. Finally, institutions such as the state planning organization (*Devlet Planlama Teşkilatı*) were created, with significant autonomy from the electoral political process. Though this was not the institutional arrangement that DP leaders envisioned in the late 1950s, it had similar effects: the new constitutional order ensured that economic policies benefiting the "national interest" could be insulated from electoral concerns. This separation, however, was no real solution either, since it allowed politically unaccountable officers and bureaucrats to be the arbiters of the national interest. For decades to come, the political leaders who successfully reconstituted the DP coalition would struggle to reassert control over autonomous state institutions, the military being only the most obvious one.

⋆

This book began with President Recep Tayyip Erdoğan's speech on the sixtieth anniversary of the 1960 coup, given on Yassıada, now renamed "Democracy and Freedom Island." In his remarks, Erdoğan reminded the youths of the nation, "You … should learn well here of dear departed Menderes's decade of 1950–60; you should learn well of the progress Turkey made in ten years."[13] He listed off dams, bridges, and roads, as well as the rise in income, and compared the attacks on Menderes and the DP with the attacks against himself and his allies in contemporary Turkey.

The line from the DP to the present day is neither as straight nor as flattering as the president would have it be. The examination of the DP in this book has emphasized the degree to which it was a product of the late Ottoman Empire and early Republic of Turkey. Its leaders were actively involved in creating and enforcing the authoritarian and secularizing policies that subsequent generations of conservative politicians have decried. Moreover, while critical of state power when in opposition and

[13] "Demokrasi ve Özgürlükler Adası'nın Açılış Töreni'nde Yaptıkları Konuşma," T. C. Cumhurbaşkanlığı, May 27, 2020, available: www.tccb.gov.tr/konusmalar/353/120308/demokrasi-ve-ozgurlukler-adasi-nin-acilis-toreni-nde-yaptiklari-konusma.

willing to reform some particularly oppressive features of the regime, DP leaders were quick to expand state authority when faced with challenges. Finally, despite upholding such formal elements of democracy as elections, the DP was generally unwilling to risk exposing itself to competitive elections whose outcomes were uncertain. Instead, it tilted an already unbalanced electoral system further in its favor.

If the DP failed to consistently defend and expand institutions that bolster democracy, then perhaps its greatest legacy is the way in which it positioned Turkey in relation to other states. While the CHP had situated the country firmly on the American side of the bipolar Cold War order, it had done so as something of a charity case, a scrappy, democratizing nation in need of aid. The DP, by contrast, presented the country as an essential part of the American order, willing to fight and, thus, deserving of significant financial support. That support underwrote the dams, bridges, and roads for which the DP is remembered. Under DP rule, the country experienced exhilarating developmental steps (if not the "leap" that Menderes and his supporters claimed). Yet securing American largesse entailed risks. For a decade, DP leaders proved adept at managing this array of challenges until, finally, it all began spinning out of their control.

Bibliography

Note on alphabetical order: the items below follow Turkish alphabetical order, so headwords with *unaccented* first letters come before those with *accented* first letters, hence those beginning with C come before those beginning with Ç, Go– before Gö–, Gu– before Gü–, O before Ö, etc.

Archives and Special Library Collections

BCA *Başbakanlık Cumhuriyet Arşivi*
(Prime Ministerial Republican Archives) (Istanbul)
010 (Yassıada Tribunal)
030 (Prime Minister's Office)
180 (Department of Education)
490 (Political Parties)

BDK *Beyazıt Devlet Kütüphanesi*
(Beyazit State Library) (Istanbul)

BNA British National Archives (London)
DO (Dominions Office)
FCO (Foreign and Commonwealth Office)
FO (Foreign Office)
T (Treasury)

DPMGMZ *TBMM Demokrat Parti Meclis Grubu Müzakere Zabıtları*
(Democrat Party Parliamentary Group Deliberation Minutes) (online)

FRUS *Foreign Relations of the United States*
Available at: https://history.state.gov/historicaldocuments/eisenhower

İBBAK İBB Atatürk Kitaplığı (Istanbul Municipal Atatürk Library) (Istanbul)

KEKBMV *Kadın Eserleri Kütüphanesi ve Bilgi Merkezi Vakfı*
(Library of the Works of Women and Information Center Foundation) (Istanbul)
Süreyya Ağaoğlu Private Archives

MKB *Milli Kütüphane Başkanlığı* (National Library of Turkey) (Ankara)
NA The National Archives (College Park, Maryland)

RG 59 (Department of State)
RG 84 (Foreign Service Posts)

RG *Resmi Gazete* (Official Gazette). Available at: www.resmigazete.gov.tr.

TBMM Türkiye Büyük Millet Meclisi Tutanakları
(Proceedings of the Turkish Grand National Assembly)
Available: www.tbmm.gov.tr/kutuphane/tutanak_sorgu.html
TBMM Albümü, 1950–80
(Turkish Grand National Assembly Album, 1950–80)
Available: www5.tbmm.gov.tr/TBMM_Album/Cilt2/Cilt2.pdf

Periodicals

Akis (Istanbul)
Akşam (Istanbul)
Anadolu Ajansı (Ankara)
Ateş (Balıkesir)
Balıkesir (Balıkesir)
Balıkesir Postası (Balıkesir)
Chicago Daily Tribune (Chicago)
Congressional Record (Washington, DC)
Cumhuriyet (Istanbul)
Demokrat İzmir (İzmir)
Demokrat Malatya (Malatya)
Dünya (Istanbul)
Fırat (Malatya)
Gayret (Malatya)
Havadis (Istanbul)
Hürriyet (Istanbul)
Indianapolis Star (Indianapolis)
İstanbul Ekspres (Istanbul)
Kadro (Ankara)
Kayseri Haber (Kayseri)
Kudret (Ankara)
Los Angeles Times (Los Angeles)
Malatya Postası (Malatya)
Milliyet (Istanbul)
New York Times (New York)
Radikal (Istanbul)
Son Posta (Istanbul)
Tasvir (Istanbul)
Tercüman (Istanbul)
The Times (London)
Türk Sesi (Istanbul)
Türk Dili (Balıkesir)
Ulus (Ankara)
Vatan (Istanbul)

Washington Post (Washington, DC)
Yeni Malatya (Malatya)
Zafer (Ankara)

Books and Articles

Abou El-Fadl, Reem. *Foreign Policy as Nation Making: Turkey and Egypt in the Cold War*. Cambridge: Cambridge University Press, 2019.

Adalet, Begüm. *Hotels and Highways: The Construction of Modernization Theory in Cold War Turkey*. Stanford: Stanford University Press, 2018.

Ağaoğlu, Samet. *Arkadaşım Menderes: İpin Gölgesinde Günler*. Istanbul: Yapı Kredi Yayınları, 2011 [1967].

Bütün Öyküleri. Istanbul: Yapı Kredi Yayınları, 2013.

Demokrat Partinin Doğuş ve Yükseliş Sebepleri: Bir Soru. Baha Matbaası, 1972.

İki Parti Arasındaki Farklar. Ankara: Arbas Matbaası, 1947.

Kuva-yı Millîye Ruhu. Istanbul: Yapı Kredi Yayınları, 2011 [1944].

Siyasi Günlük: DP'nin Kuruluşu, edited by Cemil Koçak. Istanbul: İletişim Yayınları, 1992.

Ağaoğlu, Süreyya. *Bir Ömür Böyle Geçti*. Istanbul: Ağaoğlu Yayınevi, 1975.

Ahmad, Bedia Turgay, and Feroz Ahmad. *Türkiye'de Çok Partili Politikanın Açıklamalı Kronolojisi, 1945–1971*. Istanbul: Bilgi Yayınevi, 1976.

Ahmad, Feroz. *The Turkish Experiment in Democracy, 1950–1975*. Boulder: Westview Press, 1977.

Akalın, Muzaffer. *Bir Olayın Hikayesi*. Istanbul: M. Sucuoğlu Matbaası, 1961.

Akandere, Osman. "1939–1946 Yılları Arasında Türkiye Büyük Millet Meclisinde Bir Denetleme ve Kontrol Organı Olarak Müstakil Grup'un Yapısı ve İşlevi." *Selçuk Üniversitesi Türkiyat Araştırmaları Dergisi* 7 (2000): 305–326.

Akça, Bayram, and Osman Köse. "Demokrat Parti Dönemi'nde Muğla'da Siyasi Hayat." *Sosyal ve Beşeri Bilimler Araştırmaları Dergisi* 19, no. 41 (2018): 161–185.

Akgün, Şeref Laçın. *Balıkesir Demokrat Parti İçyüzü*. Balıkesir: Türkdili Matbaası, 1950.

Akpınarlı, Kerim Kani. *Balıkesir Şehir ve Belediye Tarihi*. Balıkesir: Balıkesir Belediye Yayınları, 2009.

"Balıkesir Şehri Tarihçesi." In *Balıkesir İktisat Kılavuz*, edited by Mustafa Salman. Balıkesir: Balıkesir Ticaret Odası, 1957.

Akşin, Sina. *Kısa Türkiye Tarihi*. Istanbul: İş Bankası Kültür Yayınları, 2016 [2007].

Aktar, Ayhan. *Varlık Vergisi ve "Türkleştirme" Politikaları*. Istanbul: İletişim Yayınları, 2000.

Akün, Ömer Faruk. "Mehmed Fuad Köprülü." In *Türkiye Diyanet Vakfı Islam Ansiklopedisi*, vol. XXVI, 471–486. Istanbul: Türkiye Diyanet Vakfı, 2002.

Akyol, Taha, and Aydın Menderes. *Demokrasiden Darbeye: Babam Adnan Menderes*. Istanbul: Doğan Kitap, 2011.

Albayrak, Mustafa. "Demokrat Parti Döneminde Milli Korunma Kanunu Uygulamaları, 1955–1960." *Atatürk Araştırma Merkezi Dergisi* 23 (2007): 219–250.

Türk Siyasi Tarihinde Demokrat Parti, 1946–1960. Ankara: Phoenix Yayınevi, 2004.

Albertus, Michael, and Victor Menaldo. *Authoritarianism and the Elite Origins of Democracy.* Cambridge: Cambridge University Press, 2017.

Alemdar, Korkmaz. *İletişim ve Tarih.* Istanbul: İmge Kitabevi Yayınları, 1996.

Alkan, Mehmet. "Kahve-Kahvaltı ve Çay Tiryakiliği." In *Türkiye'nin 1950'li Yılları*, edited by Mete Kaan Kaynar, 619–620. Istanbul: İletişim Yayınları, 2015.

Alp, Ömer. *Ortak Pazar Ülkeleri ve Türkiye Şeker Endüstrileri.* Ankara: Yeni Desen Matbaası, 1963.

Alpay, Yalın. "Fuat Köprülü." In *Modern Türkiye'de Siyasi Düşünce V: Muhafazakarlık*, edited by Tanıl Bora and Murat Gültekingil, 136–149. Istanbul: İletişim Yayınları, 2006.

Alper, Emin. *Jakobenlerden Devrimcilere: Türkiye'de Ögrenci Hareketlerinin Dinamikleri, 1960–1971.* Istanbul: Tarih Vakfı Yurt Yayınları, 2018.

Anter, Musa. *Hatıralarım, 1–2.* Istanbul: Avesta Yayınları, 1999.

Arai, Masami. *Turkish Nationalism in the Young Turk Era.* Leiden: Brill, 1992.

Aras, Tevfik Rüştü. *Görüşlerim.* Istanbul: Semih Lütfi Kitabevi, 1945.

Arcayürek, Cüneyt. *Bir İktidar Bir İhtilal, 1955–1960.* Ankara: Bilgi Yayınevi, 1984.

Yeni İktidar Yeni Dönem, 1951–1954. Ankara: Bilgi Yayınevi, 1985.

Arslan, Zehra. "Trabzon'da Vatan Cephesi, 12 Ekim 1958–27 Mayıs 1960." *Karadeniz Araştırmaları* 36 (2013): 129–148.

"Vatan Cephesi Davası (Kararname, Savunmalar ve Karar)." *History Studies: International Journal of History* 4, no. 2 (2012): 1–37.

Arzık, Nimet. *Menderes'i İpe Götürenler.* Ankara: Kurtuluş Matbaası, 1966.

Asılsoy, Abdülkerim. "Mehmet Fuat Köprülü'nün İlmi Hayatı ve Eserlerinde İzlediği Metot Üzerine." In *Tarihimizden Portreler: Osmanlı Kimliği: Prof. Dr. Cevdet Küçük Armağanı*, edited by Zekeriya Kurşun and Haydar Çoruh, 213–244. Istanbul: Ordaf Yayınları, 2013.

Aslan, Ömer. *The United States and Military Coups in Turkey and Pakistan: Between Conspiracy and Reality.* London: Palgrave Macmillan, 2018.

Aslan, Senem. *Nation-Building in Turkey and Morocco: Governing Kurdish and Berber Dissent.* Cambridge: Cambridge University Press, 2015.

Aslanoğlu, İbrahim. *Sivas Meşhurları*, vol. II. Sivas: Valiliği İl Kültür ve Turizm Müdürlüğü, 2006).

Atakuman, Çiğdem. "Anatolia and Archaeology in the Early Years of the Turkish Republic, 1923–1938." *Journal of Social Archaeology* 8, no. 2 (2008): 214–235.

Atatürk, Mustafa Kemal. *Nutuk.* Istanbul: Kaynak Yayınları, 2015 [1927].

Atatürk Araştırma Merkezi. *Atatürk'ün Söylev ve Demeçleri II.* Ankara: Türk Tarih Kurumu Basımevi, 1997.

Atılgan, Gökhan. *Behice Boran: Öğretim Üyesi, Siyasetçi, Kuramcı.* Istanbul: Yordam Kitap, 2007.

Avanas, Ahmet. *Milli Mücadele'de Konya.* Ankara: Atatürk Araştırma Merkezi, 1998.

Avcı, Sedat. "Türk Şeker Sanayiinin Kuruluş ve Gelişmesinde Devletin Etkisi." *Coğrafya Dergisi* 4 (1996): 291–302.

Avcıoğlu, Doğan. *Türkiye'nin Düzeni: Dün, Bugün, Yarın 1*. Istanbul: Tekin Yayınevi, 1996 [1969].

Aybars, Ergün. *İstiklal Mahkemeleri*. 2nd ed. Istanbul: Doğan Kitap, 2018 [1975].

Aydemir, Şevket Süreyya. *Menderes'in Dramı?* 7th ed. Istanbul: Remzi Kitabevi, 2000 [1969].

Aydın, Ertan. "Peculiarities of Turkish Revolutionary Ideology in the 1930s: The Ülkü Version of Kemalism, 1933–1936." *Middle Eastern Studies* 40, no. 5 (2004): 55–82.

Ayhan, Aydın. "İzmir'in İşgali Sırasında Balıkesir." In *Milli Mücadele'de Balıkesir*, 31–52. Istanbul: Kent Basımevi, 1986.

Ayral, Alparslan. *Balıkesir'in Kültür Hayatı*. Sivas: Dilek Ofset Matbaası, 1995.

Aytürk, İlker. "Nationalism and Islam in Cold War Turkey, 1944–69." *Middle Eastern Studies* 50, no. 5 (2014): 693–719.

Azak, Umut. *Islam and Secularism in Turkey: Kemalism, Religion and the Nation State*. London: I. B. Tauris, 2010.

Baban, Cihad. *Politika Galerisi: Büstler ve Portreler*. Istanbul: Remzi Kitabevi, 1970.

Baer, Marc. *The Dönme: Jewish Converts, Muslim Revolutionaries, and Secular Turks*. Stanford: Stanford University Press, 2010.

Bağlum, Kemal. *Anıpolitik, 1945–1960*. Istanbul: Bilgi Yayınevi, 1991.

Bakiner, Onur. "A Key to Turkish Politics? The Center–Periphery Framework Revisited." *Turkish Studies* 19, no. 4 (2018): 503–522.

Bali, Rıfat. *A Scapegoat for All Seasons: The Dönmes or Crypto-Jews of Turkey*. Istanbul: The ISIS Press, 2008.

Barkey, Karen. *Empire of Difference: The Ottoman Empire in Comparative Perspective*. Cambridge: Cambridge University Press, 2008.

Başgil, Ali Fuad. *27 Mayıs İhtilali ve Sebepleri*. Istanbul: Çeltüt Matbaacılık, 1966.

Batatu, Hanna. *The Old Social Classes and the Revolutionary Movements of Iraq*. Princeton: Princeton University Press, 1978.

Bayar, Celal. *Başvekilim Adnan Menderes*, edited by İsmet Bozdağ. Istanbul: Tercüman Gazetesi, 1986.

Şark Raporu. Istanbul: Kaynak Yayınları, 2006.

Bedlek, Emine Yeşim. *Imagined Communities in Greece and Turkey: Trauma and the Population Exchanges under Atatürk*. London: I. B. Tauris, 2016.

Bein, Amit. *Kemalist Turkey and the Middle East: International Relations in the Interwar Period*. Cambridge: Cambridge University Press, 2017.

Belen, Fahri. *Demokrasiden Diktatörlüğe.*: Istanbul Matbaası, 1960.

Belge, Murat. "Menemen Olayı." In *Cumhuriyet Dönemi Türkiye Ansiklopedisi 2*, edited by Murat Belge, 573. Istanbul: İletişim Yayınları, 1983.

Berkes, Niyazi. *The Development of Secularism in Turkey*. London: C. Hurst & Co., 1998 [1964].

Bet-Shlimon, Arbella. *City of Black Gold: Oil, Ethnicity, and the Making of Modern Kirkuk*. Stanford University Press, 2019.

Bilgin, Mustafa. *Britain and Turkey in the Middle East: Politics and Influence in the Early Cold War Era*. London: I. B. Tauris, 2007.

Birand, Mehmet Ali, Bülent Çaplı, and Can Dündar. *Demirkırat: Bir Demokrasinin Doğuşu*. Istanbul: Milliyet Yayınları, 1991.

Boratav, Korkut. *Türkiye İktisat Tarihi, 1908–2009*. Istanbul: İmge Kitabevi, 2015.

Bordo, Micheal. "The Bretton Woods International Monetary System: A Historical Overview." In *A Retrospective on the Bretton Woods System: Lessons for International Monetary Reform*, edited by Micheal Bordo and Barry Eichengreen, 3–108. Chicago: University of Chicago Press, 2003.

Bouquet, Olivier. "Old Elites in a New Republic: The Reconversion of Ottoman Bureaucratic Families in Turkey (1909–1939)." *Comparative Studies of South Asia and the Middle East* 31, no. 3 (2011): 588–600.

Bowie, Robert, and Richard Immerman. *Waging Peace: How Eisenhower Shaped an Enduring Cold War Strategy*. Oxford: Oxford University Press, 1998.

Bozdağ, İsmet. *Bir Darbenin Anatomisi: Celal Bayar Anlatıyor*, 3rd ed. Istanbul: Emre Yayınları, 2006 [1991].

Bozkurt, Abdurrahman. *Tevfik İleri Cumhuriyetin İkinci Eğitim Mimarı*. Istanbul: İdil, 2012.

Brewer, David. *Greece, the Decade at War: Occupation, Resistance and Civil War*. London: I. B. Tauris, 2016.

Brockett, Gavin. *How Happy to Call Oneself a Turk: Provincial Newspapers and the Negotiation of a Muslim National Identity*. Austin: University of Texas Press, 2011.

"The Legend of 'The Turk' in Korea: Popular Perceptions of the Korean War and Their Importance to a Turkish National Identity." *War & Society* 22, no. 2 (2004): 109–142.

Brummett, Palmira. *Image and Imperialism in the Ottoman Revolutionary Press, 1908–1911*. Albany: State University of New York Press, 2000.

Buğra, Ayşe. *State and Business in Modern Turkey: A Comparative Study*. Albany: State University of New York Press, 1994.

Burçak, Rıfkı Salim. *İdamların İçyüzü*. Ankara: Demokratlar Klübü Yayınları, 1997.

On Yılın Anıları. Ankara: Nurol Matbaacılık, 1998.

Türkiye'de Demokrasiye Geçiş. Ankara: Olgaç Yayınevi, 1979.

Yassıada ve Öncesi. Ankara: Çam Matbaası, 1976.

Cem (İpekçi), İsmail. *Türkiye'de Geri Kalmışlığın Tarihi*. 4th ed. Istanbul: Cem Yayınevi, 1974 [1970].

Cesarano, Filippo. *Monetary Theory and Bretton Woods: The Construction of an International Monetary Order*. Cambridge: Cambridge University Press, 2009.

Chapman, Herrick. *France's Long Reconstruction*. Cambridge, MA: Harvard University Press, 2018.

Cillov, Haluk. *Türkiye Ekonomisi*. Istanbul: Sermet Matbaası, 1965.

Clark, Bruce. *Twice a Stranger: The Mass Expulsions That Forged Modern Greece and Turkey*. Cambridge, MA: Harvard University Press, 2006.

Cohen, Michael. *Strategy and Politics in the Middle East, 1954–1960: Defending the Northern Tier*. London: Frank Cass, 2005.

Cohn, Edwin. *Turkish Economic, Social, and Political Change: The Development of a More Prosperous and Open Society*. New York: Praeger Publishers, 1970.

Council for Economic and Industry Research, Inc. "Evaluation of Industrial Development: Turkey." International Cooperation Administration. 1957.

Cumhuriyet Dönemi Türkiye Ekonomisi, 1923–1978, edited by Memduh Yasa. Istanbul: Akbank Kültür Yayını, 1980.

Çağaptay, Soner. *Islam, Secularism and Nationalism in Modern Turkey: Who Is a Turk?* London: Routledge, 2006.

The New Sultan: Erdogan and the Crisis of Modern Turkey. London: I. B. Tauris, 2017.

Çakır, Armağan Emre. *The United States and Turkey's Path to Europe: Hands across the Table*. New York: Routledge, 2016.

Çakmak, Diren. "Türk Siyasal Yaşamında Bir Muhalefet Partisi Örneği: Hürriyet Partisi (1955–1958)." *Akademik Bakış* 2, no. 3 (winter 2008): 153–186.

Çalış, Şaban Halis. *Turkey's Cold War: Foreign Policy and Western Alignment in the Modern Republic*. London: I. B. Tauris, 2017.

Çandır, Muzaffer. *Manisa Milletvekili: Yazar Samet Ağaoğlu: Hayatı, Sanatı, Eserleri*. Manisa: Manisa İl Özel İdaresi, 2013.

Çaylak, Adem. *Osman Bölükbaşı ve Siyasal Hareketi*. Ankara: Atatürk Araştırma Merkezi, 2010.

Çelebi, Onur. "14 Temmuz 1958 Irak Darbesinin Türk İç Politikasına Yansımaları." *Electronic Turkish Studies* 12, no. 31 (2017): 41–60.

Çınar, Metin. *Anadoluculuk ve Tek Parti CHP'de Sağ Kanat*. Istanbul: İletişim Yayınları, 2013.

Çolak, Filiz. "Demokrat Parti Dönemi'nde TBMM'deki Kadın Milletvekilleri ve Meclisteki Faaliyetleri, 1950–1960." *Tarih Okulu Dergisi* 10, no. 32 (2017): 115–158.

Çolak, Yılmaz. "Language Policy and Official Ideology in Early Republican Turkey." *Middle Eastern Studies* 40, no. 6 (2004): 67–91.

Çölaşan, Emin. *Unutulmayan Söyleşiler: Tarihe Düşülen Notlar*. Istanbul: Doğan Kıtapçılık, 2006.

Danforth, Nicholas. *The Remaking of Republican Turkey: Memory and Modernity since the Fall of the Ottoman Empire*. Cambridge: Cambridge University Press, 2021.

Dann, Uriel. *King Hussein and the Challenge of Arab Radicalism: Jordan 1955–1967*. Oxford: Oxford University Press, 1989.

DeBruyne, Nese, and Anne Leland. "American War and Military Operations Casualties: Lists and Statistics." Congressional Research Service. January 2, 2015. Available: https://apps.dtic.mil/dtic/tr/fulltext/u2/1013824.pdf.

Dede, Kadir. "Forum Dergisi." In *Türkiye'nin 1950'li Yılları*, edited by Mete Kaan Kaynar, 451–464. Istanbul: İletişim Yayınları, 2015.

"İnönü'den Bayar'a Gericilik: Çok Partili Hayata Geçiş." In *Resmi Tarih Tartışmaları 7*, edited by Fikret Başkaya, 87–118. Ankara: Özgür Üniversite Yayınları, 2009.

Dedman, Martin. *The Origins and Development of the European Union 1945–2008: A History of European Integration*, 2nd ed. London: Routledge, 2009.

Demir, Şerif. *Türk Siyasi Tarihinde Adnan Menderes*. Istanbul: Paraf Yayınları, 2010.

"Van'da Siyasi Hayat 1945–1960." *Van Yüzüncü Yıl Üniversitesi Sosyal Bilimler Enstitüsü Dergisi* (2021): 133–160.

Demirci, Aliyar. "Ahmet Emin Yalman." In *Modern Türkiye'de Siyasi Düşünce VII: Liberalizm*, edited by Tanıl Bora and Murat Gültekingil, 473–479. Istanbul: İletişim Yayınları, 2005.

Demirci, Aytaç, and Yusuf Rıza Düvenci. *Bir Mücadele Gazetası! Demokrat İzmir.* Istanbul: Yapı Kredi Yayınları, 2018.
Demirel, Ahmet. *İlk Meclisin Vekilleri: Milli Mücadele Döneminde Seçimler.* Istanbul: İletişim Yayınları, 2010.
Demirel, Tanel. *Türkiye'nin Uzun On Yılı: Demokrat Parti İktidarı ve 27 Mayıs Darbesi*. Istanbul: İstanbul Bilgi Üniversitesi Yayınları, 2011.
The Development of National Banking in Turkey. Ankara: Press Department of the Ministry of Interior, 1938.
Dikerdem, Mahmut. *Ortadoğu'da Devrim Yılları: Bir Büyükelçi'nin Anıları.* Istanbul: Cem Yayınları, 1990 [1977].
Dinç, Ahmet. *Hamido: Meclis'in Son Kabadayısı İlk Faili Meçhulü!* Istanbul: Hayykitap, 2015.
Doğan, Hamdi. *Birinci Mecliste Malatya Milletvekilleri ve Siyasi Faaliyetleri, 1920–1923*. Ankara: Akçağ Yayınları, 2011.
Doğaner, Yasemin. *Türk Demokrasi Tarihinde Vatan Cephesi*. Ankara: Siyasal Kitabevi, 2013.
Doumanis, Nicholas. *Before the Nation: Christian–Muslim Coexistence and Its Destruction in Late Ottoman Anatolia*. Oxford: Oxford University Press, 2012.
Dower, John. *Embracing Defeat: Japan in the Wake of World War II.* New York: W. W. Norton, 1999.
Dressler, Markus. *Writing Religion: The Making of Turkish Alevi Islam*. Oxford: Oxford University Press, 2013.
Dunkerley, James. "Guatemala since 1930." In *The Cambridge History of Latin America*, vol. VII: *Mexico, Central America and the Caribbean*, edited by Leslie Bethell, 211–250. Cambridge: Cambridge University Press, 1990.
Eichengreen, Barry. "The European Payments Union: An Efficient Mechanism for Rebuilding Europe's Trade?" In *Europe's Post-War Recovery*, edited by Barry Eichengreen, 169–195. Cambridge: Cambridge University Press, 1995.
Emen-Gökatalay, Gözde, and Semih Gökatalay. "Was There Room for Christian Turks in Early Republican Turkey? Debates on the Migration and Turkishness of the Gagauz." *Middle Eastern Studies* 59, no. 2 (2022): 199–220.
Emiroğlu, Atiye. *Hasan Polatkan.* Ankara: Nobel Yayın, 2011.
Emrence, Cem. *99 Günlük Muhalefet: Serbest Cumhuriyet Fırkası.* Istanbul: İletişim Yayınları, 2006.
Engerman, Davis. *The Price of Aid: The Economic Cold War in India.* Cambridge, MA: Harvard University Press, 2018.
Erer, Tekin. *On Yılın Mücadelesi*. Istanbul: Ticaret Postası Matbaası, 1963.
Ergin, Murat. *"Is the Turk a White Man?": Race and Modernity in the Making of Turkish Identity*. Leiden: Brill, 2006.
Ergun, A. Yavuz. *CHPli Menderes, 1931–1945: Tek Parti Dönemi'nde Adnan Menderes'in Siyasi Yaşamı.* Istanbul: Boyut, 2017.
Eroğul, Cem. *Demokrat Parti: Tarihi ve İdeolojisi.* Istanbul: Yordam Kitap, 2013 [1970].
"The Establishment of Multiparty Rule: 1945–71." In *Turkey in Transition: New Perspectives*, edited by İrvin Cemil Schick and Ertuğrul Ahmet Tonak,

translated by İrvin Cemil Schick and Rezan Benatar Schick, 101–143. Oxford: Oxford University Press, 1987.

Erol, Emre. *The Ottoman Crisis in Western Anatolia: Turkey's Belle Epoque and the Transition to a Modern Nation State*. New York: I. B. Tauris, 2016.

Ersanlı, Büşra. *İktidar ve Tarih: Türkiye'de "Resmî Tarih" Tezinin Oluşumu, 1929–1937*. Istanbul: İletişim Yayınları, 2003.

Ersarı, Nevra. "Ellili Yıllarda Radyo ve Siyaset." In *Türkiye'nin 1950'li Yılları*, edited by Mete Kaan Kaynar, 393–422. Istanbul: İletişim Yayınları, 2015.

Evans, Martin. *Algeria: France's Undeclared War*. Oxford: Oxford University Press, 2012.

Evliyazade, Mehmet Özdemir. *Onları Anlatıyorum*. Istanbul: Yeni Doğuş Matbaası, 1960.

Eyüpoğlu, A. Cevdet. "Şeker Fabrikasyonun Tarihçesi ve Türkiye'de Şeker Sanayii." *Kimya Mühendisliği* 2, no. 23 (1967): 14–23.

Farouk-Sluglett, Marion, and Peter Sluglett, *Iraq since 1958: From Revolution to Dictatorship*. 3rd ed. London: I. B. Taurus, 2001.

Fedayi, Cemal. *Kandıralı Profesör Turan Güneş: Hayatı, Düşüncesi, Kişiliği*. Ankara: Kadim Yayınları, 2012.

Fersoy, Orhan Cemal. *Bir Devre Adını Veren Başbakan: Adnan Menderes*. Istanbul: Garanti Matbaası, 1971.

Finefrock, Michael. "Laissez-faire, the 1923 Izmir Economic Congress and Early Turkish Developmental Policy in Political Perspective." *Middle Eastern Studies* 17, no. 3 (1981): 375–392.

Frey, Frederick. *The Turkish Political Elite*. Cambridge, MA: MIT Press, 1965.

Gaddis, John Lewis. *We Know Now: Rethinking Cold War History*. Oxford: Oxford University Press, 1997.

Garapon, Béatrice, and Adnan Çelik. "From Tribal Chiefs to Marxist Activists: Kurdistan from 1946 to 1975." In *The Cambridge History of the Kurds*, edited by Hamit Bozarslan, Cengiz Güneş, and Veli Yadirgi, 229–249. Cambridge: Cambridge University Press, 2021.

Garlitz, Richard. "Land-Grant Education in Turkey: Atatürk University and American Technical Assistance, 1954–68." In *Turkey in the Cold War Ideology and Culture*, edited by Cangül Örnek and Çağdaş Üngör, 177–197. London: Palgrave Macmillan, 2013.

Gavin, Francis. *Gold, Dollars and Power: The Politics of International Monetary Relations, 1958–1971*. Chapel Hill, NC: University of North Carolina Press, 2004.

Gendzier, Irene. *Notes from the Minefield: United States Intervention in Lebanon and the Middle East, 1945–1958*. New York: Columbia University Press, 1997.

Geniş, Kaan Cem. "Demokrat Parti'ye Yapılan Bağıslara Dair Kayıtlar (1950–1960)." *Atatürk Dergisi* 9, no. 1 (2020): 73–96.

Gerolymatos, Andre. *An International Civil War: Greece, 1943–1949*. New Haven, CT: Yale University Press, 2016.

Geyikdağı, V. Necla. *Foreign Investment in the Ottoman Empire: International Trade and Relations, 1854–1914*. London: I. B. Tauris, 2011.

Gildea, Robert. *France since 1945*. Oxford: Oxford University Press, 2002.

Gingeras, Ryan. *Fall of the Sultanate: The Great War and the End of the Ottoman Empire 1908–1922.* Cambridge: Cambridge University Press, 2016.

Heroin, Organized Crime, and the Making of Modern Turkey. Oxford: Oxford University Press, 2014.

Giomi, Fabio. "Domesticating Kemalism: Conflicting Muslim Narratives about Turkey in Interwar Yugoslavia." In *Nostalgia, Loss and Creativity in South-East Europe: Political and Cultural Representations of the Past*, edited by Catharina Raudvere, 151–188. London: Palgrave Macmillan, 2018.

Goloğlu, Mahmut. *Demokrasiye Geçiş, 1946–1950.* Istanbul: İş Bankası Kültür Yayınları, 2009.

Gökalp, Ziya. *Turkish Nationalism and Western Civilization: Selected Essays of Ziya Gökalp*, edited by Niyazi Berkes. New York: Columbia University Press, 1959.

Gökçen, Ahmet, and Ertuğrul Ünal. "27 Mayıs 1960 Tarihinde Yürürlükte Olan Ceza Mevzuatımız ve Evrensel Hukuk Bağlamında Yassıada Yargılamaları." *Marmara Üniversitesi Hukuk Fakültesi Hukuk Araştırmaları Dergisi* 28, no. 1 (2022): 129–169.

Gökşen, Nesimi. *Devletin Subayı, Subayın Devleti: Cuntalar, Darbe ve İktidar Savaşı, 27 Mayıs 1960.* Istanbul: İletişim Yayınları, 2023.

Gönüllü, Ali Rıza. "Milli Mücadele ve Cumhuriyet Döneminde Hayvanlar Vergisi, 1920–1962." *Selçuk Üniversitesi Türkiyat Araştırmaları Dergisi* 1, no. 38 (2015): 69–102.

Gözel, Murat. *İz Bırakanlar: Malatyalı 44 Şahsiyet.* Istanbul: Malatya Kent Konseyi Yayınları, 2013.

Gunn, Christopher. "The 1960 Coup in Turkey: US Intelligence Failure or a Successful Intervention?" *Journal of Cold War Studies* 17, no. 2 (2015): 103–139.

Güçlü, Yücel. *The Life and Career of a Turkish Diplomat: Cevat Açıkalın.* Ankara: Ministry of Foreign Affairs, 2002.

"Turkish–German Relations on the Eve of World War Two." *Turkish Studies* 1, no. 2 (2000): 73–94.

Gül, Murat. *Architecture and the Turkish City: An Urban History of Istanbul since the Ottomans.* London: I. B. Tauris, 2017.

The Emergence of Modern Istanbul: Transformation and Modernisation of a City. London: I. B. Tauris, 2009.

Gülizar, Jülide. *Haberler Bitti Şimdi Oyun Havaları.* Ankara: Ümit Yayıncılık, 1994.

Gündüz, Alptekin. *En Sevdiği Güneşti: Dr. Suphi Baykam'ın Fırtınalı Yaşamı.* Istanbul: Piramid Yayıncılık, 2004.

Günver, Semih. *Fatin Rüştü Zorlu'nun Öyküsü: Z, Zorro Gibi.* Istanbul: Bilgi Yayınevi, 1985

Gürpınar, Doğan. "The Reinvention of Kemalism: Between Elitism, Anti-Elitism and Anti-Intellectualism." *Middle Eastern Studies* 49, no. 3 (2013): 454–476.

Gürsoy-Naskali, Emine. *Cumhuriyet Tarihi Soyadı Hikayeleri.* Istanbul: Doğan Kitap, 2013.

(ed.). *Yassıada Zabıtaları 6: Vatan Cephesi Davası.* Istanbul: Kitabevi, 2011.

Güveloğlu, Gülşah Kurt. *Demokrat Partinin Kadın Milletvekilleri*. Istanbul: Kriter Yayınları, 2018.
Güven, Dilek. *Cumhuriyet Dönemi Azınlık Politikaları ve Stratejileri Bağlamında 6–7 Eylül Olayları*. Istanbul: İletişim Yayınları, 2006.
Haggard, Stephan, and Robert Kaufman. *The Political Economy of Democratic Transitions*. Princeton: Princeton University Press, 1995.
Hajimu, Masuda. *Cold War Crucible: The Korean Conflict and the Postwar World*. Cambridge, MA: Harvard University Press, 2015.
Hale, William. *The Political and Economic Development of Modern Turkey*. London: Croom Helm, 1981.
Turkish Foreign Policy since 1774. London: Routledge, 2000.
Turkish Politics and the Military. London: Routledge, 1994.
Hasanlı, Cemil. *Stalin and the Turkish Crisis of the Cold War, 1945–1953*. Lanham: Lexington Books, 2011.
Hatipoğlu, Şevket Raşit. *Dış Ticaretimizde Ziraatın Payı*. Ankara: Yüksek Ziraat Enstitüsü, 1936.
Helleiner, Eric. *States and the Reemergence of Global Finance from Bretton Woods to the 1990s*. Ithaca: Cornell University Press, 1994.
Heper, Metin. "The Recalcitrance of the Turkish Public Bureaucracy to 'Bourgeois Politics': A Multi-Factor Political Stratification Analysis." *Middle East Journal* 30, no. 4 (1976): 485–500.
Hershlag, Z. Y. *Turkey: An Economy in Transition*. The Hague: Uitgeverij van Keulen NV, 1958.
Hiltner, John. "Land Accumulation in the Turkish Cukurova." *Journal of Farm Economics* 42, no. 3 (1960): 615–628.
Hirst, Samuel. *Against the Liberal Order: The Soviet Union, Turkey, and Statist Internationalism, 1919–1939*. Oxford: Oxford University Press, 2024.
Holland, Robert. *Britain and the Revolt in Cyprus, 1954–1959*. Oxford: Oxford University Press, 1998.
Ihrig, Stefan. *Atatürk in the Nazi Imagination*. Cambridge, MA: Harvard University Press, 2014.
Ilıcak, Nazlı. *16 Yıl Sonra Salim Başol'u Yargılıyoruz*. Istanbul: Tercüman, 1977.
İleri, Tevfik. *Yassıada ve Kayseri Günlükleri*. Istanbul: Ötüken Neşriyat, 2003.
İlkin, Selim, and İlhan Tekeli. "(Kör) Ali İhsan (İloğlu) Bey ve Temsili-Mesleki Programı." In *Atatürk Döneminin Ekonomik ve Toplumsal Tarihiyle İlgili Sorunlar Sempozyumu, 14–16 Ocak 1977*, 283–356. Istanbul: İstanbul Yüksek İktisat ve Ticaret Mektebi Mezunları Derneği Yayını, 1977.
Uygulamaya Geçerken Türkiye'de Devletçiliğin Oluşumu. Istanbul: Bilge Kültür Sanat, 2009 [1982].
İnsel, Ahmet. "Türkiye'de Liberalizm Kavramının Soyçizgisi." In *Modern Türkiye'de Siyasi Düşünce VII: Liberalizm*, edited by Tanıl Bora and Murat Gültekingil, 41-74. Istanbul: İletişim Yayınları, 2005.
İsmet (İnönü), "Fırkamızın Devletçilik Vasfı," *Kadro* 22 (1933): 4–6.
İsvan, Ahmet. *Başkent Gölgesinde İstanbul*. Istanbul: İletişim Yayınları, 2002.
Jackson, Julian. *A Certain Idea of France: The Life of Charles de Gaulle*. London: Penguin, 2018.

Jalal, Ayse. *The State of Martial Rule: The Origins of Pakistan's Political Economy of Defence*. Lahore: Vanguard Books, 1991.

The Struggle for Pakistan: A Muslim Homeland and Global Politics. Cambridge, MA: The Belknap Press of Harvard University Press, 2014.

Kara, Hamdi, and Nuri Yavan. "Türkiye'de Doğrudan Yabancı Yatırımları ve Bölgesel Dağılışı." *Coğrafi Bilimler Dergisi* 1, no. 1 (2003): 19–42.

Karakaş, Ömer. "Balıkesir'de Serbest Cumhuriyet Fırkası'nın Teşkilatlanması ve Belediye Seçimleri (1930)." *Turkish Studies* 8, no. 5 (2013): 357–375.

Karaömerlioğlu, M. Asım. "Turkey's 'Return' to Multi-Party Politics: A Social Interpretation." *Eastern European Quarterly* 40 (2006): 89–107.

Karaveli, Halil. *Why Turkey Is Authoritarian: From Ataturk to Erdogan*. London: Pluto Press, 2018.

Karpat, Kemal. "Actors and Issues in Turkish Politics, 1950–1960: Prototypes and Stereotypes." *International Journal of Turkish Studies* 17, no. 1 and 2 (2011): 115–159.

Ottoman Population, 1830–1914: Demographic and Social Characteristics. Madison: University of Wisconsin Press, 1985.

"The People's Houses in Turkey: Establishment and Growth." *Middle East Journal* 17, no. 1/2 (1963): 55–67.

"Social Effects of Farm Mechanization in Turkish Villages." *Social Research* (1960): 83–103.

Turkey's Politics: The Transition to a Multi-Party System. Princeton: Princeton University Press, 1959.

Kasaba, Reşat. "Kemalist Certainties and Modernist Ambiguities." In *Rethinking Modernity and National Identity in Turkey*, edited by Sibel Bozdoğan and Reşat Kasaba, 15–36. Seattle: University of Washington Press, 1997.

"Populism and Democracy in Turkey, 1946–61." In *Rules and Rights in the Middle East: Democracy, Law, and Society*, edited by Ellis Goldberg, Reşat Kasaba, and Joel S. Migdal, 43–68. Seattle: University of Washington, 1993.

Kayalı, Hasan. *Imperial Resilience: The Great War's End, Ottoman Longevity, and Incidental Nations*. Berkley: University of California Press, 2021.

"The Struggle for Independence." In *The Cambridge History of Turkey*, edited by Reşat Kasaba, 112–146. Cambridge University Press, 2008.

Kayış, Yasin. *Demokrat Parti Döneminde Siyasi Karikatür (1950–1960)*. Istanbul: Libra Kitap, 2009.

Kayra, Cahit. *'38 Kuşağı: Anılar*. Istanbul: Türkiye İş Bankası Kültür Yayınları, 2002.

Keleş, Ruşen. *100 Soruda Türkiye'de Şehirleşme, Konut ve Gecekondu*. Istanbul: Gerçek Yayınları, 1972.

Keyder, Çağlar. "The Political Economy of Turkish Democracy." *New Left Review* 115 (1979): 3–44.

State and Class in Turkey. New York: Verso, 1987.

Kezer, Zeynep. *Building Modern Turkey-State, Space, and Ideology in the Early Republic*. Pittsburgh: University of Pittsburgh Press, 2015.

Khoury, Philip. *Syria and the French Mandate: The Politics of Arab Nationalism 1920–1945*. Princeton: Princeton University Press, 1987.

Kılıç, Murat. *"Allah, Vatan, Soy, Milli Mukaddesat": Türk Milliyetçiler Derneği, 1951–1953.* Istanbul: İletişim Yayınları, 2016.

Kılınçoğlu, Deniz. *Economics and Capitalism in the Ottoman Empire.* London: Routledge, 2016.

Kıpçak, M. Reşit. *Turistik Ekonomik Balıkesir.* Istanbul: Acar Matbaası, 1968.

Kısacık, Raşit. *Malatya'da Toplumsal Olaylar.* Istanbul: Ozan Yayıncılık, 2012.

Kieser, Hans-Lukas. *Talaat Pasha: Father of Modern Turkey, Architect of Genocide.* Princeton: Princeton University Press, 2018.

Koca, Selçuk. "Atatürk'ü Koruma Kanunu." In *Türkiye'nin 1950'li Yılları*, edited by Mete Kaan Kaynar, 321–330. Istanbul: İletişim Yayınları, 2015.

Kocabaşoğlu, Uygur (ed.). *Türkiye İş Bankası Tarihi.* Istanbul: Türkiye İş Bankası Kültür Yayınları, 2001.

Koç, Rasim. *İdam Sehpasındaki Dışişleri Bakanı: Fatin Rüştü Zorlu.* Istanbul: Ötüken, 2010.

Koçak, Cemil. *Demokrat Parti İktidârı (1950–1960), I: Demokratlar ve Halkçılar,1950–1954.* Istanbul: Timaş Yayınları, 2024.

"Hüseyin Cahit Yalçın ve Fikir Hareketleri Dergisi, 1933–1940." In *Modern Türkiye'de Siyasi Düşünce VII: Liberalizm*, edited by Tanıl Bora and Murat Gültekingil, 246–259. Istanbul: İletişim Yayınları, 2005.

İkinci Parti: Türkiye'de İki Partili Siyasi Sistemin Kuruluş Yılları, 1945–1950, vol. I. Istanbul: İletişim Yayınları, 2010.

İktidar ve Demokratlar: Türkiye'de İki Partili Siyasi Sistemin Kuruluş Yılları, 1945–1950, vol. II. Istanbul: İletişim Yayınları, 2012.

Rejim Krizi: Türkiye'de İki Partili Siyasi Sistemin Kuruluş Yılları, 1945–1950, vol. III. Istanbul: İletişim Yayınları, 2013.

Türkiye'de Milli Şef Dönemi, 1938–1945, vol. I. Istanbul: İletişim Yayınları 1996 [1986].

Türkiye'de Milli Şef Dönemi, 1938–1945, vol. II. 3rd ed. Istanbul: İletişim Yayınları, 2007 [1986].

Umûmî Müfettişlikler, 1927–1952. 2nd ed. Istanbul: İletişim Yayınları, 2010 [2003].

Uzlaşma: Türkiye'de İki Partili Siyasi Sistemin Kuruluş Yılları, 1945–1950, vol. V. Istanbul: İletişim Yayınları, 2016.

Koçak, M. Hakan. "Ellili Yıllarda Emek Rejimi ve Emek Hareketi." In *Türkiye'nin 1950'li Yılları*, edited by Mete Kaan Kaynar, 69–95. Istanbul: İletişim Yayınları, 2015.

Koraltan, Refik. *Tek Parti Devirden 27 Mayıs İhtilali'ne Demokratlar: DP'nin Kurucusu Anlatıyor*, edited by Kamil Maman. Istanbul: Timaş Yayınları, 2013.

Koraltürk, Murat. "Ahmet Hamdi Başar Kimdir?" In *Ahmet Hamdi Başar'ın Hatıraları, Cilt I: "Gazi Bana Çok Kızmış ...,"* edited by Murat Koraltürk, 1–58. Istanbul: Bilgi Universitesi Yayınları, 2007.

(ed.) *Ahmet Hamdi Başar'ın Hatıraları, Cilt I: "Gazi Bana Çok Kızmış ...."* Istanbul: Bilgi Üniversitesi Yayınları, 2007.

Kostanick, Huey Louis. "Turkish Resettlement of Refugees from Bulgaria, 1950–1953." *Middle East Journal* 9, no. 1 (1955): 41–53.

Kubilay, Çağla, and Mehmet Pehlivan. "Demokrat Parti ve Radyo: Bir Islahat Girişimi, 1954." *ilef Dergisi* 6, no. 1 (2019): 27–60.

Kuneralp, Zeki. *Sadece Diplomat*. Istanbul: İstanbul Matbaası, 1981.

Kurt, Ümit. "Revisiting the Legal Infrastructure for the Confiscation of Armenian and Greek Wealth: An Analysis of the CUP Years and the Early Modern Republic." *Middle Eastern Studies* 53, no. 5 (2017): 700–723.

Kutay, Cemal. *Üç Devirden Hakikatler: Celal Bayar'ın Yazmadığı ve Yazmayacağı*. Istanbul: Alioğlu Yayınevi, 1982.

Lee, Yong Wook. "The Origin of One-Party Domination: America's Reverse Course and the Emergence of the Liberal Democratic Party in Japan." *The Journal of East Asian Affairs* 18, no. 2 (2004): 371–413.

Leffler, Melvyn. "The Emergence of an American Grand Strategy, 1945–1952." In *The Cambridge History of the Cold War*, vol. I: *Origins*, edited by Melvyn Leffler and Odd Arne Westad, 67–88. Cambridge University Press, 2010.

"Strategy, Diplomacy, and the Cold War: The United States, Turkey, and NATO, 1945–1952." *The Journal of American History* 71, no. 4 (1985): 807–825.

Lerner, Daniel. *The Passing of Traditional Society*. New York: Free Press, 1958.

Lesch, David. *Syria and the United States: Eisenhower's Cold War in the Middle East*. Boulder: Westview Press, 1992.

Levi, Avner. *Türkiye Cumhuriyeti'nde Yahudiler: Hukuki ve Siyasi Durumları*. Istanbul: İletişim Yayınları 1996.

Levin, Paul T. "Reflections on Şerif Mardin's Center–Periphery Thesis." *Turkish Studies* 24, nos. 3–4 (2023): 617–639.

Levitsky, Steven, and Lucan Way. *Competitive Authoritarianism: Hybrid Regimes after the Cold War*. Cambridge: Cambridge University Press, 2010.

Levy-Aksu, Noemi. "Freedom versus Security: Regulating and Managing Public Gatherings after the Young Turk Revolution." In *The Young Turks and the Ottoman Empire: The Aftermath of the 1908 Revolution*, edited by Noemi Levy-Aksu and François Georgeon, 212–233. London: I. B. Tauris, 2016.

Lewis, Bernard. *The Emergence of Modern Turkey*, 2nd ed. Oxford: Oxford University Press, 1968 [1961].

Lewis, David Levering. *The Improbable Wendell Willkie*. New York: Liveright, 2018.

Lewis, Geoffrey. *Modern Turkey*. New York: Praeger Publishers, 1974.

Lightfoot, Dale, and Halil Taş. "Gecekondu Settlements in Turkey: Rural–Urban Migration in the Developing European Periphery." *Journal of Geography* 104, no. 6 (2005): 263–271.

Lord, Ceren. *Religious Politics in Turkey: From the Birth of the Republic to the AKP*. Cambridge: Cambridge University Press, 2018.

Madanoğlu, Cemal. *Anılar, 1919–1953*. Istanbul: Evrim Yayınevi, 1982.

Makal, Ahmet. *Ameleden İşçiye: Erken Cumhuriyet Dönemi Emek Tarihi Çalışmaları*. Istanbul: İletişim Yayınları, 2007.

Türkiye'de Tek Partili Dönemde Çalışma İlişkileri, 1920–1946. Istanbul: İmge Yayınları, 1999.

Mardin, Şerif. "Center–Periphery Relations: A Key to Turkish Politics?" *Daedalus* 102, no.1 (1973): 169–190.

The Genesis of Young Ottoman Thought: A Study in the Modernization of Turkish Political Ideas. Princeton: Princeton University Press, 1962.

"Opposition and Control in Turkey." *Government and Opposition* 1, no. 3 (1966): 375–387.

Religion and Social Change in Modern Turkey: The Case of Bediuzzaman Said Nursi. Albany: State University of New York Press, 1989.

Marshal Plan in Turkey 24. The Organization for International Economic Cooperation, Ministry for Foreign Affairs. 1955.

Marshall Plan in Turkey 40. The Organization for International Economic Cooperation, Ministry for Foreign Affairs. 1959.

Massicard, Elise. "The Repression of the Koçgiri Rebellion, 1920–1921." Sciences Po, Paris, France. September 29, 2009. Available: www.sciencespo.fr/mass-violence-war-massacre-resistance/fr/document/repression-koa-giri-rebellion-1920–1921.

Türkiye'den Avrupa'ya Alevi Hareketinin Siyasallaşması. Istanbul: İletişim Yayınları, 2005.

Mat, Ertuğrul. *Demokrasi Yolunda Karınca Misali: İstanbul ve Ankara Günleri.* Ankara: Berikan Yayınevi, 2015.

McDowall, David. *A Modern History of the Kurds.* 3rd ed. London: I. B. Tauris, 2004.

McGlade, Jacqueline. "More a Plowshare than a Sword: The Legacy of US Cold War Agricultural Diplomacy." *Agricultural History* 83, no. 1 (2009): 79–102.

Meeker, Michael. *A Nation of Empire: The Ottoman Legacy of Turkish Modernity.* Berkeley: University of California Press, 2001.

Metinsoy, Murat. *İkinci Dünya Savaşında Türkiye Gündelik Yaşam Devlet ve Toplum.* Istanbul: Türkiye İş Bankası Kültür Yayınları, 2017.

Power of the People: Everyday Resistance and Dissent in the Making of Modern Turkey, 1923–38. Cambridge: Cambridge University Press, 2021.

Meyer, James. *Red Star over the Black Sea: Nâzım Hikmet and His Generation.* Oxford: Oxford University Press, 2023.

Turks across Empires: Marketing Muslim Identity in the Russian–Ottoman Borderlands, 1856–1914. Oxford: Oxford University Press, 2015.

Mikesell, Raymond. *Foreign Exchange in the Postwar World.* Maryland: The Twentieth Century Fund, 1954.

Miller, Jennifer. *Cold War Democracy: The United States and Japan 1945–1963.* Cambridge, MA: Harvard University Press, 2019.

Milward, Alan. *The Reconstruction of Western Europe, 1945–51.* London: Routledge, 2006.

Naymansoy, Günseli. *Türk Felsefesinin Öncülerinden Tezer Taşkıran.* Ankara: Atatürk Kültür Merkezi, 2013.

Neuberger, Mary. *The Orient Within: Muslim Minorities and the Negotiation of Nationhood in Modern Bulgaria.* Ithaca: Cornell University Press, 2004.

Nutku, Emrullah. *Demokrat Parti Neden Çöktü ve Politika'da Yitirdiğim Yıllar, 1946–1958.* Istanbul: Fakülteler Matbaası, 1972.

O'Donnell, Guillermo, and Philippe Schmitter. *Transitions from Authoritarian Rule: Tentative Conclusions about Uncertain Democracies.* Baltimore: Johns Hopkins University Press, 1986.

Oğuz, Mevlüt. *Malatya Tarihi ve Sosyoekonomik Durumu.* Istanbul: Kurtiş Mabaatcılık, 2000.

Okutan, M. Çağatay. *Bozkurt'tan Kur'an'a Millî Türk Talebe Birliği (MTTB) 1916–1980*. Istanbul: Bilgi Universitesi, 2004.

Okyar, Osman. "Inflation in a Mixed Economy." In *Capital Formation and Investment in Industry*, 352–370. Istanbul: İstanbul Matbaası, 1963.

Oran, Baskın. "Dönemin Bilançosu." In *Türk Dış Politikası, Cilt I: 1919–1980*, edited by Baskın Oran, 479–498. Istanbul: İletişim Yayınları, 2001.

Overy, Richard. *The Interwar Crisis, 1919–1939*. 2nd ed. London: Pearson, 2007.

Öner, Kenan. *Siyasi Hatıralarım ve Bizde Demokrasi*. Istanbul: Osmanbey Matbaası, 1948.

Örgen, Ertan. *Samet Ağaoğlu: Hayat, Hikayeleri ve Hatıraları Üzerinde Bir Araştırma*. Ankara: Milli Eğitim Bakanlığı Yayınları, 2009.

Örnek, Cangül. *Türkiye'nin Soğuk Savaş Düşünce Hayatı*. Istanbul: Can Yayınları, 2015.

Öymen, Altan. *Öfkeli Yıllar*. Istanbul: Doğan Kitap, 2009.

...Ve İhtilal. Istanbul: Doğan Kitap, 2013.

Özavcı, H. Ozan. *Intellectual Origins of the Republic: Ahmet Ağaoğlu and the Genealogy of Liberalism in Turkey*. Leiden: Brill, 2015.

Özbudun, Ergun. "Established Revolution vs. Unfinished Revolution: Contrasting Patterns of Democratization in Mexico and Turkey." In *Authoritarian Politics in Modern Society: The Dynamics of Established One-Party Systems*, edited by Samuel Huntington and Clement Moore. New York: Basic Books, 1970.

Social Change and Political Participation in Turkey. Princeton: Princeton University Press, 1976.

Özcan, Feridun Cemil. "Ellili Yıllarda Türkiye Ekonomisi." In *Türkiye'nin 1950'li Yılları*, edited by Mete Kaan Kaynar, 39–67. Istanbul: İletişim Yayınları, 2015.

Özcan, Gencer. "Ellili Yıllarda "Dış" Politika." In *Türkiye'nin 1950'li Yılları*, edited by Mete Kaan Kaynar, 97–133. Istanbul: İletişim Yayınları, 2015.

Özdemir, Nuray. "Cumhuriyet Döneminde Türkiye'de Yol Vergisi." *Tarih Araştırmaları Dergisi* 32 (2013): 213–258.

Özdemir, Zekeriya. *Balıkesir Bölgesinde Milli Mücadele Önderleri*. Balıkesir: Balıkesir Belediyesi, 1998.

Özel, Sabahattin. *Milli Mücadelede Trabzon*. Ankara: Türk Tarih Kurumu Basımevi, 1991.

Özer, Mehmet Halis. "The Effects of the Marshall Plan Aids to the Development of the Agricultural Sector in Turkey, the 1948–1953 Period." *International Journal of Economics and Financial Issues* 4, no. 2 (2014): 427–439.

Özgür, İren. *Islamic Schools in Modern Turkey: Faith, Politics, and Education*. Cambridge: Cambridge University Press, 2012.

Öztürkmen, Arzu. *Türkiye'de Folklor ve Milliyetçilik*. Istanbul: İletişim Yayınları, 1998.

Pamuk, Şevket. "Intervention during the Great Depression: Another Look at Turkish Experience." In *The Mediterranean Response to Globalization before 1950*, edited by Şevket Pamuk and Jeffrey Williamson, 321–339. London: Routledge, 2000.

The Ottoman Empire and European Capitalism. Cambridge: Cambridge University Press, 1987.

"War, State Economic Policies and Resistance by Agricultural Producers in Turkey 1939–1945." In *Peasants and Politics in the Modern Middle East*, edited by Farhad Kazemi and John Waterbury, 125–142. Gainesville, FL: Florida International University Press, 1991.

Parmaksız, Pınar Melis Yelsalı. *Türkiye'nin Modernleşmesinde Kadınlar: 1839'den Günümüze*. Istanbul: İmge Kitabevi Yayınları, 2017.

Payaslı, Volkan. "Tek Parti İktidarı'ndan Doğmuş Bir Denetim Organı: Müstakil Grup (1939–1946)." *Çağdaş Türkiye Tarihi Araştırmaları Dergisi* 14, no. 28 (spring 2014): 175–197.

Pelt, Mogens. *Military Intervention and a Crisis of Democracy in Turkey: The Menderes Era and Its Demise*. London: I. B. Tauris, 2014.

Perin, Mithat. *Yassıada Faciası: 27 Mayıs Darbesinden İdamlara Kadar İskence Altında Ezilenlerin Dramı*. Istanbul: Dem Basım Yayım A. Ş., 1990.

Pınar, Mehmet. "Van'da Demokrat Parti Teşkilatlanması." *Atatürk Dergisi* 2, no. 2 (2013): 31–55.

Pitman, Paul. "'A General Named Eisenhower': Atlantic Crisis and the Origins of the European Economic Community." In *Between Empire and Alliance: America and Europe during the Cold War*, edited by Marc Trachtenberg, 33–61. New York: Roman & Littlefield, 2003.

Polatel, Mehmet and Uğur Ümit Üngör. *Confiscation and Destruction: The Young Turk Seizure of Armenian Property*. London: Continuum, 2011.

Provence, Michael. *The Last Ottoman Generation and the Making of the Modern Middle East*. Cambridge: Cambridge University Press, 2017.

Przeworski, Adam. *Democracy and the Market: Political and Economic Reforms in Eastern Europe and Latin America*. Cambridge: Cambridge University Press, 1991.

Przeworski, Adam, Michael Alvarez, José Antonio Cheibub, and Fernando Limongi. *Democracy and Development: Political Institutions and Well-Being in the World, 1950–1990*. Cambridge: Cambridge University Press, 2000.

Reed, Howard. "Turkey's New İmam-Hatip Schools." *Die Welt des Islams* 4, nos. 2/3 (1955): 150–163.

Robinson, Richard. *The First Turkish Republic: A Case Study in National Development*. Cambridge, MA: Harvard University Press, 1963.

"Tractors in the Village: A Study in Turkey." *Journal of Farm Economics* 34, no. 4 (1952): 451–462.

"Turkey's Agrarian Revolution and the Problem of Urbanization." *The Public Opinion Quarterly* 22, no. 3 (1958): 397–405.

Rustow, Dankwart, and Robert Ward (eds.). *Political Modernization in Japan and Turkey*. Princeton: Princeton University Press. 1964.

Rüstem, Ünver. *Ottoman Baroque: The Architectural Refashioning of Eighteenth-Century Istanbul*. Princeton: Princeton University Press, 2019.

Salman, Mustafa (ed.). *Balıkesir İktisat Kılavuzu*. Balıkesir: Balıkesir Ticaret Odası, 1957.

Sarıçoban, Gülay. "Demokrat Partiden Bir Siyasi Portre: Samet Ağaoğlu." *Cumhuriyet Tarihi Araştırmaları Dergisi* 9, no.17 (2013): 77–104.

Sarol, Mükkerem. *Bilinmeyen Menderes*, vol. I. Istanbul: Kervan Yayınları, 1983.
Bilinmeyen Menderes, vol. II. Istanbul: İnkılap, 2014 [1983].
Satterthwaite, Joseph. "The Truman Doctrine: Turkey." *The Annals of the American Academy of Political and Social Science* 401, no. 1 (1972): 74–84.
Sayarı, Sabri. "Interdisciplinary Approaches to Political Clientelism and Patronage in Turkey." *Turkish Studies* 15, no. 4 (2014): 655–670.
"The Turkish Party System in Transition," *Government and Opposition*, 13, no. 1 (1978): 39–57.
Scott, James. *Seeing like a State: How Certain Schemes to Improve the Human Condition Have Failed.* New Haven: Yale University Press, 1999.
Seale, Patrick. *The Struggle for Syria: A Study of Post-War Arab Politics 1945–1958.* 2nd ed. London: Tauris, 1986 [1965].
Sertel, Sabiha. *Roman Gibi.* 2nd ed. Istanbul: Belge Yayınları, 1987 [1969].
Sever, Ayşegül. "The Compliant Ally? Turkey and the West in the Middle East 1954–58." *Middle Eastern Studies* 34, no. 2 (1998): 73–90.
Sey, Yıldız. *Türkiye Çimento Tarihi.* Istanbul: Türkiye Çimento Müstahsilleri Birliği, 2003.
Seyhan, Dündar. *Gölgedeki Adam.* Istanbul: Nurettin Uycan Matbaası, 1966.
Seyman, Yaşar. *Tarihin Deltasına Yolculuk: Sina Akşin Kitabı.* Istanbul: Türkiye İş Bankası Kültür Yayınları, 2009.
Shankland, David. *The Alevis in Turkey: The Emergence of a Secular Islamic Tradition.* London: Routledge, 2003.
Shields, Sarah. *Fezzes in the River: Identity Politics and European Diplomacy in the Middle East on the Eve of World War II.* New York: Oxford University Press, 2011.
Shissler, A. Hollie. *Between Two Worlds: Ahmet Agaoglu and the New Turkey.* New York: I. B. Taurus, 2002.
Silverman, Reuben. *Borderline Personalities: Lives at the Political, Social, and Geographic Edges of Modern Turkey.* Istanbul: Libra Yayınevi, 2021.
"Republican People's Party People: Partisan Polarization in the Republic of Turkey, 1950–1953." *The Middle East Journal* 73, no. 1 (spring 2019): 74–91.
"Show (and Tell) Trials: Competing Narratives of Turkey's Democrat Party Era." *Turkish Studies* 23, no. 1 (2022): 147–167.
"Süreyya Ağaoğlu and the Emerging Liberal Order in Early Cold War Turkey." *Middle Eastern Studies* 60, no. 2 (2023): 320–335.
Turkey's Ever Present Past: Stories from Turkish Republican History. Istanbul: Libra Yayınevi, 2015.
Singer, Morris. *The Economic Advance of Turkey, 1938–1960.* Ankara: Ayyıldız Matbaası, 1977.
Skocpol, Theda. *States and Social Revolutions: A Comparative Analysis of France, Russia, and China.* Cambridge: Cambridge University Press, 1979.
Smith, Hannah Lucinda. *Erdoğan Rising: The Battle for the Soul of Turkey.* London: William Collins, 2019.
Smith, Sarah-Neel. *Metrics of Modernity: Art and Development in Postwar Turkey.* Berkeley: University of California Press, 2022.

Smith, Tony. "New Bottles for New Wine: A Pericentric Framework for the Study of the Cold War." *Diplomatic History* 24, no. 4 (2000): 567–591.

Solak-Çakmak, Fevzi, and Aslı Şener. "Türk Basın Tarihi İçinde Muhalif Bir Gazete-Demokrat İzmir." *Belgi Dergisi* 2, no. 20 (2020): 2475–2509.

Sonyel, Salahi. "Mustafa Kemal and Enver in Conflict, 1919–22." *Middle Eastern Studies* 25, no. 4 (1989): 506–515.

Sönmez, Erdem. "A Past to Be Forgotten? Writing Ottoman History in Early Republican Turkey." *British Journal of Middle Eastern Studies* 48, no. 4 (2021): 753–769.

Sönmez, Mustafa. *Türkiye'de Holdingler: Kırk Haramiler.* Ankara: Arkadaş Yayınevi, 1988.

Steil, Benn. *The Marshall Plan: The Dawn of the Cold War.* New York: Simon and Shuster, 2018.

Stirling, Paul. *Turkish Village.* New York: Wiley, 1966.

Stone, David. "The Balkan Pact and American Policy." *East European Quarterly* 28, no. 3 (1994): 393–407.

Sunar, İlkay. "Populism and Patronage: The Demokrat Party and Its Legacy in Turkey." *Il Politico* 55, no. 4 (October–December 1990): 745–757.

Suny, Ronald Grigor. *"They Can Live in the Desert but Nowhere Else": A History of the Armenian Genocide.* Princeton: Princeton University Press, 2015.

Szyliowicz, Joseph. *Political Change in Rural Turkey: Erdemli.* The Hague: Mouton & Co., 1966.

"Political Participation and Modernization in Turkey." *Western Political Quarterly* 19, no. 2 (1966): 266–284.

Şahin, Mehmet Serkan. *Erken Cumhuriyet Dönemi'nde CHP'nin Malatya Teşkilatı, 1923–1950.* Istanbul: Libra Yayınevi, 2016.

Şenşekerci, Erkan. *Türk Devriminde Celal Bayar (1918–1960).* Istanbul: Alfa Yayınları, 2000.

Şenyapılı, Tansı. *Baraka'dan Gecekonduya: Ankara' da Kentsel Mekanın Dönüşümü, 1923–60.* Istanbul: İletişim Yayınları, 2004.

Şeremetli, Sıtkı. *Balıkesir'de Demokrat Parti Hareketi, 1946–1960: İktidardan-İhtilale.* Balıkesir: Liva Yayınevi, 2006.

Şişman, Cengiz. *The Burden of Silence: Sabbatai Sevi and the Evolution of the Ottoman-Turkish Dönmes.* Oxford: Oxford University Press, 2017.

Tanyeri-Erdemir, Tuğba. "Archaeology as a Source of National Pride in the Early Years of the Turkish Republic." *Journal of Field Archaeology* 31, no. 4 (2006): 381–393.

Taşkın, Yüksel. *Anti-Komünizmden Küreselleşme Karşıtlığına Milliyetçi Muhafazakar Entelijansiya.* Istanbul: İletişim Yayınları, 2007.

"Turhan Güneş." In *Modern Türkiye'de Siyasi Düşünce II: Kemalizm,* edited by Tanıl Bora and Murat Gültekingil, 452–455. Istanbul: İletişim Yayınları, 2009.

Taubman, William. *Khrushchev: The Man and His Era.* New York: W. W. Norton, 2003.

TBMM Albümü, 1920–2010: II. *Cilt: 1950–1980.* Ankara: TBMM Basın ve Halkla İlişkiler Müdürlüğü Bakanlıklar, 2010.

Tekeli, İhsan. *Cumhuriyetin Belediyecilik Öyküsü (1923–1990)*. Istanbul: Tarih Vakfı Yurt Yayınları, 2009.

Tellal, Eral. "SSCB'yle İlişkiler." In *Türk Dış Politikası, Cilt I: 1919–1980*, edited by Baskın Oran, 314–324. Istanbul: İletişim Yayınları, 2001.

Temür, Haydar. *Demokrat Parti'de Parti İçi Muhalefet, 1946–1960*. Istanbul: Tarih Vakfı Yurt Yayınları, 2022.

Tezel, Yayha Sezai. *Cumhuriyet Döneminin İktisadi Tarihi, 1923–1950*. Istanbul: Türkiye İş Bankası Kültür Yayınları, 1982.

Toprak, Zafer. *Milli İktisat-Milli Burjuvazi*. Istanbul: Tarih Vakfı Yurt Yayınları, 1995.

Türkiye'de Milli İktisat, 1908–1918. Istanbul: Doğan Kitap, 2012 [1982].

Toker, Metin. *Demokrasiden Darbeye 1957–1960: Demokrasimizin İsmet Paşa'lı Yılları*. Istanbul: Bilgi Yayınevi, 1991 [1966].

DP Yokuş Aşağı 1954–1957: Demokrasimizin İsmet Paşa'lı Yılları. 2nd ed. Istanbul: Bilgi Yayınevi, 1991 [1966].

DP'nin Altın Yılları, 1950–1954: Demokrasimizin İsmet Paşa'lı Yılları. 2nd ed. Istanbul: Bilgi Yayınevi, 1991 [1990].

Tek Partiden Çok Partiye, 1944 –1950: Demokrasimizin İsmet Paşa'lı Yılları. 3rd ed. Istanbul: Bilgi Yayınevi, 1990 [1970].

Tunaya, Tarık Zafer. *Türkiye'de Siyasal Partiler II: Mütareke Dönemi, 1918–1922*. Hürriyet Vakfı Yayınları, 1986.

Tunçay, Mete. *Türkiye Cumhuriyeti'nde Tek-Parti Yönetimi'nin Kurulması*. Ankara: Yurt Yayınları, 1981.

Türkiye'de Sol Akımlar, 1908–1925. Istanbul: İletişim Yayınları, 2009.

Turan, Ali Eşref. *Türkiye'de Yerel Seçimler*. Istanbul: Bilgi Üniversitesi Yayınları, 2008.

Turan, Murat. *CHP'nin Doğu'da Teşkilatlanması, (1923–1950)*. Istanbul: Libra Yayınevi, 2011.

Turnaoğlu, Berna. *The Formation of Turkish Republicanism*. Princeton: Princeton University Press, 2017.

Türkiye İstatistik Kurumu (TÜİK). *Milletvekili Genel Seçimleri, 1923–2011*. Ankara: Türkiye İstatistik Kurumu Matbaası, 2012. Available: www.ysk.gov.tr/doc/dosyalar/1923–2011-MVSecimleri-Tuik.pdf.

Türköz, Meltem. *Naming and Nation-Building in Turkey: The 1934 Surname Law*. London: Palgrave Macmillan, 2018.

Unbehaun, Horst. *Türkiye Kırsalında Kliyentalizm ve Siyasal Katılım: Datça Örneği: 1923–1992*. Ankara: Ütüpya Yayınları, 2005.

Urbinati, Nadia. "Political Theory of Populism." *Annual Review of Political Science* 22 (2019): 6.1–6.22.

Uyar, Hakkı. *Vatan Cephesi: Türk Siyasal Yaşamında Cepheleşmelere Bir Örnek*. Istanbul: Boyut, 2012.

Üzmez, Hüseyin. *Malatya Suikastı*. Istanbul: Timaş Yayınları, 2004.

Vanderlippe, John. *The Politics of Turkish Democracy: İsmet İnönü and the Formation of the Multi-Party System, 1938–1950*. Albany: SUNY Press, 2005.

Weiker, Walter. *Political Tutelage and Democracy in Turkey: The Free Party and Its Aftermath*. Leiden: Brill, 1973.

The Turkish Revolution 1960–1961: Aspects of Military Politics. Washington, DC: The Brookings Institute, 1963.

Westad, Odd Arne. *The Global Cold War: Third World Interventions and the Making of Our Times*. Cambridge: Cambridge University Press, 2005.

White, Jenny. "Islam and Politics in Contemporary Turkey." In *The Cambridge History of Turkey*, edited by Reşat Kasaba, 357–380. Cambridge: Cambridge University Press, 2008.

Wood, Robert. *From Marshall Plan to Debt Crisis: Foreign Aid and Development Choices in the World Economy*. Berkeley: University of California Press, 1986.

Yadirgi, Veli. *The Political Economy of the Kurds of Turkey: From the Ottoman Empire to the Turkish Republic*. Cambridge: Cambridge University Press, 2011.

Yalçınkaya, Ekrem. *Muhtasar Malatya Tarih ve Coğrafyası*. Istanbul: Cumhuriyet Matbaası, 1940.

Yalman, Ahmet Emin. "The Struggle for Multi-Party Government in Turkey." *Middle East Journal* 1, no. 1 (1947): 46–58.

Yakın Tarihte Gördüklerim ve Geçirdiklerim 2. Istanbul: Pera Turizm, 1997 [1970].

Yaqub, Salim. *Containing Arab Nationalism: The Eisenhower Doctrine and the Middle East*. Chapel Hill, NC: University of North Carolina Press, 2004.

Yasa, Memduh (ed.). *Cumhuriyet Dönemi Türkiye Ekonomisi, 1923–1978* (Istanbul: Akbank Kültür Yayını, 1980).

Yaşar, Beril. "Demokrat Parti'de Parti İçi Demokrasi, 1946–1960." *Tarih Okulu Dergisi* 7, no. 18 (2014): 503–541.

Yavuz, Hakan. *Erdoğan: The Making of an Autocrat*. Edinburgh: Edinburgh University Press, 2021.

Yerasimos, Stefanos. *Azgelişmişlik Sürecinde Türkiye III: I. Dünya Savaşından 1971'e*. Istanbul: Gözlem Yayınları, 1976.

Yeşilbursa, Behçet Kemal. *The Baghdad Pact: Anglo-American Defence Policies in the Middle East, 1950–59*. London: Frank Cass, 2005.

"CENTO: The Forgotten Alliance in the Middle East, 1959–1979." *Middle Eastern Studies* 56, no. 6 (2020): 854–877.

"The 'Revolution' of 27 May 1960 in Turkey: British Policy towards Turkey." *Middle Eastern Studies* 41, no. 1 (2005): 121–151.

"Turkey's Participation in the Middle East Command and Its Admission to NATO, 1950–52." *Middle Eastern Studies* 35, no. 4 (1999): 70–102.

Yeşilyurt, Süleyman. *Bayar Gerçeği*. Ankara: Stratejik Araştırma ve Kültür Yayınları, 1997.

Yetkin, Çetin. *Türkiye'de Tek Parti Yönetimi, 1930–1945*. Altın Kitaplar Yayınevi, 1983.

Yıldırmaz, Sinan. *Politics and the Peasantry in Post-War Turkey: Social History, Culture and Modernization*. London: I. B. Taurus, 2016.

Yıldız, Aytaç. *Üç Dönem Bir Aydın: Burhan Asaf Belge, 1899–1967*. Istanbul: İletişim Yayınları, 2011.

Yıldız, Nuran. "Demokrat Parti İktidarı (1950–1960) ve Basın." *Ankara Üniversitesi SBF Dergisi* 51, no. 1 (1996): 481–505.

Yılmaz, Hakan. "Democratization from Above in Response to the International Context: Turkey, 1945–1950." *New Perspectives on Turkey* 17 (1997): 1–37.

Yılmaz, Hale. *Becoming Turkish: Nationalist Reforms and Cultural Negotiations in Early Republican Turkey, 1923–1945*. Syracuse: Syracuse University Press, 2013.

Yılmaz, Şuhnaz. "Turkey's Quest for NATO Membership: The Institutionalization of the Turkish–American Alliance." *Southeast European and Black Sea Studies* 12, no. 4 (2012): 481–495.

Yorulmaz, Naci. *Arming the Sultan: German Arms Trade and Personal Diplomacy in the Ottoman Empire before World War I*. London: I. B. Tauris, 2014.

Yurdakök, Abdullah. *Balıkesir Basın Tarihi, 1886–1991*. Balıkesir: Sonsöz Gazetesi, 1992.

Yurdakul, Doğan, and F. Cengiz Erdinç. *Adalet Savaşçısı: Menderes'in Avukatı Burhan Apaydın'ın Anıları*. Istanbul: Kırmızıkedi, 2012.

Yurtoğlu, Nadir. "Cumhuriyet Türkiyesinde Elektrik Enerjisi Üretimi ve Enerji Politikaları, 1923–1960." *Atatürk Araştırma Merkezi Dergisi* 34, no. 98 (2018): 227–280.

"Demokrat Parti (DP) Dönemi'nde Pamuk Politikaları ve Dokuma Sanayisine Etkileri, 1950–1960." *Atatürk Araştırma Merkezi Dergisi* 37, no. 103 (2021): 293–335.

"Kalkınmanın Önemli Bir Unsuru, Kuruluşundan 50. Yılına Türkiye'de Çimento Sanayi, 1910–1960." *Atatürk Araştırma Merkezi Dergisi* 31, no. 92 (2015): 113–164.

Yüksel, Erol. *Milli Mücadele'den 27 Mayıs'a Bir Siyasetçi: Refik Koraltan*. Ankara: Atatürk Araştırma Merkezi, 2018.

Zakaria, Fareed. "The Rise of Illiberal Democracy." *Foreign Affairs* 76, no. 6 (1997): 22–43.

Zürcher, Erik. *Turkey: A Modern History*. 3rd ed. London: I. B. Tauris, 2004.

The Unionist Factor: The Role of the Committee for Union and Progress in the Nationalist Movement, 1905–1926. Leiden: Brill, 1984.

Dissertations and Theses

Akgümüş, Murat. "Kayseri in the Period of the Democrat Party, 1950–1960." PhD diss., Erciyes Üniversitesi, Kayseri, 2023.

Akkuş, Süleyman. "Demokrat Parti Aydın Milletvekilleri ve TBMM'deki Faaliyetleri, 1950–1954." PhD diss., Adnan Menderes Üniversitesi, Aydın, 2016.

Arslan, Zehra. "Demokrat Parti Dönemi'nde Trabzon, 1950–1960." PhD diss., Karadeniz Teknik Üniversitesi, Trabzon, 2011.

Avcı, Fikret. "Demokrat Parti (DP) İktidarı Döneminde Malatya: Şehir, Siyaset ve Toplum, 1950–1960." PhD diss., İnönü Üniversitesi, Malatya, 2018.

Aydın, Fatma. "Demokrat Parti İktidarı Uygulamalarının Bir Taşra Kenti Basınına Yansımaları: Balıkesir Örneği, 1950–1960." PhD diss., Balıkesir Üniversitesi, Balıkesir, 2013.

Ayhan, Fırat. "Demokrat Parti ve Demokrat Parti Van Milletvekilleri." Master's thesis, Necmettin Erbakan Üniversitesi, Konya, 2023.

Bal, Bülent. "Aydın Siyaset İlişkisi Bağlamında Hürriyet Partisi." PhD diss., Marmara Üniversitesi, Istanbul, 2017.

Bolat, Ercan. "Demokrat Parti Dönemi Mersin (İçel) Milletvekilleri ve Meclis Faaliyetleri, 1950–1960." Master's thesis, Ömer Halisdemir Üniversitesi, Niğde, 2017.

Çoban, Fatma Eylem. "Demokrat Parti Döneminde Hükümet-İş Adamı Ilişkileri." PhD diss., Dokuz Eylül Üniversitesi, Izmir, 2022.

Esen, Berk. "Political Mobilization and the Institutional Origins of National Developmentalist States: The Cases of Turkey, Mexico, Argentina, and Egypt." PhD diss., Cornell University, Ithaca, 2015.

Garapon, Béatrice. "Aux origines de la Turquie conservatrice: Une sociologie historique du Parti démocrate, 1946–1960." PhD diss., L'université de Bordeaux, Bordeaux, 2017.

Gemici, Filiz. "Demokrat Parti Dönemi Adapazarı-Sakarya, 1950–1960." PhD diss., Sakarya Üniversitesi, Sakarya, 2019.

Gemicioğlu, Emrah. "Demokrat Parti Döneminde Hakkâri'de Siyasal Yaşam ve Yapılan Kamu Harcamaları, 1950–1960." Master's thesis, Van Yüzüncü Yıl Üniversitesi, Van, 2021.

Gök, Hacı Veli. "Demokrat Parti Döneminin Önemli Bir Siması: Namık Gedik ve Siyasi Faaliyetleri." PhD diss., İstanbul Üniversitesi, Istanbul, 2020.

Gökatalay, Semih. "The Political Economy of Corporations in the Late Ottoman Empire and Early Turkish Republic, 1908–1929." Master's thesis, Middle Eastern Technical University, Ankara, 2015.

Karakuzu, Hasan. "Demokrat Parti Dönemi'nde Zonguldak, 1950–1960." Master's thesis, Nevşehir Hacı Bektaş Veli Üniversitesi, Nevşehir, 2021.

Karataş, Esra. "Demokrat Parti Döneminde Adana'da Siyasal Hayat, 1950–1960." Master's thesis, Mersin Üniversitesi, Mersin, 2021.

Kaya, Asıl. "Türk Siyasi Tarihi'nde CHP'nin Gençlik Kolları." Master's thesis, Dokuz Eylül Üniversitesi, Izmir, 2010.

Kaya, Ayşe Elif Emre. "Demokrat Parti Politikalarının Cumhuriyet Gazetesinde Ele Alınış Biçimleri, 1950–1960." PhD diss., Ankara Üniversitesi, Ankara, 2009.

Kıyıcı, Fatih. "Demokrat Parti Döneminde (1950–1960) Erzurum'da İktisadi Hayat." PhD diss., Atatürk Üniversitesi, Ankara, 2024.

Kocakaya, İsmail. "1950–1960 Yılları Arasında Demokrat Parti Döneminde Biga." Master's thesis, Çanakkale On Sekiz Mart Üniversitesi, Çanakkale, 2021.

Madendağ, Gülten. "Demokrat Parti Döneminde Adana'da Gündelik Hayat." PhD diss., Sakarya Üniversitesi, Sakarya, 2018.

Meyer, James. "Memory and Political Symbolism in Post-September 12 Turkey: A History of the May 27th Debate." Master's thesis, Princeton University, Princeton, 2001.

Morgil, Orhan. "The Social Structure and Economic Development of Turkey, 1950–1960." PhD diss., University of California, Riverside, 1972.

Öz, İsmail. "Demokrat Parti'nin Gençlik Politikaları ve Gençlik Teşkilatı, 1946–1960." Master's thesis, Fatih Sultan Mehmet Vakıf Üniversitesi, Istanbul, 2014.

Özçetin, Burak. "Democracy and Opposition in Turkey: Locating the Freedom Party." Master's thesis, Middle East Technical University, Ankara, 2004.

Özdurğun, Yunus. "Demokrat Parti İktidarı Hakkındaki Mali Yolsuzluk İddialarının Yassıada Yargılamalarına ve Dönemin Siyasetine Yansımaları." PhD diss., Van Yüzüncü Yil Üniversitesi, Van, 2022.

Özoral, Başak. "The Turkish Transformation and Celal Bayar." Master's thesis, McGill University, Montreal, 2004.

Öztürk, Onur. "Demokrat Parti Dönemi Basın Rejimi ve *Zafer Gazetesi* (1957–1960) *Ulus Gazetesi* ile Karşılaştırmalı Bir İnceleme." Master's thesis, Ankara Üniversitesi, Ankara, 2004.

Pişkin, Çağrı. "Demokrat Döneminde Nevşehir." Master's thesis, Nevşehir Hacı Bektaş Veli Üniversitesi, Nevşehir, 2019.

Ryan, James. "Republic of Others: Opponents of Kemalism in Turkey's Single-Party Era." PhD diss., University of Pennsylvania, Philadelphia, 2017.

Sayın, Hüdai. "Malatya'da Siyasal Seçkinler." Master's thesis, İnönü Üniversitesi, Malatya, 1996.

Şahin, Mehmet Serkan. "Cumhuriyet Halk Partisi'nin Malatya Teşkilatı, 1923–1950." Master's thesis, Dokuz Eylül Üniversitesi, Izmir, 2008.

Şenel, Aymelek. "Demokrat Parti İzmir İl Örgütü, 1946–1960: Muhalefetten İktidara Bir Siyasal Partinin Yerel Politikası." PhD diss., Manisa Celal Bayar Üniversitesi, Manisa, 2018.

Tamküpeli, Tuğba. "Edirne Siyasi Tarihinde Demokrat Parti Dönemi, 1950–1960." Master's thesis, Tekirdağ Namık Kemal Üniversitesi, Tekirdağ, 2021.

Tınal, Melih. "Bir Siyasal Kişilik Portesi Olarak." PhD diss., Dokuz Eylül Üniversitesi, Izmir, 2001.

Yücebaş, Oğulcan. "Demokrat Parti Döneminde Menemen, 1950–1960." Master's thesis, İzmir Kâtip Çelebi Üniversitesi, Izmir, 2021.

Index

Books in the Series

1 Parvin Paidar, *Women and the Political Process in Twentieth-Century Iran*
2 Israel Gershoni and James Jankowski, *Redefining the Egyptian Nation, 1930–1945*
3 Annelies Moors *Women, Property and Islam: Palestinian Experiences, 1920–1945*
4 Paul Kingston *Britain and the Politics of Modernization in the Middle East, 1945–1958*
5 Daniel Brown *Rethinking Tradition in Modern Islamic Thought*
6 Nathan J. Brown *The Rule of Law in the Arab World: Courts in Egypt and the Gulf*
7 Richard Tapper *Frontier Nomads of Iran: The Political and Social History of the Shahsevan*
8 Khaled Fahmy *All the Pasha's Men: Mehmed Ali, His Army and the Making of Modern Egypt*
9 Sheila Carapico *Civil Society in Yemen: The Political Economy of Activism in Arabia*
10 Meir Litvak *Shi'i Scholars of Nineteenth-Century Iraq: The Ulama of Najaf and Karbala*
11 Jacob Metzer *The Divided Economy of Mandatory Palestine*
12 Eugene L. Rogan, *Frontiers of the State in the Late Ottoman Empire: Transjordan, 1850–1921*
13 Eliz Sanasarian *Religious Minorities in Iran*
14 Nadje Al-Ali *Secularism, Gender and the State in the Middle East: The Egyptian Women's Movement*
15 Eugene L. Rogan and Avi Shlaim, eds., *The War for Palestine: Rewriting the History of 1948*
16 Gershon Shafir and Yoar Peled, *Being Israeli: The Dynamics of Multiple Citizenship*
17 A. J. Racy *Making Music in the Arab World: The Culture and Artistry of Tarab*
18 Benny Morris *The Birth of the Palestinian Refugee Crisis Revisited*
19 Yasir Suleiman *A War of Words: Language and Conflict in the Middle East*
20 Peter Moore *Doing Business in the Middle East: Politics and Economic Crisis in Jordan and Kuwait*
21 Idith Zertal *Israel's Holocaust and the Politics of Nationhood*
22 David Romano *The Kurdish Nationalist Movement: Opportunity, Mobilization and Identity*

23 Laurie A. Brand *Citizens Abroad: Emigration and the State in the Middle East and North Africa*
24 James McDougall *History and the Culture of Nationalism in Algeria*
25 Madawi al-Rasheed *Contesting the Saudi State: Islamic Voices from a New Generation*
26 Arang Keshavarzian *Bazaar and State in Iran: The Politics of the Tehran Marketplace*
27 Laleh Khalili *Heroes and Martyrs of Palestine: The Politics of National Commemoration*
28 M. Hakan Yavuz *Secularism and Muslim Democracy in Turkey*
29 Mehran Kamrava *Iran's Intellectual Revolution*
30 Nelida Fuccaro *Histories of City and State in the Persian Gulf: Manama since 1800*
31 Michaelle L. Browers *Political Ideology in the Arab World: Accommodation and Transformation*
32 Miriam R. Lowi *Oil Wealth and the Poverty of Politics: Algeria Compared*
33 Thomas Hegghammer *Jihad in Saudi Arabia: Violence and Pan-Islamism since 1979*
34 Sune Haugbolle *War and Memory in Lebanon*
35 Ali Rahnema *Superstition as Ideology in Iranian Politics: From Majlesi to Ahmadinejad*
36 Wm. Roger Louis and Avi Shlaim, eds., *The 1967 Arab-Israeli War: Origins and Consequences*
37 Stephen W. Day *Regionalism and Rebellion in Yemen: A Troubled National Union*
38 Daniel Neep *Occupying Syria under the French Mandate: Insurgency, Space and State Formation*
39 Iren Ozgur *Islamic Schools in Modern Turkey: Faith, Politics, and Education*
40 Ali M. Ansari *The Politics of Nationalism in Modern Iran*
41 Thomas Pierret *Religion and State in Syria: The Sunni Ulama from Coup to Revolution*
42 Guy Ben-Porat *Between State and Synagogue: The Secularization of Contemporary Israel*
43 Madawi Al-Rasheed *A Most Masculine State: Gender, Politics and Religion in Saudi Arabia*
44 Sheila Carapico *Political Aid and Arab Activism: Democracy Promotion, Justice, and Representation*
45 Pascal Menoret *Joyriding in Riyadh: Oil, Urbanism, and Road Revolt*
46 Toby Matthiesen *The Other Saudis: Shiism, Dissent and Sectarianism*
47 Bashir Saade *Hizbullah and the Politics of Remembrance: Writing the Lebanese Nation*
48 Noam Leshem *Life after Ruin: The Struggles over Israel's Depopulated Arab Spaces*
49 Zoltan Pall *Salafism in Lebanon: Local and Transnational Movements*
50 Salwa Ismail *The Rule of Violence: Subjectivity, Memory and Government in Syria*
51 Zahra Ali, *Women and Gender in Iraq: Between Nation-Building and Fragmentation*

52 Dina Bishara *Contesting Authoritarianism: Labour Challenges to the State in Egypt*
53 Rory McCarthy *Inside Tunisia's al-Nahda: Between Politics and Preaching*
54 Ceren Lord *Religious Politics in Turkey: From the Birth of the Republic to the AKP*
55 Dörthe Engelcke *Reforming Family Law: Social and Political Change in Jordan and Morocco*
56 Dana Conduit *The Muslim Brotherhood in Syria*
57 Benjamin Schuetze, *Promoting Democracy, Reinforcing Authoritarianism: US and European Policy in Jordan*
58 Marc Owen Jones *Political Repression in Bahrain*
59 Dylan Baun, *Winning Lebanon: Populism and the Production of Sectarian Violence, 1920–1958*
60 Joas Wagemakers *The Muslim Brotherhood in Jordan*
61 Amnon Aran, *Israeli Foreign Policy since the End of the Cold War*
62 Victor J. Willi *The Fourth Ordeal: A History of the Muslim Brotherhood in Egypt, 1968–2018*
63 Grace Wermenbol *A Tale of Two Narratives: The Holocaust, the Nakba, and the Israeli-Palestinian Battle of Memories*
64 Erin A. Snider *Marketing Democracy: The Political Economy of Democracy Aid in the Middle East*
65 Yafa Shanneik, *The Art of Resistance in Islam: The Performance of Politics among Shi'i Women in the Middle East and Beyond*
66 Shirin Saeidi, *Women and the Islamic Republic: How Gendered Citizenship Conditions the Iranian State*
67 Jessica Watkins, *Creating Consent in an Illiberal Order: Policing Disputes in Jordan*
68 Nora Derbal *Charity in Saudi Arabia: Civil Society under Authoritarianism*
69 Tine Gade *Sunni City: Tripoli from Islamist Utopia to the Lebanese 'Revolution'*
70 Chloe Skinner *Occupier and Occupied: Israel, Palestine and Masculinities across the Divide*
71 Miriam R. Lowi *Refining the Common Good: Oil, Islam and Politics in Gulf Monarchies*
72 Mathilde Zederman *Tunisian Politics in France: Long-Distance Activism since the 1980s*
73 Reuben Silverman *The Rise and Fall of Turkey's Democrat Party: The Cold War and Illiberalism, 1945–1960*

For EU product safety concerns, contact us at Calle de José Abascal, 56–1°, 28003 Madrid, Spain or eugpsr@cambridge.org.

www.ingramcontent.com/pod-product-compliance
Ingram Content Group UK Ltd.
Pitfield, Milton Keynes, MK11 3LW, UK
UKHW021845150226
468058UK00008B/142
* 9 7 8 1 0 0 9 6 0 4 4 5 1 *